One Drop in a Sea of Blue

One Drop in a Sea of Blue

The Liberators of the Ninth Minnesota

John. B. Lundstrom

Minnesota Historical
Society Press

www.mhspress.org

The Minnesota Historical Society Press is a member of the
Association of American University Presses.

Manufactured in the United States of America

10 9 8 7 6 5 4 3 2 1

♾ The paper used in this publication meets the minimum requirements
of the American National Standard for Information Sciences—Permanence
for Printed Library Materials, ANSI Z39.48–1984.

International Standard Book Number
ISBN: 978-0-87351-821-5 (paper)
ISBN: 978-0-87351-872-7 (e-book)

Library of Congress Cataloging-in-Publication Data

Lundstrom, John B.
One drop in a sea of blue : the liberators of the Ninth Minnesota /
John B. Lundstrom.
p. cm.
Includes bibliographical references and index.
ISBN 978-0-87351-821-5 (pbk. : alk. paper) — ISBN 978-0-87351-872-7 (ebook)
1. United States. Army. Minnesota Infantry Regiment, 9th (1862–1865).
2. Minnesota—History—Civil War, 1861–1865. 3. United States—History—
Civil War, 1861–1865—Regimental histories.
I. Title.
E515.59th .L86 2012
973.7′476—dc23
2012010518

To my Mother

Contents

One Drop in a Sea of Blue

Preface

I never thought I would ever write a book on the Civil War. For forty years World War II has been my passion, and I have written five books on the early Pacific naval campaigns. The Civil War has always interested me, but only in an abstract way. I did not expect to be able to contribute anything original in this field, which frankly seemed already heavily overworked, as opposed to in virgin territory of Second World War history. So why this book? Quite literally by accident I latched onto an intriguing and dramatic Civil War story, or more correctly, it latched onto me and would not let go. As I quickly discovered, the incident is virtually unknown in the vast literature of the war. In deciding whether to research and narrate it, three questions came immediately to mind. Is there enough surviving documentation for an adequate treatment? Is the subject worthy of further study? Does it bear broader significance in Civil War history? The answers to all three questions, I believe, are most decidedly, yes.

On November 11, 1863, thirty-eight soldiers from the Ninth Minnesota Volunteer Infantry Regiment did something noble and, in its own way, heroic. They responded to the agonized plea of an escaped slave to save his family who were being taken out of state to be sold. In defiance of direct orders from irate senior officers who were actually present, the Minnesotans conducted an armed rescue of the family. As a result the thirty-eight "liberators," as they are identified in this book, were arrested, confined, and charged with mutiny. During the entire war, so far as can be determined, nothing quite like this rescue or prosecution ever happened. Their case resonated beyond Minnesota and even caught the attention of the U. S. Senate. In the larger historical perspective, the ideas and actions of the liberators and their allies do indeed cast much fresh light on Union military occupation policy and the changing attitudes of Federal soldiers toward slavery.

Astoundingly, the reuniting of the slave family became, for the liberators, merely the opening chapter of a much larger, equally dramatic, and important saga. After their release in early 1864, nearly all the liberators, along with the rest of the Ninth Minnesota, suffered very hard service during the balance of the war. One liberator fell in battle and ten sustained wounds of varying degrees (one lost a leg, and another an arm). Eleven experienced the horrors of Confederate prisons, where six died of disease, malnutrition, or the effects of wounds. Two others succumbed in Union hospitals. Thirteen were invalided home due to wounds or ill health, and two deserted. In August 1865 when the Ninth Minnesota mustered out of the service, only fourteen liberators still stood in its ranks.

The Ninth Minnesota's first battle of any note came in June 1864 at Brice's Crossroads, Mississippi. A heavily outnumbered Confederate force led by the renowned Maj. Gen. Nathan Bedford Forrest routed the mostly veteran Federal troops. Union losses exceeded Rebel casualties by nearly five to one. That confused battlefield disaster and the calamitous retreat to Memphis constituted perhaps the Union army's most shameful defeat of the war—quite an achievement given all the competition. Certainly no drubbing embittered the humiliated losers to any greater degree.

What the Minnesotans endured and accomplished at Brice's Crossroads is little known. Equally so is the gruesome fate of those who were captured: imprisonment in the Andersonville stockade and other dire locales like Millen and Florence. The death rate for the 235 captives of the Ninth Minnesota exceeded 60 percent—among the highest of any comparably sized group in the entire Union army. A liberator was one of the very last Minnesota soldiers released by the Rebels following the war. In the meantime the Ninth Minnesota, with the other liberators, had taken part in the two victories, Nashville and Mobile, that helped end the war in the western theater.

The Ninth Minnesota honorably represented the "Boys in Blue" from their home state. Like the other survivors of America's bloodiest conflict, the remaining liberators resumed their lives the best they could despite the physical and psychological harms of the war. All bore scars of one kind or another. Their postwar fortunes have much to say, representing in microcosm (and in some cases vastly surpassing) the general range of experiences, good and ill, of all the Union veterans. One liberator in particular surmounted terrible tragedy and gross injustice that in their way reflect deeply on the liberation itself. Most lived to a ripe old age. The last one died aged ninety-three in 1936, near to the end of the entire Civil War generation.

The background, military service, and postwar experiences of all the liberators became of the greatest interest, and I researched the subject to the best of my ability. The result has been an avalanche of government records, personal papers, newspaper accounts, pension affidavits, and myriad other sources that shed more light on those thirty-eight randomly selected individuals than I could have ever imagined. Moreover, few regiments have left such a rich legacy of recollections, particularly prison experiences, as the Ninth Minnesota. Thus, it is possible to relate, in a way that is unprecedented in existing literature, the woeful odyssey of the Minnesotans through the whole Rebel prison system.

This entire project is a wholly unforeseen result of a soldier's service record that I ordered a decade ago from the National Archives in a belated look at my Civil War ancestors. A great-grandfather and three great-great-uncles were enlisted men in the Union army. They all served faithfully, honorably, and bravely, but to my knowledge with no particular personal distinction other than that one had died during the war. I was wrong. My great-great-uncle John Morrison, I discovered, was a liberator. Taken at Brice's Cross-roads, he died in the fall of 1864 as a prisoner and rests today, as do so many thousands of Civil War soldiers, in an unknown grave. Late in the war, Minnesota authorities, in the absence of any real information, selected October 31, 1864, and Savannah, Georgia, as the date and place of his death. Both guesses, as my later research has shown, were in error.

For nearly 150 years, John Morrison was simply a name in the Minnesota Civil War roster. Uncovering his service and that of his comrades has not only been personally rewarding but will, I truly hope, be of real value to others in understanding wider aspects of the war. It is of enormous personal satisfaction that the correct place and date of John Morrison's death have now been established. His name will eventually be placed on a memorial in the national cemetery where he rests with nearly three thousand anonymous comrades who died in the same Confederate prison. Most of them are also only now being identified. May they all be recognized and remembered!

CHAPTER ONE

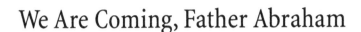

We Are Coming, Father Abraham

THE CALL

On a cold, moonless night in November 1863, the third autumn of the Civil War, an escaped slave stumbled through the gloomy countryside as fast as his tired legs permitted. He learned that day that he and his entire family—wife and five young children, brother and sister-in-law, and two younger sisters—were to be hauled off to another state and almost certainly separated and sold. In deep despair he resisted and fled his master's farm. A desperate plan seized hold of him. He knew the slave owner intended to board his human chattel on the next morning's mail train. One early stop would be a town, nearly twenty miles distant, located near a small Union army post. If he could reach that particular camp in time, and if he could enlist the help of those Northern strangers (two tremendously big "ifs"), he might yet forestall catastrophe.

Ordinarily one might have expected that a fugitive slave should have commanded the sympathy and ready assistance of any Federal troops—all the more here because President Abraham Lincoln's hallowed Emancipation Proclamation had already been in effect for nearly a year. In truth that young father's quest for justice appeared hopeless from the very beginning, for he was enslaved not in the rebellious South but in Missouri, one of the four Border States exempted from that sacred promise of freedom. The law in Missouri still favored the rights of loyal slave owners to dispose of their property at will. The army there could neither aid a fugitive slave nor interfere in any way with slavery, let alone arbitrarily free a slave and his whole family.

The man, breathless, disheveled, and distraught, attained his destination with only minutes to spare. By sheer chance the soldiers he accosted were

7

from the Ninth Minnesota Volunteer Infantry Regiment. Who they were, where they were from, and what they had already experienced in Missouri would strongly affect how they responded to his urgent call for help.

The Ninth Minnesota was formed in August 1862 as part of the North's second great summons of troops. After a shaky start in 1861, the war went well for the men in blue, especially in the western theater. In the first four months of 1862, Union victories at Mill Springs (Kentucky), Forts Henry and Donelson (Tennessee), Pea Ridge (Arkansas), and Shiloh (Tennessee) secured Kentucky and Missouri and opened the Confederate heartland to invasion. Nashville fell in February, New Orleans in April, and Memphis in June. In the East Maj. Gen. George B. McClellan inched his way up the Peninsula of Virginia to within a few miles of the Confederate capital of Richmond. By mid-June the Civil War seemed virtually won. Suddenly the Northern effort faltered. Momentum in the West dissipated once the Rebel army entrenched at Corinth in northeastern Mississippi. In Virginia during the Seven Days (June 25 to July 1), Gen. Robert E. Lee bloodied McClellan's forces and rocked him back on his heels. Seizing the initiative in East and West, resurgent Rebels plotted to regain the lost territory.

To remedy the deteriorating situation, Lincoln moved swiftly in July 1862 to muster a vast new host. "We are coming Father Abraham, three hundred thousand more" began a stirring poem by New Yorker James Sloan Gibbons that was quickly transformed into the lyrics of a popular song. Although Gibbons exulted the "sturdy farmer boys fast forming into line," in truth, despite the patriotic ardor, recruitment in July lagged far below requirements. A desperate Congress moved to tap the state militias—potentially every able-bodied man between eighteen and forty-five—for conscription, while Lincoln doubled the call to six hundred thousand men. If any state did not attain its full quota of volunteers by August 15, the government would simply draft militiamen for nine months to make up the difference.[1]

News of the impending draft caught Minnesota, as it did the other states, totally by surprise. That the federal government demanded a mere 5,362 men from the North Star State, less than 1 percent of the total, aptly illustrated its tiny population in comparison with most other states. Admitted into the Union in 1858, Minnesota completed the double tier of states that bordered the mighty Mississippi River. Much of the state's southern third comprised a vast, rolling prairie. The rest was trackless, wooded wilderness dotted with lakes. The 1860 census recorded 177,023 residents, excluding "Indians not taxed" (as the U.S. Constitution put it). Roughly two-thirds of native whites hailed from New England and the Mid-Atlantic States. Very few residents were ex-Southerners, and only 259 were free persons of color. Germans and

Irish were the most numerous foreign born, but the numbers of Norwegians and Swedes were increasing quickly. The great majority of Minnesota's inhabitants were farmers. Agriculture had rapidly supplanted the fur trade as the major industry, while the lumber industry was growing in importance. The white population clustered mostly along the Mississippi River and the shallow Minnesota River that wound through the southwestern part of the state before curving north and east to join the Mississippi near Fort Snelling. The settlements dotting the Minnesota River valley sustained the farmers who expanded across the rich grasslands and started to tame the "Big Woods" to the north.[2]

In 1862 Minnesota constituted a Republican stronghold. Lincoln had won the 1860 election by a nearly two-to-one vote. The Republicans strongly denounced the expansion of slavery into the territories and favored free western land for settlers. Democrats, who differed with Republicans on both fundamental issues, thrived in the "older commercial and industrial centers" such as St. Paul, Stillwater, and St. Anthony. Up to May 1862, Minnesota had furnished the Union army some 4,600 men in five infantry regiments, three cavalry companies, and two light artillery batteries. Claiming to be the very first volunteer regiment mustered into Federal service, the gallant First Minnesota fought in the First Battle of Bull Run and with McClellan in the Peninsula. In the western theater the Second Minnesota shared in the victory at Mill Springs and in the siege of Corinth. The Third and Fourth Regiments and most of the Fifth also went south. Organized in May 1862, the Sixth Minnesota experienced a difficult birth once the briefly favorable Union military situation rendered further recruitment "apathetic." More volunteers would step forward, moaned the *Rochester City Post* on June 28, if they could remain at home "until after the harvest." The same languid spirit prevailed in much of the North—until conscription loomed.[3]

On August 5 Governor Alexander Ramsey raised the Seventh Minnesota and threatened to fill it and the Sixth Minnesota with militia if the required number of volunteers did not step forward within two weeks. Soon afterward he called forth the Eighth, Ninth, Tenth, and Eleventh Regiments to cover the rest of Minnesota's quota. Fortunately, the War Department extended the period for voluntary enlistments to August 22. "Because the quota of the state was apportioned among the counties and towns according to the number of their enrolled militia," explains Minnesota historian William Watts Folwell, "all the communities of the state became interested at once in supplying each its contingent" to avoid "the humiliation of a draft." Prominent men raised companies of one hundred men that were to gather at Fort Snelling, where the men would be examined, elect their officers, and receive furloughs to help bring in the harvest. The state adjutant general would group the companies by tens to form infantry regiments and appoint the field officers.[4]

A frenzy of war meetings in the individual communities raised funds for enlistment bounties as an added incentive to local volunteering. To forestall the "comparative disgrace of a draft," Winona County, for one, added a bounty of $100 ($25 in advance and $75 at discharge) in addition to the Federal bounty of $25. A patriotic Mower County farmer offered $2 to every local volunteer plus five bushels of wheat for every married man to supplement the county's own $50 bounty. Each enlistee would also receive a month's pay in advance, which for a private was $13. Militiamen if they were drafted would get not only less pay ($11 per month per private) but also no bounty.[5]

Such "powerful medicine had immediate effect." According to the *Mankato Weekly Record,* the draft order elicited "universal rejoicing" that "instantly aroused" Mankato's "patriotic ardor" so that "numbers of our best citizens nobly came forward and enrolled their names." By August 16, observed the *Rochester City Post,* the rate of enlistment had reached "a perfect avalanche." Those "liable to militia duty have at once realized that their duty to themselves no less than to their Country requires them to step forward and take rank in the service of their country, rather than to be driven by the compulsion of drafting." The "rural districts," notes Folwell, "felt the appeal for the army as never before and responded to it with admirable promptness; whole companies were made up in neighborhood rallies." Not only did volunteers receive bounties, but they could choose to serve in the same units as relatives, friends, and neighbors. Those who enlisted in the summer of 1862 tended to be older and more settled than the eager volunteers of 1861, although certainly they too included many youngsters.[6]

By August 22 more than forty new volunteer companies had sprouted in counties and municipalities throughout Minnesota. The state adjutant general earmarked eight particular companies for the Tenth Regiment and two for the Eleventh Regiment, but for reasons best known to him, he shuffled the deck and incorporated them as the new Ninth Minnesota. The Minneapolis region (primarily Hennepin and Wright counties) furnished Companies A and B. To the northwest on the upper Mississippi River, Stearns County raised Company G, an interesting mixture of Yankees and Germans ("the right stamp for Soldiers," boasted the *St. Cloud Democrat,* "farmers in the summer, lumbermen in the winter") and Ojibwe Indians, who were superb woodsmen. Four companies originated in the Minnesota River valley: I (Scott County), H (Carver County), D (Nicollet County), and E (Blue Earth

County). Germans and Scandinavians were strongly represented in Company H and Welshmen in Company E. Mower County, on the Iowa border, supplied Company C, while nearby Rochester in Olmsted County recruited Company F. Winona and Wabasha counties, along the Mississippi River in the southeastern portion of the state, provided Company K.[7]

"Soon wagonload after wagonload of volunteers passed down the [Minnesota River] valley through our little city [Shakopee]," Colin F. Macdonald would recall fifty years later, "all singing, cheering, beating drums, waving 'Old Glory,' and giving vent to their enthusiasm in every possible manner." In 1861 the eighteen-year-old Macdonald had helped found the *Shakopee Argus,* but the next summer he joyfully suspended his budding newspaper career to join Company I. Too young to enlist without parental consent, he secured Capt. Horace B. Strait as legal guardian in lieu of his father, a physician in Illinois. Most underage volunteers simply lied about their age, and recruiters were only too happy to ignore their youth and enlist them. One with his parents' permission was seventeen-year-old Lorin Cray. He enlisted in Company D and later wrote his company was "made up very largely of farmer boys right from the harvest fields, dressed in denims and straw hats, some in bare feet, and we were not in first class marching order, nor very presentable. Uniforms and Government clothing could not be had." Thus Company D left for Fort Snelling "looking more like a squad of Missouri bushwhackers than Union soldiers."[8]

Representative of the uncertain fortunes of many small farmers who volunteered for what later became the Ninth Minnesota was forty-four-year-old Orsamus D. Rhoades in Company C. After farming in New York, Pennsylvania, and for the last four years, Iowa, Rhoades, his wife, Mary, five children, a yoke of oxen, one cow, and thirty-five cents in cash relocated in August 1856 to northwestern Mower County, where permanent settlement had only begun the year before. Rhoades took up 160 acres of "fine prairie" with black loam soil along the Cedar River where timber was readily at hand. On the third day after arriving, he suffered severe rheumatism and malaria and could not work, but Mary and their eleven-year-old son, Oscar, harvested enough grass to feed the stock during the winter. Then a wildfire torched everything the family owned "except the clothes they were wearing." They had to sell an ox to afford food and clothing. Kind neighbors helped them build a log cabin. During the "long and very cold" winter of 1856–57, Rhoades had to relinquish the remaining ox and the wagon for living money, keeping only the milk cow. In the spring and summer of 1857, the family hunted, fished, and trapped while plowing some fields. The next year they garnered a good crop of potatoes. By 1859 Rhoades could afford two bulls and a wagon for hauling freight. He also put more land under cultivation. In the spring of 1862, he and Oscar planted fifteen acres of wheat, which they began harvesting in mid-August. "Father cut with a cradle," recalled Oscar, "mother raked in the sheaves, and I bound, while the two girls placed it in shocks." Within a few days Orsamus enlisted in Austin, the Mower County seat, and soon reached Fort Snelling, where on August 19 he took the oath of allegiance along with the rest of Company C. "Mother and I harvested the crop," Oscar explained. "I cradled, mother raked in, and then would carry the cradle back and I would bind it. This took a long time. Father came home on a furlough and helped stack it. Then I secured a threshing machine and threshed it. We had no granary, so I laid up a rail pen and thatched the sides and roof with straw and put the wheat in." Finances were strained with Orsamus Rhoades in the army, but Oscar, who turned seventeen in September 1862, "faced the responsibility like a man," took good care of the family, and "managed to get along."[9]

The memoirs of Rev. Ole Paulson illuminate how and why certain men came to volunteer for the Ninth Minnesota.[10] Born in Norway in 1832, he came at age eighteen to Wisconsin and, after a stint in Iowa, went north in 1854 to Minnesota and became one of the first Scandinavian settlers in Carver County. In 1859 Paulson left his farm to become a colporteur (seller of religious tracts) and Lutheran lay preacher. He and wife, Inger, temporarily relocated in January 1861 to Chicago so he could attend Augustana College. They spent the summer of 1862 back on the farm before he resumed his studies in the fall. "There was great excitement bordering on panic," Paulson reminisced. "Recruiting was going on in nearly every county over the whole land. The recruiting officers traveled around with drums and fifes in cities, villages and out in the country. They drummed crowds together in meetings, and speakers made fiery and appealing speeches to the young men to arouse their war fervor. The situation on the battlefield was not bright, and the duty of every able-bodied man was to hasten to the aid of his bleeding country."

Paulson himself played a vital role in recruiting Company H. Two Chaska lawyers, William Rowe Baxter, a New England transplant, and Joseph Weinmann, a German immigrant, implored him to speak to his fellow Scandinavians, most of whom did not understand English. "I went with them and made thundering speeches appealing to their sense of duty and patriotism. The result was that many of my friends, relatives and neighbors enlisted." However, "while I was talking to others, I was also talking to myself, and I, too, became smitten with the war fever." Although excused from the draft as a theological student, Paulson "began to be a little bit anxious with the thought that so many of my warmest friends and loved ones should go." Nonetheless, he assured Inger, he had no plans to go to war: "I have greater ambitions than to be a warrior."

Retaining enough scarce labor in Minnesota in the summer of 1862 for the harvest trumped even urgent distant military concerns, but a far more serious worry erupted near the end of the volunteer enlistment period. The new crisis shook the state to its very roots. On August 18, when late annuity payments brought Dakota Indians to face starvation, factions of men from two reservations situated along the western course of the Minnesota River suddenly turned hostile. Led by Chief Little Crow, they killed most of the officials and their families at the Lower (Redwood) Agency and ambushed troops coming to their aid from nearby Fort Ridgely. Soon afterward the Indians assaulted Fort Ridgely and twice attacked the town of New Ulm. Mounted warriors raided isolated farms and settlements all along the frontier and killed hundreds of whites. Panic gripped the entire state. False rumors spread of the devastation of Mankato, St. Peter, and other communities along the Minnesota River. There were strong fears that the Ho-Chunk and Ojibwe Indians would join the Dakota to sweep the whites out of Minnesota. Huge numbers of settlers fled to St. Paul, Stillwater, Winona, and farther east. Many never returned to Minnesota. Some bold souls took refuge in hastily constructed fortifications near their homes. Cray's family lived in southern Blue Earth County southeast of New Ulm, well within range of Indian raiders. His father turned loose his stock, "hastily loaded" his wagons with the "women and children and a little food," and departed after leaving his house unlocked. At that point "no one knew where they were going" in the "general stampede." The Cray family stopped five miles away at Shelbyville and forted up with their neighbors.[11]

Word of marauding Indians killing and burning everything in their path reached Carver County on the evening of August 20. Paulson saw terrified refugees charge through the settlements on "lumber-wagons, cub carts, light wagons, buggies, sleds. Most of them drove, but many rode horseback or ox-back. An extensive gathering of frantic people fled as though the enemy was right at their heels, they drove their animals to exhaustion trying to get away. If you spoke to them, they would not take time to answer. A fugitive lying exhausted begging for help along the road would receive neither aid nor attention. This was the condition along all the roads leading into Carver, Chaska, and St. Paul."[12] The next day some Carver County settlers scoured the immediate area but turned up no hostile Indians. Men deliberated whether to join the army. Andrew John Carlson, a canny twenty-five-year-old immigrant, told his friends that "it is my duty to go, and I must." He was part of a group of sixteen Swedes who agreed to enlist if all of them did. Another was

Carlson's relative by marriage, thirty-year-old Pehr (Peter) Carlson, who had emigrated in 1854. Upon enlisting he declared to his family the "Union flag is my home, and I am ready with my life to safeguard its freedom against its enemies." However, he signed up without his wife Catharina's approval, and she never let him forget it. In April 1864, after another "well intentioned admonition," he pleaded, "Smite me kindly. You know as well as I" that "it would be better to go willingly than to be drafted."[13]

On the evening of August 22, the final deadline for enlistments, Paulson went to Chaska to bid farewell to his friends and found "excitement beyond description." Company H lacked fourteen men to fill the quota, but "no one seemed to be inclined to go." At least that many Scandinavians, mostly Norwegians, "sincere young men from the same congregation" as Paulson, proved "willing to go providing I would go along." They "argued" with him nearly until midnight when all enlistment ceased. Paulson steadfastly maintained he must return to the seminary, but "all my excuses were in vain." The men countered it was more important to "take up arms and save the country from defeat and ruin." Finally someone labeled Paulson a "slacker." His "blood commenced to boil," and he challenged them to join with him and enlist right there. "We are all ready," they replied. "Hip, hip hurrah!" Soon "fifteen of us raised our hands and swore we would be faithful to Uncle Sam unto death." After the excitement faded, Paulson agonized over forsaking his ministerial call but finally decided it was God's will. Baxter was later elected captain; Weinmann, first lieutenant; and Paulson, to his surprise, second lieutenant.[14]

The quota was met in Carver County and nearly everywhere else. "Farmers, mechanics, merchants, lawyers, priests and ministers, students young and old, had, at the stroke of the clock, taken the oath of allegiance to take up arms in defense of their beloved country," Paulson observed with pride years later. "This is no doubt a very outstanding incident in the history of war." Those who enlisted with him that day included younger brother John and their sister's husband, Bjørn ("Burn") Aslakson. Born in Rauland, Telemarken, Norway, in 1830, Aslakson had accompanied the Paulson family to the United States and settled in Carver County in 1855. "I need give no extended explanations for volunteering in the Union Army," he reminisced. "There were hundreds of thousands of others that did the same. My country was in dire need and called all loyal sons to its defense, and although I had a wife and family, I could not say no." Little if anything was said during the enlistment period of the need to end slavery. Rather, the goal was to preserve the Union and punish the Rebels.[15]

GARRISON DUTY

The Ninth Minnesota played only a limited role in the swift defeat of the Dakota in the U.S.–Dakota War. The only organized military force initially available was a battalion of the Fifth Minnesota and the raw Sixth Minnesota. Two companies of the Fifth were besieged in Fort Ridgely, while the third defended distant Fort Abercrombie on the western border. Colonel Henry Hastings Sibley, former fur trader, pioneer, and first governor of Minnesota, led the Sixth Minnesota and several hundred mounted civilian rangers to the relief of New Ulm and Fort Ridgely, whose successful defense had already discouraged the Indians. While marching against the Dakota reservations, Sibley won a decisive victory on September 23 at Wood Lake. Marching through the Indian villages along the Minnesota River, he negotiated for the release of 269 captives at Camp Release. Little Crow and many warriors fled northwest into Dakota Territory. Most of the Dakota who stayed in Minnesota were later removed, but the threat of raids persisted.[16]

Seven companies later assigned to the Ninth Minnesota were among those deployed to the frontier. West of the Minnesota River, evidence of the disaster could be seen everywhere in the deserted countryside. Particularly heartrending were the bodies of the slain men, women, and children found wherever the Dakota had struck. Company C, for one, buried more than forty settlers. Only three companies had any significant contact with hostile Indians. On September 3 Company B fought a terrifying skirmish against Little Crow on the prairie near Acton in Meeker County and lost three killed and twenty-three wounded (three mortally). Although taunted for their inglorious retreat, the men were in fact very lucky to survive their fight with fierce, more numerous adversaries. Company C joined Sibley's force immediately following the Battle of Wood Lake, while Company G helped relieve Fort Abercrombie far to the west.[17]

Minnesota met its full quota of volunteers, but all of the newly formed regiments had to stay to defend the frontier from the Dakota. It seemed therefore the state's modest contribution to the Union war effort might hardly be noticed. Charles Niedenhofen, second lieutenant of Company K, declared in a letter on September 28 that the North now wielded overwhelming strength. The South "will soon be conquered because it cannot maintain itself against such a power." If President Lincoln had only created an army that strong in 1861, he sighed, "the United States would already be at peace." The genial, thirty-year-old immigrant from the Prussian Rhineland, who was once an elite Jäger in the Prussian Army, owned a popular restaurant and candy shop in Winona. "It was very hard for me to separate from my dear wife and two little children and from my business," he explained. "But should I be fortunate enough to see my dear ones again I will be taken care of in my turn."[18]

Exiled for blunders in August in the Second Battle of Bull Run, Maj. Gen. John Pope took over the newly formed Department of the Northwest. Numerous posts, he explained to his superiors, "must be kept up all along the frontier this winter to induce the settlers to go back. They are already returning in large numbers." Pope established a string of garrisons between the upper Mississippi River and the Iowa border. The Ninth Minnesota took over those in the center, to the west of and along the Minnesota River. Four companies held Fort Ridgely, and the rest protected Hutchinson, Glencoe, St. Peter, Judson, South Bend, and distant Fort Abercrombie. Winter garrison duty proved tiresome if not particularly arduous. The rough and tumble life at Fort Ridgely strongly impressed young David F. M. Felch, a private in Company C. Born in 1844 in Racine, Wisconsin, and son of Mower County's first probate judge, the headstrong, idealistic youth had enlisted with his parents' grudging permission. His family fretted that he was "so young" and his "education was not finished," but Felch received schooling of another sort at Fort Ridgely. "There is some of the hardest boys at this place that I ever saw," he wrote home in November, and "more gambling card playing stealing swearing & getting in to the gard house than ever was to Fort Snelling."[19]

The Ninth Minnesota was most fortunate its colonel was a highly experienced combat veteran rather than a callow politician. Said to be the smallest colonel in the army, Alexander Wilkin measured a tad over five feet and weighed less than one hundred pounds. Born in 1819 in Goshen, New York, son of a prominent attorney, he studied law at Yale. During the Mexican War, he served as a captain in the Tenth U.S. Infantry but reached northern Mexico only after the great battles were over. Wilkin relocated to St. Paul in 1849 and two years later became territorial secretary. In 1853 he helped establish the St. Paul Fire and Marine Insurance Company. In 1855 during the Crimean War, Wilkin journeyed to Europe specifically to observe the siege of Sevastopol. A War Democrat and strong Unionist, in April 1861 he raised Company A ("Pioneer Guard") of the First Minnesota and fought at First Bull Run, where his bravery was recognized with a captain's commission in the regular army. In September 1861 he joined the Second Minnesota in the West as major and was at Mill Springs. Promoted lieutenant colonel in May 1862, Wilkin served on Brig. Gen. William T. Sherman's division staff at the siege of Corinth. His commission as colonel of the Ninth Minnesota was dated August 24, 1862, and he assumed command on November 26 at St. Peter.

A proud, fierce, determined, chivalrous fighter and tough disciplinarian, the diminutive Wilkin was definitely no one to trifle with. In January 1848 following a quarrel of long standing, he fought a duel in Mexico with another captain, Joshua W. Collett, who fell in the first exchange of shots. Shortly thereafter Wilkin resigned his commission. He felt "deep regret" at having to kill to defend his honor. A friend described him as "uniformly quiet and reflective; deliberate in coming to a conclusion; prompt earnest and daring in acting upon his judgment; without any showy [sic] and pretensions, and absolutely without personal fear."[20]

The new lieutenant colonel of the Ninth Minnesota, commissioned on November 20, was more typical of the newly minted officers. Josiah Fay Marsh had no military experience prior to August 1862, when he formed Company E of the Seventh Minnesota. He was the older brother of Capt. John S. Marsh of the Fifth Minnesota, killed in the U.S.–Dakota War, and that connection led to him becoming lieutenant colonel of the Ninth Minnesota. Born in 1825 in Whitby, Ontario, Canada, Marsh immigrated to Minnesota Territory in the mid-1850s. He was a lawyer and probate judge in Preston in Fillmore County. It is not known precisely how Wilkin and Marsh got along, but the enlisted men genuinely cared for Marsh, who possessed a much warmer personality than the austere and strict Wilkin. Private William Johnston Dean

Alexander Wilkin, ca. 1863

of Company I, a bright, handsome, nineteen-year-old farmer's son from Shakopee, first met Marsh on New Year's Day 1863 and wrote, "[We] cheered him and he made quite a speech to us," and he "seems like a fine man."[21]

William Markham, appointed major of the Ninth Minnesota on January 17, 1863, proved a cross between Wilkin and Marsh in that he was both experienced and approachable. Born in 1824 in New York, Markham left home with his younger brother in 1842 to become merchant seamen. In 1845, after rough voyages in Alaskan waters, they settled in California. During the Mexican War, the brothers enlisted in the U.S. Navy. Just prior to the California gold rush, Markham returned east to Oshkosh, Wisconsin, then in 1858 moved to Rochester to work as a master mason and builder. In 1861 he became captain of Company B, Second Minnesota, and greatly distinguished himself in January 1862 at Mill Springs, where he was wounded by buckshot in the left knee. In February 1862 while on medical leave, he learned of his dismissal from the army because of an adverse report by an examining board. Markham furiously sought reinstatement. Colonel Robert McCook, a former board member, soon apologized. Even before Mill Springs, McCook explained to Markham, he had become "satisfied that the board had made a great mistake," while "after the battle in which you behaved so nobly I felt

Josiah Fay Marsh, ca. 1865

that a great injustice had been done to you." With War Department concurrence, Governor Ramsey reappointed Markham a captain in the Second Minnesota, but its colonel refused to accept him until Ramsey again intervened. In June Markham was charged with being drunk on duty but was never tried. In July 1862 to Company B's great distress, he resigned his commission. A "very intelligent man," Markham "displayed great originality of character and a rare degree of companionability," according to an unsigned obituary. Throughout the war he wrote wonderful letters under the pseudonym "High Private" to the *Rochester City Post*. Private Dean warmed to Markham on first acquaintance. "He is a fine fellow, very common among the boys."[22]

That winter Colonel Wilkin and four companies (D, E, H, and K) took part in the largest legal mass execution in American history. A military commission had sentenced 303 Dakota warriors to be hanged for allegedly committing atrocities during the war. Feeling among whites ran so high that the authorities feared a massacre of all the Indians in confinement and deployed troops, including Company K, to protect them. After personally reviewing the sentences, Lincoln reduced the number of condemned to thirty-nine, one of whom was soon pardoned. His leniency toward the Dakota rankled most Minnesotans. Private James M. Woodbury, a twenty-three-year-old, recently married native of Maine, had enlisted in Company C with some reluctance. After the Dakota War he had no desire whatever to go south and hewed to

William Markham, ca. 1863

those Peace Democrats who deplored Lincoln's war. On December 15 he wrote home angrily denouncing Lincoln's clemency for the Indians and criticizing the Republicans. "I think the North is more to blame than the South and I hope that the South will maintain their rights." He took heart from the November congressional elections. "I am very glad to hear that the Democrats have done so well. I wish their triumph had been still greater. I hope that next year it will be complete all over the United States and that the Union may again [be] restored to peace and harmony." Woodbury claimed some of his comrades also "hope the administration would sink if it would not defend the frontier and if they were down South they would fight against the North. If ever Lincoln should run for President again they would not vote for him as they did before." Discontent certainly existed in the Ninth Minnesota over Lincoln's sparing most of the Indians, but there is no evidence of such antiwar, pro-Southern sentiment Woodbury describes.[23]

The hangings took place on the morning of December 26 at Mankato in temperate weather under blue skies. The huge gallows, made of "heavy, square timbers" that resembled "the framework for a barn," could execute all thirty-eight prisoners simultaneously. Over 1,400 soldiers kept order in the midst of a huge throng of enraged spectators. While drums were beating, Wilkin formed 360 men from the Sixth Minnesota and Ninth Minnesota in line of battle between the front of the scaffold and the river. Other infantry units completed the square, and a line of cavalry moved in between the execution site and onlookers. "Singing a death song," the condemned Dakota ascended the platform. Hangmen adjusted nooses and lowered hoods to conceal the condemned men's faces. "When all were ready," the signal officer "beat three distinct taps upon the drum." At the third stroke "with a crash down came the drop," recalled Lieutenant Paulson, and "our little commander's voice rang 'Attention! Battalion! About face!'" The infantrymen beheld at close range "the spectacle of thirty-eight redskins dangling in mid air in the contortions of the death struggle." To Paulson "the sight of so many poor heathens thrown into eternity sent a black wave before my eyes. Some of them kicked and squirmed for a few seconds, then it was as still as death. After a little while the 'hurrahs' broke out until they re-echoed over the hills." Once the bodies were removed, the troops were dismissed. "Thus our mission was ended and retribution completed." The crowd quietly dispersed, and "few who witnessed the awful scene," observed one reporter, "will voluntarily look upon its like again."[24]

Although the Ninth Minnesota was widely separated and likely so to remain at least until spring, Wilkin was determined to see that it was well drilled. At St. Peter, under his watchful eye, he established a regimental military school where officers and noncommissioned officers learned proper drill and military lore. The classic 1891 novel *The Captain of Company K* admirably summarized the complicated training regime of the Civil War armies:

> Handling the musket and bayonet, marching, wheeling, facing, ploying, deploying, loading, firing, charging, halting, dressing, skirmishing, saluting, parading, for days and weeks (not to say years); all for the single purpose of bringing men into a double line, shoulder to shoulder, facing the foe; knowing enough (and not too much) to load and fire until they fall in their tracks or the other fellows run away.

"Drill your men carefully in squads and in Company when you can," Wilkin directed one of his captains. "Pay great attention to skirmishing as that will be very important in fighting Indians." He devised an extensive regimen of marksmanship training far beyond the usual in other regiments. After practice in "loading and firing, kneeling & lying down," there followed "target firing, under the superintendence of an officer." The initial range of 150 yards was to be increased gradually to 400 yards. "The target should always be placed in such a position that it will be necessary to aim low— never higher than the belly." In the spring the men received proper arms, U.S. Springfield Model 1861 Rifle-Muskets. "We drill considerable now," William Dean wrote home from Fort Ridgely in March 1863. "We drill three hours out of doors every fine day and about 20 minutes in the quarters. The Major drills us in battalion drill every afternoon." Company D at St. Peter, Lorin Cray would recall, was "diligently and persistently drilled in military maneuvers throughout the entire winter, and became quite proficient." In this way the Ninth Minnesota ultimately fielded some of the best-trained soldiers in the state.[25]

In the spring and summer of 1863, while Maj. Gen. Ulysses S. Grant took Vicksburg and the Army of the Potomac lost the Battle of Chancellorsville but finally beat Lee at Gettysburg (where the First Minnesota's very desperate, very bloody charge helped preserve the Union line), all but two companies of the Ninth Minnesota remained on garrison duty in Minnesota. "Our duties the entire summer," according to Cray, "were very light for soldier life, and we had ample time to devote to pleasure and amusement." Hunting and fishing were particularly good. With families and friends not too distant, the soldiers received a plentiful flow of letters and visitors. Private Jacob Dieter of Company F, a thirty-seven-year-old former Pennsylvanian, enjoyed a pleasant summer with his family at Fort Ridgely, where his wife, Martha, took temporary employment as a laundress and cooked pies for hungry soldiers. Their daughter Martha, then five, treasured the time she shared with her father out on the prairie. He "always played on his fife for us." Many years later she recalled "the tears we shed" when it was time for the family to return home to Olmsted County.[26]

Joining Brigadier General Sibley's expedition to Dakota Territory, Companies A and H experienced a very different summer from the rest of the Ninth Minnesota. On the march the massive expedition resembled one of the wandering tribes of Israel. The "sun burned without mercy," Ole Paulson remembered. The infantry, complained Pehr Carlson, trudged twenty miles a day across the baked, arid prairie on "2 or 3 pieces of hardtack & a piece of raw meat & a bottle of 'swamp water.'" It was too hot even to celebrate the Fourth of July. It was also excellent training for the real war to come. South of Devils Lake, in the midst of "dusty prairies, alkaline lakes, locusts, heat," Sibley turned the column west toward the Missouri River. At Big Mound on July 24 and again at Stony Lake four days later, the cavalry skirmished with more than a thousand Dakota who were too wary of the infantry's firepower to draw close to the main body. Satisfied that he had badly harmed the Dakota, Sibley retired southeast to Fort Abercrombie, where Company H peeled off to join Company G in the garrison. Company A remained with the main column, which reached Fort Snelling on September 13 after a march of a thousand miles. To their surprise the men received a furlough before leaving to fight the Rebels.[27]

ORDERED SOUTH

For the men of the Ninth Minnesota on the remote frontier, Antietam, Fredericksburg, Vicksburg, and Gettysburg were only names in the newspapers. It was sometimes hard to believe a bloody civil war was being waged somewhere "down South." In May 1863 Pvt. Milton A. Stubbs of Company B received a telling lesson of just what the Rebellion was all about. Part of the vast wagon train forming up for Sibley's Dakota Expedition passed through St. Peter on its way to Camp Pope. To Stubbs's surprise "a great many of the drivers were persons of color," freed slaves whom Sibley had summoned from St. Louis to St. Paul. "It was funny to hear them run on each other," Stubbs wrote home. "They seem to be very intelligent. I got to talking with one little fellow who could tell some very interesting stories." He related to Stubbs that he was previously a slave of Confederate Gen. Gideon J. Pillow but had been "confiscated" the year before. Stubbs "asked him a great many questions, among the rest if the slaves wanted to be free." Some ex-slaves did not know how to handle freedom, the teamster replied, but "I always knowed better!" When he and his fellow slaves heard artillery fire booming at Fort Donelson, which Grant captured in February 1862, one "by the name of Mose hollered 'Hurrah for Uncle Abe.'" All the former slaves whom the teamster knew "seem to be highly pleased with their freedom." Another connection with the fighting down South was the solemn duty that Company I undertook in August while provost guard at St. Paul. The company often served as honor guard for the funerals of officers killed in battle and returned home for burial.[28]

By early September fate, it seemed, conspired to keep the Ninth Minnesota at home. Languishing at St. Peter, Wilkin despaired over the prospects of going south. "I have now been here for nearly a year and am likely to be for a long time to come," he complained to Brig. Gen. Horatio Van Cleve, his old colonel in the Second Minnesota. His regiment was "so scattered" that he had not yet seen all of the companies. Wilkin feared other regiments would go off to fight in place of the Ninth. He wished he could join Van Cleve in Tennessee. "I have an excellent Regiment, in which I would place perfect confidence under any circumstances."[29]

Writing home on September 7, Pvt. John Felix Aiton, a forty-six-year-old Scottish immigrant with Company D, agreed with his colonel that the "signs are against the 9th going South," but he personally was glad of it. "We prefer staying in Minn." A Presbyterian missionary to the Dakota and later a teacher and farmer in Nicollet County, Aiton strongly opposed slavery and had expected to be sent south to fight. The idyllic summer of 1863, however, temporarily sapped even his firm ideological commitment to the war. He was far from alone in his reluctance to leave Minnesota. When Company D departed Fairmont, recalled a wistful Lorin Cray, "we paused and looked back . . . at the beautiful landscape, and our pleasant camping ground, and I, for one allowed a deep sigh of keen regret to escape me, as I realized that the pleasant part of my soldier life had forever ended."[30]

Wilkin got his wish in September when he received orders to leave "without delay" for St. Louis. Ordered to send several regiments there, General Pope chose the Seventh, Ninth, and Tenth to fill the quota. "Will require some days," he advised his superiors on September 16, "as only parts of two regiments have yet reached Snelling. Another regiment will be sent by October 1." The troops were to receive additional directions in St. Louis. Pope expected they would be sent to eastern Tennessee, "a healthy country," to join Maj. Gen. William S. Rosecrans's Army of the Cumberland, which included the Second Minnesota. That scenario seemed certain after September 20 when Rosecrans suffered disastrous defeat at Chickamauga in northern Georgia. For his part, Wilkin would have liked nothing better than to fight alongside

Maj. Gen. George H. Thomas, his old commander at Mill Springs, now besieged with Rosecrans's army in Chattanooga.[31]

On September 23 the Ninth Minnesota (less Companies G and H still at Fort Abercrombie) received furloughs prior to going south. Headquarters and Companies A, B, D, E, and I were to reassemble at Fort Snelling, and Companies C, F, and K at Winona. The men greatly enjoyed their visits home, being regaled with banquets and other demonstrations of patriotic fervor. "Our dear brave soldiers, tired of Indian hunting and fort defending, were very much pleased with the idea of going South," explained the *Mower County Register,* "and were much more pleased when they learned that, in all probability, they were to be sent to the Army of Rosecrans."[32]

In turn John Arnold, a private in Company C who was also an ordained minister, articulated to the hometown newspaper what it meant finally to be going off to fight the Rebels:

> Some of us, no doubt, have left Mower county never to return, and it will be a matter of comfort to their friends at home to know that they have done all they could for their temporal and spiritual welfare. We have some noble wives left behind to manage, and to bring up our children, and bear the burden of

Company C, Ninth Minnesota, October 1863

husband as well as wife. To them we would say, keep up good courage, ask God to help you in the midst of your complicated trials and hardships. You are doing much to crush the rebellion at home, while your husbands are fighting it abroad, and at the same time, we are sure of your prayers of frequent letters. We remember, with tender feelings, when we separated, the quivering lip, the little tear, the parting embrace, the kiss we gave and received from the children; and well do we remember your exhortation for us to be steady, and to write often. We remember also the gray-haired sires and mothers, who, at the parting, received our promise that we would abstain from all bad habits.

Cease not to remember us in your prayers, and write to your sons at least once every week. Sisters and other relatives, we ask you to give your best wishes and advice, if you do not wish us to give way to the many temptations with which we are surrounded.

And, finally, we hope, as a Company, if called into action upon the field of carnage, which we probably will, that we shall not bring a stain upon our Country, State or County.

The good reverend, himself a husband and father, could scarcely have dreamt that barely a month after departing Minnesota, he and thirty-seven comrades would be under arrest, charged with mutiny and other crimes potentially punishable by death.[33]

CHAPTER TWO

In the Land of Secesh

DOWN TO DIXIE

After more than a year guarding the frontier from the Dakota, the Ninth Minnesota finally headed south to the "real war" against the Rebels. On October 8, 1863, after tearful goodbyes on the St. Paul levee, Colonel Wilkin with regimental headquarters and Companies A, B, D, E, and I of the Ninth Minnesota trooped on board the small steamboat *Chippewa Falls*. "Cheer after cheer" resounded when the vessel and two towed barges started down the Mississippi River bearing their cargoes of "living freight, another sacrifice to the bloody Moloch of Rebellion." An eloquent reminder of that fearsome toll appeared many years later in the recollections of Lorin Cray. Perched comfortably on the hurricane deck of the *Chippewa Falls,* Cray and seven good friends from Company D, "healthy, cheerful, light-hearted soldier boys" from the beautiful Blue Earth River valley, enjoyed the grand view beyond Red Wing where the Mississippi widened dramatically to form Lake Pepin. They speculated who among them would ever see home again. Of the group, only Cray survived the war and that with severe wounds. Five of his friends died in Confederate prisons and two in Union hospitals. The next day, after another emotional parting at Winona, Companies C, F, and K clambered on board the barges.[1]

Wilkin was to report first to St. Louis for orders. Ordinarily the Union Army shifted troops by rail, but aside from an experimental line that linked St. Paul and St. Anthony, the iron horse had not yet galloped as far as Minnesota. The nearest railhead was forty miles southeast of Winona, at La Crosse, Wisconsin, where on the evening of October 9 the Ninth Minnesota disembarked. No direct line existed to St. Louis, so the Ninth Minnesota zigzagged southeast to Chicago, then cut diagonally southwest across Illinois to the Mississippi River opposite St. Louis. "Being told that probably we would not be able to get away from there [La Crosse] before Sunday or Monday following," recounted Lt. Ozora P. Stearns of Company F, "we pitched our tents and prepared to make ourselves comfortable. Just as we were retiring to rest, the long roll sounded in our ears. Farewell to the muskrat feathers we had gathered for beds; in ten minutes, our tents were struck and everything on our part ready for a start, but somehow though we were kept up all night, we did not get under way till 4 o'clock, Saturday morning."[2]

Crowded on a Chicago & North Western Railroad train, many Minnesotans experienced their first trip on the rails. An early autumn excursion through rural Wisconsin ("pretty rough" according to Pvt. William Dean, but "still the most best and civilized country") should have been pleasant, but the weather was dreary. After only one stop with hot coffee at Janesville, the weary Minnesotans rolled into Chicago early Sunday morning. While the officers breakfasted at the Briggs House, five hundred soldiers huddled around a cook wagon outside the depot for "a plentiful supply of coffee with the usual etceteras." By 10 A.M. the men began the final leg across the flat, unrelenting landscape of the Sucker State (as Illinois was known in the nineteenth century) and finally reached Alton on the Mississippi about dawn on Monday, the twelfth. "Our trip was a tiresome one," for "the boat and cars upon which we came were crowded," one officer complained, "and the facilities for sleep exceedingly limited." Yet to Pvt. David Felch it was a "splendid ride," and Pvt. John Aiton thought "on the whole we have had a fine trip." Both he and Rev. John Arnold took great comfort that "while on the river, on the cars, and during the whole distance from Winona here, we were cheered by inhabitants with flags and handkerchiefs."[3]

Ferried back across the Father of Waters, the Ninth Minnesota trudged to Benton Barracks, at the huge fairgrounds four miles north of St. Louis. The impressive complex completely dwarfed Fort Snelling. Erected in 1861 to help keep Missouri in the Union, Benton Barracks featured living quarters, drill fields, warehouses, and hospitals capable of handling nearly 30,000 men at one time—impressive considering that Minnesota was said to have raised 24,020 men during the entire Civil War. Set in long rows, the commodious one-story barrack buildings, made of rough boards whitewashed inside and out, proved remarkably congenial for soldiers who "sought repose with eagerness." Many Minnesotans were so tired they skipped the evening meal, always a mistake in the army. That evening the Tenth Minnesota joined the Ninth at Benton Barracks. In town since the previous day, the Seventh Minnesota found less providential quarters in the city proper at the "close, damp and dirty" Schofield Barracks, christened after Maj. Gen. John M. Schofield, who led the Department of the Missouri.[4]

At Schofield's headquarters Wilkin learned to his vast dismay that the Ninth Minnesota would not be going any farther south. Having impatiently awaited his three Minnesota regiments for several weeks, Schofield would not willingly part with them. The Federal military situation in Missouri, never for the faint of heart even at the best of times, was at the time in some turmoil. Guerrilla depredations sharply increased that summer, culminating on August 21 with William C. Quantrill's destruction of abolitionist Lawrence, Kansas. Union troops in western Missouri then enforced the infamous General Order No. 11 that evicted civilians in three border counties who lived more than a mile from military posts, while Kansas radicals threatened dire retribution. Such draconian measures only exacerbated the bitterness.[5]

Thereafter the situation in Missouri really soured. In early October six hundred Confederate cavalry from Col. Joseph O. Shelby's "Iron Brigade" burst out of Arkansas to raid and recruit in central Missouri. Reinforced by six hundred Missouri Confederates, the Rebel horsemen cut the railroad to Sedalia in western Missouri and threatened to cross the Missouri River near Boonville and raise havoc in the northern half of the state. Schofield rushed what troops he could spare from St. Louis to contain and destroy the raiders. Brigadier General James Totten, his chief of staff, hastened to Jefferson City, the state capital 125 miles to the west, to coordinate the effort. As the crisis deepened, Totten repeatedly beseeched Schofield: "Have your troops arrived from Pope? Can you send me a regiment?" On October 12 Schofield offered him one of the newly arrived Minnesota regiments "if you need it or can make good use of it." Totten telegraphed back that evening: "The troops I have with me are unreliable. If you possibly can, send me a good regiment."[6]

Schofield chose the Ninth Minnesota. Wilkin hastened to Benton Barracks after midnight on October 13 to muster his sleeping troops and deliver them to the railroad station before dawn. Roused by "our fierce commander," the men learned the "exciting news that Rebel guerillas had taken, or were about to take, Jefferson City." Wilkin called the new assignment a "compliment to the Regiment." John Arnold concurred, especially as there was "a fair prospect for a fight in view; and, to tell the truth, we felt very much like it." Cold, damp weather plagued the predawn march to the depot. "The mud was worse in the streets of St. Louis than I ever saw it in Minn," complained James Woodbury, who truly did not want to be there. It was not the last time he would unfavorably compare conditions in Missouri to those at home. Soon 550 shivering Minnesotans, huddled in the open flat cars of the optimistically named Pacific Railroad, were "whirling at a rapid rate" west toward the "semi-rebel" town of Jefferson City. Somber skies revealed to the jaundiced eye of one Minnesotan "a rough, hilly and uninviting section of country" that was the epitome of hardscrabble. The "few villages through which we passed indicated that the spirit of enterprise was wanting in the people," while "the few farms, or patches of ground . . . testified only to the inherent shiftlessness of those who occupied and pretended to cultivate them." Aiton more charitably called it "a very interesting, rough country."[7]

Reaching Jefferson City on the "awful muddy" Missouri River the same evening, the Ninth Minnesota, eager for battle, found everything disappointingly tranquil. That day 1,800 Missouri state militia led by Brig. Gen. Egbert B. Brown had fought Shelby's raiders at Marshall, sixty miles to the northwest. According to Shelby, Brown "came up like a black cloud from Jefferson City, where he had been hurriedly concentrating, expecting us to attack him there under the shadow of [Governor Hamilton R.] Gamble's usurped dynasty and was thundering in my rear with disappointed hate and malice." After a sharp but surprisingly bloodless engagement, Shelby's outnumbered force scattered and hightailed it south. He claimed vast amounts of damage and boasted the diversion of ten thousand Union troops that he supposedly prevented from aiding Chattanooga.[8]

Jefferson City was safe, although the Rebels burned one vital railroad bridge forty-five miles to the west. Lacking tents and other baggage, the Ninth Minnesota dispersed among three vacant churches. Felch described sleeping that night "in an old sesesh meeting house." It dawned on the men that they had finally caught up to the War of the Rebellion. The Ninth Minnesota viewed Missouri's capital with the deepest suspicion. "We are in the land of secesh," Aiton wrote home, although Jefferson City was in fact one of Missouri's staunchest Unionist communities. Most of the Minnesotans would have gladly agreed with Rebel Colonel Shelby, who told his superiors he "found the people of Missouri, as a mass, true to the South and her institutions, yet needing the strong presence of a Confederate army to make them volunteer." Shelby's assessment proved wishful thinking because he garnered only a few recruits. Nonetheless, the Minnesotans strongly distrusted any population, even ostensibly loyal, that tolerated slavery. "There are a good many union people here, (I think a majority)," Capt. Jerome Dane of Company E opined on October 19, "but it is a little dangerous to avow secesh principles, and that makes it hard to tell what the masses would be if they dare." In Company B, Sgt. George W. Herrick, a twenty-five-year-old farmer from Hennepin County, fully concurred, commenting on October 22 that "here [the Missourians] keep very quiet at present. Well they may for our regiment destroyed the property of one man . . . for disloyalty."[9]

SETTLING IN

When their wedge tents (for four or five men) arrived in the regimental baggage train, the Ninth Minnesota set up camp on a commanding hill a mile south of the impressive Missouri State Capitol. "No doubt we shall remain through the winter, or till some unlooked for emergency occurs," observed Surgeon Reginald H. Bingham. "We shall probably have to content ourselves with hunting bushwhackers for a time," wrote Lieutenant Stearns, "a business for which hunting Indians has eminently fitted us." Sergeant Herrick related how "our men have concluded not to wish for any further change while they are in the service for they think they have been getting into a worse place every time they move. We have been told by soldiers that have been in different parts of this state that there are places where mud is more plenty and everything else more disagreeable." Those were sensible sentiments for a soldier.[10]

After a pleasant evening "as warm as an August night in Min," the Ninth Minnesota awoke on October 22 surprised to find the ground covered in white. By early afternoon snow accumulated over three inches with no sign of a letup. "Our little tents [have] no fire in them," Aiton noted. It snowed "pretty heavy" all day while he cooked for his company in the open air. This was not the "sunny South," where "autumn would glide pleasantly into the lap of the winter season." Instead, sighed another soldier, "in this, as in many other respects we were subject to disappointment." Lieutenant Clark Keysor of Company E recalled "considerable suffering and a severe strain on the English language." The men stripped a burnt building of bricks to build fireplaces in their tents. They spread rubber blankets as groundsheets and snuggled under cloth blankets and overcoats. Such rude quarters proved "pretty comfortable," judged William Dean, yet some griped they "have suffered with cold more here, than through a whole winter in Minnesota." Alternating days of rain and snow turned roads and campsites into quagmires. "Mud is worst for us, it dirties bed & clothing," Dean explained. "The weather here has been very changeable since we came here," Surgeon Bingham observed on the first of November. "We have had two pretty severe snow storms, and in fact every gradation from summer heat to winter cold." Nonetheless, the general health was "very good," most complaints being for "catarrh of throat and lungs."[11]

Wilkin christened his bivouac "Camp Brown" after General Brown, grizzled victor of the Battle of Marshall who led the District of Central Missouri. Wilkin was in a good mood. "Our Regiment is looked upon here as something wonderful," he bragged to his father on October 30, better trained "at a similar period" than either the First or Second Minnesota. "I am not afraid to go into any action with it now and feel that I can rely upon it to the last man." The men drilled "whenever the weather will permit," with schools of instruction every evening. Wilkin resolved to make the Ninth Minnesota "the crack regiment of the state." No other unit he had yet seen "can equal it in target shooting—this is generally neglected, but I have paid a good deal of attention to it." His confidence resonated with his men. The colonel "has showed himself more of a man than I thought he would," Herrick explained on November 3 to his brother. "He is just as civil to the men in the ranks as he is to officers. He wants things to go on pretty nearly right. He seems to feel quite proud of his regiment, has told some of the officers . . . this regiment are the best body of men he was ever with." The "boys think considerable of the colonel," mused Dean, while young Felch simply commented, "Our Colonel is on his taps [even] if he is a little brat."[12]

The report of Capt. Levi Pritchard, Inspector of the District of Central Missouri, reflected Wilkin's boast that the Missouri authorities "never saw any to be compared to [the Ninth Minnesota]":

This is a most excellent regiment, the field, staff and company officers are, I think, with scarcely an exception, a most efficient set of officers. Col. Wilkin is deserving of high praise for the unremitting vigilance he has exerted to make his command efficient. To give a general idea of the quality of this regiment, in a very few words, it is only necessary to say, their camp is their home, and they try to make it what it should be. I am informed by [Missouri State Militia] Col. [John] Pound, Commanding the Post, that no complaints are made against them by the citizens—a circumstance so unusual as to deserve mention.

The soldierly bearing and "gentlemanly behavior" of the Ninth Minnesota impressed Pritchard and others, in contrast with that of troops from other states, Missouri not excepted. Three weeks later different members of the Ninth Minnesota would make another kind of impression on Pritchard.[13]

Echoing soldiers from time immemorial, the Minnesotans readily found fault with their strange new surroundings. Of Jefferson City Dane wrote, "I think all agree that it is a rough place." To Aiton it was "a straggling city on several ridges." Private Frank M. Harrington of Company B bemoaned the bare clay hillsides. "If this is a specimen of Missouri deliver me from ever having to live here." Another Minnesotan, using the nom de plume "Now and Then," informed the *Mankato Union* the topography of Jefferson City, situated along bluffs bordering the south bank of the "sluggish" Missouri River, "is very rough and uneven," with as many hills as buildings. A network of "deep gulches" from "numerous narrow and deep water courses" crisscrossed the whole area, leaving the streets "generally in a very bad condition." Another correspondent deplored the lack of more than "twenty rods of respectable sidewalk" and, more importantly, the absence of public school buildings, though "in this respect she is not unlike some of her more pretentious Northern cities." Unfortunately, "inertia seems to have settled upon the people in their industrial pursuits," while "labor is considered degrading *i.e.*, labor that negroes have been accustomed to perform." After a corporal of the Missouri State Militia with whom he was on guard could not write the name of his relief, Dean noticed the paucity of "common schools." Herrick unfavorably compared the inhabitants of Jefferson City ("not a very promising looking place") to the "energetic go ahead and enterprising people that live in New England and Minnesota." Of course, he himself was from Vermont and now resided in Minnesota.[14]

The denizens of "Jeff City" appeared not to have been perturbed, or even aware, that the haughty newcomers cared little for their municipality and state. They saw the Minnesotans as just another bunch of bluecoats and poked some holes in the condescending attitude of the new garrison. Herrick was amused to learn the Missourians were "not very well acquainted with the geographical position of Minnesota." One woman "enquired of one of our guards if Minnesota was as large as Jefferson City," while others wondered "if Minnesota was in Iowa or Wisconsin." Shelby did take notice of the Minnesota troops by including them in the horde he said his raiders battled, beat back, and "eluded altogether" while escaping to Arkansas.[15]

On October 30 the Ninth Minnesota mustered for the solemn duty of hanging a Rebel bushwhacker, John S. Nichols, age twenty-two. Though lacking the horrific scale of the execution of the thirty-eight Dakota at Mankato, the event nevertheless afforded a "scene of the most imposing character." Nichols was apprehended in May for the mutilation murders of four loyal Union men during a recruiting stint gone wrong. Trial testimony described him as a "very bad man" even prior to the war, while during the conflict he emerged as the "terror" of Pettis County, west of Jefferson City. Said to have boasted of killing "many Union men," he was also accused of murdering at least one black man and raping an eighteen-year-old slave woman. President Lincoln personally approved the death sentence. On the morning of his execution, Nichols spoke at length with Chaplain Aaron Kerr of the Ninth Minnesota, who wrote out a confession that Nichols signed. Claiming occasional service in the pro-slavery Missouri State Guard, Nichols steadfastly denied being a guerrilla and committing murders and mutilations, except for killing a black man who was "piloting some men in search of me." Grimly serenaded by two bands alternately playing the "Death March," Nichols rode in a wagon while "clothed in his shroud and sitting on his coffin." To Bingham the condemned man's demeanor "gave but feeble indications of a proper appreciation of the terrible fate that so soon awaited him." After bidding farewell to his sister, "a beautiful young lady of perhaps eighteen" according to one attentive Minnesota admirer, the prisoner took his place on the gallows "with a firm step and erect position." Following a short prayer by a priest and after shaking hands with the hangmen, Nichols adjusted his own noose and spoke his defiant valedictory to the small crowd of spectators: "See how a Confederate soldier can die!" After a hood was put over his face, Nichols was "launched into eternity." Even Wilkin conceded "he died game."[16]

John Nichols shortly before his execution on October 30, 1863

Chaplain Aaron Kerr, ca. 1863

Despite his protestations Nichols truly was a bushwhacker, though merely a minor freelancer with one accomplice. Certainly, pro-Southern guerrillas (known as Partisan Rangers) represented the toughest foe for Union forces in Missouri. Their continued presence demonstrated just how near to secession Missouri came in 1861. Henry Clay Bruce, who spent most of the war as a slave in Chariton County on the Missouri River northwest of Jefferson City, contrasted such desperadoes with Confederate men "who were willing to shoot and be shot at in the open field of battle." Once the war began, "the regular confederate troops raised in that and adjoining counties went South as fast as recruited, so that only bushwhackers remained, and they were a source of annoyance to Union men and Union troops." The Ninth Minnesota had yet to fight bushwhackers but knew of their atrocities in Missouri and at Lawrence. A few days before Nichols was executed, some of the soldiers spoke with families of Missouri Union men forced to flee their homes "on account of secesh trouble." It is hardly surprising, then, that the dead guerrilla elicited little sympathy. "The country is full of just such scoundrels as he," Bingham declared, "and they are as great a terror to the quiet and peaceably disposed citizens of the State as are the [Dakota] to those in Minnesota." Guerrillas deserved "the same treatment," including "a reward of two hundred dollars for their scalps." Aiton forbore to compare Indians and guerrillas, but as for the late John Nichols, he declared, "so perish all the enemies of our Government."[17]

SERIOUS POLITICS

If the guerrilla war in Missouri was uniquely fierce, so too, the Minnesotans soon discovered, were its politics. Standard party affiliations no longer applied. Elsewhere in the North, the Democratic Party comprised War Democrats and a strong peace faction, derisively known as "Copperheads," who opposed emancipation and fervently desired accommodation with the South. That party did not exist as such in Missouri politics at that time, nor was there a distinct Republican Party on the national model. By the fall of 1863, Missouri was run by Unionists who agreed in principle to end slavery, but, split as Conservatives and Radicals, they strongly differed on the means and timing. A pro-slavery, pro-Union faction wielded little power. "People in Missouri, in 1863, took their politics seriously, and all the more were they in earnest on the emancipation question."[18]

The Emancipation Proclamation of January 1, 1863, had specifically excluded slaves held in the Border States of Missouri, Kentucky, Maryland, and Delaware, as well as in Tennessee and certain other regions occupied by Union troops. Keeping the Border States firmly in the Union was absolutely essential to victory. Lincoln was famously said to have quipped that he "wanted to have God on his side, but he *must* have Kentucky." He might have said the same about Missouri. The Confederacy was already strong enough without adding any more enemies of the United States. Lincoln justified the freeing of the slaves in Rebel hands as a military necessity to help win the war, but he believed he lacked the power under the Constitution to emancipate slaves in the states that remained in the Union. Either those states themselves addressed that issue, or the Constitution must be amended.[19]

Led by Governor Gamble, the Conservatives understood that Missouri's Provisional Government walked a tightrope. The potential for chaos existed at all times. He preached moderation so as not to inflame the tense situation. "His policies kept many loyal to the Union who might otherwise have gone over permanently to the Confederacy or at least refused to cooperate with the Northern war effort," writes Missouri historian William E. Parrish. "Many of those who had fought for the South early in the war returned to their original allegiance, as it became obvious Federal authorities would not dictate state policy." Understanding that freedom for Missouri's slaves was inevitable, the Conservatives, many of whom owned slaves, resolved on gradual emancipation that preserved the legal rights of masters who remained loyal to the Union. In a state convention in June 1863, the Conservatives succeeded in passing an ordinance calling for uncompensated emancipation in 1870 coupled with an additional period of servitude that would depend on the ex-slave's age.[20]

Gamble relied on the close cooperation of General Schofield, the top Federal military leader in Missouri. Self-described as an "anti-slavery man, though not an abolitionist, before the war," Schofield averred that he had advocated the "speedy emancipation of slaves" as "one of the necessary consequences of the rebellion, or rather as one of the means absolutely necessary to a complete restoration of the Union." That view reflected a growing sentiment within the Union army. Like the Conservatives, Schofield desired emancipation be accomplished in a legal fashion. "The loyal slave-owner demands that his rights *under the law* [Schofield's emphasis] be protected." Lincoln completely concurred, having long sought gradual emancipation with compensation to the masters, but the Border States would not agree. Thus, the president judged it necessary to "protect rights of slave-holders in the short time slavery is permitted to exist," meaning the Federal occupation forces in Missouri must not "be used in subverting the temporarily reserved legal rights in slaves during the progress of emancipation."[21]

In stark contrast, the Unconditional Unionist Radicals insisted on the immediate end to slavery in Missouri. Centered in St. Louis and within the

German immigrant communities along the Missouri River, they had long fought the good fight for emancipation and rallied to prevent Missouri's secession. In August 1861 they vigorously cheered Maj. Gen. John C. Frémont's military order that freed slaves in Missouri who belonged to Rebel masters. "So long as General Frémont is in command of this department," wrote one of his admirers, "no person, white or black, will be taken out of our lines into slavery." Understandably, then, in November 1861 the Radicals vehemently protested when Lincoln repudiated the emancipation order and fired Frémont. Only in July 1862 did Congress pass the Second Confiscation Act that finally liberated the slaves of disloyal masters. The Radicals deplored that the Emancipation Proclamation extended only to slaves in areas under Rebel authority and that Gamble's provisional government failed to act decisively against slavery. In righteous certitude that only they represented true justice, the Missouri Radicals no longer tolerated even Conservative Unionist brethren, whom they now saw as standing in the way of freedom for all. In their eyes the Conservatives were no better than Copperheads. Their rage, according to the biographer of one Radical, stemmed from "the trial and suffering" they had endured. "In no other State were the unconditional Union men wrought up to a higher pitch of bitterness against the lukewarm adherents of their cause; and in none was more dissatisfaction felt and expressed with what was thought to be the too cautious and conservative policy of President Lincoln." In September 1863 the Radical Union Emancipation Convention held in Jefferson City demanded full and immediate freedom for all slaves, Gamble's resignation, Schofield's removal, and Missouri State Militia reform. The convention chose a delegation, the Committee of Seventy led by Charles D. Drake, to present their case directly to the president.[22]

Infuriated by the Radical press and aware of disaffection within much of the state militia, Schofield appealed to Washington for permission to declare martial law and suppress seditious newspapers. On September 26 Maj. Gen. Henry W. Halleck, the general in chief, relayed Lincoln's approval but counseled caution. "Neither faction in Missouri is really friendly to the President and administration, but each one is striving to destroy the other, regardless of all other considerations. In their mutual hatred they seem to have lost all sense of the perils of the country and all sentiments of national patriotism." Lincoln himself permitted Schofield to use the military "as far as practicable, to compel the excited people there to leave one another alone." On October 1 Schofield asserted that "secession is dead in Missouri," and "as a party the secessionists are utterly without influence." Even so, "the degree of support which they will hereafter give to the government will depend upon its policy." Should the Radicals "triumph, the enemies of the government will be increased both in numbers and bitterness." Instead, if "a wise and just policy be pursued, every respectable man in the State will soon be an active supporter of the government, and Missouri will be the most loyal State in the Union."[23]

In the meantime, on the last day of September, Drake's Committee of Seventy and a like-minded group of Kansans under fiery abolitionist Senator James H. Lane descended on the White House "to get their right as they viewed it." That "ill combed, black broadcloth, dusty, longhaired and generally vulgar assemblage of earnest men," teased presidential secretary John Hay, fiercely denounced Missouri's Conservative Unionists and insisted that Schofield be replaced. Lincoln sharply rejected their demands. In private he empathized with the Radicals—their hearts were in the right place—but he deplored their methods and especially their timing. A bold strike against slavery in Missouri might be righteous but would also be politically disastrous. "I believe, after all," Lincoln told Hay later in October, "those Radicals will carry the state & I do not object to it. They are nearer to me than the other side, in thought and sentiment, though bitterly hostile personally. They are utterly lawless—the unhandiest devils in the world to deal with—but after all their faces are set Zionwards." Fortunately, the bitter Radical antipathy toward Lincoln "proved more a matter which concerned the leaders than the rank and file." On October 13 Schofield crowed that Drake's deputation "has returned from Washington very much crestfallen." Even Senator Lane appeared to relent, informing Schofield's emissary that "he had stopped the war upon me, and intended hereafter not to oppose me unless circumstances rendered it necessary." Yet if anything, political infighting in Missouri intensified. The Radicals now put all their hopes on state elections set for November 3, after which a Radical majority on the state supreme court could declare Governor Gamble's provisional rule invalid.[24]

A TERRIBLE WARFARE

This political tumult was in full course when the Ninth Minnesota reached Jefferson City on October 13, and they eagerly jumped into the fray. Among the units Totten hastily assembled to defend the capital was a battalion of the First Nebraska that had also come from St. Louis, the hotbed of Radical politics. In September 1863 one member of the First Nebraska described his regiment as "without exception staunch Radicals" who "hated" supposed Copperheads like Schofield and Gamble "more than the enemy facing us." On the morning of October 12, one Nebraskan began "hurrahing Jim Lane" out on the street. Personally nabbing the "disorderly soldier," Totten secured him in the telegraph office, only to have his comrades demand his release. Totten arrested them too and ordered the battalion confined to quarters. He dispatched Maj. Lucien J. Barnes to alert Colonel Pound, the commander of the post. Confronting two hundred men of the First Nebraska, Barnes repeated Totten's order. "The men resisted, and rescued one whom Major Barnes had arrested," with "officers and non-commissioned officers looking on without affording assistance to the officer resisted." Totten scornfully reported "a number of officers of the regiment in this state of things had the audacity to ask me to release their men, thereby upholding this mutinous spirit." He restored order, and Schofield soon removed the unruly Nebraskans from Jefferson City.[25]

The Ninth Minnesota heard all about the Jim Lane enthusiast who, as Felch stated, "was put in the lock up [and] when the boys found it out then went & broke down the door to get him out." Arrested again, the hapless bluecoat had a ball and chain affixed to his leg and was "compelled to drag them around the camp." The Minnesotans queried locals for their opinions and enthusiastically offered their own. It appears a substantial proportion of the Ninth Minnesota, possibly a strong majority, was already well disposed toward the Radical Republican cause. "Our Minnesota boys take delight in showing their freedom and independence," wrote Herrick, "by cheering Jim Lane and the stars and stripes all they please." Hearing on October 14 that Lane himself was headed to Jefferson City, Aiton wrote that day, "Radical meeting, here, in the City tomorrow night. *Jim Lane* [Aiton's emphasis] is expected here. He is the impersonation of Liberty out here. So 'Hurrah!' 'For Jim Lane' is here the cry of real Union boys & girls." The "politics of Missouri are secesh, union and radical," Aiton explained to his family. "Union is slavery abolished gradually, secesh (you know what it is) and radical is for the immediate abolition of slavery (and of course is union really). And it is expected that the Radicals will carry the state this fall." The Mankato soldier correspondent "Now and Then" described the great meeting of the "unconditional loyal men of this city," who approved the "President's proclamation of Freedom" as a "wise and necessary step in the great work of crushing the Rebellion." He denounced "with merited emphasis" the policies of Gamble and Schofield. The "blight of slavery rests upon this people," repressing "the spirit of improvement so natural to the Yankee nation."[26]

Assigned to court-martial duty in the capital, Lieutenant Stearns enjoyed the leisure to observe the Missouri legislature. The "Radical, immediate emancipation sentiments that are daily uttered, and indeed are triumphant here in Missouri would shock the sensitive nerves of some of our tender footed Republicans of Minnesota." He approved how the Missouri Radicals dealt with slavery "boldly, fairly and squarely." They "triumphed, not by the aid of Federal and military influence, but in spite of it, and against a coalition of all opposing elements." The Radicals have "resolved to finish the monster while he is down," and "so it must be throughout the country." William Dean also expressed his disgust with slavery in Missouri. "We have seen enough to still more convince me that it is of the greatest evils." In Jefferson City he discovered some slaves, mostly children, picking apples under the sinister gaze of their master, an "old tub of guts" who treated them "like dogs." The garrulous slaveholder contemptuously compared his human property to horses and avowed not even a compensation of three hundred dollars per slave would be sufficient for him to accept emancipation. He even demanded that Rebel slave owners also be recompensed for the fair value of their slaves. Dean scornfully dissented.[27]

General surveys of the attitudes of Union soldiers during the Civil War have established that the vast majority did not join specifically to end slavery but rather to preserve the Union. "The men who enlisted in our army in the first two years of the war," declared Capt. Theodore G. Carter of the Seventh Minnesota, did so "because our flag had been insulted and fired upon." Slavery "had but little to do with enlistments," for "a large portion of our soldiers were Democrats, who would not have stayed a day had it been understood that they were fighting to free slaves." Carter estimated at least half his company were Democrats. Historian James M. McPherson has confirmed how soldiers who were true abolitionists were "rare indeed" at the outset. Prior to

William Dean, May 10, 1864

the war, even anti-slavery Republicans perceived abolitionists as dangerous extremists. The strong Northern animosity against Southerners resulted not from any sympathy for black slaves but from fears that slavery itself represented an aristocratic tyranny that for whites risked economic and political subjugation if not outright bondage. Hence the territories must be kept open for free settlement.[28]

Concern for the plight of blacks in the South, however, soon became evident, at least among some Northern soldiers. In Maryland in December 1861, Brig. Gen. Willis A. Gorman, a Minnesotan who led the brigade that included the First Minnesota, declared, "if rebels or anybody else get a slave returned to their master during this rebellion, they will have to find some other instrument to perform the work other than myself. . . . Every fugitive slave that has come to my Brigade, has been fed & cared for, as we understand the orders of the War Department." Sergeant James A. Wright of the First Minnesota concurred. "Though none of us had any inclination to pose as abolitionists, I think we were all glad when a slave went free. Most certainly if his owner was a secessionist." Like General Schofield most bluecoats "eventually converted" to the need for emancipation to ensure victory. In September 1862 Lt. Col. Lucius F. Hubbard, commanding the Fifth Minnesota in northwestern Alabama, did "quite a business in the confiscation of slave property" and derived much "private satisfaction" from it. "Crippling the institution of slavery," he maintained, strikes "a blow at the heart of the rebellion." Historian Earl J. Hess, who emphasizes the importance of ideology in the North's prosecution of the war, also differentiates between "the earlier 'political' abolition of prewar days and the 'practical' emancipation advocated by the Northerners during the war." The liberation of slaves became "primarily a war tool; support for black freedom was based on what the citizenry believed could be gotten out of it." When fugitive slaves "flocked to the armies, soldiers used them as servants, cooks, teamsters, and in a variety of other noncombat capacities, relieving white men of much dreary labor." That is not to say once Northerners received a firsthand look at the manifest evils of slavery that many did not sympathize with blacks, just that such empathy had not been their initial motivation.[29]

Of course for some genuine Radicals, including Aiton, "Now and Then," Stearns, Dean, and numerous others in the Ninth Minnesota, emancipation was not merely a tool of war. They did not go south just to restore the Union. Freedom for the slaves already meant much more to them. Although it seems Radical attitudes were quite prevalent in the Ninth Minnesota, perhaps to an unusual degree, other political opinions were expressed as well. "Judging from what I have learned from good authority since I have been here,"

Captain Dane acknowledged to the *Mankato Union*, "if the people of Missouri could have their say, they would pass an act for the immediate emancipation of slavery" but "not from any sympathy for abolitionism." Instead, they "are anxious to have this war brought to a speedy close, and they see the nigger in the way, and are getting anxious to get him out, and the quicker the better." The Ninth Minnesota definitely included some traditional anti-emancipation Peace Democrats like Woodbury who loathed the war and Lincoln in particular. Then there were those who mistrusted the motives of both sides. Writing to the *Winona Daily Republican* on November 1, Surgeon Bingham warned, "a terrible warfare is now being waged between the two political parties in this State," with "both claiming to be intensely loyal, and each charging upon the other the very worst kind of disloyalty." Once the election was past, the people of Missouri must "turn their attention to their enemies in arms, and not continue to wrangle about matters and questions of State policy, that are of small importance compared with the great struggle for national existence." General Halleck would have shouted, "Hear! Hear!"[30]

The Missouri state elections on November 3 proceeded without incident. "As all voters have to take the oath before voting," Herrick observed, "it is

Surgeon Reginald Bingham,
ca. 1864

feared that if union men try to carry out this rule they will meet opposition and trouble but we shall now very soon know. The citizens here say that there are plenty of secessionists in this place and the country surrounding." The Minnesotans detected no such interference at polling places. At first it appeared the Radicals won a very close election. "The Radicals of Missouri did nobly at the election on Tuesday last," exulted "Now and Then," with no thanks to the "official representatives of the Federal Government" and their "host of rebel retainers." A certain "G. H. E." from the Ninth Minnesota commented in the *Winona Republican* that "the returns from all parts of the State give the Radicals a majority over the loyal disloyal party—a very unusual thing for Missouri; but what loyal people are left here stand up for their rights, and the last election shows that they worked faithfully." In late November the Conservatives, by disallowing supposedly suspicious ballots from Radical military voters, squeaked through by 2,436 votes. Aiton complained on November 29 that the "Conservative ticket is likely to succeed here, by rascally throwing out the soldiers votes," but such "villainy will not always succeed." Similarly, "E. R.," another staunch Ninth Minnesota Radical, deplored that the "Conservative—more properly rebel—officials have thrown out some 4,000 soldiers' votes, and thus brazenly-facedly claim to exercise authority vested in them by the voice of the people." A "more palpable swindle was never perpetrated on the ballot box." Regardless, "the Radicals—the only loyal party in the State—have achieved a signal triumph, under the most adverse circumstances and in opposition to the avowed policy of both State and National Governments."[31]

Thus, by the end of November 1863, Missouri appeared safe, for a little while, from drastic reform. Yet the illusory prospect of a Radical victory, with the possible swift emancipation of slaves without compensation to their owners, had deeply frightened one particular Missouri slaveholder. The desperate measures he took led a portion of the Ninth Minnesota to turn Radical ideology into drastic action of their own.

CHAPTER THREE

The Outrage at Otterville

GUARDING THE LAMINE BRIDGE

On October 18, two and a half weeks before the election, General Brown directed Colonel Wilkin to furnish two companies of the Ninth Minnesota to guard the railroad bridge over the Lamine River near Otterville, forty-five miles west of Jefferson City. The bridge was one of the most vulnerable points along the Pacific Railroad that supplied strategic Sedalia, the cornerstone of the Union position in west-central Missouri. Shelby's raiders had burned the span nine days before, but it was being speedily rebuilt. Wilkin selected Companies C and K, 6 officers and 147 enlisted men under Capt. David W. Wellman, commander of Company K. They were to relieve a ragtag body of 550 convalescents, artillerymen, and state militia under Maj. Richard H. Brown who had been protecting the site since shortly after the bridge was destroyed. Provided "garrison and camp equipage" and ten days' rations, Wellman proceeded on the twentieth to the bridge by train.[1]

Flowing north, the Lamine (pronounced luh-MEEN) River joined the Missouri River near Boonville. The railroad bridge was located near the Lamine's headwaters in southwestern Cooper County, where its scenic banks were heavily wooded, steep, and rocky, with higher, open terrain to the east. Just southwest of the bridge on ground rising from the river sat the remains of the massive Lamine Cantonment, a relic of the heady days of autumn 1861 when armies contended for western Missouri. Union soldiers had burned the first Lamine Bridge that September after the fall of Lexington, fifty-five miles northwest. Colonel Josiah W. Bissell's Engineer Regiment of the West rebuilt it and constructed the cantonment to protect Sedalia. "We were right in the midst of the very worst 'secesh' region in the State," Bissell would recall, "from which nearly every young man had gone into the rebel army, while the old men were sending them supplies and information." In early 1862 after the Rebel army withdrew to Arkansas, Union forces swiftly vacated the Lamine position. Since only sporadic outbreaks of irregular warfare erupted, a simple blockhouse on the west bank of the Lamine sufficed to protect the bridge and its associated water tank for refilling thirsty locomotives.[2]

That minimal defense proved unequal to the task. On the "dark and murky" night of October 9, Shelby sent one hundred men under Capt. James C. Wood to "destroy the La Mine Bridge at all hazards." Captain Milton Berry and twenty-eight men of Company D, Fifth Provisional Regiment, Enrolled Missouri Militia, manned the blockhouse. Shelby's report described how Wood's raiders, who with a "wild yell, charged headlong upon the fort," surprised and defeated the garrison after a "bloody" but "brief fight." Thereafter, the second Lamine Bridge, a "magnificent structure, reared at the cost of $400,000 [!], stood tenable against the midnight sky, one mass of hissing, seething, liquid fire" before "the last blackened timber plunge[d] into the gulf below." In fact, after ten defenders took to their heels, Berry's garrison surrendered without firing a shot. Wood's men seized "everything of value they possessed, even their clothing." The prisoners had to stack all their tents, camp gear, wagons, and supplies—whatever their captors could not carry away—onto the bridge before it was torched along with the blockhouse and water tank. After paroling the prisoners, the Rebels "stole what movable property they could lay their hands on in the neighborhood, and left." Wellman's Minnesotans heard the whole ignominious story of the pitiful defense of the bridge, to which James Woodbury remarked, "I guess that they would just as soon be taken prisoners as not, so they sent our company and Co. K to guard it."[3]

Lamenting the loss of its "expensive bridge" (valued at merely $9,000), the Pacific Railroad griped that it had been burned "for mere wantonness," as if it were not a vital military objective. The railroad had to "concentrate its energies upon rebuilding that section." Major Brown's force camped on the east bank of the Lamine River upon slightly higher ground within a loop just south of the crossing, and apparently Wellman established his bivouac there. He set a strong picket guard around all the bridge approaches. Spanning 160 feet and rising 25 feet above the water, the new bridge was the usual rickety-looking wooden trestle with, as President Lincoln once described another such structure in Virginia, "nothing in it but beanpoles and cornstalks." Vital train service soon resumed between Sedalia and St. Louis.[4]

Located on the railroad a mile southwest of the bridge, Otterville numbered perhaps four hundred souls. Known as Elkton when it was surveyed in

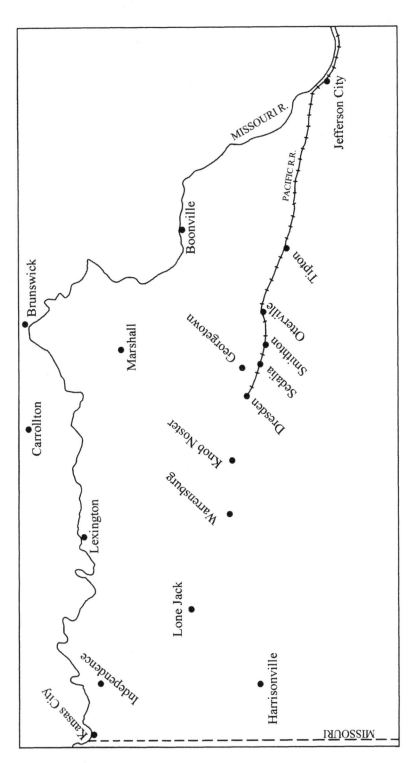

West-Central Missouri

1837, Otterville received its own post office in 1848. Notoriety and prosperity arrived in August 1860 with the advancing Pacific Railroad, whereupon the town "commanded quite a brisk trade." That November, though, when the tracks were extended six miles west to Smithton and then in February 1861 as far as Sedalia, Otterville swiftly reverted "to its original obscurity." It had little love for the North. In October 1861 when Federal troops marched through, no U.S. flags were evident, and its denizens appeared "very indifferent to the Union cause." As Bissell noted, secession enjoyed powerful support in Cooper County, and its Unionists favored the Conservative cause. No matter the side, Otterville grew very weary of being pillaged in the name of North or South. Major Brown admitted his relief force had exhibited "a considerable disposition" to "appropriate other people's property in the shape of sheep, chickens, &c., to their own use, thereby setting a pernicious example to the balance of the command." Although many of the men displayed "considerable disorder" by raucously cheering Jim Lane and cursing General Totten, their officers "did not appear to interest themselves in the suppression of these irregularities." Nonetheless, boasted Brown, he "stopped to a great extent the propensity to rob the people of their property." The locals doubtless looked with jaded eye at the Minnesota newcomers.[5]

Company C ("Mower County Rangers") was only the second company raised in Mower County, a "gently undulating prairie" perched on the Iowa border. Its sparse population mostly comprised Yankees from New York and New England drawn to southern Minnesota by the lure of excellent farmland. After just missing fighting the Dakota in the Battle of Wood Lake, Company C languished on frontier garrison duty. Captain Edwin W. Ford, thirty-one and a native of Lockport, New York, took command in November 1862. He was an accountant and dealer in farm products in Austin, the county seat. His standing with his men fluctuated according to their attitude toward military life in general. To David Felch, the new captain was "not much of a military man but he is kind to the boys & we like him." By February 1863, in the midst of a dreary winter at Fort Ridgely, Ford experienced a true crisis in command. Felch deplored how he "gets drunk quite often, quite a laughing stock for the boys." In May Woodbury declared, "There is not hardly one of the company but what hate him," for "he won't do anything for the men if he can help it." A month later Felch warned, "The company is death on him, and he may feel cold led [lead] if he is not careful not that I would do any such thing. I have always treated him well and he has treated his men like dogs. He is watched very closely lately. The Colonel has got his eye on him." The opportunity for active service dispelled pent-up frustrations, enabling Ford to start with a clean slate in Missouri.[6]

Assembled at Fort Snelling in September 1862, Company K was an unusual amalgam of recruits from the southeast corner of the state who had been among the very last volunteers prior to the deadline. Winona County supplied about thirty Yankees and immigrants and a separate contingent of eighteen Germans, while Wabasha County contributed a cosmopolitan mix of Germans and river men of French-Canadian descent. If Company C included the toast of Mower County, raffish Company K (it apparently even lacked a nickname) rated distinctly lower within Winona society, where it was overshadowed by Company K of the elite First Minnesota and the two companies raised ahead of it in August. Captain David Wellman, age thirty-seven, was another former New Yorker who relocated to Minnesota Territory in the 1850s. He was a qualified civil engineer, which explains why Wilkin picked him to keep watch over the crucial Lamine Bridge. Wellman appears not to have aroused the antipathy of his men to the extent Ford did, but he craved military opportunities to exercise his professional talents beyond just leading an infantry company.[7]

Making themselves at home at Lamine Bridge, the two companies adapted to the surprisingly changeable weather that alternated snowstorms and heavy rain, freezing cold with "pleasant" weather as "warm as September in Minnesota." The men took advantage of plentiful timber to construct stout log houses, "excellent huts" according to an Otterville doctor. The overall health of the men remained good, or at least was not any worse than in Minnesota,

David Wellman, ca. 1863

though Company C was saddened to learn that Pvt. James H. Carver, left behind in the hospital at Jefferson City, had died on November 1 from congestion of the lung. Sickness and battle were not the only hazards of the service. On November 7 Pvt. Carl Sprung of Company K, a forty-four-year-old recent immigrant from Germany, fell while crossing the narrow footway on Lamine Bridge and died from his injuries.

The poverty and instability of the Otterville region deeply impressed at least one soldier of Company K. Writing to the Winona newspaper on November 2 under the pseudonym "Volunteer," he described how "a great many of the citizens here are in very destitute circumstances, and must suffer greatly during the coming winter." The region was "poor," its people already impoverished "before the war, which has added desolation to poverty, until the country is in a truly pitiable condition," whereas the folks back in Minnesota did not realize how well off they were, living in "peace and plenty." The wartime "Citizen of Missouri, when he lies down with his family at night, knows not whether he will ever rise again, and while he sleeps, he knows not but some marauding guerilla is stealing his last horse from his stable, or lies in wait at his door thirsting for his heart's blood." The solution, according to "Volunteer," was the ballot box: "We soldiers, as well as the citizens here, realize the important results arising from the issues of the elections this fall." The anonymous Minnesotan affirmed, "Every truly loyal man is Radical to the back-bone," and "every loyal Union man agrees that slavery was the cause of the rebellion, and that it must die with it." On November 3 Wellman furnished twenty-five soldiers to guard the polling place at Otterville, where voting proceeded without incident. To the likely chagrin of "Volunteer" and the other Radical sympathizers, the Conservatives won Cooper County by a small margin.[8]

Fortunately for the Ninth Minnesota, and Wellman's two isolated companies in particular, partisan activity in Missouri declined dramatically at the onset of cold weather, which bushwhackers did not like any better than anyone else. Like migratory birds, most of them went south for the winter. "Volunteer" remarked that Lamine Bridge was "expecting a visit" by "marauding guerillas and bushwhackers," for which "we are holding ourselves in readiness to give them a warm reception." Contact with the enemy turned out to be furtive instead of confrontational. The first incident took place in mid-November. During the night, a small party slipped past the bridge pickets on the east bank, forded the river, robbed one man of over four hundred dollars and "one good horse," and helped themselves to other mounts nearby. A posse of fifteen citizens and several soldiers pursued the thieves for fifteen miles but could not close before their quarry scattered and went to ground. South of Otterville "the country is very broken," one Minnesota soldier complained, "and [the fugitives] can hide in caves where all the forces in Missouri could not find them."[9]

The apprehension of the first "bushwhacker" took place soon after, and the story lost nothing in the retelling. The incident involved 1st Lt. Jules Capon of Company K, who in Wabasha was known by his height of six feet two inches and country of origin as the "Big Frenchman." Born in 1828 in Bapaume, he left for America in 1851 and by 1854 reached Wabasha. At the outbreak of the Crimean War, he returned to France to enlist and fought at Sevastopol. Afterward in Wabasha he married in 1857. In the spring of 1861, Capon was a clerk at the Redwood Indian Agency, attacked during the Dakota War, but luckily he and his family did not stay. After serving less than three months in the First Minnesota, he joined the Second Minnesota in June 1861 as a first sergeant. In April 1862 after Mill Springs, he rose to second lieutenant but resigned in July. That September he was commissioned in the Ninth Minnesota. A "thorough military man," Capon was undoubtedly the finest soldier in Company K. He issued commands in a loud and very distinctive voice. During the winter of 1862–63, Wilkin selected him to train officers and noncoms in the special regimental school in St. Peter. Because of Capon's excellence, Company K was "one of the best drilled in the State."[10]

Jules Capon had a weakness—a fondness for the bottle. In June 1862 while with the Second Minnesota at Corinth, he had been charged with being drunk while officer of the guard and was permitted to resign rather than face court-martial. His brigade commander described him as a "good soldier but a great drunkard." Wilkin, then lieutenant colonel of the Second Minnesota, commented that "the service will be benefitted by his resignation." Capon, however, was too valuable to be lost permanently to the army, and once in the Ninth Minnesota, he worked his way back into Wilkin's good graces, though there were occasional lapses.[11]

On the night in question, Capon and one of his Wabasha cronies, a German private dubbed "General Sigel" after the famous Union General Franz Sigel, were at Otterville drinking and swapping tales with a farmer who lived within a mile of the bivouac. The three men, by now all on "very friendly terms," started back toward the river.

It seems they got along very nicely until within a quarter mile of the camp. Capon has a mania that seizes him every time he abandons his temperance principles, and that is that some one is going to shoot him. On such occasions he has more narrow escapes than any man I ever knew. Capon supposed this man was going to shoot him, and he pitched into him, seizing him by the throat and hallooing for help. Sigel came to his assistance, and while Capon held the farmer, Sigel

pounded him on the back, but was too drunk to hurt him much. The man had a
revolver, and that he threw away, fearing he might actually be killed with his own
weapon. At this time a few men came along belonging to the camp, and brought
the "miserable bushwhack" (as Capon called him) to camp. Capon tried to make
Capt. Wellman believe he was shot under the chin, the ball passing out of his
mouth, knocking some teeth out. His mouth was bleeding, caused by falling over
a fence, and the Captain supposed he was actually shot. The revolver was examined, however, and the cylinder was found to be full, and not a cap exploded.

The next morning when "Capon was sober and on the stool of repentance,"
it was seen that the "hole in his chin" had vanished, and the "teeth that he
had in the morning before" were "as safe as ever." Wellman released the innocent farmer, who "went his way rejoicing" with no hard feelings. "So much
for the capture of the first bushwhacker."[12]

If Otterville held hard feelings against the Minnesotans, there is no evidence of it. The friendliness of the locals greatly impressed Woodbury, who
perceived "a great difference in the people here and in Minn" because "here
they will do almost anything to accomodate any of the soldiers." The farmers "come and help us get up logs for our houses or any thing that we want
to do and when we offer to pay them they say that we may come and help
them a little while if we can get time[;] if not it is all right." Woodbury, the
Peace Democrat, was one of the few who truly sympathized with Southerners. Nonetheless, the feminine half of the Otterville community did prove
quite approachable. "The boys have great times going to church and going
home with the girls the first time they ever saw them and as a general thing
the girls let them go with them." One local luminary and social bellwether
was Dr. Samuel H. Saunders, who was certainly no Radical and very possibly
not even a Conservative. Yet he too took a fancy to the Minnesota troops.
Late in November upon hearing a rumor the two companies were to be
transferred, he informed General Brown that the Minnesotans "are well liked
by the citizens" and have made themselves snug for the winter. Should the
Ninth Minnesota remain in Missouri, Saunders asked that these two companies stay at the bridge. All of this was sincere praise indeed, for one can
hardly imagine the populace of Otterville desiring to retain any of the other
troops who had guarded their fair community.[13]

TWO DESPERATE MEN

For the Minnesotans bivouacked at Lamine Bridge, Wednesday, November
11, started routinely. Reveille sounded in the dark at 5:30 and roused the men

in their comfortable log huts. They fell in on company parade fifteen minutes later. The orderly (first) sergeants, Marcius Whitford (Company C) and George Hays (Company K), called the roll. Sick Call followed at 6:30. With the welcome Breakfast Call a half hour later, on this day shortly after sunrise, those soldiers not on guard duty eagerly marched to the company cookhouses, where they drew their hot coffee and meals and exchanged comments as to the quality of their fare. Next, Orderly's Call summoned the sergeants to hear new orders, followed by Police Call at 7:35, when those on the duty roster formed the daily fatigue parties. The lucky others not so instantly encumbered hied themselves elsewhere to do as much as required or as little as they could get away with.[14]

Perhaps an hour after dawn, a large black man in his mid- to late twenties, exhausted and manifestly distraught, presented himself to the guards at the entrance of the camp.[15] They conducted him to the headquarters of Company C. The evidence indicates his Christian name was John (by which he will be referred here), but his surname (if he indeed had one at that time) most regretfully remains unknown. Soldiers not otherwise employed crowded around to find out what was wrong. John declared he was a slave who lived some twenty miles west, but he was now a fugitive, on the run all night. The previous day John's master had gathered him, his wife, Emily, and their five small children; his younger brother Billey and Billey's wife, Rachel; and his teenage sisters, Anna and Patsey—eleven slaves in all—and announced he was taking them to Kentucky. The reason, the slaves well knew, could only be their sale and dispersal. John resisted and ran. Now at the Lamine camp, "the poor fellow begged of our men to save his family for him, as this was his last chance." John explained they should be on the morning mail train that would soon stop at Otterville. According to Felch, who was present, he "wanted us to take them up when they came along."[16]

To understand just why John came to be at Lamine Bridge to plead with the soldiers of the Ninth Minnesota, one must introduce his master, Charles Willis Carter Walker, another desperate man. A forty-two-year-old farmer, businessman, slaveholder, and "respectable citizen" from neighboring Pettis County, he had a farm a few miles north of Georgetown, the county seat three miles north of Sedalia and fourteen miles northwest of Otterville. Walker had come to Pettis County about 1842 from Fayette County, Kentucky. His parents and siblings joined him in 1843. The rolling prairie in western Missouri proved ideal for raising corn and wheat. The economy there was based on farming rather than huge plantations harvesting a single market crop. Few masters "owned more than one family of blacks," and "white owners and their sons labored in the same fields with negroes both old and young."

By 1850 the Walker family farmed real estate worth $3,500 and owned one young male slave. In the next decade both Walker parents died, and one of Charles's younger brothers married and went out on his own. Charles's own household included two younger brothers (one a physician) and four children orphaned after the death of the eldest sister and her husband. Walker prospered wonderfully as a farmer, trader, and freight hauler. In 1860 he and his two brothers held real estate to the value of $36,000 and a personal estate of $12,000. Despite the strong inflation in slave prices in the 1850s, he now owned seven slaves, evidently John, Emily, their two young children, and Billey, Patsey, and Anna. In July 1860 Charles married twenty-one-year-old Martha Vienna Thomson, the daughter of Milton Thomson, a prosperous farmer in neighboring Johnson County. The Thomsons were a prominent local clan of old settlers whom Gen. David Thomson, Martha's grandfather, had brought from Scott County, Kentucky, to Pettis County in 1833.[17]

In 1861 life soured for C. W. C. Walker as well as the rest of Missouri. The region around Sedalia appears to have been strongly pro-slavery and secessionist. The Georgetown area in particular was sympathetic to the Confederacy. Partisanship grew especially bitter. Two of Martha Walker's uncles split irrevocably over slavery. Milton Thomson's eldest brother, Mentor, running as a delegate to the state convention that was to rule on secession, "took the position that if the majority of the people in Missouri were in favor of seceding, he would vote for secession, but if they favored staying in the Union he would vote for staying in." Thus, he subordinated his personal views in favor of the popular mood. In contrast, Mentor and Milton's brother-in-law George R. Smith, who founded Sedalia, declared himself unreservedly for the Union and against slavery. Asked if he would vote for his brother-in-law, Smith bitterly replied, "No! If a rope were tied around Mentor Thomson's neck, and my vote would save him, I would not vote for him." In the spring of 1861, Smith freed his dozen slaves and joined the Unconditional Unionists. In August the bloody Union defeat at Wilson's Creek in southwestern Missouri opened Pettis County to Confederate attack and led to an "uprising of the enemies of Government." Consequently, "desperadoes were turned loose; Union men were in hiding; farms were deserted; slaves were fleeing from their masters; the sacredness and security of home were gone." Smith sent his family east and joined Governor Gamble's administration. That fall strong Federal forces, supported from the Lamine Cantonment, occupied Sedalia. For the next two years, ferocious foraging devastated Pettis County, stripping the property of the loyal Smith and his political opponents with equal abandon. Slave owners in particular became the targets of marauding Union soldiers and ruffians posing as them. In May 1863 Mentor Thomson's own home suffered such an invasion, and tragedy was only narrowly avoided. There is no reason to believe C. W. C. Walker enjoyed any immunity from such depredations.[18]

Living at Brunswick on the Missouri River forty-five miles north of Georgetown, Henry Clay Bruce, who was a slave until 1864, witnessed the loss of wealth among the masters. "Near the close of 1863, the Union men were on top, and the disloyal or southern sympathizer had to submit to everything. The lower class of so-called Union men almost openly robbed rebel sympathizers by going to their farms, dressed and armed as soldiers, taking such stock as they wanted, which the owner was powerless to prevent; in fact he would have been killed had he attempted." It was ironic, then, according to Bruce's personal experience, that the "master found his slave to be his best and truest friend, because it often happened that he was forced for self-protection to hide his valuables from these prowlers, and knowing that their quarters would not be invaded, he placed his precious property in their hands for safe keeping." One strongly doubts if Walker ever trusted his slaves to that extent.[19]

Bruce stuck with his master until March 1864 when it became obvious to him the farm was no longer a going concern. Then he and his fiancée escaped to the free state of Kansas. John's extended family, increased since 1860 by the addition of Billey's wife, Rachel, and three more children, likewise remained with C. W. C. and Martha Walker through thick and thin, even though thousands of Missouri slaves had already found freedom in Kansas. Why John did not flee before November 10, 1863, can never be known, but engineering a successful secret exodus of an entire family was very difficult. Many of the slaves from Missouri who reached Kansas came along with Kansas troops. Otherwise the escape route to the west was extremely dangerous. "Slaves traveling overland without military protection were vulnerable to recapture by their masters or attack by guerrillas." John Nichols, the bushwhacker hanged in Jefferson City in October 1863, had terrorized Pettis County, and others of his vicious ilk prowled the region. On August 3, 1863, Brig. Gen. Thomas Ewing Jr., in charge of the District of the Border through which John's family would have had to pass to get to Kansas, wrote that blacks "dare not travel by land lest they be murdered on the road." The "guerrillas have shown a singular and inhuman ferocity towards them." When Bruce and his fiancée made their dash to freedom, he made sure they were well mounted and that "buckled around my waist" was "a pair of Colt's revolvers and plenty of ammunition." John's family with small children would have lacked that mobility and very likely such protection.[20]

So John and Billey stayed on Walker's farm and labored in good faith to preserve their family. Kinship was for them a welcome bond that the state and their own master refused to honor. Perhaps John just counted on an eventual Union victory that must resolve everything. As Bruce recalled, "Slaves believed, deep down in their souls, that the government was fighting for their freedom, and it was useless for masters to tell them differently." They "could meet and talk over what they had heard about the latest battle and what Mr. Lincoln had said, and the chances of their freedom, for they understood the war to be for their freedom solely, and prayed earnestly and often for the success of the Union cause." Those slaves "who could read and could buy newspapers, thereby obtained the latest news and kept their friends posted, and from mouth to ear the news was carried from farm to farm, without the knowledge of masters." John, as will be seen, seems to have been particularly well informed.[21]

Unforeseen circumstances, though, conspired to place John in a terrible dilemma. The adoption by the provisional government of the principle of gradual emancipation for Missouri's slaves meant their freedom, if not imminent, was inevitable. That development much dismayed their masters, who would lose not only the labor of their slaves but all their remaining equity as property. At one time that sum was considerable. In 1860 a top field hand in Missouri easily commanded $1,300 and a young female $1,000, but those values declined radically after the outbreak of the war. No one particularly desired purchasing an asset that was prone to disappear actually as well as fiscally. As Bruce noted, "From 1862 to the close of the war, slave property in the state of Missouri was almost a dead weight to the owner; he could not sell because there were no buyers." One estimate is that by 1863 nearly 40 percent of Missouri's slaves had left their masters.[22]

In early November 1863, Walker had to reckon on two new factors that further imperiled his ownership of John's family. That fall Missouri finally edged toward enlisting able-bodied black men, not just free men of color but slaves who had fled from the seceded states and slaves of disloyal Missouri masters. As yet, none were to be taken from loyal owners without their consent, but given the Union's desperate need for soldiers, that could not be long in coming. In fact Lincoln had already issued secret orders to that effect, with the compulsory manumission of all slaves who enlisted and compensation of up to three hundred dollars to the owners who remained loyal. Then came the election on November 3 and the apparent victory of the Radical judges that boded the end of the Gamble administration and the possible immediate emancipation of all slaves with no compensation whatsoever.[23]

Walker had one last card tucked up his sleeve. "As the world closed in around them," historian Ira Berlin writes, "unregenerate Missouri masters searched for a way to salvage their investment in slavery." Their solution was

Kentucky, where "slaveholding Unionists still held the upper hand." An active slave market existed there, and the Bluegrass State barred the enlistment of blacks. To transport his slaves out of Missouri, a slaveholder needed to apply to the local army provost marshal to obtain a pass that was supposed to be issued only to those of proven loyalty. Many Missouri slave owners had already availed themselves of that last opportunity to extract some final profit from their slaves. Union officers calculated that in the fall of 1863 slave brokers in Louisville alone had sold perhaps a thousand slaves from Missouri. The Radicals in St. Louis, though, took careful notice of so many slaves passing through their city. They pressured Schofield to stop "all slave exportation from Missouri and to the slave trade with other States, which has lately been carried on pretty extensively, especially with Kentucky." On November 10 headquarters in St. Louis issued Department of the Missouri Special Orders No. 307, which stated in part, "Hereafter, no Provost Marshal nor other officer in the Military service in Missouri will give any pass or permit to any person, authorizing him to take slaves from Mo. to any other State." Thus, by the "laconic mode of a military order," crowed the St. Louis Radical German newspaper *Anzeiger des Westens Wochenblatt,* the end of the slave trade in Missouri was nigh, "stopped by the worthlessness of the property."[24]

The celebration was premature. Orders could take considerable time to be disseminated throughout an entire department, and no one in western Missouri knew of No. 307 for some while. On that same day, November 10, in distant Georgetown, Walker was preparing to ship eleven slaves by rail east through St. Louis and then by steamboat to Kentucky. Unaware that action was now officially forbidden, Lt. Warren B. Davis, the assistant provost marshal at Sedalia, issued a pass (dated for November 11) to Walker, whom he obviously had good reason to consider a loyal Union man. Walker planned to board his human cargo on the next train for St. Louis, scheduled to leave Sedalia at 8:14 on the morning of the eleventh. Walker's slaves despaired when they learned of their fate to leave the next day for Kentucky, where they could be sold and separated, possibly forever. John protested and then succeeded in escaping in a desperate attempt to get help and prevent the breakup of his family.[25]

One can only speculate why John decided to resist. When Bruce's master returned him and other slaves to Missouri in 1850 after a thoroughly unpleasant sojourn in Mississippi, he recalled, "We were once more in the *state we loved and intent on remaining whether our master liked it or not* [Bruce's emphasis], for he had brought us where it was not so easy to take slaves about without their consent, and besides some [of us] had become men." That was one factor. Another concerned changing attitudes in Missouri during that period of the Civil War. According to Bruce, "excitement, such as I had never seen, existed not alone with the white people, but with the slaves as well. Work, such as had usually been performed, almost ceased; slaves worked as they pleased, and their masters were powerless to force them, due largely to the fact that the white people were divided in sentiment." By November 1863 the end of slavery in Missouri appeared nigh, not only to Walker, who feared it, but also to John and his family who so dearly welcomed it.[26]

Another, more personal reason behind the resistance of Walker's slaves was rooted in their tight kinship. It is most significant that they were not just random purchases from different sources but one close-knit family who had managed to stay together in bondage. Although not recognized legally, the marriage of slaves in that particular region of Missouri meant something more than was usual elsewhere in the South. "There is this to be said for the slaveholders in that part of the country, at least," Bruce conceded. "They believed in having their slave women live a virtuous life, and encouraged them in getting married." A black preacher would be brought in to perform the marriage ceremony, and afterward the couple lived in a cabin the "master had built and furnished" for them. The Thomson clan followed that tradition. In the great migration of 1833 from Kentucky, General Thomson, the patriarch, brought along seventy-five slaves overseen by his son, Milton, Martha Walker's father. "The slaves had intermarried, with the neighbor's negroes, and [David Thomson] being humane in his feelings, was unwilling to separate them; so to overcome this difficulty, he had to buy where he could, and sell where he must. This was no little task among a number of thirty or forty people, but it was finally accomplished as far as possible." Nevertheless, as one historian of Pettis County has written, "the specter of the market would always hang over the lives of slaves, protected only by a paternalism that knew real bounds." Nonetheless, John's family would have seen Walker's sudden threat to sell and disperse them as dire betrayal.[27]

If Walker had hoped to snap up John near Georgetown or Sedalia, he was disappointed, for John unexpectedly took the direct road southeast to Otterville. That cold, hungry overnight trek of sixteen-odd miles from Walker's farm passed over a high plateau of farmers' fields, broken by wooded gullies and creek bottoms that gradually descended toward the Lamine River. Although risking mounted pursuit, John would have had to stay on the road or very near it on that moonless night or lose his way in the occasional thick patches of timber. Just why he went to Otterville is unknown, save that he knew his family must pass through there on the railroad between Sedalia and St. Louis and roughly when. There might also have been other reasons as well. Perhaps John was involved in the grapevine to which Bruce alluded. In late 1861 Colonel Bissell, while at the Lamine cantonment, had organized a network of slaves in the surrounding counties to watch Rebel activities. "By the time we left in the spring [1862] for the New Madrid Campaign I had every reason to believe that the colored element in Western Missouri was thoroughly organized, but the same answer was made to every inquiry, 'Please do not ask any questions,' and I never did." Bissell also ran an illegal underground railroad, secreting escaped slaves in the Lamine camp until they could be sent safely to freedom. John had to have known Union soldiers were camped there again. One wonders if he was also aware they were Minnesotans, who might be much more sympathetic to his plight than the local Missouri State Militia in Sedalia. All of that could help explain why John turned up at Lamine Bridge on that bleak November morning.[28]

WE'RE ALL OFFICERS

After listening to John relate his terrible predicament, "our men were moved by his story," recalled one member of the Ninth Minnesota. The question became what, if anything, they could or would do about it. At that time the Union army's official position regarding slaves belonging to loyal Missouri masters was clear: "absolute non-intervention." Soldiers could neither help nor hinder fugitive slaves, let alone liberate their families. In 1861 and 1862, Union generals Frémont in Missouri and David Hunter in South Carolina had been disciplined for stepping beyond the policy of the government on the question of emancipation. Since then Lincoln had issued the Emancipation Proclamation, but it applied only to areas in rebellion, and he was still sensitive about alienating the residents of Border States like Missouri. "Allow no part of the military under your command to be engaged in either returning fugitive slaves or in forcing or enticing slaves from their homes," Lincoln personally directed Schofield on October 1, 1863. Schofield himself was already on board. On August 14 he had ordered General Ewing to proceed carefully when dealing with the slaves of masters of questionable loyalty. Should troops "bring away from their masters any persons who are legally held as slaves, you will not hesitate to rectify the error whenever it shall be made to appear." The Ninth Minnesota well understood its obligations in this regard. "Father Abraham has instructed, and Gen. Schofield has commanded," one officer wrote, "that soldiers in Missouri shall neither assist in the capture nor aid in the escape of fugitive slaves." Thus, military duty dictated the Minnesotans do nothing other than politely usher John on his way. Nonetheless, many of them chose not to remain neutral. The vigorous declarations of Radical Republican sentiments uttered in the recent election had only strengthened their resolve.[29]

Among those who heard John's heartrending story was Captain Ford, who wished to help the anxious, excited black man but lacked official authority to do anything. Instead he announced to his noncommissioned officers that he and the other officers were going to "take a walk out of camp" and that "the boys could do as they pleased," recalled Cpl. John W. Hartley. The "boys" understood exactly what he meant. If the captain was not present, he could not stop them. Therefore they decided to "have some fun out of it." Francis Merchant, the tall, handsome, "generous and brave" second sergeant of Company C, took the lead. Born in France in September 1842, he immigrated in 1850 to the United States with his parents, older sister, and younger brother. The family lived six years in Oneida County in western New York and stopped a year in Wisconsin before settling in Freeborn County on the prairie just west of the Mower County line. Prior to enlisting, young Frank had helped his father work the family farm.[30]

Private John Arnold recalled how Sergeant Merchant "passed around through Company C, saying he was ordered to see how many would volunteer to assist in rescuing some slaves, which their masters were endeavoring to smuggle South on the cars to be sold." From Company C, in addition to Merchant, came Hartley, a twenty-four-year-old Mower County blacksmith

Francis Merchant, 1865

originally from Ohio, and eighteen privates, including Arnold and David Felch. Corporal John Henry Ehmke mustered seventeen privates from Company K. Age twenty-two and a farmer from Winona who left Holstein in northern Germany only in 1861, Ehmke had sewn on his stripes just ten days before. His squad joined Merchant without the knowledge and certainly without the approval, tacit or otherwise, of its own commander Captain Wellman, in charge of the post and who was busy eating breakfast at the time. The volunteers grabbed their Springfields. With the remarkably persuasive John at his side, Merchant smartly formed his detachment, crossed the bridge, and marched west on the Otterville road that paralleled the railroad track. To casual observers, including any interested officers, the orderly procession of thirty-eight soldiers, just over one quarter of the effective strength, simply looked as if it was undertaking a routine task.[31]

A mile down the road, Merchant's rescue party lined up along the platform of the railroad depot located on Pacific Avenue on the south edge of Otterville. Within perhaps fifteen minutes—at 8:55 A.M. if Pacific Railroad conductor Charles White was running on schedule—the morning mail train chugged into the station. Sliding past the rank of blue-clad men, the train halted to take on passengers and freight. Understanding that slaves would not be riding in passenger cars, the Minnesotans began sliding open the doors of the freight cars.[32]

Huddled inside a dark, frigid boxcar were Emily and Rachel, Emily's five small children, and their two sisters-in-law, Anna and Patsey, age fourteen and twelve. The two women had been tied together, leaving the young aunts to care for the frightened, hungry youngsters. The mood must have been extremely gloomy. Following John's escape the previous day, probably after the family had been taken somewhere else to spend the night nearer to the railroad depot, his younger brother, Billey, also resisted and likewise tried to run but was shot dead. Felch later heard from John's family that the master "had killed this negroes brother[;] they put six balls through him for making a noise." Another liberator recalled that one of the young women [Anna?] said that "when boarding the slaves [on a wagon?] on the previous night her brother tried to make his escape [but] his master shot him through the head three times. He was found that morning lying dead but a few paces distant." Walker's slave pass authorized him to transport eleven slaves, including the two men, but he had brought only nine, all women and children, to the train on the morning of the eleventh. Moreover, he entrained the group not at Sedalia, the departure point listed on the pass and closest to his farm, but at Smithton, the next stop seven miles southeast. That is odd because Smithton was almost twice as far from the Walker farm as Sedalia, about eleven versus six miles. The family's testimony and the unexplained absence of one of the two black men named in Walker's movement permit offer strong evidence of Billey's murder.[33]

While under restraint in the dismal boxcar, Rachel mourned her husband, Billey, and Emily had no idea what might have happened to her own dear spouse. It had looked like nothing could stop the master from selling and thereby dispersing the rest of the beleaguered family. Now, hazel eyes flashing, Merchant stepped on board the car with eight other soldiers to relieve, Arnold later quipped, "the slaveholder of the disagreeable task of selling his slaves in Kentucky, or paying their fare any further." As they were being untied, he informed the two incredulous women that they and the children were now free and politely asked if they would like to come with him. Amazed at the unexpected turn of events, "they readily complied with our request." John must have been delirious with joy and relief. What Walker's reaction might have been to see his fugitive slave standing on the platform surrounded by soldiers can be imagined. He certainly made no move to flourish his permit or otherwise identify himself to retain his precious property, but rather stayed inside the passenger car and kept silent. "The master did not make his appearance," one Minnesotan recalled, "which I think was safest for him." One wonders if Walker, when he first saw the soldiers, feared they were coming to arrest him for the death of Billey, or alternatively, he might have declined to confront what looked like an armed party of inflamed abolitionists.[34]

Instead Conductor White, a pugnacious twenty-seven-year-old professional railroad man from Massachusetts, swiftly intervened before Merchant could remove the women and the children from the car. He angrily demanded to know what right the Minnesotans had to take slaves from his train. In April 1861 White commendably assisted the Union in securing the St. Louis arsenal by secretly bringing troops to help hold it. Now, however, he deferred any possible emancipationist sentiment in favor of a fierce loyalty to the Pacific Railroad. Merchant replied that they indeed had orders. "Where are your officers?" White snapped. One bold Minnesotan retorted that they were "all officers."[35]

Riding the train were Captain Pritchard, the Inspector of the District of Central Missouri who had praised the Ninth Minnesota a few weeks before, and Capt. Oscar B. Queen of the Seventh Missouri State Militia Cavalry. A feisty forty-four-year-old former Marylander who farmed in Carroll County to the north on the Missouri River, Queen happened to be temporarily in charge of the Second Sub-District that included Otterville and the Lamine camp and was therefore Wellman's immediate superior. The commotion outside the boxcar drew the attention of the two officers, who grabbed their overcoats and stepped out into the cold air on the platform. Queen later reported,

> I then went up to the apparent ringleaders and asked them if they had an offi-
> cer with them to which they replied they had. I told them who I was, and some
> of them remarked "they didn't care a damn" for the Commanding Officer of
> the District[;] they had their orders and were going to obey them. The Con-
> ductor and myself then tried to prevail upon them, to leave the Negroes where
> they were until we got to the bridge and saw Capt Wellman. One of them was
> disposed to do this, but the others overruled him and marched the negroes out
> of the cars.

Pritchard heard Queen tell the Minnesotans "they had no orders to do it and to let the negroes alone," but "they refused to obey him and took the blacks off the train." The soldiers later disputed whether the officers ever properly identified themselves. "They informed us that they were officers, but seeing nothing that we should recognize as officers, we felt in no way under their commands." Their overcoats, the Minnesotans later claimed, "hid their shoulder straps, if they had any."[36]

While Queen took over challenging Merchant's authority to remove the slaves, White sprinted along the platform shouting to the engineer and fire-man lounging in the cab of the locomotive to get the train moving as quickly as possible. The engineer rang the bell to warn that the cars were about to start in motion. Merchant, however, had already anticipated that contin-gency by deploying a squad of soldiers ahead of the engine to prevent it from leaving. That night some passengers related to the St. Louis *Westliche Post* that the conductor had "commanded the engineer to go on, when the soldiers leveled their guns on the engineer, threatening to shoot him—whereupon he refused to obey the orders of the conductor." An outraged White later com-plained to Pritchard that "some of the men cocked their guns on him and the engineer." Felch, one of the blocking squad, confirmed they had at least aimed at the locomotive, if not the trainmen themselves. "We had to threaten as at least we did of putting a minie ball through the boiler."[37]

Once the party disembarked with the nine slaves, Merchant directed the squad in front to allow the train to proceed. Standing in the midst of the res-cuers on the Otterville station platform, John "received a wife and five chil-dren joyfully to his arms." Merchant reformed his detachment and started back toward camp, taking the family with him. They had only gone a short way out of town when suddenly, at a slight bend in the track ahead, they saw the train backing toward them. Queen had stopped the train at Lamine Bridge and along with Pritchard stormed into camp demanding to see Wellman. The bewildered Wellman "disclaimed all knowledge of the whole proceeding, said the men acted without orders and entirely on their own responsibility, and seemed much put out at their conduct." Ford, on the other hand, was strategically absent. Queen, Pritchard, and Wellman quickly repaired to a passenger car, whereupon White set the train in reverse and soon brought it up alongside Merchant's column, which, according to one account, had drawn up "in a threatening manner."[38]

By the time the train halted, John and his family had already disappeared into the timber that bordered the tracks to the south. Felch wrote home the next day:

> We saw [the train] coming and the boys told them to run in the woods and hide for we knew we would be arrested if found with the negroes but when I thought of they catching those poor negroes and taking them back to slavery I left the boys and said they take me with them. Then one more [possibly his close friend Pvt. Latham D. Stewart] went with me. We hid them in the brush as well as we could for we did not have much time to hide.

Asked by Wellman where the blacks were, the men lied by reporting they had stayed in Otterville, "where they said they could take care of themselves." Walker finally asserted himself and, according to the passengers, "endeavored to capture his 'chattels' [but] they could not be found." White had had enough. "Thinking it was useless to delay," he directed the train to resume its journey eastward. Walker stormed back on board. It was very fortunate he did not persist and that the train left so quickly, for he might have been killed. After helping stash the family out of sight, Felch impetuously "crawled back so as if to see if they were coming[,] with the intention of shooting the first man that came in sight or after them. I should of did it to[o] but presently the cars started and well it was they did." Felch was deadly serious about protecting John and his family.[39]

Felch told John to remain where he was until he could return. Before rejoining his companions, though, he heard them relate the tragic news to John of his brother's murder. The liberators returned to camp, where Felch, for one, nonchalantly "acted if I knew nothing about it." The turmoil must have been intense as Wellman, seriously perturbed, tried to get to the bottom of what had just occurred. An hour later Felch adroitly slipped away and retraced his steps to where John's family was hiding. Telling them "they had better be traveling," he led them to a more secure location deep in the forest, where he told John to stay until nightfall. Felch promised to guide them to a small dwelling where "they would be safe and comfortable." That evening "according to agreement," he and another soldier once more braved Wellman's wrath by sneaking out to deliver the family a loaf of bread and some pork, "which they were very glad to get." Again Felch's companion was very possibly Stewart, who recalled many years later that they hid the blacks in a swamp. Felch told John he would return the next evening with more food or send someone he trusted in his place. The two Minnesotans sneaked back into camp. Later Felch heard some slave takers had gone out to catch the fugitives and hunted all night, for "all the good it did." He intended personally to see John's family safely clear of the area, but he never got the chance.[40]

In the Lockup

If the liberators presumed their impromptu act of emancipation would just blow over, they would be sadly disillusioned. From his headquarters at Tipton, thirteen miles southeast of Otterville, Queen wired General Brown a blistering report describing the "high handed outrage committed on the Cars of the Pacific R.R. this morning by a detachment of about 40 men of the Ninth Minnesota Volunteer Infantry." Riding the same train all the way to Jefferson City, Pritchard personally submitted a similar statement to Brown. Walker also complained vociferously to the general. District staff digested those disturbing tidings and at 4:30 P.M. telegraphed orders to Queen to "send negroes and soldiers implicated to Jeff City under Guard." The escaped slaves were not at hand, but the soldiers were. The next morning Wellman paraded the two companies in front of camp and ordered all involved in the incident to step three paces forward. Thirty-eight did. He presented Brown's order to produce the escaped slaves or suffer arrest. "Even after fifty years," Latham Stewart wrote in 1914, "I am pleased to state every last man of us were arrested" instead of revealing the slaves' hiding place. Wellman took the men into custody. Later that day Felch wrote home the shocking news that he was "under arrest for running of negroes. We are awaiting for the cars to take us to Jefferson City to be tried. I expect tomorrow we will be in the lockup for protecting colored folks and it will go hard with me if they knew I knew whare they was and fed them. A letter or two and a few papers will be very thankfully received when I am in prison if you think a prisoner deserves news. L. D. Stewart is in the same fix."[41]

Greeted on the morning of November 13 at the Jefferson City depot by a detail from the post guardhouse, the Minnesotans learned they were to be detained while awaiting the filing of formal charges for trial. Recognizing the special nature of their offense, Brown did not clap them in the guardhouse along with the hard cases, but instead housed them in two "good-sized rooms" in the basement of the ramshackle, vacant Ransom Hotel. According to an apparently envious Minnesota officer, the prisoners were "relieved from all duty, furnished good comfortable quarters and allowed to go pretty much where they please." Things were not all that rosy. Although officially denied by Brown, the prisoners in fact received only half rations for several weeks. "Many have to buy a good share of their provisions," one of the incarcerated men complained late in November, "as enough is not given us to satisfy hunger." Their extra money came from chopping wood and other menial tasks performed for civilians in town. While guarding a railroad bridge east of Jefferson City, John Aiton heard from a fellow soldier that in addition to the "short rations," the prisoners "sleep without hay, or straw." Wood stoves in the old hotel provided heat and a convenient way to cook bacon, but ventilation was so poor that several men were soon hospitalized with smoke-inflamed eyes.[42]

Colonel Wilkin was furious over what he perceived were reckless and insubordinate acts at Otterville that resembled the mutinous behavior of the disgraced First Nebraska the month before in Jefferson City. On November 13 he informed General Sibley in Minnesota that forty of his men had "stopped a train of cars and released eleven slaves in charge of their owners," for which "they have been arrested and sent here by order of General Brown." Aside from "this exception," he again bragged the Ninth Minnesota "is much thought of by the people," who "say it is the best Regiment they have seen in this part of the State." Wilkin described "most of the men engaged in the affair" as "orderly and religious," but nonetheless, he hoped "they will be severely punished." He sought retribution for the blot upon his regiment and his own reputation. A former "zealous" supporter of Senator Stephen A. Douglas and classic War Democrat, Wilkin had little use for black people whether slaves, freedmen, or soldiers.[43]

Wilkin identified the "Ringleader" as a "Methodist preacher," an obvious reference to Rev. John Arnold, who in fact belonged to the Church of the United Brethren in Christ. Though not the actual instigator (in a certain sense Captain Ford was), Arnold's staunchly abolitionist religious teachings provided powerful inspiration. The United Brethren had decreed in 1821 that no member could own slaves, and despite its ardent pacifism, the church ultimately endorsed "direct political and even military involvement in the cause of emancipation." Born in 1816 near Poughkeepsie, New York, Arnold left in 1834 with his family for Lorain County in north-central Ohio. He married in 1837 and eventually worked his own farm while raising four children.

In 1855 he and his children experienced terrible tragedy when his wife, Harriett, "lost her mind, killed her baby and committed suicide." Arnold soon remarried, but the pain of his loss was probably decisive in his decision to be ordained in the United Brethren and preach full time. In 1858 he moved his family to Freeborn County, where he founded a small congregation that met in private homes. By 1860 they resided in nearby Austin, where Arnold's little group kept together longer than usual in those volatile religious times.[44]

In August 1862 Arnold, approaching fifty, left his second wife, Susan, and three young children in Austin to join Company C. The United Brethren Church regretted that, like Arnold, so many itinerant ministers served as common soldiers. "We can not but commend them for their patriotism; and when we meet one of them in their short blue coats and heavy shoes, we would willingly take our place at their feet. Yet, in our humble opinion, it would be better for the country if all efficient ministers would remain at their special work, unless drafted or called into the public service as chaplains." The soldiers, though, appreciated and applauded religious mentors who served in the ranks with them in furtherance of the same cause of freedom. Those soldier-ministers gained an authority they otherwise might be lacking. Arnold certainly encouraged the men that day when they, like him, demonstrated the courage of their convictions at Otterville.[45]

In addition to the influence of preachers like Arnold, the liberators were motivated by a society where direct action in support of liberty was thought not to be a crime. In background they were a diverse lot, ranging from a true blue-blooded, double-direct *Mayflower* descendant to an immigrant who may have reached American shores barely two months before enlisting. Of the twenty from Mower County's Company C, only five were born outside the United States: Francis Merchant (France), Stephen N. Chandler (Quebec), Nathan N. Palmeter (Nova Scotia), and the Watkins brothers, John Richard Jr. and Evan (Wales). The rest hailed from New York (John Arnold, George H. Bullard, Zara Frisbie, Ira W. Padden, Erastus Slocum, Latham Denison Stewart [the *Mayflower* scion], Daniel B. Vaughan, and Augustus Whitney), Vermont (Siloam Williams), New Jersey (Joshua C. Epler), Ohio (John W. Hartley and Isaac Peterman), Indiana (Noah McCain), and Wisconsin (David F. M. Felch and Joseph H. Lagree, who was of French-Indian descent). Seventeen were farmers, Hartley was a blacksmith, Arnold a clergyman, and Lagree a laborer. The oldest were Arnold at forty-seven and Peterman (also a United Brethren), who was probably forty-three; the youngest, at nineteen, were Felch, his chum Stewart, and Slocum. All enlisted in August 1862 in Mower County except for Lagree, who originally joined Company E in Mankato but transferred to Company C in late September 1862.[46]

Joshua C. Epler, ca. 1880

Siloam and Mary Williams.

By contrast, twelve of the eighteen Company K liberators were immigrants. Eight were born in various German states: Jacob Bader, Charles Dietrich, Henry Ehmke, George Frahm, Frederick Heilmann, Henry Jansen, Hens G. Lüthye, and Jacob Thielen, who possibly landed in New York in June 1862. John Morrison had departed Scotland in 1840, and John Gordon left Ireland in 1849, while Pierre Demars and Pierre ("Peter") Rodier both emigrated in the 1850s from eastern Canada. Of the Yankees, Allen Hilton and Enoch W. Pike were born in Maine, Samuel Mickel and Lyman Raymond in New York, Theobald B. Fenstermacher in Pennsylvania, and Hiram A. Buck in Ohio. The majority enlisted in August 1862 in Winona, while Bader, Demars, Rodier, and Thielen joined in Wabasha County, and Morrison in Olmsted County. Hilton signed on in February 1863 in Winona. Reflecting the somewhat more-urban conditions along the Mississippi River, just ten of the eighteen were farmers. Jansen was a shoemaker, Frahm a mason, Thielen a wheelwright, Buck and Rodier were carpenters, Demars an engineer of some sort, Mickel a lumberman, and Lüthye a laborer–stone mason. The oldest was Gordon at thirty-six; Hilton was only fifteen.

The thirty-eight Minnesotans faced trial for grave offenses under the Articles of War. Article 6 forbade disrespect or contempt toward the commanding officer, who Captain Queen no doubt was. Article 7 prescribed death or lesser punishment for any soldier who "shall begin, excite, cause, or join in, any mutiny or sedition," while Article 8 included those who were present but did nothing to stop said "mutiny or sedition." According to Article 9, "Any officer or soldier who shall strike his superior officer, or draw or lift any weapon, or offer any violence against him, being in the execution of his office, on any pretense whatsoever, or shall disobey any lawful command of his superior officer" would face the same dire penalties. The foray to Otterville was certainly armed. On November 21 district headquarters referred the case to the provost marshal, Lt. Col. Theodore A. Switzler, who enjoined his assistant Lt. Calvin S. Moore to "endorse hereon the names of the soldiers arrested and refer the papers to the proper military court for trial." Captain Alva R. Conklin, the judge advocate, confirmed that "charges against the prisoners of the 9th Minn Vols have been drawn, copy served and on file for trial." Requesting "an early trial of said soldiers," Moore submitted his list to the judge advocate of the Military Commission, Lt. J. Curtis McCain of the Ninth Minnesota, but he sloppily omitted the names of four liberators already in custody but included another under arrest in a different matter. At first the remainder of the companies at Lamine Bridge thought the men were released after twenty-four hours, but word soon came of the court-martial set to begin on the twenty-fifth. With Lt. Lyman A. Sherwood of Company C slated to be a member of the court, "we should know what they do with the boys," wrote Woodbury. Things thereafter ground to a halt. "We cannot learn that any charges have been preferred against us," one of the discouraged and disgusted prisoners wrote on the twenty-eighth. "I see nothing to cause me to believe that we are not as likely to be here for two months to come as we have been the two weeks past."[47]

CHAPTER FOUR

An Act of Humanity

REFLECTIONS ON A RESCUE

Federal military policy that buttressed slavery in the loyal Border States of Missouri, Kentucky, Maryland, and Delaware grated on some Union soldiers, most particularly those from the Upper Midwest. Historian Victor B. Howard points out that in Kentucky (as with the Ninth Minnesota later in Missouri), most Northern soldiers disdained slaveholders no matter how much the masters might support the Union. Recalling the widespread opposition in the North to the odious 1850 Fugitive Slave Act, Federal regiments in Kentucky often sheltered blacks who ran away from their ostensibly loyal owners. Ira Berlin describes how soldiers there "defied orders and welcomed runaway slaves into their camps, setting them to work at various menial tasks." If the masters turned up, "the soldiers jeered, threatened them with bodily harm, and helped the slaves elude capture." According to Howard, "the rank and file of the soldiers, often with the assistance of the lower echelon of officers, greatly damaged slavery in Kentucky and significantly influenced policy in the state."[1]

Certain Union colonels in Kentucky refused to obey orders to remand escaped slaves to their masters or simply turn the fugitives out of camp. As justification they cited Congress's injunction to the Union army in March 1862 not to enforce the Fugitive Slave Act, the July 1862 Second Confiscation Act, and Lincoln's Preliminary Emancipation Proclamation of September 1862. In the fall of 1862, Col. William L. Utley's Twenty-Second Wisconsin, the so-called Abolition Regiment, took in many slaves in northern Kentucky and smuggled several north. A former newspaperman, Utley ignored orders from his division commander to relinquish the fugitives and declared that his superior lacked such authority. The general did not pursue the matter. When the citizens of Georgetown, Kentucky (whose relatives, ironically, had founded Georgetown, Missouri), threatened to use force to retrieve the fugitive slaves, Utley vowed to torch the town. A young slave named Paul who gained refuge with the Twenty-Second Wisconsin had escaped from George Robertson, chief justice of Kentucky and a former congressman. Utley refused Robertson's demand for Paul's return. "I do not permit nigger-hunters to ransack my regiment." Nor did Utley's direct superior intervene. Robertson sought felony charges against Utley under Kentucky law for harboring a slave and assisting his escape. Served with an arrest warrant, Utley groaned, "I am in a devil of a scrape." Robertson even complained to his old friend Lincoln who offered him $500 for Paul's freedom, but Robertson refused. The army never disciplined Utley, but after the war the crusty jurist sued him and secured a judgment by default. In 1873 by special act of Congress, Robertson finally received $934.46 in compensation.[2]

In Missouri the principal emancipators were Kansas regiments and civilian Jayhawkers who freed slaves during what amounted to looting expeditions and spirited them back to Kansas. As historian Nichole Etcheson writes, "Kansas troops engaged in none of the soul-searching about whether to return runaway slaves to their rebel masters as occurred in the eastern theater." It would have required real courage, or utter foolhardiness, for a Missouri slaveholder to confront Jayhawkers and demand his slaves or possessions back. In October 1861 in Springfield, Missouri, a slave owner brashly accosted Col. Owen Lovejoy and demanded the immediate return of a fugitive who had become Lovejoy's hired servant. A clergyman, celebrated abolitionist, and serving congressman from Illinois, Lovejoy indignantly refused. He recognized no obligation on the part of the black man to resume his servitude. "By his own consent he is in my service, and I pay him for his labor, which is his right to sell and mine to buy." The "astounded" master wisely departed.[3]

The Seventh Kansas Cavalry, known as "Jennison's Jayhawkers" after its notorious first colonel Dr. Charles R. Jennison, epitomized the combination of anti-slavery idealism and a penchant for relieving Rebels of their precious goods. No less a figure than Capt. John Brown Jr. had formed its Company K, and his men in particular were truly "abolitionists of the intense sort." Transferred east of the Mississippi River in May 1862, the Seventh Kansas Cavalry cut a swath through Tennessee with the "old familiar story of livestock and feed taken, of henroosts, smoke houses, and orchards robbed, of the theft of money and watches, of Negroes enticed from their masters, and of the loyal and disloyal victimized indiscriminately." The regiment likewise refused to remand escaped slaves to their masters and on one occasion threatened an angry slave owner that if he did not desist, he would be "hung higher than Haman." Lieutenant Colonel Daniel A. Anthony, brother of suffragette Susan B. Anthony, got into trouble in June 1862 by ordering the Seventh Kansas Cavalry not to return any slave to his master. For refusing to repudiate his directive, Anthony was arrested for disobedience of orders and for helping slaves leave their masters. He never was tried, nor, apparently, for any similar charge was anyone else from the regiment.[4]

Conductor White angrily asserted to Captain Queen that the seizure of the slaves on his train by men of the Ninth Minnesota was "the first instance of the kind which ever took place on the [Pacific Railroad]."[5] In fact, the Otterville incident appears virtually unprecedented in the entire Union army. Those soldiers in Kentucky and elsewhere who refused to relinquish fugitive slaves coming on their own into camp incurred no penalty because they had enjoyed at least the implicit agreement of higher military authorities. What transpired at Otterville was entirely different. Not only had the thirty-eight Minnesota liberators illegally sheltered a runaway slave, but they had forcibly removed his family from the lawful master in direct defiance of the orders of their commander, who was present. Far from enjoying the tacit approval or benign indifference of their superiors, the Otterville liberators had stirred up a heap of trouble for themselves.

Unlike the previously described military emancipations, the actions of Sergeant Merchant and his thirty-seven followers resemble the "forcible slave rescues" that took place in the North in the decade before the war. In defiance of the federal Fugitive Slave Act of 1850, several Northern states passed what were called "personal liberty laws." In a curious reversal of the states' rights doctrine, they decreed that state law exempted their citizens from complying with the hated federal fugitive slave law. That view encouraged not only passive disobedience but active and occasionally violent support of escaped slaves. Free blacks and whites alike defied lawful authority to prevent recaptured runaway slaves from being sent back to the South. Details of the more prominent incidents demonstrate their similarity to the later Otterville "outrage." In February 1851 members of the local black community invaded a Boston courtroom and spirited away Shadrach Minkins before he could be returned to slavery. That September in Christiana, Pennsylvania, a party of blacks led by William Parker and abetted by white neighbors resisted the seizure of four fugitive slaves from Maryland and killed the slaveholder. In October 1851 a "well-organized mob" of whites and blacks battered their way into the U.S. commissioner's office in Syracuse and "forcibly liberated" William ("Jerry") Henry, a runaway slave from Missouri. In these three instances

the fugitive slaves all reached Canada. Courts indicted seventy-five participants but convicted only Enoch Reed, an African American, in Syracuse.[6]

Resistance to the Fugitive Slave Act redoubled in 1854 with the Kansas-
Nebraska Act that infuriated Northerners because of its vast potential to
expand slavery in the territories. In March 1854 in Racine, Wisconsin, a slaveholder, two deputy federal marshals, and three others apprehended an escaped
Missouri slave, Joshua Glover, and beat him when he resisted. Fearing an
uprising, the authorities removed Glover to the Milwaukee jail. One hundred
Racine men followed but found the populace there already in an uproar.
Rallied by the cry "Freemen! To the rescue! Slave-catchers are in our midst!"
a large crowd broke into the jail and liberated Glover, who was subsequently
smuggled into Canada. In an interesting turnabout, the Racine sheriff charged
the slave owner with assault and battery, but a local judge released him. The
law gave a master the right to recapture a fugitive slave and present him to
federal authorities for return to bondage. The Wisconsin Supreme Court
steadfastly ruled in favor of the rescue's chief ringleader, Sherman M. Booth,
and refused to acknowledge a decision in 1859 by the U.S. Supreme Court
that overruled them. In May 1854 a similar rescue attempt in Boston turned
tragic when a courthouse guard was killed. The federal government returned
Anthony Burns to his master in Virginia where he was harshly treated and
imprisoned, but in March 1855 Northerners purchased and freed him.
Another celebrated incident occurred in September 1858 when John Price, a
runaway slave living in Oberlin, Ohio, was seized and held in a hotel in
nearby Wellington prior to being taken back to the South. In a bloodless
assault thirty-seven residents of Oberlin and Wellington freed Price, who
went to Canada. Twenty rescuers served time in jail, while fellow residents
publicly demonstrated their support.[7]

Prior to August 1860 Minnesota saw few, if any, such incidents. That
month Eliza Winston, a slave from Mississippi, came north with her master's
family to vacation in St. Anthony as part of the increasingly popular Southern tourist trade. Abetted by local abolitionists—a small minority within
Minnesota—Winston sued for her freedom. To the intense irritation of pro-
slavery Democrats and others who feared the loss of Dixie tourist dollars,
Judge Charles Vandenburgh granted her freedom based on the Minnesota
state constitution which forbade slavery. His ruling defied the 1857 U.S.
Supreme Court decision involving Dred Scott, who certainly was the most
famous black person yet associated with Minnesota. Scott had sought his
freedom after extended sojourns in free states and territories, including stays
in 1836 and 1837 at Fort Snelling. The Supreme Court brazenly rejected his
suit by declaring slaves were merely property and no blacks could have the

right of citizenship. In the wake of Winston's emancipation, rioters in Minneapolis and St. Anthony ransacked the homes of prominent abolitionists in a vain hope of finding her and returning her to her master. Tempers stayed high until the outbreak of the Civil War eight months later.[8]

The Ninth Minnesota would have known of these highly publicized slave rescues effected by free blacks themselves and by Northern abolitionists. John Arnold, for example, had lived just outside Wellington, Ohio, for many years and left for Minnesota the same year of Price's dramatic deliverance. One can only assume with his abolitionist beliefs and close connection with that community that Arnold was fully aware of what took place there. It is also evident that a substantial portion of the Ninth Minnesota already strongly opposed slavery before the regiment went south. The political turmoil over the Missouri elections clearly added to that sensitivity. Even so, one can only theorize why thirty-eight of their number acted so swiftly and decisively in direct defiance of orders to help John and his family.

As historian Eric Foner writes, "Hostility to slavery did not preclude deep prejudices against blacks." Some ardent abolitionists seem to have opposed slavery more as an abstract philosophical exercise rather than from any deep sympathy for the enslaved. Despite growing support for emancipation among Union soldiers, the vast majority of Northerners, in and out of the military, lacked personal empathy and any fundamental respect for African Americans. Those blacks whom the soldiers most often encountered were newly freed slaves who toiled in and around the army camps. Previously forbidden an education, often possessing nothing but their clothes, such "Contrabands" were the rootless refugees of a cruel but necessary war. They also suffered from blame-the-victim syndrome. In November 1862 Pvt. Harvey Reid of the Twenty-Second Wisconsin "Abolition Regiment" harshly disapproved of the former slaves whom he observed in camp. They were "lazy, saucy, and lousy," and he wanted them ejected from quarters. Nonetheless, he chided the hypocrisy of "rabid abolitionists" who "declared with all the emphasis the language is capable of, that not one [fugitive] shall be taken out while a drop of blood remained in their veins." Yet "because [those blacks] did not prove the perfect beings they supposed them, they turn them out of their tents in the cold, not knowing or caring whether they find another place to sleep." At Jefferson City in November 1863, John Aiton recorded a specific act of prejudice by a fellow soldier of Company D whom he saw "jerk a negro's sack and scatter his apples all over." The "others did not approve of the act" and "helped to gather up the scattered fruit." That night another member of the company became angry after returning unexpectedly to find that his tentmate, Pvt. Levi Goodfellow, had invited blacks to take shelter from the cold.

As far as he was concerned, Goodfellow "could sleep with the hogs." With mock outrage Aiton responded, "Oh horrors!" but added in a serious vein that "men ought to be valued by their moral, and by natural qualities."[9]

Such noble sentiments as Aiton expressed were rare. Only in exceptional circumstances could blacks surmount the stereotype of racially inferior menials that white society imposed on them. "Our countrymen do not know us. They are strangers to our characters, ignorant of our capacity, oblivious to our history," black abolitionist James McCune Smith despaired in 1860. When whites actually did make a sincere effort to relate to blacks as fellow human beings sharing a common dignity and worth, wonderful things could happen. As Reverend Lovejoy commented in 1861 in Missouri, "How can a man establish a stronger claim to the sympathy and protection of a stranger than that which tyranny, misfortune, and misery have given to this poor negro upon me?" On the morning of November 11, 1863, John swiftly and decisively established such a direct connection with soldiers of the Ninth Minnesota. Like them he was a loving and loyal husband, father, and brother, and they perceived him as such. It says volumes about John's strength of character, fortitude, and courage that he fought so hard for his loved ones in the only way left open to him. Many years afterward H. C. Bruce mused of the time when he and his fiancée actually undertook their perilous journey to freedom in Kansas: "I am satisfied, even now, that I was braver that night than I have ever been since." John could certainly have said the same. He had no idea whether the Northern strangers would even bother to listen to his cry for help, but he went ahead nevertheless. Indeed, even when compared to the magnificent forcible rescues in the North, the "Outrage at Otterville" stands in stark relief. That quiet morning at Lamine Bridge beheld no searing symbol of a chained and brutalized fugitive slave, a fellow resident of a free community cruelly recaptured by his ruthless master and unjustly bound over to an uncaring authority for return to bondage. Nor did an eloquent abolitionist orator deliver an impassioned speech that emboldened his audience to rise up and act. Instead John, wholly and humbly alone, presented his own case to his potential rescuers and enlisted them to save his family. Miraculously, he succeeded, and to their eternal credit Sgt. Frank Merchant and his thirty-seven comrades in the Ninth Minnesota stepped forward in what indeed became a wonderful and unique event of the Civil War.[10]

ELABORATIONS AND RATIONALIZATIONS

After their arrest the liberators enjoyed plenty of spare time to contemplate their serious predicament and to mull in their own minds just how they had gotten into it. Everything had happened so quickly that morning at Lamine Bridge and on the train at Otterville that most of them knew little of what exactly had transpired other than there were slaves to be rescued. Nevertheless, they now had to mount a legal defense against the serious charges looming over them. Not until the Minnesotans reached Jefferson City did they learn the slaves were actually being transported by military pass. C. W. C. Walker had never identified himself to the soldiers who absconded with his slaves, let alone brandished his official movement permit. Only afterward had he waved the pass in front of Queen and Pritchard and the other passengers. A second salient fact ascertained later was that the pass was not even valid, given Special Order No. 307 forbidding the transport of slaves out of Missouri. In St. Louis the conservative *Daily Missouri Republican* reported the incident under the headline "Attack on a Railroad Train," while the Radical *Westliche Post* exulted, "Another Nigger-Driver prevented from exporting his 'Chattels'—This time without orders."[11]

Although new facts came to light, rumor and supposition soon embroidered the simple truth. On November 13 a certain "R. M. W.," an anonymous soldier of the Ninth Minnesota stationed at Jefferson City, wrote the *St. Paul Press* to describe the event for the first time in print in Minnesota. The slaves, he charged, were being taken to St. Louis "'under military orders' for sale by, no doubt, some secesh master." It was also asserted that the slaveholder was himself "a man now in the rebel service" or even "an officer in the rebel army" who was taking the slaves to the Confederacy to be sold. Such conditions would mitigate the offense of the rescue. Soon it was stated that the escaped slave [John] had voiced that fable when he beseeched the Minnesotans for help, and that he himself claimed his master had killed at least one other slave who resisted. Those inaccurate embellishments constituted the first attack on John's credibility that others later exploited. The evidence shows that John never said Walker was in the Confederate army or was even a Rebel sympathizer. Nor did he ever assert his family was to be sent across enemy lines. In fact he did not know of the death of his brother, Billey, until one of his sisters told him after the rescue.[12]

The swift evolution of the Otterville story is reflected in a letter to the *Rochester Republican* written on November 15 at Jefferson City by Lieutenant Stearns. Noting "some big cock and bull stories" concerning the incident, Stearns offered his own interpretation:

> Certain negroes represented to the boys that a certain Secesher, after having killed one or two of his slaves, was about to remove some eight or ten others to Kentucky for the purpose of selling them; that the said slaves were to pass on a

certain train of cars whereupon some forty of the boys repaired to the depot, all "armed and equipped as the law directs." When the train came along, they sent the first mentioned negroes to tell those on the train that they were at liberty to cut sticks for the woods. Whereupon they did *cut sticks* and have not since been heard of.[13]

Stearns's use of the term "represented" is significant considering the way the story would be spun.

A subsequent adornment to the basic tale was that Captain Wellman himself gave the order or at least condoned the removal of the slaves. Arnold came to believe that was so. In freeing the slaves, the liberators "had obeyed the law, both civil and military, as well as the laws of justice and humanity." Writing to the *Religious Telescope,* the newspaper of the United Brethren, he claimed the "commander of the post signified his wish that the slaves might be taken from the train and liberated" and had ordered Merchant to assemble volunteers. An anonymous Company C liberator wrote to the *Mower County Register* under the pseudonym "C. E. M." and also to Missouri Radical state legislator H. J. Fisher, who kept the correspondent's name confidential. His accounts described the commander at Lamine Bridge going through Orderly Sergeant Whitford, who assigned the Otterville mission to Merchant. In that version the escaped slave supposedly told the post commander that his master was in the "rebel army" and had directed his "son" to take the slaves out of state to sell them. The son tried to embark his slaves at Sedalia, but the "troops would not allow it" and instead sent the fugitive slave to warn the garrison at Lamine Bridge. In the meantime, the son boarded his human cargo at "Residence," the next station six miles down the line. Once Merchant solicited volunteers, the "boys" readily complied, "anxious to proceed to a deed we believed to be our responsible duty as soldiers to perform." The anonymous liberator further explained to Fisher, "It had been for several months the habit in our camp of getting men for any excursion by volunteering in preference to detailing, and in this instance we supposed, did we not volunteer, we would be detailed."[14]

The claim that the soldiers acted under direct orders obviously arose from the hands-off attitude that Ford expressed to the Company C noncoms. Wellman, his immediate superior, never knew what was afoot, much less approved of liberating the slaves. Had he known of and sympathized with John's plight, he could simply have flagged down the train at Lamine Bridge and removed the family. Walker, moreover, had no grown son. The "troops" at Sedalia would have had no reason to hinder him, for he possessed a pass from the local provost-marshal to transport his slaves. Nor had they dispatched John to alert the men at Lamine Bridge. There was no town named "Residence," a confused reference to Smithton where the slaves actually did board the train. Another unresolved question was how a fugitive slave who was on foot could have possibly managed to race a train to Lamine Bridge. Writing the day after the incident, untainted by later fables, David Felch best described the circumstances behind the rescue. "So forty of us took up our guns without orders and went up to the depot and stayed there till they came a long."[15]

ATTITUDES AND PERCEPTIONS

If the letters of Arnold, Felch, and the anonymous "C. E. M." are representative, the rescuers believed they were being persecuted for a simple "act of humanity" by those "fighting for free and equal rights." To "C. E. M.," liberating the slaves was simply "an act we believed only our duty as soldiers in the service of our country and our God, to do." In the *Religious Telescope* Arnold articulated to his fellow churchmen that "we are not ashamed of the crime of giving liberty to the slave, any more than we are ashamed of persuading sinners or the slaves of sin to run away from the degrading service of the devil, and engage in the noble and elevating employment of serving God." He trusted that with the Lord's help "we may bear our trials with the same fortitude that two of the apostles did when they were thrust into the inner prison, and their feet made fast in the stocks for no other crime than that of doing good." Such sentiments echoed the famous "Higher Law" speech made during the debate preceding the Compromise of 1850 when Senator William Henry Seward of New York repudiated slavery by invoking a "higher law than the Constitution."[16]

Soldiers of the Ninth Minnesota who had not participated in the rescue mainly offered their support to those who had. "Most of the officers are our friends, as well as the whole Regiment," Arnold opined. "R. M. W." insisted "there is not an enlisted man, nor more than three or four officers in the regiment, who will not, in their hearts, justify the act as between man and man." Those "who rescued the slaves" had "acted under the noblest impulse of nature," and "whatever punishment is meted out to them, will be a crown of glory on their heads, should God in his mercy vouchsafe their return from the army." Evidently hearing of the slave hunters at Otterville, "R. M. W." regretted the actions of other soldiers, "only a few" who "are as fierce on the track of a poor fugitive mother and her child as would the blood hounds of Jeff. Davis' on his Mississippi plantation." An anonymous soldier wrote on November 18 from Lamine Bridge that the men there "generally approve of the rescue, despite the irregularity of the proceedings," but "not so with a few of our officers, who would not soil their delicate hands, nor sully their conservative reputations, by engaging in any act, no matter how inherently right, if it had the taint of the 'nigger' about it." On December 1 yet another Lamine correspondent, "Volunteer" from Company K, elucidated events as he knew them so the citizens of Winona could "judge for themselves how much our men are to blame, at least in a Christian point of view, whatever legal authorities and conservative shoulder straps may think of it." Confident of "the feelings of every soldier, and some of the officers," he declared that "whatever punishment the poor fellows may incur, they will have the heartfelt sympathies of every Christian man and woman" in the North. Yet opinion at Lamine Bridge was not unanimous in favor of the liberation. Still bitter over going south to fight what he thought was an unnecessary war over slavery, James Woodbury remarked on November 25 in a letter home that his friend Nate Palmeter "is still down to Jefferson [with] all the rest of the niger lovers. I guess it will go pretty hard with them and perhaps it will be a good thing if it does it may learn them something."[17]

It would be valuable to know what Wellman and Ford personally thought of the Otterville "outrage" (and how Wellman viewed Ford's role in it), but no written record has come to light. The "boys were very naughty" to have disobeyed orders and freed the slaves, Stearns admitted, but he sympathized with how "hard" it was "for those who have breathed the pure air of Minnesota to disregard appeals to their generosity in behalf of liberty, even tho' prudence would deny them." He deplored such insubordinate behavior, "as all must who would maintain military discipline," but admired how "the thing was cooly and handsomely done, just as Minnesota soldiers know how to do things." In turn Chaplain Kerr remarked that the prisoners received "much public sympathy," their "act being regarded as impulsive and prompted by feelings of humanity toward the oppressed." Furthermore, "some acts of slaveholders, secesh sympathizers and Provost Marshals need ventilation and a few months' imprisonment of such would not injure the cause of freedom one whit."[18]

Soldiers understood that the liberators, although serving a higher cause, acted contrary to military regulations and government policy. Republican newspaper editors in Minnesota and elsewhere, however, predictably raged against those who ordered their arrest. The *Mower County Register* could not "see but they did perfectly right" and blamed "the mean, contemptible proslavery officers in Missouri" who condoned the illegal transporting of slaves out of the state. "The soldiers who rescued these blacks, simply put a stop to this wrong." Minnesotans "are not fighting to maintain slavery—they fight for the Union and Freedom. Does not General Schofield understand this, or will he not?" The *Religious Telescope* took dead aim at the "Schofield-Gamble rule in Missouri," which "in too many cases" served the "interest of the rebels." General Brown "deserves the contempt of all humane men" for incarcerating the Minnesotans. "Had [the soldiers] not promptly delivered the poor blacks, they would have deserved arrest." The *Central Republican* of Faribault, Minnesota, even linked the "Copperhead" Schofield with long-detested "Copperhead" General Sibley, whom the paper accused of sabotaging the 1863 Indian Expedition in order to retain troops who could otherwise fight in the South. The newspaper also faulted Lincoln for permitting Copperhead officers to dominate the Union army. Of course, the Radicals were indulging in their usual hyperbole. None of the officers whom they labeled "Copperheads" were in any way Peace Democrats.[19]

Enter the Radicals

The Missouri Radicals followed their supposed victory in the state elections of November 3 by urging the General Assembly to choose their leader Benjamin Gratz Brown for the U.S. Senate. On November 13, the same day the arrested Minnesotans reached Jefferson City, he defeated James O. Broadhead, a Conservative Unionist who was Schofield's provost marshal general. "Whoever dreamed," exulted famed abolitionist William Lloyd Garrison, "that Missouri would elect [Brown], a thoroughgoing Abolitionist, to the Senate of the United States?" The Ninth Minnesota soldier correspondent "R. M. W." completely concurred, writing that the Missouri legislature had "covered itself with glory." At the same time Senator John B. Henderson, an astute Conservative who earned Lincoln's respect as a "hearty Emancipationist," received a full term as an Unconditional Unionist. Lincoln hoped that by this action the two Missouri factions might finally cooperate. "Nothing that happened in our politics," he averred, "has pleased me more."[20]

The tale that Schofield's Department of the Missouri had arrested soldiers simply for freeing slaves was red meat to the Radicals in Jefferson City. Arnold wrote delightedly on December 2 that many members of the Missouri state legislature "sympathize with us, and offer to do all they can in our behalf." The next day "C. E. M." penned his letter to legislator Fisher, who commented, "It is generally acknowledged by all who have come in contact with these men that they are of the most quiet and orderly character." After he canvassed his fellow Radicals in the General Assembly, fifty-nine state legislators signed a petition to General Brown on behalf of the prisoners. It related the events of the rescue according to the now familiar elaborations. The slave owner was said to be "in arms against the Govt of the U.S."; the soldiers did not stop the train or detain it "beyond its usual time"; they did not recognize Queen and Pritchard as officers, "as no insignia or badge of office was visible upon these persons"; and "though not acting under regular orders at the time," the men "had the sanction of at least some of their superior officers" (which was true in the case of Ford). Several factors "may to some extent mitigate the offence for which these men are held under arrest." The Ninth Minnesota, "having but recently been organized," could hardly be expected to have acquired "the strict orderly bearing and dicipline [*sic*] which characterizes the old soldier." The men themselves "are of high moral stand[ing] in the community in which they resided." Having come from a Free State, "it is but natural that they should hate slavery—the cause of the Rebellion—as it should be hated!" The petitioners entreated Brown to weigh all these factors and, if it should "meet with your approval," to free the men.[21]

Brigadier General Egbert Benson Brown, a forty-seven-year-old native of New York, sat squarely in the center of the controversy. Restless at an early age, he spent four years on a whaling voyage to the Pacific Ocean. Prospering afterward in business and politics, he was briefly mayor of Toledo in 1852 before coming to St. Louis as a railroad manager. An ardent Unionist, he helped organize the Seventh Missouri in June 1861 to save the state from secession and rose to brigadier general of Missouri Volunteers. His gallant defense of Springfield on January 8, 1863, against regular Confederate forces

Egbert B. Brown

saved the town, but his shoulder was severely wounded. He lost full use of his left arm, which was spared amputation only by a radically new surgical procedure. His victory at Springfield earned him the thanks of the Missouri legislature and promotion to brigadier general of U.S. Volunteers. Brown took over the District of Central Missouri in June 1863. Bald and sporting a chin curtain beard, he was a moderate, even kindly man, a cautious plodder, but also dogged and determined. Not notably a political intriguer, Brown appeared more comfortable with the Conservatives than with the Radicals, who certainly showed him no sympathy.[22]

On December 7 Brown replied to the legislators by declaring bluntly the prisoners were "mutineers." Although affirming his "abhorrence of the institution of slavery," which was the "cause of the war," he did not condone flaunting army regulations "in order to give expression to any individual views, nor can I recognize the right to do so by soldiers under my command." Far from newly formed, the Ninth Minnesota, he pointed out, had over a year's service. "Its soldierly appearance, and strict discipline, as well as general reputation shows that it has been commanded by Officers who knew and have done their duty." Queen and Pritchard, "both in full uniform," had properly identified themselves as officers and vainly "used all the authority and force in their power to stop the mutinous conduct of these men." Brown had not arrested the prisoners "for their participation in the release of slaves, for the Army is engaged in doing that duty as one of the means of conquering a peace," but instead "for their violations of the 6th, 7th, 8th & 9th Articles of War." Those offenses were "of so grave a character" and "so clearly set out in the reports of the officers who witnessed them, that I do not feel authorized to order their release, but will refer the question with your petition for the decision of the Secretary of War." As will become evident, Brown's stern posture was a bluff, for he personally, unlike Wilkin, did not intend the wayward Minnesotans to suffer severe punishment. Given such an inflammatory issue in volatile Missouri as the forcible freeing of slaves, it seems he felt he must maintain the appearance of strict discipline.[23]

If General Brown could not be made to see reason, perhaps newly minted Radical Senator Gratz Brown would see that he did. On December 10 Fisher wrote Gratz Brown summarizing the legislators' petition and General Brown's reply. After interviewing the "mutineers" and some officers of the Ninth Minnesota, he concluded the charges were "trumped up." Noting General Brown's intention to buck the case up to the Secretary of War, Fisher sought to "enlist" Gratz Brown's "sympathies and attention in behalf of the accused." With the battle shifting from Jefferson City to Washington, senatorial action could prove decisive in freeing the Minnesotans. Fisher also understood that the new senator would eagerly welcome any additional ammunition to use against Schofield and other Conservative-minded army leaders in Missouri. It was high time to settle old scores.[24]

Following regular channels, General Brown submitted the Otterville case to the headquarters of the Department of the Missouri in St. Louis. He expected Schofield to endorse the papers and forward them in timely fashion to Secretary of War Edwin M. Stanton for disposition. Until the authorities in Washington or St. Louis resolved the issue, the liberators would continue to bunk in the smoky bowels of the Ransom Hotel. Schofield, though, had many other weighty matters on his mind, and the case of the Minnesota mutineers got lost in the process. The excessive delay in fact violated the rights of the accused who were supposed to receive a speedy trial. According to the 79th Article of War, "no officer or soldier who shall be put in arrest shall continue in confinement more than eight days, or until such time as a court-martial can be assembled." There had already been much more than enough time to have done so.[25]

An End to the "Farce"

In the meantime Wilkin endured another uprising by his men. Beset by "cold, wet and disagreeable" weather, the Ninth Minnesota eagerly stoked the brick fireplaces inside its tents. Consequently, the "neighboring rail fences and all kinds of combustible material began to disappear," eliciting strong civilian complaints, recalled Sgt. Colin Macdonald of Company I. On November 25 a regimental order prohibited the destruction of fences and other wooden structures on pain of severe punishment. "That night, while the guard's back was conveniently turned, a grass sod was neatly adjusted on the top of Col. Wilkin's tent stovepipe." The next dawn as "the boys were peeking from their tents toward headquarters," the orderly who started the customary morning blaze "rushed out in a cloud of smoke, gasping for breath." He was "followed by the colonel, rubbing his eyes." To the delighted men, "the spectacle was ludicrous in the extreme," and they "broke into a hearty cheer." Swallowing his pride, Wilkin astutely ignored the "practical joke." He directed parties to go into the woods that afternoon to cut firewood that enabled the men "thereafter to enjoy their fire-places undisturbed." It was a rare victory, for the Ninth Minnesota did not often get the best of its pugnacious, pocket-sized colonel.[26]

On the Tennessee-Georgia line, Confederate Gen. Braxton Bragg, conducting a supposed siege of Chattanooga, was thrown back from his position atop Missionary Ridge and driven south into Georgia. The Rebels also broke off the siege of Knoxville. Those two successes completely reversed the Union disaster incurred at Chickamauga two months before. Thereafter, the armies settled in for the winter in anticipation of Federal offensives in the spring of 1864 in Virginia and Georgia that could decide the war. The Ninth Minnesota had no idea whether it would ever participate directly in achieving that long-sought final victory.

After briefly running the First Sub-District, Wilkin departed for St. Louis on court-martial duty. There he encountered the balance of his regiment, Companies G and H under Major Markham, on provost duty in the city. At Jefferson City Lieutenant Colonel Marsh took command of the Ninth Minnesota as well as the First Sub-District. On December 7 Capt. Horace Strait led Companies A, B, E, and I in a long circuitous route by rail to Rolla, the terminus of the southwestern branch of the Pacific Railroad fifty miles southeast of Jefferson City. While Companies C and K still guarded Lamine Bridge, only regimental headquarters and Companies D and F stayed in the state capital. To Chaplain Kerr the old camp "brings to mind the story of the deserted village." The two companies stripped lumber from dwellings abandoned by the others to make "themselves comfortable here thro' the winter." Digging in a couple of feet, the men "built up with timber or plank sufficiently high for two bunks, one above the other, and then fastened the tent on top." These tents proved "more endurable in severe cold weather than I had supposed." Thus situated, wrote Kerr, "We will likely remain as now posted until spring fairly opens, and then be 'off to the wars.'"[27]

The worried but bored prisoners in the decrepit Ransom Hotel wondered if they too were to be left in limbo for the winter. Felch gladly chopped wood for four days at a dollar a day to earn enough cash to buy a pair of boots. On December 16 he advised his father that new charges had been preferred, but they were "nearly the same" as before. Disgusted, he could not say when the trial would take place, "nor do I care." On the twenty-ninth he complained, "I am yet in the gard house and we don't have the best of fare." He was "getting tired of laying around this place" and declared the whole brouhaha "a disgrace to the Regiment." Zara Frisbie, another Company C liberator, took the whole experience much more philosophically. The twenty-nine-year-old farmer, who was Felch's neighbor in Mower County, had two children, daughter Ella who just turned four and son Willis who was two. He wrote his wife, Mary, to say that he was "well as usual and feel thankful for all things. Our food is good now, for a while they did not give us what rashions was due to us." Moreover, "I am cook today. I expect I shall be most anything you want for a man when I get home. I am cooking, washing, and mending and I expect when I get home I must try and help you more than I used to." Frisbie's greatest regret was being separated from his family. "I think of my visit often and long to be with you to leave no more, to war no more, but to live in peace." He asked Mary to "do the best you can. Keep up courage. Talk to the little ones. Show them early that God loves good little children. . . . This from your affectionate husband until death."[28]

Up to mid-December, the weather, despite occasional precipitation and chill, was "very mild and pleasant," more like October in Minnesota. Then the harsh winter of 1863–64 struck with a vengeance. On December 16 after a "long, cold night" on guard at Lamine Bridge, Woodbury found "it is snowing as fast as I ever saw it in Minn." After a massive New Year's snowstorm blanketed the Upper Midwest, the temperature at Jefferson City plunged to twenty-two degrees below zero and by the seventh to twenty-six below. Frozen out of the tents of the regimental hospital, the patients, including several ill liberators, took refuge in the brick comfort of the Jefferson City General Hospital. The weather "verily reminded us of Minnesota." Kerr had "feared there would be much suffering among the men in their tents, but with the exception of some frosted ears and fingers of those on guard, there was no complaining."[29]

Things heated up, though, with regard to the prisoners. General Brown was in a particularly good mood. Friday, January 8, 1864, was not only the forty-ninth anniversary of Gen. Andrew Jackson's triumph at New Orleans, but was precisely one year after his own signal victory at Springfield. Despite bitter cold the day witnessed a gala of joyous events. On the Capitol square, Brown conducted a feu-de-joie national salute of thirty-four guns. Risking frozen mouths and fingers, military bands played outdoors. Companies D and F paraded in front of Brown's headquarters, where he "felicitously addressed" them. In the evening Brown was "tendered the compliment of a serenade" at his home by a "large number of his friends" in honor of the Battle of Springfield.[30]

That same happy day, headquarters of the District of Central Missouri quietly issued Special Order No. 7 that sparked tremendous relief and special rejoicing among the reluctant tenants of the Ransom Hotel. "The enlisted men of Cos. C and K Ninth Infantry Minnesota Volunteers at present under arrest are returned to duty with their respective companies." For certain it was drinks all around in celebration of their own liberation, as the "loyal citizens gave the boys great praise, and quite an ovation upon their discharge."[31]

According to Stearns, the release of the prisoners finally brought "the farce" to an end. In the absence of any direction from either the War Department or headquarters in St. Louis, Brown finally acted on his own to free the men, at least temporarily, pending future developments. As the "proper authority" who ordered the court-martial in the first place, he had the right under military law to reject any findings and return the men to duty. On January 21 he informed the authorities in St. Louis why he decided to release the prisoners. His investigation revealed that although Charles Walker, a "loyal citizen," had lawfully transported his slaves, the men of the Ninth Minnesota were "under the impression that an act of injustice was being done." Brown asserted they were "misled by a story of a negro" who falsely claimed "the master of the slaves was in the rebel army." He also established to his own satisfaction that "no orders were issued by the commanding officer of the detachment to release the slaves," and that Queen and Pritchard "were in uniform" when they confronted the soldiers on the train. In mitigation of these offenses, he found the Minnesotans to be "good soldiers" who "cheerfully performed their duty" and "obeyed all orders except in this case." Moreover, they had "acknowledged the fault they had committed," although no actual record of such newfound contrition has been found. L. D. Stewart, for one, was not cowed. "I was never Court Martialed," he wrote in 1914 to a pension board of review, "was never tried in any way, never even reprimanded, nor was the time of my arrest ever deducted from my pay. If charges were ever preferred against me they must have been dismissed."[32]

Brown declared the "punishment the men had received would prevent future offences of this character." Deterrence was his principal motive for holding the men as long as he did. Having forwarded the case to the Secretary of War, he "ordered them to duty with their regiment, and discharged them from arrest to await his decision." He seemed confident Stanton would simply let the matter drop. No doubt he also noticed, with the Radicals increasingly in the ascendant, which way the political wind now blew both in Jefferson City and Washington. The untruthful assertion that John himself lied and thereby beguiled the Minnesotans into rescuing his family under false pretenses enabled the authorities to sweep the whole sticky issue under the rug without confronting the fundamental injustice of continuing to tolerate slavery in Missouri.[33]

General Brown's release order directed the men from Company K to "proceed without delay" to Lamine Bridge, but he retained those from Company C in Jefferson City, where the rest of Ford's men were now expected. Otterville was no longer receptive to soldiers, Minnesotans or otherwise. In late December Brown had brought in the Fourth Regiment of Missouri State Militia Cavalry to protect against a suspected raid by "Quantrill and his cut throats," who in truth were hundreds of miles away in Texas. The troopers soon reminded the populace of the bad old days, particularly when the extreme cold weather forced some of them to take temporary refuge in town. Companies

C and K were snug in their own shelter, luckily camped where firewood was abundant. According to Woodbury, "it has been awful cold standing guard" in temperatures as low "as any time last winter in Minn." On January 4 Dr. Saunders, Otterville's self-appointed spokesman, demanded that Brown immediately remove all troops from the town even though the Missouri cavalrymen had already left. Brown refused to transfer the two Minnesota companies, especially "when there is no special cause of complaint," but did promise "as soon as the weather will permit" to "move the troops into cantonments removed from any town." The first step was to cut the garrison at Lamine Bridge to just Wellman's Company K.[34]

POST HOC FIREWORKS IN WASHINGTON

On Monday, January 11, the same day the last of the former prisoners rejoined Company C in Jefferson City, Republican Senator Morton S. Wilkinson of Minnesota rose at his mahogany desk in the U.S. Senate to offer a resolution:

> Resolved, That the Secretary of War be, and he is hereby, instructed to inform the Senate whether he has any official information in his Department relating to the arrest and imprisonment by the military authorities in Missouri of a large number of the private soldiers belonging to the ninth Minnesota regiment; also, as to the cause of their arrest and imprisonment, how many have been so arrested, and how long they have been confined in prison.

The Senate, by unanimous consent, proceeded to consider the resolution.[35]

Elected to the Senate in 1859, "Wilk" Wilkinson was an able lawyer and fine orator. Tall, spare, and elegant with "thin, marked and intellectual" patrician features, he had migrated to Minnesota in 1847 from New York and sat in the first territorial legislature. A former Whig and committed opponent of slavery, Wilkinson helped found the Minnesota Republican Party. His election to the Senate was said to have "surprised everybody," having occurred only because of "competition between prominent men." Charles Francis Adams Jr., who met him in 1860 while campaigning for Lincoln, rated him "not a man of any considerable ability" whom only a "new state" would elect. A quintessential backbencher who just happened to sit in the front row (despite his relative seniority he never did chair an important senate committee), Wilkinson consistently voted with the most radical Republicans, the "Jacobins," who proved such a thorn in Lincoln's side, although he always treated them with careful respect. Lincoln's clemency toward the Dakota following the U.S.–Dakota War had particularly enraged Wilkinson. So did the often dismal performance of the Union army high command. Unfortunately, he displayed an otherworldliness in often-futile dealings with the practical side of life. "It is to be regretted," wrote one commentator, "that his speeches were always better than his practices." Wilkinson also committed the fatal political error of ignoring his constituents, at least those who actually mattered. General Pope, a bitter critic, gleefully informed the War Department in August 1863 that, in addition "to his other disqualifications and unpopularity," Wilkinson "has of late added bad personal habits" and was in "desperation at the certainty of falling into total obscurity after his term expires."[36]

Given Senator Wilkinson's anti-slavery sentiments and open antagonism toward the top military authorities, the case of the Minnesota "mutineers" was right up his alley. Based on letters and newspaper articles from home, he presented in varying degrees of accuracy the much-elaborated, now familiar story of how the soldiers rescued the slaves from "the hands of the traitors who were conveying them out of the State." He read from a letter from a Ninth Minnesota soldier, quite possibly Orderly Sgt. George Hays of Company K who was also very likely "Volunteer" in the *Winona Daily Republican*. The arrest, Wilkinson's correspondent declared, was "an act of military official baseness that certainly demands inquiry beyond the jurisdiction of the pro-slavery tyrants who have caused this incarceration." Wilkinson himself denounced the military bureaucracy and General Brown in particular for "demoralizing our soldiers" in Missouri. "I shall insist, as the representative of the State of Minnesota, that our soldiers shall be treated differently in the

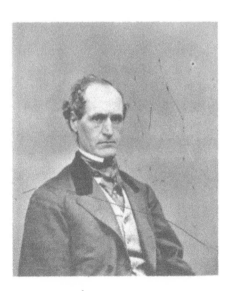

Senator Morton S. Wilkinson

future." He would "never consent that they shall be made the tools of the slavery-loving tyrants of Missouri."[37]

Wilkinson also related the tale of the luckless soldier forced to wear a ball-and-chain for "having hallooed for Jim Lane," though he erred in attributing that miscreant to Minnesota rather than Nebraska. Taking the floor, Senator Lane of Kansas himself righteously asserted that "scores, if not hundreds of soldiers have been confined in the guard-houses of Missouri for no other offense than hallooing for Jim Lane." Two such unfortunates, he alleged, were even "bayoneted for no other offense than that," although history has not confirmed such shocking allegations. Lane thanked Wilkinson for raising the case of the Minnesotans, which, he had learned, a committee of the Missouri legislature had also investigated. The flamboyant Kansas senator tarred the "Gamble régime" with the usual wide radical brush. "The officers appointed by the Governor of the State are the criminals; the soldiers are unconditional Union men, anti-slavery all of them, with scarcely an exception." It is likely Lane suggested to Wilkinson the tactic of a senate resolution. That ploy had worked in July 1862 when both Kansas senators asked the Senate to look into the arrest of Lieutenant Colonel Anthony of the Seventh Kansas Cavalry. As a result the military had buckled and released Anthony without a trial.[38]

Senator James Lane

Next to speak was Senator Henderson of Missouri, who earlier that very day had introduced a resolution that ultimately led to the Thirteenth Amendment, outlawing slavery in the United States. He did not "for a moment think there is any correctness in the inference drawn here that General Brown has mistreated the soldiers from Minnesota in consequence of any pro-slavery feeling on his part." Though desiring "to have the facts," he said he would support the resolution. That set the stage for his new colleague, Gratz Brown. It was due to Governor Gamble and General Schofield, Gratz Brown charged, that "no State in its military affairs has been so disastrously managed as my own." He had received "communications from loyal members of the Legislature at Jefferson City, setting forth the facts in regard to the case to which has been alluded to by the Senator from Minnesota, and they confirm the statement which he has made." The "resolution will pass," Gratz Brown prophesied, "and I trust we shall have an opportunity to take a full review of the acts of oppression and of hostility to the loyal, freedom-loving sentiment in that State, and that we shall be able before long to take such action as to preclude its continuance here." The Senate did pass Wilkinson's resolution and submitted it to the secretary of war.[39]

Stung by the hot potato the Senate tossed in his lap, Stanton contacted Schofield, who had stewed in Washington ever since mid-December awaiting the president's pleasure. Up to that time, Lincoln had been confident of a compromise that would ease the tense situation in Missouri. The Senate was to confirm Schofield's promotion to major general of volunteers, followed by his welcome transfer to a significant field command. That would make room for General Rosecrans, who, although in disgrace after the defeat of Chickamauga, was thought to be acceptable to the Missouri Radicals. However, Schofield's recent intransigent opposition to Gratz Brown and the Radicals threatened the amity Lincoln hoped to achieve from the Missouri senatorial elections. Egged on by Gratz Brown, the Radical Republicans adamantly refused to see Schofield promoted. "Very much displeased," Lincoln summoned Schofield to the capital to answer for his actions. The battle lines were already drawn when Wilkinson presented his resolution.[40]

Schofield did not recall the circumstances behind the arrest of the Minnesota soldiers and had to telegraph headquarters in St. Louis for the details. On January 13 his adjutant forwarded a sheaf of documents with the gentle reminder that the papers had been laid on "your desk for your action," but "nothing has been done." Schofield passed the papers to Stanton with the excuse "they were received by me only a short time before I left St. Louis and had not been acted upon in consequence of my been suddenly called away." Further communications from St. Louis late in January, including General

Brown's letter of January 21, informed the War Department the soldiers had indeed been returned to duty.[41]

Meanwhile the fight continued in the Senate over Schofield's promotion. On January 20 Gratz Brown presented a petition from members of the Missouri General Assembly charging that Schofield favored "disloyal elements" and had disenfranchised Missouri soldiers. Citing the Minnesota soldiers who were punished for their "hostility to slavery in Missouri," he invoked the teary image of the "blue-eyed northern boy marching from his far-away home to confront a rebellion contending for mastery of the State—his heart aglow, perhaps, with traditions of freedom—[who] finds transgression against the slave code visited with unrelenting harshness while oblivion drapes a corresponding breach of the articles of war." Approval of Schofield's confirmation languished in the Committee on Military Affairs and the Militia. Wilkinson asserted years later that he was primarily responsible for getting the confirmation through the Senate. His ardent defense of the Ninth Minnesota's liberators had made him a minor player in Missouri politics. At some point—it is not certain when—Lincoln requested Wilkinson and Senator Zachariah Chandler of Michigan, a prominent Radical, to meet with him privately and broker a deal with the Missouri Radicals. As Wilkinson remembered it, Lincoln's clarification of Rosecrans's suitability and the urgent need for Schofield to join General Sherman in the field swayed him and Chandler. When they raised the matter in the Senate Republican caucus, "Schofield was confirmed without difficulty—on[ly] the Missouri senators (I think) voting in the negative." The actual vote on the senate floor (twenty-five ayes, nine nays) took place in May 1864, long after Schofield had moved on and Rosecrans had replaced him. The record shows that Wilkinson and Chandler, along with the most ardent Jacobins, actually voted *against* confirmation. Perhaps the most Wilkinson accomplished, if he indeed accomplished anything at all in that regard, was to help get the confirmation out of committee for a vote.[42]

In Jefferson City General Brown soon learned of the calumnies that Gratz Brown and the others had spread about him in the Senate. On January 26 he wrote headquarters in St. Louis angrily demanding a court of inquiry in light of the charges that he had abused soldiers and civilians for "releasing the slaves of rebels and for 'hurrahing for Jim Lane.'" He also insisted the court investigate all his activities since he took command in June 1863. Rosecrans, settling in his new command, had no wish to open that can of worms. On February 1 he forwarded Brown's letter to the adjutant general along with his disapproval: "I think the interests of the service do not require any further steps to be taken in the matter." Stanton replied to Vice President Hannibal Hamlin on February 27 in fulfillment of the Senate Resolution and provided copies of papers that "present all the information on record in this department." The "soldiers referred to having been released and returned to duty," he concurred with Rosecrans that no further action was necessary. On March 4 Hamlin delivered Stanton's report to the Senate, which ordered it to "lie on the table and be printed." That was the last official examination, except a brief one in 1914 regarding L. D. Stewart's pension, of a case that had served as a convenient sideshow in the relentless Radical assault against the Conservatives in Missouri.[43]

Fortunate that he had freed the thirty-eight Minnesota liberators prior to Wilkinson's resolution, General Brown thus unwittingly stole the Senate's thunder—not that he ever received any of the credit.[44] It came to be believed in the Ninth Minnesota and in Minnesota, too, that the Senate, at Wilkinson's behest, compelled Stanton to order the immediate release of the prisoners. "If Minnesota soldiers, who have been in the habit of breathing an atmosphere untainted by the stench of the putrescent carcass of slavery, are to be arrested and incarcerated in prison to gratify Missouri slaveholders and rebels," editorialized the *Rochester Republican,* "our noble Senator insists upon knowing the facts in the case at once." Moreover, "when our representatives in the National Council stand up manfully not only for the dignity and rights of our own State, but also for the principles of an enlightened humanity, they do imperishable honor to themselves and confer lasting benefits on their constituency."[45]

There is no indication in surviving sources that Lincoln ever took direct notice of the actions of the Ninth Minnesota's liberators and their defenders other than to recognize Wilkinson's resulting connection to the Missouri Radicals. Unanswerable is what he might have done had the trial gone on and convicted the soldiers of mutiny. Through his friend Maj. Gen. Joseph Holt, Judge Advocate General of the Army, Lincoln closely followed significant military trials. He pardoned numerous condemned soldiers, declining to intervene only where defendants had demonstrated "meanness and cruelty." A trial of the Minnesota liberators would have cast a unique light on the fundamental contradictions of Lincoln's anti-slavery policies: Union soldiers judged guilty for freeing slaves. It is hard to believe that Lincoln would not have intervened where the motives of the wrongdoers were so selfless. Political expediency might have dictated that he sustain a guilty verdict, but a presidential pardon would have most likely ensued.[46]

In any event no hard feelings existed between General Brown and the Ninth Minnesota, except perhaps among those whom he had arrested. On February 8 he expressed to Marsh that he was "highly gratified" with the "soldierly bearing and the high position [the Minnesotans] have attained in the confidence of the people." It afforded him "great pleasure to commend the inhabitants of the county to their care, remembering always that though temporarily estranged, yet they are our brethren." In turn Marsh tendered the "sincere thanks" of the regiment and assured Brown, a "brave, just and noble Officer," of "our ambition as soldiers to do our whole duty faithfully having in view the restoration of peace and harmony to our distracted, yet much beloved country." That fall and winter, Pvt. Edward L. Clapp of Company C, a twenty-nine-year-old former New Yorker who resided in Rochester, had served on detached duty as a clerk at Brown's headquarters. Years later he recalled Brown "with much pleasure for his many kind acts and good advice to me. He was an officer and a gentlemen." Certainly Brown's approbation aided Clapp's sudden rise in March 1864 from private to sergeant major of the Ninth Minnesota. Things did not work out as well for two of the three liberator noncoms. When Orderly Sergeant Whitford left Company C in February to accept a commission in the Sixty-Seventh U.S. Colored Infantry, Ford should have chosen his replacement, but still in Marsh's doghouse, he had no say in the matter. By Marsh's direct order, Second Sergeant Merchant was passed over for Whitford's old slot, which was given to 4th Sgt. Alonzo Avery, while Hartley lost his corporal's stripes without any explanation. In Company K Corporal Ehmke did get to retain his rank.[47]

The story of the rescue of the slaves engendered only brief interest even in Minnesota and remains virtually unknown in Missouri and elsewhere. For the Ninth Minnesota it proved simply an interlude, for sterner trials in the War of the Rebellion lay ahead. The boost in popularity that Senator Wilkinson received at home was only temporary, for he continued to offend his constituents. The Missouri Radicals had a right to feel pleased. Schofield was gone, and so in another sense was their other great adversary, Governor Gamble, who was injured in December and died on the last day of January 1864. Major Markham saw improvement in the military situation in Missouri from the new leadership. On February 17 he observed how Rosecrans "has said nothing to indicate that he intended to side with either of the parties here—Radical or Conservative—but he has quietly commenced reorganizing the Department; and the interests that have heretofore been wholly controlled by the pro slavery faction, is now being quietly transferred to the other side." The tide had turned decisively in favor of the Missouri Radicals, who never truly forgave Lincoln during his lifetime.[48]

THE GREAT MYSTERY

The one missing piece of the puzzle is the ultimate fate of John and his family. Felch wrote on November 12 at Lamine Bridge that he had hoped to see them that night while they hid nearby, but "today as I am under arrest I could not go with them." He promised to bring them food or to send someone in his place, but whether that ever happened is not known. Felch assumed they "have gone north to sleep in the cold forrest." On December 28 while in Jefferson City, he commented, "We are in here well and the negroes are free." Likewise, Stewart recalled in 1914 that the blacks were "never found." Yet there is a cryptic entry dated November 24, 1863, in the letter book of the District of Central Missouri summarizing a communication from Wellman at Lamine Bridge: "In compliance with orders from Sub District Hqtrs [Wellman] sends negroes taken from train by soldiers at Ottersville." Yet no account of the arrest and confinement of the Minnesota soldiers ever remarked of the terrible irony if the same unit that freed the slaves subsequently recaptured them. It is very hard to believe such news would not have reached prisoners like Felch and Stewart, who certainly had a big personal stake in the matter. Most unfortunately, Wellman's letter itself is not among the surviving district correspondence, and maddeningly, there is no indication whether he seized all, part, or, in truth, any of John's family. It may have even been a case of mistaken identity. No one at Lamine Bridge on November 24 had ever seen any of those slaves except John.[49]

Years later Hartley stated regarding the freed blacks, "I never saw them afterward but I understood they staid about [Ottersville]." It is not known if he learned they might have been retaken, or whether he had gained any direct knowledge of their true fate. If John's family had actually remained close to Lamine Bridge for nearly two weeks, it would have been during cold weather, with little food and only rudimentary shelter. Circumstances, especially for the young children, could have been dire. Very likely the family would have had no other place to go or any means of getting away. Their supposed capture, if such actually took place, or perhaps even their surrender might have seemed a relief. Had the two captains not been on the same train, the rescuers would have brought the family to the protection of their camp as they intended. Walker would have had to cut his way through layers of military bureaucracy to reclaim his slaves, during which time the Minnesotans could have seen John's family safely away. The direct involvement of Queen and Pritchard and the swift arrest of the soldiers ended all chance of a merciful conclusion.[50]

One can only speculate what might have occurred had John and his family indeed been taken to Jefferson City. The logical assumption is that the authorities would have returned the ten slaves to Walker's tender care and that they stayed with him on the farm near Georgetown until at least spring 1864. By then slavery in Missouri had largely collapsed, although the state did not formally abolish it until January 11, 1865. Walker, however, could have sent at least some of his slaves to Kentucky and separated the family after all. On December 9, 1863, Schofield shamefully succumbed to the blandishments of Broadhead and the Conservative slaveholders by modifying Special Order No. 307 to permit "loyal" masters to take "female Slaves and males not fit for military duty" out of the state. That proviso was "subject only," as Ira Berlin writes, "to the virtually unenforceable restriction that the removal be made *with their* (the slaves) consent." Slave owners found many ways to compel such "consent." Only on March 1, 1864, did Rosecrans, citing "humanity, justice, and Missouri's need to retain all the slave and other labor she has within her own border," renew the earlier order.[51]

Other than by escaping again, the only way John might have materially altered his circumstances had Walker regained him was to join the Union army. On November 12, 1863, Schofield issued General Order No. 135 that decreed, "All able-bodied colored men, whether free or slaves, will be received into the service, the loyal owners of slaves enlisted being entitled to receive compensation." Moreover, "All persons enlisted into the service shall forever thereafter be free." Thus, as Berlin notes, "Black recruitment offered legitimate access to freedom for the first time to slave men whose owners were loyal. Unionist slaveholders quickly perceived that recruitment doomed gradual emancipation, and they took steps to obstruct the enlistment of their slave men." The compensation of three hundred dollars that the federal government promised eventually to provide owners for each slave who enlisted did not, in the slaveholders' minds, balance the loss of their property.[52]

Missouri's own black regiments most certainly drew on black men recruited in Jefferson City. In December 1863, for example, Sgt. Francis J. Heller of Company F escorted sixty recruits from Jefferson City to familiar Benton Barracks in St. Louis, where several regiments of "Americans of African Descent" were being organized. Markham carefully observed one of those units being put through its paces:

> They drilled nearly as well as a white regiment of equal experience in the movements, but were much more awkward with the gun. I never saw a cleverer, more contented and happy regiment in my life. I asked one sable Sergeant if he intended to fight? And if so, how hard? He said, "I'se goin to pitch in as long de officers stay wid us, and if dey go soon, may be I stay longer; any way, I'se not goin' to be tuken prisoner, so dey hang a feller, if I can help it."

"Everyone that has seen those Regiments," Markham added, "have their faith increased in negro troops," but he personally remained skeptical of their prowess in combat.[53]

Should John have indeed worn the proud Union blue (without his actual surname there is no real way of knowing), his wife, their five children, his two sisters and widowed sister-in-law would still not have been free. Sifting through contemporary military documents, Berlin catalogues the horrors endured by the enslaved families of many Missouri black soldiers. Some masters expelled them from their land. Lieutenant William Argo, the provost marshal at Sedalia, warned in March 1864 that "large numbers of black women and children, many of them are the wives of soldiers that have been enlisted in my district," were being "driven from their masters homes after their husbands enlisted." He declared that "humanity demands that something should be done in their behalf." Other slaveholders, Berlin notes, "required the soldiers' kin to perform unaccustomed chores, including back-breaking work previously reserved for slave men," or "resorted to open terror." A few masters even hustled women and children across the Mississippi and sold them in Kentucky. In many cases families accompanied the men to the military posts, where they gained "a precarious de facto liberty." Even then, instances occurred of slave catchers apprehending escaped slave women and children and returning them to their owners. Black soldiers and their white officers complained bitterly of such terrible offenses but were powerless to accomplish much in the way of relief.[54]

John and his family have disappeared into the mists of time. It is only possible here to recognize John's courage and his family's sacrifice and to honor their memory alongside the thirty-eight liberators, who would endure their own agonies during the balance of the war and afterward. Perhaps someone reading this account of the "Outrage at Otterville" will joyfully recognize John and his family as beloved ancestors. Only in that way might the rest of the story become known.

CHAPTER FIVE

From Missouri to Memphis

Working on the Railroad

In January 1864 the thirty-eight Otterville liberators gratefully resumed the anonymity of the ranks. Thereafter the Minnesotans engaged in no confrontations with higher authority over escaped slaves or, apparently, anything else. To garrison key points along the Pacific Railroad, the Ninth Minnesota was spread across the breadth of central Missouri along two broad axes, one southwest of St. Louis as far as Rolla and the other west from Jefferson City. "Our Regt. is about as much scattered as it was before we left Minn," moaned Private Frank Harrington. Over the winter the few remaining bushwhacker bands settled for sporadic raids against soft targets such as stagecoaches, recruiters, and loyal Union men on isolated farms. Only well-mounted troops ever had a prayer of catching such elusive marauders; infantry could only protect specific points. With such static soldiering, tedium was more of a threat than Confederates. Guard duty at the huge railroad span at Osage east of Jefferson City inspired the poet in John Aiton: "I am a Union Soldier / I battle for the right / I lounge about in daytime / I watch the bridge at night." Chaplain Kerr supposed the Ninth Minnesota was "doing good service in Missouri, though the men have felt that this guarding of property and preserving the peace of a *loyal* State is not precisely the object for which they enlisted." With the big armies in Virginia and Georgia in hibernation, wintering in Missouri was not the worst duty, but nothing better loomed on the horizon.[1]

On January 8, the same day that he released the Otterville mutineers, General Brown was delighted to learn that his District of Central Missouri was being enlarged all the way to the Kansas line. General Ewing and the Kansas troops who so fervently enforced the mandatory evacuations under General

Order No. 11 were to be removed. Utterly opposed to the terrible dislocation and cruel hardship imposed in the border counties, Brown invited all loyal refugees to return to their abandoned homes. Another cornerstone of his policy to normalize the district was to complete the Pacific Railroad all the way to Kansas. Its western branch extended only as far as tiny Dresden, seven miles west of Sedalia, and the last long stretch to Kansas City would entail passing through the worst bushwhacker country in Missouri.[2]

In February Brown shifted his headquarters from Jefferson City west to Warrensburg, on the railroad right-of-way thirty miles west of Sedalia and sixty-five miles southeast of Kansas City. Marsh left Jefferson City on February 8 with Companies C (with half the liberators), D, and F bound for Warrensburg. At Lamine Bridge he picked up Captain Wellman's Company K (with the remaining liberators) and relieved Otterville of its now onerous Yankee garrison. Though situated on a pleasant prairie—a nice contrast from hilly, muddy Jefferson City—Warrensburg was "a miserable looking place" of "charred ruins" and despoiled buildings. The local population was, if anything, less inspiring. Even Aiton, ordinarily so tolerant, finally had his fill. "I do not, certainly, feel very much prepossessed in favor of Missouri or its citizens. Nor does the appearance of its rustic citizens increase my admiration." Private Jacob Dieter of Company F was profoundly glad his own children attended school back at home despite the hardship caused by his absence. "I want the children to learn all they can," he wrote his wife, Martha. "There is the most ignorant lot of people in this country that I ever seen[;] children ten or twelve years old cant read and some of them don't know how old they are[;] there is but very few people here that can write."[3]

Brown needed good infantry to garrison "some of the more important posts in this sub-district" to allow the cavalry to patrol and chase guerrillas. The hilly, overgrown country at the headwaters of the Snibar and Big and Little Blue Rivers required "dismounted troops in connection with the cavalry for scouting operations." On February 19 he asked St. Louis if he could keep the part of the Ninth Minnesota that was still in his district. "Their soldierly bearing and well merited reputation for good conduct would make them very desirable troops for the service on the border," and they "would have a great influence in counteracting the bitter sectional strife that now exists."[4]

In early March regimental headquarters and Companies D and F marched in easy stages from Warrensburg northwest toward Kansas City. The devastation wrought on such scenic country by years of constant warfare shocked the Minnesotans. "This region has been overrun by guerillas, rebels and federal forces,—what one party did not burn or destroy, another would endeavor to do," wrote Lieutenant Stearns. The population removed by General Order

No. 11 had not yet returned. "From almost any elevation, chimney stacks are seen in all directions; houses, barns, fences, all burned. Beautiful yards and lawns, and thrifty orchards, laid waste; hogs in large number, running wild." In Lone Jack, thirty miles southeast of Kansas City, Dieter found "not a single inhabitant; windows and doors broken in, many buildings burnt, nothing but [a] chimney left standing." The only enemy contact occurred one day out of Warrensburg. About twenty-five horsemen formed ominously on a knoll overlooking the road a mile ahead of the column. Company F fanned out as skirmishers and closed in, but the riders galloped away before firing a shot.[5]

Passing through a "rich and beautifully undulating country" that was William Quantrill's favored stomping ground, Company F, the "Olmsted County Tigers," under Stearns peeled off to join a detachment of the Second Colorado Cavalry stationed at Independence, ten miles east of Kansas City. Marked by broad, "finely graded" streets, a "beautiful public square," and formerly sumptuous residences, Independence ("twice as large as Rochester") had definitely seen better days. Once a source of "Border Ruffians and Rebels," the city had "suffered a fearful retribution." Eager for a "pop" at "old 'Quant,'" the "Tigers" declared if he "comes in here he will find a different reception than he did at Lawrence." Marsh took Capt. Asgrim Skaro's Company D farther west to Kansas City. A rugged blend of hills and valleys, Kansas City appeared less elegant than Independence but bustled with activity and commerce.[6]

The two companies with the Otterville liberators remained behind at headquarters in Warrensburg under Brown's watchful eye. He had plans both for their vigilance and their muscles. While Company K garrisoned the town, Brown assigned Wellman a task worthy of a crack civil engineer. Using Ford's Company C as labor, Wellman designed and built a new bridge over Blackwater Creek a few miles north of Warrensburg. The poor nature of the ford there had barred heavy vehicles ever since Union forces burned the original structure in 1861. While at the bridge, Pvt. Isaac Peterman, one of the two eldest Company C liberators, sought his discharge for medical disability. Unable to read or write, he had, shortly after enlisting, "picked on" young Nathan Palmeter, his neighbor in Mower County and fellow liberator, to read him his letters and draft his replies. Peterman's hearing had faltered ever since a severe head cold in the winter of 1862–63. "I remember of his having to get very close to hear me read them," Palmeter later testified, "as they contained some times private things from home. I can well remember yet of saying to him why Peterman you are getting deaf at which he would say I don't want everyone to hear my letters." One tragic letter conveyed word of the death of his eldest son, Cpl. Barnabas Peterman, Thirty-First

Ohio, who was killed on November 25, 1863, at Chattanooga. By early 1864 the "boys" were teasing Peterman for "playing of deaf," making him "mad about it." He earned extra money by selling fruit to his fellow soldiers. During card games at Blackwater Bridge, they often called to him for apples, but when he failed to respond, Pvt. Daniel Vaughan, another liberator, stepped in with his own stock "and so took a good many ten cts from Peterman." Amusement notwithstanding, his comrades understood that he could no longer serve effectively in the ranks and petitioned for his honorable discharge. Marsh's endorsement called Peterman "a brave, patriotic and faithful soldier." As usual the military bureaucracy would require months to decide on the discharge.[7]

After completing the Blackwater Bridge, the versatile Wellman took on another specialist post as Topographical Engineer of the District of Central Missouri, leaving Lieutenant Capon in command of Company K. Progress on railroad construction west of Dresden was slow. Labor was scarce, frightened away by the threat of guerrillas. Brown moved Company C and part of Company K ten miles east of Warrensburg to Knob Noster, along the right-of-way. He had hoped to use Missouri black troops as laborers, but pleas to St. Louis proved unavailing. Consequently, he authorized all but the "necessary camp guard" to volunteer to cut railroad ties and lay track at the additional wage of two dollars per day. The Minnesotans jumped at

Daniel B. Vaughan

the opportunity. They camped at their work site, moving their tents forward when necessary, and marched to work with their rifle muskets, which they kept handy. Soon they were helping to lay about a half mile of track a day. Bushwhackers prowled the area, but none threatened the railroad project. "There are some of them around and some of them have been caught," James Woodbury informed his wife, "but don't you feel any unease about us for I don't think we will have any trouble with them. We are on the look out for them so if they do come we will be ready for them." Even so, as David Felch reported, it was "getting dangerous to be out after dark." On April 28 bushwhackers killed an officer and three Missouri militiamen on their way to Warrensburg.[8]

The additional wages proved a godsend, particularly for privates with families. Army pay was only thirteen dollars a month, with disbursements at irregular, widely separated pay days. Like many others, including the Otterville liberators, Dieter took on work in Missouri when he could get it and sent home as much money as he could spare. While stationed at Osage in the early winter, he garnered twenty-eight dollars chopping wood and splitting rails, but at Warrensburg and Independence, he found "no chance to earn anything or place to do it." By mid-March the pay of the Ninth Minnesota was four months in arrears. Chronic delays in being paid caused much soul-searching. "If Uncle Sam can't pay up better than that," Woodbury opined, "he had better send us home." Corporal William Doyle of Company B at Rolla also worried that his wife had run out of money. "It is not pleasant to be a soldier," he wrote. "I could stand it without a murmur, but when I have a family dependant upon my wages for all support, and I don't get paid more regular than this it doesn't create very pleasant reflections, but still we must be patient and hope this does not long continue." His solution was to prosecute the war as vigorously as possible. "If Old Abe thinks of trying for the next Presidency," he must remove "some of these copperhead officers of his." Doyle did not think Lincoln would "for he is rather slow for the armies. I hope they will get an honest and out and out Radical for the next four years. I still have hopes and believe this summer will end the Rebellion." Then "we shall have a free country in reality as well as name." In contrast William Dean much desired Lincoln's reelection as the "best chance" to "forever kill American slavery and cleanse the Republic." The pay finally appeared in late April.[9]

In April Marsh and regimental headquarters embarked at Kansas City, cruised the Missouri River as far as Jefferson City, and proceeded from there by rail to Rolla. Following the breaking up of Markham's small battalion at St. Louis, Lt. Charles H. Beaulieu's Company G guarded Franklin at the main junction of the Pacific Railroad, forty miles west of St. Louis, while Capt. William Baxter's Company H reinforced Rolla. Markham briefly led the Rolla detachment, but when Marsh turned up, he took over the four companies (C, D, F, and K) spread across Brown's District of Central Missouri. One hundred and three recruits for the Ninth Minnesota reported to Rolla from Fort Snelling for a couple months of drill before joining their respective companies. Lieutenant Paulson of Company H supervised their training.[10]

Thirty-five of the new soldiers, over one-third of the total, came from the home regions of the two liberator Companies C and K. The experiences of four recruits reflect the varying motivations behind the enlistments. Private Chauncey Ira Hill, a twenty-six-year-old former New Yorker, farmed eighty acres at Saratoga near St. Charles, in western Winona County. Through his diary and letters to his wife, Sarah, Hill, a sincere, devout, and articulate man, provided a candid and detailed look at life in the Ninth Minnesota. Sarah later wrote that because her husband had been "raised in adversity," he "knew what it was to work hard" and sought every opportunity to learn. Married one month before enlisting in February 1864, Hill willingly accepted sixty dollars, the first installment of a three-hundred-dollar bounty. Yet it was not money or the threat of conscription that led him to volunteer. "The country needs and must have our help in the army," and now was "a good time to go while arrangements can be made to let our farms and arrange matters for the coming summer." Hill's father, Warren, would work his son's farm as well as his own. "If we rise freely now," Hill wrote, "we may hope to crush the traitor nest before another new year and return home to put in our next year crop." Ties of kinship also played a vital role. His brother-in-law, Albert T. Downing, was a private in Company K, which Hill hoped to join along with his good friend and fellow recruit Joseph E. Harvey, "a bright, jovial young man" who had married another Downing sister. A third Saratoga recruit for Company K was Pvt. Martin Shortt, a forty-one-year-old, Canadian-born tenant farmer who had grown up in Vermont. It seems an urgent need for the bounty money cinched his decision to enlist. He had brought his impoverished family to Minnesota in 1861 after losing everything when the crop failed in Illinois. "Very reluctant, having no desire for war" but "fearing to be drafted," Shortt is said to have enlisted "expecting to fight Indians" but instead went south. Years later his family claimed some "well-to-do neighbors" had "selfishly persuaded" him "it was his duty to enlist in the war, thinking to so lessen their chances of being drafted." They "promised all protection" for his wife and four children should he be killed. Fear of the draft certainly influenced the enlistment of Dudley Perry, a teenage farmhand from Wisconsin who signed on in Olmsted County hoping for

Chauncey and Sarah Hill, 1864

Company C. He enlisted as a substitute, hired to take the place of someone liable for the draft. Listed as eighteen years of age, Perry was actually not more than fifteen or sixteen.[11]

At Last We Are United

May marked the traditional opening of the campaigning season, and Union armies east and west prepared to launch new invasions that could at last crush the Rebellion. Yet according to a rumor related by Hill, the Ninth Minnesota "will go up the Missouri River with General [Alfred] Sully into the Indian Country." A summer jaunt into Dakota Territory was the last thing Wilkin desired. It would take him and his regiment even farther from the real war—the one they had signed up to fight. The *Rochester City Post* reported on May 14 that "Col. W. is fretting like a caged tiger because he cannot go to the front. Some of his boys, we know, are equally anxious to see more active service, and we hoped they may be gratified." Wilkin tried in vain to have the Ninth Minnesota redirected to George Thomas's Army of the Cumberland, one of three armies under William Sherman that were poised to invade Georgia. Before they could be released from Missouri, though, other troops must replace them. Word of their colonel's efforts filtered down to the scattered elements of the Ninth Minnesota. At Rolla, Harrington waxed enthusiastically about the prospects of going to Tennessee. "I hope so for I have got all I want of Missouri and I am ready to leave at anytime." Not everyone felt that way. "Wilkin is trying to get us down further south," complained Woodbury, the Peace Democrat. "He wants to get us down there and get us in to a fight, then he is in hopes to get promoted. If he does get us down there I hope he will be the first man that is shot."[12]

After speaking with Rosecrans, Markham had come away convinced "there is little prospect of either of the Minnesota regiments leaving this State for a long time; and except, perhaps in the case of a few shoulder-straps who are getting snug positions with some extra pay and no extra work, the prospect is distasteful." He did not count on Grant's determination to strip most of the Federal infantry from garrison duty for the front. In May Grant sent Maj. Gen. Napoleon J. T. Dana, an old regular and former colonel of the First Minnesota, trolling for troops in Missouri to reinforce Maj. Gen. Frederick Steele in Arkansas. Dana secured approval to replace the Ninth Minnesota with an Illinois militia regiment and directed Rosecrans to send the Minnesotans "without delay" to Steele at Little Rock. Rosecrans telegraphed Rolla and Warrensburg on May 18 releasing the Ninth Minnesota to St. Louis "to be sent to the front at once."[13]

Dramatic Union advances in Virginia and Georgia in May seemed to presage the imminent end of the war. Grant accompanied Maj. Gen. George G. Meade's Army of the Potomac across the Rapidan River to inaugurate a bloody campaign that would last six weeks and take the Federals to the gates of Richmond. In northern Georgia, Sherman feinted at the main Rebel position with one of his armies and sent another around to the right to cut the Rebels' supply lines. All this caused the Minnesotans to feel very hopeful about the prospects for victory. Beginning on May 19, the various elements of the Ninth Minnesota filtered into Camp Gamble, a "most beautiful campground" two miles west of the "dust & turmoil of St. Louis." First to arrive was Marsh from Rolla with Companies A, B, H, and I and Paulson's newly minted soldiers. The latter included Hill, who proudly informed Sarah that she no longer needed to address her letters to "Recruit." He found the scenery at Camp Gamble to be idyllic. "In the shade of fine old chestnut oak trees, on undulating ground, whose grassy slopes are smooth and dry, our little shelter tents show their diminutive white roofs."[14]

At Camp Gamble a long-brewing crisis in Company H, with its precarious balance of New England Yankees, Germans, and Scandinavians, came to a head. Captain Baxter had long ailed with tuberculosis. "With an ardent desire to serve his country in the field, and true soldierly impulses," he nevertheless "was so frail in health as to be almost helpless." When Company H had left Minnesota in November 1863, Baxter remained behind because of bleeding in the lungs. His own health shaky, Second Lieutenant Paulson reluctantly assumed temporary command, but Markham kept close touch, becoming "much esteemed." The major was "a whole-souled man [who] knows his business and attends to it." After Baxter rejoined in December, Markham feared "his health will not allow him to remain with us long." By mid-January 1864 Baxter had "not recovered sufficiently from his last hemorrhage of the lungs, to perform the duties required of a Captain at this post. He expects to leave the Company soon, as he will not be able to endure field duty, and is probably an invalid the rest of his days." Baxter grimly hung on, but on May 19 First Lieutenant Weinmann led Company H into Camp Gamble. The next day during drill, Weinmann bridled at the surly attitude of Pvt. Johannes J. Stor, a burly Swede who was the largest man in the company. An encounter with the end of Stor's rifle musket put Weinmann in the hospital. "The clock had struck," Paulson sadly realized, and once Baxter finally became too sick to serve, "I was thereby doomed to be alone again with the company." That prospect greatly troubled him. Wishing to complete his seminary studies and be ordained, he always felt uncomfortable exercising command. Soberly realizing his limitations, Paulson immediately submitted his resignation and departed for home three days later. "All who were acquainted with him regretted very much to have him leave," wrote Baxter. Orderly Sergeant Allen W. Tiffany rose to acting lieutenant in Paulson's place.[15]

On May 21 when Company G arrived at Camp Gamble, the *St. Louis Republican* became fascinated with its Ojibwe contingent, whose number the newspaper vastly exaggerated to one hundred. Counting nine new recruits, Company G actually included some twenty-three Ojibwe, about one-third of its strength. "These men of the forests," wrote an admirer in the Ninth Minnesota, "make fine soldiers—ever ready and willing for duty." Like Charles Beaulieu, a well-educated man newly promoted to captain, most were of mixed Indian and white descent. In an article entitled "Big Injuns," the newspaper conceded the Ojibwe hailed from "mainly a civilized tribe." They "have fallen into soldier ways, so as to get along as well as any in drill and other routine duties." Even more amazing, "several of these Indian soldiers could read and write," and one "possessed the accomplishment of writing an elegant clerical hand." Despite its highly condescending tone, the article accurately predicted the Ojibwe "will no doubt give a good account of themselves in action."[16]

At dusk on Sunday, May 22, Ford's Company C and Company K under Capon, with the Otterville liberators, entered Camp Gamble. Alerted at the close of the evening Sabbath service when "martial music told of something unusual," Hill was delighted to see his other brother-in-law file into camp. He slipped behind Downing "just as he was unloading himself, grabbed his hand & we had a hearty shake." Old friends from St. Charles and Winona, "all in excellent spirits," crowded around. Acerbic as usual, Woodbury observed, "our Col. says if he cant get us down where we will have some fighting to do he will resign. There is nothing that will suit the Regt. any better than to have him leave us." It seems true at that time a large segment of the Ninth preferred that the strict Wilkin not return. Marsh, "a splendid officer" who was "well liked by the officers and men," according to Sergeant Macdonald, certainly ruled with a lighter hand. It would take a battle to change their minds about their colonel's true worth and the value of his hard training regime.[17]

Captain Dane's Company E reached Camp Gamble on May 23, followed two days later by Company F from Independence. Lieutenant Milton J. Daniels now led the "Tigers" after Stearns left for Virginia to become colonel of the Thirty-Ninth U.S. Colored Infantry. On May 26 Capt. Asgrim Skaro's Company D arrived by steamboat, having come all the way from Kansas City. Astoundingly, it was the very first time in its nearly two years of existence that the entire Ninth Minnesota actually assembled in one place. "It has been our fate to be separated," wrote Macdonald (the new regimental color sergeant), "but at last we are united, and all look forward with eagerness to the time when we will have a chance to try our muscle in a contest with the hated foe." That evening, with Wilkin present but still on detached duty, Marsh conducted the very first regimental dress parade. Proudly overseen by Principal Musician Joel Handy, the "bugles, drums & fifes, all combine to make a scene enough to fill any head that's not entirely hollow," quipped Aiton. Putting forth a "fine appearance," the Ninth Minnesota proudly maneuvered "with a precision that pleased [Wilkin] greatly."[18]

THE *B. M. RUNYAN*

On May 28 the Ninth Minnesota received orders to proceed without delay to Memphis and "from that point to such other point as may be indicated by Major-General [Edward R. S.] Canby, commanding Military Division of West Mississippi." Resuming command that day, Wilkin understood that Memphis was to be just a brief stopover before Little Rock. On Sunday morning, May 29, Camp Gamble witnessed "all confusion and hurry," wrote Hill, "for we are packing for St. Louis & expect then to take a boat for some port down the river. It is but a short time after breakfast, but the boys are mostly packed. Wagons are loading and men are moving to and fro." By 10 A.M. the eight hundred officers and enlisted men of the Ninth Minnesota, their baggage, wagons, horses, and mules, had started trooping on board the steam packet *B. M. Runyan.* Years later Macdonald recalled how the regiment enjoyed its first tour in Missouri, never quite realizing how very fortunate it was to not experience firsthand the less-charming aspects of guerrilla warfare that erupted worse than ever that spring. In particular the region east of Kansas City became "full of bushwhackers." That was due, historian Albert Castel charges, to Brown's "badly watered down Order No. 11," which had allowed Confederate sympathizers to return there in large numbers.[19]

On embarkation day Pvt. Pierre Demars of Company K became the first Otterville liberator to separate from the Ninth Minnesota. In the midst of the hubbub, he quietly slipped away, evidently the only member of the regiment to desert successfully in Missouri. In February the twenty-nine-year-old Quebec native had gone to Minnesota on furlough, but after returning to Warrensburg, he spent considerable time in the hospital. Regimental returns listed Demars as "believed struck out for Canada," despite having a wife in Mendota near St. Paul. Given his profession of "engineer" (presumably involving steam propulsion) and knowledge of the river, Demars evaded any attempts to apprehend him. There is no record of him ever residing by that name thereafter in the United States.[20]

At 3 P.M. the *B. M. Runyan* started down the Mississippi River. Built in Cincinnati in 1858, the large side-wheeler had sunk in December 1862 in shallow water off Alton but was raised, repaired, and brought into Federal service in the spring of 1864. Despite the spartan appointments, Dean thought her "a fine large boat" that should offer a "pretty good ride." Officers and invalids moved into the main cabin, while the individual companies spread out on deck. Company D rode the guard—the part of the main deck that overlapped the hull—"it being the best place outside the cabin," according to a pleased Aiton. Felch likewise thought the trip was a "splendid ride," but Hill was less impressed with Company K's exposed vantage on the upper deck. While cruising the river, the men particularly enjoyed observing the ironclads on picket duty and were impressed with the maneuvers required at Cairo to move the *B. M. Runyan* a short distance up the Ohio River and to go alongside the wharf for coal.[21]

After sunset on May 31, the *B. M. Runyan* tied up on the levee at Memphis, the gateway to the Deep South. Little was visible of the ex-Rebel city, situated on higher ground, other than "torches flaring in the darkness." Although the "dust, turmoil and heat combine to make us uncomfortable," observed Hill, the Ninth Minnesota was "full of noise and frolic." The steamboat tarried while Wilkin stepped ashore to call on Brig. Gen. Ralph P. Buckland, in charge of the District of Memphis. "For some days quite ill and scarcely able to get about," Wilkin expected the interview to be just a formality to transmit orders to continue to Little Rock. Instead what he heard surprised and pleased him immensely, for Buckland alerted the Ninth Minnesota for combat. The regiment was to leave Memphis at 6 the next morning by rail.[22]

The *B. M. Runyan* resumed her busy schedule plying the lower Mississippi River. On July 21 while traveling between Vicksburg and Memphis, she struck a snag and sank on the Arkansas side with perhaps as many as 150 military and civilian passengers. In the meantime the luck of the Ninth Minnesota had proven only marginally better.[23]

CHAPTER SIX

An Easy Happy-Go-Luck Kind of March

Going after the Rebel Forrest

Wilkin's surprise orders on May 31 added the Ninth Minnesota to a large expedition organized at Memphis by Maj. Gen. Cadwallader C. Washburn. He tasked Brig. Gen. Samuel D. Sturgis to find and defeat Maj. Gen. Nathan Bedford Forrest's formidable cavalry force lurking in northeastern Mississippi.[1] The long rail line through Middle Tennessee and south from Chattanooga into Georgia was vulnerable to raids that could cut off Sherman's supplies and endanger his assault on Atlanta. Tying down Forrest, therefore, was "more important than any new operations that can be undertaken immediately in the country west of the Mississippi." Glad to get more infantry in fit condition (those from the disastrous Red River excursion in Louisiana had arrived in sad shape), Washburn informed Major-General Canby that "as good luck would have it, the Ninth Minnesota arrived last night, 600 strong, and I have sent them out with the expedition."[2]

Bedford Forrest was one of a handful of Rebel generals whom the Minnesotans instantly recognized, though his notoriety stemmed as much from alleged atrocities as achievements. On May 31 the *B. M. Runyan* glided by a narrow point on the Mississippi River forty river miles north of Memphis where a high, steep bluff marked the location of Fort Pillow, its "earthworks torn down" and structures "now in ashes." Seven weeks before, on April 12, Forrest and 2,500 dismounted troopers had stormed the fort and killed 248 out of the garrison of nearly 600, including 186 of 262 black soldiers. The federal government vehemently accused him of the wholesale slaughter of prisoners, both black and white, and sources do support the likelihood of a massacre.[3]

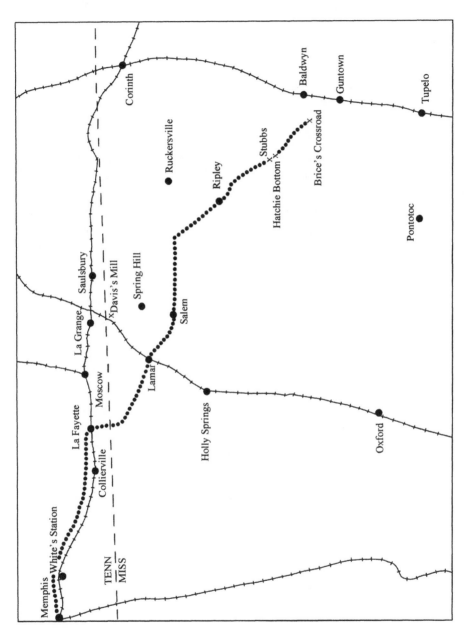

Northern Mississippi

Forrest epitomized the ultimate secessionist villain. Tall, strong, and ruggedly handsome, the forty-two-year-old former slave dealer and self-made business magnate was a superb soldier, charismatic leader, and implacable foe. A veritable Confederate Achilles, he personally killed more opponents in single combat than any other Civil War general and regularly embarrassed whole Union armies. Minnesota had already felt his sting. In July 1862 Forrest bluffed a brigade defending Murfreesboro in central Tennessee into ignominious surrender. The captives included nearly all of the Third Minnesota led by Col. Henry C. Lester, Captain Wellman's business partner in Winona. The enlisted prisoners were soon paroled and sent to the frontier to fight the Dakota, but the army cashiered Lester and most of the officers who voted to surrender. The Ninth Minnesota never doubted it would lick Forrest's dastardly Rebels and gain long-awaited revenge. David Felch, the young Company C liberator, declared to his folks that "no quarter is the word," but that was mere bluster. Forrest and his myrmidons would prove tougher foes than the green Minnesotans could ever have imagined.[4]

Washburn told Wilkin to take only fit men in light marching order, sans knapsack, tent, change of clothes, and cloth blanket. Only two army wagons, two ambulances, and the medicine wagon would go along. The surgeons rapidly sorted out over 100 sick and convalescents and those "to whom there was the slightest doubt of their being able to stand a long and fatiguing march." The winnowing left 30 officers and 635 men available for duty. Wilkin thought they might only be away two or three days. Those going included some 31 Otterville liberators. It appears that 5 privates from Ford's Company C stayed behind. Although proud to be an acting orderly to Quartermaster John Owen, Felch was "a little vexed to think I did not go with my company but I am not to blame." Severe hemorrhoids ended Reverend Arnold's marching days, deaf Peterman awaited his disability discharge, and Lagree and Williams were sick. Capon's Company K apparently contributed sixteen liberators, the sole known absentee being Pike, who had yet to report from detached duty as a commissary clerk in Missouri.[5]

At 3 A.M. on June 1, a bugle roused the Ninth Minnesota. A brisk predawn tramp through dark streets offered glimpses of their first true Rebel city. Pehr Carlson admired the "well-built and beautiful landscaping." At the Memphis & Charleston Railroad depot he discovered "troops in the thousands of both black and white." Like its fellow western regiments, the Ninth Minnesota wore the more practical wide-brimmed, black slouch hats instead of the small forage caps of the eastern armies. Long frock coats gave way to short, dark blue woolen blouses (the fatigue jacket or sack coat) worn with coarse white wool flannel shirts, sky blue wool trousers, and black, square-toed brogans. Nine pieces of hardtack bread (three days' ration) plus salt pork and coffee were jammed in each cloth haversack, a "bag about a foot square, with a broad strap for the shoulder, in which soldiers soon learned to bundle all their food and table furniture, which after a day's march were always found in such a delightful hodgepodge." Rolled and slung over the shoulder, rubber blankets served as a poncho or groundsheet. The round, flat Pattern 1858 tin canteen, hanging by its own strap, held about three pints of water. Suspended from a broad shoulder band, the heavy leather cartridge box, emblazoned with an oval brass plate lettered "U.S.," weighed eight pounds when filled with forty rounds of ammunition. The black leather waist belt, secured by a brass U.S. plate, bore a pouch for percussion caps and a leather scabbard for the Model 1855 socket bayonet whose narrow, angular blade stretched nearly nineteen inches. A "great many" Minnesotans lugged heavy fighting knives so beloved by rookies, and a fair number carried small pistols. Strictly personal possessions included smoking gear, handkerchief, pocket knife, cards, testament, photographs, and pen or pencil and paper.[6]

The Ninth Minnesota valued their U.S. Springfield Model 1861 Rifle Muskets, considered the finest and most reliable military muzzleloader. Of percussion ignition, .58 caliber, and an overall length of fifty-six inches, the Springfield featured a bright steel forty-inch barrel and weighed ten pounds. Even in the dawn of breechloaders, the single-shot rifle musket was a powerful tool in well-drilled hands (the Ninth Minnesota, for the most part, was), with a sustained rate of fire of up to three aimed shots per minute. The complicated loading procedure involved nine primary commands and fifteen motions. From a standing position with rifle musket held butt to the ground, the soldier would tear open the paper cartridge with his teeth, pour the powder charge into the barrel, position the cartridge with its massive conical lead bullet ("Minie ball") inside the muzzle, draw the steel ramrod from its channel beneath the barrel, ram the powder, bullet, and wadding firmly to the breech, return the rammer to its slot, elevate the rear of the piece ("cast about"), and prime by placing a percussion cap onto the nipple. There followed the commands "ready," "aim," and "fire." All of this takes longer to describe than an experienced soldier actually required to load and fire, but to accomplish it while tightly packed within the ranks in the midst of intense noise and smoke and being shot at can only be imagined. The maximum effective range was 600 yards, although infantry combat took place much closer, often within 150 yards. The Ninth Minnesota, coming from the frontier, already had the advantage of being familiar with firearms in general and had received marksmanship training well beyond the average Civil War regiment, particularly in estimating ranges. Officers carried revolvers and straight swords, the latter mainly as symbols of command.[7]

The infantry started boarding train cars at 7 A.M. to be shuttled thirty-three miles southeast to the staging point at La Fayette, near the Mississippi border. The cavalry, artillery, and massive supply train of 250 wagons and ambulances (with the five Ninth Minnesota vehicles) left by road. Rolling through the countryside, the Minnesotans noticed comely homes in stately plantations, along with several villages that looked largely empty. Although cotton plants were four to six inches high, the farmer's practical eye deplored the "worn out" soil and the "poor" corn. Taking "a good while" on a journey marked by "stopping, retreating, advancing," the train eventually disgorged its passengers that afternoon at the burned bridge over Davis Creek, five miles shy of La Fayette. Within fifteen minutes heavy showers soaked the men, and the rain continued into the night—a portent. Marching in the rain while covered by a rubber blanket became routine in the next ten days. Being so encumbered was a "comical sight," recalled a sergeant of the First Minnesota, "each man with his head through the opening in his blanket, his hat pulled tightly onto his head and the brim turned down; carrying his rifle under the crook of his right arm with the muzzle down, and the lock and breech under the blanket to keep them dry."[8]

The town of La Fayette was "nearly gone," just a few scattered chimneys surrounded by land "abandoned & growing up to woods & bushes." The chosen camp ground was "wet land, level and poor." On June 2, another rainy day, the Minnesotans remained in camp. Seeking potable water, Chauncey Hill and friends in Company K conversed with an elderly woman in her garden. She had sold out of onions but not of grief, having "experienced many hardships & trials & longs for a time of peace." During the day, more regiments came down from Memphis, raising the total to 8,300 men: 5,150 infantry, 2,800 horsemen, and 350 artillerymen with twenty-two cannons. After dropping off the supply train, the cavalry clattered eighteen miles southeast to Lamar, Mississippi. "From all these indications," Hill wrote home that day, "it would seem that quite a formidable expedition is forming, but we have no means of knowing with certainty where we go, probably some movement in favor of Sherman, it is thought by way of Corinth [95 miles southeast of Memphis]. When we started we expected to be back to Memphis in a few days, now we think differently, but of course we don't know. The soldier is not permitted to know about these movements & many of the officers seem to know as little. The head commanders of course understand what is intended, but they know as little of the future as the private soldier."[9]

Private Hill would have been shocked to realize the "head commander" was nearly as clueless as he about what the expedition could or should do. A native of Pennsylvania, the forty-one-year-old Samuel Davis Sturgis graduated from West Point in 1846 and fought in the Mexican War and on the frontier. In August 1861 after Brig. Gen. Nathaniel Lyon was killed at Wilson's Creek, Major Sturgis safely withdrew the Federal force. Promoted brigadier general in 1862, he led an infantry division at Antietam and in the terrible assault against Marye's Heights at Fredericksburg. The next year he served as chief of cavalry in the Department of the Ohio. A fellow general described Sam Sturgis as a "handsome fellow, with full, round features, sharp black eyes, and curly black hair and mustache." He was brave but "never really comfortable with the responsibilities of command," particularly independent command. His bluster concealed a strong want of self-confidence made manifest by a love of the bottle remarkable in an army where inebriation was far from rare. In April 1864 shortly after coming to Memphis, Sturgis went on a "protracted drunken spree" at his headquarters in the Gayoso House, the city's finest hotel, and "smashed looking glasses, crockery and furniture to his heart's content." The night of June 1 witnessed another binge, with Sturgis "raging like a madman."[10]

Samuel Davis Sturgis

In an earlier foray in early May into the northeast corner of Mississippi, Sturgis failed to corner Forrest's cavalry. Now Washburn directed him to approach Corinth from the southwest. Should its capture fail to provoke the desired battle, Sturgis was to advance south along the Mobile & Ohio Railroad fifty miles to Tupelo, destroying the railroad and supplies. If necessary he should push even deeper into Mississippi's grain belt before returning through the center of the state. Largely picked clean of food and fodder, northeastern Mississippi was a barren no man's land that neither side could secure. Sturgis's massive wagon train hauled rations for twenty days but had only inadequate forage for horses and mules. Washburn believed Corinth held a huge store of feed that would remedy that shortage.

Sturgis's present expedition comprised a cavalry division with ten pieces of horse artillery and three brigades of infantry supported by twelve guns. Brigadier General Benjamin H. Grierson, age thirty-seven, a former Illinois bandleader and merchant, led the horsemen. In spring 1863 during the Vicksburg campaign, Grierson earned great praise by slicing through the length of Mississippi, an exploit portrayed in John Wayne's motion picture *The Horse Soldiers.* He came to know Forrest and his tactics well after another deep raid in February 1864 ended in defeat at Okolona, Mississippi. On June 2 Sturgis formed his infantry into a division under Col. William Linn McMillen, the senior brigade commander, and put him in charge of the wagon train as well. Passionate and aggressive, "apparently something of a glory hound," the thirty-four-year-old McMillen was a politically well-connected Ohio physician. On August 30, 1862, less than two weeks after he raised the Ninety-Fifth Ohio Volunteer Infantry, he lost nearly the whole regiment captured in a great defeat at Richmond, Kentucky. McMillen distinguished himself the next year at Vicksburg and in January 1864 assumed command of the First Brigade, First Division, Sixteenth Army Corps. Another senior officer who drank far too much, he staggered on the night of June 1 and fell "drunk as hell," according to one private. To the surgeon of the Seventy-Second Ohio, McMillen was a "vain drunkard and a soulless scoundrel," but one member of the Ninety-Fifth Ohio dissented. "Many did not understand him, but I did, and knew him to be a true and brave man."[11]

Wilkin took over the First Brigade of 2,340 officers and men including the Ninth Minnesota. Indeed, he wrote his father that "if my commission had been a week earlier, I should have had command of all the Infantry." Wilkin relinquished the Ninth Minnesota to Marsh. Lieutenant Lyman Sherwood of Company C became acting regimental adjutant. Pleased the big Ninth Minnesota brought its numbers "up to a respectable figure again," the rest of the First Brigade—confident and experienced, together since April 1863—worried about their new bantam-sized leader, who was "an entire stranger to us." The Seventy-Second Ohio Volunteer Infantry fought in 1862 at Shiloh and Corinth and the next year at Vicksburg and upon re-enlisting in 1864, added the coveted title "Veteran." The remainder of the First Brigade comprised the Ninety-Third Indiana, Ninety-Fifth Ohio, and 114th Illinois, which had also helped take Vicksburg, and two veteran batteries, Company E, First Illinois Light Artillery (four guns) and the Sixth Indiana Battery (two guns).[12]

Colonel George B. Hoge's Second Brigade (1,670 officers and men) comprised five Illinois regiments, all of which had fought at Vicksburg. The Eighty-First Illinois and Ninety-Fifth Illinois only just reached Memphis following the ill-fated Red River expedition and desperately "needed a season of rest to recruit us up" but did not get it. The Memphis garrison provided a 145-man detachment of the 108th Illinois, Hoge's own 113th Illinois, the 120th Illinois, and Company B, Second Illinois Light Artillery (four guns). Colonel Edward Bouton's Third Brigade (1,350 all ranks) included the Fifty-Fifth U.S. Colored Infantry, the Fifty-Ninth U.S. Colored Infantry, and Battery F, Second U.S. Light Artillery (Colored) with two guns. The black enlisted men, nearly all freed slaves, were led by white officers. Neither regiment, although well-drilled and splendidly motivated, had seen much combat. Derided as "cotton field negroes," they had much to prove to themselves and others. They vowed revenge for Fort Pillow, where a detachment from Battery F lost two guns and many men missing and feared dead.[13]

ADVANCING TOWARD CORINTH

Before dawn on June 3, after a breakfast of soggy hardtack, the infantry division started southeast for Lamar. It "rained a good deal," the mud being "ten times more disagreeable than dust" to Pvt. Melville Robertson, a medical orderly in the Ninety-Third Indiana. The foot soldiers tramped through what Cpl. A. J. Carlson called "quite a thickly settled country, but now laid waste by the horrors of war." His relative Pehr Carlson noticed "nothing but women and small children and old men." He contrasted the fine homes of well-to-do masters with the "sheds or open stables of logs" where their slaves dwelt. After lunch the rain came "down in earnest." Soon the mud was "about shoe mouth deep," letting sand seep in and irritate wet feet. That evening after passing devastated Lamar, the First Brigade camped in an old, sloping cornfield, just a "mud hole" according to James Woodbury. McMillen set guards to prevent soldiers from dismantling "old buildings" and "fence rails & planks" to make shelters, "but men wet and cold were not to be easily managed." Private Alexander Almond, a recent recruit of the Seventy-Second

Ohio, complained of being "wet through" and having "to sleep with our wet clothes on all night" in the rain. Even a grizzled old campaigner like his fellow Ohioan Pvt. William B. Halsey marveled at "the hardest day and night I have seen in the war except one at Corinth in 1863."[14]

The wagon train straggled badly and by 11 P.M. was still four miles short of Lamar. Soggy roads were agony for its hapless horses and mules. To improve travel conditions, Sturgis directed McMillen to organize a pioneer corps from the Ninth Minnesota "where I learned there was a company of artisans especially suitable for that duty." They came from Company A, pioneers in the 1863 Dakota campaign. McMillen tactlessly placed the experienced loggers under Lt. David M. Tate from his own Ninety-Fifth Ohio. The pioneers labored mightily, cutting tree trunks and laying corduroy roadbeds, but extreme conditions often rendered their efforts largely useless. "All night," according to 1st Sgt. John Merrilies of Company E, First Illinois Light Artillery, "the rain fell in torrents, and morning found the roads impassable ahead." McMillen impatiently waited until noon on June 4 when the exhausted wagon train finally attained Lamar. The weather cleared, and Colonel Hoge's Second Brigade left for Salem a dozen miles east. The other two brigades stayed in camp.[15]

On Sunday, June 5, the rest of the infantry and the wagon train trudged toward Salem. That morning, although sweltering, was at least dry. The condition of the road improved rapidly, but heatstroke killed or incapacitated numerous overworked horses and mules. Despite the "broken, hilly country," there was "plenty of water at hand," ever, as Corporal Carlson noted, "a great blessing for a soldier on the march." At noon the First Brigade, in the rear of the wagon train, passed through Salem (one of Forrest's boyhood homes) and continued two miles east to Big Sand Springs, where the water was excellent. That evening Chaplain Kerr conducted Sabbath worship and chatted with John Aiton and other old Nicollet County friends in Company D. Artillery Sergeant Merrilies "indulged in the luxury" of a "'Turkish Bath, that is—sand, and Government soap, and moderately dirty water." Other Yankees sought "pigs & chickens," likely with little success, although one party made the grisly discovery of a "dead Union soldier hanging in an old building, captured on previous scout."[16]

Given the snail-like rate of advance, young Melville Robertson could ascertain "nothing of the object or destination of the expedition." Nor apparently yet did General Sturgis. In addition to transforming roads into quagmires, the torrential rains flooding the nearby rivers and creeks threatened to wash away any prospect of Union success. Certain that chances were virtually nil for the far-ranging campaign that Washburn envisioned, Sturgis wondered if the Rebels might still be found in strength to the east. Only time would tell if wily Bedford Forrest could be located before logistics forced Sturgis to retreat.[17]

McMillen got the infantry moving at dawn on June 6 east toward Corinth. The rain poured sporadically the whole day. When the sun did emerge, the air was extremely hot and humid. Beyond Salem the country was, according to Aiton, "very rolling, pines, but few houses." Corporal Carlson found the inhabitants "very poor," with "only women and young children at home in their small rude log cabins." It "rained like hell all the time we stopped for the waggons to come up," noted Alec Almond, "but they did not catch up until night." After plodding fourteen miles, the First Brigade camped at the crossroads of the Saulsbury road six miles shy of Ruckersville, where most of Grierson's cavalry waited.[18]

A CHANGE OF DIRECTION

On the hot, rainy morning of June 7, the infantry brigades again loitered until 11 A.M. to enable the tormented wagon train to come up. Having just learned that cavalry patrols found no enemy troops near Corinth, Sturgis decided, in defiance of Washburn's wishes, to turn the infantry column southeast onto the Saulsbury road to Ripley. The supply of animal fodder in the wagon train was long since exhausted. Indeed, the poor horses "have commenced dropping off." To the disgust of the soldiers, Sturgis also reduced the daily ration of hardtack by half and meat to a quarter. Although hilly, the country proved more level than near Salem, a relief to the infantry, and was more open and settled. Pehr Carlson rated the land excellent for raising corn, wheat, and rye: "Haven't seen better." Late that afternoon the infantry entered Ripley, the seat of Tippah County. Pleasantly situated "in small groves of beech and sycamore trees," Ripley, once "very pretty and flourishing," was now "a small, dilapidated town." Its courthouse had been "burnt and all the places of business deserted, windows broken in and doors bursted open." Nonetheless, a "good many families" lived there. The "fair sex," Merrilies discovered, was "as usual decidedly predominating, and taking no pains to disguise their sympathies, which are anything but Union." The Third Brigade, the first black soldiers ever seen in Ripley, caused an uproar among the locals, who complained of their insolent behavior. The First Brigade camped in comfortable settings in town, close to the Ripley Female Academy.[19]

That night, as usual, the rain came down in buckets. Because of short rations, the regiments unleashed parties of foragers. Those from the First Brigade garnered "eight or nine beef cattle, among them three or four large steers." In response to citizen complaints, Sturgis brusquely ordered the cattle returned to their owners and forbade foraging on threat of cashiering the commanding officers. Furthermore, he ordered the First Brigade to be "searched for citizen's clothing and contraband generally, which had been taken from houses in town last night." That action "took a good many by surprise," wrote an amused Merrilies, "and they had to deliver their ill gotten gains, but some of the knowing ones smelt the rat, and 'lit out' for the woods with the plunder in time to save it." The inspectors gathered the loot at head-quarters for civilians to claim. "Damn Sturgis!" fumed a veteran forager in the Seventy-Second Ohio. One light-fingered Hoosier was tied to a tree by his thumbs. No one from the Ninth Minnesota was singled out—at least nothing was recorded. Slipping out of camp to "confiscate some fresh meat of some kind," Corporal Carlson and a friend scared up a small calf and a couple of scrawny chickens alongside an old cabin. "We agreed to take the calf, but when I saw the tears in the woman's eyes and the two small children looking at us, and the oldest said to the mother they are taking our calf, I abandoned the attempt." Afterward Carlson heard some hardhearted Mis-sourians "took all she had."[20]

While Wilkin was left to punish plunderers, Sturgis convened a council of war with Grierson, McMillen, and Hoge. Given the delays imposed by the horrible weather and the lack of animal forage, Sturgis considered whether to turn back to Memphis. By now Forrest, who it seemed had to know every Federal move, would have had plenty of time to mass his forces in the direc-tion of Tupelo. Grierson preferred to withdraw, but he urged that if they did advance, the wagon train, their ball and chain, should remain at Ripley. Appalled by such pessimism, McMillen vehemently urged they execute Wash-burn's orders to find and fight Forrest. Only if rebuffed should they relent. Responding to McMillen's "emotional appeal," Sturgis elected to resume ad-vancing southeast while promising to keep his force concentrated and always ready for battle. Grierson merely shook his head in disgust.[21]

Despite their general's restored enthusiasm, not until early afternoon on June 8 did the infantry and wagon train venture southeast from Ripley along the road to distant Fulton, the seat of Itawamba County. The day proved "excessively hot and sultry, the road dry and dusty, and enclosed on each side by a very thick growth of underbrush, shutting out the little air there is stirring, and rendering the march very oppressive." Later "a splendid thunderstorm" cooled things off. The column crept just six miles over undulating terrain before halting for the night in "beautiful open timber" near New Harmony Church. Grierson's cavalry bivouacked a mile ahead of the infantry. While the men prepared supper, drums suddenly "beat the long roll, the bugles sounded the 'To Arms,' and in ten minutes the Brigade was in line of battle all ready for any emergency." The Rebels were said to be attacking, but it was a false alarm caused by a brief clash of patrols. Rain that night again drenched weary sleepers.[22]

To lighten the expedition, Sturgis ordered emptied wagons to be loaded with soldiers who were too ill to proceed. They were to be sent with the played-out horses and mules back to Memphis. Those who were selected numbered about four hundred in forty-one wagons. The Ninth Minnesota provided one wagon and thirty-six men (ten from Company H alone), but so far as is known, none were Otterville liberators. The detachment departed on the morning of the ninth. Further easing the burden on the train, the remaining soldiers filled their haversacks with five days' rations. Some of the infantry, including the Ninth Minnesota, also stuffed their pockets with twenty paper cartridges in addition to the forty rounds already lodged in their cartridge boxes.[23]

While waiting in camp, the Minnesotans reflected on their situation. Despite the nine-day march of more than a hundred grueling miles over terrible roads, often in the rain, Wilkin, for one, felt much better. His health was once so precarious that Sturgis had advised him to return to Memphis. Nonetheless, "I put my Brigade in the best shape I could, considering that I was a stranger to all but my own Regiment." Wilkin was gratified to hear that Sturgis had "no complaints" and that he "knew I understood my business." He surmised the expedition was bound for Tupelo where "they say Forrest is concentrating a large force and will give us battle." Marsh was proud of the Ninth Minnesota. "Up to this time the weather had been very wet, and the roads heavy, and my regiment being unaccustomed to long marches, were very much fatigued," he wrote in his report, "yet not a murmur was heard, but all appeared anxious to meet the enemy." Hill advised his wife, Sarah, that he had "come through so far in good health & spirits" despite "mud & rain" and "some warm weather when it seemed like melting a fellow down." Occasionally "a rich plantation farm now no longer rich" could be seen, "but much of the land [is] running to waste." The war "is making sad havoc with much of the southern country. God grant it may soon end."[24]

Elsewhere that day the National Union Party (made up of Republicans and War Democrats) notified President Lincoln that its convention had unanimously nominated him for reelection. The party platform demanded Confederate unconditional surrender and proposed a constitutional amendment to end slavery forever. In place of Vice President Hamlin of Maine, the convention had selected Andrew Johnson of Tennessee, a staunch War Democrat senator who had become military governor of his state. Decisive results appeared nigh on both major battlefronts. At Cold Harbor only ten miles east of Richmond, the exhausted Army of the Potomac rested following the staggering losses of the Overland Campaign. Grant already planned to turn Lee's right flank, cross the James River, and sever Richmond's main supply line at Petersburg. In Georgia, Sherman had maneuvered within twenty-five miles of Atlanta and prepared to assault the next line of defense sited around rugged Kennesaw Mountain. Grinding through the wretched mud of northern Mississippi in search of Forrest ranked merely as a sideshow in the vast western theater, but success would earn Sturgis's men a share of the eventual victory.

THE "COTTON CAMP"

"In heavy rain with the mud about a foot deep," the infantry column set out at 1 P.M. on June 9 southeast on the Fulton road. Assigned as rear guard, the Ninth Minnesota and a section of Company E, First Illinois Light Artillery, could not start moving for nearly two hours. Wagon duty was particularly onerous for the escort. The jerky stops and starts made it difficult to keep a proper pace, a problem the rolling terrain only intensified. Falling farther behind the main body and bereft of supporting cavalry, Marsh deployed flankers and pickets. "Marched till dark," Merrilies commented in his diary, "when it commenced raining very hard. As the troops began camping, the train closed up very fast, compelling us to trot to keep up. This, with the darkness, was the means of our missing our camp altogether." Only at 11 P.M. when fourteen miles southeast of Ripley did the Ninth Minnesota grope its way back to its brigade camp in a rare, large open field belonging to a plantation established in the 1840s by Thomas B. Stubbs, a planter from Georgia. "Wet to the skin," the weary Minnesotans "stacked arms by fixing bayonets and sticking the bayonets into the ground" to prevent the barrels from filling with water.[25]

Nearby was a cotton gin in an old wooden structure filled with neatly stacked bales of cotton. Heedless of its value of a dollar a pound, the Minnesotans eagerly stripped away the bands and seized the cotton "for bedding to rest our weary and worn-out beings on the ground," reminisced William Franklin ("Frank") Lyon, a twenty-one-year-old private in Company C. Prior to enlisting in February 1864, he had worked on his father's farm in High Forest in Olmsted County and taught school part time. After Lyon and his mates scavenged plenty of cotton padding, he thoughtfully asked Ford if he, too, might like some. Gladly, Ford replied, if there was any to spare. "So I handed it over to him and went back to my *downy* couch" and "slept well in the 'land of cotton.'" Early the next day, "you ought to have seen our appearance, the white cotton sticking to our wet woolen pants and coats," recalled Corporal Carlson. "We certainly did not come up to military regulation that morning." Orders came down that "every man who had anything to do with that cotton will at once, without delay, put it back where he found it." Lyon quickly collected the cotton he used and what he gave the captain and returned it. Soon he heard "every man who had anything to do with that cotton, will be put under guard and marched in the rear of the regiment in disgrace." Standing during roll call fully exposed in the front rank, Lyon "was covered with cotton from head to foot. It wouldn't come off." Walking along the line, gravely inspecting each man, Ford confided to him in a low voice: "You look pretty well." It was a "compliment" Lyon accepted "gracefully without a word." When Ford simply walked on, Lyon "didn't go to the rear because he didn't tell me to."[26]

BATTLE PLANS

Dawn on Friday, June 10, was already "excessively warm and oppressive" and the day only got worse. As the hot sun emerged through the clouds, recalled one Confederate, "the steam from the rain-soaked earth was almost unbearable for men or horses." At sunrise Grierson started his cavalry division southeast along the Fulton road after a "gloomy and irritable" Sturgis had rejected his earnest advice to keep the main body where it was and await certain attack. "Our chances for victory would be greatly strengthened if the Infantry and Artillery could be quietly put into position for battle," Grierson proposed, "while the Cavalry, unencumbered, continued to operate in such manner as to fully develop the enemy's strength and draw him forward to a general engagement." Although uncertain where the Rebels actually were, Sturgis was confident they were not anywhere nearby in strength. He told Grierson to "attack the enemy wherever he might be found." After going nine miles on the Fulton road, the cavalry was to turn northeast and proceed another six miles to Baldwyn, a small town located on the Mobile & Ohio Railroad. In turn McMillen would "follow promptly with the Infantry well closed up," keeping to the Fulton road for sixteen miles to Guntown, situated on the railroad six miles south of Baldwyn. Upon breaking camp, McMillen formed his division in the order: Hoge's Second Brigade, Wilkin's First Brigade (with the Ninth Minnesota), and finally the huge wagon train, guarded that day by the African American infantry of Bouton's Third Brigade. The Minnesota axmen took their accustomed place at the head of the column. At 7 A.M. the infantry started out "with light hearts" in confident anticipation of a fight that day at Guntown. Cheering them was a false rumor, more credible in that it was said to have come from the Rebels, that Sherman had seized Atlanta. Upon leaving the campsite, recalled Lyon, "someone went to the spring to fill his canteen, and as he passed the house, he lighted a match and threw it into the house and hurried into his place. As we passed over the hill we saw the smoke. The speculating officers who had hoped to get that cotton to market were doubtless disappointed." So, too, was the Stubbs family following another calamitous visit by the infernal Yankees.[27]

In a little valley a mile and a half beyond Stubbs's farm, the swollen headwaters of the Hatchie River had inundated about two hundred feet of bottomland through which the Fulton road passed. Grierson's cavalry splashed across at the cost of one horse drowned. Riding out ahead of the infantry, Sturgis and his cavalry escort soon reached that "unusually bad place in the road" that, he saw, "would require considerable time and labor to render practicable." Both Grierson and Sturgis blundered terribly, for a little scouting would have revealed a perfectly dry detour on higher ground that bypassed the swamp a half mile to the west. The direct route appears to have been a shortcut the locals used only in dry weather, which this decidedly was not. Encountering "much delay occasioned by bad roads," Hoge's and Wilkin's brigades slogged across the morass, but the wagons and their escorts could not follow until the pioneers finished laying a new roadbed. Laboring in the hot sun, the Minnesotans placed logs lengthwise in the road, crisscrossed them with smaller poles and filled the gaps with brush. Nonetheless, given the heavy traffic that had already passed, McMillen judged the road now "almost impassable" and "impossible to put it in good condition." Not only was the infantry advance significantly delayed, but such an appalling obstacle in the rear could gravely threaten the Yankees if they encountered real trouble that day.[28]

Continuing south a short distance along the Fulton road, Hoge's brigade halted in front of a "double log farm house that had a front porch." When some Yankees pillaged its "well stocked garden," an "old woman, gray haired, about seventy five or eighty years old" began "marching up and down the porch." Private John W. Bartleson of the Eighty-First Illinois saw her "praying so loud that all could hear her, that God would take vengeance upon us and destroy us all!" He "felt sorry for this old grandmother." By the time Company E, First Illinois Light Artillery, came up with Wilkin's brigade, the plunderers, using the excuse of finding a cavalry saddle and military gear, had ransacked the old woman's home. Merrilies heard her unleash "a storm of wrath, calling down all sorts of vengeance on the heads of the Yankees, shouting away till she became perfectly frantic." No one paid her much notice until an intruder upset a hive of honeybees that became "the means of clearing the lot and house much more than the old lady's anathemas." The avenging bees stung the battery horses, forcing their swift evacuation to safer ground. From well down the road, Merrilies could still hear the "shrill notes" of the old woman thanking the Lord "for the bees that drove off the Yankees."[29]

Markham subsequently described the trek from Memphis as "an easy happy-go-luck kind of march" that gave "the rebs time to get any force they liked to meet us in any position they chose." Truly Sturgis had stirred up a nest of gray avengers, a swarm of human hornets led by the Confederacy's fiercest warrior. By the time Forrest learned of Sturgis's departure from Memphis, he and a picked force had already started for northern Alabama to raid Sherman's supply line in Middle Tennessee. Now instead he summoned what strength he could—roughly six thousand cavalry and mounted infantry—and kept careful watch on the likely Federal routes of advance. In that respect Sturgis already accomplished his primary objective of keeping Sherman free of possible interference. By June 9 four Rebel brigades and a horse artillery battalion were distributed along the railroad south of Corinth. Once Forrest discovered that Sturgis had halted at Stubbs's farm, he correctly deduced the Yankees would next make for Baldwyn or Guntown on the railroad. Forrest's superior preferred to meet the enemy farther south in open ground near Tupelo, but Forrest himself boldly determined to fight on the tenth somewhere along the narrow roads where thick woods would mask his numbers. That was vital, for he estimated there were ten thousand or more Yankees. The Confederates faced all of the same drawbacks of rain, heat, lack of rest, and muddy roads, but their overall mobility was much greater. Well mounted as cavalry, Forrest's horsemen could also fight adroitly and comfortably afoot. About half carried muzzleloading rifles, the rest carbines, mostly Sharps breechloaders. Many also sported Colt revolvers, very handy for close-in work. Forrest's horse artillery was efficient and well led, while the Federal gunners lacked an overall commander or any real coordination.[30]

Near 11 A.M., Sturgis read a message from Grierson locating enemy forces seven miles ahead. Skirmishing ensued near the point where he was to veer northeast. There the Ripley-Fulton road intercepted the so-called Wire Road (telegraph poles ran alongside) that ran northeast from Pontotoc to Carrollville, near Baldwyn. That crossroads was known by the name of a nearby resident, William Brice. Grierson reported six hundred Rebel horsemen on the Baldwyn road northeast of Brice's Crossroads. Sturgis ordered him to leave six or seven hundred horsemen at the crossroads to await the infantry and to push vigorously with the rest of the cavalry through to Baldwyn. From there he was to drive the enemy south along the railroad toward Guntown. In the meantime Sturgis expected McMillen's infantry, moving briskly, to reach Guntown in time to block the Rebel retreat. Earlier that day he had also emphasized to McMillen how important it was for the infantry to keep in supporting distance of the cumbersome wagon train until it cleared the obstacle at Hatchie Bottom, but that would take hours. In fact Bouton's Third Brigade required over three hours just to exit the old campsite at Stubbs's farm. The two orders grossly contradicted each other. Tied to the pace of the wagon train and hampered by the very warm, humid weather, the foot soldiers could not be expected to move quickly. Yet the eager if mercurial Sturgis did not seem concerned his force was no longer concentrated and ready for battle but was strung out badly. To him, at least, everything boded well for a sharp Confederate defeat on the railroad south of Baldwyn. That day, however, the Ninth Minnesota and the rest of Sturgis's little army faced the fight of their lives.[31]

CHAPTER SEVEN

The Battle of
Brice's Crossroads (I)

DOUBLE-QUICK INTO DANGER

The Ninth Minnesota was fifth in order within the First Brigade, behind the Ninety-Fifth Ohio, the two artillery batteries, the 114th Illinois, and the Ninety-Third Indiana. The Seventy-Second Ohio and the brigade ambulances brought up the rear. With Marsh on horseback at its head, the Ninth Minnesota, 630 strong, marched in the customary four abreast—the "column of fours." Markham was the only other mounted officer. This day the regiment moved "by the left flank," to use the technical term. In the lead was the "Field Music" of twenty drummers, fifers, and buglers under Principal Musician Handy, a forty-one-year-old professional musician and proprietor of a book and music store in St. Anthony. Private DeWitt C. Handy, his nineteen-year-old son, was one of the drummers. No one recorded whether on this excessively hot, humid morning Handy's musicians played light tunes to encourage their fellow plodders. The seniority of the captains (present or absent) dictated the order of the ten companies. On that occasion Markham's left wing of Companies E, C (with fifteen liberators), G, H, and A was in front, followed by Marsh's own right wing with the color guard (Sergeant Macdonald and eight stalwart corporals) and Companies I (the color company), B, F, K (with sixteen liberators), and D. When in the field, the Ninth Minnesota, like most other western regiments, carried only the stars and stripes of the national color and not the regimental (or state) colors. The two regimental ambulances (with Dr. Bingham, acting brigade surgeon, and Dr. John C. Dixon, second assistant surgeon) and the medicine wagon traveled behind in the First Brigade's medical contingent. The one remaining army wagon crept along in the brigade supply train still negotiating Hatchie Bottom.[1]

Close to noon after the First Brigade had slogged four miles beyond Stubbs's farm, Wilkin learned of trouble with the cavalry skirmishing at Brice's Crossroads five miles ahead. At that time most of the supply wagons had yet to clear the unnecessary crossing at Hatchie Bottom. Before leaving for the crossroads, Sturgis directed McMillen to bring Hoge's brigade forward "as rapidly as possible—without distressing the troops," while Wilkin and Bouton were to advance as swiftly as they could without separating from the wagon train. That meant slow progress given the circumstances, while Hoge's brigade pressed on ahead. A few minutes after twelve with the boom of distant artillery now audible, another courier galloped up to Wilkin with more details of the cavalry fight. Within an hour he received permission to leave the Third Brigade to protect the train and move the First Brigade ahead more quickly. The pioneers rejoined the Ninth Minnesota after their futile effort to bridge the morass.[2]

Marching that day proved agonizing under a sun that was, according to Capt. Egbert O. Mallory of the 114th Illinois, "as hot as ever shone in Mississippi." It was "the hottest day I ever experienced," recalled William Dean of Company I. The temperature exceeded one hundred degrees, with the brutal tropical humidity magnifying its debilitating effect. Not a breath of wind stirred the broiling air for the men whose blue woolen blouses turned black with sweat. Nearly everywhere along the narrow, hilly Fulton road a "dense pine forest rose like an impenetrable wall to a height of from sixty to eighty feet, and most effectually shut out even the slightest motion of the atmosphere." Only at infrequent intervals around homesteads did clearings or small fields break the barrier of trees and brush. "The men who marched that day will never forget how hot it was in that woods," wrote Sgt. John W. Lacock of the Ninety-Third Indiana. "The very sand under our feet was as if we were treading in hot ashes. The perspiration poured off like rain." Furthermore, the wretched road stayed "fearfully muddy" in low spots.[3]

A shocking number of men soon straggled. On route marches the captains watched for those who fell out of the ranks. Frank Lyon from Company C dropped out around noon. "In consequence of my weakened condition, the sun so affected my head and back that my legs refused to work and I was obliged to lay down by the road side and wait for the wagon train to come up." Taking one look at the limp soldier Captain Ford raised no objection. During recruit training at Rolla earlier that spring, Lyon had been hospitalized with fever and weakness in the legs and back. On the march out from Memphis, he struggled manfully to keep up "but made no complaint thinking that I would get stronger." He never did.[4]

Out in front with Hoge's brigade, McMillen received "repeated and urgent orders to move up as rapidly as possible." At that time Wilkin neared a fine large white house belonging to Dr. Enoch Agnew three miles short of Brice's Crossroads. He relayed to his regiments McMillen's order to proceed at the "double-quick," 165 steps per minute to advance 150 yards each minute as long as the men could keep it up. The First Brigade "sprang forward with a will," declared an officer of the Ninety-Third Indiana, but sustaining that tempo "seemed impossible" to Sergeant Herrick of Company B. "We had been marching all the forenoon in the hot sun; it was very sultry." The Minnesotans double-quicked a mile, but thereafter "kept marching and double quicking alternately." Laden with weapons, ammunition, haversacks, and rubber blankets, the "hungry, hot, fatigued footmen," recounted John Aiton of Company D, could do no more.[5]

As the sound of far-off firing grew louder, the First Brigade encountered "many men" from Hoge's brigade "who had fallen out sun struck & exhausted." Modern medicine defines heatstroke (sunstroke) as when the victim is no longer able to sweat and faces mental impairment, unconsciousness, and even death. Most of those afflicted suffered heat exhaustion, a lesser though still profoundly debilitating ailment. Lieutenant Colonel John F. King of the 114th Illinois in Wilkin's First Brigade estimated that he passed four hundred to eight hundred overheated soldiers sitting or prone "on the sides of the road begging for help and asking for water." To Col. De Witt C. Thomas of the Ninety-Third Indiana, "so thickly were the dead or dying scattered along the road that it presented the appearance of a running fight having taken place." In turn an artillery officer counted about three hundred of Hoge's Illinoisans "lying in the road." He later concluded the Second Brigade was "beaten before they went into the fight at all."[6]

The many casualties because of the heat and pitiless pace soon included substantial numbers of the First Brigade, at least two hundred men from what acting Adjutant Sherwood heard, but very likely many more. Lieutenant Colonel Jefferson Brumback of the Ninety-Fifth Ohio proffered no number for the heat-related casualties in his regiment, stating only "they went into action very much fatigued." King reckoned one hundred from the 114th Illinois, "just over one quarter," were absent. "From the remarks of my officers," Thomas believed the Ninety-Third Indiana lost at least forty men from "exhaustion." Lieutenant Colonel Charles G. Eaton of the Seventy-Second Ohio, in the rear of the First Brigade, averred "quite a number of my men fell out before we arrived there, being overcome with heat and fatigue."[7]

Those stricken in the Ninth Minnesota were numerous. "We were obliged to 'go in' on the double quick," wrote Lieutenant Daniels of Company F, "and as it was very hot, many of our men fell in the road *sunstruck.*" For Pvt. Nicholas H. Schreifels of Company G, "the indescribable heat of the midday sun was more than human beings could endure. All along our route men lay strewn around gasping for breath and fainting." Chauncey Hill recorded how "many fell by the way, exhausted by the heat and travel." After Hill's friend Pvt. George O. Jenkins gave out with severe chest pains, Dr. Dixon brought him into his ambulance. Lieutenant Keysor of Company E decided once he heard the distant boom of artillery he "could remain in the ambulance no longer." Feverish the last several days, he nonetheless got to his feet after hearing the bugle call sounding the "double-quick." He soon caught up with his company after passing several of his men "overcome by intense heat." Pehr Carlson suffered severe heat exhaustion. "I wasn't able to raise my head for a while, but became better afterward and came in in a wagon soon afterward." Private Dominick Mompher of Company K ailed from such acute sunstroke that his comrades feared he would soon die. How many of the liberators also gave out from the heat cannot now be determined. Hens Lüthye fell out with five other soldiers from Company K. "I dropped down unconscious, and when I came to I found myself under a tree & was attended by a soldier of the company." An ambulance retrieved Lüthye. The hospital steward treated him because the surgeons were busy with other sun victims. Lüthye would be extremely fortunate his ambulance remained at the very rear of the long wagon column. Another liberator who faltered was Samuel Mickel.[8]

Emerging from the timber, the panting Minnesotans breasted a low ridge about a half mile northwest of Tishomingo Creek. The bottomland to the west was largely forested, with open fields to the east. An old wooden bridge bisected the creek, which flowed north to south and was now swollen from the recent rains. On the east bank, the Fulton road rose past a wooded knoll to the north and sharply inclined toward the high plateau on which sat Brice's Crossroads a half mile east. A ribbon of men in blue, the Ninety-Third Indiana, was already making that hard climb. The Minnesotans bent down to refill their canteens in the muddy water. On both sides of the creek and to the left (north) beyond the knoll, lines of dismounted cavalry from Col. George E. Waring's First Brigade faced north. They comprised the extreme left of the Union position. To the right (south) of the road, four horse artillery pieces belonging to Col. Edward F. Winslow's Second Brigade rested in a field west of the creek, and hundreds of cavalry mounts, grouped in fours by the horseholders, milled just beyond.

After crossing the creek, the Ninth Minnesota halted briefly to strip for action. Most of the men tossed their rubber blankets, haversacks, and other extraneous gear into company piles alongside the road for the musicians to watch. In battle the drummers and fifers, armed with swords, carried wounded back to the ambulances. Dean wisely chose to keep his haversack with his rations, as did Herrick, who noted such foresight "proved judicious after." Herrick doffed his sodden woolen blouse—"it was so warm I could not keep it"—but not before, he wrote his wife, Salome, five days later, retrieving his handkerchief. "It was the one you sent me," and "I did not want to lose it." At the time Herrick enjoyed a quick word with his father-in-law, Joel Handy, it being "the first time I had seen him during the day." His young brother-in-law, DeWitt, greeted him too. The musicians were filling canteens as fast as they could and handing them out. Joel gave one to Herrick. When Pvt. Samuel Ennerson of Company C, "overheated and partially sunstruck," keeled over, Pvt. Charles C. Stewart bathed his head with water from the creek. A little later Ennerson recovered sufficiently to "'toddle' along and try and find the Regt. again." Many other heat victims did also.[9]

AT BRICE'S CROSSROADS

After 2:30 P.M. Marsh led the Ninth Minnesota past the knoll overlooking Tishomingo Creek and up the steep rise toward the crossroads. Once on top of the hill, he deployed from marching column into line of battle facing the direction of march. The regiment moved by files left into a field north of the road, halted, and turned right to face east. Standing shoulder to shoulder, the men formed into the customary two ranks, the second by regulation a cozy thirteen inches behind the first. Two paces behind the rear rank, an attenuated third line of "file-closers," lieutenants and sergeants, ensured everyone ahead stayed in their proper place. From the front the regiment presented a saw-toothed appearance. By hallowed military tradition, a soldier's height determined where he actually stood in line, marched, and fought. Within each company the tallest corporal and tallest private formed the first file on the right, with the corporal in the front rank. That arrangement by height continued all the way across to the last file on the left of each company, made up of the shortest corporal and shortest private. Thus, Evan Watkins (height 5 feet 10½ inches), a Company C liberator, did not get to stand alongside his older brother, John Watkins Jr., also a liberator. Only 5 feet 4 inches tall, Jack Watkins customarily mustered on the far left flank of the company, with his much taller brother in the right half. Nor could Evan Watkins team up with his own tentmate Pvt. Arad Welch, who was 3 inches shorter. He recalled that as they reached the creek, Welch was "about three files behind the one I was in." He saw Welch fall out from fatigue but could not help him. According to Evan Watkins, "Each file took care of its own men," meaning the four men of each pair of adjacent files, who were known as "comrades in battle," always cooperated closely.[10]

McMillen posted the Ninth Minnesota some distance behind William Brice's house. That large, two-story white structure occupied the northwest quadrant of the crossroads formed by the Ripley-Fulton road, oriented northwest to southeast, and the Wire Road that ran northeast from Pontotoc to Carrollville, near Baldwyn. The house sat in a clearing on higher ground, flanked to the north, east, and south by a dense wall of blackjack oak and overgrown brush. The roads supplied the only openings into those thickets. A short way northeast up the Wire Road was Bethany Associated Reformed Church. The Ninth Minnesota discovered the clear space around Brice's house to be "very contracted" and "very much" cluttered with ambulances, led horses, and artillery caissons "scattered about, mixed up" or "stuck in the mud." The roar of rifle and cannon fire and clouds of white powder smoke revealed the battle being waged out of sight northeast and east beyond the barrier of woods. Wounded soldiers, either carried or afoot, hobbled down to the knoll adjacent to the creek where surgeons set up a field hospital in a double-log cabin that was Brice's slave quarters.[11]

Three artillery pieces from Hoge's brigade, in battery close to the woods just north of Brice's house, blindly fired shells northeast over the trees in the general direction of the enemy. Three of four guns of Capt. John A. Fitch's Company E, First Illinois Light Artillery, rested in reserve between Brice's house and the Fulton road. Fitch deemed the ground around the crossroads, although the highest in the immediate vicinity, to be poor for artillery—"no position at all." He "could not see for any distance" or "judge the distance the enemy were from me, or whether the ground rose or fell in our front." One of his twelve-pounder Napoleon cannons, planted in the center of the crossroads, aimed straight down the Fulton road. Even there, Fitch perceived no direct targets "on account of the brush, which was distant about forty feet from my gun." However, "judging by the firing of the enemy's position I timed my fuses at a second and a half, which gave me a distance of about 450 yards." With the one cannon, he kept a slow, steady fire "with shell and shrapnel."[12]

Marsh had the Ninth Minnesota "sit down and rest until we were needed." The tired men required no prompting. There is no way of knowing how many of the 630 Minnesotans who left Stubbs's farm were still actually in the ranks—perhaps 450. According to Corporal Carlson, the men "were nearly all used up" and "certainly not in a very good condition to meet an enemy in regular line of battle." Sergeant Herrick was shocked to find only "about 20 able to go into action" out of the forty-nine that Company B mustered that morning. Other companies were not reduced to that extent, but the shortfall was bad enough. Marsh directed each company to detach a corporal "to try

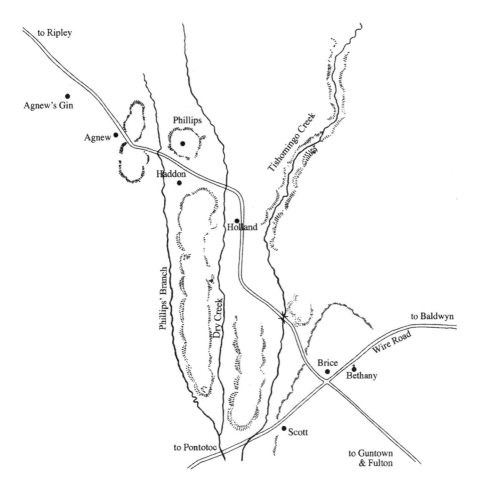

to Ripley

Agnew's Gin

Agnew

Phillips

Haddon

Phillips' Branch

Dry Creek

Holland

Tishomingo Creek

to Baldwyn

Wire Road

Brice

Bethany

Scott

to Pontotoc

to Guntown
& Fulton

Area around Brice's Crossroads

and gather up those that had fallen out along the road and report at the Brigade Ambulances." Captain Baxter detailed Carlson for Company H. "I went a short distance back and the first comrade I found was [Pvt. Bjørn Aslakson]. I brought him to the ambulance." Aslakson was "so weak he could hardly walk."[13]

The Seventy-Second Ohio stumbled up the slope behind the Minnesotans. Sturgis observed the scene from the steps of Brice's nearby dwelling while taking periodic pulls from a long-necked black bottle. Because Rebels could be glimpsed off to the north extending their lines west toward Tishomingo Creek, McMillen directed Wilkin to double back with the Seventy-Second Ohio and the two guns of Capt. Michael Mueller's Sixth Indiana Battery to the knoll that overlooked the creek. From there they could support Waring's cavalrymen covering the Federal left flank and also protect the all-important Tishomingo bridge. Bouton's brigade with the wagon train had not yet reached the battlefield, leaving the Ninth Minnesota as McMillen's only infantry reserve. Soon a column of nearly seven hundred dismounted cavalry troopers, Iowans from Winslow's Second Brigade, emerged from the woods around the crossroads and filed past the Ninth Minnesota to remount in the rear, near the stream. Word went around that the "Rebels were gaining on us," but there seemed to be no particular disorder or panic. In truth the whole Union position faced great peril.[14]

The Fighting up to That Point

When the Ninth Minnesota crossed the Tishomingo bridge, combat at Brice's Crossroads had raged and sputtered for over four hours. The "ball" opened around 9:30 A.M. when Grierson's vanguard encountered a few gray horsemen west of the creek. Against little resistance the Union cavalry soon reached the road junction and discovered evidence of a Rebel force lurking off to the northeast toward Baldwyn. A patrol sent in that direction encountered the enemy a mile or so beyond the crossroads. Grierson started Waring's brigade toward Baldwyn as planned but kept Winslow's brigade in reserve for the time being behind the creek. Around 10 A.M. Waring's advance guard found Confederates posted across the Wire Road in a "remarkably thick growth of blackjack oak" broken only by a few small fields. Supposedly weak in numbers and seeking only to delay the Federal juggernaut, the Rebel cavalry reacted with surprising truculence. At the edge of a large field about a half mile northeast of the crossroads, Waring dismounted his brigade and unlimbered six artillery pieces in line across the road. Every fourth man took his own horse and three others back to safety. About six hundred troopers

deployed across the road in single rank in loose line of battle, with skirmishers in front. A regiment was in reserve.[15]

Suddenly, Rebel infantry or dismounted cavalry swarmed "out of the
woods to the east of us like bees out of a hive." Waring's men fended off two
"desperate" charges that certainly persuaded Grierson the enemy was much
stronger than expected. He told Waring to "hold the position as long as
possible," but if "necessary" to retire "to the edge of the timber this side of
the clearing, where his reserve was formed, with the open ground in front."
About 11 A.M. Grierson brought Winslow's brigade to the crossroads after
Winslow took the trouble to repair the old bridge, "a thoughtful precaution,
subsequently, of much importance to the command." Deciding that pushing through to Baldwyn was now "entirely impracticable," Grierson resolved
"obstinately" to "obstruct" the Rebels in "the position which I deemed advan-
tageous" while awaiting the infantry he supposed was "near at hand." Equally
impressed by the fierce opposition, Waring completely concurred. "Pending
the arrival of the infantry it would have been folly for us to attempt a further advance." Although heavily engaged, Grierson informed Sturgis that he
could hold if the infantry was "brought forward promptly." He also detached
a cavalry battalion from Winslow's brigade to return and take over guarding
the wagon train.[16]

Thus, Grierson, "a raider and not a fighter" according to the distinguished
historian Edwin C. Bearss, surrendered the initiative—precisely what Nathan
Bedford Forrest desired. However, it is difficult to see given the terrain and
stiffening Rebel resistance what else Grierson could have done under the
circumstances. Definitely present in some strength, Forrest was, as usual,
more than eager to fight. With as many as 1,200 tough Kentuckians, mostly
mounted infantry, Col. Hylan B. Lyon's Third Brigade was the first substantial Confederate force on the field. Forrest himself brought his elite personal
escort and that of Brig. Gen. Abraham Buford—about 120 well-armed, crack
horsemen under Capt. John C. Jackson. Eager to "develop the enemy" while
awaiting the rest of his troops, Forrest dismounted most of Lyon's men and
lined them up across the Wire Road to put up a brave front to deceive the
Yankees. Subtracting the horse holders, his available force roughly equaled
the troopers in Waring's front line. Within an hour Col. Edmund W. Rucker's
Sixth Brigade of nearly a thousand Mississippi and Tennessee cavalry had
arrived. Most of them moved out afoot on Lyon's left to extend the line
southward toward the Fulton road.[17]

Reacting to the warning by his pickets of the threat to the Fulton road,
Grierson dispatched seven hundred dismounted Iowans from Winslow's
brigade to connect with Waring's right and extend his line south beyond the

road. There the "small trees and underbrush were so dense, the enemy could not be seen until within less than a hundred yards distance." Thus, Grierson troopers, arrayed in a loose single line, held an arc stretching from north to east roughly a half mile out from Brice's Crossroads. To watch the right flank, Winslow furnished two hundred Missouri and Illinois cavalry under Capt. Amos P. Curry to patrol the Wire Road south of the crossroads.[18]

With the arrival of Col. William A. Johnson's brigade of perhaps seven hundred Alabamans, Forrest's available strength exceeded Grierson's. That demonstrates the wisdom of Grierson's decision to assume the defensive, but not necessarily total passivity. Going into line on Lyon's right north beyond the Wire Road, Johnson demonstrated against Waring's left flank, causing Waring to draw forces from his right near the junction with Winslow's brigade. Charging that now tender spot after 12:00 P.M., Lyon and Rucker drove back the Seventh Indiana Cavalry as well as the Second New Jersey Cavalry, previously in reserve. Winslow had to refuse his endangered left flank, leaving a second gap that the Rebels also exploited. The whole Union line recoiled about four hundred yards. Aided by horse artillery firing from Brice's Crossroads, the Federals held, barely, but Waring's men were badly shaken.[19]

Shortly after 1 P.M., Sturgis himself reached Brice's Crossroads with his own escort of one hundred Pennsylvania troopers, whom he strung out as a backstop behind Waring's crumbling center and right flank. Advised by Grierson that Waring was hard-pressed and needed relief, Sturgis curtly replied the infantry was nearby. He ordered Grierson to prepare to "withdraw and reorganize" and to hold his horsemen "in readiness to operate on the flanks." Grierson overheard Sturgis remark "in a petulant manner" to a staff officer that "if the damned cavalry could only be gotten out of the way," he would "soon whip the enemy with his Infantry." From the commanding general's brusque behavior, Grierson deduced he "did not, even then realize the fact that the rebels were in large force in our front." Sturgis, though, did not care. He believed stalwart infantry could stop any dismounted cavalry and never comprehended how the grueling forced march had shredded the endurance of his hapless foot soldiers and how the thick brush would reduce their formidable firepower. The obvious course of action, had he truly understood the situation, was to post the infantry and artillery on one of the ridges west of the creek and let the cavalry fall back to them. Alternatively, if he had stayed at the crossroads, he could have kept the cavalry well in hand in reserve rather than simply count on winning without them. Instead, Sturgis let the battle slip totally out of his control.[20]

Beginning at 1:30 P.M., a lull descended over the battlefield. In the searing heat, both sides welcomed the opportunity to rest and regroup. Private John

Milton Hubbard of the Seventh Tennessee Cavalry in Rucker's brigade gladly scooped water out of puddles in the rain-soaked fields and later avowed he "never tasted better." After a long, rapid ride, General Buford reached the field with most of Col. Tyree H. Bell's big Fourth Brigade and two batteries of artillery (eight pieces) under Capt. John W. Morton. The presence of their own artillery greatly raised Rebel morale. Morton positioned two guns near the Wire Road to keep the Federals busy, while Forrest determined his plan of action.[21]

While marching his brigade to the battlefield, Hoge heard from Sturgis that the "enemy was gaining ground" against the cavalry and that the "only thing that could save us was the infantry." Within fifteen minutes of taking the double-quick pace, Hoge's overtaxed men had, as the First Brigade discovered, dropped out in droves. "As I rode along the moving column from regiment to regiment," wrote Dr. Lewis Dyer, surgeon-in-chief to the infantry and artillery, "I saw numerous cases of sunstroke, and scores and hundreds of men, many of them known to me as good and true soldiers, falling out by the way, utterly powerless to move forward." He warned the colonels if the men did not slow down they could not "handle their muskets." Colonel Thomas W. Humphrey of the Ninety-Fifth Illinois fully concurred. "You can place me under arrest," he snapped to one of McMillen's aides, "but you cannot hurry me or my men into this fight." Private James Mooney of the 113th Illinois later recalled how "nearly every hundred feet," some of his comrades gave out from "over heat, sun stroke & want of water." They "would take 2 or 3 staggering steps, fall down and commence crying & calling for water. We would tear their shirt collars open, pour water on their necks & heads, carry them to a shade tree & run for our place in the ranks." It appears nearly half of the Second Brigade succumbed to the heat, at least temporarily, before reaching the crossroads.[22]

When McMillen brought up Hoge's lead infantrymen shortly after 1:30 P.M., he encountered a portion of Waring's brigade "falling back rapidly in disorder." The "roads at Brice's house were filled with retreating cavalry, led horses, ambulances, wagons, and artillery, the whole presenting" to Hoge "a scene of confusion and demoralization anything but cheering to troops just arriving." Furthermore, "the enemy was also shelling this point vigorously at this time and during the arrival of my troops." When the weary, "jaded and forlorn" 113th Illinois in the lead briefly halted at the crossroads, the "tongues of many hung out of their mouths, and they couldn't bite a cartridge." The acrid taste of gunpowder only intensified their thirst. McMillen deployed the foot regiments as they came up one at a time to replace Waring's wavering cavalry northeast of the crossroads and to relieve a portion of Winslow's cavalry brigade as well. The 113th Illinois went into line with its left resting on the Wire Road. From the hard-pressed Seventh Indiana Cavalry, "such a cheer as went up drowned all the rebel yells I ever heard," wrote Lt. James H. S. Lowes. Corporal Henry Dillenberger, with the Fourth Missouri Cavalry spread west of the Wire Road, thought the new reinforcements were "a sorry looking lot of soldiers" who were "nearly exhausted with running the double-quick so far through the heavy dust and heat."[23]

To relieve the rest of the cavalry, McMillen placed in succession the 120th Illinois, 108th Illinois detachment, Ninety-Fifth Illinois, and Eighty-First Illinois to the right of the 113th Illinois. Hoge's brigade thus extended in an arc southeast toward the Fulton road. The infantry disappeared into "very thick timber with quite a heavy undergrowth." Once in line Hoge counted perhaps 1,200 exhausted men at the very most, with the rest straggling far back up the road. His skirmishers exchanged brisk fire with Rebel sharpshooters who took umbrage at the presence of infantry, ordinarily more to be feared than horsemen afoot. Waring's discouraged cavalrymen switched over to the far Union left where the Ninth Minnesota later saw them. Winslow, though, wisely kept his Iowans in position close behind the Federal right until more infantry could come up, but he soon received peremptory orders from Sturgis to withdraw immediately.[24]

Wilkin, unlike Hoge, did not get to fight his command as a unit because McMillen threw each regiment of the First Brigade into line where he thought it was needed. The first to arrive, the Ninety-Fifth Ohio, trudged northeast along the Wire Road and shifted into line in the woods immediately to the left (west) of the 113th Illinois, with the road in between. McMillen detailed the next two regiments all the way to the opposite flank. The 114th Illinois continued along the Fulton road 300 yards beyond Brice's Crossroads to the cavalry line and filed north into very thick brush. McMillen desired the left flank of the 114th Illinois to join the right of the Eighty-First Illinois on the extreme right of Hoge's brigade to carry the infantry line solidly from the Wire Road to the Fulton road, but Lieutenant Colonel King lacked the men to fill that gap. After his own right flank had come fully 150 yards north of the Fulton road, he halted without ever connecting with the Eighty-First Illinois still farther off to the northwest. "The rebels were found to occupy the slopes on an extensive ridge, semi-circular, and covered with dense growth of scrubbly 'Black Jack,' almost impenetrable." Worried by indications that the enemy was massed opposite his right flank, McMillen rushed the Ninety-Third Indiana down the Fulton road to the point where the 114th Illinois disappeared off to the north. The Hoosiers formed south of the road, relieving the last of Winslow's cavalry. Employing a favorite phrase, he told Colonel Thomas to hold his position "at all hazards."[25]

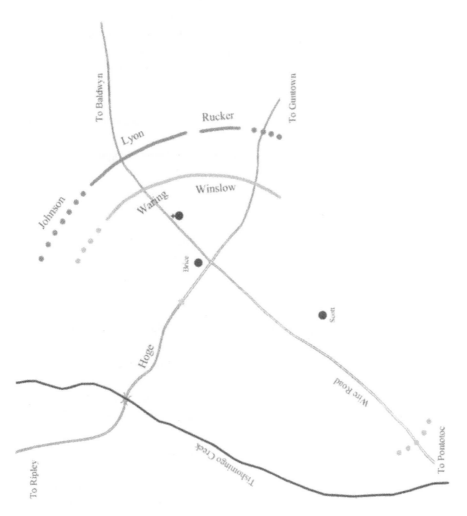

Brice's Crossroads Battle: Cavalry Lines

"The infantry was a long time in getting into position," according to Grierson, but finally, nearly the whole cavalry division came off the line. However, by taking up the regulation two ranks, less skirmishers, the foot soldiers proved too few to cover the same length of front once held by the single loose line of dismounted cavalry. Gaps consequently emerged that the Rebels could exploit. Fearing a powerful assault against what he, at least, realized was overtired infantry, Winslow had withdrawn his cavalry brigade with the greatest reluctance and only at Sturgis's repeated orders to leave. Sturgis would later claim falsely that Winslow had demanded his brigade be relieved immediately. Indeed, one of Sturgis's many errors, and arguably one of the most serious, was to remove Winslow's brigade from behind the right flank, which up to that point was ominously quiet. According to Cpl. Louis Bir, the Ninety-Third Indiana "Run in a thicket and Laid down thought to get Some Breath." Such respite was not to be.[26]

In the meantime, after discerning weakness on the Yankee right, Forrest decided on a dismounted attack. Buford would use Lyon's and Johnson's brigades and Morton's artillery to pin the Union left along the Wire Road, while Bell's and Rucker's brigades punched through the enemy right wing to the crossroads and beyond to seize the all-important Tishomingo bridge. Forrest had already arranged for other forces to maneuver far around each enemy flank and raise havoc at the proper time. In the roughly one hour during which Union infantry replaced the cavalry, Forrest prepared his main thrust with great care. First he inspected Rucker's brigade holding the center with about 500 troopers of the Seventh Tennessee Cavalry and Eighteenth Mississippi Cavalry Battalion. "Mounted on his big sorrel horse, sabre in hand, sleeves rolled up, his coat lying on the pommel of his saddle," Forrest looked to Private Hubbard "like the very God of War." Forrest next dismounted Col. William L. Duff's Eighth Mississippi Cavalry and shifted them and a reinforced squadron of the Twelfth Kentucky Cavalry led by Capt. Henry A. Tyler farther south beyond the Fulton road. Into the gap they left, he inserted two fresh regiments (some 1,200 men) from Bell's brigade. Colonel Robert M. Russell's Fifteenth Tennessee Cavalry moved into line adjacent to Rucker's left flank, while Col. Andrew L. Wilson's reinforced Sixteenth Tennessee Cavalry, forming on Russell's left, straddled the Fulton road. When Forrest greeted Capt. John W. Carroll's company in Wilson's regiment, he "had something to say to each man as he passed along the line—some word of encouragement. We could all see with what intense feeling and anxiety he regarded the issue. This made the men more determined." Subtracting the horse holders as a quarter of the strength gave Rucker, Bell, Duff, and Tyler together possibly 1,500 dismounted troopers in one long single rank, with skirmishers out in front. It is likely Bell, at least, made even more men available for combat. In his memoir he recalled setting aside every eighth man in this battle as a horse holder rather than every fourth. The opposing Ninety-Third Indiana and 114th Illinois together counted perhaps 600 muskets, the Eighty-First Illinois and Ninety-Fifth Illinois another 500 or so, giving the attackers a superiority of about a third over the number of defenders. Moreover, the defenders were exhausted from their scrambling run to the front line.[27]

South of the Fulton road, Colonel Thomas noticed a "solid line" of men emerge out of the brush ahead of the Ninety-Third Indiana and also overlap his right flank to the south. At first glance they appeared to be clad in blue and displaying U.S. cavalry guidons. Word had passed that more Union cavalry was still out in front. When scattered shots rang out from suspicious Indianans, both Thomas and Lt. Col. John W. Poole shouted, "Cease fire!" The enemy, for that is who it was, replied with a "deadly volley." Several officers including Poole went down, and "enlisted men fell like grass before a mower," wrote Sergeant Lacock. "We were suddenly astounded by a raking fire on the right flank, where the rebels, having no opposition in their front, stood fast, and, owing to the thick brush, we were unable to see them. At the proper moment they rose and poured into us a destructive volley, forcing us to retire to avoid capture, as they were already beginning to close up in our rear." Boxed in by Wilson's regiment to its left and front and Duff's Mississippians and Tyler's Kentucky squadron swarming on the right, the Ninety-Third Indiana fought "one of the hardest contested battles I have ever witnessed," wrote Thomas, "the enemy flanking me every few moments and my men changing their front, contesting for every foot of ground." Tyler saw it differently. "We soon drove the enemy out of the black-jack thickets in our front and soon had them on the run."[28]

North of the Fulton road, Lieutenant Colonel King's 114th Illinois also briefly wondered whether men perceived out ahead were friendly. Then a "rebel line advanced in plain sight" and, according to Captain Mallory, "opened a destructive fire on our right." Part of Wilson's Sixteenth Tennessee Cavalry flowed into the 150-yard gap between the 114th Illinois and the Fulton road to the south. King faced the 114th Illinois to his right toward the Tennesseans. "Our boys poured volley after volley into them at not more than 20 paces, which drove them back in confusion," Mallory wrote, "but being reinforced they rallied, and pressed us so close that right and left they poured volley after volley down our column and from our rear." Adding to the misery, Russell's Fifteenth Tennessee Cavalry flooded the open space between the 114th Illinois and the Eighty-First Illinois to the north and likewise turned

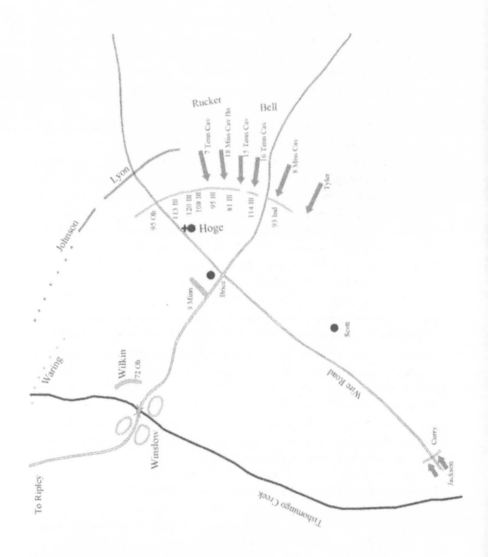

Brice's Crossroads Battle: Bell and Rucker Attack

King's left flank. Together Wilson and Russell pushed the stubborn 114th Illinois back. King formed a second line in the woods closer to the crossroads, but his flanks were open. He doubted he could remain there very long.[29]

In the center Rucker's brigade pitched into the Eighty-First Illinois and Ninety-Fifth Illinois of Hoge's brigade, but there the contending numbers were close to even. At first the fierce combat went well for the Yankees. Colonel Franklin Campbell's Eighty-First Illinois captured the bright, new battle flag of the Eighteenth Mississippi Cavalry Battalion after its color bearer incautiously came too far forward. Part of Russell's Fifteenth Tennessee Cavalry then flanked the Eighty-First Illinois on its right and rolled it back. At the same time, the Seventh Tennessee Cavalry slammed into the Ninety-Fifth Illinois. Pugnacious Colonel Humphrey, who had refused to double-quick the Ninety-Fifth Illinois to the battlefield, was mortally wounded. After intense fighting, which cost many casualties and most of their ammunition, the Eighty-First Illinois and Ninety-Fifth Illinois slowly fell back toward Bethany Church and the Wire Road.[30]

COUNTERATTACK

McMillen was behind the right flank when "notwithstanding the efforts of officers and men to regain and hold that ground," the Ninety-Third Indiana and 114th Illinois gave way to Bell's fierce assault. To make matters worse, to the south near where the Wire Road crossed Tishomingo Creek, the first of Forrest's deep-flanking elements stormed into action. After a cross-country march toward the southwest, Captain Jackson, with two elite escort companies and part of the Twelfth Kentucky Cavalry, perhaps 150 men, struck the Wire Road a mile south of the crossroads. He loosed a mounted charge that ripped into Curry's 200 Missouri and Illinois cavalry pickets guarding the far Union right flank. After a "short skirmish," the blue horsemen scurried north to the crossroads. Sturgis dismounted the 150 Missourians to help protect the direct approach to the bridge and sent the Illinoisans with all their horses back across Tishomingo Creek.[31]

Fearing the whole Federal right was about to collapse, McMillen spurred his horse across the Fulton road to his only reserve, the Ninth Minnesota waiting in two-rank line of battle behind Brice's house. He ordered Marsh to deploy along the Wire Road just south of the crossroads and to hold "at all hazards." Marsh moved up to the road, faced the regiment to the south by "files right," and advanced at the double-quick. After passing Fitch's one firing cannon, the Ninth Minnesota halted and again faced east. The men "fixed bayonets and laid down in the road." Within a few minutes, McMillen directed Marsh to continue south far enough to clear the right flank of the Ninety-Third Indiana fighting unseen ahead in the trees. The Minnesotans pounded 150 yards down the gentle slope toward Samuel Scott's farm and again faced east. With a breadth of perhaps two hundred files, the regiment's line of battle was roughly 100 yards long, ranged from north to south:

LEFT WING   *Major Markham*
Company E   Capt. Jerome Dane
Company C   Capt. Edwin W. Ford (with half the liberators)
Company G   Capt. Charles H. Beaulieu
Company H   Capt. William R. Baxter
Company A   Lt. Benjamin P. Shuler

RIGHT WING   *Lieutenant Colonel Marsh*
Company I   Capt. Horace B. Strait (with Sergeant Macdonald's color guard)
Company B   Capt. William A. Clark
Company F   Lt. Milton Daniels
Company K   Lt. Jules Capon (with half the liberators)
Company D   Capt. Asgrim Skaro

Acting Adjutant Sherwood assisted Marsh, and Sergeant Major Clapp stood by Markham.[32]

From his vantage on the extreme right flank, Aiton beheld only "brush and timber as far as I could see." Sherwood discovered undergrowth "so thick that we could not see two rods [eleven yards]." Torrents of bullets erupted from ahead in the timber. According to Lieutenant Keysor with Company E on the left, "the balls [were] whistling around us very thick." The "underbrush being so thick," Markham wrote, "we knew nothing of the position of the enemy except the direction the bullets came from, and there were times they came in showers from the front and both flanks." The Rebels had launched a major attack, but blinded by the foliage, the Minnesotans could not tell exactly where. "At last we reached the place where the storm of balls answered the roar of cannon," wrote Hill. "I cannot say I felt much excitement." Similarly, Sergeant Herrick was surprised to feel "perfectly calm; I did not seem to be more excited than I do now." He simply unbuttoned his shirt, "put my trust in God and went in." So did William Dean, who recalled, "if I ever prayed in my life it was as I went into it."[33]

Grimly aware the right flank to the south along the Wire Road was now totally exposed by the flight of Curry's cavalry pickets, McMillen ordered Company D to "discover the enemy's position and his movements to our right." Accordingly, Skaro deployed his men as skirmishers at the edge of the woods. McMillen directed Marsh to move the rest of the Ninth Minnesota forward into the timber to support the faltering Ninety-Third Indiana. Thick foliage forced Marsh and Markham to dismount and relinquish their horses. As another precaution, Marsh sent Company F, the "Olmsted County Tigers," to advance out in front as skirmishers. After dressing the line to the center, Marsh shouted, "Battalion, Forward." Macdonald's color guard stepped out six paces in front and guided the Ninth Minnesota into the brush. "Not withstanding the obstructions that met us at every step," Marsh proudly observed, "my men moved forward steadily, preserving a good line, so that not a moment was lost." The regiment breasted a slight slope into one of Farmer Scott's cleared fields. Beyond loomed a second band of timber.[34]

Captain Tyler's two dismounted Kentucky companies led the pack that hounded the retreating Ninety-Third Indiana. "We went with a rush, I well on the flank and my extreme left was within 200 yds of the Pontotoc [Wire] Road, with my right extending back east and north keeping in touch with the main line." Suddenly Tyler saw that a "full Brigade of Federal Infantry had double quicked down the Pontotoc Road until within one hundred yards of Scotts farm and then fronted east and charged us. They were in double line close formation and advanced directly upon us." The "full Brigade" was the Ninth Minnesota. Out in front, the Company F skirmishers "went in lively." Ordinarily individual skirmishers were five to ten yards apart, but the undergrowth forced them closer together. When Rebels appeared close at hand, the "Tigers" took cover behind the trees and brush. Tyler's troopers assumed the scattered Yankees glimpsed in the trees ahead were merely demoralized stragglers from the regiment they had forced off the field. It was a deadly mistake. The overconfident Kentuckians "ordered us to surrender several times," joked Lieutenant Daniels, "but the boys kept up such a fire that I couldn't get the chance to surrender." Two Rebels demanded Pvt. Lewis Moses give up, "but, as they got in right position he blazed away, and killed them both with one shot." Although "many of the rebs tumbled," Daniels bragged, "not a man of Co. F was hurt." Tyler ruefully admitted that he "lost here in two minutes more men killed and wounded than in all the day besides." When the rest of the Ninth Minnesota crashed through the brush behind them, the skirmishers drew off, one platoon to the north and the other to the south, so not to mask their fire. Daniels rallied his men behind the main line and at Marsh's order quickly moved Company F up alongside Company E to take the extreme left of the regiment. "My greatest work," Daniels wrote of the Tigers, "was keeping them *back*; they wanted to '*go for them*.'" Marsh halted the Ninth Minnesota on a low ridge, whereupon the color guard and guides dropped back into the ranks. While the noise of combat drew closer,

Marsh had his men lie down and dispatched a messenger to let Skaro know where he was.[35]

Company D had its own troubles. "Mindful of my instructions to protect the flank at all hazards," Tyler had not simply withdrawn his outnumbered Kentucky squadron. Instead he gallantly led his men to his left (south), jumped a fence on Scott's farm, and ran along it west toward the Wire Road. They soon came across Skaro's men spread in a skirmish line off to their right in the direction of the crossroads. "We dropped to the ground and, pushing our guns through the cracks [in the fence] near the ground, opened fire upon their flank." That volley, from Rebel sharpshooters "secreted in the brush," tore through the center of Company D. After shooting back Sgt. James W. Holtsclaw had started to turn around when a Rebel bullet struck him in the face near his nose and eye. He "fell backward, seemed to open his mouth 2 or 3 times, and appeared quietly to die." Sergeant Albert C. Albee ran over and turned Holtsclaw on his side "to let the blood flow," but discovered he was dead. Under heavy fire, Albee could not recover his comrade's "pistol, watch & money, such was the hurry and heat of battle." Holtsclaw, an athletic thirty-five-year-old farmer and early settler of Nicollet County, was the first member of the Ninth Minnesota to fall against the Confederates. He was an "excellent, good man," and his "loss is deeply felt by his comrades," wrote Chaplain Kerr. They had last spoken "the morning before the battle, under a tree, and I left him reading his testament. I hope he was prepared for the christian soldier's death."[36]

At first Skaro's skirmishers dueled only Tyler's dismounted Kentucky squadron firmly ensconced behind the fence at Scott's farm, but soon another foe pressing north along the Wire Road threatened Skaro's own right flank. After driving away the cavalry pickets, Jackson had dismounted the two escort companies and warily approached the main Union position at the crossroads. To deal with the new threat, Skaro led the First Platoon back across the Wire Road to confront Jackson, leaving Lt. Henry R. Walker's Second Platoon (which included Aiton) to deal with Tyler. Although badly outnumbered, the fifty or so men of Company D fought very well. The veteran Skaro "boldly repulsed the enemy who was attempting to flank us on the right" and gallantly "maintained his position" in a prolonged firefight to protect the Union right.[37]

In the meantime, while perched on the shallow ridge south of the Fulton road, Marsh spied a line of Confederates "extending along our whole front, advancing cautiously upon us." They were the dismounted troopers of Duff's Eighth Mississippi Cavalry and the left wing of Wilson's Sixteenth Tennessee Cavalry cautiously pursuing the routed Ninety-Third Indiana. Calmly waiting until the nearest Rebels had approached within thirty yards, the Ninth

Minnesota stood up and smoothly brought their Springfields up to their shoulders. At Marsh's order, "Fire by Battalion," they loosed a "most terrific volley" such as "had not been heard before that day," wrote Markham. "Our men were cool and steady, took good aim," recalled Keysor, "and I could see the rebels falling like autumn leaves." It was a "terrific scene." Wilkin "had drilled the men a great deal in target firing and their fire was very effective." He learned later that twenty Rebels had popped up in front of two of the companies who "fired killing or wounding everyone." Tyler recalled how the Eighth Mississippi Cavalry "immediately to my right broke in wild disorder, my men shouting to me 'Look out Captain, the damned Mississippians are running,' and they did run like the devil was after them." Staggered by the deadly ambush, the Eighth Mississippi Cavalry disappeared to the rear for the rest of the day. Out of apparently two hundred rank and file actually engaged (evidently not counting horse holders), the Mississippians sustained the highest loss (eight killed, forty-eight wounded) of any Rebel unit in the battle.[38]

When Wilson tried to interpose his Sixteenth Tennessee Cavalry between his foe's left flank and the Fulton road, he suffered a similar defeat. Taking advantage of the flight of the Mississippians, Marsh quickly shifted the Ninth Minnesota a short way to his right for a better field of fire. "The enemy fought desperately for some time," he related in his report, "but finally gave way and was thrown into disorder and confusion by the destructive fire of my brave boys." Recounted Captain Carroll of Wilson's regiment, "We moved to the assault through a deep underbrush in which the enemy was concealed. The onslaught was terrific and repelled with equal vigor." According to Nathaniel Cheairs Hughes, Bell's biographer, the Tennesseans were "flanked and enfiladed" and, "struck by murderous volleys," they "broke to the rear." Marsh's men delivered "a good Minnesota yell," wrote Markham, a "*whoop* such as only Minnesota soldiers can give." The "rebs," boasted Daniels, "probably knowing that sound by contact with the First, Second, Third, Fourth, and Fifth regiments, couldn't stand it and broke, with the Ninth close upon their rear." The "rebels were thick on the hill opposite us," Herrick recalled, "and after firing a few volleys we started for them." Cheering loud enough to be heard clearly back behind the crossroads, the Ninth Minnesota executed a bayonet charge with "an impetuosity" the veteran Markham "never before saw." Herrick stepped over "dead and wounded rebels to give us evidence that our firing had been telling." With Company K on the far right flank, Hill "went down into a ravine, driving the enemy at a rapid rate, they leaving the ground strewn with guns and equipments and an occasional dead or wounded man."[39]

Brice's Crossroads Battle: Counterattack

Ignoring the heat and intense fatigue, the jubilant Ninth Minnesota raced eighty rods (a quarter mile) through "thick woods" and "very uneven ground" pursuing the fleeing enemy. After pivoting nearly ninety degrees in the process, the winded Minnesotans crossed the Fulton road heading northeast. When Markham's left wing breasted a slight rise on a direct line from the crossroads, his men were suddenly hit by "grape from our own guns, which, on account of our advanced position, were now flying thick through our left flank." Three men swiftly went down. The offender was Fitch's twelve-pounder Napoleon blindly firing down the Fulton road. In its hasty retreat the Ninety-Third Indiana had emerged from the brush at the crossroads "terribly cut up" and in "considerable confusion" after losing sixty or more killed and wounded. McMillen rode among the men and rallied them "with great gallantry," according to First Sergeant Merrilies. McMillen then ordered Fitch to "sweep" the Fulton road "with grape and canister." Yelling at the Hoosiers to lie down, Fitch blasted canister rounds over their heads as fast as he could reload. Falling under friendly artillery fire gave the Ninth Minnesota pause. With no Rebels in sight, the weary men fell back across the road and dropped to the ground.[40]

The wild counterattack cost the Ninth Minnesota four killed and perhaps twenty wounded, but specific circumstances are known for only a few. On the extreme right flank, Capon's Company K had swung farthest along the arc as the regiment pivoted to the left. Liberator George Frahm, a twenty-five-year-old German immigrant mason from Winona, was hit in the breast and hand. Thought to be mortally wounded, he had to be left where he fell on the bleak battlefield. The only other Company K liberator known to have been harmed at that time was Hiram Buck, a twenty-six-year-old carpenter from Dresbach in Winona County. While reloading after the first great volley, Buck, who stood in the front rank, was suddenly dazed by a terrible pain in his head. Too eager to take a bead on the approaching Rebel line, Sgt. William G. Brown, one of the file closers, had leaned his rifle musket over the shoulder of a man in the second rank in violation of procedure and fired with the muzzle only a few inches from Buck's left ear. Capon, who witnessed the incident, reprimanded Brown, otherwise a good sergeant, for "gross negligence." Shaken and suffering permanent hearing loss, Buck remained in line with his comrades. Their ordeal this day had only just begun. In Company B next in line, the first to fall was Cpl. William Doyle, who had fretted in Missouri when his pay was long delayed and had hoped President Lincoln would win the war that summer. A bullet struck him in the body during the very first exchange of fire on the ridge. Herrick saw him pitch over obviously dead. At the same time, Pvt. Enoch Frank, a young Swede, collapsed with a minor head wound. He "raised himself up and I asked him if he could walk," Herrick recalled. "He thought he could. I could not stay with him, so I told him to go to the rear if he could." Corporal John Burns, a tough Irishman who was Company F's representative in the color guard, had his groin torn from scrotum to left thigh by a bullet. He limped to the rear to get help.[41]

Because of stiffer resistance by Wilson's Tennesseans, Markham's left wing had suffered more than the right wing. Shot through the body, Cpl. Daniel Hutchins of Company A died where he fell. In Company H next in line, Pvt. Godfrey Hammerberg, a young Swedish immigrant, took a bullet through the head. Covered in blood, he also remained where he lay. In the midst of the left wing, Captain Ford's Company C, with the other liberators, sustained the heaviest casualties of all. "Four privates of our company were shot in the first charge and were seen to fall." Private Nicholas Swab, a thirty-seven-year-old farmer from Germany and recent recruit, was killed outright. His seventh child would be born three weeks after his death. Private Pliny S. Conkey, age thirty-eight and a pioneer settler of Mower County, was wrongly thought to be mortally wounded, while James Woodbury, the ardent Copperhead Democrat, sustained a head wound that also looked much worse than it actually was. The fourth member of Company C to fall in the charge was the first Otterville liberator to die. Shot in the head and instantly killed

Asgrim Skaro, ca. 1863

was Augustus Whitney, a twenty-eight-year-old married farmer from Lansing in Mower County. "Augustus was a noble young man well educated & capable of doing any kind of business," Whitney's mother, Anna, later informed the government's pension board. She had been widowed twenty years before, and her son was "the last one of my family then living at the time of his death. In him were centered all my hopes and all I cared for in this life." Company E lost two or three men wounded in the first exchange of fire. Ailing Lieutenant Keysor found himself in charge after Captain Dane unaccountably failed to come forward from behind a large oak tree. Keysor

John Burns, 1863

next saw him days later in Memphis. In Company F, which had come up on the far left, Pvt. Syvert Ellefson, a young Norwegian, sustained what was evidently a "friendly" canister ball in his hip. He made his own way to the rear to find treatment.[42]

Saving the Army?

With the Ninth Minnesota halted along the west edge of the Fulton road, Markham considered the situation. Flanks open, the regiment was completely on its own behind enemy lines. No friendly units were in sight nor did it seem any were coming. Hastening over to the right to speak with Marsh, he earnestly counseled withdrawing immediately to the shallow ridge to regroup. "Reluctantly" concurring, Marsh retired the Ninth Minnesota the way it came. No one disputed the wisdom of the order, but the turn of events disgusted him. "At this juncture," he grumbled, "had our right been supported by only a part of a regiment, we could have turned the enemy's left flank completely." Winslow's cavalry brigade was sorely missed. In the meantime McMillen had ordered the Ninety-Third Indiana to charge and regain the ground it had lost. After rallying, the Hoosiers advanced back into the brush south of the Fulton road and soon reached their former line of defense. Not realizing the Minnesotans had already driven off the Rebels, Colonel Thomas was very surprised his counterattack met virtually no resistance. "The enemy giving way left us in comparative quiet for a short time." He rested his men who were hardly in shape to penetrate the Rebel rear even if he had known of the Ninth Minnesota in the trees a few hundred yards ahead. A "hasty count" revealed fewer than two hundred men in the ranks of the Ninety-Third Indiana, less than half than at the start of the day.[43]

Although the Ninth Minnesota had not finished off the fleeing enemy, it earned McMillen's deep, even if only temporary, gratitude. "My extreme right, after a sharp and bloody contest, was forced back," he wrote in his report, "and I was obliged to throw in the only regiment I had in reserve to drive the enemy back and re-establish my line at that point. This work was gallantly performed by the Ninth Minnesota, under the heroic Marsh, and I desire here to express to him and his brave men my thanks for their firmness and bravery, which alone saved the army at that critical moment from utter defeat and probable capture." The "brief limits of an official report," he later explained to Marsh, "do not offer ample room to express the great and lasting admiration I felt for you and your heroic regiment on the unfortunate field of Brice's Cross Roads." Ensuing events soon nullified the Ninth Minnesota's signal success. Sturgis omitted the counterattack in his report, but then again he only expressed his strong disappointment with the infantry and never acknowledged *anything* the foot soldiers had accomplished at the crossroads.[44]

McMillen subsequently changed his tune. In late July he testified to an investigating board that he had ordered the Ninety-Third Indiana and Ninth Minnesota "to charge the enemy which they did in the most gallant style, regaining all of the ground we had lost and driving that portion of Buford's division on our right of the Guntown [Fulton] road from the field." Including the Ninety-Third Indiana in the part of the charge that actually swept the enemy back and even giving it priority was more expedient than accurate. By that time the Ninth Minnesota was no longer in his brigade, whereas the Ninety-Third Indiana never left it. Thomas was even less generous, only conceding the "assistance" of the Ninth Minnesota during the Ninety-Third Indiana's successful counterattack. In truth the Ninth Minnesota alone routed the Rebels. McMillen's original fulsome praise of the Ninth Minnesota is little reflected in histories of the battle. In by far the most comprehensive analysis, historian Bearss describes how after Bell's brigade had pushed back the Union line, "reinforced on their right by the Ninth Minnesota, the Hoosiers turned on their tormentors." The Confederates swiftly rallied, Bearss explains, the "crisis eased, and Bell's men resumed their attacks on the 114th Illinois, 93d Indiana, and Ninth Minnesota." Thus, in his eyes the counterattack was no big deal.[45]

So in truth had the Ninth Minnesota "saved the army"? According to historian Hughes, Bell's situation (and the whole Confederate left flank) suddenly turned "desperate" when the Eighth Mississippi Cavalry and Wilson's Sixteenth Tennessee Cavalry recoiled in complete disarray across the Fulton road. Their precipitous retreat cleared the ground in front of the Ninety-Third Indiana and also disrupted the attack of Russell's Fifteenth Tennessee Cavalry against the stalwart 114th Illinois and Eighty-First Illinois. Writing on June 15, an anonymous Confederate complained, "The greatest injury inflicted upon us during this engagement was by an ambuscade. Wilson's and Russell's regiments, of Bell's brigade, suffered severely. It is unfortunate that more caution was not exercised to prevent such unnecessary damage." That punishment was mostly the Ninth Minnesota's doing. "Forrest's men say the 9th Minn whipped them & drove them & they thought from their fire that it was a Brigade," an escaped prisoner of the Ninety-Fifth Ohio told Wilkin a few days later. According to the authoritative 1868 history of Forrest's cavalry, not only had Bell's assault failed, but after "Wilson's Regiment, flanked and enfiladed, gave back," the "issue seemed inevitably unfavorable for a time." Captain Morton later declared that Bell's brigade was "sorely pressed" after being "flanked and compelled to fall back," but by "rallying his valiant troopers," Bell "with pistol in hand drove back the enemy and held his ground on a line with Rucker" to the north. It must be stressed that no one "drove back" the Ninth Minnesota. In this brief instance, the dense blackjack timber worked greatly to its advantage. Bell never realized how much he outnumbered the Ninth Minnesota. At that crucial moment, Lt. Col. Dew M. Wisdom with 250 men from Col. John F. Newsom's Nineteenth Tennessee Cavalry fortuitously appeared after riding the farthest of any Rebels to reach the battlefield. Dismounting his men, Wisdom strengthened the tender left flank of Bell's brigade as it reformed east of the Fulton road.[46]

By the time the Ninth Minnesota counterattacked, Forrest, worried that his holding attack against the Federal left wing might have "miscarried," had hastened north toward the Wire Road looking for Buford. Bell rushed a courier in his wake informing him the Yankees "have flanked us and are now in our rear." If reinforcements were not forthcoming, Bell warned, "I could not stay where I was." Forrest reacted entirely in character. "We'll whip these in our front and then turn around, and won't we be in their rear? And then we'll whip them fellows." He would simply smash the Union troops arrayed alongside the Wire Road and then finish off whatever remained. After personally ensuring that Buford's attack was going well, Forrest returned to his imperiled left flank. "Stay on the field," he assured Bell. "I am here and I will stay as long as you live." Only after some time, though, did Bell's reorganized brigade resume its advance along both sides of the Fulton road. Bearss errs when he asserts that Bell again engaged the Ninth Minnesota and Ninety-Third Indiana east of Tishomingo Creek and drove them back. As will be seen, by that time those two regiments had already been withdrawn from Bell's front. Thus, the Ninth Minnesota's stunning counterstroke had knocked Forrest's biggest brigade out of action for an appreciable interval and thereby prevented the immediate storming of the crossroads and the seizure of the Tishomingo Creek bridge. Their timely shutting of the front door, a handsome feat of arms, certainly did "save the army" at that particular instant. Sergeant Merrilies, with the Illinois artillery positioned at Brice's Crossroads, fully comprehended the true situation. "It was evident now," he explained in his diary, "that the enemy, unable to force our position in front [*i.e.* along the Fulton road], were going to try their success at turning it."[47]

CHAPTER EIGHT

The Battle of Brice's Crossroads (II)

LAST IN, FIRST OUT

In the past half hour the Ninth Minnesota, in a sharp counterblow, had driven back Bell's reinforced brigade, thereby relieving the perilous situation of the Union right wing along the Ripley-Fulton road. Lacking visible support from friendly troops, Marsh marched the Minnesotans back through the brush to the low ridge from where he had counterattacked. A staff officer galloped up with urgent orders from McMillen to retire to the Wire Road. Re-emerging from the woods southwest of the crossroads, Marsh discovered the Ninety-Third Indiana was nowhere in sight. He placed the Ninth Minnesota behind the Wire Road, with two of Captain Fitch's cannons positioned to his left at the crossroads. To the west, Captain Skaro's stalwart Company D effectively shielded the Federal right flank. Rebel Captain Jackson's elite escort troopers were ranged behind a fence about four hundred yards from the main Federal position, with "a clear open field lying between." They and Captain Tyler's Kentucky squadron at Scott's farm laid a galling fire on the Minnesotans, who also absorbed bullets and shells from the fierce fight that was raging north and northeast beyond the trees. "We had not long to wait," wrote Markham. "They poured such showers of all kinds of missiles on us it seemed not a man to escape." Sergeant Merrilies likewise marked "bullets beginning to come over from both flanks crossing the [Fulton] road at almost right angles, and taking our line of battle directly in flank." Marsh had the Ninth Minnesota lie down. Some stragglers previously hobbled by heat exhaustion stumbled forward to rejoin the ranks there. "At that time," recalled one, Pvt. Samuel Ennerson, the regiment "was in the hottest part of the battle."[1]

"Before being fairly engaged" in the new position, Marsh was surprised, indeed astonished, by peremptory orders from McMillen to withdraw immediately to an unspecified point beyond Tishomingo Creek. For the time being, Skaro's men had to fight on alone. Moving by the left flank, the Ninth Minnesota passed Brice's house. The road was still obstructed by "a mixed throng still going toward the front,—soldiers singly and in squads, stragglers, camp-followers, servants,—all hurrying over the bridge and toward the crossroads," forcing the Minnesotans into the adjacent fields that sloped toward the bridge.[2]

"As we were falling back to get to another position," remembered acting Adjutant Sherwood, "the rebels turned our own batteries and gave us hell and repeat." When "we crossed a field," wrote Keysor, "the shell and solid shot seemed to fill the air and strike on all sides of us, yet we moved on in good order, passed by the dead and dying, and leaving them to fall into the hands of the enemy." Private John Allen wondered why they did not simply retake the lost guns. But "we had to 'get out o' that,' which was done as quietly and cooly as on company drill," wrote Lieutenant Daniels. "Not a man broke, but each marched in his proper place." Though no Minnesotans appear to have been killed during the move, several were wounded. "While we were leaving the battlefield a shot from a cannon knocked down a slab or piece of bark or limb of a tree against [Pvt.] Arad Welch's face," recalled liberator Nate Palmeter. Head bloodied and shirt torn, Welch nonetheless "did not seem to think it was anything serious." Many years later the wound turned cancerous and killed him. Wood splinters from a tree branch gouged out by a cannonball tore up Lieutenant Capon's left leg. Orderly Sergeant Hays loaded the "Big Frenchman" into a convenient ambulance and sent it racing ahead to the bridge. Lieutenant Niedenhofen, the former Prussian Jäger from Winona, took over Company K. Although sick upon arriving at Memphis, he had begged his superiors to be allowed to go along. Shell fragments temporarily blinded Pvt. Joel D. Chamberlain. He, too, was fortunate to leave the field. A few wounded had to be left behind.[3]

Waiting west of Tishomingo Creek for the rest of his cavalry brigade to mount and cross the bridge, Winslow happened to be standing with Grierson when a shell burst "within 50 feet." The cannon that fired it, Winslow observed, must be sited near the crossroads. "Do you not know we have been beaten," Grierson shot back, "and will soon be in full retreat?" As confirmation, Winslow noticed the Ninth Minnesota pounding down the hill. "The infantry not yet in disorder but in full retreat came from the woods and along the road hurrying toward the bridge, passing cavalrymen while shells from the confederate cannon burst over them or crossed over the field." Ignoring the piles of haversacks and other baggage dropped on the way in—there was no time to retrieve them—the Ninth Minnesota smartly crossed the bridge and continued up the Ripley road. Grierson was correct. The disintegration of the Union position had begun, and the rout trailed the perplexed Minnesotans like the tail of a comet. Immediately after they were across, Winslow galloped over the bridge to retrieve the rest of his brigade. He was shocked to see "one indiscriminate mass of wagons, artillery, caissons, ambulances, and broken, disordered troops" racing down the slope directly toward him. Nothing in the world could have stopped them.[4]

THE COLLAPSE AT THE CROSSROADS

Forty-five minutes before, it seemed the Union situation had finally stabilized. From his vantage at the crossroads, Fitch heard "a heavy volley," followed by cheering as the Minnesotans "seemed to be driving the enemy although I could not see them." The Rebel assault on the Ninety-Third Indiana and 114th Illinois suddenly slackened. Accosting Grierson and Winslow west of the creek, Sturgis fussed about how slowly Winslow's cavalry brigade was executing his orders to redeploy on the west bank. Before riding off he "remarked that Colonel McMillen was driving the enemy." At the same time, Colonel Hoge, whose infantry brigade held most of the line north and east of the Fulton road, grew increasingly concerned. His right wing (Ninety-Fifth Illinois and Eighty-First Illinois) had come under furious attack, while other Rebel forces maneuvered along the Wire Road opposite his left wing (113th Illinois, 120th Illinois, and 108th Illinois detachment). Hoge feared the thrust along the Fulton road was the feint and the "main object of the enemy" was "to turn our left flank and get into the rear."[5]

Hoge's left wing stretched southeast from the Wire Road into the woods. To the northwest, across the Wire Road from the 113th Illinois, stood the Ninety-Fifth Ohio from Wilkin's First Brigade. Hoge's left wing plus the Ninety-Fifth Ohio numbered perhaps eight hundred muskets. Opposing them was Colonel Lyon's dismounted Kentucky brigade deployed astride the Wire Road. Though Lyon had somewhat fewer men than the Federal troops in front of him, his Kentuckians, despite having fought for several hours, were infinitely more fresh and confident. Farther north, spread out to the west toward the creek, Colonel Johnson's Alabama brigade effectively pinned not only Wilkin's Seventy-Second Ohio and Sixth Indiana Battery on the knoll that overlooked the bridge but also Waring's cavalry brigade covering both sides of the stream. In the distance among the trees, Johnson's skirmishers glimpsed the white canvas tops of the wagons as the head of the main Federal supply train approached the creek.

Forrest's second-in-command was forty-four-year-old Gen. Abe Buford, a West Point graduate and distinguished Mexican War veteran. The "genial, jovial" man "weighed something over three hundred pounds" and was "of powerful frame, [with] a round, ruddy face covered with a short, stubby, red beard." A Union prisoner recalled that he "often chuckled in the course of his remarks." Buford orchestrated a clever two-pronged assault to support the main attack along the Fulton road. He ordered Lyon's brigade to thrust southwest along the Wire Road aiming for Bethany Church and Brice's house beyond, while Johnson's brigade did an "oblique to the left and rear" to double back to the Wire Road and flank the Federal left. The attack was late in getting started. By the time Forrest reined up to ask Buford about the delay, Lyon's brigade was only just going into action. Long engaged in fierce skirmishing, the men of Lt. Col. George R. Clarke's 113th Illinois had already expended most of their cartridges without any resupply despite desperate calls to Sturgis for ammunition. Posted in thick timber ahead of Clarke's line, James Mooney noticed the Kentuckians steadily approaching "in a single rank, at a fast walk." Along the Wire Road, more of Lyon's men struck Lieutenant Colonel Brumback's Ninety-Fifth Ohio in front while part of Johnson's brigade sliced in from behind. Spying only two cannons firing in support of Lyon's brigade, Forrest sharply ordered the other six guns pushed forward to point-blank range. Captain Morton eagerly obliged. He loaded his artillery with double rounds of canister, turning them into huge shotguns. Employed in two groups of three guns behind Hoge's left wing, the Union artillery never replied effectively because of badly restricted fields of fire.[6]

The assault by Lyon's brigade split the Union line, which had no ready reserve to halt the Rebel advance. The right flank of the exhausted 113th Illinois simply melted away. Falling back to "where our regiment had first formed," Mooney discovered only "12 or 15 of our own men" who were "loading & firing at the advancing rebels, for dear life." After a few volleys, Brumback's Ohioans hastily retreated into the woods north of Brice's house. On their right, the beaten 113th Illinois drifted back toward the church and cemetery beyond. Very quickly Lyon's men swarmed the first trio of guns (Lt. Francis W. Morse's Fourteenth Indiana Battery and one cannon from Capt. Fletcher H. Chapman's Company B, Second Illinois Light Artillery) set on a low wooded ridge a quarter mile north of the crossroads. The triumphant Kentuckians seized two artillery pieces, while the surviving gun careened down the Wire Road in wild flight. The shattered 113th Illinois tumbled back through the woods north of Brice's house. Flanked because the 113th gave way on their left, Col. George W. McKeaig's 120th Illinois and Lt. Col. Reuben L.

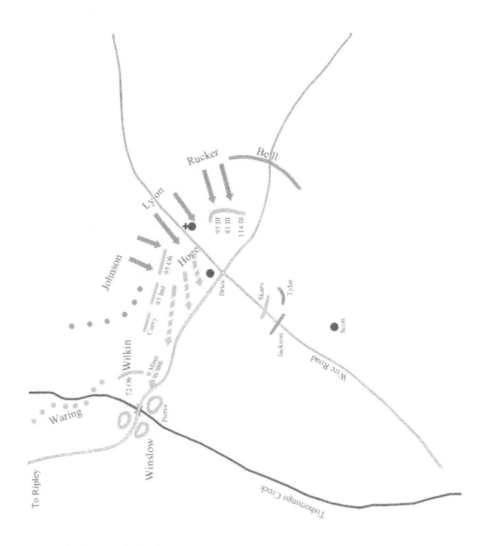

Brice's Crossroads Battle: Retreat

Sidwell's 108th Illinois detachment also retreated toward Chapman's three guns firing blindly over the trees just north of Brice's house.[7]

Buford's attack exceeded all expectation. To his horror McMillen discovered "all the regiments on the left [north] of the Guntown [Fulton] road" were suddenly "driven back to the vicinity of the crossroads in confusion." He sent word to Sturgis that he was "hard-pressed and that unless relieved soon, I would be obliged to abandon my position." Sturgis replied he had nothing to send and told McMillen to "use his own discretion." In turn McMillen "endeavored to get the regiments to move out to their original positions, but neither the most positive orders nor the most urgent entreaties could accomplish that object." Only the 114th Illinois "made any effort to regain the lost ground," aided unwittingly by the Ninth Minnesota's earlier repulse of Bell's brigade. The other regiments were "exhausted and dispirited" from "the excessive heat of the day and the rapid march that they had made to reach the field," as well as the "universal" belief that the Rebels were superior in number. They also became frantic for cartridges as inexplicably no ammunition was brought up. McMillen hastened another messenger to Sturgis warning that unless reinforced, "I must abandon the position," but that rider never found him. After a shell detonated near him at Brice's house, Sturgis hastily led his cavalry escort back toward the creek. He feebly explained later that he had gone back to find Bouton's Third Brigade and use it to organize a stand somewhere farther back along the road to Ripley. On the way he snatched Captain Mueller's Sixth Indiana Battery (two guns) from the knoll and left Wilkin without artillery support.[8]

Confronted by the breakthrough in the north, McMillen hastily fashioned a plan to retreat in stages to the west bank. By gathering the Ninety-Fifth Ohio, which was falling back, and Captain Curry's 150 dismounted Missourians covering the bridge, he cobbled together, out in front of Wilkin's knoll, a new emergency line facing north. The repulse of Bell's attack had released the Ninety-Third Indiana and Ninth Minnesota. McMillen intended for them to pass behind the new line and cross the bridge, to be followed by the 114th Illinois, Hoge's brigade, the emergency line itself, and finally the Seventy-Second Ohio on the knoll in that order. To see the infantry safely on its way, McMillen counted on the rest of the artillery, remaining briefly in position near the crossroads, to hold off the enemy by rapid fire of "grape and canister."[9]

McMillen's first step was to recall the Ninety-Third Indiana from its position south of the crossroads and start it back along the Ripley road toward the creek. Ambulances, artillery caissons, and wagons from the cavalry division and Hoge's infantry brigade train clogging the road forced Thomas's Hoosiers to parallel the road to the north. He noticed farther north "some of our men coming out of the woods, followed a few minutes later by the Rebels." Instead of retreating any further, Thomas alertly inserted the Ninety-Third Indiana between the Ninety-Fifth Ohio and Curry's Missouri cavalrymen. The orderly retreat of the Ninth Minnesota occurred next. To the north out of direct sight of the crossroads, the Confederates turned the two captured cannons against nearby Federals and rolled their own guns forward to give the Ninth Minnesota its warm sendoff. With Lyon's Kentuckians bearing down on them, the 120th Illinois and the 108th Illinois detachment simply followed the 113th Illinois "in inevitable retreat." An "effort was made to rally the men," Lieutenant Colonel Sidwell lamented, "but it proved of no avail." A "perfect stampede ensued." Curry's dismounted cavalry protected the three Illinois regiments fleeing toward the bridge. At the same time, Chapman hurriedly limbered up his three guns and escaped the trap by racing past Brice's Crossroads and down the Ripley road to the bridge. The two guns of Fitch's second artillery section, in reserve, joined their precipitate retreat.[10]

Surgeon Bingham of the Ninth Minnesota had set up shop with two ambulances and the medical wagon in a narrow ravine on the slope leading up from the creek. Ahead "a line of battle formed, and too plainly visible, I thought, for my own comfort." Hoisting "a piece of red flannel as a hospital sign," Bingham "had a patient in about a minute with a bullet in his thigh, which I easily and quickly removed." He was attending to another soldier who had "just limped up, when I heard the balls singing about my ears. This made me a little nervous and I stepped to the road to survey things, and just then a battery of artillery went to the rear on full gallop and carelessly collided with my medical wagon, the result being a broken axle." Accosting the colonel of one of the broken Illinois regiments, Bingham "modestly asked him if we should be properly supported for a hospital, or had we better climb, too, for the rear. He expressed himself in a way that settled the question in my mind very speedily, and after directions about getting my ambulances to the rear, and in case of greater speed being necessary—unhitching the horses and abandoning the ambulances—I commenced a retreat." The two ambulances got over the bridge, but Bingham, on horseback, had to jump the creek. "In my hurry I did not notice a tree on the opposite bank, and my leg became impinged between the tree and horse, bruising it and adding very much to the discomforts of the retreat."[11]

To Chief Surgeon Dyer, "it was now obvious that no preparation had been made in anticipation of possible defeat." His field hospital in the double-log house on the knoll beside Tishomingo Creek was now in danger. Hospital stewards and musicians frantically removed the wounded in ambulances and by stretcher. "Very active in looking after the wounded, bringing them water,"

Chaplain Kerr did all he could "under the circumstances to relieve their suffering." He found Pvt. John Summers of Company D from his home county crippled by a gunshot wound in the small of the back above the left hip. Kerr barely got him to the field hospital when the rout began, but he ensured that Summers got away. "Few of the fallen had been brought off," Dyer sadly observed. "The dead and wounded alike must be abandoned to the victors." Corporal Carlson decided that "his mission" seeking stragglers from Company H "was at an end" and that "it now became a question to me of how I was to save myself. I saw but few footmen near and could not find any of our regt. or Co. so I concluded to turn my steps back like the rest and started down the road."[12]

When everything suddenly fell apart, the Fourth Iowa Cavalry (less one battalion) under Maj. Abial R. Pierce was waiting patiently for its turn to cross Tishomingo Creek. The bridge became "blockaded with broken-down teams," while "the steep banks of the creek in my immediate rear rendered it impossible to cross with horses." Pierce's men proceeded to "upset the wagons, mules and all, into the creek and gave a chance for the led horses to go over the bridge." Turning around, the Iowans rushed part way up the slope to defend the direct approach to the bridge in concert with Wilkin and the Seventy-Second Ohio on the nearby knoll. The feeble pursuit of Johnson's Alabama brigade enabled the Ninety-Third Indiana and Ninety-Fifth Ohio to break free and wade the stream, while Curry's dismounted Missouri troopers escaped over the bridge.[13]

Still planted at the crossroads with two cannons, Fitch could not yet see Bell's brigade, which had finally renewed its attack up the Ripley-Fulton road. Nonetheless, he "judged from their firing that they were very near" and "immediately gave them canister with both pieces and as fast as I could load and fire." Suddenly some of Lyon's relentless Kentuckians appeared in Brice's garden only seventy-five feet behind Fitch. "I saw it was useless to remain longer and I limbered my two guns to the rear." Cut off from the bridge, Fitch led his section through a field south of the road, ran down the slope to the creek, and audaciously jumped his guns over the bank. One cannon overturned in the stream, but its determined gunners pulled it out. Now nearly surrounded and with the direct escape route to the bridge already gone, the troops that had been left in the immediate defense of Brice's Crossroads—the Eighty-First Illinois and Ninety-Fifth Illinois mixed together and the 114th Illinois on their right—withdrew south across the Ripley road and mixed in with Skaro's Company D straddling the Wire Road. "We all had a very narrow escape from being captured," wrote Pvt. Frank Curtis of the Ninety-Fifth Illinois. "They flanked us and got on three sides of us giving

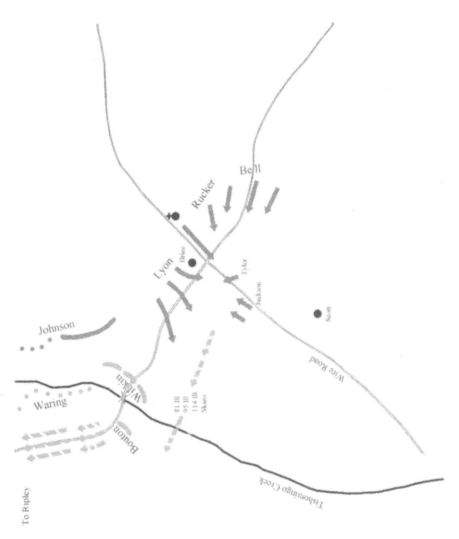

Brice's Crossroads Battle: Collapse

us a crossfire mowing our men down like grass. May God spare me from ever getting into such another hot nest." The "rebels pushed our men back," explained Sgt. James W. Dodds of the 114th Illinois. "Everything was there together on a few acres of ground, and it was impossible to reform. The men fell back to the creek, and went into it like hogs (for they were dying for water)." The Fourth Iowa Cavalry covered their tumultuous crossing south of the bridge. The lengthy firefight with Tyler and Jackson and the precipitous retreat cost Company D the lives of Sergeant Holtsclaw and Pvt. Francis Kaus, a thirty-two-year-old hotelkeeper from Austria, and wounded Summers and two or three others.[14]

From his vantage at Scott's farm, Tyler exulted as the Federals "fled in wild disorder" in "such a panic I had never witnessed." Rushing his squadron forward across the Wire Road, he first noticed Lyon "at the head of the Kentucky brigade pushing up to the Brice house." Next "Captain John Morton, of the artillery, appeared and soon his artillery opened up at close range upon the seathing mass of disorganized Federal soldiery. His shot came so near my men that I was compelled to cross back to the east side of the road." Soon afterward he "saw Colonel Rucker and Colonel Bell both leading their brigades up to the cross-roads and General Forrest. It was about a few minutes when we all met at the cross-roads. We were certainly a happy and enthusiastic band but little organization."[15]

THE TRAIN'S TRAVAIL

Wilkin's stalwart defenders—the Seventy-Second Ohio and Fourth Iowa Cavalry—not only protected the Federals escaping over Tishomingo Creek but also shielded the whole supply train that Sturgis negligently allowed to come right up into the bottomland instead of just sending ahead a few vital ammunition wagons. Spread out among the train's wagons, Maj. Edgar M. Lowe's Fifty-Fifth U.S. Colored Infantry (perhaps 650 strong) hustled by individual companies into battle. Lieutenant Lowes of the Seventh Indiana Cavalry watched the first black soldiers approach at the double-quick, "throwing away blouses, blankets and caps, many of them bareheaded and with bare backs," shouting "Remember Fort Pillow! Remember Fort Pillow!" Under withering fire the two lead companies of the Fifty-Fifth under Capt. Frank M. Ewing crossed to the east bank of the creek and stubbornly held their ground alongside the Seventy-Second Ohio and Pierce's Iowans. Bouton deployed seven more companies of the Fifty-Fifth near the west bank in support. Four horse artillery cannons buoyed the defense until wagons "got in front and so close to the pieces, that the guns could not be fired without endangering our men," and they withdrew. The vast supply train also prevented "the running of ambulances to bear off the wounded" on the narrow Ripley-Fulton road and interfered "with any necessary movement of troops to the rear."[16]

From the high ground near Brice's Crossroads, Morton turned his guns on the distant wagon train. Desperate to escape his fire, the lead teamsters "ran into stumps, crashed through fences and jammed their wagons into ambulances loaded with wounded." Suddenly the whole train started turning around despite being hemmed in by trees and swampy ground. "You have heard teamsters yell at their mules, crack their whips, and sometimes— swear," recalled Chief Surgeon Dyer. "Well, they did all these things, and whatever else teamsters may lawfully and properly do. At any rate, 'Bedlam let loose,' could hardly excell in the noise and commotion you would have witnessed had you been there, in the efforts of these men to get out of harm's way." Frank Lyon, who had dropped out of Company C around noon with heat exhaustion, rode a wagon near the head of the supply train and witnessed the disaster. "Get those mules out of here!" the wagon master bellowed. "If you can't get them out any other way, cut them loose and let them go." Lyon "stepped behind a tree and watched the performance. The mules came tearing and the drivers came swearing. The air was full of circus language." A "worse smash-up" Corporal Carlson had "never seen." As "the shells exploded in every direction I had to take my chances in getting over. About half way across, a mule driver came on a gallop riding through and on to some of the struggling men on foot. In the rush I stumbled and landed somewhat in the mud." A shell "struck one of the hind legs of the mule" the driver "was riding" and threw him "headlong in the mud," reducing him "to a footman same as the rest of us." Private John Stack, a Company H wagoner, was killed about that time.[17]

The wounded were laid in a grassy field about three-quarters of a mile west of the creek, but soon "the poor mangled fellows" had to be lifted back into ambulances to flee. Several wounded of the Ninth Minnesota escaped on mules and horses. "Everybody seemed to be in a hurry," Dyer remembered. "The road was not wide enough. It was filled up to overflowing from fence to fence, with wagons, ambulances, artillery, horsemen and footmen—everybody trying to get ahead of everybody else!" To the left, moving parallel to the road were "two columns of cavalry," their "files not very well dressed, to be sure, but making good time. The infantry, poor fellows, seemed light of foot by the way they plodded along on either side of the road, dodging through the brush, over logs and gullies, constituting a dense body of flankers to the column that filled the road." Refreshed after his rest, Lyon "fell in with the Infantry and was able to keep with them as I had thrown away all my luggage."[18]

Within the fleeing mass, Corporal Carlson encountered two stragglers from Company H: first his friend Pvt. Andrew Wallace, who fought in the battle but lost track of the regiment in the retreat, and then Pehr Carlson, his relative by marriage. Pehr was "sitting bareheaded, leaning against a big stump near the road very sick" and not eager to move. "Never mind the gun," A. J. told him. "We will each one of us take you by the arm and help you along." Pehr only desired that they deliver his farewell to his wife. "If I die I rely on the promise of God through Christ to save my soul, good-by." They were not about to leave him behind. A. J. seized Pehr's gun, "knocked [it] against a tree to make it useless and threw it away with his 60 rounds of ammunition." They kept Pehr's food to share, for they had dropped their own haversacks prior to the battle.[19]

The mass of stragglers and broken regiments "fell back into the woods; officers were no better than men, and men weren't so good as horses, because they couldn't go as fast." The tail of Bouton's Third Brigade, Lt. Col. Robert Cowden's Fifty-Ninth U.S. Colored Infantry with about 550 men, confronted wagons, cavalry, infantry, and artillery in utter confusion blocking the road ahead of them. A quarter mile or more short of the creek, he moved to a ridge to the right where the timber was slightly less thick and tried to cover the retreat. In the meantime Grierson had told Waring and Winslow not only to fall back but also to "check the flying infantry troops who were spreading out on either side of the road, without any apparent order or organization." Near the head of the rout (the Ninth Minnesota had already gone past), Waring's troopers encountered the second of Forrest's two deep-flanking elements— part of Col. Clark R. Barteau's Second Tennessee Cavalry from Bell's brigade. Hours before at Carrollville, near Baldwyn, Forrest had unleashed Barteau and 250 men on a wide detour around to the north and west to strike the Ripley road several miles west of Tishomingo Creek. Approaching the creek, Barteau spread his force along the north edge of the road to harass the fleeing Federals. "With drawn sabers and revolvers," the Fourth Missouri Cavalry quickly brushed away the scattered Rebels "without serious opposition" and forced open the road. Instead of dealing the knockout blow on the *east* bank of which later Confederate histories would boast, Barteau's presence well beyond the *west* bank was in fact barely noticed in the profound Union rout.[20]

FUTILE ROADBLOCKS

After reorganizing, Forrest's main body, "in beautiful style, and with their banners flying," swept down toward the knoll overlooking the Tishomingo

Creek bridge, while Morton vigorously shelled the area around the bridge and the wagon train beyond. Wilkin's outnumbered defenders hastily crossed the narrow bridge or plunged "waist deep across the deep muddy waters." Swiftly remounting, the Fourth Iowa Cavalry departed to find its brigade. Bouton directed the two companies of the Fifty-Fifth U.S. Colored Infantry to rejoin their regiment deployed in line just across the creek. That action inaugurated a series of stands by the rear guard, as one part held the Rebels until another line could be formed farther back. On the first hill beyond the edge of the timber, Grierson began the process by placing Wilkin and the Seventy-Second Ohio to the left of the road to cover Bouton's inevitable retreat.[21]

Aided immensely by Morton, who swiftly got four guns over the swollen creek, Jackson's elite escort severely pressed the black soldiers, whose very presence infuriated them. Bell's Tennessee brigade followed on foot. For a time the stalwart Fifty-Fifth U.S. Colored Infantry, giving ground slowly, stalled the Rebel advance. Replacing wounded Major Lowe was Capt. Arthur T. Reeve, who soon had to retire the Fifty-Fifth at a run to the protection of Wilkin and the Seventy-Second Ohio. "Those colored troops were on the borders of hell," recalled cavalry Lieutenant Lowes. Eventually "their lines broke and many threw their guns away flying for their lives. The expressions on their faces will be remembered a lifetime." After the black soldiers "had gone through us like a cyclone," reminisced Cpl. Robert W. Medkirk of the Seventy-Second Ohio, "we were ordered to move on and clear the road ahead of us." The Ohioans only withdrew a short way before some teamsters "began destroying their wagons, thus blockading the road so that all those behind had to be abandoned." The "fighting was going on at a furious rate on all sides, and our men were coming back by regiments," recounted an Illinoisan in the First Brigade train. "Now we ordered the teams cut loose and told the men to jump on the mules. The third wagon in the rear was already in the hands of the rebs, who came up with a shout and a volley at the same time." Hungry Rebels grabbed food from abandoned wagons. In another of Sturgis's terrible blunders, most of the ammunition wagons were also left at that point. Reeve paused to reorganize the Fifty-Fifth U.S. Colored Infantry "in the edge of the timber on the brow of a small hill" and put "every man in line that was able for duty." The Seventy-Second Ohio passed through Reeve's line last of all. Buoyed by ammunition that Grierson provided, the valiant Fifty-Fifth kept "the rebels from crossing the field in our front until a force of them came around our left." Finally, Reeve testified, "nearly all of our officers and many of our men were unable to do their duty from sheer exhaustion."[22]

About a mile by road north of the Tishomingo Creek bridge and just below where the Ripley-Fulton road curved northwest, Bouton organized the next roadblock. On a rise adjacent to Henry Holland's "old house," he placed the two guns of Capt. Carl Adolph Lamberg's Battery F, Second U.S .Light Artillery (Colored), supported by the reserve company of the Fifty-Fifth U.S. Colored Infantry. Cowden's Fifty-Ninth U.S .Colored Infantry withdrew to a wooded ridge on the right but ended up too far away to support the position near the Holland house. Bouton promised McMillen he would "fight the enemy as long as I had a man left." Encouraged by his spirit, McMillen exclaimed, "That's right; if you can hold this position until I can go to the rear and form on the next ridge you can save the entire command. It all depends on you now." The whole caravan of defeat filtered past Bouton, last of all the hard-pressed Fifty-Fifth U.S. Colored Infantry, which he formed across the road to the left of Lamberg's guns. Barely had Reeve's men got into line when Morton's relentless gunners targeted them. The Confederates advanced first against Bouton's right, then infiltrated the woods alongside the road and poured a devastating fire into the exposed Fifty-Fifth and the battery. Lamberg lost several horses and one caisson before he could limber up and flee. About 5:30 P.M. the battered Fifty-Fifth U.S. Colored Infantry fell back along the road, "which was considerably blocked up with wagons and teams; most of the wagons were without mules; some tipped over" and others "with covers on fire." At least three-quarters of the train, though, had already passed that point. Beyond on the next ridge stood a new line that included the Ninth Minnesota.[23]

HOLDING HADDON RIDGE

During the previous hour, Marsh's Ninth Minnesota, maintaining what liberator Jack Watkins called a tiring "dog-trot," had retraced its route up the Ripley-Fulton road and past the Holland house. Seeing black soldiers sprinkled among the wagons of the massive supply train that was then still rolling toward the crossroads, Markham felt "some misgivings, some fears that they would fail us in this trying emergency." After splashing through inappropriately named Dry Creek, the Minnesotans reached John Haddon's "large white house," situated in the saddle of a ridge a half mile beyond the Holland house. There the ground provided "a strong natural position for defensive operations," according to Rebel Captain Morton. About 5 P.M. one of Sturgis's aides halted the Ninth Minnesota, Mueller's Sixth Indiana Battery, two hard-used regiments from Hoge's brigade, Clarke's 113th Illinois, and McKeaig's 120th Illinois. Sturgis ordered Colonel McKeaig, who was senior,

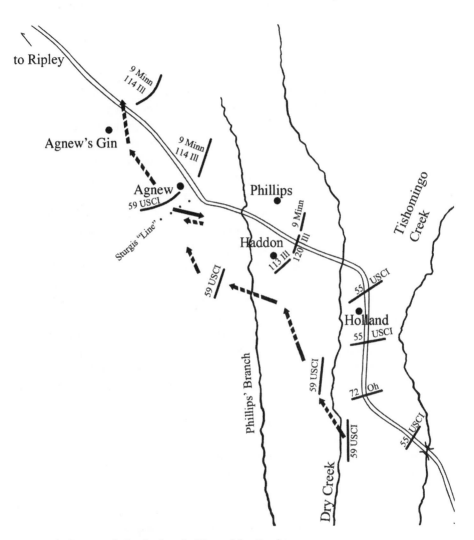

to Ripley

9 Minn
114 Ill

Agnew's Gin

9 Minn
114 Ill

Agnew
59 USCI

Phillips

Sturgis "Line"

9 Minn
120 Ill

Haddon

113 Ill

59 USCI

Tishomingo Creek

USCI
55

Holland

55 USCI

Phillips' Branch

59 USCI

72 Oh

59 USCI

55 USCI

Dry Creek

Brice's Crossroads Battle: Stands West of the Creek

to "form his regiment in the road" alongside the guns and place one regiment on each flank. "If you can hold [the Rebels] in check here for a short time," he exhorted, "we will be even with them." The 120th Illinois straddled the road. Moving by the left flank, the Ninth Minnesota filed up the hillside to the left (north) of Mueller's two cannons into dense brush on the farm of William Phillips. What was left of the battered 113th Illinois went into line on McKeaig's right south of the road.[24]

Spurring over to the Ninth Minnesota, Sturgis explained to Marsh that he held an "important position" and asked how long he could stay there. "As long as they could hold the battery on our right," replied Marsh. "Colonel, all depends on your noble regiment now," Sturgis proclaimed. "*You* can rally when no one else can make a stand and give us time." Affirmed Marsh, "I will do so." Color Sergeant Macdonald observed with disdain as the general took a healthy swig from a bottle his orderly handed him. "That it was *whiskey* there was no doubt, and that liquor was to some extent responsible for our defeat there is little less doubt." Sturgis "left for the rear," Sherwood recalled, "and that was the last we saw of him until we met him [in Memphis]."[25]

Marsh ordered his men to "hold the ground as long as possible." From his right flank he detailed Niedenhofen's Company K, with half the liberators, as skirmishers in the timber ahead. Ford's Company C, with the other liberators, stood in the left wing. The heat finally got to Markham, who passed out and had to be sent to the rear in an ambulance. "My excuse for all these shortcomings," he explained on June 22, "is brief and easily summed up. I am, and have been for three weeks sick; in fact so weak that like the celebrated Frank Pierce (once President of the U.S.), I fainted on the field of battle. I had no sympathy for Frank, when the matter was talked of freely during his canvass for the Presidency, but I admit a change of sentiment in that particular. I think that there are times when a man is justified in fainting." It's not clear which captain took over the left wing. Jerome Dane of Company E had long before "given out and left the field." It appears William Baxter of Company H succeeded Markham, but how, fatally afflicted with tuberculosis, he ever made it so far on such a day on foot was nothing short of miraculous.[26]

Within the hour the rest of the Federal force—wagons, artillery, cavalry, and infantry—swept past the Haddon house but largely out of sight of the Ninth Minnesota, ensconced in the woods north of the road. Skaro and half of Company D went on with all the rest, but Lieutenant Walker's platoon luckily discovered and rejoined "our Regt. which," as Aiton wrote, "was holding the enemy in check while all else seemed to retreat as best each could." Next to last in the weary column, the Seventy-Second Ohio skirted the northern edge of the road. To Corporal Medkirk the Ninth Minnesota, "standing in line" waiting to take over as rear guard, was "looking pretty blue," while "our boys were laughing and joking with each other." One Minnesotan "wanted to know if we could not keep the Rebels back?" Private Charles F. M. Guernsey, the renowned regimental "talker," snapped back, "No!" With "a long face and a voice like a child," the Minnesotan retorted, "Well, if you veterans can't keep them back, how do you expect us to?" Guernsey, "as quick as a flash," replied, "Oh, that is easy enough explained, you green troops don't know when you are whipped, and we veterans do, and we know that we are whipped like hell, and we are going to the rear." According to Medkirk, "This raised a laugh which cheered us up for a while." Last of all, Reeve's Fifty-Fifth U.S. Colored Infantry limped past Haddon's white house, where it thankfully took refuge behind the line of Illinoisans. Several hundred yards to the south, separated by fields and thick brush from the Ripley road, the Fifty-Ninth U.S. Colored Infantry floundered in frustrated isolation. The wooded, hilly terrain had prevented Cowden from linking up with the rest of the Third Brigade defending the Holland house position. Instead he had to ford Dry Creek through a "dense growth of underbrush which completely concealed it" and caused "considerable delay."[27]

Close behind Reeve's men swarmed Bell's Tennessee brigade, spread out behind a strong skirmish line, and Jackson's two reinforced escort companies on horseback. Four of Morton's ubiquitous "Bull-Pups" went into battery near the Holland house. "Soon driven back to the line by the enemy who came in on our right" in the direction of the road, observed Chauncey Hill, the Company K skirmishers "again went back to our proper place in the regiment." The fighting became severe, "a most desperate struggle," according to Marsh. Although the Ninth Minnesota held its ground on the left, the attack overwhelmed the Union right. "A few well-directed shots from the artillery stationed near the Holland house and a charge by our cavalry across Dry Creek," bragged Morton, "readily put [the Federals] to flight." There was, though, much more to it than that. The 113th Illinois, explained Lieutenant Colonel Clarke, "fought the enemy until our ammunition was entirely exhausted, when we were compelled to retreat, knowing it would be useless to contend against odds of four to one. I am sorry to say our retreat was in great confusion." The sudden flight of the 113th Illinois uncovered the right of McKeaig's 120th Illinois holding the center. "As the enemy came up we opened fire and repulsed them," recalled Capt. Parker B. Pillow, "whereupon they commenced swinging in on us again." Unfortunately, explained Cpl. William S. Blackman, "we had nothing much to fight with" and "were soon outflanked again." The two Illinois regiments, one in much greater disorder than the other, retreated along the road. Ahead of them went Mueller's artillery and the Fifty-Fifth U.S. Colored Infantry, who "moved back as [the white infantry] were forced back." At the same time, learning the Fifty-Fifth was no longer on his left, Cowden sought to join the white troops and artillery fighting near the road. He marched the Fifty-Ninth U.S. Colored Infantry north by the left flank. "Just as the head of my column emerged from the bush into the open wood I discovered a rebel battle-flag occupying the place [Haddon house] our troops had just left." Cowden had no choice but to retreat.[28]

"From this time," testified Captain Reeve, "I saw nothing that acted very much like an organization, but it looked like a regular stampede." Engulfed in the tide, however, he never realized that the actual rear guard never faltered. The sudden collapse of all the troops on the right had surprised the Ninth Minnesota still fighting in the brush north of the road. "We had been holding our ground pretty well," recalled Pvt. Lyman Raymond, a Company K liberator. Hill supposed the retreat of the others "was only a falling back of our advance line," but "it became obvious that we were defeated." Noted Sherwood, "Our right gave way and a general stampede ensued." Marsh retired from Haddon ridge. Moving by the right flank, the Ninth Minnesota marched "in good style" parallel to the road. The men soon discovered wagons "left along the road while others were crowding to the rear mixed with cannons and caissons all in confusion." Having not yet witnessed the full measure of the chaos, all the Minnesotans finally fathomed the true magnitude of the defeat.[29]

The terrible heat and oppressive humidity exhausted pursuer and defender alike. While busy setting up his guns on Haddon ridge, Morton was shocked to see cannoneers "drink with apparent relish" the black water in the buckets where the sponge end of the staffs were dipped after swabbing gun bores. At the end of the "dog trot" jog that had brought the Ninth Minnesota to Haddon ridge, Pvt. Taliesin Williams of Company F passed out. By the time he awoke, still in helpless condition, Company F was about to depart the field. Lieutenant Daniels saw that he was placed on a mule and assigned a steadfast comrade (unfortunately unidentified) to stay with him. Previously wounded in the face, Arad Welch of Company C succumbed again to heat exhaustion and was helped to an ambulance. William Dean noticed Cpl. Josiah Cooper from his own Company I sitting alongside the road, gasping, "Leave me alone." Dean and Pvt. Frederick Merrill, both considerably taller and stronger than Cooper, "took hold of him and lifted him from the ground, hung on to him, and pulled him along for some distance." Dean toted Cooper's weapon as well as his own. Cooper fortuitously stayed in the ranks. When Pvt. Albert Downing of Company K suffered sunstroke, Hill and Pvt. Joseph Harvey, his two brothers-in-law, ran to Orderly Sergeant Hays, who emptied his own canteen on the unconscious Downing's head but failed to restore him. Downing "begged to be left alone, he wanted to lie down," recalled Hays. "He was very hot." Hays pointed to some wagons moving out ahead on the road and told the two privates to put Downing into one "if they could get him in." They succeeded and rejoined the ranks but soon lost sight of that wagon.[30]

As the Ninth Minnesota left Haddon ridge, Captain Baxter went missing. Years afterward Macdonald averred he was killed "while gallantly encouraging his men," but in truth the regiment never saw what befell him. Later a Confederate officer confirmed his death and courteously delivered his personal effects to a captured Minnesota officer. A couple of days after the battle, some soldiers from Company F who had been taken prisoner found Baxter's body and buried him. He had been "shot through, near the lungs," and they surmised that "when he was wounded he betook himself to this tree and died in a sitting posture." The pension affidavits of Pvt. Andrew Bangston of Company H provide a plausible explanation. He stated that during the retreat some three miles from the battlefield proper, beyond Haddon ridge, Baxter called to him for assistance to an ambulance, but the Rebels overtook them. Baxter was killed, and Bangston was shot in the right leg

William R. Baxter, ca. 1862

and briefly taken prisoner. Despite his terrible affliction, Capt. William Rowe Baxter faithfully did his duty "until," in the words of his friend Col. William R. Marshall (later governor of Minnesota), "the enemies' leaden messenger of death cheated fell consumption of its prey. It was such a death, I doubt not, as he coveted."[31]

With the setting sun shining over their left shoulders, the Ninth Minnesota retired "slowly and in good order" along the north edge of the Ripley road, waded Phillips's Branch, and crossed an open field bound for a line of woods on a small hill. South of the road, but not visible to the Minnesotans, the Fifty-Ninth U.S. Colored Infantry also pulled back. Brutal fire blasted both regiments on their way. The four guns on Haddon ridge, according to Morton, poured "rounds of double-shotted canister upon the demoralized Federal ranks, as they hastily retreated through the open fields on either side of Phillips's Branch." Ahead was the plantation of Dr. Enoch Agnew, where the First Brigade had inaugurated its fast march to the battlefield a mere six hours before.[32]

GOD BLESS THE BRAVE BLACKS!

While McKeaig's three regiments briefly held Haddon ridge against the Rebels, Sturgis and McMillen labored to form another line of defense about a half mile back on the slope in front of Dr. Agnew's splendid white mansion. "By dint of entreaty and force, and the aid of several officers, whom I called to my assistance, with pistols in their hands, we succeeded at length in checking some 1,200 or 1,500, and establishing them in a line," explained Sturgis. What was left of the Ninety-Fifth Ohio and Ninety-Third Indiana of Wilkin's First Brigade rested in a field south of the Ripley road, with the Eighty-First Illinois and Ninety-Fifth Illinois from Hoge's Second Brigade slightly to their right and rear. The 114th Illinois from the First Brigade stood apart farther back up on the road. McMillen kept the wagon train moving until its rear passed the Agnew farm. Two regiments did elude his grasp. "Seeing no line being formed" and "having no orders," Lieutenant Colonel Eaton kept his Seventy-Second Ohio moving, as did Reeve's Fifty-Fifth U.S. Colored Infantry. Of all the artillery that had clattered past, McMillen could only snag Mueller's two guns, which he put into position at Agnew's front gate. The rest of the demoralized Illinois infantry never stopped their hurried retreat.[33]

Thus, the only Union forces remaining in direct contact with the enemy were Marsh's Ninth Minnesota, withdrawing north of the Ripley road, and Cowden's Fifty-Ninth U.S. Colored Infantry, falling back through fields and timber south of the road. The commanding general's histrionic testimony notwithstanding, no officers "with pistols in their hands" compelled those two regiments to their duty to protect the rest of the force.

Before exiting the scene with his cavalry escort, Sturgis advised McMillen that he was retiring to Stubbs's farm six miles back. One cavalry brigade was to corral the fugitives there, while the other pressed on to secure Ripley. He directed McMillen to leave the rear guard in front of Agnew's farm in good hands and to hie himself to Stubbs's place to "reorganize and resupply his troops." McMillen was about to turn over the First Brigade to Colonel Thomas when Wilkin rode up. McMillen informed him that Hoge's Second Brigade and Bouton's Third Brigade held the right flank south of the Ripley road and that he had personally deployed the Ninety-Third Indiana and Ninety-Fifth Ohio between Hoge's troops and the road itself. He ordered Wilkin to "contest the ground if possible until dark," but if the other two brigades "should be obliged to retire through his line," they were to relieve "each other as they retired." Who in the absence of the division commander would coordinate such very difficult maneuvers McMillen left unclear. Things also were not as rosy south of the Ripley road as McMillen had portrayed them, for half of Bouton's brigade and Hoge and most of his brigade had already disappeared up the Ripley road. The white troops who remained were in sore shape. Sergeant Lacock of the Ninety-Third Indiana, for one, "*fell into line without officers or a single cartridge* [Lacock's emphasis]," and he was far from the only one without ammunition or hope.[34]

Told erroneously the right flank was in good order under Bouton and Hoge, Wilkin attended to the left flank of his brigade positioned on the road north of the Agnew farm. There he found only Lieutenant Colonel King and eighty to one hundred men of the 114th Illinois. When his own regiment appeared, he greeted the Minnesotans warmly and placed them on the left overlooking an open field. The Ninth Minnesota numbered fewer than four hundred even counting the stragglers it reabsorbed. The 114th Illinois filled the short gap between Marsh's right and the road. Informed the Illinoisans were nearly out of ammunition, Wilkin detailed Lt. Edward H. Couse, the Ninth Minnesota's adjutant seconded to his staff, to fetch cartridges from the train. Couse returned holding a ninety-pound pine box with a thousand infantry rounds across his saddle. That was not much, but Couse alone could transport only one heavy crate at a time.[35]

In the meantime the Fifty-Ninth U.S. Colored Infantry, after crossing Phillips's Branch a good distance south of the road, lined up behind a rail fence bordering a wood. Cowden relished the clear shot at pursuing Rebels, that "being the first opportunity I had of doing any execution." Observing the Yankees from Haddon ridge, Morton quickly discovered "another strong line had formed behind the fence in the skirt of woods just westward of Phillips's Branch." His gunners started "plying shell and solid shot" at those Federals, but Cowden's infantrymen returned fire "thick and fast" at the battery. Their "leaden balls were seen to flatten as they would strike the axles and tires of our gun-carriages," wrote Morton. "Trees were barked, and the air laden with the familiar but unpleasant sound of these death messengers."[36]

Forrest organized a two-part attack. He personally led a mounted charge by Captain Jackson's elite escort companies over Phillips's Branch well south of the road and through a field to circle around the Federal right flank. Perceiving the threat, the Fifty-Ninth U.S. Colored Infantry retired northward "in good order" through an "open wood" toward the Agnew farm. Despite a severe wound in the right hip, Cowden, its brave and able commander, remained in the saddle in charge of his regiment. Before Forrest's horsemen could trap them, most of the Fifty-Ninth U.S. Colored Infantry retreated into the Agnew farm. Bouton himself happened to be on the far right flank when Rebel cavalry forced its way in between him and the rest of the regiment. He had to cut his way out and detour through the woods, leaving his command behind. Only hours later did he regain the Ripley road several miles north. Cowden ran his line from the "large white house" to eight cabins, the "negro quarters," that still housed most of Agnew's slaves (he had forty-eight in 1860). "I saw no other troops near me," wrote Cowden, "but determined on holding this point as long as possible." His men fended off the enemy horsemen trying to get around his right and temporarily stabilized the situation there.[37]

At the same time Forrest charged, four of Morton's guns, supported by Bell's dismounted brigade, audaciously bounded down Haddon ridge onto the road and moved closer to pound the bluecoats arrayed on the far slope. When Thomas returned to the fields in front of Agnew's house looking for his Ninety-Third Indiana, he was shocked to discover only a few stragglers. All the white troops there had abruptly fled the area. Private Bartleson of the Eighty-First Illinois had been surprised to see "a body of rebel cavalry and artillery," 150 yards distant, "crossing the Ripley road, hoping to station their guns to catch us at the next turn of the road at the top of the hill." That movement elicited a "well distinct volley" from the Eighty-First Illinois and Ninety-Fifth Illinois that failed to dissuade Morton's gunners from wheeling their pieces into position. Their fierce cannonade swiftly sent the Illinoisans reeling after the demoralized Ninety-Fifth Ohio and Ninety-Third Indiana, all of whom skedaddled. "After remaining in line till the Rebels were nearly to us and *had yet no orders*," Sergeant Lacock explained, "we began to look for Sturgis, but he had 'limbered to the rear' and left *no orders to retreat or surrender*, and we were forced to fly to the woods for safety" [Lacock's italics].

It appears Mueller's Sixth Indiana Battery never got off a round before flee-ing. After his third shot, Bartleson happened to glance around, but "not one of our men was in sight. If I ever ran it was then, I did not stop to load." Pri-vate Lawrence Sheehan of the Ninety-Fifth Ohio ended up "among a mob of infantry, cavalry and artillery, mules, etc., with officers begging and entreat-ing all who had a gun to form a line and try to check the advance. But with rebel shell bursting among us and rebels yelling like demons, no one paid heed to anything but getting as far away from his present location as possi-ble on the road toward Ripley."[38]

By 6:30 P.M., a little more than a half hour before sundown, Wilkin had consolidated his line behind the crest of a small wooded hill just north of the road and roughly opposite the Agnew house. Repulsed by the black soldiers holding the Agnew farm, Forrest left Cowden alone for the time being and redoubled his efforts to break through the Union position directly along and north of the road. Unlimbering on the road just short of Agnew's farm, four cannons under Lt. Tully Brown and Lt. H. H. Briggs raked Wilkin's line from short range, while Bell's Tennesseans, screaming Rebel yells, "poured" into the field to its front. "They came on," wrote Marsh, "only to be slaughtered, for my men, although very much fatigued, stood up to the work like veter-ans." Hill described the "balls, shot and shell flying all around." The Min-nesotans "loaded and fired lying down," recalled Sergeant Herrick. "This let many of the bullets and shells pass over us. Capt. [William] Clark and I were lying within three feet of each other. We had our heads raised up, when a bullet came between our heads and cut a bush that was just behind us. The ground was plowed up with large solid shot, and trees were crashing all around us." The "noise was terrific. It seemed almost a miracle that more of us did not get hit." During this "very sharp firing," wrote Dean, "we lay down and poured it into them across the fields. The regiment would have lost far more, but they over fired us always, their shell and shot from cannon hardly ever hurt as much for they fired too high." Having fallen back "to what is called the 'White House,'" wrote Sergeant Dodds, the 114th Illinois and the Ninth Minnesota "formed and fought there as long as they could." The two regiments "took advantage of a ridge in front of an open field," according to Captain Mallory, "and amid the confusion of retreating cavalry, artillery, infantry succeeded in checking and holding back the exulting foe, who was bearing down almost irresistibly on our retreating columns, threatening us with utter annihilation."[39]

After a "severe" fight with "considerable loss" that lasted almost to sun-down (7:07 P.M.), Wilkin finally ordered his two regiments to break free and retreat. He had no specific knowledge of any perceptible support on his flanks, which the enemy now threatened. It must be remembered the thick timber and hilly ground greatly restricted what could be seen from most places. The 114th Illinois and Ninth Minnesota withdrew "in good order, frequently facing to the rear and firing" and "contesting every inch" despite suffering severe "enfilading" fire. "About sunset," Aiton lamented, "we took the road, then the brush, then the road, bullets thick around our ears, one poor fellow fell all blood just before me. He was left. We hurried on mid *balls & bullets*" [Aiton's italics]. On the back slope beyond the Agnew house, Wilkin came across a line of thirty or more abandoned wagons, several of which were set afire. Just after crossing a small creek, he glimpsed off to the south a formation of black soldiers "retiring with skirmishers out." Fighting magnificently, the Fifty-Ninth U.S. Colored Infantry had just given the arrogant Rebels their second big scare of the battle.[40]

While Wilkin held the road against Morton's guns and Bell's brigade, Cowden had welcomed the respite to consolidate his position on the Agnew farm. His men unfortunately completed the pillaging of Agnew possessions the white troops began. Near sunset after a half hour of relative peace, Cowden noticed Rebel horsemen approaching his left flank from the direction of the road. Forrest was concentrating his forces to dislodge Wilkin, while Morton readied another "artillery charge." Seizing the opportunity, Cowden suddenly counterattacked with most of the Fifty-Ninth U.S. Colored Infantry. Morton clearly heard the Union officers "giving orders to their men to stand steady." Shouts of "'Remember Fort Pillow.' 'Charge, charge, charge,' rang along their lines and on they came." Ridiculed by the Rebels as the "negro avengers of Fort Pillow," Cowden's infantry in fact drove Jackson's two reinforced companies back several hundred yards. Wheeling to their left (north) toward the road, the black soldiers "steadily moved upon our guns," wrote Morton, "and for a moment their loss seemed imminent. Our cannoneers standing firm and taking in the situation drove double-shotted canister into this advancing line. [Jackson's] cavalry rallying on our guns sent death volleys into their ranks, which staggered the enemy and drove them back, but only to give place to a new line that now moved down upon us with wild shouts and almost got within hand-shaking distance of our guns." Private Joseph J. Vernon of Wilson's Sixteenth Tennessee Cavalry never forgot "how those negroes looked; they looked like a big black cloud coming." He and his compatriots waited until the enemy was forty to fifty yards off, then fired a volley and charged "at the same time."[41]

Wielding "bayonets and clubbed muskets," the Fifty-Ninth U.S. Colored Infantry had disrupted Forrest's attack and unknowingly protected Wilkin's men while they retreated. Once Colonel Lyon's dismounted Kentucky brigade reinforced Bell's Tennesseans, the greatly outnumbered blacks faced grave danger and recoiled. The last line that Lyon's brigade stormed that day, recalled Pvt. Henry Ewell Hord of the Third Kentucky Mounted Infantry, comprised "the negroes," who, he claimed, "did not put up much of a fight." With Rebels close on their heels, the Fifty-Ninth scurried past the Agnew house and halted to get its breath on a low ridge near Agnew's cotton gin. In the fading twilight, Cowden, "feeling faint" from his hip wound (his boot was filled with blood), finally relinquished command to Capt. Henry W. Johnson, an older officer of Lincolnesque appearance. Trotting up to the road and back another two hundred yards, Cowden sighted Wilkin's men forming yet another line at the edge of a thicket facing open fields. "This was the nearest support I had during the entire engagement," Cowden commented in his report. The rest of the rear guard appreciated the achievement of the heroic black troops. "They fought with the bravery and coolness of the oldest veterans," wrote Markham. "I heard many a 'God bless the brave blacks!'" That good feeling was not reciprocated by some officers in the Third Brigade. Learning later that Wilkin fell back about the same time the Fifty-Ninth U.S. Colored Infantry charged, Bouton, who had not been present, unfairly disparaged the "demoralized" white troops who, he scoffed, left his men in the lurch. Nothing was further from the truth.[42]

Last Out

Spotting the beleaguered Fifty-Ninth U.S. Colored Infantry retreating rapidly north toward the road behind the Agnew house, Wilkin directed Captain Johnson to form his men to the right of the 114th Illinois. The Ninth Minnesota held the left. "Shortly after sunset, when twilight was rapidly giving way to darkness," reminisced Macdonald, "the Ninth made a halt a little in the rear of a slight eminence, and, kneeling down, awaited the pursuer. Again the Confederates came on rapidly, the Ninth holding its fire until they were in close range, the enemy not perceiving us in the gathering darkness until the flash of our guns illuminated the thickets, and the roar of our musketry broke the silence." Marsh especially commended the conduct of Captain Strait's Company I with Macdonald's color guard, which in the past hour had lost three men wounded, one mortally. The black troops whom Wilson's Sixteenth Tennessee Cavalry eagerly chased with pistols in hand took shelter behind a reserve line of whites "on the other side of the hill," remembered Private Vernon, who was surprised it turned into a "hard fight." The Rebels recoiled. Morton brought up his guns to shell the defenders but failed to move them. Brisk firing continued until after the end of twilight at 7:36 P.M., when, wrote Captain Mallory, "night lowered her sable curtain between the combatants and put a stop to that day's hostilities." The 114th Illinois led off down the road, followed by the Fifty-Ninth U.S. Colored Infantry retiring "in good order, but without ammunition," with, finally, the steadfast Ninth Minnesota in the extreme rear. The tired Confederates gladly rested while their mounts were brought up.[43]

The fighting from Haddon ridge until the last stand after dark cost the Ninth Minnesota Captain Baxter (Company H) and Pvt. Henry Zarn (Company I) killed and more than a dozen (two or three of whom had replaced fallen or missing corporals in the color guard) seriously wounded. Again details can only be found for some of the wounded. Three were liberators. Shot through the right shoulder, Evan Watkins managed either to get to an ambulance or to grab a horse or mule and exit the battlefield, as did Jacob Bader, who was struck in the knee. Likewise Charles Dietrich suffered wounds, but how extensive they were is not known. Also, from Company K, Pvt. Myron Tower, a recent recruit from Saratoga, was hit in the left thigh and ankle. He crawled into the brush hoping the pursuers would go past and give him a chance to get away. From Company F, Pvt. Henry H. Howard kept walking despite being shot in the knee, but in the very last action, Pvt. Hiram Brooks received a dreaded wound in the abdomen and had to be left where he fell. A ball from a double-canister round tore the hip of Pvt. Walter S. Ross of Company E, but his comrades delivered him from the battlefield along with two brothers, Sgt. Wesley Maxfield (severe hand and knee wounds) and Pvt. George Maxfield (lacerated arm). Near sunset, while falling back from the Agnew mansion (the large "two-storey white house"), Pvt. Henry E. Seelye of Company A took a bullet in his left thigh near the knee. He succeeded in grabbing a loose cavalry mount and joined the crowd hastening up the road. Private Matice Scherrer of Company I, a young Alsatian immigrant with a similar bullet wound in his left leg, was not so fortunate and was left behind.[44]

Of the final phase of the battle, McMillen reported that the "the Ninth Minnesota again took a conspicuous part, and the colored regiment fought with a gallantry which commended them to the favor of their comrades in arms." He told Wilkin on June 16 that "the Ninth Minnesota, by holding the hill and keeping the enemy in check until dark, was the only thing that saved the command from being captured." Wilkin himself praised the Ninth Minnesota's behavior in the last action. "If they had been as much disorganized as the other Regiments they would have lost many more men, but they took all advantages and retreated facing the enemy frequently." The men, too, were proud. "We never started on the retreat until we were ordered to," wrote Herrick right after the battle. Dean concurred. "The ninth never moved without orders to the rear. All was cool. Col. Marsh was cool and is brave, every officer and likewise. I fired and held my gun steadier than if firing at ducks." Boasted Macdonald, "Never during the day's battle was the Ninth compelled to retire before a force in its front. It was lack of support on its flanks which forced it back each time."[45]

Chaplain Kerr heard Sturgis himself declare "the Ninth Minnesota acted like veterans; they never flinched under fire. They behaved well, and deserve all praise." Yet the commanding general's report condemned the entire rear guard. "The new line, under Colonel Wilkin, also gave way soon after, and it was now impossible to exercise any further control." Seeing only those troops who had been shelled out from in front of the Agnew house, but not—because he had already fled the battlefield—the valiant soldiers, black and white, who never broke, Sturgis affirmed, "no power could now check or control the panic-stricken mass as it swept toward the rear." Speaking to Winslow that night, he disparaged his troops as hopelessly undisciplined. "Although good soldiers when successful, when unsuccessful they were perfectly worthless" and "nothing but a mob." Given how well these "perfectly worthless" men fought and won every single one of their other battles, what might have transpired at Brice's Crossroads had Sturgis shown a scintilla of real leadership, grit, and proper judgment will never be known.[46]

CHAPTER NINE

Our Poor Exhausted, Foot Sore Boys!

The Terrible Marsh

"The labors were fast overcoming me, and I was glad when darkness closed the scene," recalled a sick and worn-out Lieutenant Keysor. Sergeant Dodds of the 114th Illinois spoke for all that day on the Union side: "Dear, oh dear! Such a time was never seen by mortal man—such a defeat—such confusion— such suffering!" A crescent moon faintly illuminated the narrow, hilly Ripley road leading northwest away from the Agnew farm. Wilkin's rear guard of the 114th Illinois, Fifty-Ninth U.S. Colored Infantry, and Ninth Minnesota passed another half dozen wagons whose "luried flames," recalled Nicholas Schreifels, "reddened the evening sky." Utter defeat and fatigue exacted a dreadful toll on spirit as well as body. During the "fore part of the night," forty-six-year-old Lt. J. C. McCain of Company B eased gingerly onto a log, intending to go no farther. Sergeant Lucius A. Babcock loyally stayed with his officer, as did several privates. It was said they "preferred to be taken prisoners to killing themselves in running in such a climate, and under such unfavorable circumstances." Many others also gave out.[1]

About 10 P.M. Wilkin bumped into the rear of the supply train, whose lead wagons, he was told, were "slowly passing through the bottom land and creek." The tragedy that unfolded at Hatchie swamp exceeded anything that yet befell Sturgis's incredibly ill-led force, but it was completely avoidable. Never realizing that the dry detour circled a half mile west, two cavalry brigades, two horse artillery batteries, Sturgis's cavalry escort, and a horde of infantry churned the two-hundred-foot-wide slough into muddy soup. Seven or eight ambulances (one with liberator Hens Lüthye) and one wagon made it across, but more than a hundred vehicles and a dozen artillery pieces waited their turn. Then a caisson "stuck fast in the mud" and "completely obstructed the passage." Vehicles trying to go around became mired up to their axles. Utter chaos ensued. Sergeant Merrilies discovered "a gulf of mud and water, the whole passage jammed with a mass of men, horses, wagons, ambulances and artillery plunging and floundering in the abyss, carriages dashing recklessly into each other, getting smashed up and turned over, the drivers yelling, lashing, swearing, and making [the] night hideous, and getting the passage so hopelessly blockaded that it was impossible to get either one way or the other, except on foot or on horseback." Frank Lyon compared the confusion to the Tower of Babel. "Every man was calling for his regiment and company, and so many were calling at the same time that a person couldn't understand himself." Gratified to hear shouts of "95th this way!" Private Sheehan of the Ninety-Fifth Ohio found "quite a squad" of men, but most belonged to the Ninety-Fifth Illinois! In the intense darkness after the moon set at 10:42 P.M., observed Merrilies, "numberless lanterns and candles twinkled all the way across, where the line of men were eagerly picking a way out, the imperfect light adding to the dismal character of the scene." Going barefoot, Corporal Carlson's little party from Company H made "but slow progress" in the "deep and sticky mud." Some of the infantry tried to work around the slough, but "in the woods," wrote Capt. Edmund Newsome of the Eighty-First Illinois, "it was all a swamp and thick with under-brush and running briers. We got through but the consequence was that the various regiments were mixed together."[2]

On the high ground at Stubbs's farm a mile and a half beyond Hatchie Bottom, Winslow's cavalry brigade held the fugitives until Sturgis ordered them "to push for Ripley [fourteen miles north] as fast as possible." Sturgis hoped to reorganize a short way past the town, although he already wrote off the artillery and wagon train. Grierson was to see to "the abandonment of all things" at Hatchie swamp and withdraw last of all. "For God's sake don't let us give it up so," Bouton pleaded with Sturgis. He promised the Fifty-Fifth U.S. Colored Infantry would hold if supplied with "the ammunition that the white troops were throwing away in the mud," and if given help, he pledged to save the artillery and the train. "For God's sake," Sturgis whined, "if Mr. Forrest will let me alone I will let him alone. You have done all you could and more than was expected of you, and now all you can do is save yourselves." Sturgis clattered off to Ripley with McMillen. The wounded who could ride or walk followed, including liberators Evan Watkins and Bader. The surgeons reluctantly left behind patients who could not cross the marsh on their own. "There in the wilderness, in the darkness and gloom of midnight," wrote Chief Surgeon Dyer, "our wounded companions were taken out, and gently laid upon the bosom of mother earth—the precious trust left to the tender mercies of the advancing foe!"[3]

It is astonishing that none of the brass thought to inspect the train, for Wilkin faithfully guarded its rear. James Mooney, a straggler from the 113th Illinois, stumbled into Wilkin's brigade, whose very organization encouraged him to feel "safe" because "every move & word" of its "very energetic" leader "seemed to say 'Brace up boys, Keep right on, We will come out all right yet.'" Wilkin still hoped to "form a line of battle just beyond the train and possibly save it." It took Capt. James C. Foster, the twenty-two-year-old acting major of the Fifty-Ninth U.S. Colored Infantry, "three hours to convince him that we had been abandoned" and that they should retreat to Ripley. That Wilkin's brigade was "left in the position mentioned, without orders, or even a notice to look out for himself," Foster wrote in 1882, "should be sufficient to dismiss Gen. Sturgis from the service." Only near midnight, after much futile effort, did Wilkin reluctantly abandon the train. He directed the wagons be burned and the batteries to dispose of their dozen cannons. The artillerymen spent a frantic hour "cutting up cartridges, chopping wheels, spiking the guns, and rendering the battery generally unserviceable," and mounting, they crossed the "dismal swamp." Private Tal Williams of Company F and his devoted caretaker sloshed through the morass with their borrowed mule. Private Thomas L. Buxton saw Williams at midnight "in a semi-conscious and critical condition."[4]

Finally the sleeping infantrymen were "quietly awakened and called into line" to make the crossing. After 1 A.M. on Saturday, June 11, the weary Ninth Minnesota, last of all, filed past the long string of wagons leading down to Hatchie Bottom. "The sight which met our eyes beggars description," recalled Color Sergeant Macdonald. "Abandoned wagons, which had been set on fire by the 'mule whackers' lined the road. The horses or mules had been cut loose and ridden away by the drivers or soldiers. As we moved on our men applied the torch to wagons which were not already burning. Many pieces of artillery were observed spiked, and dismantled." The "rout became more obvious than ever," wrote Chauncey Hill. "Wagon after wagon, cannon after cannon and caisson after caisson were abandoned in the mud." In the gloom Pvt. Frank Lohr was shocked to spy wounded Lieutenant Capon, his commander and old friend, "lying near an oak tree unable to move." After the driver had run his ambulance down the slope and wrecked it, Capon crawled back up to the roadside. Lohr and his fellows quickly hoisted him on an "old horse" and took him along. Nearby, Markham, mounted again, waited patiently for the regiment to arrive. Still woozy, he had forgotten to buckle on his fine presentation sword from the Second Minnesota and had left it in the ambulance. When he discovered his loss, he ruefully prophesied, "some Grayback will read his name on the beautiful Damascus blade with great satisfaction no doubt."[5]

Aiton bemoaned the "Terrible Marsh!" An appalled Wilkin found horses "floundering about & men were rushing past each other in the wildest confusion." That "fearful sight," recalled Lt. Seth Wheaton of the Fifty-Ninth U.S. Colored Infantry, "showed us the full extent of the calamity. There, in that great pool of mud & water dismantled, overturned, thrown about in every conceivable shape, intermingling with the carcasses of horses & mules lay all our hope of safety; (our Artillery). It is an actual fact that I crossed this pool

George W. Herrick

Colin Francis Macdonald, 1881

(dry shod) on the artillery wagons & the carcasses of animals." Alongside
the swamp "the wounded were begging for water and asking us to help them
along," remembered Sergeant Herrick. "Oh, what a sight! It was not in our
power to help them; we could scarcely drag ourselves along. We had to
wade through mud and leave them. I went in mud half way to my knees. I
saw others in the whole length of their legs; it was awful to see them struggle,
but here we were." Macdonald described the ground as "strewn with broken
and abandoned muskets, and all kinds of accouterments, clothing and other
articles." Hill, too, observed how "worn out soldiers" discarded "their guns
and equipment that they might keep along with the tide." One was Pvt. David
Dackins, a twenty-nine-year-old Welshman in Company E. "I broke my
gun and threw it away, together with my blanket and everything else except my clothes. I drew off my shoes and threw them away. I knew what
was coming."[6]

THE MARCH TO RIPLEY

At the rear of the entire army, the Ninth Minnesota, "a few hundred, not over
three or four," reassembled on the north bank of Hatchie Bottom. Hearing
of a "better and shorter road to Ripley," Wilkin turned the First Brigade onto
a new route, but soon, "worried about getting lost," he returned to the old
road. In the process the brigade, especially the Ninth Minnesota, "became
mixed up and we scattered us a considerable and fled north fast," remembered liberator Raymond. "We kept to the road which was filled up with soldiers from different companies." Gathering most of the left wing and small
groups and single men from the other companies, Markham stepped out
ahead of Wilkin and Marsh. Thus, the Ninth Minnesota separated into two
parts and never did reunite short of Memphis. Ahead on the ridge behind
Stubbs's farm blazed numerous small fires built from stacks of fence rails.
"The tired men of the Ninth thought at first that this must be 'camp,' but
it was only a ruse to deceive the enemy into thinking that the Union forces
had halted for the night." Winslow had set the blazes before departing for
Ripley. Bitterly disappointed, Wilkin and his men finally comprehended
they were completely on their own with "a large [enemy] army close upon
us." Schreifels saw "no ray of hope lighted of deliverance." He and his fellow
soldiers were "footsore, sick and exhausted," with "ammunition wanting."
There was not "a morsel to eat in the whole command," grumbled Sherwood,
who possessed nothing but "a rubber blanket and blouse lashed to Colonel
Marsh's saddle." Although Sergeant Major Clapp personally toted "plenty of
rations," he lacked an appetite. "Wearied and foot-sore, down-hearted and

almost discouraged by our shameful defeat," he wanted only to rest. "We then began our weary pilgrimage. What a prospect for infantry soldiers. One hundred miles from the nearest [friendly] point," wrote Markham. "Our poor exhausted, foot sore boys! Many a poor fellow I looked at, and wished I had it in my power to help him." Once past Stubbs's farm, he warned his men "it was probable that nearly all the infantry would be captured" and advised them "in the last extremity, to break into squads and seek the woods for safety." Only the "thought of being taken prisoner nerved us for the chase," observed Keysor, but increasing debility dampened that fear for more and more weakened men.[7]

Just trudging the Ripley road became agony in itself. Occasional rain showers kept the muddy track gooey. Not only had shoes "filled with sand," recalled Raymond, but "our legs had been chafed from our woolen pants." The mud-encrusted garments inflicted "so much pain and inconvenience" that he too discarded his shoes and "cut the bottoms of my pants off to prevent their chafing my ankles." He was far from unique. Hacked-off trousers became the trademark of Sturgis's woebegone infantry. When safely back in Memphis, Herrick still could not fathom "why we did not all fail" that fearful night. He thanked God his strength endured. "Sometimes I would get almost blind; I could just stagger along." At one time those few still with Company B possessed only six rifle muskets, "but two more of the boys found guns and brought them along afterwards." Herrick himself had no thought of parting with his Springfield. "I had my mind made up to go with my gun when it went. I intended to go into the woods and lay down when I could stand it no longer, and after resting try and bushwhack my way in."[8]

Others showed spirit as well. Left behind with a leg wound during the retreat from Haddon ridge, Matice Scherrer of Company I suddenly reappeared around 2 A.M., riding a mule. He asked Pvt. Peter Brown for water, saying that "he was suffering great pain on the right side of the groin" and that it "hurt more than the leg." After refreshing himself, Scherrer gamely trotted ahead hoping to overtake a surgeon. About that same time in the derelict train at Hatchie Bottom, Albert Downing of Company K suddenly awoke "with water falling in his face" after rain leaked through the canvas wagon cover. He had no idea how he got there, having no memory of being overcome by the heat some eight hours before and being placed in the wagon by his brothers-in-law, Hill and Harvey. Discovering "the mules had been cut from the wagon," Downing set off alone and afoot in the dark, determined not to be captured.[9]

A few hours after midnight, not long after Downing sloshed through the slough, Rucker's Rebel brigade, rested and fed, approached Hatchie Bottom.

"Don't you see the damned Yankees are burning my wagons?" Forrest raged. "Get off your horses and throw the burning beds off!" Profanity notwithstanding, he was "in great good humor," having "put the skeer" on Sturgis. "I meant to kill every man in Federal uniform," he recalled in 1865, "unless he gave up." On the way to Hatchie Bottom, Private Hubbard found "many Federal soldiers, now thoroughly exhausted, were sleeping by the roadside, while others, armed and unarmed, willingly surrendered. They were invariably told to go to the rear." The mass of wagons and artillery pieces strewn around the "slough of despair" amazed Rucker's men. Lieutenant William Witherspoon was amused to see "Yanks perched as close as they could be" on floating logs, "for there were more Yanks than logs." They looked like "chickens at roost, except each Yank had a lighted candle holding above his head saying 'Don't shoot, don't shoot.'" Witherspoon heard that 275 prisoners were taken on the road, as well as an incredible amount of stores and equipment. Forrest led the pursuit around the swamp over the dry detour that he certainly knew.[10]

"Grey dawn" at 4:12 A.M. found Wilkin with Marsh's half of the Ninth Minnesota and portions of the Ninety-Fifth Ohio, 114th Illinois, and Fifty-Ninth U.S. Colored Infantry still six miles short of Ripley. They had briefly stopped at a creek to fill their canteens when "a party of the enemy's Cavalry dashed out of the woods and across the road, calling out Halt! Halt! and firing their pieces among the crowd." The Rebels killed one man, "but a good many of the men had their guns loaded, and returned the fire, forcing them to leave as suddenly as they had come on us." Herrick was acutely aware of how vulnerable they were. "We had no cavalry to protect our rear, and were so worn out [we] could show but little resistance. We had but little chance to hope; it seemed as though we should very soon be prisoners." Yet "our little colonel was full of pluck; he had not deserted us as the commanding general had done." Wilkin "encouraged us to keep on and fire on the advancing enemy what we could. He said we must not give up to a little band of bushwhackers."[11]

Soon a company of the Fourth Iowa Cavalry trotting down the road on patrol was very surprised to encounter an organized body of friendly infantry between them and the enemy. Wilkin deployed the horsemen to protect his rear. Equally astonished to hear of Wilkin's men behind him, Winslow formed the rest of the Fourth Iowa Cavalry across the road and waited until the foot-sloggers went past. "This relieved the Ninth, for the first time, from rear guard fighting." Impressed how Wilkin and "the remnant" of his brigade kept their composure in the face of the enemy, Winslow wrote in his report they were "entitled to much praise." To Lt. William F. Scott, the Fourth Iowa Cavalry's adjutant, "this incident shows, as indeed do many others, that, if it was a lack of courage and spirit that caused Sturgis' failure, the lack was not wholly that of his troops."[12]

The Fight at Ripley

Plodding into Ripley about 7 A.M., Markham's left wing joined a horde of bedraggled Yankees. Soon after sunrise, Chief Surgeon Dyer had arrived to find "already there" a cavalry brigade, "as well as great numbers of the artillery and infantry." Yet "everything was out of joint, and in a sad plight. Some men had hats on, and some hadn't—some rode horses and some rode mules, some with saddles and bridles, and some without!" An Illinois soldier watched as "our boys came pouring in from all regiments, white and black, some without hats or coats, shoes or guns. They had thrown away every thing weighing an ounce they could do without. Their pants were covered with mud wet from crossing streams, and very heavy. Some cut them off at the thigh, and the negro boys threw them away altogether. Everyone was asking for his regiment and officers, but nobody could tell anything about them." Corporal Medkirk of the Seventy-Second Ohio showed up "coatless and in my bare feet" sharing a mule with a black soldier. After wolfing down some "cracker soup," he collapsed under a tree. Amazingly, only nine men from the veteran Seventy-Second Ohio were missing. The other regiments were in far worse shape. Sturgis later claimed, "The army presented quite a re-spectable appearance," but in fact it was a hollow entity desperately short of weapons, ammunition, and hope.[13]

Sturgis intended to press on immediately to Salem, seventeen miles north-west. A staff officer directed Markham's detachment west of town where the First Brigade reformed along the Salem road. There he discovered a host of stragglers, including Corporal Carlson's small party, Lyon and Dackins. Raymond was resting behind a fence when George Jenkins, his good friend in Company K, rode up on an "old artillery horse." Jenkins had fallen out the previous afternoon. When Raymond lamented that he "was played out and didn't know whether to go on or not," Jenkins magnanimously gave him the horse. Eventually Markham's detachment swelled to nearly three hundred. From his left wing were parts of Companies A, E, and G, most of Ford's Company C (with maybe ten liberators) and H, plus Company F, Skaro's half of Company D, and much of Company K (perhaps eight liberators) under Niedenhofen. Also present were Adjutant Couse, Chaplain Kerr, Surgeon Bingham, Capon, Clapp, and Principal Musician Handy.[14]

After dawn when the remaining few "ambulances with our groaning wounded men came pouring into the village," numerous "women, who had so recently given only evidence of a horrified hatred, pressed round to offer every aid that lay in their power." It seemed "quite a number of men with only flesh wounds had managed by the aid of horses and mules picked up on the road, to keep along with their friends to this place." Henry Seelye on his borrowed horse had fallen in the previous night with men of the Fourth Iowa Cavalry, but they jostled him on the narrow road and "hurt my wounded leg terribly." Reaching Ripley, he "couldn't ride farther on account of loss of blood and fell from my horse." When "two of our wounded boys rode up on horses," Pvt. Thaddeus L. Matthews of Company E was detailed to take them to the surgeons. With Sturgis about to decamp from Ripley, the "graver cases," more than fifty, had to be left behind. The "citizens to whose houses they were taken," wrote Dyer, "gave every assurance that our wounded, whether white or black, should be well cared for." Two assistant surgeons were supposed to stay to treat them, but only Dr. Dixon of the Ninth Minnesota, a "kind hearted, worthy man" who was "greatly loved by the Regiment," actually did. A dozen Minnesotans remained, including Corporal Burns, Scherrer, Summers (from whose lower back Dixon removed a rifle bullet later that day), Seelye, Howard, and liberator Bader. Dixon also treated liberator Evan Watkins's severely wounded shoulder, but Watkins very fortunately secured a mount and went on.[15]

While Markham reorganized his detachment, the famished soldiers lit fires to cook their breakfast. Events soon interrupted the repasts. Abruptly starting for Salem with Waring's cavalry brigade, Sturgis ordered the First Brigade infantry to keep close behind the horsemen. When the Seventy-Second Ohio formed up, Medkirk sadly realized it had been a mistake to stop. "We were so sore and stiff we could not stand alone for some time, but finally got so we could fall into line." Parts of the Ninety-Fifth Ohio, 114th Illinois, and most of the Ninety-Third Indiana followed, with Markham's half of the Ninth Minnesota in the rear. The exhausted men marched silently. The organized portions of Hoge's Second Brigade, Bouton's Third Brigade, and McKeaig's 120th Illinois were to follow in that order, with Winslow's cavalry brigade as rear guard.[16]

Near 8 A.M., as Markham's men slogged west on the Salem road, Wilkin, with the rear guard that included the rest of the Ninth Minnesota, entered Ripley from the east. He sent Foster's Fifty-Ninth U.S. Colored Infantry ahead to rejoin its brigade but retained Marsh's part of the Ninth Minnesota and the rest of the 114th Illinois and Ninety-Fifth Ohio. Working through narrow streets "very crowded with troops, in considerable confusion," they frequently halted to clear the way for cavalry to pass. While his aides vainly sought Sturgis and McMillen for orders, Wilkin rested his rump brigade at

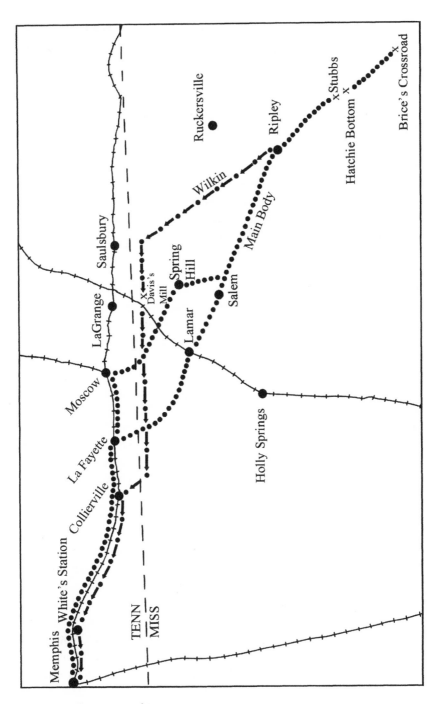

Retreat: Ripley to Memphis

the junction of the Saulsbury road, the same route by which the army had entered Ripley four days before. "We were like all the rest," Wilkin ruefully understood, "nearly out of ammunition and many of the men, being exhausted, had thrown away their arms & everything else."[17]

Not far behind, Forrest pushed hard for Ripley. Substituting Bell's fresh brigade for Rucker's tiring troopers, he sent part of Wilson's Sixteenth Tennessee Cavalry ahead to pressure Winslow's cavalry, while skirting the town to the south with the rest of the brigade. Dismounted Rebels infiltrating streets from the south surprised the Yankees still in Ripley after most of Hoge's brigade and Bouton with about 170 men had also departed. Grierson halted Reeve's Fifty-Fifth U.S. Colored Infantry, Foster's Fifty-Ninth U.S. Colored Infantry, and McKeaig's 120th Illinois to hold the enemy until the rest of the army could get clear. "This was done, and more," wrote Foster, but "we found a fearful ordeal." McKeaig led his men "on the double-quick to the south street of the town and formed in the street." The two black regiments drew up on his right. "By lying down," wrote Corporal Blackman of the 120th Illinois, "we could get at the approaching foe by shooting under the dwellings, which seemed to be on pillars two feet high."[18]

Halted some distance away toward the center of town, Wilkin heard heavy firing abruptly break out to the west. At the same time, he learned of a strong force of Rebel cavalry rapidly driving in the Fourth Iowa Cavalry toward his left. He briefly considered rushing ahead to support the regiments battling on the Salem road but sadly realized he had little with which to fight. "All of you who want to come with me fall in," Private Mooney heard the Minnesota colonel (who wore a "straw or Panama hat") call out. "I will do my best to bring you through safe." Mooney, too, saw the "advancing enemy & our cavalry falling in line & preparing for a fight." Wilkin's "look was that of a man whose duty was to turn his back on the enemy leaving his companions to fight while he & his men marched off in safety, but whose every feeling revolted at that thought." He led his men north to the Saulsbury road to escape to the north. Herrick understood the Rebels "were around the town in large numbers; a hard battle was going on," but "our regiment was so worn out covering the retreat all the day before and all night, they did not call us into action." In truth, as Keysor confessed, Wilkin's men just "skedaddled." Private Ludwig Klos of Company H, a young immigrant from Hesse, Germany, was shot from a house and left for dead. Also cut off from the Salem road, half the Fourth Iowa Cavalry under Capt. William W. Woods followed Wilkin north. Riding the length of the hapless infantry column, the Iowans protested they had no ammunition, "then left us," related Captain Mallory of the 114th Illinois, "saying that we were sure to be captured in the next hour. This was by no means encouraging. Still we did not despair, but with renewed energy pressed on (determined to escape), and in this resolve performed almost impossibilities."[19]

Grierson understood why Wilkin could not help him, but he never forgave Sturgis for not releasing Waring's relatively fresh cavalry brigade to his aid. It did not take long for the Rebels, recounted Corporal Blackman, "to advance so as to fire lengthwise of the street and rout us in short order. Our colonel, while on his horse directing our attention to a most dangerous squad to the east, received a ball through the breast and right arm, breaking it in two and bringing him to the ground." The men carried McKeaig, thought to be mortally wounded, into a nearby house, "where the lady promised to treat him right." The 120th Illinois retreated, "as we saw we had no chance to stay the progress of the enemy." Barred from the Salem road, most of the 120th and a host of stragglers, among them Private Matthews who had helped the wounded, fled north toward the Saulsbury road. At the same time, Grierson with the bulk of Winslow's cavalry brigade took to the Salem road, leaving behind most of the black brigade that had charged and forced the Rebels back a short way. "As the last shot had been expended, and we were under a galling fire," recalled Foster, the black troops "fell slowly back, in line of battle, until a thick wood, north of the road, was reached, where a halt was made." Conditions "seemed hopeless." He and Reeve "agreed that each should take his own course, and immediately separated" with the core of his regiment and many men from the other. The two captains "struck out for the north" on different paths, leaving Ripley to the jubilant Rebels.[20]

DISASTER ON THE SALEM ROAD

The main body of the army, perhaps five thousand men, fled northwest on the Salem road, the direct route to Memphis ninety miles distant. At their head, Sturgis and his escort, Waring's cavalry brigade, a horde of teamsters, artillerymen, and fortunate stragglers, and the few remaining ambulances (with Lüthye) formed a "great mass of mounted men, marching in tolerably good order." Among the lucky riders were liberators Evan Watkins and Raymond, Bingham nursing his bruised leg, and Capon astride his "old horse." Sturgis impatiently set a rapid pace, gradually increasing it so much that the weary foot-pounders could not stay up. Winslow's cavalry brigade guarded the rear. Forrest unleashed Buford with two brigades directly up Salem road in hot pursuit and led most of Bell's brigade by a different route hoping to cut off the fleeing Yankees.[21]

Passing through rough, thickly timbered country, the Salem road, as historian Bearss explains, "ran along a ridge that fell off into deep ravines to right and left." About five miles beyond Ripley, the route "broke down off the ridge and crossed North Tippah Creek by a narrow bridge." That span, Merrilies noted, quickly became "blocked by a crowd frantically endeavoring to get across, cutting off the column of Ambulances with the wounded, and at last crowding one completely off the bridge into the creek, where it was disabled and had to be abandoned." That calamity forced the horsemen to vault the steep, muddy banks on both sides of the creek and rejoin the road farther northwest. "Scattered about the bridge and banks of the creek" were, Winslow's rear guard discovered, "many infantrymen, sitting and lying down, apparently utterly exhausted. They had stopped there for water or to rest, but they were now so worn out and dull and hopeless in mind that they could not be moved" despite the urging of the cavalry. Adjutant Scott of the Fourth Iowa Cavalry condemned the "pitiful spectacle of broken spirits," but one of the Ninth Minnesota later retorted, "You fellows with horses had the cinch on us poor devils who were afoot, about getting back to Memphis."[22]

Coming soon upon the scene, Rucker's Rebel cavalry brigade nabbed several hundred prisoners, so many that the Kentucky brigade had to take the lead. Captain Ford, who had encouraged the liberators at Lamine Bridge, was taken there. "Ford got about five miles this side of Ripley and gave out," learned Sherwood, who was with Wilkin on the Saulsbury road. From all accounts the captain had "done first-rate, and managed his company well." Lyon was another "Mower County Ranger" who finally had enough. "I was partially sun-struck the day before, and about noon, when the sun was pouring down upon us, my head began to hurt, and I left the line." Spying 1st Lt. Christian Becker of Company G, he called, "Lieutenant, let us take to the woods and wait until night." Becker replied, "No. I can't stop here; I must go on." Lyon slipped into a ravine "and lay down in its shady depths" on his rubber blanket near a small spring. Hearing the "hubbub pass by," he knew he was isolated and fell asleep. Later he discovered Becker "lying in the road, dead. He was shot from behind while going up a hill. I probably should have shared his fate if I had stayed with him." Some Minnesotans heard from Rebels that Becker, "refusing to surrender and firing his revolver at short range, was shot and killed." A. J. Carlson, Pehr Carlson, and Andrew Wallace also left the line of march near North Tippah Creek. Hiding in the brush "20 rods from the road," they saw several men killed, including Becker, and thirty taken prisoner. Going "a little further," the three "laid down and soon fell asleep as we had, had no rest for 40 hours." Near there Chaplain Kerr last saw several Company D friends from his hometown. Nursing his arm with "a flesh wound," Pvt. Patrick Connell, a short, tough Irish seaman, "was cheerful, and said he could still handle his gun, and would try and push through," but Cpl. Thomas Pettijohn "seemed a good deal exhausted but cheerful. I understand that he and several others took to the timber soon after this."[23]

Little Tippah Creek, about three miles beyond, proved the final straw for the ill-fated infantry on the Salem road. After cutting across country, Winslow's cavalry ended up ahead of the foot soldiers, leaving part of Waring's cavalry brigade guarding the rear. The head of the column came up against a "very bad slough for cavalry or infantry to cross." While the few remaining vehicles and the mounted contingent started working their way across the obstacle, the infantry waited its turn on the confined, tree-lined road. Having ridden hard along side roads from Ripley, Colonel Barteau and part of his Second Tennessee Cavalry reached the vicinity of Little Tippah Creek before the Union infantry could cross. Drawing unseen within sixty yards of the writhing blue column, they loosed a volley, "one sheet of fire." Part of Hoge's brigade "simply, in a body, with one accord as though by command, stepped to the left a few paces down hill," where the "ridge sheltered us," and stumbled down the steep banks of the creek. Barteau heard no evidence of Buford's pursuit and, thinking he was cut off, withdrew. He thereby missed a wonderful opportunity to bag the demoralized infantry that crowded the ford on Little Tippah Creek.[24]

Enormous tumult soon erupted in the stalled Yankee rear when the Twelfth Kentucky Cavalry from Lyon's Rebel brigade furiously assaulted the Fourth Missouri Cavalry. "We tried to rally and make a stand," explained Corporal Dillenberger, "but it was no use." The Missourians "stampeded pell-mell, screaming and yelling with fear, while the Confederates charged into and through them with their hideous yells." Blowing right through another part of Waring's brigade that tried to halt them, the frantic horsemen slammed into the tightly packed infantry of Hoge's brigade already disordered by Barteau's ambush. Trampled by the Missourians, the desperate Illinoisans tried to push past the First Brigade halted ahead of them, beginning with the Ninth Minnesota. Markham attempted to get his men out of the way but "was knocked off my horse once with the butt of a musket." Bellowing "The enemy is coming!" the frenzied Fourth Missouri Cavalry erupted out of the horde of infantry clogging the narrow road. "With hardly strength to stand up," recalled Clapp, "we could not resist this additional burden of frightened cavalrymen, and I was struck by a horse and thrown into brush by the road-side." The whole horrible cavalcade rippled through the rest of the First Brigade. One of Hoge's regiments "went through us with a rush," related Corporal Medkirk, "throwing away their arms as they ran. We used some pretty forcible language to them, but it had no effect. They said they were instructed by their officers to do so." Next the Fourth Missouri Cavalry "scattered us in all directions." Most of the Ohioans took refuge in "a heavy growth of small pine" to the left of the road. "Struck by a horse, and hurled into the pine," a furious Pvt. John Furry "brought his musket to his shoulder and was about to drop a damned cavalryman, as he expressed it," but Medkirk "persuaded him not to do it."[25]

For the Union infantry at Little Tippah Creek, the hour of doom had struck. Once, the veteran Seventy-Second Ohio had been in the best shape of all of the infantry, but now, explained Lieutenant Colonel Eaton, "My men, being wholly out of ammunition, and seeing that it was absolutely necessary to rid themselves of all incumbrances in order to avoid being captured, broke their guns and destroyed their accouterments by cutting them to pieces." Some of the panicked infantry pounced on mounted stragglers still waiting to cross the slough. "If a poor negro was found upon a mule he was at once dismounted and a pair of white boys took his place; those who could not procure mules clung to the tails of horses and mules and were dragged for miles on the double-quick." Large numbers of foot soldiers, though, "being overcome by the excessive heat of the day and the long and rapid march were compelled to leave the road and seek safety in the woods." Colonel Thomas related how "many of the regiments, being out of ammunition, took to the brush," scattering "into the woods in every direction, each endeavoring to save himself." Recalled Sergeant Lacock of the Ninety-Third Indiana, "Our condition seemed desperate, but at the time we were in a dense forest of heavy timber[,] we 'skedaddled' into its darkest recesses, and the cavalry skurried after, followed by the rebels in hot pursuit." The game turned into "'hide and seek,' we doing the hiding while the rebels did the seeking." The delighted Twelfth Kentucky Cavalry rounded up several hundred more prisoners.[26]

For his own part, Markham "advised the boys to take to the brush, trust in the Negroes, and 'work in nights'" to Memphis on their own. Company C, which included ten or so liberators, threatened to dissolve, and Niedenhofen's Company K with perhaps eight liberators did split up. "Exhausted and out of ammunition," unable either to fight or run, "many of our men broke for the brush to escape being picked up," wrote Lieutenant Daniels of Company F. They hoped to "work their way through as best they could." The "Tigers" who fell out included Lt. Alfred M. Hall and twenty men, none of whom "were injured in any way when they left for the woods." Jacob Dieter was one. Another was Pvt. William Williams, older brother of Tal Williams, who himself had recovered enough to make his own way back through "swamps & woods." Much of Company H under acting Lieutenant Tiffany, a portion of Company G led by 1st Sgt. Frank Weber, and some of Company A under Lt. Leonidas M. Lane also sought refuge in the timber. Sergeant Herrick (who was with Wilkin's column) learned later that his father-in-law, Joel Handy, his brother-in-law, DeWitt Handy, and Sgt. Ernest Hainlin from Company B were last seen "to go into the woods; the enemy was pressing them so closely they could not keep out of their way." Joel "was inquiring for me and said I must have been captured." Herrick thought they "may go into the [forest and rest] and avoid the road and [they] had, I think, something to [eat in their] haversacks. DeWitt, I learn, had [been] shot into his clothes, but was [fine]." Clapp, who hid nearby, recalled lying "still as I could until all the rebels had passed by and it was quiet as a Sabbath morning." Having discarded mud-soaked "boots, stockings and blouse, and "with pants rolled up to my knees, a-la-cowboy, I hurried through the brush into the woods and began to look for a place of rest." Clapp settled on "an old burned log, and, in company with another unfortunate like myself, lay down beside it and threw a large rubber blanket over us, using my haversack for a pillow and intending to lunch from it when I awoke."[27]

Winslow's brigade halted the rout and enabled such infantry who could to cross the slough and continue toward Memphis. They were sadly reduced in numbers, consisting now of only "a few stragglers" whom Thomas advised to strike north for the Memphis & Charleston Railroad just above the Tennessee state line and to follow it west to La Fayette. Of nearly three hundred men of Markham's detachment, perhaps a third regained the road. Sergeant Merchant, who led the liberators at Otterville, reorganized Company C and magnificently inspired those who could keep moving. Nearly all his liberators got back onto the road. Jack Watkins, struggling with a failing right hip, "had to be forced along by his comrades to keep him from falling into the hands of the enemy." The Company K liberators fared poorly without such decisive leadership. Most of the company ended up lost in the brush. Hill and brother-in-law Harvey did take up the relentless pace, as did the Welshman Dackins of Company E.[28]

Out ahead with those of the mounted party who first crossed Little Tippah Creek, Merrilies "hardly credited at first" the tales of the rout, but the news created "a perfect panic among the stragglers, crowds of whom commenced galloping to the front, believing there was nothing now to hinder the enemy's cavalry from dashing in and gobbling up the whole column. Their stories as they passed spread the fire, and in a short time nothing remained of the column but scattered squads extending for miles ahead, some on the roads and others cutting across the fields, all hurrying wildly to get as far to the front as possible. All day long this continued." Raymond rode his borrowed horse "as long as I could stand it," but that afternoon he gave it to another comrade ("I don't remember who") and "continued on foot as fast as I could." Although afoot, Dackins kept up with a mounted party for twenty miles beyond Little Tippah Creek, where "the weakest of us had to fall back into the woods." At times, he took "hold of a horse's tail and hanging on for miles, determined to keep up as long as my legs would let me. But the enemy had better horses than our cavalry, so they kept us on a tight run all the time. Then our horses would fall down, and the riders had to foot it." Finally about 5 P.M., after trotting and walking what he estimated was fifty-seven miles in the last twenty-five hours, Dackins could no longer go on. He "ran in the brush and staid till dark."[29]

The mounted men reached Salem just ahead of Forrest. Fortuitously, most of the remaining infantry had already turned north onto the Spring Hill road four miles east of Salem and headed for Moscow, on the railroad forty miles southeast of Memphis. The last leg proved to be the worst. "The retreat had been through a hilly country hard to travel," recalled Hoge, "the roads being very muddy and the men being without provisions . . . keeping up with the cavalry reduced them to an exceedingly exhausted condition, and many fell unavoidably into the hands of the enemy." At times, Hill recorded, "Many would shout to make a stand but so many went on that little could be effected. Finally, several miles on, a number of us made a stand on a hill in the woods but it was of short duration and again we were on the move. At last [Harvey] and I, tired and far behind the main body, went into the woods, threw aside our guns and got under cover. While lying there in an old tree-top over a little brook, two of the enemy passed close by but did not discover us. Here I threw away all my trappings but haversack and we were able to start barefooted at any favorable time. Meanwhile the rebel cavalry were stringing along the road, some in pursuit of our flying troops." Dieter had also pushed for the state line. "It seems impossible for men to endure such fatigue," a comrade wrote Martha Dieter, "for they had not had anything to eat all day before they commenced to retreat. The last that I can hear from Mr Deiter he had got back within 20 miles of the railroad and I do not know the reason why he has not come in. I am in hopes that he will be in yet for he did not get a scratch in the battle. He might have straggled into the brush and is waiting for the excitement to be over a little. Then he will not be as likely to be picked up by the bushwhackers. You must keep up good courage for I think there is a very good chance for him to come in yet." In fact Dieter was already in Rebel hands.[30]

Around 11 P.M. at La Fayette (thirty-three miles southeast of Memphis), a few mounted stragglers who had made the best time bumped into the camp of the four hundred sick men and forty-one wagons that left Ripley two days before. Shaken by stories that the Rebels had "gobbled up" the entire expedition and were in hot pursuit, the wagons immediately lit out for Memphis, stopping on the way only to water the teams. At first light on Sunday the twelfth, after an indescribable all-night march, the lead elements of the main column beheld the railroad a few miles east of La Fayette. "The horses were nearly jaded out," wrote Chaplain Kerr. "The infantry which had kept up were very foot sore and exhausted. Many, however, had fallen out by the way. Guerillas infest the woods, and many a noble fellow will meet his death with none to tell where he fell." An Ohio officer was amazed any infantry even kept up with the mounted men. "I never saw such powers of endurance exhibited." Markham "rejoiced" to find seventy Minnesotans who came through the ordeal with him. "It seems as though the human system could not endure such an immense strain, but the thought of [the Confederate prisons at] Belle Isle and Castle Thunder will do much to aid one in finding resources he never before thought himself possessed of." There was a terrible price. Among the "brave dirt begrimmed and suffering soldiers" were, according to the Ohio officer, many swollen legs and feet "bruised, blistered, black and blue and bursting open."[31]

Amid the bedraggled infantry, Markham's Minnesotans stumbled west along the tracks to Collierville, twenty-five miles from Memphis. It was estimated they had marched almost ninety miles in the last forty-eight hours, nearly all without food. Stragglers and a few wounded at Collierville raised the detachment to about one hundred men. "Only think of the wounded riding upon mules or in the ambulances for one hundred miles, without having their wounds dressed," wrote a chaplain. "Yet there was scarcely a murmur from a wounded man. They endured it as only the warrior can endure such things." Sergeant David Ellis of Company A, badly wounded in the arm, was one of many who "suffered greatly" on the retreat. At Collierville they met Col. Edward H. Wolfe's infantry brigade and a hundred troopers of the Seventh Kansas Cavalry with rations, forage, and ammunition. "Oh Joy!" recalled Schreifels. "Many of us were so overcome with joy of being again in God's country, that we could not repress the tears that freely stole down our haggard cheeks." Told to board trains, "many of us were so maimed, that we did so on all fours. Scarcely had we entered the car, the unexpected order reached us to clear it again, to make ready for another engagement." It was a false alarm. "Fortunately, our aid was not needed, nor could we have done so for the little rest had so benumed our sore and swollen feet that we could not move about." That evening trains reached Memphis with "a large number of the defeated force." Raymond found upon alighting from the car "my legs and feet were so badly swollen that I, with others, could not march to camp, and I was carried up in an ambulance." Capon, Evan Watkins, Lüthye, and the other wounded or disabled men went to hospitals.[32]

No one at Collierville knew the fate of the rest of the army. Fearful of being attacked, Sturgis ordered the entire command to withdraw that evening seventeen miles to White's Station on the outskirts of Memphis. Grierson vehemently disagreed. More stragglers were "constantly coming in," and cavalry patrols could rescue those still on the road. Moreover, he learned from Captain Woods of the Fourth Iowa Cavalry that Wilkin had gone north from Ripley "with a considerable column" and might be near La Grange, fifty miles from Memphis, or even closer at Moscow. To relinquish Collierville risked their destruction. Sturgis refused to listen. If Wilkin and his men had indeed escaped, which he strongly doubted, they were on their own.[33]

REDEMPTION ON THE SAULSBURY ROAD

Marching north on the morning of June 11 from Ripley, Wilkin's column swelled to over a thousand, including perhaps 250 men of the Ninth Minnesota under Marsh. From the right wing were Walker's half of Company D, the rump of Company K (with maybe a half dozen liberators) under Orderly Sergeant Hays, the core of Clark's Company B, Company I under Strait with Macdonald's color guard, and Lieutenant Schuler's Company A. Representing the left wing were parts of Captain Beaulieu's Company G (with most of the Ojibwe) and Company E led by Keysor, plus eleven men of Company C (with L. D. Stewart and possibly one or two other liberators) whom Sherwood, their first lieutenant, took under his wing. There were also portions of the 114th Illinois, Ninety-Fifth Ohio, 120th Illinois, Ninety-Fifth Illinois, and a host of stragglers from other commands that either started out with Wilkin or caught up. A motley assortment rode horses and mules. Many had no arms or ammunition. The strangers soon warmed to their new leader, a "grand little man" according to Sgt. George A. Woodruff of the 113th Illinois. Woodruff appreciated that when "we would get strung out," Wilkin halted the column to let the laggards catch up—a stark contrast to the attitude of Sturgis and other top leaders of "every man for himself." Fortunately, after Woods's Iowa cavalrymen disappeared, no Confederates followed in their wake. Every Rebel was currently busy on the Salem road, but Wilkin did not know that.[34]

The familiar route north along the Saulsbury road proved embarrassing for some Minnesotans. A story later enjoyed around the campfire related how on June 11 they had returned to a "nice residence" they last visited four days before on the way to Ripley. On that earlier happy occasion they greedily stripped "a number of cherry trees, loaded with ripe fruit" without asking permission of the owner. Stepping out her door, the "lady of the house" had cheerily called out, "Boys, help yourselves to the cherries; you have more time to pick them now than you will have when you come back." Now sadly that circumstance "was literally true." Ashamed to face the inevitable "I told you so," those particular Minnesotans "made a wide detour to the rear of the premises and passed out of sight of the occupant of the place."[35]

Late that afternoon Wilkin's column passed the Salem-Ruckersville road and kept going northwest toward Saulsbury. At dark after another half dozen grueling miles, Wilkin halted five miles shy of Saulsbury in a woods near the Tennessee line, sixty miles from Memphis. Foster soon came up with over four hundred black soldiers. The Saulsbury road was "pretty thickly strewn with ammunition and guns," he wrote. "The latter we broke and the former carefully gathered and with full cartridge boxes and twenty rounds extra. Confidence returned, and never again left us." Much later Foster claimed he found Wilkin "utterly discouraged" and fearful "we could not hope to escape," and he greeted Foster "very coolly." Said to have "Fort Pillow on his mind," where Forrest massacred whites as well as blacks, Wilkin supposedly "expressed regret that the colored troops had found him." Outraged, Foster "promptly offered to relieve him of our presence" and make his own way to Memphis, but Wilkin changed his mind when told the black soldiers had kept their guns and had "plenty of ammunition," and he "concluded that we would be a good thing to have between him and the enemy." Although Foster conceded that Wilkin was a "brave man," he was "not strong physically, and on this occasion fatigue and starvation had taken the pluck all out of him." Yet very credible evidence, including Foster's own testimony of the previous night at Hatchie Bottom, where capture seemed just as imminent, decisively contradicts his contention that Wilkin, always an extraordinarily determined man, ever lost his "pluck" or was in any way panicky.[36]

Wilkin's men truly enjoyed their rest. Macdonald "enfolded the colors in my arms, pillowed my head upon 'Old Glory,' and was asleep." When "a familiar voice shouted in my ear, 'Wake up, Sergeant! Chicken!'" Macdonald awoke "in an instant! The only one left of my color guard had gone 'foraging,' had found a setting hen, had cooked it, and sought me out." The "recollection of that tough old Mississippi rebel hen will live in my memory as long as life shall last as the most toothsome morsel that I ever ate." Others divided what rations they had toted such a long way. Herrick shared out not only some hardtack but his mother's favorite tea. "No one can imagine how good it was here, after our long weary march and fasting." Like many others he wore nothing "but my pants and a thin shirt. The ground was damp and I soon commenced to shiver. I thought I had the ague, but was so worn out soon went to sleep and slept dearly all night."[37]

Herrick and the others slept till dawn on June 12 only because Wilkin courageously let them. Several officers, including Foster, urgently advised pushing on at midnight. The discussion turned quite "stormy" according to Foster, but around 11 P.M. while the brass walked "among the men, who were sleeping and snoring to beat the band," Thad Matthews overheard Wilkin say "There is no use asking these men to march." They must have "one good night's rest." The worn-out men included Foster's own guards. That night when a party from the 120th Illinois reached the bivouac, the black pickets were "so wearied that only one of them could be awakened at all." At first light on Sunday, the men awoke "much refreshed" but in appalling shape. "It was difficult to stand," Herrick explained, "but after hobbling around for a while [we] could walk along quite well." Many were already barefoot, and more discarded their shoes, including Keysor, whose "feet were perfectly raw." Like so many others, Wilkin's men had "cut up their pants to wrap around their feet" or had removed their trousers altogether. "Perhaps you never saw such tired mortals as we," sighed Aiton. "Of 26 of us [in Company D's Second Platoon], only 12 had guns. It was to give up or lighten and try to escape. I chose the latter." Dean noted that many tired men of the Ninth Minnesota finally "broke guns, threw everything away, that is about one-third threw guns away. I brought mine in."[38]

After stumbling two miles northwest toward Saulsbury, Wilkin met "Union people" who urged him to leave the road. Turning west, moving carefully by lanes and fields—the "most obscure route known," according to Woodruff—Wilkin approached Davis's Mill on Wolf Creek at noon only to find the bridge partly dismantled. While repairs were under way, Wilson's Sixteenth Tennessee Cavalry rushed in from the rear and fired into the column from both sides of the creek. "Everything was in confusion," wrote Wilkin. "The stragglers from other Brigades, who had joined us, having thrown away their arms & the men on the horses & mules embarrassed me. I formed a line as best I could in the dense swamp & threw out flanking." Macdonald unfurled the colors, and the Ninth Minnesota prepared "to resist an attack." In the rear Foster swiftly marshaled his black soldiers and faced the enemy.

According to Herrick, some of the black soldiers "got into a panic, and most of them were out of ammunition." The Minnesotans handed over "some of our ammunition from some of us that had more than they needed." The black infantry "again formed in as rear guard and we marched ahead." They valiantly covered the column while it crossed Wolf Creek. Woodruff watched one squad calmly hold their fire until the enemy drew near and give the Rebels "a surprise that they little expected." Afterward he "always had a very kind feeling towards the Colored Soldier." Another who praised the black infantry was Chaplain Thomas R. Satterfield of the Ninety-Fifth Illinois. "All honor to the darkies. They displayed great bravery and coolness, both in the field and on the retreat." Wilkin had personally thought little of black troops, but he changed his mind and praised the "imperturbable coolness and steadiness of the colored troops under command of Captain Foster." They "behaved splendidly" and "are the coolest and most indifferent men I ever saw in action."[39]

Among Wilkin's flankers were Beaulieu and perhaps twenty Ojibwe from Company G—"my Chippewa half-breeds," according to Wilkin. "They were bare footed," wrote Mooney, and "had their pants rolled up." A few Ojibwe supported the advance guard from the Ninety-Fifth Ohio, but most of them spread out around the bridge in the rear. It was good that they did. Observing Rebel cavalry trying to get between the retreating black troops and the bridge, Foster urged his men to double-quick to escape, but they shouted "I won't run!" and "I'll be damned if I run." Foster faced a rough time, but Beaulieu's Ojibwe "posted themselves behind trees and bushes, and whacked the enemy, holding him in check until we had crossed the bridge and thrown the planks in the water." Foster grudgingly acknowledged the "unlooked for assistance" from Wilkin.[40]

Skirmishing persevered throughout the afternoon. Making good time while marching west near the state line, Wilkin's column bypassed Moscow and La Fayette. At one point the Ojibwe sniffed out "Guerillas in our front" and "shot some & chased others who left behind their arms." Late that afternoon they slipped up to a house near the road. "Three of them got taken," Herrick learned, but inexplicably the Rebels let them ago. "How they happened to parole the Indians I do not see, but it was all the same to the Indians." They came back, "drove the few rebels away from the house, and shot two or three. How they yelled when they saw a rebel fall. They got possession of the house, took what they could find to eat and a mule that was in the yard and came on. We passed safely on while they were maneuvering." Macdonald also heard their shouts and "war-whoops." The Ojibwe by "their cunning and proficiency with their guns kept the enemy at a safe distance." The last sharp action took place after sunset when the Tennesseans lunged at the rear guard, only to receive "a warm reception" when Foster's black soldiers and the Ojibwe "tumbled" several "from their saddles." Mooney declared "the cool col. [Wilkin] & his braves was to much for [the Rebels]." The Ojibwe dropped "down behind rocks, stumps or in holes and wait[ed] until the pursuers was almost upon them, then with one accord they would all fire, leap in the air and yell every time they tumble a rider. This was more than our pursuers could stand for long. They learned to keep off at a respectful distance." Captain Pillow of the 120th Illinois likewise praised the "great service" of the "light footed Indians."[41]

Wilkin kept going until after midnight on Monday, June 13, when only four miles from Collierville. He let the men rest until first light. "We were growing hungry now," recalled Herrick. "Some had eaten nothing but green apples and raw dry corn since the battle. You could hear them offering all the way from 25 cents to $2 for a piece of hardtack. It was not to be had. I had some coffee left and that helped me some." At dawn Wilkin started for Collierville. Some of the black soldiers were so tired Foster had to threaten them with a revolver to get them up. Sherwood made it his mission to bring in all eleven men from Company C, including liberator Stewart. Private Lewis Andrews "was the hardest one I had to get along. The last day he gave up several times. Every time he would lay down I would put him on his feet and give him a damning and he would march on again." Despite his own rapidly failing strength, Hays in Company K, an "efficient & faithful soldier," similarly exerted "great effort to save lives of men under his charge," among them a few liberators. Slaves from nearby farms warned that a brigade of Rebel cavalry had passed nearby. Soon the column came across the tracks of the Memphis & Charleston Railroad twenty-five miles from Memphis. No help was in sight. "I confess my courage began to run low, as did many others," Herrick admitted. "I did not think my life was worth saving. My left knee was so weak I could scarcely drag my leg along, but I kept along." Foster asked Wilkin to order white soldiers on horses and mules to surrender their mounts to his own wounded and disabled men. Wilkin "didn't have the heart" to force them to dismount, but he gave his own horse to an incapacitated black soldier, as did Foster. Such deep concern by the leaders meant that few with Wilkin ever straggled and became lost. "We all felt safe with the Col.," explained Mooney. "He was brave, energetic & self possessed though several times closely pressed by the enemy. He never run & left us."[42]

Wilkin was deeply disappointed not to find "cars, rations or reinforcements" at Collierville. A few leftover boxes of hardtack fed a fraction of the men. "How they leaped for joy, at the sight of food," wrote Chaplain Satterfield. "I heard some boys say, whose wants had not yet been supplied, 'I wish I had a piece of hard tack,' the big tears trickling down their cheeks." Wilkin warned his forlorn band two Rebel cavalry brigades prowled close by. If they appeared, "we could do nothing but surrender." He placed his hope in Lt. Harvey P. Hosmer from his staff, who volunteered to ride a strong mule seventeen miles west to White's Station and contact Sturgis. His trust was not misplaced. Hosmer pounded into White's Station around 10 A.M. Certain that Wilkin was dead and his men already taken prisoner, Sturgis was "thunderstruck." General Washburn dispatched a train loaded with the Twenty-First Missouri to Collierville and sent seven hundred cavalry by road.[43]

Wilkin let his men rest until noon and then led them west along the tracks toward Memphis. Two miles beyond, the Ojibwe "discovered the enemy's scouts." A "brisk" firefight broke out. "We began to despair of ever getting through," Keysor wrote. Suddenly, a whistle sounded and a train materialized ahead. "Again the colors of the Ninth were flung to the breeze, and sent up the track to signal the train that we were friends." The train cautiously approached, but recognizing friendly troops, its passengers let out whoops of joy and relief. "Could you have witnessed the scene that followed and heard the shout of welcome that went up from the throats of about 1200 [actually 1,600] starving human beings and heard their cries for bread, you would have been capable of forming some idea of our sufferings." Keysor had "never appreciated the stars and stripes as I did that day when I saw about 1,000 well armed men bearing the flag of our country to our relief." Sherwood heard that when Wilkin "saw that we were reinforced he shed tears."[44]

While the men were eating hardtack from the relief column, some Rebels appeared. Disembarking, the Twenty-First Missouri "swore they would protect us to the last, and bid us rest." The train itself could not hold all of Wilkin's men. Those who "felt as though they could do a little fighting," he announced, "had better remain and let the cripples go on." About fifty stalwarts from the Ninth Minnesota volunteered to "see it out" with Wilkin, Marsh, and Macdonald. "Seeing the cars come up and fresh troops," Herrick explained, "my courage somewhat revived, so I thought I could fight a little if they would come where I was, so concluded to act 'tough' and stay." So did Lieutenant Colonel King and the "tattered colors" of the 114th Illinois. "Come on, Mr. Rebs," taunted Chaplain Satterfield. "We are ready for you. We would not now have to fight you with empty guns, while yours are full. We would not now have to stand up like sheep, and be shot down, with no way to defend ourselves. It is an eye for an eye and a tooth for a tooth now." After the train departed, Wilkin warily led the combined force west along the tracks.[45]

At 4 P.M. the train loaded with survivors from Wilkin's column (including Foster and most, if not all, the black soldiers) rolled into White's Station. When a delighted Sturgis approached the cars, he "seemed to rouse a slumbering demon in nearly every man on that train," according to Mooney. "Some were calling him 'You dirty old cowardly Son of B.' Others were hissing and spitting at his face, some commenced picking up their guns & saying 'Let us shoot him, shoot the damned old coward down in his tracks.'" Mooney watched Sturgis "wheel suddenly on his heel and make good time for a safer locality." Lieutenant Henry M. Austin of the Fifty-Fifth U.S. Colored Infantry also witnessed Sturgis's humiliation. "I heard private soldiers accuse him to his face of selling out to Forrest and heard taunts and epithets hurled in his teeth which no soldier would take as quietly as he did." Obviously shaken, Sturgis telegraphed Washburn requesting "a personal interview with you in regard to the propriety of my being relieved from command."[46]

Sturgis had other worries. The second train sent toward Collierville should have returned by now with the rest of Wilkin's men and the rescue force. His "last news was to the effect that they were in line of battle." But everything turned out well. The remainder of the column eagerly embarked for the ride back to Memphis. Although the battered Ninth Minnesota "had but few men with it, the colonel was there and the colors," Herrick proudly related. "We never moved or retreated without orders." At White's Station, Sturgis warmly greeted Wilkin and his men, who showed none of the rancor of the first batch of survivors. "I have been highly complimented," Wilkin wrote home. "The men praised General Sturgis and cheered me." He discovered that he "brought in the largest body which came together and in the best order." Gladdened by Wilkin's unexpected appearance, Washburn informed his superiors that the overall loss was "not as bad as first reported."[47]

In the streets of Memphis, the returning troops received a lively reception of a different sort from the many "savage rebel" citizens. Children jeered, "Oh, the Yankees is licked:—the Yankees is licked!" Adults laughed at the bedraggled Federals. "I guess you got enough this time!" was probably the most polite comment. The "dejected" men, "silent, sullen, with downcast eyes," simply hobbled on. However, "the negro women came down," observed Chaplain George W. Gue of the 108th Illinois, "and were ready to help our suffering boys and give them a cool drink of water. God bless them; my prayers will be for their freedom. They are our friends." It was another stark reminder that the Emancipation Proclamation had not freed the slaves in

Union-held Tennessee any more than in Missouri and underscored just why the North was fighting this war.[48]

Great joy erupted in Markham's camp when Wilkin, Marsh, and the balance of the Ninth Minnesota unexpectedly turned up. "They supposed we were all captured," wrote Herrick. Keysor, so ill he could barely move, considered the whole retreat with Wilkin an "almost miraculous escape." Felch, who had so fortuitously remained in Memphis the whole time on quartermaster duty, was appalled by the radically different appearance of his close friend and fellow liberator L. D. Stewart. The once sturdy, blond-haired and blue-eyed six-footer "looked like a skeleton," being shoeless, his feet "all raw," and his "pants and shirt nearly all tattered off." Even so, most of the other returning Minnesotans, it seemed to Felch, had "suffered worse than him. A great many had only their drawers on and a part of a shirt. It was a horrible sight." Such was the end of the "first fighting campaign of our hopeful and gallant Ninth Minnesota!" deplored Quartermaster Owen. "It is a sad record for our brave boys; but they have the satisfaction of knowing that it was no fault of theirs that their names are thus recorded on so dark a page of the history of this war."[49]

CHAPTER TEN

Picking up the Pieces

RATHER A FRIGHTFUL HOLE

The Union called the bitter defeat at Brice's Crossroads the Battle of Guntown, after the small town five miles southeast. The subsequent retreat was, according to Wilkin, "probably the most severe of the war." A survivor of the First Battle of Bull Run, he knew of such things. The Ninth Minnesota regained Memphis in "pitiable condition," mainly "barefooted, their feet badly blistered and swollen, and in some cases poisoned. Most of them had eaten nothing for three days and all had suffered for want of food." Dean humbly thanked the "Almighty God and Preserver," who "gave me such physical strength when strong men gave out and lay down by the road side to be taken by the enemy." Of 629 officers and enlisted men who left Stubbs's plantation on June 10, only 342 (54 percent) had regained Memphis five days later. The others if not dead, wounded, or taken prisoner, lamented Owen, "are yet wandering in the woods in a starving and destitute condition."[1]

In succeeding days, a steady stream of evaders and escapees filtered back to Memphis with their own stories to tell of hardship and perseverance. Taliesin Williams, who collapsed the evening of the battle, limped in on June 16 "in an exhausted condition clad in a worn out pair of pants reaching to the knees and ragged shirt, having neither hat cap coat shoes or socks." His older brother, William, was still missing, having taken to the woods on June 11 with much of Company F. On June 17 twenty-six men rejoined the Ninth Minnesota. One was Albert Downing of Company K, the sunstroke victim whom brothers-in-law Hill and Harvey placed in a wagon the evening of the tenth. After waking up alone at the Hatchie marsh early the next morning, Downing adroitly avoided the pursuing Rebels for six days despite once being chased by bloodhounds, and he fortuitously encountered Union scouts. He came in, like so many others, "with pants off at the knees." Orderly Sergeant Hays "did not at first recognize Downing so greatly had he changed from the hardships he had gone through." Downing was very saddened not to find Hill and Harvey in camp. Privates George Sherman, James Reynolds, and Frank W. Warner of Company F also returned that day. Splitting five hardtack crackers and "such forage as green apples," they "hid by day and traveled by night and lived on."[2]

On Monday, June 20, eight more stragglers turned up. David Dackins of Company E, twice captured, never gave up. In 1851 at seventeen, he had come from Wales with his parents and settled in Minnesota five years later. In the spring of 1857 when the Dakota threatened the white community, the local community chose Dackins, a pleasant and resourceful young man, to join a parley with the Dakota in their village at Swan Lake. Chief Red Iron "gave the messengers full assurance of peace and friendship." Compared to the Dakota, the Rebels did not appear so intimidating. The evening of June 11, on the road northwest of Salem, Dackins fell out exhausted. The next dawn he ran afoul of four enemy horsemen. "I saluted them with 'good morning, boys,' and they returned the salute. They appeared to be real gentlemen, but still I did not want their company." He decided "to make myself as agreeable as I could, gain their confidence, and run the first chance. I then commenced cooking breakfast for us all." Three Rebels suddenly galloped off, and the one watching Dackins became distracted when his horse shied. "I dropped the meat and ran as fast as I could into the woods, soon followed by my guard." All four troopers tore after him. "They [hollered] and swore they would shoot me if I did not come out." Five other Yankees surprised everyone by rising out of the brush and surrendering. That night Dackins blundered into a marsh. "As I was barefooted, my feet were badly scratched and bleeding. I had nothing on me but a shirt and a pair of pants. I had to swim a river, and recrossing it on a log, I fell off a distance of fifteen or twenty feet, hurting my right arm so that I could not use it to swim. But I was not discouraged. I worked myself out of the sloughs."[3]

On Sunday morning Dackins warily approached an isolated dwelling. "To my astonishment, who should come out the house but a rebel soldier, and I was 'gobbled' again" and held by an elderly man who ran a still. Dackins spun a tale of being a down-on-his-luck Alabamian who had lost his horse and wagon. Despite living briefly in Memphis, he did not sound enough like a Southerner to fool the crusty Mississippian, who told him he "lied like hell." Complaining the "damned Yankees had stole all he had," the old codger ordered his sons to turn the fugitive in. Dackins noticed a muzzleloading gun leaning on the stash of whiskey. After washing his hands, he cleverly contrived to pour water down its barrel. Grabbing a "bucket in one hand and the rifle in the other," the old man set off for breakfast, followed by Dackins. "He kept about ten paces in front, and eyed me closely. I looked for an opening in the woods, and soon made a dash into the timber. I could hear him crack the cap, but I knew it would not go off. In a few moments four horsemen were in pursuit, but I hid under a large log. They hunted me all day, but it was no go."[4]

"Feet all torn" and "clothes in an equally bad condition," Dackins kept on the move all the rest of the week. "I did not have anything to eat for several days, except occasionally a few apples, green corn," and "at times sought to appease my hunger by eating grass." On Sunday, June 19, ten miles from Memphis, he met "an old man, lady and little girl coming from church. Although Rebel sympathizers, they showed true Christian sentiments." Worried "more substantial food might hurt him," they wisely allowed Dackins only a biscuit. He cautiously worked his way west through guerrilla-infested country toward Memphis. Suddenly a train roared into sight. "As it passed I waived my hat. The soldiers pointed guns at me, probably thinking that if anything happened to the train to shoot me. After going probably a half a mile, the train was stopped and came back to me." The soldiers "took me to their camp and wanted me to stay with them," but "anxious to get back to my old comrades," Dackins politely "declined their kind invitation." At 1 A.M. on Monday, he crept into camp looking for a quiet bunk, but "Captain Dane was so rejoiced that he woke up the boys and I had to tell them my story. They gave me food to eat and I was so hungry that I ate everything, and especially hearty of cold beans. Almost instantly I was attacked with pains and became insensible in my sufferings." After a week in bed, he reported to the convalescent camp and later left on furlough. His health "badly shattered," Dackins remained home until December 1864 and thereafter saw only limited duty at Fort Snelling.[5]

The last of the eight who came in on the twentieth was the trio of Cpl. A. J. Carlson, Andrew Wallace, and Pehr Carlson of Company H.[6] About noon on June 11 when everything fell apart on the Salem road, they hid in the brush, where A. J. Carlson and Wallace finally tossed away their weapons. While traveling that night, the three startled a lone private from the 113th Illinois. "You can form some idea how glad he was that we had taken him prisoner in place of the Rebels," wrote A. J. Carlson. The four deliberated whether to head east to Decatur, Alabama, but determined to keep on to Memphis. They elected one of their number as guide, and the others promised to "follow him without raising any objections. In order to succeed we had to keep very quiet and travel nights." The winner also got the Illinoisan's shoes. A resourceful man who "united sound sense with strong convictions and a candid outspoken temper," A. J. garnered three votes in "one of the most honest elections ever held in the south. We certainly had a fair count." The little party stumbled a few more miles that night. "We had poor blankets and the night air was cold. We could not sleep very much." The next day they rested in a small lean-to. Horsemen and baying bloodhounds drew alarmingly close, and A. J. even glimpsed horse's legs through the brush. The four fugitives feared being shot on sight. A. J. took solace in his testament, "which I always had with me during my 3 years' service and very suddenly all fears seemed to disappear and I was ready to die." Wallace panicked and crawled through the thicket hoping to get away. "I grabbed hold of one of his legs and held him; in a few moments he cooled down and came into our hole again for such a move at this time would certainly have cost us our liberty if not our lives. The Rebs did not find us and in a short time everything became quiet again. If ever I sent an earnest praise to my God for his protection it certainly was at this time."

The next several days they made steady progress despite moving cautiously at night through rough terrain and brambles that left "scratches and blood on feet and legs." By June 15 when a few miles shy of Lamar, they risked stopping at a slave cabin, where for a greenback dollar they bought several pounds of raw cornmeal, a little corn bread, and a small piece of bacon. A party of Rebels on their trail with bloodhounds forced them to take shelter in a swamp. The next day they were aided again by slaves. After an elderly black man called out "God bless you," A. J. went over and shook his hand. On June 17, again near to starving, they paid for supper cooked by a poor white family headed by a one-legged man. The meal was wonderful despite having to stomach a "sermon" from the matriarch, who railed against them "for fighting on the wrong side and against God and Jesus Christ himself." The next day after buying more food from slaves, they ran into Federal pickets near White's Station. Glad to be back in "God's Country," the trio enjoyed a feast of beefsteak, coffee, and crackers courtesy of the Fourth Missouri Cavalry. On June 19 they rode a train into Memphis where they bade farewell to the Illinoisan, "a true friend and comrade." Reaching camp the next afternoon, the three drew the attention of a "large number of the Regiment" who "flocked around to have a look at us." They certainly were a sight: "our clothing all torn to rags (what was left of them) our bare feet and legs all sore and bleeding."

A daring escape enabled two Minnesotans to return among the last of all the Guntown refugees. In the battle Pvt. Joseph K. Gould of Company A suffered a grazed head, and Pvt. Thomas Butts, a Company G Ojibwe recruit, was hit so severely the others thought he must have died. Nevertheless, the two slogged to within twenty-five miles of Memphis before being snatched along with thirty others. The Rebels hastily marched them one hundred miles south to Grenada and confined them on the second story of a brick guard-house. Learning they were very shortly to be sent to Mobile, Gould contrived with Lt. James M. Miller, a twenty-two-year-old Iowan of the Fifty-Fifth U.S. Colored Infantry, to escape. On the night of June 23, despite the guard on their floor, "they managed to loosen two of the bars in the windows, tied a rope and quilt together, and sprang out and let themselves to the ground." Butts and three very grateful Rebel deserters followed them down. Gould and Miller lit out westward for the Mississippi River. They "received uniform kindness from negroes, during their flight," wrote Aiton. "God bless the negroes." With "little clothing" and "utterly exhausted," the two paddled a plank out onto the river nine miles above the mouth of the White River and hailed a gunboat that fetched them to Memphis on the Fourth of July. Butts reached Union lines on his own, but it is not known exactly when or where. The escape of the three deserters (who faced the death penalty), two "Yankees," and one "Yankee Indian" enraged Grenada's provost marshal. The guards, reported the local newspaper, "took their places in prison next morning but have been released since."[7]

"Rather a frightful hole" the Guntown expedition "has made in the regiment," observed Markham. Many were hospitalized, and nearly all the others required medical treatment. "It will be some time before they are fit for service." Although somewhat fewer than first feared, the final tally of casualties proved bad enough: 262 of all ranks, or 41 percent. One officer was wounded, and 9 (2 of whom were dead) did not return. Eight enlisted men died in battle, 15 sustained wounds, and 229 were missing (at least 26 of these also wounded). The Ninth Minnesota mustered just 400 men. "Shattered and broken," sympathized Colonel Marshall of the newly arrived Seventh Minnesota, "the Ninth has still done nobly in keeping the field with so many officers and men." Active campaigning reduced fighting strength very quickly when there was, as in the Federal army as a whole, no organized system for replacements.[8]

The two companies with the Otterville liberators suffered appallingly. Company C lost 2 privates killed and 1 wounded, and Captain Ford, 3 sergeants, 2 corporals, and 26 privates (including 2 wounded) missing. Thirty-six total casualties represented the most of any company in the Ninth Minnesota. Of Company C liberators, Whitney was killed; Chandler, Frisbie, and Palmeter went missing. Merchant, Bullard, Epler, Hartley, McCain, Padden,

Slocum, Stewart, Vaughan, Evan Watkins (wounded), and John Watkins reached Memphis. Merchant, who saved the main body of Company C on the Salem road, rose to acting first sergeant in place of Alonzo Avery, who was reported captured. Evan Watkins was one of five wounded of the regiment invalided out of the service. On June 10 Lieutenant Capon's Company K numbered 67 present for duty (2 officers, 5 sergeants, 6 corporals, and 54 privates). Thirty-five, including 3 wounded, eventually returned to Memphis. Lieutenant Niedenhofen, 3 sergeants, 2 corporals, and 26 privates were missing. Thus, Company K tied Company H for second place on the casualty list. One missing private died from sunstroke, and at least four others suffered wounds. Half of the Company K liberators in the battle did not return: Bader (wounded), Dietrich (wounded), Frahm (wounded), Gordon, Hilton, Morrison, Rodier, and Thielen; while Corporal Ehmke, Buck, Fenstermacher, Heilmann, Jansen, Lüthye, Mickel, and Raymond regained Memphis.[9]

CONTRASTING REPUTATIONS

The terrible toll sustained by the Ninth Minnesota reflected the catastrophic attrition inflicted on the expedition as a whole. No loss figures are completely reliable. The initial report was 2,240 (223 killed, 394 wounded, and 1,623 missing) of just under 7,900 soldiers engaged, whereas a later calculation exceeded 2,400 (at least 132 killed, 427 wounded, and 1,859 missing). Forrest claimed he captured "no less than 2,000" Yankees, but that appears high because a proportion of the missing were dead. In 1867 the army recovered the bodies of 132 unidentified soldiers killed during the Sturgis expedition and reinterred them in the Corinth National Cemetery. Aside from the horrific cost in men, Sturgis lost 16 of 22 artillery pieces, 190 wagons, 25 ambulances, hundreds of horses and mules, and nearly 5,000 small arms, as well as vast stores of ammunition and food. By contrast Confederate losses were given as 492 (96 killed and 396 wounded) in what ranks as Forrest's greatest victory. His highly aggressive nature, superb leadership, and tactical skill, along with the high quality of his troops, were the keys to his success.[10]

It was precisely how Sturgis's splendid little army of mostly Vicksburg veterans actually met its doom against the weaker foe that infuriated its survivors, who were unused to losing. Not to take anything away from Forrest, but Sturgis wrote a virtual primer on how to lose a battle. One gross blunder followed another. The rainy advance from Memphis was hesitant and uncertain. At one point Sturgis wanted to turn back, but he persisted against his better judgment and Grierson's. On the day of the battle, despite Sturgis's stated intention to keep the column closed up for mutual support, he sent the cavalry far ahead. When the horsemen encountered a strong Rebel force, instead of withdrawing them to the infantry, or at least to a more defendable position, he rushed the infantry forward at the double-quick, heedless of the brutally hot weather.

Once Sturgis personally reached the field, he did not seem even to have a plan on how to fight the battle. He failed to employ his superior artillery properly and committed the exhausted infantry piecemeal in circumstances that further restricted its firepower. Instead of keeping the cavalry nearby and ready to fight, he simply pulled them out. Much of Winslow's fine brigade was completely wasted. Other than the Ninth Minnesota, there was no immediate reserve. Despite having the whole wagon train brought so far forward as to constitute a real impediment, the cavalry and infantry both received little replacement ammunition, thereby hurting their ability to continue fighting. Once the line broke north of the crossroads, most of the foot soldiers could not be rallied. "This was the first and only time" the victors of Vicksburg "ever yielded to a panic." An officer of the Eighty-First Illinois was mortified to describe that precipitous retreat as "something like we had seen the enemy do at Champion Hill" (the May 16, 1863, Union victory that helped isolate Vicksburg). The abandonment of the artillery and the train at Hatchie Bottom was completely avoidable because of the dry detour that the most cursory scouting should have discovered. At Ripley the next morning, Sturgis failed to rally his troops, then disgracefully abandoned them. The indefatigable Forrest pursued the disorganized Yankees nearly all the way to Memphis, gobbling up hundreds of exhausted prisoners. No Union survivor ever forgot what he endured and why. Asked in 1890 what the most important event he personally experienced in the Civil War was, Capon replied, "The miserable retreat of Guntown, Miss." He made that choice despite some later personal adventures that could have been thought to overshadow the debacle of Brice's Crossroads.[11]

Leadership was the greatest problem. As Markham complained, the army "was a great, powerful body feeling the need of a head." The top leaders, with the sole exception of Wilkin, either lost control or simply ran and forsook their men. Sturgis was the first to leave the battlefield, and he and McMillen were the first to set out from Ripley for Memphis. "Everybody blames the General (Sturgis) for our failure," wrote Aiton right after the retreat. Herrick bristled that Sturgis had announced all the infantry "fell into confusion" and had been captured. "This was a base falsehood." Dean heard that "Old Sturgis is under arrest and is going to be tried for the way he handled us. I believe we were sold, for he run the train of supplies right up to the battle field." On June 15 Grierson learned that Sturgis, "being subjected to the fierce maledictions of the soldiers," had been relieved of command and, "possibly fearing bodily injury," fled Memphis. He recalled Sherman stating the "great mistake" he made was in assigning Sturgis to go after Forrest, but in fact Sherman was not entirely unhappy about Sturgis's command. For all his blundering, Sturgis had at least kept Forrest from assailing Sherman's critical supply line in Georgia. Sherman vowed that he "will have the matter of Sturgis critically examined, and, if he be at fault, he shall have no mercy at my hands." A board of investigation in Memphis elicited highly condemnatory testimony. Nonetheless, by August 24 with the capture of Atlanta imminent and still no interference from Forrest, Sherman offered excuses for Sturgis. Against a "bold and daring foe, misfortunes may befall us all, and these are rendered more likely in wood countries, with narrow roads and deep mud." Grant asserted in 1865 that Sturgis did valuable service during the war and made only the one mistake.[12]

Unemployed for the rest of the war, Sturgis reverted to his regular army rank of lieutenant colonel. In 1869 he rose to colonel of the famous Seventh U.S. Cavalry but did not lead it in the field until after the Battle of the Little Bighorn, where he lost a son. He served creditably if not spectacularly in the 1877 Nez Perce War. In 1882 Sturgis became governor of the National Soldiers Home in Washington, infuriating many Guntown veterans. In an unprecedented action, fifty former officers and five hundred ex-enlisted men who had fought at Brice's Crossroads signed a petition urging Congress to investigate his conduct there. They included several from the Ninth Minnesota. A. J. Carlson considered Sturgis either a "fool or traitor." It was the "generally expressed opinion of our boys," wrote John Allen, "that Sturgis was a traitor." John W. Jenkins of Company E, a former prisoner of war, could not decide if Sturgis was simply drunk or "sold us out to the rebels." To Noah Grant of Company G, another Rebel prison camp alumnus, Sturgis's conduct was "shameful and cowardly from beginning to end." Congress refused to act. Colonel Sturgis retired in 1886 and died three years later in St. Paul. He is buried at Arlington. "May God for the future keep such men from our army," was Grierson's epitaph. By contrast, Maj. Gen. Jacob D. Cox, who served with Sturgis during the Civil War, acknowledged that his "military downfall was a severe lesson, but he gave every evidence afterward of having learned it, and 'lived cleanly' through many years of service after the Civil War was over."[13]

If Sturgis's reputation plummeted, at least temporarily, Wilkin's rose sharply. "Everybody praises Col. Wilkin," wrote Aiton. It was "by his good management and Gods care did we weary fellows all get home." Herrick also gave Wilkin "great credit for bringing this command off with as many men as he did." Others besides the proud Minnesotans concurred. Quartermaster Owen remarked how "wounded officers, from [an] Illinois regiment, here lying in the same hospital ward in which I write, speak in highest praise of our Colonel's courage, practical energy and untiring exertions in getting the men together, and staying by them after they were together until they were safe in Memphis." Surgeon Stacey Hemenway of the Ninth Illinois Cavalry stressed it was "principally by [Wilkin's] courage, skill and bravery our command was saved from being entirely annihilated." To the 114th Illinois, Wilkin was simply "the little fellow who stayed with the infantry on the retreat from Guntown." On June 24 Wilkin noted to his father, "I have never had such a reputation since I have entered the service as I have now. Everyone here knows me & my conduct in the battle and particularly my conduct of the retreat is highly spoken of." The "privates in particular think a great deal of me. I have been amused to overhear some of them talk about me and my size."[14]

The whole Ninth Minnesota briefly basked in unaccustomed glory. "A source of great satisfaction to us," wrote Markham, is that "we are complimented publicly and privately by every one who saw us under fire. 'Hurrah for the true Minnesota Boys.' 'You saved us all at Gunn Town, &c.,' is what we hear every day." Wilkin, too, was very proud of his regiment. "Everybody talks of [the Ninth Minnesota's] conduct. Lt. Col. Marsh managed it admirably & was perfectly cool under fire. Not an officer was killed or wounded [on the firing line]. They were so well disciplined[,] fought in such good order & obeyed orders so well that the officers did not have to expose themselves to the sharpshooters, to keep them in order & get the Regiment through." Wilkin noted that before the battle the men thought he had "been too particular about little things & too strict," but "they now see the advantages of it." Hearing of the praise in McMillen's report, Minnesota Governor Stephen Miller was "gratified to learn that the reputation of the regiment is so firmly established" in the Union army. The Ninth Minnesota truly fought well despite the devastating defeat, but ultimately it was of limited consolation, like hitting three home runs in a game your team lost twenty to six.[15]

CHAPTER ELEVEN

Lost in the Confederacy

THE GREAT ROUNDUP

While the Ninth Minnesota licked its wounds in Memphis and prepared to fight again, 7 officers and 228 enlisted men fell into Rebel hands. Just the year before at Vicksburg, General Grant had accepted the parole of 30,000 Confederates who were told simply to go home and await news that they had been formally exchanged for Union prisoners before returning to the fight. By 1864 the war had entered a new and far less tolerant phase regarding prisoners.

Confederate forces pursued the demoralized Federals almost sixty miles, and opportunistic bushwhackers harassed them nearly all the rest of way to Memphis. "The whole route was strewed with arms, cartridge boxes, bayonets, sabers, their dead and live Yankees," wrote one Rebel shortly after the battle. "The truth beggars any description." Working southeast from Salem back to Ripley through "ridgey, broken country," Lieutenant Witherspoon hugely enjoyed the "big sport" of trolling "up and down the hollows" for Union stragglers. "We scattered in small bodies on both sides of the road, just exactly as we would have done had we been hunting rabbits in deep snow time." Forlorn Yankees appeared "in squads ranging from a half a dozen to twenty or more. Up would go their hands, exclaiming, 'We surrender!'" Most of the "foot-sore, tired and hungry" bluecoats "had thrown away not only their arms, but their haversacks, clothing and blankets." The hunting of fugitive Federals proved great fun not only for Forrest's enthusiastic troopers. "The upper counties of Mississippi were for days traversed by the stragglers from Sturgis' command," recalled Maj. Gen. Dabney H. Maury in Mobile, "many of whom were captured by Confederate soldiers who happened to be at their homes on furlough from their commands, and by the old men and youths exempt from service because of age; and even by that noble class of able-bodied Southern men who claimed exemption under the twenty-Negro bill, but who could sometimes do valiant service on a thoroughly routed and panicked enemy." Spurring the frenzy were scurrilous rumors of rapes and other atrocities supposedly committed by black soldiers to avenge Fort Pillow.[1]

On June 11 alone the Confederates nabbed at least five hundred prisoners along the Salem road. Resting in the woods near Little Tippah Creek, Sergeant Major Clapp and a comrade abruptly awoke late that afternoon to the sight of a Rebel "sitting on a mule with a two-barrel shot-gun demanding us to rise." In a letter Clapp knew would be censored, he related how his captor "spoke very kindly" and that he had "received the best of treatment since." A pamphlet he published soon after returning home told a very different story. "Instead of receiving the respect and sympathy due him as a brave soldier, even from the hands of the victors themselves, [the prisoner] is treated like a traveler who is waylaid; almost the first thing he hears is a demand for his watch, money, rings, or any jewelry he may have about him." The captors even "take the Photographs of friends, and of his family, and tear them up before his eyes." George Jenkins of Company K fully concurred. "The prisoners were all robbed of their money, watches and article of clothing the rebels happened to fancy." Captured the next day, 1st Sgt. John E. Warren of the Seventh Wisconsin Light Artillery took the whole experience more philosophically. Briefly a Rebel prisoner in 1863, he understood his "valuables" were automatically forfeit. The Rebels "didn't have horns," and "we were while with them as well treated as we could expect to be under the circumstances."[2]

In his refuge near North Tippah Creek, Frank Lyon awoke alone after dark on June 11 realizing he must effect his "own salvation," a task he "proceeded to do with fear and trembling." First he hacked off his mud-caked trouser legs. "I soon found I was cutting too high, so I cut down a way, then up and then down, until the circle was completed. I proceeded with the other in like manner, with about the same result. When I looked at those legs in the morning, I smiled, and I think you would have smiled too. But the load was gone and I could travel better." That night, after fumbling several miles in the dark, Lyon encountered a lone horse tied to a tree. He leapt on its back, but the animal would not move. Suddenly he heard "Who's dat?" and the click of a rifle being cocked, so he shouted, "I surrender!" His captors graciously allowed him to roll himself in his blanket with a saddle as pillow to sleep comfortably. At daylight he woke to find three others from Company C in the same fix. The Rebels took his rubber blanket, four dollars, and all personal effects except his testament. "I showed that to the head man and said to him, 'I suppose you will let me keep this.' 'Yes,' he said, 'if you will read it.'" Someone switched the fine broad-brimmed slouch hat that had cost him two dollars in St. Louis for another "that wasn't worth ten cents." It was a "quick trade and no talking back, but I thought some things." Another Rebel eyed the excellent boots that Lyon's father had made, but the mud hid their quality. Lyon turned them into much-needed cash in prison.[3]

After giving out on the afternoon of June 11, brothers-in-law Chauncey Hill and Joseph Harvey encountered a black soldier who exclaimed, "I'm mighty glad to see you gemmen." The three cautiously worked their way west until nightfall and then rested near a creek. At dawn on the twelfth, they attempted to cross the Salem road but had to hide from a Rebel scout. While trying to get clear, they discovered concealed in the brush seven Union soldiers who waved them over. From the road came the shout "Halt!" and a pair of "well armed Kentuckians rode quickly up." The unarmed Yankees all surrendered. "Our captors were quite kind and gentlemanly to us, not offering to rob us of anything, which I afterwards appreciated still more." Back on the road, "we marched on as cheerfully as we could under the circumstances, being foot sore, tired and hungry."[4]

On that rainy morning of June 12, guards started several batches of prisoners southeast toward Ripley. After trudging six miles, Lyon's small party overtook about five hundred fellow unfortunates. "Almost the first man I met that I recognized was my captain [Edwin Ford]," a "dejected looking object." In place of "his fine uniform of the day before, he had on an old ragged suit, such as worn by privates, an old hat and he was barefoot." Lyon sympathetically offered Ford his "good woolen socks," which he gratefully accepted. "So I pulled off my boots and gave him my socks and put on my boots without them. He marched beside me all that day in his stocking feet. For once I outranked the captain." The prisoners "made quite an imposing spectacle," Lyon observed, "that is we felt quite imposed on to say the least." Hill remembered "four of our men, stiff and ghastly, shot, all of them I think, through the head. How have I been kept through all these dangers. I have not been touched. How good is God to me." At Ripley the column halted hoping to be fed, but they were greatly disappointed to learn no food was to be had short of the abandoned wagon train at Hatchie Bottom sixteen miles away. In town Lyon was fascinated to see Forrest, "who impressed me as being a very bright officer. If he had been on our side, I think I should have been quite proud of him."[5]

The Rebels set up Dr. Dixon in a makeshift hospital on the first floor of the scorched Ripley courthouse, a "little dinkey building" that was a "verry dirtey place." Among the fifty wounded were eleven from the Ninth Minnesota, including liberator Jacob Bader, shot in the knee. The good citizens of Ripley doted on Dixon's patients, pouring in "more delicacies and comforts to the wounded than were needed." To the joy of an orderly, Pvt. Rollin W. Drake of the Seventh Indiana Cavalry, the "guards generously allowed those who had assisted the wounded to have a square meal out of the food sent in by the citizens." The other able-bodied prisoners were not fed or were given only a little to eat. The customary search cost Drake his "lead pencils, memorandum book & fine tooth comb." The Rebels left his "pocket Bible, which they had no use for," but missed a "good pocket knife" hidden in his hair. At some point Dixon lost a treasured heirloom to a plunderer. Years later Solomon N. Brantley, a former private in the Seventh Tennessee Cavalry, recalled being "detailed to guard the Federal doctor we captured. I know he had a very fine gold watch which I could have taken but wouldent do it and if he is still living I would like for him to write to me as I know he recollects the incident that happened to him later on. I never robbed a prisoner under no circumstances as I never thought it was right."[6]

Drake and perhaps 150 captives swelled the main column of prisoners at Ripley to 650, over half just from the Seventy-Second Ohio and Ninth Minnesota. Among the nearly 150 forlorn Minnesotans were Ford and four other officers; Clapp and father-son musicians Joel and DeWitt Handy; Lyon, Peace Democrat James Woodbury (with a minor head wound), Orsamus Rhoades (the hardy Mower County pioneer), and liberator Stephen Chandler from Company C; Jacob Dieter from Company F; and Hill, Harvey, Martin Shortt (the reluctant Saratoga recruit), and liberators Charles Dietrich (wounded), Peter Rodier, and Jacob Thielen of Company K.

That rainy evening the prisoners glumly trudged four miles southeast on the Fulton road and slept where they had camped under such different circumstances four nights before. "We started hungry for Guntown the next morning [June 13], discouraged almost to death," remembered Pvt. Jacob F. Hutchinson of the Seventy-Second Ohio. The route to Brice's Crossroads was a Yankee Via Dolorosa. "Never shall I forget that march," wrote Lyon. "The road was strewn the whole length with guns, sabres, clothing of all kinds, broken wagons, dead mules, horses and men—everything that belongs to and goes with an army." Walking the "tiresome dusty 'mud pike,'" Drake too recalled being "heartsick and sore." At the gate of a "rather pretentious mansion," a matron, "dressed very like a lady of wealth and refinement," mocked the prisoners. "Why didn't you 'rally round the flag' boys, why didn't you rally round the flag?" She could not, she taunted, distinguish between white and black Yankees. "The burned powder and dust together with the excessive heat had bronzed us considerably," Drake admitted, but not nearly as much as later in prison. Hill, who sprained his left foot, had an easier time. "There

W. Franklin Lyon, January 1864

being no conveyance I must walk, but at last I gave out and was left by the road, Joseph [Harvey] being sent on. After a rest I got in with a Kentuckian who had left his horse and we were well matched, he not walking fast."[7]

Approaching dreaded Hatchie Bottom, the Union prisoners were shocked to be led over the short detour to the west that completely avoided the morass. To Lieutenant Wheaton of the Fifty-Ninth U.S. Colored Infantry, that alone testified to the "wretched incompetency if not down right treachery of Gen'l Sturgis." Beyond the slough each prisoner received two hardtack crackers from the abandoned wagons. The famished men devoured biscuits turned "sour" by dampness. A small field hospital tended twenty or more Union wounded who had survived being left behind at Hatchie. "Experienced the kindest treatment from the rebels in charge of us," wrote Melville Robertson of the Ninety-Third Indiana, one of the medical orderlies.[8]

Near Dr. Agnew's farm were the first actual signs of battle. On June 12 Agnew's slaves started burying black soldiers who had fallen around the house, but completed few graves in the heavy rain. That evening the guards provided four Union prisoners, including one Minnesotan, to help deal with the Federal dead. Dr. Agnew's son Samuel, a clergyman, wrote in his diary that the prisoners were "down upon their officers, saying that in a fight they are always in the rear, and on a retreat at the front." He noted the "Yankees are buried shallow, the negroes especially so." Slaves and prisoners interred more dead on June 13, but the scene remained horrific. Sergeant William B. Woolverton of the Seventy-Second Ohio deplored that bodies of black soldiers left lying in the road had been "horribly mangled by the heavy artillery wagons" after no one had "the decency to remove them or turn their teams an inch from their course to avoid a body." Reverend Agnew chatted with prisoners, including Minnesotans, who filed past his gate. "It is impossible to find one that ever acknowledged that he ever plundered. One remarked as he came up here's the man that caught your Turkeys. Another was heard to say here's the place we got the wine." Others eagerly recounted the battle. "The prisoners pointed out their positions here. One was in the yard, one in the road, another in the woods & one pointed to a tree and said I shot at a big fat rebel from behind that tree."[9]

At Brice's Crossroads about two hundred Union prisoners were penned in a yard. The day after the battle, their guards "called for volunteers from us to bury our dead," wrote Pvt. Alfred Nash of the Ninety-Fifth Illinois. "Although we were almost worn out, this we cheerfully did, and saw that our more unfortunate comrades were decently interred in the rude trench we dug for that purpose." The mass grave was sited northwest of the Bethany Church graveyard on the west side of the Wire Road. Very likely the anonymous dead there included liberator Augustus Whitney, Sergeant Holtsclaw killed on June 10, Dominick Mompher of Company K who had died the next day from sunstroke, and Hiram Brooks of Company F who had succumbed on the twelfth to his abdominal wound. The dead buried near the church were among those, all unknown, moved in 1867 to the Corinth National Cemetery. In the meantime, Holtsclaw's wife, Jane, had placed a tombstone for him in the local cemetery in Nicollet County and inscribed it according to Mary Magdalene's words in John 20:13: "And I know not where they have laid him."[10]

On the afternoon of June 13, the guards added the 200 prisoners already at Brice's Crossroads to those who had come down from Ripley, increasing the column to 850 men. The doleful caravan proceeded to Guntown, five miles southeast on the Mobile & Ohio Railroad, where at sundown the authorities registered the prisoners and issued "Secesh hardtack & bacon." Afterward the men were crammed into dirty boxcars. John Bartleson of the Eighty-First Illinois counted eighty-two occupants in his car, which was "tight and hot, no space for air." A profane Irish bully forced him to battle for enough room to sit. The train departed at 10 P.M. "What our destination was we did not know," recalled Lyon, "and [we] didn't care much if they would only let us rest." For Bartleson it was the "most miserable night of my whole life."[11]

Hill and his amiable escort reached Brice's Crossroads at nightfall, too late to continue to Guntown. Instead he was detailed to the Brice house, which served as a Confederate hospital. Also under care there were about thirty Yankees with "wounds generally severe, several with legs taken off." The only two from the Ninth Minnesota were Company K liberator George Frahm, with wounds in chest and hand, and Godfrey Hammerberg of Company H, with "a terrible looking wound." A bullet had pierced his face beneath the left eye and exited under the right ear. To Hill's astonishment Hammerberg "seemed to be smart and free from pain, walking around, talking and eating." On June 11 Hammerberg had made the same deep impression on some prisoners from Company H who did a double take when they saw him "sitting on a porch of a farmhouse eating a piece of pie a short distance from where he was left for dead the day before." Badly riddled Bethany Church, where liberator John Gordon of Company K was an orderly, sheltered the other Federal wounded. Gordon had gone lame the evening of June 10 and was taken the next day.[12]

Robertson and some of the Federal wounded from Hatchie Bottom reached Brice's Crossroads on the evening of the thirteenth. He found "sixty men here suffering wounds in almost every part of the body." The charity of local women in providing "delicacies for our wounded" greatly impressed him. "God bless them for their kindness to our poor boys." Fortunately for the wounded of both sides, the Rebels had recovered a superbly stocked medicine wagon on the battlefield, very likely the one Surgeon Bingham lost near Tishomingo Creek. Robertson and Reverend Agnew observed a Confederate surgeon remove the right foot and part of the left hand of one of the Northerners, who mercifully lay "insensible being under the influence of Chloroform." Agnew "felt sorry when I looked on the poor fellows, dieing so far from the dear ones at home."[13]

Hill worked nearly all night tending Union wounded and helped bring more injured men from a "cotton house" near the battlefield. On the morning of June 14, he "got a tolerable breakfast, crackers, fried meat and coffee." Another large batch of about 275 prisoners, taken mostly on June 12 on the Salem road, passed through bound for Guntown. Among perhaps 35 from the Ninth Minnesota was liberator Zara Frisbie of Company C. Hill and some of the others joined them. "As my name was not put in the nurse-list, I got away with our boys and left the scene of woe. I think several of the men will die of exposure and neglect but their condition was improved at time of leaving." That evening after being fed at Guntown, 311 prisoners crowded into boxcars. Hill gladly clambered onto the roof, where he enjoyed "a fine view of the country" on the ride south.[14]

JOURNEYING TO REBEL PRISONS

The captives of the Ninth Minnesota had only a hazy understanding of what might befall them in Rebel hands. Hill expected to be sent to an "exchange camp," as did most of the others. The prisoners, Chaplain Kerr wrote to Minnesota, "in due course will find their way home by exchange or otherwise." Indeed, for much of the war each side swiftly traded its captives for those held in enemy hands. Once paroled, the ex-prisoners were not supposed to be mobilized for military duty until declared exchanged according to a set formula by rank—so many privates for a colonel, and so forth. Thus, in July 1862 Forrest had immediately paroled the enlisted men of the Third Minnesota captured at Murfreesboro. They were sent home to Minnesota and fought in the U.S.–Dakota War. Their officers were released some months later. The process worked reasonably well, resulting in relatively short stays in prison camps.[15]

In the summer of 1863, however, the whole system broke down primarily for two reasons: a dispute over the status of the 30,000 prisoners whom Grant had immediately paroled after the fall of Vicksburg and the introduction of black soldiers into the Union ranks. The South branded the white officers of black regiments as renegades who incited slave revolt and therefore deserved summary execution. The black soldiers they simply regarded as recaptured slaves rather than legal combatants. Except in a very few instances, the impasse halted all prisoner exchanges, with tragic implications for many thousands on both sides. One consequence in particular was that Union prisoners began overfilling the prisons in Virginia, such as Libby and Belle Isle, and consumed resources far beyond the limit of what the Confederate government thought necessary or moral to devote to their care. A society that was hard-pressed to feed its own soldiers had little incentive to provide food and care for enemy prisoners. As a result there was rampant starvation, disease, and death in Southern prisoner-of-war camps. New camps constructed in more remote areas of the South were supposed to relieve the congestion. One such prison was Camp Sumter, located at tiny Andersonville in southwestern Georgia, where most of those captured at Brice's Crossroads were being sent.[16]

The train from Guntown carrying the lead group of 850 Union prisoners chugged south all night. After sunrise on June 14, the men saw lush rows of corn plants stretching out to the horizon and huge "fields of ripe wheat being harvested by slaves" in Mississippi's treasured grain belt. That morning at a stop at Okolona, prisoners bought copies of Mobile newspapers and shared the good news that not only were the Union armies still advancing in Virginia and Georgia, but the Republicans had again nominated Lincoln for president.[17]

Early on June 15, the train finally rolled into Meridian, 160 miles south of Guntown. Set in a deep pine forest, the village was an important rail hub from which lateral lines snaked westward to Jackson and Vicksburg and eastward into Alabama. Wrecked engines, burned cars, and newly rebuilt buildings were reminders of Sherman's devastating visit in February 1864. Under the baleful glare of Lt. John J. Fitzpatrick, the hard-bitten "transplanted Yankee" provost marshal of Meridian, the tired and sore prisoners rested in an open field, happily under fair skies. While being put into cattle pens, another infamous pat-down "robbed" them of most of their remaining "rubber blankets, haversacks, canteens, cups and knives and forks." The only way to save their goods from pillage was "to secrete them from their crafty searchers." The bedraggled Yankees (called "Forrest's Pets") were, according to the Meridian *Daily Clarion,* "about as motley a set of human beings as we ever saw." To one onlooker, "three-fourths of them at least [have] the scoundrel plainly stamped on their face."[18]

That afternoon, after Fitzpatrick promised to forward letters by truce to Vicksburg, prisoners wrote to hometown newspapers or to their comrades in Memphis the names of their fellow captives. Clapp estimated about 150 men of the Ninth Minnesota were in Meridian, with more "expected today." He listed Ford and 18 others from Company C and the detainees of Company F, which hailed from his hometown, Rochester. Private Charles Newton, a forty-six-year-old farmer and former county clerk, set down on the "very coarsest brown note paper" for the *Winona Republican* the names of 17 comrades of Company K and related what little was known of a few of the others. Some prisoners also wrote loved ones. "We fought for about four miles and the enemy being too much we were obliged to retreat . . . about thirty-five miles before we were captured," Stephen Chandler, a twenty-four-year-old Canadian-born liberator from Austin in Mower County, informed his wife, Abigail. "We had quite a bunch that was killed out of our Co. C." He, too, identified those captured with him. "Dear Wife, You must not worry and frett on my account for I trust we will come out all right and I have not arrived to our destination yet [and do not know where] it will be." Chandler promised to write when he finally reached there. "Good bye, I love you dearly, From your loving husband."[19]

Around 5 P.M. the second prison train from Guntown, bearing Hill and his companions, chuffed up to the pens at Meridian and stopped briefly before continuing south. The two groups of prisoners shouted greetings across to each other. Near sundown on June 15, the captives who remained at Meridian were issued a pound of cornmeal per man, along with kettles and pans. The mood in the enclosure lightened. Some sang while eager guards offered to buy "watches, knives, hats of the boys and paying in Secesh money." In turn some prisoners forked over $1.50 in Confederate money for small cakes that Sgt. Harkness Lay of the Seventy-Second Ohio valued at only five Federal cents.[20]

Before dawn on June 16, as the closely packed prisoners at Meridian rose for breakfast, a Rebel guard accidentally shot and killed one soldier of the Seventy-Second Ohio and wounded two others. Suddenly sobered, the men drew more corn bread and boarded boxcars. By sunrise they were rolling eastward into Alabama through a "damed rough country," according to Lay. "One minute we would be riding as high as the tree tops the next minute in total darkness in some deep cuts." No bridge existed over the wide Tombigbee River. At McDowell's Bluff, forty-six miles from Meridian, the prisoners embarked on a "wheezy old steamboat" filled with corn that they unloaded at Demopolis, five miles upriver, before boarding more rail cars. Warren, the Wisconsin artillery sergeant, joked how "all the devious windings and turnings" looked "like an attempt to lose us in the Confederacy." At sundown, after riding fifty miles, the prisoners reached Selma, "a nice town" situated in "level, sandy country." The *Selma Daily Reporter* likewise took note of the "wretched creatures" who were "dirty, illy clad and very miserable in appearance." Lay wondered why Selma's inhabitants "acted as though they had never seen a live Yankee before." Indeed, a substantial crowd, fired up by the rumors of atrocities in Mississippi, jeered the transients, who according to an outraged Clapp suffered the taunts of those "cowardly puppies" in "silent disgust." After an elderly citizen shouted "Look at the poor devils, I could lick any six of 'em," Lyon particularly enjoyed one guard's response. "Old man, if you think you can lick six of 'em, you'd better take your gun and go to the front. You'll soon find out how many you can lick."[21]

By midnight on June 17, the prisoners, jammed on board the steamboat *Comedfar,* started up the winding Alabama River. It took all day to traverse the eighty miles to Montgomery, the first capital of the Confederacy. That boat ride, recalled Corporal Medkirk of the Seventy-Second Ohio, offered the "first experience in what we were to endure for want of food." He and his fellow prisoners "stood around the roustabouts while at their meals and eyed their food like famished wolves, and every scrap they would cast away was scrambled for." The captives slept on the Montgomery levee until dawn on June 18, when they received their first ration since leaving Meridian, two pieces of hardtack per man. One of Medkirk's friends "would draw a ration, hand it to me, slip into some other part of the line and draw again. He repeated that several times and by that means we had quite a supply." Later in prison camp, they learned that common practice was known as "flanking."[22]

Loaded onto a train of the Montgomery & West Point Railroad, the men lurched eastward in the rain through a "poor and hard country" to Columbus, Georgia, eighty-eight miles away. There Medkirk "spent the most miserable night of my existence. We were corralled, as the rebels called it, on a commons in the city, without food or shelter. It rained torrents the entire night." At daylight on Sunday, June 19, with rain still falling, the prisoners crowded into open cars for the fifty-mile trip east to Butler. The right of way passed through what Harkness Lay called "the damdest poorest country I ever did see," nothing but patches of blackberries and wild cherries. The locomotive, wrote Rollin Drake, suffered from "asthmatic breathing and frequent coughing spells." To the cheers of the "boys" who got off to lighten the cars, the engine faltered on steep grades and had to reverse to "get a head of steam & nobly try it again." Its "rate of speed would decrease, the wheels revolve slower and still more slowly until in sheer desperation, it seemed at our taunts and jeers, by one supreme effort it would gain the summit and go down the other side much more easily." During halts, the prisoners eagerly gathered tasty berries. At Butler they switched to the South Western Railroad, whose equipment functioned much more smoothly. Making good time, they reached Fort Valley, twenty miles east, and that afternoon rode the southbound route thirty-two miles through "an interminable forest of pine trees" to Anderson Station, or Andersonville, a small settlement ten miles north of Americus. At the depot the guards separated the men from their officers, who were to be taken to the special prison eighty-eight miles northeast at Macon. Ford, "with tears streaming down his cheeks," recalled Lyon, grasped each of the eighteen members of Company C "by the hand and we said farewell."[23]

The second large shipment of 311 Union prisoners had, as noted, briefly stopped at Meridian on June 15 before going on to Mobile, 135 miles south. Among their number were roughly 35 from the Ninth Minnesota, including liberator Frisbie, as well as Hill and Lieutenant Niedenhofen, captured late on June 11 near Salem. Niedenhofen had befriended a severely wounded fellow *Deutschsprecher*, Lt. Sigmond von Braida, an Austrian count in the Second New Jersey Cavalry. The Rebels had thrown the captives into a "filthy cow-yard," without "overcoats and blankets—or any other means of shelter

Routes to Andersonville and Cahaba

from the rain." Niedenhofen "begged" the officer commanding the guard for a blanket to cover von Braida, but the "chivalrous son of Kentucky replied only with a volley of curses and a blow from his sword." Not long after the war, Niedenhofen accosted the same officer in a St. Louis hotel. Stating the ex-Rebel's name and rank, he "asked him to take a drink." After denying he knew Niedenhofen, the Kentuckian "with a blush of shame acknowledged his wrong and begged forgiveness." Niedenhofen "told him frankly that he harbored no feeling of malice against him, and the two men shook hands in token of reconciliation." Even so, "some of Mr. Niedenhofen's friends were indignant at his letting his persecutor escape so easily, but Charley always insists that he punished him more severely by thus heaping the fires of forgiveness on his head than he would have done by knocking him down."[24]

The country south of Meridian was "poor, low and piney; streams sluggish and dirty and land little used," but the "trees having gray moss of the south hanging to their branches" fascinated Hill. In particular the magnolia's "dark glossy leaves and white blossoms looked strange to our northern eyes." After "much restlessness and grumbling," the prisoners finally rolled on June 16 into Mobile, on the Gulf of Mexico. "The country is low and uninviting and even the suburbs of the town were covered with brush and water." The men delightedly moved into a comfortable "old warehouse" and wolfed down "a supper of corn bread, meat and molasses." As usual the dejected Yankees, largely "shoeless and ragged," proved an irresistible object of curiosity. "After floundering through the swamps until their shoes and pantaloons were loaded with mud," a Rebel guard explained to the *Mobile Evening News,* "the [Yankees] threw away the former and cut off their trowsers legs half way up to the knees, to facilitate their running, which it did; for thus lightened of their extra weight they ran into the net that Forrest had applied to their rear."[25]

At Mobile the seventeenth proved a welcome quiet day. "It is with something of pleasure & also something of pain I pencil these lines," Hill wrote his wife, Sarah. "It is a pleasure to find myself still in health & looking forward with a cheerful hopefulness to the time when I can once more see the faces of dear ones at home. It is painful to know that I am farther than ever before from those dear ones knowing they are in anxious suspense longing for tidings of the missing. However I am here healthy & hopeful. God has mercifully spared me in the hour of battle[,] sustained me in all trials, & I am in the hands of those who have treated me with kindness & care." Noting that the weather was "very warm for us" and that "we get enough to eat & dry quarters," he expected to leave soon for the "exchange camp" near Americus, Georgia. "Dear Wife, let us trust in the God of all truth & justice. He only knows what is for our best good. He orders the affairs of this world; let us have faith in him. I trust, hope & pray that we may soon meet forth with, but if not given His pleasure, let us hope & pray that we may have happier meeting in heaven."[26]

On June 18 the Mobile prisoners each drew six hardtack and a pound of meat—food intended to last five days—and that afternoon rode a packet across Mobile Bay. The vessel ascended the Tensas River 22 miles to Tensas Station, terminus of the grandly named but short of length Mobile & Great Northern Railroad. Fifty miles northeast at Pollard, the prisoners switched to the cars of the Alabama & Florida Railroad for the final leg of 114 miles to Montgomery. Riding all night was "tedious," but Montgomery proved surprisingly "fine and pleasant, shady and well built." The weather did not cooperate. After receiving more food, the men left the next day in the rain following the same route taken by the first shipment. The boxcars were "wet and dirty and our surroundings bad enough as we sped on toward Columbus," wrote Hill. The captives spent the night there outside in the rain. The next morning they boarded flatcars and so enjoyed "a better view of the country." Hill was surprised to see "corn and small grain" under cultivation instead of cotton. The ubiquitous blackberries "looked very tempting," but he did not get to pick any. On June 21, after changing locomotives at Butler, the train proceeded "at a spanking rate" to Andersonville. Once again, the officers were culled out, and 282 luckless enlisted men went into the stockade.[27]

Niedenhofen's group reached Macon on June 22 and entered Camp Oglethorpe, the officer prison. For some reason the larger party that included Ford, Hall, Lane, McCain, and Tiffany did not get there until the next day. After leaving Andersonville on the nineteenth, they were kept on their train for three days without rations other than what little they could buy from guards. The poverty and ragged condition of all the Guntown "fresh fish" (as newcomers to any Civil War prison were inevitably called) made a strong impression on their fellow Macon inmates. One wrote how the new arrivals "had been robbed of every thing, clothing, money, watches, rings, diaries, and even the photographs of their friends at home, and, not content with robbing them *once*, every time they changed hands they were plundered again. They were destitute indeed, yet were cheerful-looking and only asked to be exchanged that they might settle up their accounts with the villains who had thus treated them."[28]

Camp Oglethorpe comprised a three-acre compound built around an old building that once served as the floral hall in the state fairgrounds. Life was tolerable if not particularly pleasant. A stream and three wells supplied sufficient good water not only for drinking but for cooking and washing. The grounds were cleaned every morning. Rations consisted of "cornmeal, some rice, beans, bacon, molasses, vinegar & salt," but the quantity was "not more than half enough" for those who lacked funds to buy additional food from sutlers. The newcomers were allowed to go outside under guard and secure wood to construct their own sheds. "It may interest some to know how we killed time during our dreary captivity," wrote Lt. Zelotes Perin of the Seventy-Second Ohio. "Some had obtained French and German books and were studying these languages; others had made some rough wooden swords and were learning fencing from the German officers, and many of the Eastern officers having procured a large ball indulged in a game of wicket-ball, and the more despondent prisoners would do nothing but lay around and talk of our hopelessness and bemoan the (to them) probable failure of our army to crush the rebellion."[29]

Two more shipments with 210 doleful "Sturgis raiders" took the same route as the lead group: Meridian, Demopolis, Selma, Montgomery, Columbus, Fort Valley, Andersonville. Among the third batch of 100 men were perhaps 10 from the Ninth Minnesota, including Company C liberator Nathan Palmeter, captured on June 13 near Salem, and 2 privates from Company B, William R. Lovell and William B. Atwater. Lovell, an eighteen-year-old farmer from England, tended Atwater's wound during the retreat. They were befriended by the family of a Confederate colonel who made their captors give back their money, Lovell's knife, and their photographs. Enjoying an easier trip than the first contingent—even a ride in a passenger train—they arrived at Andersonville on the twenty-fifth.[30]

Traveling a day behind the third convoy, the remaining 110 prisoners reached Andersonville on the twenty-sixth and were the last large transport of "Sturgis men" sent there. It is likely that 10 hailed from the Ninth Minnesota. John M. Kerlinger of Company I, a thirty-six-year-old corporal from Shakopee, had faltered on the harsh double-quick march and missed the battle, but he evaded the Rebels for a whole week. When one prisoner weakened on the trek to Guntown, Kerlinger heard a Rebel captain tell a guard to "take him to one side and take care of him. The guard, however, did not obey the brutal suggestion." Myron Tower of Company K had been shot in the left thigh and ankle during the rear-guard fighting. Crawling into the brush, he broke up his firearm, buried the parts, and subsisted six days on rainwater. The Rebels found him on June 16 only "partially conscious" and "more dead than alive."[31]

Another from Company K in the same transport to Andersonville was Tower's Saratoga neighbor, liberator John Morrison, a thirty-three-year-old farmer from Paisley, Scotland. Morrison would have missed the Guntown expedition had his thirty-day furlough been granted only a few days later than April 26, for upon his return from Minnesota, the regiment was already in St. Louis. Even so, he nearly got away, being one of the last liberators captured. By the end of July 1864, his family had still not received any word from or of him. His half-brother, James Strachan, who served in the Fifth Iowa Cavalry, had looked into the situation as best he could from Nashville. On August 3 he wrote their parents that he was "very sorry that you had not received any word from John yet, as I had expected that you would have heard from him by this time. I cannot bring my mind to think that he has either been killed or wounded, for if he had he would have been recognized by some of the Regiment. I have therefore come to the conclusion that he must be a prisoner, and am in hopes that he will turn up all right in good time."[32]

It took considerably longer for the Federal wounded to reach their ultimate destination within the Confederate prison system. On June 15 Surgeon Dixon and some forty hurt prisoners (eleven Minnesotans) weathered a rough wagon ride from Ripley to Guntown, where they joined another hundred injured collected from around Brice's Crossroads. Dixon advised his superiors in a letter passed by truce through the lines that the wounded "are comfortable, and that Gen. Forrest had promised to release him in a few days." That promise would not be honored, but it was not Forrest's fault. The wounded, laid on straw in boxcars, went south in two groups. In the middle of the night, the train carrying the first batch derailed, overturning two of the six boxcars packed with wounded. The cars careened down an embankment, causing further injuries and even a few deaths. It is not known if any Minnesotans were affected. The second group had a much easier time but still endured over forty hours in miserable circumstances on board their train. By June 19 nearly all the surviving Union wounded, 136 in Dixon's care and their orderlies, had reassembled at Mobile. Fifteen were Minnesotans, including Bader and Frahm, with Gordon and Pvt. Pliny Conkey of Company C (wounded at Brice's Crossroads) as orderlies.[33]

The Garner House, an old hotel facing Mobile Bay, served as temporary hospital and prison. After being cleaned up in the "wash house," the Yankee wounded were "arrayed" either "in C.S.A. shirts and drawers" or "rigged out in calico shirts." Thus "made presentable," they were introduced to the Mobile citizenry who were "clamoring to get in and see the Yanks." For two to three hours, recalled Pvt. Ira F. Collins of the 114th Illinois, a multitude of people of all ages and sexes "inspected each wounded prisoner with about the same curiosity that a crowd has for the animals in a circus tent." Confederate surgeons assessed more than fifty of the captives as "permanently disabled from wounds." General Maury sought permission on June 29 to send them through Union lines, but Richmond obstinately refused. The Yankees must be formally exchanged at Vicksburg if the Federal authorities allowed it or otherwise kept in confinement. The North remained equally adamant against general exchanges unless the Confederates relented in their harsh policy regarding captured black soldiers.[34]

The new quarters proved inadequate for the needs of all of Dixon's charges. On July 1 about seventy wounded were transferred a short distance to the Mobile General Hospital, the former U.S. Marine Hospital. It was a "pleasant place," wrote Robertson, one of the orderlies, with the "benefit of a strong breeze from the bay nearly all the time during the day." Bader's wounded knee became infected, forcing Dixon to amputate the leg. Gangrene set in, and he died on the Fourth of July. Born in Wurttemberg, Germany, about 1844, he came to the United States while still very young. By 1860 his father John farmed in Houston County in the extreme southeastern portion of the state. The second liberator to die, Jacob Bader was the first to succumb in captivity.[35]

On July 16 Dixon, much against his will, had to leave his patients once the Rebels at Mobile judged his services were no longer necessary. Incensed at being treated like a prisoner of war instead of released as a noncombatant, he was remanded to the officers' prison at Macon. Robertson remarked in his diary that "most patients are fast recovering, will probably be sent to camp." An idyllic interlude quickly neared its end. "The majority of our patients are now able to be up most of the time," he wrote on July 24, "and we are inclined to be the most sociable crowd imaginable. The confederacy is most shamefully ridiculed at times." On the last day of July, the authorities dispatched thirteen recovered wounded (including Frahm) and three medical orderlies (including Gordon and Conkey) to the "prison camp in Georgia." The situation at Mobile grew perilous on August 5 when Rear Adm. David Farragut stormed past the outer forts to win a great naval victory in Mobile Bay. Three days later the Confederate command, anxious to be rid of the prisoners at Mobile, placed them on board the steamer *Ariel* for a trip up the Alabama River. The shipment comprised the last of the Guntown wounded, nearly 100 men (13 from the Ninth Minnesota) and 7 orderlies, including Robertson. Many of the wounded were "nearly well." Three days later the party fetched up at Cahaba prison, ten miles south of Selma, where they discovered about 150 comrades from the Sturgis expedition who had been there since late June. Five were from the Ninth Minnesota, including the youngest liberator, Pvt. Allen Hilton of Company K. They were fortunate, for the most part, to have been captured too far north or too late to join one of the four large shipments to Andersonville.[36]

"What will be my fate I cannot tell," Clapp wrote his wife, Lou, on June 15, "but I shall keep up good courage and hope for the best." His sentiments reflected those of the vast majority of the Ninth Minnesota's captives, who in their wildest nightmares could not have imagined what was in store for them.[37]

CHAPTER TWELVE

Andersonville (I)

A Despairing and Dying World

On the dismal Sunday afternoon of June 19, the first trainload of 824 Union enlisted men (including about 150 from the Ninth Minnesota) from Sturgis's failed expedition entered "Camp Sumter," the prison at Andersonville.[1] Formed in the "drenching rain" into a ragged column of fours, the weary, hungry captives, already soaked to the skin from riding in open flatcars, tramped east across sandy ground that rose toward the large stockade in the distance. "When we got within a short distance of that place," recalled Pvt. William N. Tyler of the Ninety-Fifth Illinois, "we smelt something rather strong." To his question as to the source of the odor, a guard answered, "You will soon find out what it is," and, Tyler added, "You bet we did."[2]

The guards halted the new arrivals near camp headquarters, an "old log cabin" set atop a hill. Across an adjacent valley the huge compound stretched southward toward them, extending down one steep, bare hillside, hurdling a little creek, and climbing the nearer, shorter slope. "God help us, what a sight!" recoiled Bjørn Aslakson of Company H. "On both sides of the stream we could see thousands of prisoners, ragged and crippled, sitting on the turf and walking around. It looked for all the world like an ant hill." In place of barracks or any substantial accommodations bloomed a sickly garden of thousands of small "crude tents," with a very few log huts in their midst. The "stench, noise and disorder" of the stockade, "a despairing and dying world," represented "a death call to us." To Corporal Medkirk of the Seventy-Second Ohio, "the mass of seething, hot, starving, diseased and dying humanity" visible inside the camp "seemed to daze us; we did not comprehend what it was and what was before us. I aver now, after the lapse of years, that if the prisoners could have realized what they would have to endure when they were once turned in there, they would have fell upon their guards and settled the question then and there whether it should be liberty or death."[3]

The shout "Prisoners, Attention!" in a guttural German accent introduced the newcomers to the "Dutch Captain," as the inmates dubbed Capt. Henry Wirz, in charge of the inner prison. "While the counting was going on," remembered Pvt. Andrew C. McCoy of Company F, a twenty-one-year-old farmer from Rochester and Hamline University student, "Capt. Wirz and other officers and men mounted on horses, stood in our front and rear with long pistols in hand apparently ready for any emergency." A forty-one-year-old Swiss immigrant and onetime homeopathic doctor from Louisiana, Wirz had long served in Confederate prisons. His right arm was permanently crippled from wounds received, he claimed, in the 1862 Battle of Seven Pines. Perched on an old, white mare and wearing his customary warm-weather garb of gray army cap, white shirt, and trousers of white cotton duck, he personally oversaw registering the new intake.[4]

"We were worn out and hungry," recalled Aslakson, "but forced to stand in line for many hours." When John Bartleson of the Eighty-First Illinois plopped down in the mud, Wirz snapped, "Stand up you damned Yankee or I will shoot you." Actually, that was a mild reaction, for Wirz often cursed creatively and vehemently, dismounted, flourished his, in fact, broken revolver, and shoved men back into line. One Rebel guard called him "very profane, one of the profanest men I ever saw. He had a very severe temper." A Connecticut soldier testified how Wirz was often "violent in these moments, cursing and swearing, as he always was with us," but he added with insight that Wirz "seemed harder than he was." To the prisoners the "Dutch Captain" came to personify all the terrible sins of the Rebel prisons, despite the fact he truly had little power to improve their living conditions. According to Aslakson, Wirz (the "evil spirit") was "slim in stature," with a "rat-like face," a "stiff bristly beard," and a "terrible temper that bordered on insanity." Frank Lyon described him as "stoop shouldered; complexion dark; hair black; mustache, black; eyes, black," with a "heart as black as the fires of hades could burn it." In stark contrast, Orderly Sgt. James Madison Page of the Sixth Michigan Cavalry, who came to like and respect Wirz, offered a much more sympathetic portrait: "Good height, perhaps 5′ 8″, slim in build, handsome face, aquiline nose, even features, high forehead, gray eyes, short, partially full beard; quiet, subdued expression of sadness particularly in his eyes."[5]

For roll call and distribution of rations, Wirz organized the camp into detachments of 270 men divided into three squads of 90 each. On that particular day, he first counted out eight groups of 90 from the Guntown prisoners and formed the Third Squad of the Eighty-Fourth Detachment (Squad 84/3 by his notation—the first two squads were created the day before with men from Lynchburg, Virginia), the Eighty-Fifth Detachment, Eighty-Sixth Detachment, and the First Squad of the Eighty-Seventh Detachment. Squad 84/3 included at least one stray from Company K. Within Squad 85/1 were Medkirk (Seventy-Second Ohio) and 1st Sgt. John Warren (Seventh Wisconsin Light Artillery). Squad 85/3 began incorporating men from the main body of the Ninth Minnesota contingent, starting with about 18 from Company B (including Joel Handy and son DeWitt) and 10 of Company F (with A. C. McCoy and Jacob Dieter). Most Minnesotans went into the Eighty-Sixth Detachment. Squad 86/1 included Sergeant Major Clapp, about 18 men of Company A, 18 from Company C (with Lyon, liberator Stephen Chandler, James Woodbury, and Orsamus Rhoades), 10 or so from Company D (including Cpl. Thomas Pettijohn and Pvt. Levi Goodfellow, who had befriended blacks in Jefferson City), and part of the 20-man contingent of Company H (with Aslakson and another father-son pair, Jacob and Jesse Pericle). The rest from Company H and about 4 men from Company I joined Squad 86/2, while Squad 86/3 absorbed a dozen from Company G. Finally, over a dozen from Company E (mostly Welshmen) entered Squad 87/1. Liberator Peter Rodier of Company K was most likely in one of these four detachments.[6]

Wirz appointed sergeants from among the prisoners to lead the new detachments and squads. The only such prison leader known from the Ninth Minnesota was 1st Sgt. Frank Weber of Company G, who received the Eighty-Sixth Detachment. A lean, sinewy farmer and part-time schoolteacher from St. Joseph in Stearns County, the well-liked twenty-two-year-old Bavarian immigrant was, at six feet two inches, hard to miss. To enable a Rebel sergeant to verify the count, the detachment sergeant was to muster his men for roll call every day at a particular time and place in reference to a specific point, such as a certain guard post on the wall. He would also draw the rations for his detachment and distribute them to the three squad sergeants, help the squad sergeants take men to sick call, and fulfill "sundry other light duties." For that work each detachment and squad sergeant received an extra daily ration of food. The guards distributed paper and pencils to the new squad sergeants to set down the names, regiments, and companies of those placed in their charge. Paroled prison clerks did the same for camp records. The only known squad leader in the Eighty-Sixth Detachment was William Woolverton, a twenty-one-year-old sergeant from the Seventy-Second Ohio, who took over Squad 86/1 with many Minnesotans.[7]

Subtracting the 720 men in the new squads left 104 waiting to be enrolled. They were joined by 49 captives taken in Grant's bloody Richmond Campaign and brought from Petersburg. Those newcomers arrived during the count-ing. Wirz regularly allocated a portion of each new intake to fill out old detachments whose strength had dwindled because of illness or death. Thus, he scattered the tail end of the contingent, including as many as a dozen from Company K, among total strangers. Some who ended up in the very old-est detachments included liberators Charles Dietrich and Jacob Thielen, as well as Joseph Harvey (Chauncey Hill's brother-in-law), Martin Shortt (the reluctant Saratoga recruit), Charles Newton (the Meridian chronicler), and George Jenkins. Harvey even landed in Squad 1/1 with prisoners who had been in Andersonville the longest. "This disposition of the men was much against our wishes," wrote Clapp, "and we thought it proper to protest, our reason was, we wished to remain together as regiments, that we might keep an account of the number who were sick, who died, or were exchanged, &c. But we soon learned [from an irritated, sarcastic Wirz?] we had no voice in the matter. If we refused to obey an order, our fate was worse than death itself."[8]

IN THE STOCKADE

Only after 4 P.M. did Wirz release the exhausted men to enter the prison through the two gates that pierced the west wall. As they marched off, 1st Sgt. Beverly C. Bonham of Company A heard him remark, "You won't be so damned fat when you come out of there." The sun, at least, emerged "clean and bright" out of the clouds. Passing "two converging lines of Rebels" bris-tling "with muskets in 'charge bayonet,'" the ragged column was separated into two groups, one bound for the nearby South Gate and the other sent across the stream and up the steep slope to the North Gate. As the men drew near the stockade, recalled Sergeant Woolverton, the "fumes which were arising from that filthy place compelled us to cover our nostrils." They were the rankest odors he would ever smell in his entire life.[9]

The path leading to the South Gate passed the prison dead house, a "cheap, open shed" that utterly failed to conceal the horrible contents overflowing outside. Aslakson gagged at the "long rows of dead bodies" that "were lying entirely naked." They were "full of terrible sores and covered with flies and maggots." Corporal Abraham B. Towner of the Ninety-Third Indiana thought it a particularly "terrible introduction" to prison life. For added security a small enclosure surrounded each gate. After about ninety prisoners jammed into the structure protecting the South Gate, the outer gates were closed. Only then did the main gates open inward. "Oh! What a sight met our eyes as we entered the prison," recalled McCoy. "The terrible stench that greeted our nostrils—men half naked—complexion colored by sun and pitch pine, smoke-haggard countenances, flesh shriveled and drawn tight to the bone, eyes sunken and glassy—it was difficult to believe that they belonged to the same race of beings as ourselves." Thrust onto "Main Street," a narrow lane that extended east across the sharp incline, Aslakson was immediately "surrounded by thousands of prisoners all barking questions at once." Bartleson heard cries such as "Hotel Anderson!" "Fresh Fish!" "This is the place, order what you want." "Where are you from?" and "What regiment?" The befuddled newcomers disappointed those eager for news of the outside world. "They are not very well posted in regard to current events," sniffed Sgt. William F. Keys of the 143rd Pennsylvania, already there for nearly a month. Only later did stories circulate rapidly through camp of how drunken General Sturgis had blundered at Guntown and abandoned these men.[10]

The new arrivals could not believe how incredibly crowded the prison was. "The great question which presented itself to us at that time," McCoy reminisced, "was where we could find a place to stand or sit down, to say nothing about unoccupied ground to lie down on, at this end of the prison. Every inch of space seemed to be taken, but after awhile we separated and found places to lie down in the narrow spaces left for the men to walk in." Incoming prisoners who were mathematically proficient sadly realized that Andersonville could be holding well over 20,000 inmates (87 detachments of 270 equal 23,490). The tally for June 19 indeed placed 21,849 prisoners in a stockade originally designed for 6,000 to 10,000. The camp had opened in late February 1864 to relieve congestion in the Virginia prisons. With the exchange cartel in shambles, the flow of prisoners far exceeded all expectations, with no end in sight. The hospital compound, located southeast of the stockade, treated another 1,271 sick, and the graveyard contained 2,206 graves, including 49 buried that day. An extension to the stockade being erected farther up the hillside offered hope of more elbow room in the near future.[11]

Those who entered by the North Gate experienced a similar gruesome greeting. "As the gates swung on their heavy hinges," recalled Lyon, "they looked like the jaws of some huge monster opening to gather us in." The newcomers were "marched in as freely as though there was an abundance of room," according to Clapp, but, as Warren noted, the "crowd about the gate was so dense that one could hardly find standing room, let alone a chance to sit upon the ground." Near the front of the column, Lyon, Chandler, and their Company C comrades started up "Market Street," a ten-foot-wide avenue leading east into the midst of "thousands of hungry, ragged prisoners, all eager for news." Considerate old hands cautioned the "fresh fish" that "we should have to make ourselves at home and look out for ourselves."

Hence finding a "small space apparently unoccupied" roughly halfway between the gate and the east wall, the Company C contingent took root. "It
became our abode for some weeks." The street led past the camp sutler's log
hut and numerous crude stalls and stores run by prisoners. Warren noticed
the brisk trade in food and how "each man seemed intent on his own business." Things appeared especially agitated because the daily delivery of rations
had been delayed. "Finding a little space not quite so densely packed," he "sat
down on the muddy ground, thoroughly sick and disheartened."[12]

The prison, as one thirsty newcomer soon learned, was not only thoroughly unpleasant but downright dangerous. Looking to drink from the
stream that flowed between the two gates, Pvt. John Frederic Holliger of
the Seventy-Second Ohio discovered a thin wooden railing set on average
about twenty feet inside the west wall. Unaware it was the infamous "deadline" beyond which guards shot to kill without warning, he leaned over to
draw water from as close to the wall as possible, where the stream was cleanest. A shot rang out from the nearest sentry post. The bullet missed Holliger
but struck two other prisoners, killing one. The bystanders were so incensed
they turned on Holliger and "beat him nearly to death, for having drawn the
fire of the guard."[13]

Having discovered no relief around the South Gate, Aslakson and his Company H comrades wandered north across the mucky stream and climbed
toward the North Gate searching in vain for adequate living space. Eventually "we were so weary that we lay down on the ground and slept." The "awful
hub-bub" that erupted when the food wagons finally entered the North Gate
soon roused them. The rations provided there, Warren judged, were "ridicu-
lous had it not been for our pressing need. The thought that we were expected to live with such a contemptible bit of meat served to us once a day,
did not seem at all funny at the time." Medkirk and his associates were about
to wolf down all their food "when some of the old prisoners advised us not
to do so, as there was no telling when we would receive any more. So we
took their advice and divided our rations, putting half for the five of us in
my sack." In turn Aslakson's party drew corn mush that was scooped from
a wagon bed and "dished out in buckets to the mess." If the recipients owned
no containers or even a blanket to hold them (Aslakson and his comrades had
preserved no such assets), the rations were simply dumped on the ground.
Nonetheless, "due to the insatiable animal hunger, we gulped our food the
first day without investigating or caring what it was."[14]

"When night came on and this living, moving mass became quiet and laid
down for rest," wrote Clapp, "then it could be seen how much spare room
there was." With their crudely cut-off pants and with most sans shoes, blouses,

and accoutrements, the miserable Sturgis men were already impoverished, even by Andersonville standards. The leader of Squad 42/1, Sgt. David Kennedy of the Ninth Ohio Cavalry, confided in his diary that night how those particular newcomers "came in strip[p]ed. they have to make their beds on the cold wet ground. thay geather in groups along the street to keep each other warm. When they are tired thay lie down on the ground to rest their half starved bodeys." Warren "lay down blanketless on the sodden, reeking earth," while Bartleson and his comrades "slept in small streets, small walkways" that in fact proved a nightmare. "Our sleep was not one of rest for body or mind," recalled McCoy, whose group remained near the South Gate (and went hungry because of it). "To add to our discomfiture, we were trampled on by men going back and forth to the creek and slough and what a terrible tongue lashing we received for being in the way." In stark contrast at least some of the prisoners from Petersburg who also had arrived that day enjoyed unimaginable luxuries. Not only had Sgt. John L. Hoster of the 148th New York and his companions retained all their money, clothing, rubber blankets, canteens, cooking gear, and haversacks stuffed with food and coffee, they even had pup tents, which they snuggled in that night.[15]

Clapp found the "groans of the miserable and wretched from all parts of the camp" to be "so unusual and their cries so heartrending, that it disturbs the sleep of those unaccustomed to them." Medkirk and his five companions suffered from yet another peril of life at Andersonville. Along with the rations they saved, his canvas sack held their precious stash: "a half canteen plate, spoon, and one tin cup." Medkirk secured the bag beneath his head when he lay down. "Notwithstanding the rain we slept sound, and in the morning found that our valuable sack, with all we had in it, was gone. Some thief had stolen it in the night. Now we were poor indeed." A "Raider" from the gangs of prisoners who preyed upon their fellow inmates, and even murdered some, had victimized the Ohioans. When he entered the South Gate, prime Raider country, Rollin Drake of the Seventh Indiana Cavalry had noticed a fair number of attentive, affable prisoners who seemed "well fed & hearty." One such individual lurking around the North Gate obviously stalked Medkirk until the time was right to make off with his goods. Ironically, the Raiders troubled few other Guntown prisoners. No one from the Ninth Minnesota recorded any direct harm at their hands. "As we had been thoroughly robbed by the more eminent freebooter Forrest," explained Drake, "we did not present a very attractive spectacle to the raiders and consequently suffered but little from their depredations." Private Henry Devillez of the Ninety-Third Indiana counted himself "lucky at being robbed by the first soldiers, those who captured me, and was saved going through the ordeal" of Raiders.[16]

"We got through the night without any broken bones or serious scars," wrote McCoy, "but morning found us possessed with an awful gnawing for something to eat, it being 48 hours since we had tasted food." According to orders, his party met a Rebel sergeant on Main Street who "escorted us north over the creek and slough to a point northeast of the north gate" where the Eighty-Fifth Detachment took up its assigned residence. Such concentration made it easier for the detachment's sergeants "trying to locate us the best they could so that we could be provided with food at the time of issuing rations." Beginning that day, June 20, Wirz suspended formal roll calls because of congestion in the stockade and simply distributed food to the detachment sergeants without requiring a detailed count. Ordinarily, if a detachment could not account for all of its members, it went hungry until the missing men were located.[17]

On June 21 Wirz accepted the second shipment of 282 ex-Guntown prisoners, those who came via Mobile. He selected 180 men for Squads 87/2 and 87/3 and reserved the remainder, including about 34 from the Ninth Minnesota, for the next scheduled intake of 452 men (415 from Petersburg and 37 from Marietta, Georgia) who arrived two days later. They became the Eighty-Eighth Detachment and two squads of the Eighty-Ninth Detachment. Squad 88/1 would include liberator Zara Frisbie and at least 3 more members of Company C, about 6 of Company F, and several more from Company H. Chauncey Hill went into Squad 88/3. The Marietta contingent and some Minnesotans became part of Squad 89/2 under Orderly Sgt. Thomas J. Sheppard of the Ninety-Seventh Ohio, a Baptist minister. He recalled they were "turned like a wild beast" into Andersonville, with "no shelter, no cooking utensils, no soap, no kettles for washing our clothing, no system of police to prevent crime or secure cleanliness, nothing save what we carried in on our backs." On June 25 and 26, the third and fourth Guntown shipments, totaling 210 prisoners, disembarked at Andersonville. The 20 or so newly arrived Minnesotans included liberators Nathan Palmeter (Company C) and John Morrison (Company K), as well as William Lovell and William Atwater from Company B, who were "greatly surprised" to find so many of their mates already there. Adding 67 more prisoners from Atlanta and Florida, Wirz composed Squads 89/3 and 90/1, sprinkled some of the rest among old detachments (Cpl. Francis Rafferty of Company C, for example, joined the sympathetic Sergeant Kennedy's Squad 42/1), and retained the balance to mix with new convoys expected shortly. From June 27 to 30, an additional 1,577 prisoners (nearly all captured in Virginia) and the last of the Guntown prisoners comprised Squads 90/2 and 90/3, the entire Ninety-First through Ninety-Fifth Detachments and the First Squad, at least, of the Ninety-Sixth Detachment.[18]

Andersonville, Southwest View, August 1864

Thus, from June 19 to 30, some 204 members of the Ninth Minnesota, in-cluding liberators Chandler, Dietrich, Frisbie, Morrison, Palmeter, Rodier, and Thielen, entered Andersonville prison. Perhaps 20 to 25 other Minne-sotans had already experienced the charms of Camp Sumter. One was Pvt. Uriah S. Karmany, a thirty-seven-year-old Mankato grocer who was a med-ical orderly in the Second Minnesota. He had been taken in September 1863 while tending the wounded at Chickamauga. After spending four grueling months imprisoned in a tobacco warehouse in Richmond, he reached Ander-sonville on February 25 in one of the very first shipments. "The prisoners were greatly demoralized and hardened," Karmany reminisced, "each caring for no one but himself. Many, even when well, would be disheartened, and resolve to die, and they generally would." At least three Minnesotans already rested in the graveyard. There soon would be many more.[19]

LEARNING THE ROPES

During their first several days in prison, Clapp and his comrades engaged in "much speculation, doubt, worry & and introspection." Within a week, though, "we became more resigned to our fate" and took positive measures to alleviate their condition. Likewise Warren "soon came to accept and make the best of it; but for the first few days, it required all the fortitude I could

muster to keep from yielding to despondency." One key to survival was to set
and hold a daily routine. Lyon remembered "with gratitude" a Pennsylvanian who advised on the first day, "'You will soon have a tired, languid feeling
and want to lie around and sleep. Don't do it, exercise; get up and walk and
shake off your drowsiness.'" Thus, Lyon got into the habit of walking "a great
deal up and down the hill up to the north and back to the south end."[20]

"Our time at first was spent in studying our surroundings," recalled McCoy.
The dominating feature was the stockade itself. Constructed of "hewn logs,
so well jointed that no person could scale them," noted Pvt. Augustus Arndt
of Company H, the 17-foot walls ranged 1,010 feet north to south and 780
feet east to west. The outer face bristled with "pigeon roosts," covered stalls
set 100 feet apart from where sentries watched the interior. Every hour each
night, the posts would sound off in order, stridently shouting the time and
"All is well!" The enclosed area comprised sixteen and a half acres of mostly
steeply sloping terrain. Because of marshy ground around so-called Stockade Branch, only about twelve acres were livable. Flowing west to east, the
shallow creek slid "along very slowly over its bed of yellow sand." From its
north bank, "a heavy swamp, a veritable quagmire" extended a few hundred feet before the hillside inclined abruptly. The mire was smaller south of
the stream. Aside from using a foot bridge set only a dozen feet or so from
the west wall deadline, the only way to cross the morass entailed plunging
"knee deep in mud and filth." Because the "slough was used for the offal of
the prison or dumping place for all who could get there," raw sewage saturated the muck, particularly to the east where the stream was sluggish. That
represented the worst source of the terrible smell that pervaded the camp and
its environs. No better for the environment was the habit of those either too
sick or too slovenly, who defecated in and around their living spaces instead
of going down to the sink.[21]

For the most part, there was little to see within the dreary stockade. Of
what was once heavily forested hillside, only two tall pines in the southeast
quadrant remained as landmarks. The rest of the site, bare without shade of
any kind, featured a "vast assemblage of huts, blankets and old tents" whose
occupants "cowered with grim but pathetic defiance." It had rained every
day for nearly three weeks, and the ground was mucky. The two principal
avenues, Market Street, situated north of Stockade Branch, and Main Street,
located south of the stream, teemed with "gamblers, sutlers, thieves, black-
legs, speculators, buyers and spectators," according to Karmany, all hearken-
ing to the "many loud cries" of proprietors hawking goods and services for
sale or trade. Fueling the markets were extensive Federal funds brought into
camp in early May by the so-called Plymouth Pilgrims, some 2,228 prisoners

who when captured at Plymouth, North Carolina, had just been paid. As part of the surrender terms, their original captors let them keep not only their greenbacks but all their fancy accoutrements and elaborate uniforms. That embarrassment of riches rendered the "Pilgrims" easy prey for Raiders and the other sharpers.[22]

"Fresh fish" were irresistibly drawn to window-shop at the rude emporia. The current rate of exchange in camp was four Confederate dollars to one Federal dollar. Within a day or two after reaching Andersonville, Hill recorded prices in Yankee dollars of "beans 25 to 40 cts. a pint, molasses $1.50 a pint, sour beer, made of sour meal, water and molasses or a sprinkling of sassafras, 10 cts. a cup, flour 75 cts. a pint, a large onion $1.00, small one 25 cts., apples, three small green ones, for $1.00, coffee 15 cts. a spoonful, tea 75 cts., honey $2.00 a cup, 3 eggs $1.00." Other establishments sold clothing, gear, or wood or offered such services as barbering and gambling. "An onion or a cake of soap was prized most highly and was literally worth its weight in gold," Aslakson recalled. "Pieces of canvas, old or ragged clothing, not to mention such articles as cups, canteens or new clothing, were objects that a prisoner longed for and prized as much as Jay Gould would another railway system." A "prisoner trader," Clapp learned, "would start by selling rations, get enough to buy a small stock from the sutler," and "set up a stall." The top establishments featured goods attractively laid on "a board with clean cloth, papers cut in fancy manner"; although most enterprises, "much cruder," simply sat under "rough tent poles." He approved of the system, which he thought "kept men busy & healthier," but many ached to see the food that could save them from starvation or disease being sold at prices they could never afford.[23]

The newcomers soon had to consider how to ensure the essentials of life: water, food, and shelter. The available clean water proved totally inadequate. Shallow Stockade Branch provided nearly all the potable water, but runoff from the cookhouse and guard camps contaminated even that indispensable source. Weber recalled seeing "rebel soldiers wash their filthy clothing in the very stream that was to bring [the prisoners] their supply of water." The farther the stream extended in from the west wall the fouler it became. Corporal Daniel McArthur of Company F, McCoy's friend in Squad 85/3, always endeavored when his time came to fetch water to get the cleanest possible. That entailed waiting in line to be allowed access to the narrow space between the foot bridge and the deadline and then taking the risk of reaching under the deadline to fill the container. Springs and wells dug inside the camp supplied a limited amount of "quite good water," but distribution depended on the goodwill of those who controlled them. No matter the source of water, one had to transport it. There were, recalled McCoy, "all kinds of ingenious contrivances imaginable for carrying water, some with shoes, old boot tops, bags made from rubber blankets" and "small buckets made from material got inside of staves with hoops, splices, the ends of which were riveted together with zinc nails taken from the heel of an old boot or shoe."[24]

The issue of food became a matter of the greatest interest. During afternoons, closely guarded wagons entered the North Gate with the daily ration to be parceled out among the detachment sergeants. They in turn divided their allotted food into three equal parts for their squads of ninety, whose individual messes generally numbered ten men each. Within the messes, rations were "carefully divided into ten parts," wrote Warren, "anyone present being at liberty to criticize or advise . . . until all seemed satisfied." According to a method of random distribution sacred from time immemorial, the leader of the mess "would ask another to turn his back; then place his knife on one of the rations and call 'Who takes?' or simply 'Who?'" That individual "would respond by name or number; each took his ration in silence and went on his way until all were called." The "din and confusion of the calls and answers, and the hawking about of rations by those who wanted to trade, made things lively and did much to keep up our spirits." Each day, for example, seven friends from the 114th Illinois traded one-seventh of their combined daily ration for tobacco that they personally used rather than sold. Prisoners exacted severe penalties for theft or deception. One day "one of the cavalry boys" filched the salt ration for Weber's Eighty-Sixth Detachment. "We found out about it," wrote Sergeant Lay of the Seventy-Second Ohio in Squad 86/2, "marched the chap out for a raider & sheered one side of his head close off."[25]

Rations at Andersonville came in two types, cooked and raw, which were often issued to half the camp on alternate days. Cooked rations included corn bread baked of unbolted meal "ground extremely coarse" and "hard to digest." A daily serving might comprise a piece of bread three inches square and a two-ounce slice of bacon "the size of an egg." Beef was occasionally substituted for bacon, but, as Clapp explained, it was usually "such horrid stuff" that the men much preferred bacon, "if we could get it." At times a pint of mush ("simply chicken feed warmed through"), beans, or boiled rice took the place of the bread, but they were "cooked very foul," with "many bugs & impurities." Weber recalled how a "cart would be shoveled full of the smoking paste, which was then hauled inside accompanied by an army of the loathsome maggot flies hovering over it, and issued out to the detachments who received it on blankets, hats, pieces of shelter tents, or for want of these on the bare ground." The day after they arrived, Lovell and Atwater

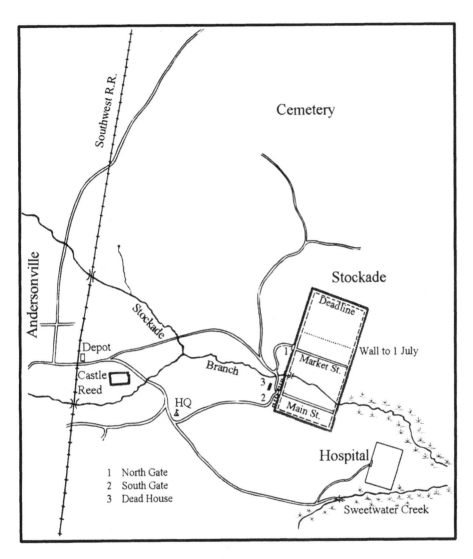

Andersonville

could not stomach such slimy rations and gave their food away to others in Company B, but McCoy, who had been there a few days longer, felt no such compunction. He simply "tore out the sleeve lining from my blouse to hold the rations of my mess." The mush could not be saved for later "as it would sour inside of 2 hours," but "our corn bread ration we tried to make last as long as possible for us to restrain our knowing stomachs." Lyon cut out his pants pockets, "putting my bread in one and my meat in the other. This was my *pantry*."[26]

Raw rations regularly included a pint of cornmeal mush ("often with the husks left in"), rice, beans, a small piece of uncooked meat, and a pinch of salt. Clapp insisted the men actually preferred raw rations, which each prepared himself. "Our cooking outfit usually consisted of one or more half canteen, a tin cup and a case knife which some one of the mess brought into the enclosure or was lucky enough to find strolling from its rightful owner." The "raw meal," McCoy recalled, "we wet up with water and cooked it on the ever handy half canteen. The beef we stewed in the same dish." After lighting a fire "with sliver of pine & root shavings," the one cooking would "add more shavings "until he could blow no more or until his fuel was exhausted, when he would call it done and eat it." The lack of firewood was a severe drawback. "It was necessary for us to economize in its use—while not more than 30 rods from where we were we could see hundreds of cords standing in the tree." Each detachment supposedly received three sticks a day, giving each mess "hardly enough just for light." Often, though, the wood ration was not forthcoming for days at a time. More firewood could only be had for money or by trading. Those who carried the dead from the stockade could also forage outside for sticks. Some prisoners even paid fellow inmates two or three dollars to be able to take bodies from the camp, Karmany explained, "as this would afford a chance for bringing in wood which could be sold at a profit."[27]

The rations were often too little to satisfy. "The pangs of hunger were at times terrible," wrote McCoy. "[We] would tell of the good meals we had helped to stow away, of what they consisted and how cooked. [We] would even remember crusts of bread we had seen floating around in our folk's swill barrel and think what a feast we would have if we could get at it." Woolverton was tormented by vivid dreams of grand feasts that disappeared when he awoke. Others were more fortunate. "I must say," McArthur stated, "I never seemed to suffer from hunger." Moreover, the purity and nutrition of the food itself was highly questionable. According to regulations, the prison ration was to be "the same as that issued to Confederate soldiers in the field," but if that were true, the Rebels would have shot their own quartermasters. "The stuff that was furnished [the Andersonville prisoners] was of the poorest quality," attested Weber, "infested with "all kinds of living and crawling things." The bread and other grains "were contaminated in a manner that gave the unmistakable impression that it had been stored in old sheds and barns, where the rats, mice, cats and dogs had free access." Often the bread was poorly baked. On June 20, for example, it proved so dank and smelly that some messes threw theirs over the deadline. Aslakson observed that when cooking the mush, rice, or beans, one had to "skim off the maggots and insects all the time it was boiling." However as Lyon noted, "those that did not float we cooked and ate. Nothing eatable was allowed to go to waste." After long scientific observation, Woolverton, their squad sergeant, asserted there were on average four bugs per spoonful of beans. Just having to eat in the open exposed the men to "swarms of flies" that forced them to gulp their food.[28]

"Many of the men became so overcome with nausea during the first few weeks of their confinement that they could not eat," wrote Aslakson. "Our stomachs many times would not retain the food and at other times the sight of it would sicken us." McCoy remembered how "many times in my own case while standing in the ranks for roll call, I became dizzy with weakness and could not see an object 20 rods in front of me, and had to sit down to keep from falling, but this feeling wore off as the day advanced and would be able to take considerable exercise and feel quite well considering." Clapp emphasized the importance of regular mealtimes, preferably three times a day. Lyon usually ate half his rations in the evening and saved the rest for the next morning. If he had bread, he would "mark a stopping place," but "it was mighty hard stopping sometimes." The old hands strongly cautioned against eating the whole ration right away and going hungry the rest of the day, but Clapp did remark that one Minnesotan regularly consumed all his food on the spot and left the prison in November still "enjoying very good health."[29]

Shelter was another essential component of life at Andersonville, but most Minnesotans had none yet, mainly because the ground on which they camped was so crowded. "For weeks I had no regular place to sleep," Lyon recalled, "but lay down wherever I could find a clear place and a bedfellow." McCoy's group from Company F likewise lived for a time "without any shelter of any kind." Weber deplored "the blazing sun, which beat down into the faces and upon the heads of the suffering captives with a torrid intensity that was alone almost enough to destroy life." Torrential rains brought a different kind of torture, forcing those without shelter "to lie and sleep in the mud, like so many hogs in the wallow."[30]

Other Minnesotans blessed with more resources did construct "shebangs," tents made up of "an old shawl" or a "few old sacks" that had been "sewn together" and held up by small poles or sticks set over holes in the ground. A few days after Hill entered the prison, he was overjoyed to encounter his brother-in-law Harvey, Newton, and another friend from Saratoga living near the northwest corner of the stockade. They were among those of Company K who on June 19 had been assigned to the oldest detachments. "A small piece of carpet had to do for the four of us; [at night] we lay on that to keep us from the ground," though by suspending the cloth overhead, "we gladly lounge under our blanket-tent during the middle of the day." Just getting wood for tent poles could be a major undertaking. Aslakson teamed up with three friends in Squad 86/1: fellow Norwegian Nils Johnson and Swedes Magnus Bengston and John Larson. Their tent was a Rebel coat they "ripped apart and sewed together." Using their only cash, a dollar that Johnson had managed to hide, Aslakson "was elected" to purchase "the needed poles." He had "made many purchases and trades in my life, but never have my wits been put to such a task as I had in obtaining these tent poles for the money I had at my disposal." It took him a whole day to find three suitable sticks they could afford. That evening the four savored sitting in their own little dwelling.[31]

Andersonville North Gate, August 1864

Body lice ("gray backs") and fleas were another grim fact of life in prison that hitherto had not plagued the Minnesotans, even in the field. "The ground was alive with the vermin," reminisced McCoy. "It was no unusual thing to have the outside of our clothes covered in the morning so thick that we could scrape off these pests with a knife or rather a stick with the edges sharpened." Their removal was known as "skirmishing," a "sordid occupation" according to Aslakson, "yet the only necessary one and it served to while away the unending hours in this terrible place." McCoy's group would start "with the shirt and then the pants and go over each article carefully—usually twice a day—and if there were any in our mess who were unable to look over their own clothes someone would do it for him. These little demons increased in number and size most the best of anything I ever saw or heard of in all God's creation—I know they sapped the life's blood from many a poor fellow's veins." Lyon rated fifty a "good kill" and added, "It was considered a breach of etiquette to neglect this important duty, and he who would not do it was put out of his mess." Karmany even asserted that "neglecting this most important duty four weeks was sure death." Some strove to wash their bodies and clothes regularly in the pools created in Stockade Branch upstream of the latrines. Lyon and his companions endeavored to wash "first thing in the morning." McCoy and his comrades did their "laundry" once a week. Many or even most others, though, never did. On June 30 a report by one Confederate surgeon deplored the "great lack of cleanliness on the part of the prisoners." That was ludicrously unfair because the authorities did virtually nothing to facilitate it. Karmany wryly suggested the absence of soap and enough good water to clean their clothes did have one advantage, "else we surely would have washed them to pieces."[32]

Yet another comfort denied most of the impoverished prisoners because of the cost was writing home. Dorence Atwater, a young prisoner clerk, judged the handling of mail a "total depravity." A one-page letter, all that was allowed, required two envelopes: the inner one (addressed home), with a U.S. three-cent stamp (cost one dollar Confederate); and the outer, with a C.S.A. ten-cent stamp, marked to the Confederate Commissary of Exchange. Wirz's headquarters censored the letters and arbitrarily destroyed those thought to malign the Confederacy. On June 22 Dieter sent the only known Ninth Minnesota letter from Andersonville. After listing all his Company F comrades, he advised he did not "know how long we will have to stay here but I hope it wont be long." He acknowledged his folks would have to help support the family "till I get out of this for I cant draw any pay til I am exchanged." That was just a hint of the financial woes the families of imprisoned soldiers faced until their loved ones were finally exchanged or, sadly, declared dead. Dieter closed with "love to you all." The camp did post notice of the rare arrival of letters from home, and at least one Minnesotan received one while in camp.[33]

RAIDERS AND RELOCATION

Most days in Andersonville passed with a terrible sameness only occasionally interrupted by events of note, usually unpleasant. "Nothing of excitement in camp," Hill scribbled on June 27. Noticeable, though, was a growing unruliness. Sergeant Lay recorded numerous fistfights among the dangerously overcrowded prisoners. "Rows are on the increase; all the devilish spirit seems to come to the front," observed Pvt. George A. Hitchcock of the Twenty-First Massachusetts, a June 16 arrival grouped with the Eighty-Third Detachment quartered near most of the Minnesotans. "First a few loud words; then a rush of several men at each other and a sound of murderous whacks; when the crowd dissolves, bloody faces or blackened eyes show us how companions in misery can treat each other." The Saratoga group "banded together to protect ourselves," noted Jenkins. "Other men scoff and dare us—our bunch drove them off." The unrest was attributed, not always accurately, to the mysterious predatory Raiders. The Ninth Minnesota's Andersonville memoirs all dealt at length with their crimes, apprehension, and eventual punishment, but only from the vantage of distant spectators with no direct involvement. "It seemed to us," recalled Aslakson, "that Raiders were everywhere and would soon compose the majority of the inmates of the prison," but "to many of us newcomers who had nothing of value this condition did not seem to matter much."[34]

Toward the end of June, some of the old-timers organized their own police force, the Regulators, whose leaders secured permission from Brig. Gen. John H. Winder, in overall command at Andersonville, to deal with the Raiders. On June 29 matters came to a head when Wirz demanded order be maintained in the camp. The Regulators led guards in search of Raiders and seized eighty-four who were removed from the stockade. The enforcement was not gentle. That afternoon seventy arrested Raiders were readmitted and forced to run the gauntlet of enraged prisoners who delivered "a beautiful pelting with clubs," according to Sergeant Hoster. Three were said to have died from the beatings. Wirz held the other Raiders for trial by the prisoners. The turmoil continued into the next day. After a "sleepless night; fights with raiders ongoing," wrote Hitchcock, "morning found the camp in the wildest excitement." The Regulators stormed the Raider stronghold in the southwest corner of the camp and uncovered much loot and evidence of murders. Snug within a crowd of spectators "packed as tightly as we could stand along the north slope," Aslakson watched in rapt attention. "We stood as if fastened to the ground. Seldom have I witnessed such a tense moment." When the Raiders broke and ran, "a mighty shout went up from twenty thousand of us that witnessed the battle from the hillside. Now that we dared to express ourselves, there was no longer any doubt as to which side our sympathy was with." The Regulators replied "with a mighty 'Hurrah!'" They grabbed "a ring leader," and "only by the fiercest struggle could the police get him outside the stockade unharmed." Wirz summoned to the South Gate all sergeants of detachments and squads and chose from their ranks a jury of twelve newcomers to try the Raiders. They were to render sentence that, if approved by the authorities, the prisoners themselves would carry out. One of the jury was Reverend Sheppard of the Ninety-Seventh Ohio. Ultimately six Raiders were convicted and sentenced to hang.[35]

On June 30 the detachment sergeants learned news that was of much more real importance than Raiders: the new addition to the stockade was finally ready. Lengthening the walls 510 feet along the hillside to the north added ten acres to the living space. Most of this new high ground either rose gently or was nearly level. Half the detachments, those numbered 49 and above, were to move in the next morning when drums sounded. At dawn on July 1, the entire camp erupted as those who were to go into the new space, including nearly the whole Ninth Minnesota contingent, made ready to move. "Tents were struck," wrote Clapp, "and with the sticks and poles that supported them; were hastily rolled up, and shouldered by the healthiest and strongest of inmates; others carried bundles of wood, cooking utensils, and rations stored in little bags, wooden buckets, and every conceivable kind of vessel. The sick and wounded crept, crawled, hobbled on crutches with the help of canes and were carried on the back of the more fortunate and able tent mates." Directed to proceed in numerical order, the lucky detachments were to be assigned "definite lots, which we were expected to occupy, and on which we answered to roll call each morning."[36]

When the movement finally began at 10 A.M., "such a crowd and rush to get through was never before witnessed." All were "eager" for "clean, purer air & more room." During the "huge rush" there was barely "room to move," and the "crowd" literally "trampled" some of their comrades who were waiting their turn. Never anticipating the immense trouble it would cause, the Rebels thoughtlessly opened a space in the old north wall just twelve to fourteen feet wide. Only later, it appears, did additional openings ease the flow. Even so it took until long after sundown to get the last of the men inside the new space. "I was on Main street during the exodus," wrote Hill, "and could not help observing what a motley mass it was. It would have been amusing under other circumstances. Here one staggered along with rough tent poles and wood bound up in an old blanket; another with an armful of trashy wood; another hobbling along with a crutch and a piece of tin for a plate; a poor fellow pale and thin, supported by his two comrades; another with a dry bush for his moveable property beside his scanty clothing; some barefooted, some with a piece of dingy cloth for a cap, some coatless, some shirtless with blouse, a mass of 12,000 men, thus moving was a strange sight." Hill, who elected to stay with his Saratoga friends instead of joining the Eighty-Eighth Detachment in the new quarters, noticed "the thinning out in the old camp is very marked."[37]

The lowest-numbered detachments making the move occupied the ground adjacent to the new North Wall. The rest formed up in order south of them. Thus, the detachments containing most of the Ninth Minnesota's prisoners ended up alongside the old stockade wall, roughly halfway across or a little farther to the east. McCoy's mess of twenty prisoners in Squad 85/3 received a space measuring some ten feet east to west and thirty feet north to south, with the south edge abutting the old wall. Although not far in physical distance, the move represented a real improvement in living conditions, especially in the sense of actually possessing the ground they lived on. "We are now in more tolerable comfort," commented Private Hitchcock about the Eighty-Third Detachment's new habitat. "Some regularity in arranging streets was attempted, but as there was not half room enough, the streets were all taken up so that by night we are as in as great a confusion as ever." Clapp's Eighty-Sixth Detachment delightedly discovered the "new stockade abounded in small shade trees, plats of green grass and an abundance of wood." The "heavy pines had been felled & were left lying on the ground." Such plenty seemed miraculous given the previous terrible shortage. Sergeant Lay secured pine boughs for beds and enough wood to cook for two weeks.[38]

All that first night the "immense camp was like a disturbed hive of bees," with "much sound of chopping," wrote Clapp. The prisoners used axes they stole, borrowed, or rented (for fifty cents to three dollars) to remove the rest of the old stockade wall. By morning it was entirely gone. McCoy and his friends "managed to get out one of those pine timbers by considerable digging with the tools nature had given us—our fingers, took it to where we had dug a hole about 16 inches deep and wide enough to permit 8 of us to lie down spoon fashion, and by the use of an old hatchet we got out six stakes and material in shape and strong enough to hold up 8 inches of dirt above this hole when completed." Because they lacked "nails to fasten them together," McArthur recalled, "we tore strips from the lower part of our trousers and shirts and tied the sticks together, and covered the thing with a light layer of earth." McArthur "slept at the north end of our shade, beside Andrew McCoy," who kindly "allowed me to use a part of his blanket when the nights were chilly." Their structure, McCoy noted, "afforded a good shelter from the hot rays of the sun by day and dew at night. But in hard rainstorms the roof would wash off and we were obliged to pull out and stand and take it. The hole filled up with water and mud but usually in a few hours the water soaked into the ground—the soil being a mixture of clay & sand. After the storm had passed over, we re-covered the roof."[39]

Many likewise used the sun-baked red clay soil to make dugouts and to construct "monitor" cooking ovens. Once set in the hot sun, the pits became "hard as brick" and lasted "a long time." Dieter, Bill Williams, and another comrade from Company F shared a blanket and covered their own tiny dugout with brush. Clapp and two others built a tent shelter set down into the fresh ground. Four feet wide by six feet long, their shebang was "shaped very much like one half of a hogshead or immense barrel cut into lengthwise. It was only about three feet high, and was our home and storehouse combined. Here we lived through that dreadful summer." The shebang "kept out the sun, heavy dews and protected from the rain far better than we expected." The view from a little higher up the north slope also proved more scenic than in the old quarters. Clapp could "look over the stockade, in the lower places, and see over to the Depot, and watch the cars as they came and started." Aslakson and his companions brought their makeshift tent with them.[40]

Not everyone, though, enjoyed constant protection from the elements. Lyon, for one, still possessed "no blanket, no shelter of any kind day or night save when I begged the privilege of sitting in my friend's mud shanty during the hottest part of the day." At night he, Chandler, and their Company C comrades "would lie down together upon the ground spoon fashion. I would take off my boots and put them under my head for a pillow." At times "as many as a dozen men would spoon together, so that those in the middle could not turn over, but when the bones next to the ground ached too hard the word would be passed to flop, and the whole line flopped together." Private Edward A. Todd of Company A was another who made do with so little. Years later Pvt. George W. Pomeroy, his "bunk mate or rather ground mate," recalled that Todd spent the whole time exposed "through the days in sun without any shelter only as he could sit in the shade of a more fortunate comrade's blanket."[41]

Securing water in the new area became more difficult than before. Whereas wells near the creek often reached "very good water" at only four or five feet, sites much farther up the hillside could require digging eighty feet or more. Often this excavation was "done with an old broken shovel and the dirt handed up in a common water bucket with a rope made of old rags." Such hard-earned water, though, remained "the property of a few." The Company C mess benefited from Lyon's friendship with someone "whose uncle I knew in Minnesota." That person's well down near the creek produced "good water." Grabbing Company C's "ten-quart wooden pail snagged by someone on the way to prison," Lyon went to the well one morning and "carried home a treat for the boys. In a day or two I introduced one of my comrades, then another and another until all had been introduced. From that time on we were supplied with well water." Most others continued to trek to the foul creek.[42]

More generous amounts of food than usual appeared on the first two days of July. "There has been quite a surplus of rations dealt out for two or three days, and we have had more meal than necessary," wrote Hill. "The raiding business however has interfered and we have a chance to fall back on our extras." On the third, the warmest day yet, Wirz resumed regular formal roll calls. A drum roll would sound at 8 A.M. to alert the detachment and squad sergeants to begin assembling their men. Each Rebel roll call sergeant was responsible for counting six detachments of eighteen squads made up of 90 men each, or 1,620 men. After July 10 William D. ("Willie") Hammack, a personable twenty-two-year-old private from the Fifty-Fifth Georgia, handled six detachments that included most of the Ninth Minnesota contingent. His testimony at the Wirz trial in 1865 offered a rare look at the process from the other side. Notebook in hand, a Colt Navy revolver belted to his waist, Hammack would enter the South Gate each morning by 9 A.M., cross the foot bridge, and make his way up the north slope to where his charges waited. Up there, he recalled, the smell was better than down near the fetid branch. He would go to each squad as it stood in line four ranks deep and have the sergeant of ninety account for all of his men. Hammack was supposed to call the roll himself, but he soon discovered he "could not pronounce the names of so many." Instead he quickly sized up his eighteen squad sergeants. "I did not always take their word for it; I would sometimes when it was a man I could trust and had great confidence in. He would tell me his men were all right, and I would mark it so and go along; and I knew there were some making false reports. I did that to save myself labor and trouble because it was a disagreeable place in there."[43]

Hammack could usually finish off a single squad in five minutes and let those men stand down. He often completed his daily task by 11 A.M. and submitted his report to headquarters, although it could take longer as "I would get talking to the men." He certainly made friends among the prisoners and, as it transpired, customers, too. In the evening he would return to the stockade his pockets stuffed with "onions, peppers and eggs" and in violation of dire orders sell them much more cheaply than the camp sutler. A dozen of his onions would go for two or three Confederate dollars. Hammack was far from the only roll call sergeant who ran an illicit business. He admitted at the trial that he sold food to the prisoners "to enrich myself, and not from motives of humanity," although he did give food and goods to "particular friends" who perhaps included Minnesotans. Hammack later became a well-known, beloved Baptist minister in Georgia. He confessed that during the war "his light was under a bushel," but he must have made a good impression on his particular group of prisoners. Although condemning most of the guards, Woolverton, one of his squad sergeants, specifically praised the men of the Fifty-Fifth Georgia. There were "no grounds of complaint against them. They undoubtedly treated us as well as their instructions would permit." That testimonial is remarkable because other prisoners singled out those same Georgians for their quick trigger fingers and harsh treatment.[44]

The daily count was very important because any squad with unauthorized absences was supposed to be denied rations until the missing men were found. A squad sergeant also risked severe punishment if it was thought he concealed an escape. Inevitably on July 3, given the tremendous dislocation of the previous several days, many squad sergeants could not round up all of their men, even though Wirz insisted the count be done twice. To the prisoners' great disgust, he ordered no rations at all be distributed that day. That particular denial of food became an issue at Wirz's trial and a factor in his conviction.[45]

The hot, rainy Fourth of July proved no real holiday for the confined Yankees. In place of another roll call, Wirz reorganized the prisoners and compiled new rolls. He consolidated the oldest detachments by abolishing some and filling gaps in the numerical sequence. The Forty-Second Detachment (with Sergeant Kennedy's Squad 42/1), for example, became the Twenty-Fourth Detachment, and the Sixty-Sixth Detachment (formed on June 1) emerged as the Forty-Fourth Detachment. The highest-numbered detachments, with nearly all the Ninth Minnesota's prisoners, simply subtracted twenty from their old number without shuffling personnel. Thus the Eighty-Fifth Detachment became the Sixty-Fifth Detachment, Weber's Eighty-Sixth Detachment the new Sixty-Sixth, the Eighty-Seventh Detachment the Sixty-Seventh, and so on. For some unknown reason, a few detachments received much higher numbers. The Sixteenth Detachment (which included Sergeant Hoster of the 148th New York as well as Pvt. Franklin C. Wilson of Company C) became the Seventy-Ninth Detachment. The food issued on Independence Day was particularly bad. "Our rations were delayed and exposed so long," Hill wrote, "that the mush was fly-blown and was refused by the prisoners; the beef, some of which was cooked, was bad enough, so we were not all in the best of humor." The prisoners defiantly "filled the night air with patriotic songs," wrote Hitchcock. "'We will hang Jeff Davis to a sour apple tree' was sung with great unction, but the chorus 'Glory, glory, hallelujah!' rolled gloriously from all parts of the camp." With "particular vigor" the "'Star-Spangled Banner' waved in a mighty chorus of song across the stockade into the *ears* if not the faces of the dastardly rebel hordes outside." Overhead, according to Hill, "the heavens thundered with heavy volleys and the lightning flashes were vivid. This was our celebration or rather one for us to appreciate."[46]

On July 6 the Confederates finally issued tools to the detachment sergeants. Weber drew an axe, a shovel, and two pails. The impatient prisoners got to work to improve their lot. Many used the temporary bounty of wood in the new area to carve little buckets to barter for food. Clapp and his comrades baked corn dodgers and whittled rings from beef bones to trade "for something more palatable." On Market Street one could see "some of the finest bone rings and ornamental carvings made from bone and wood." Another soaring business in the July heat was brewing, actually "brewery and saloon combined" that offered sassafras beer made from fermented cornmeal and sassafras bark. Selling for five or ten cents a glass, the libation, it was claimed, could prevent scurvy. Lyon never heard of anyone getting drunk on the product because "no one could afford more than one glass at a time." An enterprising entrepreneur from the Seventy-Second Ohio, Pvt. Henry W. Miller of Squad 66/2 (formerly 86/2), described a serious drawback beyond the exorbitant price. He parlayed a plug of tobacco purchased at the cost of a daily ration into a stash of molasses ("sour sorghum") that brewers desired as a sweetener for their product. One delighted beer baron offered Miller a free sample. Holding the glass up to the sun, Miller found the murky beverage was "thick with flies' legs and wings, the other parts of their bodies being dissolved so one could not see through it." Thanks, but no thanks. He used the seven dollars he had earned to buy a robust artillery jacket salvaged from a corpse and was very glad to have it.[47]

Another business effort by two Minnesotans did not turn out so well. Private George Henry Knapp of Company C approached Lyon with a proposition. A thirty-seven-year-old bachelor originally from Vermont, "G. Henry" was a well-known merchant from High Forest in Olmsted County who had enlisted in February 1864 with Lyon. He told Lyon "he thought he could sell some stuff if he only had some start-up funds." Lyon had garnered "a little money" selling the fine boots made by his father. He "bought some beans and had them cooked, and Knapp set up his stand." The first customer was a "young fellow" who "ordered a plate of beans, ate them, and then said he had no money to pay for them. Knapp was very much chagrined at being taken in, but we had a good laugh over it, which perhaps did us as much good as the money would have done." Lyon "felt very sorry for Knapp," who had "always lived well, had always made money, and was accustomed having what money would buy."[48]

July at Andersonville continued excessively warm. In faraway Virginia the assault on Petersburg had turned into a deadly siege, and Sherman knocked on the door at Atlanta. New arrivals continued to flood the camp. From the sixth to the twelfth, 3,337 men, mostly from Petersburg, swelled the numbers to 28,647. The Minnesotans behaved the same way toward those "fresh fish" as those who had first greeted them. "When the new arrivals came in the boys in their eagerness to gain news would gather and stand around them in great immense crowds." Only now, as old hands, they got to see the "sudden change" on the faces of the newcomers "the moment they stepped inside, as if they then realized the horrors of the situation."[49]

On July 11, upon learning Richmond had approved the Raider death sentences, the Regulators hastily erected a crude gallows near the South Gate. "Every living soul, inside and out who could move," wrote Hitchcock, "was watching for the entrance into the camp of the six 'raiders.'" When they pleaded for mercy, Aslakson was startled by the "savage shout" that "broke from the thousands of throats, 'Hang them! Hang them!'" One of the condemned, Charles Curtis, ran free and barreled his way north into the swamp. "The mob surged back and forth and all order seemed to have disappeared." Regulators grabbed Curtis as he crawled out the far edge of the morass and pulled him, "covered with mud and slime" and with blood coming from his ears, back to the gallows. "He was taken past where I was sitting," Lyon wrote, with "a desperate look on his face," but "there was no escape." It was a "scene to make one sad," thought Hill, to see "six men in line, waiting the moment for launching them into eternity; condemned by fellow soldiers for preying upon and killing their suffering comrades. Their caps [hoods] were fully adjusted and soon the drop fell and five were suspended between earth and sky." The rope holding William Collins, the burly Raider known as "Mosby," gave way, but it was quickly replaced, and he "was soon struggling beside his companions." The hangings afforded a horrified Hill a "scene such as I have never seen before and hope never to see again."[50]

LEARNING TO SURVIVE IN ANDERSONVILLE

"A strange excitement had occupied our minds during the struggle between the Raiders and Regulators," Aslakson explained, but "we now felt the reaction from this feverish excitement. Our resistance had diminished and we became negligent and careless of everything." The "uppermost thought always to be considered," recalled McCoy, "was the opinion of each one as to the length of time he thought our stay would be there. This opinion was asked for many times a day—anxious to know of home, of the outside world and what our armies were doing." Despite incessant rumors stoked by Confederate authorities of imminent prisoner exchange, the prison population swelled. The new arrivals far exceeded even the escalating numbers of the dead. Nor was escape a viable option. Numerous tunnels, some quite long and deep, were being dug under the walls, but there is no evidence anyone from the Ninth Minnesota took a direct part in their excavation. Such work necessarily required resources largely unavailable to the ragamuffins from Brice's Crossroads. The diggers, moreover, tried fiercely to keep their work secret lest informers tell the guards in return for some trifling favor. On July 18 Sergeant Hoster observed one such miscreant, who had betrayed a tunnel for a plug of tobacco, being shaved and branded on the forehead with a "T" in India ink. Wirz maintained a pack of bloodhounds and skilled trackers to run down those few prisoners who succeeded in tunneling out and the far greater number who simply walked away while on outside work details. Nearly all were recaptured within a short time in worse shape than when they left and were subjected to severe punishment including being confined in stocks and wearing a heavy ball and chain. Thus, the Minnesotans understood quite well they were not likely soon to go free.[51]

On the fateful eleventh of July, Hill pondered in his diary the "strange being" who is "man!" The prison environment revealed in particularly intense and vivid ways the fundamental struggles of human life. Andersonville inmates represented "all kinds of character, from the firm christian, upright, honest, conscientious, to the most depraved villain, brutal, fiendish, stained with the blood of his fellow men." Such conditions of utter destitution and high mortality engendered extremes of morality and behavior. Death and the real fear of death were evident everywhere. "It was a very easy matter to die in prison," affirmed Clapp, and death occurred in especially horrible ways as the result of starvation and wasting diseases like dysentery and scurvy. Indelible images of the dying haunted the living. The worst were those who could do nothing to help themselves. "During the hot season," remembered Weber, "the entire swamp was a mass of creeping, crawling, wriggling life! Out of it came the maggots and other vermin, which spread over every foot of ground of the pen. The poor fellows fought them desperately but the sick and dying suffered tortures, and they were literally devoured alive." Clapp recalled seeing many such victims stranded "on the very bank of the creek in the mud and filth, with their untouched rations beside them, too sick to eat. You would implore them to get up, and if they must lie down to go to a cleaner spot. But no, no; I shall die any way; let me lie, was the answer, and too true, they would die, and so easily, and without a struggle. It seemed more like going to sleep."[52]

Up to that point those who suffered the most were strangers to the Minnesotans, but the guilt, even so, was crushing. "Why did we not lend assistance in some way?" agonized Clapp. The reason, he wrote, was "simply because we *could* not. None of us were so situated that we could render aid and comfort in those extreme cases." No effective medicines were at hand. Food and clothing were insufficient. No one could clean up the infirm or shelter them properly. In many instances, the victims were too sick even to be moved. The overriding concern among the still relatively healthy was how long they themselves could count on remaining so fortunate. They only had to look at the decreasing vitality of others who had been in captivity even just a little longer. Could they, if or when they too deteriorated to living skeletons, rely on the support of their own, or would nothing, too, prevent a miserable, lonely death?[53]

Such total immersion in misery and mortality corroded even good friendships. Life in Andersonville, Lyon observed, "tended to make us selfish, desperately so," even among close comrades. "Many who at home and in camp were cheerful and companionable, after being in prison for a time, became morose and irritable. Many who were generous at home, as prisoners were penurious. Again, men who never used an oath, especially in the company of others, became profane. Men seemed to vie with each other in making their profanity terrible." An "old acquaintance" admitted to Lyon he had "stolen a tin cup. I had known him for years and at home he was a good Methodist. I never laid it up against him, and I think, under the circumstances, the good Lord forgave him." Clapp decided proper attitude was the key to survival. "It requires all the energy and will one can muster, keep up good courage, to move around and exercise, and so to occupy his time as to keep his mind in the right channel, and to worry away the dreary hours to the best advantage." The question for many was where such "good courage" could be found.[54]

One vital source of fortitude was religious faith. "God help us in mercy, for through Thee we may receive the needed wisdom," Hill prayed the day the Raiders were hanged. Christianity exerted far more of a public presence in nineteenth-century American life than in today's secular age that tends to ridicule the profound influence of the Christian faith and usually filters out any mention of it in historical sources. In any era, though, the degree to which society is truly religious is questionable. Public expressions of piety, the sanctimony of the "long face and a solemn drawl" were one thing, but keeping steadfast belief in God and love for one's neighbors in the face of terrible trials were entirely different. The impact of religion in Andersonville is strongly debated. Historian Gerald F. Linderman avers that "religious sensibility" there "seemed almost to disappear" and that "prayer diminished." In his opinion the admittedly common practice of reading testaments served "primarily as reminders of home" rather than for inspiration. As evidence he cites John Ransom, a famous prison diarist who wrote on April 7, 1864, "There are some here who pray and try to preach, very many too who have heretofore been religiously inclined, throw off all restraint and are about the worst, tried and found wanting it seems to me." On the other hand, Steven E. Woodworth finds Linderman's declaration to be "incredible." Quoting other prisoner testimony regarding religious meetings, Woodworth emphasizes how "obviously, my findings do not support [Linderman's] assertion."[55]

In fact it seems both viewpoints are valid. The war, which so vastly increased one's odds of being killed, dying of disease, or being maimed, provided a crucial test of faith. Elijah E. Edwards, the astute chaplain of the Seventh Minnesota, estimated just a third to half of his regiment were truly "religious" men, but all the more did they prove "zealous and warmhearted." The hardships Andersonville prisoners faced either drew them closer to God or by deepening doubt and despair pushed them farther away. "Many infidels have been made in here," one anonymous memorist mordantly commented. About half of the Ninth Minnesota's Andersonville accounts made no mention of faith in God. The rest did testify firmly to the vital sustaining role of their faith in Jesus Christ. "In the midst of this distress and wretchedness," wrote Aslakson, "we were not entirely left without a word of comfort and consolation, for quite often we would hear a word of comforting solace, and seldom has the Word of God found more willing listeners. The message of Him who made the blind see, cleansed the lepers and made whole the lame and the halt was especially a Gospel for the poor and miserable and was like a drink of living water to those thirsty and starved souls in this place of despair."[56]

The means of fostering such inspiration in Andersonville were limited. Captured Union army chaplains were excluded or only allowed in briefly. Risking death from disease, a few valiant Roman Catholic priests from Southern parishes did minister to the prisoners and earned their heartfelt respect. Prominent was sixty-two-year-old Father Peter Whelan, who arrived on June 16 and remained four grueling months. On the day of the hangings, he comforted the Raiders, five of whom were Catholics. Father Henri Clavreul, another priest, came to Andersonville later in July and stayed until disease nearly killed him. Though eager to speak about God with anyone who approached them, the priests could not preach or hold large services. Each day they moved about the stockade primarily attending sick call and visiting the hospital to administer the sacraments of penance and extreme unction. They generally attended to the Irish and German Catholics, with little direct contact with Protestants, who included most Minnesotans. Only Pvt. Lewis Young (Ludwig Jung) of Company I, a twenty-four-year-old Bavarian immigrant, is known to have received extreme unction, that from Father Clavreul on July 27 in the hospital, and he died twelve days later.[57]

Most prisoners who sought religious inspiration looked to those already in their ranks who voluntarily stepped forward to lead prayer meetings. There was no humbug. "No audience is more severely critical than an audience of soldiers," wrote Chaplain Edwards, and "no men see more quickly through a sham." They had "no reverence" per se for "the cloth." All the more then did the hell of Andersonville magnify such critical evaluation of spiritual mentors. "Like David of old, 'out of the depths,'" recalled 1st Sgt. Horatio B. Turrill of the Seventy-Second Ohio, "we cried unto the Lord. There was an earnest-ness and pathos in these supplications, born of our wants and helplessness, far different from the cold and formal petitions too frequently offered by assembled Christians."[58]

Perhaps the first true prisoner preacher, certainly the one, according to Turrill, who most "preached regularly and continuously," was the previously noted Orderly Sgt. T. J. Sheppard from the Ninety-Seventh Ohio, who led Squad 69/2. In 1861, while studying law, Sheppard became a licensed Bap-tist preacher and enlisted in August 1862. He was ordained in May 1863 at Murfreesboro in a regimental chapel made of evergreen boughs. For two weeks following his arrival on June 23 at Andersonville (the day after his thirtieth birthday), Sheppard sought in vain within the crowds for true "reli-gious company," though he noticed many reading testaments. Finally on the hot evening of July 8, while resting on the north side near where he and many of the Minnesotans lived, he heard hymns being sung. A "large and attentive congregation" had "gathered in a prayer and conference meeting." By "the faint light of the feeble fires," Sheppard witnessed the "emaciated forms clothed in rags, begrimed with dirt and disfigured by disease, their faces pinched with hunger" and yet "radiant with the presence of God." Deeply moved, he felt as if he never before "attended religious meetings where song and speech and prayer more fervently and fittingly expressed the riches of Christian experiences." Private Hitchcock was there. "I found a largely attended prayer meeting near us in the evening," he wrote of that night in his diary. "It was a most impressive sight to see the poor sick fellows crawl up to catch the words of earnest prayer which went up to our common Father. Men, who never had framed words into prayer, felt that a higher than human helper must be appealed to." Hill, too, was present and noted the participants were "very attentive and many serious."[59]

Sheppard preached his first sermon on Sunday, July 10, near his bivouac "on the North Side, about half-way from east to west." His text was Psalm 51:10: "Create in me a clean heart, O God, and renew a right spirit within me." Hill rejoiced over the "good and plain" sermon. Once "so weak from loss of appetite and heat," he had lost the "ambition to stir out as I should, and have not enjoyed the meetings as I might otherwise. May God help me to live more devotedly a christian." To Aslakson, Sheppard was an "earnest, serious Christian man" whose "words of comfort were to many of us like balm on open sores." He felt "a blessed longing to hear the soul saving Word. 'All that thirst come to the Waters' and we experienced even here in this living hell that above all things it is blessed to belong to the Lord and to know that He is mindful of man."[60]

After the first four nights, Sheppard's little group endeavored to hold nightly prayer meetings in "some vacant spot," while reserving formal preaching for Sundays. "A little before dark those who took a leading part, especially in singing, would repair to the place and 'ring the bell'" and open the service with a "familiar hymn. Upon this the prisoners would gather often to the number of three or four hundred. We had the most beautiful singing, led by a trio of fine voices and joined by all present." Those hymns, "full of Christ and heaven," recalled Turrill, "were sung by a hundred voices, while outside our company hundreds more caught up the strain and reechoed the words around the prison." The choir also belted out "patriotic songs to intensely appreciative audiences" until the guards made them stop. Hospital Steward Solon Hyde of the Seventeenth Ohio was impressed with how "they prayed for the nation and the President, I thought sometimes with an eloquence I never heard excelled."[61]

One favored location was near the two tall pine trees in the southeast corner. "Just after one of our quiet sunsets," wrote a "Plymouth Pilgrim," Sgt. Maj. Robert H. Kellogg of the Sixteenth Connecticut, "we gathered together and [Sheppard] gave us a splendid discourse upon the text 'Fight the good fight of faith.' He drew a *comparison* between the *Christian* and the *soldier,* and carried it through in an admirable manner." Kellogg exulted, "no earthly foe could interrupt our communion with the *heavenly world*," but that is not to say that some "earthly foes" did not try. A minister who interviewed Andersonville survivors learned that religious meetings were "often disturbed by wicked men. Some of the reckless even took this occasion to jostle and rob their fellow prisoners on the outskirts of the congregation, and the sounds of blasphemy and mockery often mingled with the voice of worship; but still the meetings were attended and sustained by sincere and earnest men, whose labors were not in vain." In addition to the meetings, Sheppard and his colleagues organized Bible study, brought water to the sick and dying (although they were barred from the hospital), and read over the dead.[62]

One of Sheppard's close associates in the spiritual work, who on occasion also led the service, was Pvt. George Atkinson of Company F, a forty-one-year-old farmer from Yorkshire, England, and the father of eight children. Brother Atkinson was a "local Methodist preacher" much loved in his community of Orinoco, north of Rochester, and in the Ninth Minnesota. In July 1863 William Dean wrote home from Fort Ridgely how Atkinson "is shouting religion yet and he is in good health. He is ever at his post on the Lord's side & our meeting still continues regular." Although quite sick during the advance to Brice's Crossroads, Atkinson had "insisted on fighting in the battle" and was snapped up along with much of his company the next day. He shared the eight-man dugout with McArthur and McCoy in Squad 65/2. George Pomeroy of Company A was one of the "golden voices" who provided such sweet music for the services. A twenty-six-year-old farmer from Hennepin County who originally hailed from Maine, he was, as noted previously, Edward Todd's "bunk mate or rather ground mate" in Squad 66/1.[63]

In discussing preaching by prisoners at Andersonville, historian George C. Rable avers, "For many Christians, what counted were conversions, or more to the point, counting the conversions." Truly though, it was the manifest devotion of so many in such horrible circumstances that bolstered one's own faith. Sheppard knew of "no test of real piety more severe than that applied by life in Andersonville and other prisons." He thought it was a marvel "that any considerable body of men should have kept up Christian faith, hope and zeal. And that they not only did not give up in despair, 'curse God and die,' but lived and labored, and when death did come, even in most horrid form, 'Crossed the River of Jordan/Triumphant in the Lord.'" To him "one of the grandest testimony that the religion of Christ is the power of God and the wisdom of God [is] that it can sustain men amid the darkest woes of earth and fit them for the brightest glories of heaven." For Sheppard and the other Christian stalwarts, including in the Ninth Minnesota, the trials became far more terrible, but they kept up their work as long as they could. Solon Hyde discerned "a majesty in that little band that challenged the admiration of all who heard. Many a poor soul was comforted by them, and when he became too weak to care for himself they ministered to him as far as they were able. Though the aid afforded may not have been more than the bringing of a cup of cool water, it was that much given in the spirit of kindness and love. They were a noble set of men, true alike to their country and their God."[64]

THE FIRST OF MANY

On July 14 the Ninth Minnesota suffered its first death in Andersonville. A twenty-one-year-old native of Pennsylvania, Pvt. Orlando Geer had worked on his father Alphonso's farm in High Forest in Olmsted County. He enlisted in Company F in August 1862 with his older brother Elisha, a corporal. They came to Andersonville via Mobile, along with Hill, and shared a shebang in Squad 68/1. "We had been there less than a month," McCoy, their fellow "Olmsted Tiger," recalled, "when our boys commenced to die of dysentery and bowel troubles caused by the quality of food received, from exposure and impure water." When the one brother fell deathly sick, the other cared for him, wrote Clapp, "as well and faithful as a prisoner of war can nurse another." Early that morning Elisha awoke to discover Orlando, lying beside him, had "quietly and without a murmur passed away."[65]

In camp parlance, Orlando Geer had "died in quarters," that is in the stockade rather than the separate hospital compound. Soon after dawn, at the direction of their squad sergeant, his brother and their comrades carried him, probably in a borrowed blanket, down the hill and across Stockade Branch to Main Street. They laid him at the deadline near the South Gate, alongside others who had died the preceding afternoon, evening, and night. "In the morning that portion of the prison, near the gate," recalled Woolverton, "would be entirely covered with dead men, whose friends were waiting until the gates should be opened to give them the opportunity to deposit them in the 'Dead house,'" the flimsy structure located fifty yards outside the west wall. Many strangers waited "eagerly and clamorously asserting their right" to carry out bodies that were merely dropped off. That was desirable duty, for once outside they could forage for a few sticks of valuable firewood. At times claimants, though strangers to the deceased, even battled for the privilege. Others scavenged the few items of clothing left on the remains. "I have seen the ragged soldier, animated with scarcely life enough to stand," wrote Woolverton, "beg of the guard to be allowed to take the shirt from the dead, and that the only rag left him for a shroud."[66]

Once the South Gate opened at 8 A.M., the bodies went out on stretchers to the dead house. Such doleful processions continued as necessary throughout the day. Elisha said his final farewell to Orlando at the rude mortuary. Each body bore a ticket bearing name, company, regiment, and prison squad (if those details were known), which was pinned to any garment still worn by the deceased. If standard procedure was maintained, three men seized the corpse, "two by the shoulders and one by the feet," and tossed it into a "common army wagon," one of the same pool of vehicles that also brought rations into the stockade. The bodies were "piled up as a farmer would load in a quantity of butchered hogs." After twenty or more of the dead were hoisted unceremoniously on board, the wagon bearing Orlando Geer departed in the first load that particular morning. The sorrowful caravan creaked its way toward the cemetery situated beyond the top of the hill in a pleasant grove a half mile north of the stockade. "Not a day passed," recalled Father Clavreul, "that I did not meet the gruesome sight of these wagons, piled with bodies, heads, feet, or arms dangling from the vehicle transporting them to their final rest."[67]

Paroled prisoners unloaded the corpses from the wagons, placed them on stretchers, and bore them to the gravesite. Oriented north to south, a trench seven feet wide, four feet deep, and long enough for seventy-five bodies awaited Orlando and his companions in death: Pvt. Joseph Chapman, Eighty-Fifth New York, a "Plymouth Pilgrim," and Pvt. David Smith, Seventh Ohio Cavalry. Lacking coffins or shrouds, they went into the red soil shoulder to shoulder, in whatever tattered garments remained to them. A gravedigger set a wooden board branded with the number 3287 into a small mound behind Orlando Geer's head and scribbled that number onto the piece of paper taken from his body. That information was subsequently entered in the hospital and dead registers. The cause of death was also supposed to be recorded. The notation for Orlando was "unknown," probably because no surgeon took time that busy morning for the customary cursory examination before his body was removed to the graveyard. Fifty-seven men were buried that day. Some had actually died the day before but only reached the dead house after the previous day's transport to the cemetery had ceased. The camp registers could only attest to the number of the grave, the identity (if known) of the deceased, and day of the interment, which was not always the actual date of death. Nonetheless, First Sergeant Warren conceded the Rebels credit for "as decent a burial, and as complete a record as were under the circumstances possible." That was little enough satisfaction for a process at Andersonville that ultimately accounted for over 12,900 lives, including at least 84 Minnesotans.[68]

CHAPTER THIRTEEN

Andersonville (II)

Waiting for Abraham

The hideous first four weeks at Andersonville were just a foretaste for the Ninth Minnesota prisoners of the rest of their captivity. Their strength and health swiftly deteriorated. "During the latter part of July the heat became so terrific that sickness and death increased to an alarming extent," recalled Aslakson. "Every day around about us we witnessed such indescribable scenes of human misery, despair, sickness and death that we sank back into a state of nonresistance, mental and spiritual carelessness and neglect that it did not seem to matter what became of either ourselves or the others." Hill fervently prayed, "May God speed the day when we may be free to breathe the untainted air and roam the boundless fields of God's free earth."[1]

Beyond Andersonville, the war expanded. Grant's bloody assault on Petersburg turned into a long-term siege, while the North repulsed a massive raid that reached the very gates of Washington. One hundred and fifty miles north of Andersonville, after Gen. Joseph E. Johnston retreated south of the Chattahoochee, the last river line before Atlanta, President Jefferson Davis finally replaced him with the aggressive John Bell Hood. In northern Mississippi the Ninth Minnesota experienced further adventures, to be related later, with Bedford Forrest.

Andersonville itself appeared on the verge of a mass escape. On July 14, the same day Orlando Geer was laid in the ground, Wirz vowed should the prisoners rush the walls, his artillery would blast "the stockade with grape and canister so long as a man were left alive within it." That afternoon while rations were being divided, he fired blank cannon rounds over the prison, while guards loosed "rattling volleys of musketry." So "great was the tumult inside the camp," wrote Pvt. Eugene Forbes of the Fourth New Jersey, some of the issuing sergeants "dropped their cups or knives and fell flat to the ground" and others "plunged headlong into their 'dug out tents,' the brook, or any place that [looked like shelter]." It was a "hell of a demonstration," thought Sergeant Lay. He heard a rumor that Wirz even threatened to shoot "any unusual" crowds."[2]

The Rebels had good reason to worry. Discontent in Andersonville soared as more inmates poured into the camp, and living conditions, such as they were, declined even more. On July 14 the stockade held 27,568 inmates, with 1,683 more in the hospital. By the end of the month, an additional 3,600 had entered as against 1,102 recorded deaths (96 on July 31 alone). Shootings markedly increased. "No one who has not been in so crowded a place," wrote George Hitchcock, "can realize the fascination of the clear space beyond the dead-line." Inflaming feelings all the more was the false rumor that every guard who shot a prisoner earned a thirty-day furlough. Wirz especially feared the vast crowds that gathered every time more prisoners entered camp. The urge to talk to newcomers, "to hear and see their cheery voices and words, like a breeze from God's land," was irresistible. Nothing ever came of the rumors of imminent exchange. "We are waiting, patiently waiting, waiting for the prison gates to [be] opened," pleaded Pvt. Samuel Melvin of the First Massachusetts Heavy Artillery, "& for Abraham to say, 'Come.'"[3]

The Rebels fretted as much about a possible rescue as a mass escape. On July 18 and 19, Union cavalry raiding between Montgomery and Columbus destroyed a thirty-mile section of track one hundred miles northwest of Andersonville, the same stretch over which the Minnesotans had passed. Rail service was tied up for weeks. "Events seem to thicken," Hill wrote on the twentieth. "The war clouds seem to come slowly nearer, and today the enemy are commencing earthworks at headquarters in plain view from our prison pen. They seem to fear a visit from some of our cavalry who are scouring the country. Oh, I earnestly pray that they may come and relieve the suffering, dying prisoners here." Although Hill personally had "got along quite well so far," the previous week he was "troubled with want of appetite and slight diarrhoea" and "felt very weak."[4]

That thirty thousand starved Union prisoners might break out or be freed to swarm the countryside panicked General Winder. Hundreds of slaves and off-duty guards dug around the clock to construct around the stockade an elaborate network of earthworks, including a fort near the North Gate and the big "Star Fort" overlooking the southwest corner. The singing of the slaves while toiling at night was "inexpressibly mournful" to Private Forbes, "as if the wail of the oppressed was rising to heaven." On July 28 the "rebs fired a solid shot over our heads which lodged in the marsh just outside the stockade," wrote Hitchcock. "It caused a big scare, and the crowds which were greeting the new prisoners were instantly dispersed." The next day a line of white flags placed inside the camp marked the space "beyond which no crowds must collect or [they] will be shelled." In early August the arrival of over a thousand prisoners recently nabbed after a disastrous cavalry raid south of Atlanta stoked rumors of imminent attack. Any rescue, though, must come quickly or those who were desperately sick, including many Minnesotans, would not survive very long.[5]

PILGRIMAGE OF PAIN

Hill grieved over the "vast cauldron" that was Andersonville, with "many dying in the streets, neglected, dirty and almost unknown." By July 31 three more Ninth Minnesota prisoners had "died in quarters." One was James Clabaugh, a twenty-year-old private in Company D, who was buried on the nineteenth. He was the first to die of the eight "healthy, cheerful, light-hearted soldier boys" who in October 1863 stood on the deck of the *Chippewa Falls* speculating about their future. Although the official cause of death was remittent fever, Clabaugh had in fact never recovered from the effects of sunstroke incurred on the fearful final march to Brice's Crossroads. He was honored after the war when his comrades in Winnebago City (Faribault County) christened their Grand Army of the Republic post for him.[6]

Those who died in quarters had received little medical treatment other than what their impoverished friends could provide. When sick call sounded in the morning, the squad sergeants were supposed to lead their ailing men to the South Gate and have those who could not walk carried there. Sick call represented one of the very worst of all Andersonville experiences. Sergeant Major Clapp could only stand to witness the process "a very few times, and each time resolved that I would not go again." The misery evident everywhere in the camp was hard enough to stomach, "but at sick call the sight was 'horrid,' every grade of disease, and every kind; from the strong robust man, to the poor creature that hardly bore any resemblance of a human being." Numerous Minnesotans were among the sick of Squad 66/1 whom Sergeant Woolverton regularly took there. "Hundreds of persons [were] in attendance at the sick call, morning after morning," he explained, "many of them unable to sit up, exposed to the intense heat of the sun for from two to three hours, awaiting their turn to get medicine." Reverend Sheppard, sergeant of Squad 69/2 with some Minnesotans, likewise brought sick men there nearly every day. "My blood never boiled hotter than when I saw daily the

Burial at Andersonville, August 1864

long line of cripples crawling along, or the still more helpless borne on the backs of comrades or on blankets, while every movement was agony, and many died on the way. Yet this daily torment was the price of a Rebel prescription."[7]

When called in order of detachments, the squad sergeants led their charges through the South Gate into the adjacent "sick yard," a fenced enclosure around the gate complex. An informal triage took place so those who seemed less sick were seen first. In a dozen examining stations, each furnished with desk and cabinet and covered by an awning, surgeons briefly looked over the sick and recommended treatment. Most often they simply turned the prisoners back into camp after little or no care. One such unfortunate, very likely in Woolverton's own squad, was seventeen-year-old Pvt. Ludoviso Bourgard of Company C. Barefoot like nearly all his Guntown comrades, he had stubbed his toe against a root, and the wound festered and turned gangrenous. He could only "hop on one leg to and fro" while leaning on a long stick. At repeated sick calls, surgeons refused to amputate or otherwise treat the toe. Finally a Rebel hospital steward took pity and cauterized the wound, a kindness Bourgard believed saved his life. Some prisoners were prescribed medications that their squad sergeants fetched after 4 P.M. at the South Gate. Those remedies, served as herbal teas, were "mostly barks or roots" with little if any therapeutic value. Sixteen-year-old Pvt. William E. Walker of Company K, another recent Saratoga recruit, suffered severe sciatica in his back. His comrades had to carry him outside. Reduced to offering only a few pills and sumac berries, the surgeon who saw him "expressed regret he was unable to furnish medicine more applicable to my case." Some prisoners did not even get that much. During the retreat from Brice's Crossroads, a horse had stomped the right leg of Sgt. Henry A. C. Thompson of Company A. When the wound became infected at Andersonville, the only advice he could get from the "old timers" was to treat it with tobacco juice, an old folk remedy.[8]

Forcing frail, ailing men to report under such conditions for so little healing effect was to Woolverton "so barbarous and inhuman, that I declined to present the sick of my detachment who could not walk." Instead he "went personally to the physicians and represented the ailments of such persons, asking medicine for them. I was very promptly informed that no medicine would be given unless the patient was produced. I remonstrated and insisted that the exposure worked more injury to the patient than all the medicine could do good, and absolutely refused to comply with the order." Even worse, complained Sheppard, "frequently from some cause no doctors would be at the gate. In that case I never knew any notice to be given to prevent the pilgrimage of pain, but the sick would come and lie around in the hot sun for hours, only at length to go groaning back to their miserable huts." He and fellow believers organized parties of prisoners to clear the way for the sick and bring them cool water, "a boon indeed."[9]

DEATH HERE REIGNED SUPREME

Woolverton soon discovered it was "very hard to get a man admitted [to the hospital], for I have often tried and failed." Until August only a set number of sick were allowed in each day, generally corresponding to the deaths that occurred in the hospital the previous day. Clerks drew up yet another ticket with personal details and pinned it to the clothes of the patients designated for admittance. The sick would sit or sprawl on the ground until a wagon could convey them to the hospital. The first Ninth Minnesota patient was Lewis Young from Sheppard's squad, admitted on July 3 with acute diarrhea. During the rest of the month, seven more were hospitalized—two because of Woolverton's persistent efforts. One in his squad was James Woodbury, the ardent Peace Democrat, with acute diarrhea, fever, and terrible chills in the "uncomfortably cool" nights in later July. Sunday, July 24, was "very cool all day and at night," a shivering Woodbury noted in his diary. "I'd liked to fraze with the cold." The next night was the "coldest night yet," according to Hitchcock. On the morning of July 26, Woodbury surrendered his pocket diary to liberator Nate Palmeter, his good friend, who recorded therein: "J. M. Woodbury went out to the hospital; the weather dry and hot; in the afternoon it looked as though it had set in for a long rain, [I] got no tent or blanket nor coat nor boots." Four of the eight hospital patients had died by the end of July. On August 2 Woodbury joined them in the cemetery.[10]

During the first few days of August, the number of sick allowed in the hospital greatly increased. Four were from the Ninth Minnesota. "Quite a movement is being made today in moving the sick and lame from camp," Hill wrote on the third. "If there is an opening tomorrow I think of trying it too, on account of my swollen feet and sickness, diarrhoea. I hope the time will speedily come when we shall all be relieved from this confinement and once more breathe freely in our own home. God grant the day may come soon." On August 4 three more Minnesotans were admitted, including liberator Zara Frisbie. The next day the authorities temporarily suspended the general sick call and only accepted patients according to unit order, beginning with the first eight detachments. Hill bid farewell to two tentmates, his brother-in-law Harvey and Newton, who were in Squads 1/1 and 1/2 respectively. Their neighbor from Saratoga, Martin Shortt in Squad 2/2, also left that day. Hill trusted they "are having better fare and treatment. I have not yet had any opportunity [to go into the hospital], as they go out by detachments." By August 6 the hospital compound bulged with nearly 1,150 more patients than on the first, but thereafter sick call was sporadic, with many fewer allowed in. During the balance of August, only two more from the Ninth Minnesota were admitted, a tiny percentage of the Minnesotans who were severely ill.[11]

Hill would never learn how Harvey, Newton, or Shortt fared. No account of their hospitalization or that of Woodbury, Frisbie, or anyone else from the Ninth Minnesota has apparently survived. Thirty-five of its prisoners eventually became patients, but only two ever walked out again, and they both died in 1865, almost immediately after returning home. In fact, only a relatively few patients ever lived to tell of being hospitalized. Wisconsin artillery sergeant John Warren was a rare survivor. Shoeless after Brice's Crossroads, he had developed an open sore on the sole of his right foot. After it became badly infected, he was only too aware of what would likely ensue from the unavoidable exposure to the "saturated, poisonous earth." The "dreaded gangrene would set in, and amputation would soon follow, only to make another wound for a fresh attack of gangrene."[12]

On August 19, feeling lucky to be selected for the hospital, Warren waited in the sick yard most of the day in the company of another fortunate prospective patient. Once the advancing sun removed the shadow cast by the stockade wall, Warren "crawled across the yard, on my hands and knees, and lay down in the little patch of shade made by the awning where the surgeon stood when examining patients." His companion gladly crept after him. The two dozed in the heat. "I well remember the happy, peaceful expression on the man's face as he rolled up his coat for a pillow and lay down in the sand to sleep." Despite "pain and hunger," Warren savored an extraordinarily pleasant afternoon in "the pure air" outside the gate. "Whatever might be ahead, the Bull Pen with its horrors was behind; and although I knew nothing of the hospital, from which, it was said, none ever returned to the stockade," his "hope revived." Later in the afternoon when water was furnished, Warren took a cup from his sleeping companion's haversack and filled it for him for when he should awake. Finally, when the wagon rumbled up to take them to the hospital, Warren gently shook him, only to find he was dead. "Like one who gathers up the ammunition of his fallen comrade to help him in the fight, so I hastily removed his haversack with the battered tin cup, and went my way."[13]

The hospital compound lay a few hundred yards southeast of the stockade in the midst of a swamp. A six-foot-high barrier, with the gate set in the west wall, surrounded its five acres. Wells furnished drinking water, while the Sweetwater Creek that flowed slowly through a ditch in the south end served as a privy. There were nineteen wards, each containing seventy-five to one hundred patients sheltered within more than two hundred "simple tents or rather flies of canvas stretched among the grateful shade of oaks which had been left standing." Warren and a half dozen others shared a tent open at the sides and perched on a "rude bank or platform, raised some two feet above the sand." There were no board bunks, bedding—even pine boughs—or soap or clean clothes. Even so, Warren rejoiced over the "room, pure air, better water, and better though not more abundant food." Since the surrounding swamp emitted a terrible stench, in truth the air was "pure" only in comparison to the even fouler stockade. The hospital cooked its own rations, and although of more variety, the fare still comprised rough, hard-to-digest corn bread, along with a bit of beef and "rice soup" on occasion.[14]

A hospital steward and six attendants staffed each ward. All were fellow prisoners serving on parole. Some were skilled and highly devoted to their charges; others were scoundrels and thieves. The Rebel surgeons, Warren conceded, "in the main did what they could for us, with their limited advantages and few medicines." The worst wards were for those afflicted with gangrene, and that was where Warren went. "We are compelled to fold our arms and look quietly upon [gangrene's] ravages," one surgeon lamented on September 5, "not even having stimulants to support the system under its depressing influence." Any available medication had to be reserved for those going "under the knife." Surgery rarely did any good, for the patients rapidly developed what was known as "hospital gangrene." Warren knew men who suffered "three amputations in rapid succession, all performed in the old way: the patient strapped to a table without anaesthetics, and, need I add, then die in consequence."[15]

Miraculously, Warren's foot got better, but he hobbled on crutches the whole time and never returned to the stockade. In contrast, all of his immediate companions swiftly died. "Six others were brought from the stockade, one after another, to remain but a short time, and then to be carried out," to be replaced by more. "Death here reigned supreme." Appearing "every morning along the street" was a "single rank of men, lying straight and stiff, with an old soldier's cap placed reverently over their faces to keep the light from the sightless eyes. Somebody's hope, somebody's dependence, waiting for [the] detail to carry them out the gate on a stretcher."[16]

Often the only word received in the main stockade about friends in the hospital was of their passing. "Many times when our young Johnnie [Willie Hammack] came inside to call the roll," McCoy recalled, "he would report to

A. C. McCoy

us the death of this and that one of our detachment who had left for the hospital but the day before." As the hospital filled with new patients, the authorities released a few convalescents back into the camp. They "report an awful condition of affairs there," Hitchcock noted on August 7, "no medicine, no proper care and nothing to relieve the dying. They prefer to be in camp where they can be near friends." Likewise, Henry Miller of the Seventy-Second Ohio, the erstwhile molasses entrepreneur in Squad 66/2, heard from "the old prison boys" that patients "lay all day without even a drink of water, and scarcely any of them came out alive." That dire description was not necessarily true for everyone in the hospital, but incidences of good treatment were rare enough to be exceptions that proved the rule. Such tales of terrible neglect forced a hard decision within many close-knit groups. "We kept our sick with us," wrote Miller, "that if we were deprived of all the necessities to properly care for them, we could give them our sympathy at least. Often when we saw them suffering and could not help them, the tears would fill our eyes and at the same time it would take all our manhood and strength and we would turn our faces away from our sick comrades until we could dry our tears and would then turn and give them our attention again."[17]

PROVIDENCE SPRING

Even though all the new defensive earthworks were worrisome, the prisoners did heartily approve of different sorts of construction. The long-anticipated clean up of Stockade Branch finally began in early August. Boarding up of the foul banks and creek bottom on the east side created a "kind of reservoir" that promised "purer and cleaner water" suitable for washing if not yet for drinking. That "fine thing," according to Clapp, "ought to have been done before the stockade was considered complete." On August 8 paroled prisoners brought in lumber to construct, starting at the northwest corner of the stockade, the first of four barracks (actually sheds), each of which would house one detachment. It appeared the Andersonville authorities were finally making some effort to create a better infrastructure for the prison population.[18]

Tuesday, August 9, proved particularly special in the long, tragic history of Andersonville. The daily count revealed 33,006 prisoners in the stockade and hospital—the most ever. In the previous nine days, 1,982 men had entered and 750 died. More remarkable events were in store. The day's weather was "exceedingly hot," so much so that it seemed things were "burning up." Late in the afternoon, before the rations could all be distributed, a "terrific" thunderstorm blew in. Fortunate prisoners with access to shelter disappeared inside them, but others, like Lyon, with no place to go simply watched in awe. "All at once the clouds seemed to break open and the rain poured down in torrents. Never before or since have I seen so much rainfall in an hour in my life." A "rushing flood of maddened water" washed down the steep hill "in a great sheet." Stockade Branch "soon overflowed its banks and spread out over the swamp. In about an hour this stream, which was originally ten feet wide, had spread out until it was three hundred feet wide and six feet deep." A sound like a "cannon shot" thundered forth, followed by another. "The stockade is broken!" echoed the cry. "Sure enough," wrote Lyon, "the flood had carried away a hundred feet of the western stockade, and as the timbers rushed down they carried with them about as much of the eastern stockade." Hearing "the report of heavy guns," Clapp and his companions "crawled out of our huts, and surely, on the west and east sides, on the creek, the barrier between us and liberty was gone. The creek was very high and completely overflowing the bottom land and looked like a small lake." Winder frantically mustered the entire guard force and sixteen field pieces to cover the breaches. "Before anyone could take advantage of the opportunity for escape, there was a heavy guard posted at both openings, and it being daylight shut out all prospects of a 'run.'"[19]

Rain and flooding persevered that night and all the next day. Only by the evening of August 12 did Winder have the situation at Andersonville fully under control. His men furiously rebuilt the sections of walls that had been swept away and began erecting an entire second stockade set roughly two hundred feet beyond the inner one. "We watched them," Clapp wrote, "wondering what they were all about, and only found out when we saw all around us a double enclosure." The logs in the second wall were "not hewn, but put up rough," which enabled the prisoners to see yet "a third stockade going up about 30' from middle one. We were now completely nonplussed, what could induce them to erect a third stockade, was a problem we could none of us solve."[20]

Nothing that was occurring outside could overshadow what had taken place inside the camp. "When the water fell," Clapp wrote, it was "found that all the fine improvements [in Stockade Branch] just had been carried away. Notwithstanding all of this we could not help being thankful, for the rain had perfectly cleaned our camp, and the air was so fresh and pure, that it really imparted new life to us." To Lyon the effect was nothing short of "marvelous." The "whole surface was washed, and the swamp, which before was almost beyond endurance, looked now as if it had been scrubbed. We were indeed in a new world." The Rebels resumed "flooring and siding the run with boards." With the "banks of creek boarded up," noted Hitchcock, "we can dip for water without stirring up the mud." The privies were also greatly improved.[21]

The thirteenth saw the "greatest marvel of all." Flowing "out from under an old pine stump which stood near the dead line just below the north gate," recalled Lyon, "we saw a stream of water as large as a man's arm pour forth and run down the hill between the dead line and the stockade." The "clear, cold, pure, spring water" collected in a "little pool" just beyond the deadline. At first the prisoners could only reach it by attaching a cup to a long pole. But in a few days, "to our great surprise," camp workers "nailed two boards together, forming a leader like an old-fashioned eaves trough. Then they placed it so as to lead the stream to our side of the dead line. Then we could go and get the pure, sweet water." The phenomenon became known as "Providence Spring." According to Aslakson, "next to obtaining our liberty, nothing could have been more welcome. Nearly every man in the prison had acquired such an unconquerable loathing and distaste for the water in the old stream that they suffered the most severe thirst rather than to drink the stinking contaminated water. This God-sent fountain was soon taken over by the prison police to guard against contamination, and the men went there and waited in line to get their supply of clean cold water which seemed like nectar from heaven." That "River of Life," wrote Lyon, "revived our sinking spirits and filled us with new hope."[22]

DEATH DAYS

Unfortunately, in hot, overcrowded Andersonville that "hope" swiftly melted away. In August "our rations became wonderfully less," Clapp recalled, "and before the month was out, we drew of corn bread a slice about two inches square and one inch thick; bacon comparatively not any; rice or cooked beans, say half a pint. Hardly a man in the camp but what would have eaten all at once and still been hungry." Sergeant Hoster of the 148th New York noticed the sharp decline in quality (although it is difficult to imagine how it could be any worse) as well as quantity. "My ration smelled bad enough," he wrote on August 10, "to drive a dog out of a tan yard," but he still managed to trade it for bread. The authorities occasionally substituted molasses for meat, but no longer a desirable treat, it acted, wrote Hitchcock, "like poison on all who are troubled with diarrhea." Poor diet was not the only problem. The hot weather, he explained, "is driving men to idiocy. Many have been sun struck and died. The effect of starvation combined with the fearful heat first makes us childish, then stupid."[23]

In the midst of the staggering daily numbers of dead, the Ninth Minnesota prisoners themselves confronted an unusually high rate of mortality in their own ranks. On August 13, the day Providence Spring spurted out of the hillside, some 191 of the original 204 prisoners remained after fifty-six days in prison. The following week 11 died and then 15 more between August 21 and September 7 (four on the fourth alone). The deaths up to that point reached 39: nearly 1 in 5 had died. The other Guntown prisoners who entered Andersonville at the same time were not dying at anything like the high percentage of the Ninth Minnesota, which made up less than a fifth of their overall number. Up through August 13, for example, the Seventy-Second Ohio, with at least 213 and possibly as many as 225 men in Andersonville, suffered only 3 dead. Six more Ohioans died between that day and September 7, for a grand total of 9 dead. In another instance, of about 90 prisoners from the 113th Illinois at Andersonville, apparently 5 died between June 19 and September 7.[24]

The official cause for 70 percent of the deaths in the Ninth Minnesota during that time was diarrhea or dysentery, both acute and chronic forms. As yet, fatalities due to scurvy (scorbutus) were quite rare among the Minnesotans, although that particular deficiency disease was taking grim hold. Some fellow prisoners ascribed their greatly increased mortality to the fierce Southern summer. At Guntown the Ninth Minnesota, which came from "the far

North," had been "full and the men large and strong," First Sergeant Turrill of the Seventy-Second Ohio would later remark, but "the change of climate and conditions were severe." Thus, in Andersonville "their mortality was excessive." Sergeant Woolverton witnessed at close hand the dire fate of the numerous Minnesotans among the ninety prisoners in his Squad 66/1. Nine of the squad's ten known deaths between June 19 and September 7 were from the Ninth Minnesota. "While I was a prisoner," he commented, "I was intimately associated with quite a number of the Ninth Minnesota men, the healthiest, best looking, and apparently as able bodied soldiers as I ever saw; all in prime of life and in perfect health, when made prisoners. After two or three months' confinement, they began to die off, and before six months there were but two left out of fourteen [by which he evidently meant just in his own particular mess], and I think neither of them ever lived to tell of the horrible sufferings and miserable death of their comrades."[25]

In the absence of a detailed diagnosis, one can only speculate why the Ninth Minnesota proved so vulnerable. Prior to the trek to Brice's Crossroads, the regiment had not experienced truly severe field conditions. No hard marches, lengthy exposure to very hot and humid climates, and other wants and trials had weeded out those who were unfit for a strenuous campaign. That contrasted sharply with the seasoned veterans of a regiment like the Seventy-Second Ohio. The oldest and youngest Minnesotans seemed in the greatest peril. In addition, their previous relative isolation in the Northwest may have made them less resistant to common diseases.

Four of the nine fatalities in Squad 66/1 were from Company H. Jacob Pericle, who was probably fifty-two years old, died in quarters on August 13 from chronic dysentery. His seventeen-year-old son, Jesse, was there to comfort him. Frederick Sauter was also present when younger brother Charles passed away a week later from marasamus, a sort of progressive emaciation that meant in essence being starved to death. Aslakson lost two tentmates: Magnus Bengston, who died on the twenty-third from dysentery, and fellow Norwegian Nils Johnson, who succumbed on September 4 from diarrhea. That left of the original four only him and John Larson (Johannes Larsson), a thirty-one-year-old Swede from Carver County. "Lonely, forgotten, half starved, as well as half-dead, we were in that condition of transition when a person gets toughened to holding on to his reserve strength and holding out against death, no matter what the odds."[26]

Others shared such terrible feelings of isolation. Palmeter thought enough of an especially vivid dream about his mother to record on August 7 in Woodbury's diary how he "awoke crying." Severe depression was deadly. Lyon recalled the circumstances surrounding the death of Franklin Wilson, "who had lived in our family at home." A thirty-six-year-old farmer from New York and, like Lyon, a recent recruit to Company C, Wilson "was married and had one child [Mary], a beautiful girl of five years. To see the anguish written on that man's face was most pathetic. It would not do for me to sympathize with him. I must divert his mind, if possible; but my efforts were in vain. His poor heart was breaking, and one morning we closed his weary eyes." Wilson died from diarrhea and was buried on the fourteenth.[27]

Between August 13 and September 7, a group of just eleven men from Company G, mostly German immigrants led by their First Sergeant Weber, accounted for six of the nine known fatalities among the ninety men of Squad 66/3. One died in the hospital and the others in quarters with their comrades. On September 7 the four survivors bade farewell to Pvt. John Monthy when he, too, left for the hospital. (He died there on September 18.) The loss of so many close comrades in his charge devastated Weber. He particularly remembered the terrible death of Pvt. Henri Schiefer, a thirty-nine-year-old married immigrant from Prussia. "Writhing in agony," with "maggots, worms and lice" that crept "from mouth, ears and eyes," Schiefer perished on August 29 from diarrhea. It was a vision Weber swore could "paralyze the soul of the most stone-hearted observer," let alone a friend. Moreover, he had to strip Schiefer's emaciated corpse. "Henry's shirt was a good one while [Weber's] was like a fish net. So I made an exchange." Such activities, Weber recalled much later to another ex–Company G comrade, "could be seen everywhere, as not a good piece of clothing was left on a dead one to be taken away. Thus the prisoners had to do to help themselves as they were not given any clothing from the rebels even if they didn't have any. Many wore the costume in which God created them . . . not a particle of clothing even to cover up modestly, while others ran around totally insane."[28]

Six of the eight recorded deaths in Squad 65/3 during that same period came from the Ninth Minnesota. On August 16 George Atkinson, the beloved Methodist preacher in Company F, died in quarters from enteritis. Corporal McArthur, his neighbor in Olmsted County, had taken special care of him at Andersonville. The first night after being captured, McArthur had wisely sewn "about ten dollars in greenbacks and postal currency" in the waistband of his trousers. When Atkinson became sick "soon after we reached the prison," McArthur used these funds to buy "tea and other luxuries" to help keep up his spirits. "After he became unable to walk, I carried him on my back from where we were located, just a short distance east of the north gate, to the south gate, where he had to go to attend sick call. The doctor could not help him and I carried him back to our camping ground." McArthur helped bring Atkinson's body out the South Gate, but he was not actually buried until the

Frank Weber

next day. "Before his death he gave me his bible to take home to his wife." In his personal regimental roll, Chaplain Kerr uniquely described Atkinson as "an earnest chr. [Christian] Man." Principal Musician Joel Handy was another fatality in Squad 65/3. While "out under the open sky," he died on the night of August 22 from "debilitas," an antique medical term for overall weakness, and was buried the next day. Young DeWitt was with his father to the end. "Before he drew his last breath," wrote a family historian, "Joel Handy exacted a promise from his son that he would make every attempt to escape the stockade."[29]

Dying after two weeks of hospitalization, Zara Frisbie (from Squad 68/1) was buried on August 19 in grave 6191. He was the first liberator to pass away in Andersonville. No cause of death was recorded, although the original reason for his hospitalization was hepatitis. As was common in the hospital, he most likely departed alone and friendless, with no opportunity to write his wife, Mary, another wonderful letter like the one he sent in December 1863 while being held in Jefferson City. Two of the three members of Company K who entered the hospital on August 5 fared no better. Martin Shortt, who was buried on August 16, became the earliest recorded death from scurvy in the Ninth Minnesota. Succumbing to diarrhea, Charles Newton joined him in the graveyard on August 27, leaving only Joseph Harvey, Hill's brother-in-law, tenuously holding onto life until September 18, when he, too, died of diarrhea.[30]

Although Hill never got to join Harvey and their friends in the hospital, in his final days he was truly comforted by devoted companionship. On August 7 he wrote what became the last entry in his diary: "Sabbath; still inside and fast getting weaker; God help me to be resigned to His will, make me more mindful of Thy goodness, Oh Father. Help me to pray earnest for support." Despite the lingering effects of his leg wounds, Myron Tower, yet another of the Saratoga neighbors, started to help take care of Hill.

> I found that he was reconciled to die. His countenance was pleasant & calm. The day before he died we walked to the gate together to see the Dr. He was weak & supported himself by putting his arms around me. We had a good chat that evening. He appeared to think he should recover & that we should [*sic*] good times at home. His last words to me were "How shall I ever repay you for your care & kindness to me" & we parted by shaking hands—when he closed by saying "May God bless you."

Chauncey Hill passed away on August 17, "some time between the hours of 2 & 4 o clock A.M." He "died without a struggle, so that the man sleeping with him did not know he was dead until morning. [The other man] got up at 2 o clock and went out of the tent." At the mortuary a surgeon gave the cause of death as dysentery. The day Hill died, no fewer than 114 men were interred in the cemetery. Such a huge number of deaths day after day overwhelmed the burial squad, which finally placed him in grave 6064 the next afternoon when they interred 88 corpses. Soon after Hill's death, by a remarkable circumstance, Tower chanced to speak with a certain Mrs. M. W. Manning "who is visiting with the prisoners here & loves to give information to friends." She kindly forwarded a letter Tower wrote on U.S. Christian Commission stationery that informed Sarah Hill of her husband's death. Most Andersonville widows never received such a timely notice. George Jenkins, yet another good friend from Company K, saved Hill's diary and eventually gave it to her.[31]

In the midst of so much death, pain, and privation, the daily grind of life in camp, for good and ill, went on. Palmeter recorded that his comrade William W. Rice, a twenty-four-year-old private in Company C, received a rare letter from home. A few days later, Palmeter was delighted to note that he himself finally bought a blouse, and soon after he "got some paper to write a letter," although it is not known if he ever mailed it. On August 28 he enjoyed "a good dinner of rice" and on September 1 a "late dinner" of "baked beef" and a "hot corn dodger." All through the next night, though, he was again hungry. Palmeter discovered that Cpl. Frank Rafferty of Company C, in another squad, was so injured and weak he "could scarcely crawl about." Sometime "after the spring broke through," Rafferty was crossing the log bridge set over Stockade Branch and the slough when he "was pushed off to strike on top of one of the short stakes." The "Boys from Co C heard about this & came to see Rafferty, found him badly hurt, struck on right side." They took care of him. In addition to his injury, Rafferty, like so many others including, it is recorded, liberator Stephen Chandler, suffered from "rheumatism." Such severe pain, along with bruising in muscle and joints and distress of the gums, was also a symptom of scurvy.[32]

About that time Pvt. George Saville, a cheerful thirty-one-year-old transplanted Englishman in Company F, helped take a body out of the inner stockade to the dead house. While outside he borrowed an axe from a slave to trim tree branches for firewood, but instead of returning the valuable tool, he smuggled it back into camp. A short time later, an officer and some guards, with the terrified black man in tow, pushed their way through the crowded North slope to Saville's squad bivouac. Forced to pick out the Yankee to whom he loaned the axe, the slave pointed to Saville. Justice in Andersonville was rough. Just outside the South Gate, easily seen from Saville's vantage, were the stocks and other devices where prisoners, particularly recaptured escapees, were bound "laying on their backs with the hot southern sun beating down on them, their wrists tied to stakes driven in the ground & in such a position that it was impossible for them to shift their position in any way." Other miscreants were chained to huge iron balls that they had to drag with them. After being taken outside, both Saville and the slave were summarily sentenced to be flogged with a "rawhide whip of 3 strands." The guards played a cruel trick. They tied Saville to a post, bared his back, and forced the black man to either give him thirty "hard lashes" or suffer an even more severe beating. Then the guards reversed their positions and sternly ordered Saville to whip the slave thirty times. "To this poor Saville demurred stoutly, and instinctively shrank from the execution of so infamous and barbarous an act. He was told, however, that if he refused to obey, the negro would be compelled to whip him the same number of lashes as before, when Saville, fearing for his life, inflicted on the poor negro the punishment ordered."[33]

The number of Ninth Minnesota prisoners at Andersonville increased by three with the arrival on August 24 of Company K liberators George Frahm and John Gordon, along with Pliny Conkey of Company C. They were part of a small group of prisoners who had left Mobile on the last day of July and traveled upriver to Selma and across to Montgomery, where they waited until the railroad was repaired before being forwarded to Macon and eventually to Andersonville. At Mobile Gordon "made some money while working in the hospital and, as his captors had not searched him [upon entering Andersonville], he was much better off than most of the other prisoners, as he had the wherewithal to purchase rations from the guards." Such advantage did not make a sojourn at Camp Sumter much easier, but in fact Gordon's stay would be much shorter than he probably expected.[34]

LEAVING

The news on September 4 that Sherman had finally seized Atlanta elicited joyous response from the prisoners but sobered the guards. On the evening of September 6, Rebel sergeants entered the stockade to tell the First to the Eighteenth Detachments to prepare to move out. "Skeptical jeers" resulted, but the railroad cars they saw waiting at the depot argued those orders were genuine. Word was of an exchange to take place in Charleston. The "lucky detachments" became "extremely excited." Palmeter heard "great shouting and cheering," and Hitchcock confirmed the "whole camp is wild with excitement." In fact Winder, fearing the Yankees at Atlanta would next come after Andersonville, had simply determined to transfer the prisoners elsewhere.[35]

The prisoners grew more exhilarated on September 7 when the first four detachments actually marched out the South Gate. They included liberator Charles Dietrich and about nine others from Company K who on first entering Andersonville on June 19 had been put, much against their will, into the lowest-numbered detachments. Now they were among the first to leave the cursed place. Trains carrying nearly 1,500 men chugged off to the north in the direction of Macon. Almost 3,000 more departed on the eighth. That day Palmeter himself exited "the bull pen in great glee of being exchanged," but most reluctantly he had to return "because there is no transportation." Another thousand got away on September 9, but not Palmeter, who stood in line for over four hours before being sent back in for his supper. His turn finally came before dawn on September 10 when he joined the 2,000 who departed Andersonville that day. In the next three days, nearly 9,300 more prisoners said goodbye. The area around the South Gate when the men marched out was chaotic. Hundreds of other prisoners tried with varying degrees of success to force their way into the "lucky detachments" before they could get out of the gates.[36]

The week beginning September 7 witnessed an amazing 16,783 prisoners vacate Andersonville. They left by detachments, not only the most senior but also some of the highest numbered with most recent arrivals. It seemed the Rebels were working from both ends toward the unhappy middle. Very likely 35 inmates from the Ninth Minnesota departed that week, including liberators Palmeter, Dietrich, and John Morrison. Most of the rest of the Ninth Minnesota contingent were in the Sixty-Fourth through Sixty-Eighth Detachments, but no one knew when or even if they would be going, too. On the evening of September 13, the Sixty-Third Detachment, at least, was told to get ready, but the order was canceled after the last train that day derailed only three miles north of Andersonville. Many prisoners were killed in the wreck, and the survivors had to stagger back down to the camp.[37]

Except for 578 sick prisoners from the hospital who departed on September 16, the general transportation of prisoners from Andersonville ceased indefinitely. Instead it was learned there would be a special exchange of 2,000 prisoners. The only catch was that they had to be recent captures from Sherman's current army around Atlanta. That ruled out anyone from Brice's Crossroads, although many of its veterans did not see it that way at all. They had proudly served under "Uncle Billy" at Vicksburg and that was that. Thus, nearly 150 former "Sturgis raiders," many from the Seventy-Second Ohio, were among 1,800 prisoners who left Andersonville on September 17 and 19, bound toward Atlanta. Perhaps two or three Minnesotans went along, but the only one known to go for certain was seventeen-year-old Pvt. Dwight Card of Company E, a former Pennsylvanian. A comrade would remember that one day in mid-September Card, who was very sick, left his shebang alone to seek medicine at the South Gate but never returned. His mysterious disappearance only reinforced warnings never to go unaccompanied to the gate![38]

Discouraging word finally reached the Andersonville prisoners that all the previous shipments had just gone to different camps, not an exchange. The Rebels had lied to keep the prisoners calm while they emptied Andersonville lest Sherman's cavalry sweep down from Atlanta and free them. Such a raid evidently never occurred to "Uncle Billy," who was mindful of the potential mischief of Hood's army, which remained at large. On September 22 Sherman even opined that the ongoing transfer of prisoners from Andersonville "will improve the condition of the balance." Considering what life was really like at Andersonville, that would have seemed a grotesque joke to those still imprisoned there. As of September 21, two weeks after the exodus commenced, only 8,861 prisoners remained in the stockade, with another 2,070 in the hospital. The interior of the prison resembled a vast anthill with but few ants. "It is very lonely and seems very drear to see so many deserted burrows and dens all over the camp," wrote Hitchcock. Inmates swarmed into the abandoned sites seeking anything of use and "gleefully" appropriated empty shebangs that promised better shelter.[39]

One unforeseen horrible consequence of the rapid evacuation was the plight of those who lacked the strength to make the move with their detachments. "A great many sick men have been left, and suffered terribly," Eugene Forbes of the Fourth New Jersey wrote on the tenth. "Some cases have been found of men not having anything to eat for three days." The prison police scoured the camp for abandoned men and removed them to the four new barracks, which were open sheds, along the North Wall. Their assigned detachments had barely moved in before being ejected to make room for the invalids. Each shed constituted two "floors," actually long wooden racks, with the lower level eighteen inches off the ground and the upper just three feet above. "Into these," recalled Lyon, "we carried these helpless fellows and laid them close together." To Hitchcock they resembled codfish "spread out" along the shore "to dry." Conditions in the barracks were particularly bad. The food supply was uncertain and medical care sparse. Many sick were robbed or otherwise mistreated or neglected. Three privates from Company K who died in quarters at that time were almost certainly victims of the barracks, being too sick to accompany their detachments, which had hurriedly pulled out on the seventh. One was twenty-three-year-old Jacob Thielen, who was buried on September 17 in grave 9003. He was the second liberator to die in Andersonville. A German immigrant and wheelwright from Wabasha, he may have been in the country only two months when he enlisted in August 1862.[40]

The appalling conditions in the barracks, where "thousands of men [were] absolutely unable to care for themselves," impelled other prisoners to volunteer to care for them. Beginning about September 10, Lyon joined them. The sheds were divided into wards of sixty men, and as a ward master Lyon's duty was to "direct and assist the nurses in drawing rations and distributing to the sick, and to do all that he could to relieve their suffering until death came." Each morning he would remove several dead men and fill their places with others. Patients who looked to be on their last legs he tried to identify and attach to their clothes a small piece of paper bearing name, company, and regiment, but so many of the sick were unknown. A Confederate surgeon who inspected the barracks in mid-September described the "haggard, distressed countenances" of its "miserable, complaining, dejected, living skeletons." Within a week or so Lyon, himself seriously ill, hobbled back to the company bivouac just beyond the old North Wall only to find his old "mud shanty" was completely empty. Lacking the strength to search for his absent comrades, he huddled alone in the shebang very fearful of what would happen to him.[41]

Although Lyon's service in the barracks was brief, two paroled prisoners stepped up to play important roles in the camp administration. Somehow Clapp happened to catch Wirz's attention as a likely prisoner clerk. On August 31 he took the oath of a paroled prisoner not to attempt to escape, to stay during the day within a mile of camp headquarters (but not to go into the stockade), and to remain at night only in his assigned quarters. Detailed to the chief surgeon's office, a log cabin outside the hospital's west wall, Clapp was delighted to discover that his new boss, Dr. R. Randolph Stevenson, was an old schoolmate. A Kentuckian by birth, Stevenson was practicing in Indiana when the war broke out, but he joined the Confederacy. He put Clapp in charge of the hospital register, the death register, and all his official correspondence. Sergeant Julian W. Merrill of the Twenty-Fourth New York Independent Light Battery, a friend in the hospital office, recalled that when Clapp arrived he was "terribly afflicted" with "scurvy sores" as well as "rheumatic pains in knees & lower limbs." Treatment by Stevenson "forced the disease to the surface" for at least temporary relief.[42]

While still in the stockade, Clapp took "special pains to enquire often of the members of different companies, as to the welfare of their comrades, and when any one died, took their names, and tried to keep a correct record that could be published for the information of their friends." Now in the chief surgeon's office, he studied the actual death register, which, he was satisfied to discover, "compared very nearly with the memorandum I kept." From that point on, Clapp kept close track of the deaths of all Minnesotans and, as best he could, prisoners from the other Upper Midwest states. "After the rest of the surgeons, stewards and clerks had retired for the night," he copied names from the death register. Clapp may or may not have known that another hospital clerk, Pvt. Dorence Atwater of the Second New York Cavalry, the actual compiler of the death register, had begun the same doleful task in August. Atwater, though, endeavored to record *all* of the prisoner deaths that took place in Andersonville, a herculean task. Like Clapp, he feared the official record might somehow be lost or deliberately destroyed. Word of their clandestine efforts did reach the stockade. "The clerks at rebel headquarters are Union soldiers on parole," an anonymous prison diarist recorded on October 16, "and some of them are keeping a record of the dead carried out, and occasionally encourage us by sending in their grim statistics. Their object in doing so is doubtless to make sure that these figures will finally be carried North."[43]

The second paroled prisoner of the Ninth Minnesota who came to fulfill important duties in Andersonville was thirty-four-year-old Alonzo Avery. The sturdy six-footer, a former New Yorker and a farmer from Grand Meadow in Mower County, was first sergeant of Company C. About September 10 he received charge of the "grave squad" in the prison cemetery after the original burial detail either ran off or were transported out. The regular Confederate foreman ("supervising sexton"), one U. W. Byram, was sick in the Fort Valley Hospital and evidently never returned to Andersonville. Avery's new squad comprised mostly slaves ("Confederate colored") and captured black Union soldiers, but it appears he was also assisted by at least one white prisoner, Pvt. George A. Kenney of Company A. In just two weeks, from September 10 to September 24, Avery's squad buried 1,398 bodies, including 130 on September 18, the highest single day total at Andersonville. Three of the dead interred on the eighteenth were from the Ninth Minnesota. Thereafter the daily number of burials tailed off.[44]

The eminent Andersonville historian William Marvel asserts that in September when "predominately illiterate blacks" superseded the original burial detail, "record keeping instantly disintegrated," resulting in a much higher percentage of "unknowns." As evidence of this deterioration, he cites the testimony in the Wirz trial of Pvt. Frank "Maddox" (actually Mardix) of the Thirty-Fifth U.S. Colored Infantry, one of the burial detail from September 1864 to February 1865. "No one was over us or in charge of us," Mardix claimed. Marvel does concede the wholesale abandonment of so many of the sick in the barracks and elsewhere after their comrades precipitously left camp greatly contributed to the number of "unknown" burials in September and October 1864; nonetheless, he condemned the later burial practices as a whole.[45]

Testimony by Avery himself and by Hospital Steward Hyde of the Seventeenth Ohio casts doubt on Marvel's conclusions. On April 5, 1865, Avery provided newspapers in Minnesota a list of all the state's soldiers who died at Andersonville through March 24, 1865 (the day he left), as well those survivors currently with him in the exchange camp at Vicksburg.

> The foregoing list of deaths I can vouch for as being correct, as I had charge of the graveyard, and made the death report each day. It is needless to say anything in regard to the manner in which they are buried, as the public are aware of the fact, ere this, that they were stripped of all their clothing, and buried without coffins, or anything but two feet of Georgia soil for a covering; such is the manner of treatment our brave soldiers receive when in the hands of the rebels, after long suffering, and at last dying the death of all deaths, starvation.

Avery rendered "this brief report as there are many families of our State who have near and *dear* friends, which they look for daily, or for their names to be among those that are paroled." He asked the newspapers to "oblige a friend and soldier" and publish his list. Hyde, a prisoner druggist in the hospital dispensary, recalled that he learned the number of deaths each day from Atwater, who "received [the daily report] from Mr. Avery, who superintended the burying of the dead at the cemetery." Each evening Avery handed in the papers he retrieved from each corpse. "The burying," Hyde explained, "was under the immediate supervision of Alonzo Avery, of Rochester, Minnesota, who was a member of the Ninth Minnesota Volunteers and a prisoner. He had a squad of negro prisoners to assist in digging and filling up the trenches. Much credit is due to Mr. Avery for the masterly and careful manner in which he performed this sad rite for our martyred, heroic dead. His task was an onerous one. From morning till night, rain or shine, he was to be found at his post, using every care in his work that there might be no mistakes."[46]

More Departures

In chilly, wet weather on September 22, Wirz consolidated the remaining prisoners into the existing detachments Forty-Five through Seventy-Three— evidently those that had not yet gone out. Six days later the evacuation of prisoners resumed, and 3,661 more departed between September 28 and October 5. About 90 were from the Ninth Minnesota, including liberators Chandler, Frahm, Gordon, and Rodier. Thus, out of roughly 165 prisoners of the Ninth Minnesota present on September 7, around 125 subsequently went elsewhere and about 20 died. Those who remained in Andersonville after October 5 included Clapp, Avery, and Kenney on parole, 9 from Company E, 2 hospital patients, and possibly 5 or 6 invalids abandoned in the barracks.[47]

Frank Lyon was fortunate to have left Andersonville rather than being consigned to the notorious barracks to die. Instrumental in his exit was Cpl. Thomas H. B. Vandegrift, a twenty-four-year-old former Pennsylvanian, also from Company C. "For some reason Tom had taken a liking to me," Lyon explained, though Vandegrift himself was not particularly popular. In February 1863 at Fort Ridgely, Joseph Lagree (a future liberator) had allegedly while "under the influence of liquor" cussed Vandegrift, grabbed him by the throat, and struck him. Considering the serious nature of the crime, the court, led by Major Markham, sentenced Lagree to a paltry five-dollar fine. Perhaps his rough behavior was thought to be partly justified. One day at Andersonville when Vandegrift groaned he was too sick to fetch water up from the well near Stockade Branch, Lyon offered to take his turn. "He ain't any sicker than you are," griped some of their comrades. "He's playing off. You don't know Tom." A few days later when Vandegrift was "sick again," Lyon once more toted the water. "The other fellows were furious. They swore at me, called me a fool, etc."[48]

Thus, about sunset on September 28 as a forlorn Lyon "lay in the mud shanty," he was "greatly surprised at seeing Tom coming toward me." Vandegrift exclaimed, "By George, Lyon, I am sorry to see you in this fix!" He volunteered to buy some food, and Lyon gave him a quarter. "After a while he came back, bringing a ginger cake three or four inches square." The next day Vandegrift returned and announced, "Lyon, I'm going out tomorrow night." Lyon expressed pleasure at his good fortune. "He looked at me in a peculiar way," Lyon wrote, and Vandegrift said, "I want you to go with me." When Lyon explained he was too weak to walk to the depot, Vandegrift heartily responded, "Well, I can help you. You be ready tomorrow night just after dark, and I'll be here." Lyon found that "true to his word, just after dark he made his appearance. He helped me to my feet, put his arms around me and together we went down the old hill and crossed the bridge for the last time." Vandegrift carefully conveyed Lyon over to the depot and onto the waiting train. "It pays sometimes to be a 'fool,'" Lyon affirmed with deep feeling.[49]

Another remarkable act of personal salvation took place on the same train that carried Lyon, Vandegrift, Aslakson, and many of the ninety departing Minnesotans north toward Macon. Given his chronic diarrhea and "a touch of scurvy in my lower limbs," Cpl. Daniel McArthur "concluded that if I was taken to another prison I would never get out of it alive." He tried to enlist his good friend McCoy to escape with him, but McCoy, barefoot, "was afraid he could not get through to our lines." On the "dark and cloudy" night of October 1, while the train slowed on an upgrade, McArthur leapt through the open door of the boxcar. "I made the jump with a forward spring over the end of the ties and struck the ditch, lay down on my face as close to the ground as I could and waited until the train had vanished." He hid that night and much of the next day before striking north. "I found a cornfield, took an ear of corn and ate all I wanted of it. I walked until I became tired then laid down and rested until I became cold or chilly when I got up and walked again." After a couple of days, wet and chilled to the bone, he chanced stopping at a plantation. Despite announcing himself as "an exchanged Union soldier," he received a good meal from a kind Southern woman. The only other time he spoke to anyone was to a black family who also fed him well and gave him directions to Atlanta, only twenty miles away. Otherwise he "ate nothing but corn and sweet potatoes and at one time a part of a pumpkin." On October 16 McArthur walked into Union lines. "To say that I was pleased and thankful is putting it mildly. I am sure I could not have been more pleased had I been entering the 'Pearly Gates.'"[50]

McArthur was the first prisoner from the Ninth Minnesota to make a successful escape after being in a Rebel prison. His adventures were far from over. On the morning of October 19, he and about thirty other escapees left Atlanta on a train for Nashville. Near Ruff's Station fifteen miles north, "our train stopped and a lot of men commenced shooting at us. We, the escaped prisoners, had no guns and there were no guns on the train, so we jumped off and ran as fast as we could and the bullets were whizzing very close to me for awhile. I dropped my bundle containing my new army blanket and a few other articles and George Atkinson's bible. I kept on running until I got into a swale and under a large brush heap, where I remained until about ten o'clock at night." Working his way back south, McArthur encountered a Federal post near the Chattahoochee River bridge. "Here I was told it was a band of bushwhackers that had attacked the train, that they had torn up the track, killed, wounded and captured some of the escaped prisoners and train men, taking everything they wanted from the train after which they burned it. My reasons for running were that I would rather be killed than recaptured." McArthur made it safely to Nashville a few days later and was granted home leave. Afterward he reported to Fort Snelling, where he was told he would receive his orders to return to the Ninth Minnesota. Those orders were never issued, and he stayed at Fort Snelling till after the war.[51]

"So you will observe that I have no reason to be very proud of what I accomplished in the government service," McArthur reflected in 1913, four years before his death at age eighty-five in Lake Benton, Minnesota. "When I enlisted I determined at all times, to perform the duty of a soldier, which is to obey orders. I became almost an expert as a drilling master. I put in nearly three solid months in 1864 drilling and teaching raw recruits how to become good and efficient soldiers. I expected when we went south we would perform wonders; but the only engagement I was in was a failure on our part. I was not able to accomplish anything while in Andersonville, and in making my escape, although guided most of the time by the north star, I am satisfied that I was guided by an Invisible Hand. So, probably it is just as well that I was not allowed to take the lives of many, if any, of those misguided Brothers."[52]

DOWN TO TWO

After the latest round of evacuations in early October 1864, only about 4,000 prisoners occupied the Andersonville stockade, with 2,000 more in the hospital. On October 9 all the prisoners residing north of Stockade Branch were herded down among the "South Siders" across the creek, a move that "seriously incommoded" those who had built their shelters on the northern slope. "The North hill looks curious, with its holes in the ground and its remnants of deserted shebangs," wrote a prison diarist. Wirz yet again reorganized the camp by breaking up the old detachments and forming new divisions of 500 prisoners, each with five 100-man detachments. About 1,000 sick who languished in the barracks were brought into the hospital. None evidently were from the Ninth Minnesota. When an Illinois soldier, one of 370 men recently captured at Ackworth, Georgia, entered the prison on October 11, he was shocked to be "engulfed in an ocean of black, grimy, emaciated beings covered with sores, vermin, rags and filth." Wirz obsessively tinkered with the physical layout between Stockade Branch and the South Wall and eventually grouped the prisoners within a compact area of about three acres, where they again burrowed in as snugly as they could to protect against the extremely cold nights. Rations were no better or more plentiful than before. The sick who remained in the barracks died at a great rate until about November 1, when the dilapidated buildings were finally evacuated.[53]

Prisoners who happened to be in the Andersonville hospital were no more fortunate. In 1889 in an address to his old comrades in the Seventy-Second Ohio, Robert Medkirk, who had been one of them, poignantly described the horrifying conditions there late that autumn:

> One of those cold days in November I was walking through the hospital when I heard a voice calling me; I went to where it was and there in an old tent as nude as the day he was born, without a rag to lie on or cover his nakedness, the ground covered with frost and the wind blowing a blast that made the rebels wrap their coats more closely about them and hug the fires at their post, laid poor Patsy. It was a horrible sight even to me, accustomed as I was at that time to human misery in all its forms. When I came up to him I saw he was nearly gone, he was slowly freezing to death. He beckoned me down to him, and in a ghastly whisper said, "Bob, you see that big fire down there at the end of the street with a lot of our boys around it; well [Elijah] Purdy is down there (Purdy belonged to Co. K, I believe), you go and tell him that I am up here freezing, freezing, and that I want him to send me two or three of those nice blankets he has; he will do it, will you go quick, Bob?" "Yes," I answered him as I tore myself away to go back in an hour and find the poor fellow dead.

Private Patrick Donahue of Company K, Seventy-Second Ohio, died on November 22 of scurvy. He was "an Irish boy, a model soldier, as neat as a pin in his dress and in the care of his accoutrements."

Medkirk next told of Cpl. Ferdinand Statler, Company E, Seventy-Second Ohio, who died on November 4 of scurvy:

> You remember Ferdinand Stodler [who] too went like poor Donahue. He begged me for the sake of his wife and little ones to get him home. "Get me home Bob," was his cry, "and I will give you all I possess. I have some little property, some bounty money, my pay—all shall be yours if you will only get me home, I only want to get home to die with my wife and little ones. I don't ask to live, but oh! Bob, I don't want to die here." I cheered him up as much as I could and left him, as I could do nothing to help him. I returned the next morning, but poor Stodler had indeed gone home.

Unquestionably few if any of the Ninth Minnesota's remaining hospital patients were any better off than Donahue or Statler. At any rate the final result was the same in every case.[54]

Shipments each of 1,000 men left Andersonville on October 31 and November 2, but so far as is known neither included anyone from the Ninth Minnesota. Finally on November 10, the last organized body of Ninth Minnesota prisoners, the small Company E contingent, went out with 841 prisoners. Only 3 had the strength to go; the other 3 had to be left in the hospital—a virtual death sentence. Another prisoner in the same transport was Reverend Sheppard of the Ninety-Seventh Ohio. Jammed into freezing boxcars with only one day's ration, they sat at the depot a full day before finally pulling out on the eleventh. The next day Pvt. William Bruce and Pvt. Edward S. Evans jumped from the moving train as it traversed northeastern Georgia and successfully made their way to Federal forces eight days later. Both rejoined the Ninth Minnesota in March 1865.[55]

Sergeant Major Clapp went out on November 15 with a party of 513 sick men, including First Sergeant Warren. When he left, he thought, as he wrote in January 1865, that only four of the Ninth Minnesota remained at Andersonville. Orderly Sergeant Avery and Private Kenney "were on parole and were in 'good health' comparatively," but the same was not true of Cpl. Ferdinand Sherrer and Pvt. Andrew Ulvin of Company E. They "were inmates of the hospital, and in such a deplorable condition that I can give no encouragement to their friends in regard to their recovery." Sherrer indeed perished from scurvy on November 17, and Ulvin succumbed to the same dire disease three days later. Since October 5 seven other men from the Ninth Minnesota (including Levi Goodfellow of Company D, who had sheltered blacks in Jefferson City) are known to have died at Andersonville, but as many as four others might have been buried as unknowns. One was Jesse

Pericle of Company H, whose father had died there in August. Diarrhea and dysentery continued to be the main cause of death. Of those who died between September 8 and November 17, where the cause is noted, eighteen succumbed to intestinal diseases and six from scurvy. It is certain, too, that scurvy had taken a potentially deadly hold on nearly all of the survivors.[56]

Despite all his careful concern, Clapp was unaware of yet another Minnesotan who had gone into the hospital on November 11, the day his comrades in Company E finally departed Andersonville. The son of an immigrant from Wales, Pvt. Lewis Lewis Jr. had been born in Pittsburgh in 1848 and came nine years later to Minnesota and the Welsh community in Blue Earth County. In August 1862, at the age of fourteen, he enlisted in Mankato. Three weeks later his father suffered a crippling wound inflicted by a Dakota. Lewis junior died from scurvy on November 26 in Andersonville. His community eulogized him as a "brave and faithful soldier," who "like his father, was of genial and friendly disposition and much esteemed by all his acquaintance." Lewis Lewis rests today in grave 12,165 in the Andersonville cemetery. Since July 14 when Orlando Geer's body was interred, 8,877 other prisoners had also been buried there. At least 66 and possibly as many 70 were from the Ninth Minnesota. On November 26 the prisoners in Camp Sumter numbered a mere 179 in the stockade and 1,211 in the hospital, including Avery and Kenney. Andersonville's usefulness as a Confederate prison had seemingly neared its end, but the Ninth Minnesota's ordeal in that horrendous place was in fact far from over.[57]

CHAPTER FOURTEEN

Spreading the Misery

To Savannah

By August the vastly overcrowded Andersonville prison, where nearly all the Ninth Minnesota prisoners were held, was a festering sore, impossible in current circumstances to improve and under increasing threat from Union forces. With Sherman tightening his noose around Atlanta, General Winder desperately required a larger prison in a safer location. Early in August he initiated construction of a huge new camp in northeastern Georgia near Millen, where rail lines linked Macon, Augusta, and Savannah. The fall of Atlanta in early September forced Winder to begin evacuating Andersonville at once, but Millen was not yet ready. The interim solution was to dump the prisoners on the two largest cities on the lower Atlantic coast, Savannah and Charleston. Both had strong garrisons, but since they were under siege, neither city could tolerate large numbers of captive Yankees for any length of time. By October 5 roughly 22,000 prisoners had been sent out of Andersonville to Savannah or Charleston, the destination depending mainly on which detachments the prisoners had been in while at Andersonville.[1]

Beautiful old Savannah, situated on the Savannah River, was known for its many parklike squares. Federal troops held the river's mouth less than twenty miles away. Since the end of July, Savannah had custody of 600 Union officers (no Minnesotans) transferred from the Macon prison camp. Thousands more enlisted prisoners were the last thing Col. Edward Clifford Anderson, the Confederate officer in charge, desired. He built a stockade for 4,500 inmates on the southwest edge of town behind the castle-like Chatham County and Savannah City Jail. "High walls of thick pine plank" enclosed an area of roughly five acres. On September 8 the barely completed facility

Prison Camps in Georgia and the Carolinas

received the very first 1,500 men shipped out of Andersonville. That "beggarly set of vagabond[s]" included liberator Charles Dietrich and as many as 9 other orphans from Company K. The next day another 3,300 captives (probably none from the Ninth Minnesota) arrived, but Anderson soon foisted 900 of them on Charleston. A few days later all the officer prisoners left for there as well.[2]

The "dirty and half-clad" newcomers were, according to Anderson, "altogether the most squalid gathering of humanity it has ever been my lot to look upon." He sincerely deplored that the "stockade is entirely without shelter and the burning sun bakes down on them from daylight til dark." Yet to the prisoners, the "cool, pure air" and delightful ocean breezes of Savannah alone were tremendous improvements over fetid Andersonville. Though the holding ground was merely a "bare common," there was a large amount of wood left lying around for tent stakes and fuel. Most importantly, to the starved men the daily ration of a half dozen hardtack crackers with "meat or a little molasses," plus vinegar, salt, and "a little tobacco," constituted nothing less than "riotous luxury," according to Pvt. John McElroy of the Sixteenth Illinois Cavalry. The guards were mostly sailors who were much friendlier than the hard cases at Andersonville. Compassionate local citizens donated food and goods to the destitute Yankees. More pleasant surroundings did not dissuade the new guests from tunneling through the soft soil. After numerous escapes, Anderson dug a deep trench around the compound and flooded it. The stagnant moat eventually "filled the air with a terrible stench" that often overwhelmed the sea breezes, and the tunneling ceased.[3]

On September 25 Savannah received a new batch of prisoners who were thoroughly disgusted even beyond the normal. "The boys are very downhearted, and still are very sick and don't think will live long," wrote one, Pvt. Simon Peter Obermier of the Seventy-Second Ohio. On September 19 during the "special exchange" that took place behind Union lines at Rough and Ready near Atlanta, things had gone very wrong for 140-odd prisoners from Andersonville. While awaiting his turn to be processed, Pvt. Jacob Hutchinson of the Seventy-Second Ohio had wandered across the "neutral ground" to the camp of some Michigan soldiers from Sherman's army who eagerly fed their grimy, threadbare, and gaunt comrade. A little later, despite the protests of his new friends who urged him to stay, Hutchinson crossed back to the other side just to make things official. To his utter horror, he was shunted off to a group of infuriated and heartsick Federal prisoners who included Obermier, young Dwight Card of Company E, and First Sergeant Turrill of the Seventy-Second Ohio. "I had, like a foolish rat, rushed right into the trap again after being free. With all those remaining I was marched back into the rebel lines, and exchange being refused to us, we had to go back to Andersonville or some other horrid prison." The unlucky men, either 132 or 137—the figure varies— were all former "Sturgis raiders" from Brice's Crossroads. "Some tall swearing" erupted "among [the] boys," Obermier noted in his diary—surely an understatement if there ever was one. "We thought very hard about being taken back again," Turrill testified in 1865 at the Wirz trial. A shocked Union officer who saw the "poor, emaciated boys" before they disappeared back into Rebel lines noted, "Many of them were utterly broke down and wept like children." A few made a run for it. "Of course it was our duty to stop them," wrote one of the Union guards, "but our boys were very dilatory about it and some got away. The Johnny officers threatened to have their guards fire on them and it looked as though we might have serious trouble, but it was quieted down." At Macon where the miserable captives briefly stopped on their way back to prison, a sympathetic Iowa prisoner wrote, "Oh the horrors of war! that their liberty almost within their grasp should thus be snatched from them."[4]

Stung by horrendous losses in the spring and summer of 1864, the top Union generals had become increasingly reluctant to swap relatively fit Confederates for broken-down Yankees. "To exchange their healthy men for ours, who are on the brink of the grave from their hellish treatment," General Halleck told Grant on August 27, "of course gives them all the advantage. Nevertheless it seems very cruel to leave our men to be slowly but deliberately tortured to death. But I suppose there is no remedy at present." Grant could not think of one either. "It is hard on our men held in Southern prisons not to exchange them, but it is humanity to those left in the ranks to fight our battles. Every man we hold, when released on parole or otherwise, becomes an active soldier against us at once either directly or indirectly. If we commence a system of exchange which liberates all prisoners taken, we will have to fight on until the whole South is exterminated." Sherman had sanctioned the special exchange with the understanding he would receive in return men from his own armies at Atlanta who only briefly were Rebel prisoners and thus were still strong and hearty. He was adamant that such was the only type of prisoner he would accept, and the criterion ruled out the Guntown ragamuffins. "To illustrate the justness of my terms," he informed Halleck on September 20, "I need only mention after our agreement General Hood sent me 137 men belonging to Sturgis' command, captured last summer in Mississippi. Hard as it was my representative, Colonel [Willard] Warner, had to decline to receive them and see the poor fellows sent back to the disgraceful pen in Andersonville. I have sent word to our prisoners to be of good cheer, for the day of their deliverance and revenge is fast approaching." Thus in a way perhaps unprecedented in the history of the U.S. Army, freedom was snatched from Card and the other rejected Union prisoners of war. It is doubtful they took much encouragement from Sherman's exhortation to "be of good cheer," for he had condemned them to up to eight more months of imprisonment or a painful, lingering death.[5]

Between September 28 and October 4, Andersonville unloaded 3,600 more prisoners on Savannah, with 90 or so captives from the Ninth Minnesota, including liberators Chandler, Frahm, Gordon, and Rodier. Passing through Macon with them, Aslakson was "encouraged by the sight of women and children fleeing with their household goods," a flight he erroneously took to mean Sherman's troops were still advancing. In Savannah, though, "everything" appeared "quiet and still." Hoping finally to be exchanged, he instead found "great disappointment" at just entering another prison. "We were crowded in there almost to the point of suffocation," wrote McCoy, another new arrival, but the "rations were better in both quality and quantity." Aslakson's party drew "some pieces of fresh meat which we certainly relished, even though the hide and hair was left on the portions we got." Lyon was more enthusiastic. As his train chuffed into Savannah one evening at dusk, it passed a "large brick residence where I could see a gentleman sitting in a well lighted, well furnished room," a rare view of normalcy that affected him deeply. The new stockade, moreover, was a "very comfortable place, clean and plenty of water, and much better food."[6]

The relatively few Yankees admitted to the hospital located outside of the Savannah stockade were surprised to be "well treated, washed regularly," and even fed a diet that combated scurvy. Nevertheless, over two hundred perished. "None die through neglect here; all is done that could reasonably be expected," wrote John Ransom, one of the patients. That could never have been said of Andersonville or the other prisons. Yet many who had "walked away from Andersonville" were "too far gone to rally, and die." Three members of Company K succumbed in the Savannah prison hospital, including Pvt. John G. Frederick, who received extreme unction from Father Clavreul on September 27, five days before his death.[7]

Even more prisoners died in the Savannah stockade, perhaps as many as three hundred, but the exact number is unknown. The advent in October of "terrible cold" nightly winds caused much suffering, particularly among the weakest. Ludoviso Bourgard of Company C "came near to perishing from ill treatment and cold." Twenty-six "Yankee prisoners died in the stockade last night," Colonel Anderson noted on the ninth. "The cold weather has been fatal to all those cases of diarrhea which have been lingering for the past fortnight, thus accounting for the large increase of mortality among the prisoners." He recoiled at the "sickening" sight of "those wretched strangers—stretched off stark & stiff in the death line awaiting transportation to their place of burial. The flies were swarming over their faces & a crowd of prisoners had gathered nearby looking on in callous indifference & jesting among themselves as though there had never existed a feeling of pity in their hearts." Personal perspective meant everything. Aslakson happened to be in that wretched "crowd," but rather than feeling "callous indifference & jesting," he was completely crushed. One of the dead displayed in such indignity was his tentmate John Larson, who had died the previous day from diarrhea. "Here I lost my last comrade," Aslakson recalled, "and I was now the only one left of those that banded together at Andersonville for mutual help and protection. A longing to die and follow my comrades out of this evil world would come over me at this time, but He who ordains our lives had other plans, and my cup of gall and wormwood was not yet empty."[8]

At least seven prisoners from the Ninth Minnesota, including Larson, perished in the Savannah stockade. One of three from Company K was twenty-year-old liberator Charles (Karl) Dietrich, who died on October 17 after nearly all his comrades had left Savannah. In June 1859 following the death of his mother, he and his father, Wilhelm, a shoemaker, had come to America from Hasserode, Prussia, looking for a fresh start. They bought a small farm near Fountain City, Wisconsin, across the river from Winona. Despite the poor soil, they made a go of it until 1861, when Wilhelm's health failed. The dutiful son not only worked their farm alone but hired himself out on other jobs to make enough money for the two to survive. He gave his invalid father all his bounty money and thereafter sent home the larger portion of his army pay. Charles Dietrich finally lost to starvation, disease, and the lasting effects of a wound incurred at Brice's Crossroads. He and the other dead Union prisoners were buried "without shroud or service" in unmarked graves hastily dug alongside Ogeechee Road just southwest of the stockade. They rest there today unknown, as there is no indication their bodies were ever recovered and interred in a national cemetery.[9]

When notified that Camp Lawton, the new prison eighty-four miles to the northwest near Millen, was ready, Anderson rapidly removed the prisoners from Savannah in the order in which they had been received. The first group left on October 11, and in a few days nearly all were gone. By the end of the month, only a few who were too sick to be moved still lingered in the hospital. Despite the many deaths, the sojourn at Savannah had offered the Andersonville captives a short interlude of hope before they returned to the same kind of hellhole as before.[10]

During the transport of prisoners from Savannah to Millen, Jacob Dieter somehow escaped from his train car. Eventually apprehended well to the north, he ended up in Salisbury in western North Carolina. The prison there was a former cotton factory compound centered on a large brick warehouse. In October 1864 Salisbury, built for 2,500 inmates, held over 10,300 unfortunates in horribly overcrowded conditions. Most had no shelter other than a hole in the ground. Rations and water were poor, and sanitation appears to have been even worse than at Andersonville. Few Minnesotans were ever held at Salisbury, a repository for captives taken in Virginia, and while Dieter was there, he was almost certainly the only one from the Ninth Minnesota. "The most pitiful objects among the prisoners are those men who have no friends or particular associates in the prison," one Salisbury inmate wrote in his diary on November 13, because they are "compelled to bear their grief and endure their sufferings alone." Dieter died six days later from pneumonia. His daughter, Martha, recalled many years later the family had only "heard that he had died when he was being moved from Andersonville to Libby Prison. He was so nearly dead from starvation that he could not stand the trip. He was buried in a trench in the South. The neighbors took Mother and us children to the old Fitch school house and held prayers for our dead father."[11]

MILLEN

Sited adjacent to the Augusta & Savannah Railroad five miles north of Millen, Camp Lawton had pretensions, Winder proudly observed, for the title of "largest prison in the world." The huge stockade, 1,398 feet by 1,329 feet, encompassed forty-two acres. Winder reckoned there was enough space for 40,000 prisoners, although only slightly more than a quarter of that number ever went there. Savannah furnished Millen about 7,600 prisoners, of whom perhaps 88 were from the Ninth Minnesota, including liberators Chandler, Frahm, Gordon, and Rodier. In late October and in November, another 3,350 prisoners (2 from the Ninth Minnesota) went to Millen directly from Andersonville. Six hundred more captives (less 1 from the Ninth Minnesota who died on the way) traveled all the way from the Cahaba prison camp in Alabama.[12]

Camp Lawton was oriented roughly northwest to southeast, with the main gate, set in the east wall, facing the railroad. Like Andersonville, the Millen stockade occupied the side of a large hill, but the slope was gentler, with grassy areas instead of bare ground. Magnolia Springs, which cut through the lower third of the Millen stockade, was a spring-fed, "beautiful stream of pure water" with sturdy banks "down to the very edge"—nothing like the foul morass of Stockade Branch. With "some fixing up which was done before [the camp] was occupied," the latrines at Millen were, according to McCoy, "more healthy and in accordance with true sanitary rules." Along the stream the numerous trees, deliberately left uncut, offered a "cool retreat" from the sun. Lyon praised the "new and clean" stockade with "much timber left, plenty for cooking." As usual Aslakson was less excited. Though deeming Millen "very much the same as Andersonville," he did allow that "the water was fairly good and firewood was more plentiful."[13]

The stockade at Millen was so big that the authorities concentrated the prisoners in just the upper portion nearest to the west wall. The streets and lanes there were more or less carefully laid out, with sutler shops and a very active market. Once in their assigned patch of sandy hillside, Lyon, Cpl. Tom Vandegrift, and two comrades excavated a square hole eighteen inches deep and wide enough for all four to stretch out comfortably. The top cover was a blanket that Lyon purchased with the last of the money earned from selling his boots. Pine needles served as the floor in the dry soil. Aslakson likewise "got myself a new partner [Sgt. Andrew Mattson of Company H, one of only two Ninth Minnesota survivors from the Andersonville hospital], and when we learned that we would have to stay here over the winter, we dug a hole or dug-out in the hillside." Private Hitchcock of the Twenty-First Massachusetts, who came to Millen three weeks later, thought "the men who arrived here first have made very comfortable winter quarters of logs." Sergeant Major Clapp, who was in Millen only briefly in mid-November, judged conditions there "far superior" to Andersonville. "A prisoner of war could possibly live at Millen with sufficient food and shelter." Sergeant Merrill, his companion, considered Millen a "paradise when compared to Andersonville."[14]

Such unalloyed good fortune, inevitably, was not to be in the Confederate prison system. The food issued at Millen proved woefully insufficient to forestall hunger and privation, especially for those already severely malnourished and wracked with dysentery and scurvy. Private Washington Kays Latimer of Company D was another of Lorin Cray's friends who had speculated in October 1863 about their respective futures. He could scarcely have imagined that a year later he would be languishing in a prison camp in Georgia following a horrific summer at Andersonville. Although the ration at Millen was supposed to comprise "½ lb. meal; ½ lb beef and three fourths lb beans or rice," Latimer wrote his family on November 14 that "we do not get near that much, and not half enough wood to cook that with." Consequently, "every night and always in my dreams I find my way to the cupboard. Last night I dreamt of eating a whole loaf of bread and butter and then did not get half enough. I expect I will eat you out of house and home when I get back."[15]

Once the frigid rains and night frosts began in mid-October, the haphaz-
ard homemade shelters at Millen no longer served to ward off chills. "Our
clothing is rather thin for this season of the year," Latimer observed. Lyon
concurred. His woolen shirt was "nearly gone," its sleeves extending only
to the elbows. He was without shoes, and even his poor "old Rebel hat" was
only a memory, replaced by one that was too small that he had salvaged from
a dead comrade. When the cold rain soaked his clothes, Lyon, like most of
the others, found no relief from the biting wind. By November he was down
to one hundred pounds and so crippled by scurvy he could barely open his
jaw and eat the food Vandegrift and other devoted friends cooked for him.
Soon he needed two or three tries just to get on his feet and then had to rest
and gain his balance before chancing a step. "I just shut my teeth and vowed
that I would not die there."[16]

Even just a little good food, though, made a real difference when it came
to the ravages of scurvy. When Sgt. Ernest Hainlin of Company B reached
Millen in mid-October, his two front central incisors were so loose that
he could remove them at will. "The last time I had them out I was going to
throw them away, but my uncle [Pvt. Charles Kingsley] persuaded me to
put them back and try them once more." About that time Hainlin "had the
good fortune to obtain a raw sweet potato; this he scraped and ate at intervals. In November, the teeth began to get a trifle firm in their sockets." Eventually after his parole at the end of November, "the teeth became firmer and
firmer," Hainlin's amazed dentist later wrote in a dental journal, "until in
February or March 1865 his recovery was entire and permanent."[17]

Medical care at Millen was even less evident and effective than at Andersonville. "Men dyes verry fast hear now on a count of the cold knights," Sgt.
James Dennison of the 113th Illinois wrote on October 24 in his diary. Aside
from a small hospital outside the grounds that admitted very few prisoners,
the Rebels often shifted those who were desperately sick to the far corner of
the stockade and abandoned them there. With no shelter, blankets, or medical care, they died alone in the cold. One prisoner recalled the "horrid spectacle" that sunrise would reveal in that dreaded place: the "dead and dying
could be seen on every hand, having perished of cold during the night." Their
bodies were randomly strewn about like the dead on a battlefield.[18]

Of about ninety members of the Ninth Minnesota who were confined
in Millen, at least a quarter, perhaps as many as twenty-five, perished there.
One was liberator Stephen Chandler, who died on or about October 31. A
friend who was with him at the end told the family that "he suffered dread-
fully from hunger, from the treatment of the Rebels and exposure, which
brought on jaundice and inflammatory rheumatism. He dwindled away to a

living skeleton." Private Duane Philes of Company C recalled to the pension board how Chandler "took sick at Andersonville with rheumatism and chronic diarrhea—sick all the time at Savannah and Millen, not treated." Another member of Company C who died at Millen was forty-seven-year-old Pvt. Orsamus Rhoades, whose young son, Oscar, ran the family farm in Mower County. Rhoades passed away in early November.[19]

The burial process at Millen was the same as at Andersonville, with numbered graves and a death record. According to Pvt. Robert Knox Sneden of the Fortieth New York, who in November 1864 took over compiling the dead book, 1,330 Union prisoners (including 478 as unknown) died at Millen. Unfortunately, the entire death register was not preserved, and the record that remains does not always include the date of burial. Nineteen men from the Ninth Minnesota, including Chandler and Rhoades, were thus registered in surviving Millen Cemetery records, but as many as 6 others remain unidentified. Sneden recalled that the dead were buried in two trenches west of the stockade, but it appears the federal government only located one of the burial sites. In February 1868, some 685 Millen dead (293 as unknown), including the 19 from the Ninth Minnesota, were reinterred in the National Cemetery at Beaufort, South Carolina.[20]

The prisoners of the Ninth Minnesota held at Millen were painfully aware of the terrible toll Rebel imprisonment was exacting from their ranks. "Out of 220 from our regiment," Latimer estimated on November 14, "not 100 are alive now." That was a slight but wholly understandable exaggeration. "We all think we will be exchanged soon or at least hope so for prison life in this southern Confederacy is anything but pleasant." Rather, "We, the 9th Regiment, think it is perfect Paradise to see the Old Flag and get to our lines. It will be the happiest day I ever saw. May it soon come is my hope and prayer."[21]

CHARLESTON

Charleston, unlike Savannah, was under active siege by aggressive Federal forces. The North was eager to capture the city where the Rebellion started in April 1861, but found it an unexpectedly difficult task. Supported by an ironclad fleet, Union troops occupied Morris Island in the outer harbor. Batteries of heavy artillery that even included a monster three-hundred-pounder cannon known as the "Swamp Angel" shelled not only Fort Sumter to a pile of rubble but pounded Charleston itself. Finally, in late July 1864, the Rebels, in a desperate effort to halt the barrage, quartered Union officer prisoners, eventually numbering 1,800, in threatened areas within the city to serve as hostages to their own guns. The North retaliated by crowding Rebel officer prisoners (the "Immortal Six Hundred") onto a barren harbor island where they were in peril of their own artillery. All of the needlessly endangered prisoners were merely pawns in a dangerous game.[22]

Thus, the first prisoners from the Ninth Minnesota to reach Charleston were not enlisted evacuees from Andersonville but rather all seven of its captive officers: Ford, McCain, Lane, Hall, Niedenhofen, Tiffany, and Dr. Dixon, who had come from Camp Oglethorpe at Macon. Although directly in the line of fire, they continued to live, if uneasily, at least reasonably well with regard to food and shelter. Allen Tiffany "escaped a great many close shots" from the Federal artillery. "Some of the time we sojourned in that ungodly city the cannonading was very exciting, more especially during the nights," wrote Lieutenant Perin of the Seventy-Second Ohio. "We could see the burning fuse of the shells as the three hundred pounders went plunging into the heart of the city and exploded with a report almost deafening. The prisoners would watch these destructive missiles by the hour and at every explosion shout 'Glory to God,' 'Give the Rebs another, Foster' [Maj. Gen. John G. Foster, the Federal commander]." The truce boat seen shuttling between the lines was a source of hope, and some officer exchanges did take place. On September 3 Dixon and thirty-one other doctors and chaplains passed through the lines by flag of truce and left for New York. No other Minnesota officers were exchanged. Writing home from Charleston, Alfred Hall of Company F described the poverty he and his fellow prisoners endured there, the lack of proper clothing and funds, and their fear of a yellow fever epidemic. "I have given up all hopes of exchange and expect to remain a prisoner during the war unless Abraham gets the Negro 'out of the fence' and agrees on a general exchange." That, of course, was the main sticking point in the prisoner negotiations: the South's refusal to treat black soldiers as legitimate prisoners of war. All the remaining officers departed Charleston on October 5 for Columbia, South Carolina, without any contact with the wretched enlisted prisoners who had started arriving there in early September.[23]

Although Charleston briefly held as many as ten thousand Andersonville prisoners, fewer than twenty, it seems, were from the Ninth Minnesota. Nate Palmeter and John Morrison were probably the only liberators, and Palmeter stayed just three days. The Rebels corralled the enlisted prisoners on the "broad, grassy flat" racecourse in the old fairgrounds northwest of the city— a scenic locale that offered a safe view of the Union bombardment. There was no stockade, and the deadline was just a plowed furrow. As in Savannah, the overall treatment and rations were far better than in Andersonville. Local citizens and charity groups generously provided additional food and some clothes, a kindness that helped many prisoners recover some strength, at least briefly. Forty-six-year-old Pvt. Noah Grant of Company G, at six feet three inches one of the tallest in the regiment, suffered severely from scurvy at Andersonville. A month's stay at Charleston, with "more wholesome food & vinegar," arrested the disease sufficiently to enable him to survive two more months of captivity.[24]

No deaths of anyone of the Ninth Minnesota are noted in Charleston at that time, but there was an escape by at least one and possibly more. In early September, despite his unhealed leg wound, Myron Tower helped four other prisoners dig a shallow tunnel using oyster shells to cut through the soft ground. His compatriots were soon recaptured, but Tower, who concealed himself under a wagon, reached the safety of the woods. Hiding by day, he pushed north through swamps and other difficult terrain. Initially he could only find raw sweet potatoes and grapes, but eventually he risked stopping at slave cabins, whose "hospitable inmates" kindly gave him hoe cake and whatever else they could spare. After a week or so of freedom, Tower was finally retaken in eastern North Carolina, sent to Wilmington, and returned to Charleston.[25]

FLORENCE

By October 1 the threat of yellow fever, the nearness of the enemy, and the overcrowded conditions made it imperative to evacuate the enlisted prisoners from Charleston as soon as possible. Within ten days nearly all were transferred by rail a hundred miles north to the small town of Florence, South Carolina, an important rail junction linking Charleston, Wilmington, Augusta, and Columbia. In September, after the first Andersonville prisoners had already arrived, Maj. Gen. Samuel Jones, the commander in Charleston, took it upon himself to construct a prison stockade outside of Florence and with amazing recklessness soon shipped a substantial number of prisoners there even though work had barely begun on the new camp.[26]

Thus, on September 14 and 15, nearly six thousand prisoners descended on Florence without any proper preparations for them. About half came from Charleston and the rest directly out of Andersonville. The trains simply dumped them in an open cornfield a mile west of the unfinished camp. A few days later, a makeshift hospital was established nearby for severely sick men from Andersonville. Private John Ryan of Company I was one of the orderlies. The Rebels provided relatively little food and water, probably deliberately. Only the half-starved and feeble condition of most of the prisoners restrained them from charging the nervous guards in a mass escape. Palmeter reached Florence on the evening of September 14 from Charleston but was not let out of his boxcar until morning, by which time, as he recorded in Woodbury's old diary, he was already "pretty hungry." The next day he still had "got no rashions yet—see hard times and hungry to[o] I think." On September 17 Palmeter finally received "a mite of grub—not a quarter enough to make a meal—draw a little rice to go to bed hungry—sleep—cold and uneasy." By the next day, discontent was so evident to the local Rebel commander that he warned Jones "he may be overpowered" and rioting prisoners might destroy the railroad. For the next two weeks, Palmeter and his companions endured very poor rations and chilly nights. On September 28 he drew "a little beef and 3 spoons full of meal and two of flour; eat it all for supper and want more; lay down for night hungry." The prisoners, "rendered desperate by starvation," wrote Eugene Forbes of the Fourth New Jersey the same day, "commenced running out this afternoon, and for an hour there was almost incessant popping [of the guards' rifles] along the line." The next day Pvt. George Cummings of Company I, whom Ryan devotedly tended, died of chronic diarrhea in the makeshift hospital.[27]

On October 2 the Florence stockade finally opened, and within ten days its population swelled above thirteen thousand. About twenty-five were Ninth Minnesota, including Palmeter and Morrison. Aligned on an east-west axis, the stockade, 1,400 feet by 725 feet, comprised about twenty-three acres. In stark contrast to Millen, the ground was low lying and poorly drained. About a third was marshy, particularly the swamp that surrounded Pye Branch, a "bold, running branch of pure water" that flowed through the compound just west of the center. The only way to the creek was through deep, black mud. Thus, despite the stream and numerous wells, clean water was scarce at Florence. Poor sanitation soon turned the swamp as repulsive and malodorous as Andersonville's Stockade Branch. Earth ramped up all along the outside of the walls provided a complete palisade for the guards and enabled cannons at the corners to command the interior of the prison. The prisoners fashioned dwellings as best they could in the sticky soil. One Rebel inspector noted the numerous "small huts, built partly of wood and dirt, of every variety and form, some over holes dug in the ground, with little dirt chimneys—some comfortable and others very uncomfortable." All the remaining loose timber inside the camp disappeared for supports and firewood, and soon wood was in short supply. As usual the impoverished Minnesotans, who for the most part lacked even basic resources, lived at the low end of the scale.[28]

The daily ration was supposed to comprise one and a quarter pound of cornmeal, or its equivalent in beans and rice, and a cup and a half of molasses,

"Drawing a Shirt" at Florence, South Carolina

but even that trifle amount was seldom issued. Meat of any kind was very scarce for everyone except certain favored prisoners (prison police) or those few sufficiently prosperous to pay sutler prices. Some days no food was issued at all. Cooking—the food was always issued raw—was essential for nutrition as well as taste, but cooking was often very difficult because of the lack of proper gear and firewood. Corporal Kerlinger of Company I assessed the rations at Florence as "of a little better quality but less in quantity" than at Andersonville. William Walker of Company K, who had turned seventeen while in Andersonville, agreed the food in the new camp was "somewhat better." His severe sciatica abated, and he regained some strength at Florence but not an ounce of weight.[29]

In October the authorities at Florence distributed a quantity of clothing furnished by the U.S. Sanitary Commission. Apparently half the prisoners got at least one item based on their perceived level of "destitution." Issues to Ninth Minnesota personnel included a pair of pants to liberator Palmeter, a woolen shirt to liberator Morrison, drawers, shirt, and socks to Corporal Rafferty, woolen socks to Cpl. Elisha Geer, a set of drawers to Noah Grant, and a shirt and drawers to Myron Tower. Kerlinger outdid the others in "flanking," that is, taking unauthorized turns in line. Using variant spellings of his name, he evidently went through three times to acquire two woolen shirts, a set of drawers, a pair of pants, three pairs of socks, a pair of shoes, and a blanket. The new clothing was not much help in the increasingly cold weather. "Ice formed quarter of an inch thick on a running brook in October," Kerlinger recalled in 1868. "The effect of these cold nights and especially cold rains could be seen in the morning by the increased number of the dead." On October 21 the authorities cleared out the northwest corner of the stockade and the next day brought in the sick from the outside hospital. At first no shelter was provided for the patients, who "lay on bare ground in cold and rain." Only after about ten days was the first of five hospital sheds erected. As at Andersonville, the hospital stewards were paroled prisoners. Even the devoted care given by some of them meant little without proper medicines and living conditions.[30]

In November at least three prisoners from the Ninth Minnesota died in Florence, but whether in the hospital or the bivouac is not known. The first was John Morrison, who succumbed on November 11 to scurvy and dropsy. It was a year to the day after he helped free John's family at Otterville. Just as with Chauncey Hill at Andersonville, Tower carefully nursed his dying neighbor. Not long afterward he or another comrade managed to get word of the date and place of Morrison's death to his wife, Jane, who with their three young children was staying at her parents' home in Oneida County, New York. The government later reckoned the start of her widow's pension from November 11, 1864, the date of death she had been given. In the meantime, in April 1865 the Ninth Minnesota arbitrarily assigned Morrison the date of October 31, 1864, and place of death at Savannah. Another Florence fatality was Pvt. G. Henry Knapp, Lyon's erstwhile Andersonville business partner, who died on or about November 15.[31]

The protocol for burials at Florence was also very similar to that at Andersonville. Every day the grave detail, supervised by Pvt. William M. Mitchell of the Tenth New Jersey, collected the corpses that had been deposited either at the deadline near the main gate in the southwest corner of the stockade or in front of the nearby hospital. Personal details, if known, were recorded on slips of paper and written in the death register. The bodies were carted to the cemetery situated alongside the road to Florence about a quarter mile north of the stockade. After 416 burials took place at that site, subsequent interments were made in a field four hundred feet to the west, where eventually another 2,322 prisoners were buried. Each grave had a wooden marker numbered to correspond with the entry in the death register. Tragically, the death register was later lost and with it any official record of those who perished at Florence. The effort to identify all of those who died there continues today for the Florence National Cemetery.[32]

After the brutal summer at Andersonville, the prospect of having to spend the winter starving, freezing, and very possibly dying in the cold muck of Florence deeply discouraged the gaunt, wasted survivors of the Ninth Minnesota. "All things taken into consideration," Corporal Kerlinger decreed, "Florence was worse than Andersonville." Years later Pvt. Frederick F. Field, also of Company I, recalled how in Andersonville, "by reason of want of medicine or other relief," he had lost any "hope of life" and that he came to Florence "with car loads of other prisoners who were so emaciated that they were not expected to live." It seemed only a miracle could prevent them all from joining Morrison and the others in the Florence graveyard.[33]

CHAPTER FIFTEEN

With Smith's Guerrillas

REVENGE

In the summer and fall of 1864, the Ninth Minnesota, though sadly reduced, continued to do its part to win the War of the Rebellion. At Memphis in late June, while most of its prisoners were being introduced to the culture of Andersonville, the regiment itself gladly found a home in Maj. Gen. Andrew Jackson Smith's "Right Wing of the Sixteenth Army Corps, Army of the Tennessee." The crusty forty-nine-year-old regular, veteran of the Vicksburg Campaign, the Meridian Raid, and the ill-fated Red River expedition, was perhaps the finest Union combat leader in the western theater. His long-ranging, hard-fighting westerners proudly bore the moniker "Smith's Guerrillas," earned on the Red River when snooty eastern troops derided them as "gorillas, coarse, uncouth, ill-dressed braggarts and chicken thieves." The Ninth Minnesota joined the First Division's Second Brigade, which Colonel Wilkin now commanded. It was known as the "Eagle" Brigade because of "Old Abe," the Eighth Wisconsin's famed bald eagle mascot. Brigadier General Joseph A. ("Fighting Joe") Mower, in charge of the First Division, gallantly led the brigade in numerous battles from 1862 to early 1864. The Second Brigade also included the Forty-Seventh Illinois, Fifth Minnesota (temporarily a small detachment until its veterans returned from furlough), Eleventh Missouri, and Second Iowa Light Battery. The Seventh Minnesota and Tenth Minnesota joined the other brigades, giving the First Division a Minnesota character unmatched in the entire army.[1]

On July 5 Smith headed into Mississippi with fourteen thousand men. The object again was to find Forrest and "whip him if possible" but "at all events to hold him where he was and prevent him from moving upon the communications of Major General Sherman." Marsh's Ninth Minnesota went into the field with fifteen officers and three hundred men, including fourteen liberators (Company C: acting First Sergeant Merchant, Felch, Hartley, McCain, Padden, Stewart, and Williams; Company K: Buck, Fenstermacher, Heilmann, Jansen, Mickel, Pike, and Raymond). The expedition camped the first night at Davis's Mills on Wolf Creek, where Wilkin fought on June 12, and the next day followed the road linking Salem and Ripley. They soon discovered evidence of the terrible retreat the month before, including the unburied bodies of some of their comrades. A fence post on one farm brazenly displayed a human skull, and a woman there foolhardily taunted passing troops that her pigs had dined on Yankee corpses. "Vengeance was swift and predictable." On July 8 Ripley "was nearly all burned down, the negroes [U.S. Colored Troops] marched through the streets with a brand of fire in one hand and a gun in the other." Some soldiers, including from the Ninth Minnesota, honored the kindness previously afforded their wounded and protected several homes. Nevertheless, the pillaging and destruction of goods such as cotton far exceeded anything done on the prior visit.[2]

Smith turned southwest. In extremely warm but dusty and very dry conditions, David Felch, a newcomer to Mississippi, sighed that the temperature was "hot enough to roast eggs in the sand." Many fell out, but Smith carefully collected the stragglers. The Rebels noticed another signal difference from

Andrew Jackson Smith

feckless Sam Sturgis when Smith kept his force well in hand and gave For-rest no opening to exploit. By July 11 Smith reached Pontotoc, twenty-eight miles southwest of Brice's Crossroads, from where he menaced the Mobile & Ohio Railroad at Okolona, twenty-five miles southeast of Pontotoc. Lieu-tenant General Stephen Dill Lee, the top Rebel commander, was all set to fight between Pontotoc and Okolona, but Smith surprised him on July 13 by slipping east through "rough and timbered" terrain toward Tupelo, nineteen miles distant. Grierson's cavalry pushed ahead, followed by the wagon train closely protected by the infantry. Forrest scrambled his forces to strike the rear of the column and its flank.[3]

In just one of several sharp actions that afternoon, General Buford caught up with the head of Mower's division as it passed a crossroads east of Coone-wah Creek, about seven miles from Tupelo. He rashly thrust two dismounted regiments through the timber to seize the wagons, saying, "Boys, do not kill the mules, but turn them down this way." Colonel Barteau's Second Tennes-see Cavalry "furiously assailed" Colonel McMillen's First Brigade, while to his left Colonel Russell's Fifteenth Tennessee Cavalry hastened to cut the road in McMillen's rear and, eager to capture the cannons, assaulted the Second Iowa Battery.[4]

Help was at hand. The Ninth Minnesota, leading the Second Brigade, alertly stepped out on the double-quick toward McMillen's endangered troops. Wilkin rushed the Minnesotans south through a cornfield into thick woods. "Suddenly," wrote Markham, "a line of troops appeared in front of the three companies [on the left], in the open ground." They halted "when nearly even with our left, and not more than twelve rods [sixty-six yards]" distant. The strangers were two companies of Russell's Fifteenth Tennessee Cavalry, old Guntown acquaintances bent on storming the Iowa battery. Wilkin and Markham "shouted to them to know who they were, and before any reply was given, one raised his gun and fired at our battery just in our rear." Both officers responded, "Fire!" "They are rebs!" "Give it to them!" A deadly volley struck down most of the Confederates. The rest "fled in utmost confusion, leaving many killed and wounded on the field." When the Forty-Seventh Illinois came up, Wilkin ordered the two regiments to charge. "In passing hurriedly" over where the Rebels once stood, Markham "counted seventeen [casualties] without moving to the right or left. They were well clothed and well armed. I picked up a Burnside rifle, and there were several of the Sharps pattern among them. They all had spurs on, indicating that they were cavalry or mounted infantry."[5]

Together Wilkin and McMillen pushed Russell and Barteau back "in dis-order" over a half mile. The rest of Bell's brigade and the Kentucky brigade never got into the fight. The Ninth Minnesota suffered no loss at all. McMillen acknowledged his debt to the Second Brigade, especially the Ninth Minnesota "who did effective service." In turn Buford ruefully praised his opponents who were so obviously better led than before. "At no time had I found the enemy unprepared. He marched with his column well closed up, his wagon train well protected, and his flanks covered in an admirable manner, evincing at all times a readiness to meet any attack, and showing careful generalship." The rebuff near Coonewah Creek stung the Tennesseans harshly. Much later Captain Carroll of Colonel Wilson's Sixteenth Tennessee Cavalry recalled that Bell's brigade was "considerably damaged and forced to retire; many of our men shed tears."[6]

That night the Federal troops camped near the ruins of tiny Harrisburg, two miles west of Tupelo. "Gen. Smith expected the ball to open in the morning," explained Markham, "and was bound to have a position that suited him." Dawn on Thursday, July 14, another scorcher, revealed Union forces facing west along a long, shallow ridge with only "occasional small skirts of woods" between them and Rebels massing beyond. Colonel David Moore's Third Division and Colonel Bouton's separate black brigade were south of the Pontotoc-Tupelo road. Two brigades of Mower's First Division held that portion of the ridge extending north and northeast beyond the road. Behind in reserve waited Wilkin's Second Brigade with the Ninth Minnesota on the right. To the east McMillen's First Brigade covered the wagon train sheltered in a valley. Mower placed boxes of ready ammunition all along his line. "This does not look like Guntown!" marveled the delighted Minnesotans.[7]

With at best three-quarters the number of Smith's troops, S. D. Lee nonetheless chose frontal attack. Still savoring their stunning success against Sturgis, his men were grossly overconfident. A coordinated assault against Smith's left wing miscarried soon after sunrise when the Kentucky brigade jumped off too soon and withered away in intense fire from Moore's division. At 7:30 A.M. it was Mower's turn. Two batteries opened a heavy cannonade that largely overshot his front line but tore into Wilkin's brigade on the reverse slope. About a thousand Mississippians from Col. Hinchie P. Mabry's brigade emerged from the timber north of the road aiming for Mower's line. Badly stung by Union artillery, they drifted northeast while continuing to advance, in A. J. Smith's words, "gallantly" but "without order, organization or skill." The combination of fierce defensive fire and broiling sun (many Rebels fainted from heat exhaustion) devastated the brave Mississippians. "Howling like Comanches," they dashed within sixty yards of Mower's line, only to take shelter behind a fence. Bell's Tennessee brigade moved into the gap that opened on Mabry's right and suffered the same dire fate. Seeing

Mabry in desperate straits, Colonel Rucker's brigade charged through a corn-field north of Mabry's left flank. Rucker pressed ahead about a mile before faltering, again within sixty yards of Mower's steadfast infantry. That dis-mounted horsemen actually dared to assault a superior number of staunch infantry simply flabbergasted William Dean. "They could not have done [it] as they had no bayonets." Nicholas Schreifels was amazed how the Rebels "tried again and again to charge us but were as often repulsed by the wither-ing volleys we poured into their ranks. Their fury knew no bounds and had they become masters of the situation and captured us, they would, undoubt-edly, have flayed us alive."[8]

Though the Ninth Minnesota was not in the direct line of fire, a "leaden hail fell thick and fast in and about my ranks for over two hours," wrote Marsh, "yet not a man moved from his place without orders." Felch wrote, "We lay there some time, and if I ever hugged the ground it was there[;] some of the balls come so close I could feel the warm air rush past my face. Then presently General Smith rode up in the thickest of the fire with a black pipe in his mouth and said now is your time boys give it to them. In an instant the cannon belched forth their messengers of death and the whole line of infantry [ahead] gave one yell and fired." So "hot was the enemy's fire at this point," noted Marsh, "that, although my men were lying flat on the ground I had one man killed and five wounded." A shell splinter pierced the chest of liberator E. W. Pike, a twenty-two-year-old farmer from Utica in Winona County who had not been with Sturgis. He rode by ambulance to Memphis. The only other liberator known to have suffered harm at that time was Sam Mickel. While in line of battle, he got sunstroke just as he had the month before at Brice's Crossroads.[9]

Around 8:30 A.M. Wilkin happened to be "sitting on his horse, immediately behind our regiment talking with a member of his staff," wrote Markham, "when a musket ball entered his left side, passing out on the right, and going through or near the heart. He never spoke after being struck." Markham thought, "A purer patriot, a better or braver man, does not live." Wilkin "often" said "he wished to die on the field of battle at his proper post of duty. We buried him within a few rods of where his life blood oozed away, and many a silent tear was dropped as the regiment passed the spot." Smith observed that Wilkin's "many noble traits had endeared him to all," while Mower praised his "high-toned bearing and gentlemanly conduct." Wilkin "was my fast friend," wrote Governor Miller. "A braver soldier never drew a blade in defense of his country's rights, and he died with his face to the foe." The "boys all feel pretty bad about losing him since he done so well," wrote Frank Harrington, but he admitted that "before we left Mo. he was not

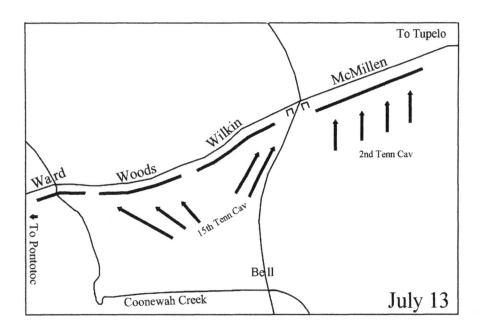

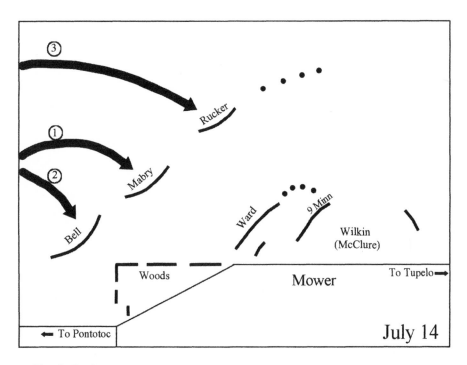

Tupelo Battle

very well liked." In "one respect," opined Dean, "some are not sorry Col. Wilkin was killed. Col. Marsh is a very feeling man for his men. And I think is not running after honors." Alexander Wilkin was the senior Minnesota officer to fall in battle during the Civil War. His family eventually recovered his body and buried him in his hometown. In 1868 a sprawling county in northwestern Minnesota was named for him, and today Wilkin's statue graces the rotunda of the Minnesota State Capitol.[10]

Colonel John D. McClure of the Forty-Seventh Illinois took over the Second Brigade. On the far north flank, Companies C (with half the liberators) and D spread out as skirmishers in the same cornfield where Rucker's brigade took such a pounding. "The Rebbel skirmishers tried to drive us back but did not make out so they shelled us," explained Felch. "That's what we did not like. We retreated a short distance but soon took our old position & kept it till they broke far afterwards. . . . We could tell very near where the shells would strike or burst. I heard one coming through the air and knew it would strike very near where I was standing & jumped over in the next row of corn and fell. It struck in the row I was standing in about six feet ahead and passed on without bursting. If I had stayed where I was it would of surely of hit me. Another burst over us filled with musket balls."[11]

Around 10 A.M. the battered Rebel brigades in front of Mower's division suddenly pulled back, in Felch's words, "in disorder, leaving a great many of theyr wounded in the field." Mower counterattacked with all three brigades—the Ninth Minnesota taking the extreme right of the whole line. "What a sight met our eyes," wrote Felch. "The ground was so covered with dead and the wounded were groaning and asking for mercy which they would not give to our wounded." He estimated "between four and five hundred killed & we did not go half a mile. The most of them was shot through the head. I saw several officers on the field. I have got a button of a rebel colonels coat." Smith's men counted 270 enemy dead in addition to many wounded and prisoners. Confederate casualties on July 14, never properly totaled, were horrendous. Forrest's horsemen never again fought with the same reckless abandon they had shown at Brice's Crossroads and Tupelo.[12]

Smith was confident he inflicted a sharp reverse on Forrest. When he learned he was running out of food—most of the hardtack had gone bad, and the men were already on quarter-rations—he resolved to return to Memphis. On the morning of July 15, after most of the cavalry, the wagon train, and Moore's Third Division left the battlefield, Bouton's black brigade retired into the line held by Mower's First Division. When the Confederates boldly seized the high ground that Bouton's troops had relinquished, Mower struck back. Bouton led with the Sixty-First U.S. Colored Infantry and part of the

Sixty-Eighth U.S. Colored Infantry. McClure's brigade formed on his right, with the Ninth Minnesota immediately adjacent to the black troops. Lieutenant Capon's Company K, with half the liberators, fanned out ahead on the flank as skirmishers. Charging with a vengeance, Bouton's black troops advanced over a mile as the Rebels gave way. They "fought like Tigers," admired Felch. The "negroes run their bayonets [at the enemy] as if they liked the fun[.] The rebs hollered no quarter to the blacks and the blacks gave no quarter nor took any prisoners. They killed every reb they got a hold of and I don't blame them. They have been slaves like dogs and they swear they will kill every reb and the officers cant help it. Nor do they dare to—in battle." The Sixty-Eighth U.S. Colored Infantry (formerly the Fourth Missouri Volunteers of African descent) had been recruited from Missouri slaves. If John, the slave whose pleas precipitated the Otterville liberation, ever enlisted he easily could have been in that regiment. A chance reunion of the principal participants of the Otterville outrage under those circumstances would have been an astounding historical coincidence.[13]

On July 21 Smith's men gratefully marched into La Grange and then rolled into Memphis the next day. Total casualties had been 674, with only 38 missing. On the way back to Memphis the Yankees "took everything eatable, clear and clean," wrote Dean, "burnt all the cotton, drove along all the beef cattle and burnt a large number of rebel houses. We stripped everything serviceable, mules with horses, chickens, meat and some clothing was taken, beehives robbed, potatoes dug, orchards was [illegible] and a host of darkies came in." Smith praised his men "for the manner in which they endured the hardships and fatigues of the campaign; marching over dusty roads with only one-half or one-third rations, under a broiling sun, with little water." The delighted Ninth Minnesota took the measure of their new generals as "veteran and hard fighters." Markham called Mower "the most dashing and the best officer to head a charge I have seen since joining the service." Just "one such man" was "worth a whole battalion of the desponding, chicken-hearted kind, of which we have too many." Surgeon William W. Clarke of the Tenth Minnesota crowed that "old A. J. Smith is the trump. He outgeneraled Forrest every move he made."[14]

Smith has been criticized for withdrawing instead of pushing deeper into Mississippi to crush the Confederates. Nonetheless, he accomplished his objective of "whipping" Forrest and preventing him from going after Sherman's supply line. The Rebels suffered more than twice the number of the Union losses and could much less afford them. The expedition, Washburn bragged to his superiors, "has thoroughly retrieved the disaster to Brigadier General Sturgis." If not removing the bitterness felt for Brice's Crossroads, the Ninth Minnesota drew great satisfaction over finally getting the better of the dreaded Forrest. "The 9th boys I think feel better over the victory than we do," observed Dr. Clarke. "They got their revenge."[15]

THE TERRIBLE MARCH

In August 1864 the Ninth Minnesota joined Smith on another soiree into northern Mississippi. They advanced as far as Oxford (fifty miles west of Tupelo) on the twenty-second, only to learn that Forrest had secretly slipped to the west and surprised Memphis the previous morning. Smith was recalled to Memphis. The war grew even rougher. "We burnt nearly the whole town of Oxford, almost as big a place as Shakopee, only two or three stores but public & private buildings far ahead of it," wrote Dean. "We ransacked everything in town almost." It was "pretty good country through which we passed," and "we destroyed everything along the road that was eatable." The Ninth Minnesota fought only one minor skirmish and lost no one on the expedition, but a considerable number were sick with "fevers contracted in the Tallahatchie Swamps."[16]

With Atlanta in his grasp, Sherman dismissed any mischief Forrest might cause. He summoned Smith's troops to Georgia, but a crisis brewing west of the Mississippi forced a drastic change in plan for Mower's First Division. Rebel raiders had crossed the Arkansas River and threatened General Steele's hold on Little Rock. To "reestablish Steele's communications" with Memphis, Mower was told to steam down the Mississippi to the mouth of the White River and proceed up that stream to the region east of Little Rock. No one thought the diversion would delay for long the deployment to Atlanta. The troops were to travel light, minus knapsacks and excess gear. On his return from veteran furlough, Col. Lucius Hubbard of the Fifth Minnesota (later governor of Minnesota) took over the Second Brigade and would lead it bravely and ably for the rest of the war. By that time it was technically no longer called the Eagle Brigade, for "Old Abe," the celebrated bald eagle, was already in Wisconsin on well-earned retirement.[17]

On September 3 the Ninth Minnesota boarded the steamer *John Raine*. Newly promoted to lieutenant colonel (the absent Marsh was now colonel), Markham kept command despite poor health. The liberators who journeyed to Arkansas were Merchant, Epler, Hartley, McCain, Slocum, Stewart, and John Watkins from Company C; and Buck, Fenstermacher, Heilmann, Jansen, Lüthye, and Raymond in Company K. Noxious swamps along the narrow, twisting White River meant slow going in the hot, humid weather. Bad water gave many soldiers severe gastrointestinal trouble. On September 6 when the little flotilla got word of the fall of Atlanta, "three hearty cheers was given of those that were able to raise their heads." Five days later the Second Brigade entered Brownsville, about twenty-five miles east of Little Rock.[18]

General Rosecrans's weakened Union forces in Missouri were in serious trouble. Not only had the guerrilla war exploded worse than before, but a large, mostly mounted force, the so-called Army of Missouri under Maj. Gen. Sterling Price ("Old Pap"), hastened north through rugged northeastern Arkansas to invade the state. Steele ordered Mower's infantry to chase the Rebel horsemen despite their already substantial and constantly increasing lead. On September 17 Mower started north. The effective strength of the Ninth Minnesota had declined through illness and incapacity to just 11 officers and 244 enlisted men. Among the many too sick to march were Epler and Jansen. The trek of Mower's division "was a rapid and severe one, through a country much of which resembled a wilderness," recalled Color Sergeant Macdonald. "Heavy and frequent rains fell; the roads were of the most miserable character, through swamps, over mountains and across swollen streams." The troops "forded Little Red Rock River, crossed Black River three times, crossed St. Francis River, passed through Pocahontas, Ark., on September 25, entered Missouri on the 29, and passed through Poplar Bluff the next day." At the outset the weather, during daytime at least, was "excessively hot," wrote Colonel Marshall of the Seventh Minnesota, but the nights "grew cold so that the men suffered" from being "thinly clad, and without woolen blankets." Even worse, "shoes and other clothing failed on the march, producing a great amount of suffering. I believe ten per cent of my command—the same of other regiments—were barefoot, when we got to Cape Girardeau. It was pitiable to see the poor fellows—true heroes— crippling along over the stony hills of southeast Missouri with blistered and bleeding feet—some with naked legs, some coatless, some shirtless, some hatless." For the Ninth Minnesota, it was a reminder of the bitter retreat from Brice's Crossroads, but even so, Macdonald averred, "The men came through in good condition and fine spirits."[19]

On October 5, after hiking 312 miles in nineteen days (an average of 16 and a half miles a day), "a dirtier, raggeder set never marched into any town than Mower's men were when they reached Cape Girardeau," wrote the adjutant of the Twelfth Iowa. In the meantime Price's great raid bore down on St. Louis but stalled after September 26 because of the spirited defense of Pilot Knob, 86 miles south of the city. Smith and his Third Division, traveling in comfort by boat, reached St. Louis before the Rebels could get there. After the disappointment at Pilot Knob, "Old Pap" bounded off to the northwest toward Jefferson City. He threatened the capital on October 7 but did not attack because it was already too strongly defended. Hoping to salvage something from his Missouri odyssey, Price set his sights on Kansas City. On the way he snapped up Boonville and Sedalia and, just as in the glory days of 1861, moved against Lexington. Rosecrans assembled units from Kansas to cover Independence, while cavalry and Smith's troops pursued Price.[20]

After resting two days at Cape Girardeau, Mower's bedraggled troops took passage to St. Louis and cruised up the Missouri River. The many sandbars slowed progress on the "Big Muddy," and it took until October 16 to reach Jefferson City. There Mower turned over the First Division to Col. Joseph J. Woods and left for a command under Sherman in Georgia. The men were very sad to see "Fighting Joe" depart. The still ailing Markham relinquished the Ninth Minnesota to newly promoted Maj. Horace Strait, who formerly led Company I. Buck went into the hospital, too, cutting the number of liberators still in the ranks to ten.[21]

Riding the Pacific Railroad west out of Jefferson City on October 18, the First Division soon arrived at yet another locale very familiar to at least part of the Ninth Minnesota: Lamine Bridge and nearby Otterville. Both places recently endured unwelcome visits by bushwhackers, and Shelby's cavalry had burned down the bridge yet again. They also torched the Otterville railroad depot where the actual liberation had occurred. Adding to the division's difficulties, wrote Marshall, was the "really cold, wintry weather," with "snow storms, and chilling rains and winds that pierced to the marrow. Remember, we had no tents, no shelter for the men, except such as they improvised in the nightly bivouacs." There was no winter clothing either.[22]

Well before dawn on October 19 began the next installment of "The Terrible March of the Minnesota Regiments in Pursuit of Price"—a sixty-mile jaunt northwest to Lexington. Marshall described the circumstances:

> One stormy, wintry night,—the rain driven in our faces by a keen northeastern wind,—we were marched into the night. The 3rd division had been some days in advance of us; that morning we marched from La Mine to Sedalia, sixteen miles, where we joined the 3rd division, and were then required to make a full day's march further—about eighteen miles—with the 3rd. We tried to do it. By some unaccountable delay we lost three hours at Sedalia, in the best part of the day. Night came on, with storm and darkness; men could not see their footing, which made the marching doubly hard. It was bleak prairie, and the road could not all the way be kept. When we came to fences at intervals, their friendly shelter and fuel were sought by the men, whose strength was gone; and gradually the ranks were thinned, until only the officers and a corporal's guard of men remained. . . .

At last we came to a fence lining the road a little way on the left. All along it were little bivouack fires made from the dry rails by the stragglers—weary, exhausted men—of regiments that had preceded us. . . . Part of the 1st Division, Col. Hubbard of the 5th Minnesota commanding the 2d Brigade, was just reaching camp, not fifty men of any regiment in the ranks. The Colonel of one of the regiments of our brigade had five men.

Macdonald called that day's slog "the hardest march that the Ninth or any other regiment of the corps had ever participated in." Thousands straggled. By another incredible historical irony, the line of march took the Ninth Minnesota north of Sedalia through Georgetown and thus very near C. W. C. Walker's farm where, though highly unlikely, John and his family might still have been enslaved. Some lost, lagging Federal troops might even have taken refuge there to escape the icy rain.[23]

On the night of October 21, the First Division stumbled into Lexington, which Price had already evacuated. McCain gave out there. That day Price had captured Independence, thirty-five miles to the west. Fearing that Union forces shielding Kansas City might be overwhelmed, Rosecrans blundered by sending "Smith's Guerrillas" straight to Independence instead of southwest across Price's likely line of retreat. Therefore, on October 23, while Smith's nine thousand men neared Independence, "Old Pap" was losing the Battle of Westport, a dozen miles to the southwest. The routed Rebels fell back out of any possible reach of Smith's disappointed troops. "Price owed his salvation—such as it was—to the fact that Smith's force had been diverted to a sector where the least use could be made of it," explains historian Leslie Anders. "We came up pretty near old Price," wrote Dean, "but he kept moving on in spite of all the cavalry. But they gave him thunder. We came on the battle[field] a day after they fought at Big Blue River about 12 miles from Independence & also at [another] place [where] they fought." The frustrated infantry hastened south to Harrisonville in futile pursuit. Between October 19 and 26, the Ninth Minnesota had covered 177 miles, with several frigid night marches, all for nothing. Marshall deplored "the vain effort of our Generals to overtake with an infantry command, General Price, whose command was mounted on the best horses they could gather in Missouri from friend and foe."[24]

Although no longer a pursuit, the "Terrible March" was far from over. On October 28 Grant ordered Rosecrans to return Smith's borrowed divisions as soon as possible. Rosecrans insisted that they could not go by water—the Missouri River was now too low for most vessels. Nor could the overtaxed Pacific Railroad bear them, so they must march all 285 miles to St. Louis!

Many cynically suspected that Rosecrans was unwilling to waste scarce rail-road resources for troops that he must soon relinquish. Ground down to 12 officers and 165 enlisted men, the Ninth Minnesota left Harrisonville on October 30 and tramped through more familiar places: Warrensburg, Knob Noster, and Dresden. In Sedalia, Brig. Gen. John McArthur assumed command of the First Division. The tough, thirty-seven-year-old, Scottish-born businessman from Illinois, who customarily wore a Scot's bonnet and clan badge, was fully as fine a combat leader as "Fighting Joe" Mower.[25]

The frigid, often stormy weather, recalled Macdonald, made "the march very laborious, and the camps at night more than unusually uncomfortable, especially as the men were lightly clothed, and had only an army blanket and rubber to wrap up in. But by clearing away the snow and building up big log fires they managed to get a much-needed rest." The stretch on November 3 from just outside Sedalia east to Lamine Bridge proved especially arduous and memorable because of a heavy snowfall. One Wisconsin soldier, writing soon afterward to a comrade, called it the "worst storm it was ever my fortune to be caught out in" and the "toughest time you or I ever saw in the service." Just to keep warm, many slogged the whole seventeen miles without halting. Even so, complained the Wisconsinite, "I surely thought I would freeze to death before we got to the timber, or get a fire going before we got there." The next day, east of Lamine Bridge, the men plowed through snow a foot deep. A few days later, warmer weather turned the roads muddy to an "unfathomable" depth. Fording the wide Osage River east of Jefferson City meant going waist deep in near-freezing water.[26]

Finally on November 15, Smith's two divisions staggered into Benton Barracks following an epic journey that had "few if any parallels in the history of the war." Since leaving Memphis on September 3, the First Division had traveled 772 miles by boat, 50 miles by rail, and 950 miles on foot. Just the distance marched since October 19 (from Lamine Bridge west to Harrisonville and back to St. Louis) amounted to 462 miles. The sojourn in St. Louis brought not only rest and ease but long overdue pay. Even after sending money home, wrote Marshall, "there was plenty left to buy gloves, comforters, and the innumerable little things that soldiers need, to say nothing of the pies and cakes and apples, and oranges, and peanuts and chestnuts, and cider and beer, and everything else that a man's fancy and appetite crave after he has been away from city shops and stands six months."[27]

Colonel Marsh resumed command of the Ninth Minnesota in St. Louis. Most of the sick from western Missouri came by boat and train to rejoin the regiment. A party of convalescents from Memphis brought knapsacks and other regimental gear. In that manner liberators Epler, McCain, Vaughan, and Williams reported to Company C, and Ehmke, Jansen, and Pike to Company K. Epler and Jansen had been among five hundred ailing men of the First Division left behind in mid-September in Arkansas. Roughly one-third of the sick, those in the worst shape (about twenty from the Ninth Minnesota), went into government hospitals at Little Rock, where they were "well taken care of." The rest, including fifty-three from the Ninth Minnesota, ended up in what Corporal Carlson called "the most God-forsaken place I ever saw used for habitation." It was a "sort of Cavalry Barracks" made up as a "long row of log cribs—horses stalls." The dirt floors teemed with lice. Within a few days, Carlson got out to see Little Rock, which was "nicely located a hundred feet or more above the Arkansas River." Chaplain Kerr arrived on October 1 from Memphis bearing many articles to delight the sick. "I can never forget the venerable old man," Carlson explained, "always kind and ready to do all he could to lessen the sufferings and hardships of the soldier." Kerr liberated a party of 250 convalescents, including Carlson, from the "lousy old log huts" and took them to Memphis.[28]

Sad news from Memphis concerned David Felch, one of the true heroes of the Otterville liberation. Suffering intermittent fever on the Oxford expedition, he had gone at the end of August into Adams General Hospital. On September 10 a comrade penned a letter on his behalf advising his family that he had been sick since the Tallahatchie River, but adding, "I think I am getting better." Kerr himself wrote Felch's father on September 21 telling of frequent visits during which he found David "cheerful" and "anxious to be a christian." Kerr, too, believed he was improving. On September 30, while enjoying a meal, Felch unexpectedly "dropped to his knee, fell back and soon expired." His swift death, ascribed to "congestive chill," surprised even his surgeon, who wrote the parents that their son was fondly remembered as a "friend to a soldier" and "esteemed by all who knew him." A letter that Felch wrote in the summer of 1864 revealed his evolving attitude toward the war: "You can't think how homesick the most of our recent recruits are. They think they are enlisted for three yrs in the sunny South. I am glad I enlisted when I did it will soon be nearing on the last year." It seemed "this war has got to end[,] will soon cease shedding its blood through our land. I think myself it will not last much longer. I wish I was old enough to voat. I would vote for old Abe, if he is not elected this election the war is again to last a long time yet the rebs say if Abe Lincoln is reellected there is no use fighting any longer." Just twenty, David F. M. Felch was the youngest liberator to die during the war.[29]

On November 23 the Ninth Minnesota, battle hardened and toughened by adversity, trooped on board the steamboat *Victory*. The sojourn of "Smith's

Guerrillas" in St. Louis had been brief because their services were desperately required elsewhere. They were still pawns of an uncertain and hesitant Union high command that could react to Confederate threats but was not yet capable of quashing them. "No one complained when the order came to march again," wrote Marshall. "Everyone would have been glad of a little longer rest. The sore feet were not all healed. But as we marched from Benton Barracks to the boats—the division filling the way about as far as the eye could well see in the hazy, dusty atmosphere, the men in their bright, new uniforms, the battle-flags floating gaily and the martial music playing cheerily—brighter, happier faces, more erect forms, firmer steps or more soldierly ranks have rarely been seen. It was quite a war pageant. And row, away, away, with the speed of steam—no great speed either on these transports—to a new field of operations."[30]

CHAPTER SIXTEEN

Back to God's Country

Momentous Events

In early November, as the ever-shrinking Ninth Minnesota plodded east to St. Louis, their imprisoned comrades wondered if they would spend the whole winter, if not longer, in captivity. The first bright spot was the presidential election on the eighth. Not realizing the fall of Atlanta had sealed Lincoln's victory, the various camp commanders ran elections among the inmates. The Rebels anticipated the majority of disgruntled captives would mirror a national repudiation of the Republicans. Yet in Andersonville, Millen, and Florence, Lincoln won by substantial margins. At Millen the Rebels retaliated for the "boys hurrahing for Old Abe" by cutting off their rations. The results at Andersonville made First Sergeant Warren especially proud of his fellow hospital patients. "No more telling blow was ever given the tottering confederacy, or a greater honor ever conferred on President Lincoln, than the clear majority" cast by those "worn-out, starved and rotten men." At Florence the guards' attitudes made it obvious they believed the South's last real chance for independence was gone. Sergeant Major Kellogg of the Sixteenth Connecticut could not resist remarking in his journal that "the rebels were blue indeed. Such a set of sour, gloomy-looking fellows."[1]

After the election, the second highly significant event was the reinstatement of a limited prisoner exchange. Under great pressure to free its men in Southern prisons, the North sought to avoid restocking the Rebel armies with healthy ex-prisoners by proposing in September to exchange "all sick and invalid officers and men who from wounds or sickness shall, in the judgment of the party holding them, be unfit for duty and likely to remain so for 60 days." The Confederate government accepted. The point of exchange for Georgia and South Carolina was to be Fort Pulaski, near Savannah. On September 25 the Confederates agreed to swap at least five thousand Union prisoners for a like number of disabled Southerners. Such complicated arrangements took time to finalize. Eventually thousands of sick and wounded Rebel prisoners were conveyed south along the Atlantic coast to be traded for all the prisoners the Confederates supplied at the exchange. No one was to be turned back, unlike in the special exchange near Atlanta. On November 4 General Winder received orders to send sick and wounded prisoners to Savannah. If Millen and Andersonville could not supply enough in that category (little chance of that), he could also include Yankees whose terms of service had already expired. Florence (which at that time was not yet under Winder's control) would also participate. The Union army advised it would be handing over at least ten thousand prisoners for exchange. In mid-November Lt. Col. John E. Mulford, the Federal agent in charge, contacted Rebel authorities near Savannah to arrange the transfers at Point Venus on the Savannah River, three miles upstream from Fort Pulaski.[2]

Hints of these developments appeared in Southern newspapers seen by prisoners at Florence and Millen, but after so many disappointments, they took the news with a large grain of salt. Thus, around November 13 in the Andersonville hospital, Warren, with great surprise and delight, noticed "a squad of rebel officers and surgeons, accompanied by a clerk, passing rapidly from tent to tent, selecting men. I promptly put myself in their way, and put my best, or rather, worst foot foremost; it was acceptable, and my name and description were recorded." Early on November 15, "the call blew, and hastily snatching up my old blanket and saying good-bye," he "hobbled through the gate. We were marched to the station, loaded into cars, and with the notable Wirz to see us off and wish us good success in getting home, started on our way." Among that group of 513 fortunate prisoners was Sergeant Major Clapp, who brought along his secret record of Andersonville deaths. That evening they entered the Millen stockade for only a brief stay before continuing to Savannah to be exchanged.[3]

The Andersonville sick would not be the only ones leaving Millen. The day before they arrived, similar cursory examinations there selected candidates from the multitude of prisoners who were sick or at least in visibly worse shape than others. McCoy recalled in an address in 1898:

> A rebel sergeant and surgeon came in and called for all the sick to fall in line.
> The boys were a little slow about it as they had been fooled so many times that
> they thought there was some game in it, but I said to my mess, "I'm going to see
> what's in it anyway."

I had no more idea I would pass or that it meant exchange than I have of owning this hall. I took a place in line and when the surgeon came to me, he looked me squarely in the eye and said gruffly, "What's the trouble with you?" I answered "bone scurvy." He pinched my right arm midway between the shoulder and elbow joint, turned to the sergeant and said: "Put his name down."

Lyon's friends urged him to submit his name, but he, too, doubted the offer was authentic. Nonetheless, leaning on his crude cane, he shuffled over to the Rebel party and queried the officer, who responded, "Young man, what is the matter with you?" "Scurvy, I suppose," Lyon replied. "Turning to his clerk," the officer said, "'Put his name down.'"[4]

Disappointed too often in the past, Lyon thought no exchange would happen. In fact, of the sixty-six or so of the Ninth Minnesota prisoners at Millen, twenty-one were selected for exchange. Some prisoners bribed Rebel officials to be put on the exchange list, but that ploy was beyond the capacity of the impoverished Ninth Minnesota contingent. One of the first groups alerted to go on November 15 included Lyon. He bid farewell to Vandegrift, who was slated for exchange on a later day. Vandegrift subsequently remarked that when Lyon "went out I did not think he would live to get home." Lyon rode a rickety wagon three-quarters of a mile to the depot, but no train appeared. Two days later he was called out again. This time the train did come, and August Arndt of Company H, for one, got on board, but there was not enough room for Lyon, who spent the night at the depot. On the nineteenth another batch of prisoners that included Warren, Clapp, and McCoy joined him. It had taken McCoy "a half day to walk that distance and I did my best."[5]

That evening Lyon's group of prisoners was herded into open cattle cars "and rode all night in an awful cold rainstorm." By the time they reached Savannah early the next morning, they were "wet through and so chilled we could hardly move." Some like McCoy were immediately presented paroles to sign. "While waiting my turn I noticed that there were some dead bodies carried from the cars." At the same time, Lyon and some of the others were marched over to "an old cotton boat" tied up on the Savannah River. It was one of several vessels the Confederates provided to transport the prisoners to the exchange. "Upon the dock stood a table upon which lay a large sheet of paper. We were required to write our name upon this paper. What the paper signified I did not know, and cared less. After signing the paper we passed on to the boat." Soon afterward McCoy's group also boarded one of the boats.[6]

The Rebel transports steamed slowly downriver toward Point Venus. Because the morning was "dark, cloudy, chilly," the passengers on board

Lyon's boat "huddled around boilers to keep warm." Clapp noticed Lyon was shivering and gave him a new shirt, which he donned under his old tattered garment. Suddenly, around noon, Lyon observed "quite a stir forward." Shifting his gaze ahead, he saw a ship "flying stars and stripes." It was one of the large fleet of Union vessels Mulford had assembled to accommodate the soon-to-be ex-prisoners. "It's the old flag!" one man exclaimed. To Lyon the sight was "a glorious sunburst after a storm," for "never before did that emblem mean so much to us." Prisoners "shouted, some laughed, some even tried to dance." Yet the long delay before the two ships came together occasioned "much frustration and fears" among the captives. Finally, McCoy recalled, "a gangplank was laid down between the two boats[;] a Federal stood at one edge, a Butternut on the other of the plank, and counted us as we passed from one boat to the other." As Lyon "eased across and onto the deck," he thanked the Lord. "My whole soul went out in a song of praise. My thoughts and feelings were beyond the power of the human tongue to express." Corporal Thomas Pettijohn of Company D remembered when he stepped on board one of the Union transports at Point Venus it was his eighteenth wedding anniversary "to the very hour." The "happiness occasioned by this transfer from rebel authority, was greater than ever caused by any other event in his life."[7]

"Cheering the Stars and Stripes" on board an exchange vessel, November 1864

"Once on God's boat (for so we felt it to be)," Lyon wrote, "our next thought was for something to eat." Warren savored the air "fragrant with the aroma of boiling coffee." In a warm cabin below, the men were fed "Yankee food"—"fresh hardtack and boiled pork and great tin cups of delicious chocolate. Never was a feast more heartily enjoyed." Lyon gobbled down eleven hardtack, a half pound of pork, and all the chocolate he could hold and was very lucky he did not get sick from it. "Joyfully we sang far into the night the long neglected, almost forgotten songs of former days," wrote Warren. The next day on their different ships, the men were taken below, "stripped of our rags—which were thrown overboard—put into large bath-tubs with plenty of soap and scrubbed." Once their hair was cut and beards trimmed or shaved, they were outfitted with new clothes and then shown to beds that hitherto had been off limits to prevent the spread of vermin. Mulford noted the "returned prisoners are in bad condition, particularly in regard to clothing, though on the whole their physical condition is not so bad as I had expected to see." He (and subsequent Confederate apologists who quoted him) did not take into account the selection process that had automatically excluded the many sick prisoners thought too infirm to survive the trip to Savannah.[8]

"Serving out Rations" on the *New York*, November 1864

Medical examinations determined if the ex-prisoners were up to the week-long voyage to Annapolis, where they would be hospitalized or, if medically fit, paid and furloughed home before being returned to their regiments. The seriously ill were transferred to hospital ships. Twenty exchanged men from the Ninth Minnesota left for Annapolis, but learning of Clapp's clerical skills, Mulford detailed him to his headquarters on the flag-of-truce vessel *New York.* Weighing 167 1/2 pounds before capture, Clapp tipped the scale at 103 pounds when exchanged. Years later Merrill, his friend from Andersonville, recalled Clapp "was confined to his berth nearly the whole time we were with Lt. Col. Mulford, by what the doctors told him was inflammatory rheumatism & for which he administered strong liniment to bathe & rub the lower limbs. I performed this part of the work during my stay with Col Mulford on account of his disability to do it himself." The "inflammatory rheumatism" was actually scurvy. Clapp and Merrill remained on duty until December 22, when Mulford released them in New York.[9]

Up through November 25, Mulford received about 3,600 prisoners from Millen. Thereafter the exchange was interrupted because of the effect of a third momentous event—the March to the Sea. On November 15 Sherman stormed out of Atlanta on his way to Savannah. His left, or northerly, wing aimed for Milledgeville, the state capital, and beyond along the railroad, ninety miles from Millen. The Confederates rapidly apprehended the danger to Camp Lawton. By November 20, during the initial prisoner exchange near Savannah, Winder ordered Lawton's immediate evacuation and the relocation of all prisoners to southwestern Georgia. On November 22, as the last captive was hurriedly removed from Millen, Sherman's left wing approached Milledgeville and occupied the capital the next day. On November 26 Union cavalry raiders scouted Camp Lawton hoping to rescue the prisoners and were very disappointed to find the huge stockade empty. After finally reaching the town of Millen on December 3, part of Sherman's left wing passed through abandoned Camp Lawton, the first large Rebel prison to fall. The reaction of the horrified bluecoats to dead bodies left unburied in the haste of the evacuation and to the pathetic shebangs and holes where the prisoners had to live was akin to what their grandsons and great-grandsons would feel eighty years later when they liberated Nazi concentration camps. In retaliation "for starving our prisoners," Sherman wreaked special havoc ("tenfold more devilish") on the town of Millen, including burning the railroad station and the hotel.[10]

In the meantime Winder had funneled all the remaining Millen prisoners into Savannah, but once there, things went awry. As intended, by November 24 most of those approximately five thousand prisoners had ended up at

Blackshear, ninety miles southwest of Savannah. At least twenty were from the Ninth Minnesota, including liberators Frahm, Gordon, and Rodier, as well as Aslakson, who would shudder years later when recalling the night spent in front of the Savannah railroad station reclining in several inches of frigid rainwater. "We were then so indifferent both to our health and life, that we all despaired of holding out any longer." The next morning "guards at bayonet point drove those who could stand into freight cars and packed them in like cattle." An overnight trip southwest in open railway cars through blustery winds became so cold for those prisoners "without blankets, and clothed in rags" that, according to Cpl. Alexander McLean of the 117th New York, "stout men cried like children." Once at Blackshear "many of the men were so chilled that when they jumped off the cars they had no use of their legs," wrote Jacob Hutchinson of the Seventy-Second Ohio, "and almost everyone would drop right down on the railroad track, and then crawl on their hands and knees until they got warmed up." Hutchinson, like young Dwight Card of Company E, also present, had been one of the unfortunates turned back in September near Atlanta. Blackshear was only meant to be a temporary holding place. There was no stockade. Under heavy guard the prisoners camped in a grove of pines north of town.[11]

A different group of Millen evacuees, approximately 1,500 prisoners who likewise included nearly twenty from the Ninth Minnesota, stewed at Savannah for three nervous, uncomfortable days before being sent north on November 25 to Charleston and from there directly to Florence. They entered the stockade at Florence on the twenty-seventh. Meanwhile, on November 26 the prisoners at Blackshear were told that exchanges were being resumed at Savannah. To a "great commotion, hurrahing and throwing up caps for joy," over a thousand, including a few from the Ninth Minnesota, were given parole papers to sign. Afterward they were dispatched to Savannah on a train without guards, but once they arrived, they were taken back into custody. "Like fools we did not escape and make for Fort Pulaski," recalled one infuriated captive. The disgruntled prisoners were immediately stuffed into rail cars, without food and with only a little water, and sent via Charleston to Florence. They went into the stockade on the twenty-ninth. Thus, about twenty former Millen prisoners from the Ninth Minnesota found themselves at Florence with Palmeter and fifteen or so survivors from the original contingent. Perhaps another twenty Millen evacuees, including Frahm, Gordon, and Rodier, remained at Blackshear.[12]

The exchange at Savannah broke down because of confusion caused by Sherman's sudden, relentless advance through Georgia. Refugees flooded into the city, and trains had to be rerouted to move troops. Those severe dislocations prevented all but the first group of Florence prisoners from reaching Savannah. The selection of suitable sick or injured prisoners at Florence had only begun on November 24. Among the first batch of one thousand "paroled men" were Corporal Kerlinger, Ryan, Field, Tower, and young William Walker. On December 1 they became the last repatriated prisoners accommodated at Point Venus. Other groups of paroled prisoners did leave Florence during the next several days, but it proved impossible to get to Savannah, and they were all turned back into the stockade. At the same time, the thousand deeply disappointed prisoners who had come up from Black-shear to Florence spread dismal word that all exchanges had ceased ("knocked in the head"). "Things look very strange indeed to all of us," a Michigan private complained.[13]

Fortunately, Mulford succeeded in shifting the point of exchange to Charleston. Led by the steamship *New York* (with Clapp on board), he brought his fleet of transports into the battle-scarred harbor and anchored close to what was left of Fort Sumter. When the exchange there finally ended on December 17, another 6,300 prisoners from Florence had been released, raising the grand total for the Savannah and Charleston exchanges to 10,916 men. Twelve prisoners from the Ninth Minnesota had started from Florence, but two died before reaching Union custody. Freed at Charleston was Nathan Palmeter, the only liberator to survive Florence. He left the camp on December 13, was paroled the next day, and boarded one of the transports for the standard routine of being bathed, clothed in new garments, and fed the hearty meal of hardtack, boiled salt pork, and hot coffee. George Hitchcock of the Twenty-First Massachusetts, who was paroled about the same time, recalled that his old rags were so noxious the bath attendant only deigned to touch them with a tip of a bayonet and hastened to drop them overboard.[14]

After a stormy voyage past Cape Hatteras, Palmeter landed on December 22 at Annapolis, where snow and ice testified to the real winter. There at Camp Parole, wrote an Illinois soldier also taken at Brice's Crossroads, "were officers representing each State waiting to receive us, who called out their State in a loud voice." The newcomers "were fed, given paper and envelopes to write to our families, stript and washt by two men, given clean new clothing and turned loose to enjoy our novel sensations." A paymaster tendered Palmeter crisp greenbacks covering two months' pay (thirty-two dollars), plus "commutation" money of twenty-five cents for each day in prison to cover the Federal rations he would have received during that time. "Starvation and disease" endured in Rebel prisons had reduced the twenty-one-year-old's slender six-foot-one-and-a-half-inch frame to a "mere skeleton," and he was sorely troubled by chronic diarrhea. Nonetheless, he had regained enough strength after nine days of good food to be cleared to travel to Camp Chase at Columbus, Ohio, where soldiers who hailed from the western states were furloughed. Accompanying him were two close friends from Company C, Sgt. David Pratt and Pvt. William Breckon. They had been with him for nearly three months at Andersonville and every day since late November after again meeting up at Florence. At Camp Chase the three received a month's leave and orders to report afterward to the parole camp at Benton Barracks prior to being sent to the Ninth Minnesota. Thus, at the end of the year, Palmeter enjoyed a wonderful homecoming at his father William's farm in Red Rock Township in Mower Country. Among the greeters was his neighbor Isaac Peterman, who finally received his disability discharge on September 3 at Memphis. As they shook hands, Palmeter asked Peterman, "Are you deaf as ever?" to which Peterman "said he never expected to see me a gain [as] he thought the rebs would lay me a way down in Dixy." Allowed an extension of leave through a surgeon's certificate, Palmeter repaired on March 17, 1865, to the "Draft Rendezvous" at Fort Snelling and soon afterward left for St. Louis.[15]

Palmeter was the first liberator to be freed from Rebel captivity and the only one from Company C ever to return home. Zara Frisbie died in Andersonville and Stephen Chandler in Millen. Word of their deaths had reached their families before Palmeter made it home. In late December Chandler's widow, Abigail, held a funeral for him in Austin and placed a tombstone in the local cemetery. Palmeter did get to turn over his friend James Woodbury's diary to his widow, Amanda. She had learned in early December of her husband's death on August 1 in Andersonville from a comrade who had received the shattering news in a letter from Captain Ford. How Ford, still in Rebel prison, ever heard of Woodbury's demise is not known. Amanda wrote on December 4 to her parents that she could not "make up my mind to give him up as dead, it seems as if he must come back, and when I think that I will never meet him again on this Earth, I want to go where I can meet him. O, how can I ever give him up, he who was always to kind and loving to me." She wished she could have taken care of him in his final illness and lamented, much more accurately than she could yet have known, the tragic circumstances "where he could see none of his friends and die alone and uncared for." That was exactly how he must have died in the Andersonville hospital. James Franklin Woodbury was born only two weeks after his father had been captured. "Little Jimmy is pretty well and is as good as he can be," Amanda wrote. "He is more comfort to me than any thing in this world, he looks so much like his father. Poor man, he never knew he had a little son to be a comfort to his mother." She closed her letter, "Pleas write soon, I am so lonely."[16]

THE FEBRUARY EXCHANGE

Sherman's March to the Sea had interfered with one prisoner exchange, but his subsequent grand offensive through South Carolina actually compelled another. In late January 1865, his troops erupted out of Savannah, but instead of following the coast northeast to Charleston as the Confederates expected, they struck north toward the state capital at Columbia. Ford, McCain, Lane, Hall, Niedenhofen, and Tiffany had been there since early October, the only Minnesotans in that particular prison. At first the officers were held in "an old worn out cornfield, partially covered with second growth pines." No stockade was built, and only the inevitable deadline marked the outer boundary. They lived either in the few tents smuggled in or in what other shelter they could improvise. Good water was plentiful and firewood was on hand. The main drawback was the issue of food, which was exclusively cornmeal and sorghum. Indeed, the prisoners dubbed the place "Camp Sorghum" because of the "large ration of sorghum that was given us in place of meat." It was "brought to us," noted Lieutenant Perin, "in old turpentine barrels thus flavoring the syrup so that none were injured by overeating." Meat could only be had at high prices from sutlers. The bad diet quickly wore down the less fortunate inmates like the Minnesota contingent. Too, the clothing of those penniless officers captured at Brice's Crossroads had been reduced by that time nearly to rags.[17]

By mid-November lax security at Columbia led to numerous escapes, including one by Hall, though he was soon recaptured. Unless the captive officers would give their parole and promise no more escapes, the Rebel commander threatened to stick them "in a *pen* in the same manner that the privates now are." The escape attempts nevertheless continued unabated. Consequently, on December 11 the authorities shifted the officers back across the Saluda River to a big yard adjacent to the South Carolina Lunatic Asylum, where a formal stockade awaited them. They were told to erect the framework for thirty-two "rough board houses," each of two rooms and its own fireplace. Only thirteen were completed; therefore, most of the captives spent the winter under canvas. Good water, though, was again made available for drinking and washing, as was generally adequate wood for cooking and heat, though the rations were still monotonously meatless. As before, anyone with access to funds, whether supplied from home, borrowed, or won (gambling there was "lively"), could do comparatively well at Camp Sorghum.[18]

The Confederates dithered while Sherman's troops plowed through swamps and otherwise made remarkable time closing in on Columbia. Only on the night of February 14, with Union forces just a few days away, did the Rebels begin evacuating the 1,200 captive officers. "We were hustled out of our quarters and marched to the depot of the S. C. railroad and put on hog cars in hot haste," Perin recalled. The rail line that connected Columbia with Florence and Wilmington was already in peril. The only direction the officers could be taken was north to Charlotte, North Carolina. The last of them, including Tiffany, left on February 15, with bluecoats just outside of town. The bacon the prisoners received at Charlotte was the first meat some had eaten in four months. Many escaped from Charlotte, including two from the Seventy-Second Ohio who were soon caught and sent to Richmond. Their comrades in the Seventy-Second, "being nearly barefoot concluded to take our chances on 'exchange' which we began to hear talked about now every day." It proved a wise decision.[19]

Sherman's advance also threatened Florence prison, seventy-five miles northeast of Columbia. After the paroles in December, about eight thousand prisoners occupied the stockade, which although less crowded was certainly no more habitable. The blustery winds, cold rain, and occasional freezing nights were even harder to stomach because of inadequate shelter, which for most inmates was only a hole covered with branches. Wood remained scarce for heating as well as cooking the raw food. The months of scanty rations of cornmeal, beans, and a little salt, only rarely supplemented with rice and molasses, wore down even healthier, relatively prosperous prisoners, like Sergeant Hoster of the 148th New York, who could afford occasionally to buy some meat and sweet potatoes. The effect of that unhealthy, monotonous diet on the weak like those in the Ninth Minnesota was devastating, especially for the many already suffering from scurvy.[20]

In Florence during that time were about twenty-five prisoners from the Ninth Minnesota. Nine or so, including Elisha Geer (Orlando's brother), George Saville, and Bill Williams of Company F, had arrived in late September or early October. Geer and one other from Company F died in December. The others had reached there in various ways in late November from Millen. First Sergeant Bonham of Company A testified in 1867, shortly before his death from the effects of his imprisonment, about conditions at the new camp:

> We received no meat at all for two months. Our corn meal was issued raw, and we were often for days without wood to cook it, while the stockade was surrounded by timber. If a man got so sick that he could not get up he was nearly sure to die. I have seen three men lie down under a piece of blanket to sleep and all found dead in the morning, starved and frozen to death. . . . I was at one time without a shirt, but made one out of a meal sack stolen from the rebels at the

risk of being whipped with a negro whip or confined in the stocks. I cut a hole for my head and made sleeves out of the [lining] of a blouse. Many envied me my shirt.

Years later George Pomeroy, one of the "golden" choir voices at Andersonville, described the travails of his friend Edward Todd, who was

getting quite badly reduced in vitality and the exposure he endured those winter months told on him badly. He was getting more reduced in strength as time passed on until about the middle of Jan he gave out entirely he had no appetite and could not eat the rations they gave him. He happened to have a little money, so I got a little piece of beef and a few other things, and made him some beef soup and nursed him the best I could. For a while he could not do anything, but he did not seem to rally very fast but after he got so he could get round a little and by pluck and good courage he pulled through.[21]

Two particularly noteworthy incidents at Florence involved men of Company F. In late 1864 Pvt. Alpheus Merritt, a forty-two-year-old farmer from Olmsted County, succeeded in escaping "by climbing over the stockade." He lit out to the north, was recaptured, and, like Jacob Dieter, was consigned to dismal Salisbury prison, completely among strangers. Merritt entered the prison hospital on December 27 suffering from intermittent fever and died on January 18. His wife, Mary Jane, had passed away two weeks earlier in Minnesota, leaving their orphaned children in the care of her parents. The second incident took place on January 15 when Sgt. Frank Heller became the only prisoner from the Ninth Minnesota known to have been killed by a prison guard. Just why the shooting occurred is not entirely clear. The word around camp was that the thirty-two-year-old farmer from Rochester was shot "merely for bidding a guard 'Good morning.'" The more likely explanation is that he had inadvertently brushed the deadline while leaning over to hang up his blanket, and the sentry gave him no mercy. Heller's death at the hands of a Rebel guard was such an unusual occurrence that it was widely remarked not only among Minnesotans but other prisoners as well.[22]

Sherman's rapid advance through South Carolina left Winder scrambling for a safe place to stash the Florence prisoners. He would have preferred to send them back to Andersonville but had no easy way to slip them past the Yankees. Instead, they, too, must go to North Carolina. On February 6 Winder died of a heart attack while visiting the Florence stockade. On February 11 the Confederate government proposed an immediate general exchange, and Grant, with the end of the war looming, agreed. Wilmington would be the transfer point in North Carolina. In anticipation of an exchange, the Rebels began shipping prisoners out of Florence on February 15 without telling them the reason or the destination. Within three days over seven thousand reached Wilmington, 107 miles to the east. Had Bill Williams known of the pending exchange, he might not have risked jumping from the train on February 16 when about twenty-five miles outside of Florence. He made his way east to the coast and attained Union lines six days later at old Fort Johnston, thirty miles south of Wilmington. At that time he weighed 103 pounds, a drastic contrast to his solid 226 pounds at enlistment. Another seven hundred Florence prisoners deemed too sick to be moved were left behind. The only one known from the Ninth Minnesota was Pvt. William Stanley Reese, a twenty-seven-year-old musician from Company H. Privates John Arndt and Goveneur K. Ives, his close comrades, reported that when they last saw Reese, he was very sick and not expected to live. They were able to bring along another friend, Pvt. Henry Etzell, whom Arndt helped carry out in a blanket. In 1866 Ives married Reese's widow.[23]

Like Corporal Kerlinger, First Sergeant Bonham condemned Florence as "the worst place I was in." Oddly enough the percentage of deaths there for the Ninth Minnesota, at least nine out of roughly forty-nine, or 18 percent, was actually less than at either Andersonville or Millen.[24]

At Wilmington the former Florence prisoners were confined in fields and exposed to the elements, but at least their rations included some bacon and beef as well as cornmeal. The Confederates had planned to conduct the exchange at Wilmington immediately but ran into a snag because Union forces under the much-traveled Gen. John Schofield were in the process of capturing the city. Having received no orders relating to an exchange (though Grant had sent them), Schofield refused to accept the prisoners in the midst of a battle until he could clear it with Washington. That left the local Confederate commander little choice. On February 20 he shifted the Florence prisoners by rail eighty-four miles north to Goldsboro, where no provision at all had been made for them.[25]

Goldsboro proved to be the low point. The hapless prisoners were simply dumped in a pine forest without any shelter. Worse, they were given no food for three days. In the meantime, many of the officers from Columbia, whom the Rebels had sent around to the east in a loop through Greensboro and Raleigh, also ended up at Goldsboro in close proximity to some of the men from Florence. The terrible suffering of the enlisted prisoners on that "bitter, cold, damp" February night profoundly shocked those officers. Clearly visible on the flat cars that brought the enlisted men were the bodies of several who had died that night. Moreover, it seemed not one of the survivors huddled in the nearby field "had a whole garment on, while nearly all were destitute of shirts or coats. A ragged or patched pair of pants, and a piece of an old blanket, constituted the wardrobe of the majority" of the enlisted prisoners. Unshaven and unshorn, their heads were so "blackened by the pitch-pine smoke" from fires that one officer likened them to blacks. "Yet all of this was nothing compared to their diseased and starved condition." The "sunken eye, the gaping mouth, the filthy skin, the clothes and head alive with vermin, the repelling bony contour" reflected "starvation, cruelty, and exposure." The officers could see that "many of them were unable to walk, or stand even, and would fall upon their knees as soon as they touched the ground." Some of the officers "gathered everything we had with us that was eatable or wearable" and moved toward the enlisted men, but the guards would not allow the two groups to mix. "Doubling clothes and rations into one bundle," one group of officers "pitched them over the guards' heads, and oh! Such a sight! Never were dogs more ravenous for a bone than were those poor boys for something to eat and wear." Some highly emotional reunions took place in those desolate surroundings. "Here we met some of the 72nd men that we had not seen or heard from since our capture in June 1864," wrote Perin. "The meetings and greetings may be imagined but not described." It is not known if Ford or any of the other officers also spotted old comrades, but likely some did. When those enlisted prisoners were marched away, three were left dead on the field. It was a stark reminder of the better treatment of officer prisoners. Their death rate at Columbia was less than 1 percent.[26]

Beginning on February 23, the enlisted men finally received good rations, including bacon. For the rest of their stay at Goldsboro, they were comparatively well fed but still completely exposed to the elements without proper clothing. The actual exchange began on Sunday, February 26, at North East Ferry on the Northeast Cape River, nine miles north of Wilmington. It lasted until March 4. Among the nearly 7,700 prisoners from the Florence and Salisbury prisons and 992 officers from Columbia were 20 enlisted men and all 6 officers from the Ninth Minnesota. The Union troops welcomed them with music and plenty of food, but the pitiful condition of so many of the enlisted parolees was staggering. One onlooker felt "mingled surprise, pity, disgust, and indignation." According to one doctor, "many of the men were in a state of mind resembling idiocy, unable to tell their names. . . . Some of them moved about on their hands and knees . . . looking like hungry dogs. . . . Some hitched along on their hands and buttocks. . . . Others giggled and smirked and hobbled like starved idiots." A huge percentage of enlisted prisoners had to be hospitalized, and as many as several hundred died there, many remaining unidentified. The others were taken by ship to Annapolis as in the earlier exchanges at Savannah and Charleston. By that time each state had its own barracks or portion of a barracks at Camp Parole and an agent to facilitate the process. Four of the twenty newly freed enlisted prisoners from the Ninth Minnesota died either in Wilmington, at Annapolis, or in nearby facilities, while all six officers reached home safely.[27]

Sources offer intimate glimpses of the fortunes of two young Florence parolees who exemplify the terrible ordeal all the Ninth Minnesota prisoners and their families endured.

Private William Henry Carlton of Company D was born in New York in 1842. At the time he enlisted in August 1862, he was living with his parents on a farm in remote Martin County in southwestern Minnesota. Captured on June 10 at Brice's Crossroads, he entered Andersonville on the nineteenth with the main body of prisoners. On October 1 he was transferred to Savannah, then to Millen and Blackshear, and ended up on November 29 in Florence. Carlton was paroled on March 4, 1865, and arrived in Annapolis ten days later, where he was found to be severely debilitated from diarrhea.[28]

In the spring of 1865, "Mary," one of Carlton's female relatives, wrote a moving account of his return for a local newspaper. The family had learned of his capture in the June 30, 1864, issue of the *St. Paul Press* that listed all of the casualties of the Ninth Minnesota. "Days grew into weeks and weeks

"Coming into Union Lines"

into months, and still no tidings of the lost Willie. The public journals were full of accounts of our brave boys' sufferings in those terrible prisons, where starvation, disease, and death reigned." During the winter of 1864–65 an exchanged prisoner from the Ninth Minnesota told the family that he had last seen Carlton at Andersonville. "Then hope beat high in each heart, but as weeks passed and prisoners were exchanged from one prison to another, [the family] began to think, 'He is dead.' But to the careworn mother, they spoke only words of hope, for her anxiety had almost deprived her of reason."

It was at the supper hour during one of the first really warm spring days, the article reported, that one of the daughters noticed the stagecoach was stopping on the road alongside the farm.

> Soon a young man wearing the familiar blue uniform was carefully lifted out by two of his fellow travelers. . . . It was their own dear Willie! . . . With a heart nearly bursting with joy, the mother's arms were thrown 'round the neck of her long lost son, while the sisters hung around him with tears, laughter and caresses. But, oh how changed was our Willie!
>
> Sickness and starvation had done their fearful work, and pale and emaciated, he looked a mere wreck of the robust youth who left us so hopefully. When we look upon him, our hearts ache with pity for him, and for the poor fellows he has left behind in the land of hard hearts and hard fare. But we ask our Father to spare him to us, and that soon this cruel war will be over.

William Carlton returned to the regiment to be mustered out in August 1865. He died on April 2, 1866, having never recovered from the long-term effects of his imprisonment.[29]

Born in 1844 in La Porte, Indiana, Henry Niles came to Minnesota in 1856 with his older brother Sanford, later a famous Rochester educator. He enlisted in August 1862 and was a corporal in Company F. Nabbed on June 12 near Ripley, he reached Andersonville via Mobile on June 21. Sent in September to Savannah, he escaped in mid-October while en route to Millen and hid in the woods for several weeks before being recaptured and remanded to his original destination. Like Carlton, Niles was one of the former Millen prisoners who were fooled at Blackshear into thinking they would be paroled at Savannah, but instead were sent to Florence.[30]

At North East Ferry, as the lines of freed prisoners threaded their way through the Union camps, the waiting soldiers eagerly sought old comrades among them. One was Col. Ozora Stearns, the former lieutenant of Company F who last saw the "Tigers" in April 1864 in Missouri when he left to take command of the Thirty-Ninth U.S. Colored Infantry. He led his regiment valiantly on July 30 at the disastrous Battle of the Crater outside Petersburg, Virginia. At his recommendation, his color bearer, Sgt. Dorsey Decatur, became one of the first African American soldiers to receive the Medal of Honor. More recently the Thirty-Ninth had come to North Carolina to fight at Fort Fisher and Wilmington. On March 1 Stearns was shocked to recognize Niles, his former corporal, being carried past on a stretcher. He had known Niles in Minnesota before the war and came to value him as a "temperate, sturdy and faithful soldier." Stearns later testified that Niles "came into our lines nearly dead." Suffering from chronic diarrhea, he was "much emaciated and debilitated [weighing ninety-six pounds] and very weak being just able to walk." Once a "bright intelligent young man," his "intellect and senses seemed very much impaired and he seemed dull restless and stupid." Stearns brought Niles to regimental headquarters and "had him cleaned up and nursed up the best I could." After three days Stearns "could not discern any apparent improvement. I then gave him a little money & sent him to Wilmington and saw no more of him."[31]

Niles landed in Annapolis on the tenth. Treated at the College Green Barracks, he (like Carlton) was sent to Benton Barracks in due course. In April he received a furlough to La Porte, where his mother, Roxana, and sister, Esther, cared for him on the farm of A. F. Talmadge, Esther's husband. A local physician described Niles as still "very emaciated" and covered with scurvy sores. After incurring several broken ribs during the retreat from Brice's Crossroads, Niles had been repeatedly injured on the right side of his chest "from being dragged and thrown into cars." Back at home he was still "unable to feed himself alone" and had to be "waited upon from April to August on account of diarrhea same as you would a babe." Niles regained his mental acuity and physical strength "very slowly." He returned to Minnesota in mid-August 1865 for his discharge, but he proved incapable of manual labor until the spring of 1866. That year he married Elizabeth Willard, and they had a daughter and a son. "Very ambitious naturally," Niles tried several times to make a go at farming, and despite the inevitable "ups and downs," he was always "conscientious" and "energetic," with a "great deal of willpower." Completely exhausted, Henry Niles died on June 14, 1876, in Canton, Dakota Territory, just across the state line from Minnesota. He finally succumbed to the abdominal diseases picked up during his captivity.[32]

The sense during the exchange in March 1865 at North East Ferry was that the long war was rapidly nearing its conclusion. Yet for the Ninth Minnesota liberators there were more battles to be fought and more prisoners to be freed before they all returned to "God's country."

CHAPTER SEVENTEEN

Andersonville (III) and Cahaba

A Sorrowful Christmas

By early December 1864, almost four thousand wretched former Millen prisoners—those not exchanged at Savannah or removed to Florence—had fetched up in remote Blackshear in southeastern Georgia. About twenty were from the Ninth Minnesota, including liberators Frahm, Gordon, and Rodier. Isolated from Savannah by Sherman's march, the prisoners would have to stay at Blackshear until Winder made other arrangements. The captives, camped in the tall timber outside of town, for once enjoyed plenty of firewood and tree branches for improvising shelters. The food got better as well, with a little fresh beef and sweet potatoes added to the inevitable corn bread. "Our rations were fair after the first three or four days," wrote Ohioan Jacob Hutchinson. "I seemed to improve a little and a part of the time was able to get around on my feet." Although Aslakson's chronic diarrhea, which he first experienced at Millen (and which plagued him for the rest of his life), worsened at Blackshear, he did get some anti-scorbutic value for inflamed gums and loose teeth by chewing Southern pine needles. Any improvement was a blessing, for he and his companions would soon need all their strength.[1]

On December 5 as Sherman closed in on Savannah, the authorities began shuttling the Blackshear prisoners by train 114 miles southwest to Thomasville, terminus of the Atlantic & Gulf Railroad, not far from the Florida line. A mile northwest of town, slaves had hastily excavated a deep ditch around a five-acre site where big fires blazed all night to mark the perimeter. By December 13 all prisoners capable of being moved from Blackshear were concentrated there. Unusually cold weather gripped Thomasville despite its proximity to the Gulf of Mexico. At night a substantial number of prisoners froze to death. Aslakson was surprised not to be one of them. "My clothes were torn and literally worn out, and my shoes were so worn that I was about barefoot." The plentiful "needle-like thorns" proved useful for mending garments, such as they were. On December 17 Winder ordered the prisoners at Thomasville moved to Andersonville, which was what they most feared. No direct rail link existed. The already frail prisoners would have to trod sixty miles north through rough country to Albany, endpoint of the Southwest Railroad, from where they could ride the remaining forty-seven miles to Andersonville.[2]

On December 19 nearly 3,600 starving, poorly clad prisoners, in groups of 500, started trudging toward Albany. Perhaps as many as 300 more had died either at Thomasville or on the trains that brought them. Never identified, they were buried in a mass grave in the Old City Cemetery. It is quite possible a few of the unknown dead were from the Ninth Minnesota. The fate of several prisoners who were thought to have been at Millen, such as Pliny Conkey and young Dudley Perry of Company C, remains unknown. "Now commenced the hardest march I ever made," wrote Hutchinson. "I was able to walk about a little, but was not fit for a long march." Uriah Karmany, the hospital orderly of the Second Minnesota, concurred. "The suffering on this march was intense. Many were very feeble and without food or shoes. Officers would force them on with bayonets until they staggered by the way side unable to rise, when they would be left to starve." Hutchinson soon dropped out, but his Rebel guard, "an old soldier," turned out to be "a whole-souled man" who kindly and patiently kept him going, even giving him a ride on his horse. Hutchinson was truly fortunate. In a few days he felt "better than I had for weeks." Simon Peter Obermier observed in his diary that "those that couldn't keep up [were] killed on the spot" and that "many drowned crossing creeks and rivers." Some exhausted stragglers were brought in by wagons, as Karmany noted, like "so much inanimate baggage."[3]

The gruesome trek lasted between four and five days, part of the time without rations. The last two days, moreover, were especially cold during which bare feet—many of the prisoners were shoeless—bled profusely. Aslakson well understood by that time how "hunger drives one to the unbelievable." During halts he "found strength enough to gather up some corn among the litter where the horses and mules had been fed, rinsed it in water and ate it with a relish I have seldom experienced." Corporal McLean of the 117th New York marveled that some famished prisoners became so absorbed in picking up those precious leftover (or worse) kernels of corn that guards had to resort to "an actual piercing with the bayonet to induce them to leave the spot."[4]

Following a brief stay quartered around the depot at Albany, the first group reached Andersonville on December 23. At that time the vast stockade held merely 210 inmates. One was Corporal Medkirk of the Seventy-Second Ohio. At the end of November, he had simply bolted in desperation out of the hospital but barely got beyond the gate. Hustled over to Wirz's headquarters, now near the railroad depot, he "sat around there until evening, with visions of the stocks before my eyes, when I was taken to Castle Reed," a nearby guardhouse in a small stockade. "There I found about twenty of my comrades who had escaped from the hospital and whom we supposed had reached our lines, but the rebels had been quietly gathering them in and putting them in that place." When the first prisoners from Albany arrived, Medkirk and his companions were put in the stockade with them. The appearance of the newcomers, who may have included old comrades, deeply shocked him. "They were if anything a more frightful sight to me than the prisoners were when I first entered the stockade. They had been in the pine woods for some time and had had all the fire they wanted and the smoke from the burning pine, together with the dirt had made them as black as soot."[5]

During the next three days, nearly all the rest of the prisoners from Albany rolled into Andersonville. "Oh what a sick looking lot of boys we are," Obermier wrote on Christmas Eve, "tetotally [sic] disgusted on arrival." Just as in the old days, Captain Wirz, mounted on his old white mare, conscientiously greeted each new contingent. "You damned Yanks, what brings you back?" he inquired of McLean's group on Christmas Day. Aslakson did not get in until late that day and found "as usual, [Wirz was] angry and ill-tempered." About one hundred prisoners in his contingent petitioned Wirz to be allowed to camp together, "but the answer was a string of foul and insulting oaths and an absolute and decisive 'No!'" Wirz marched Aslakson and his companions to the South Gate, where "again we were to enter the portal through which so many thousands had been carried out dead." When Aslakson went inside, "it was now late in the evening. It had rained unceasingly for three days, and we were nearly naked and had not had a bite to eat since the evening before." His group arrived too late to be issued any rations at all, although some of the others ate a holiday dinner of a "pint of cooked rice and a small slice of cornbread." For certain, it was a "sorrowful Christmas."[6]

Wirz reorganized old hands and returnees alike into new detachments of one hundred men, grouped, as before, in divisions five hundred strong. Eventually, in January after more prisoners arrived from Meridian, there were ten divisions in all. The returnees, particularly those who had left Andersonville prior to October 9, noticed definite changes. In December Wirz had the ground inside the stockade plowed over, not only destroying the old shebangs but masking holes and old wells, which could be dangerous. All the loose wood inside the stockade was gone. "We were all put on the south side of the creek," recalled Hutchinson, "and had plenty of room to run about in." Another surprise was that after the heavy autumn rains and the subsequent lack of pollution the "atmosphere was sweet." Once in their assigned bivouacs, the inmates hurriedly dug into the bare ground as best they could in the chilly rain. Near where the gallows that hanged the six Raiders once stood, Aslakson and Sergeant Mattson erected a ragged tent that was "very small and so low that we had to crawl into it. Morning came at last and we crawled out of our tent in the hope the corn mush wagon would soon make its rounds." Medkirk and four others enlarged a "hole in the sand and by some means we got rags enough to cover the top and we would crawl in there and freeze the night away the best we could. It seemed as though I always froze out first in the morning and would crawl out as soon as the sun was up so as to get warm." At least two prisoners desperate for shelter died on the cold Christmas night when their hole caved in and suffocated them.[7]

The biggest physical alteration was the new site of the hospital compound, which Chief Surgeon Stevenson had finally succeeded in moving west out of the swamp to the sloping ground just beyond the South Wall. His original intention had been to erect one shed for each ward of fifty for a total of forty structures, but only twenty-two were ever built. By the end of 1864, some patients were still in tents. As of December 23, there were 1,047 patients and paroled prisoners quartered in the hospital. They included First Sergeant Avery, who ran the burial detail, and his assistant George Kenney; both were about to get busy again. The hospital soon swelled with new patients who had barely survived the trip from Thomasville. Sick call took place in the old barrack sheds situated along the inside of the North Wall. Any prisoner not admitted to the hospital had to return immediately south of the creek. On January 4, 1865, Pvt. W. K. Latimer of Company D and Sgt. Moses Chamberlin of Company K went through sick call and entered the hospital. They became the last two patients from the Ninth Minnesota. Latimer, another of Lorin Cray's ill-fated friends, died on January 23 from acute diarrhea. Chamberlin, though, like Mattson before him, would survive his stay in the fearsome Andersonville hospital.[8]

Life at Andersonville went on much as before, but in place of stifling heat, the hungry men shivered. "We had more room than in the summer," recalled Medkirk, "but no more or better food and no clothing other than the rags we had been wearing. My shirt and pants by this time were mere rags. By the death of a comrade I got an old coat, but I was still in my bare feet and remained so all winter." Hutchinson remarked of the rampant illness and

"many deaths" that "occurred during the winter. The men had so little shelter, food and clothing that they soon became chilled on a bleak, frosty night,
and such chills were generally followed by death. Scurvy was on the increase,
no vegetables or vinegar being allowed." Aslakson, too, noted, "Our clothes
were nearly all worn out, and we had to go around and seek out the dead and
rob them of the clothes they had in order to keep from freezing to death
ourselves."[9]

One of the three liberators who returned to Andersonville was Pierre
"Peter" Rodier of Company K, who hailed from Wabasha. A "typical French-
Canadian," albeit at five feet nine inches somewhat taller than most, he turned
thirty in January 1865 while in Andersonville. Rodier had come to Wabasha
in 1856 as a carpenter "when the country was just opening up" and the lumber industry beginning to boom. He went into captivity on June 11 on the
Salem road along with two Wabasha friends, Cpl. Octavo "Bob" Barker, a
thirty-seven-year-old river pilot from Maine, and Pvt. Alois Spitzmesser, a
thirty-six-year-old German immigrant who had served in a Missouri artillery unit in 1861. The three went through the various prisons together. By
the time Rodier entered Andersonville the second time, he was in very poor
shape. Years later Spitzmesser recalled that Rodier suffered terribly from
rheumatism, which was very likely a symptom of severe scurvy. His badly
swollen legs made it "very difficult for him to stand or walk; part of the time
he was obliged to crawl about on his hands and knees." Barker averred that
"it was only by great energy courage and indomitable patience & persistence
that [Rodier] lived to be exchanged." Rodier was very fortunate that two
more comrades from Company K came to his aid. Sergeant George L. Wheelock was a thirty-two-year-old native of Barnard, Vermont. Corporal Patrick
Murray had left Tipperary, Ireland, in 1847 at age nine with his mother during the Potato Famine, only to be orphaned the next year in New York. Both
were farmers from Saratoga in Winona County. They had occasionally seen
Rodier in Andersonville during the summer of 1864 but never encountered
him at Millen. In December back at Andersonville, they found him "a mere
living skeleton," just 80 pounds instead of his former robust 175 pounds.
"We took much interest in him the poor fellow," Wheelock later testified,
"& by nursing & furnishing him with a few comforts in the line of meal &
tobacco a blanket &ec we succeeded in bringing him out of that cursed place
just about alive when we were exchanged."[10]

In January conditions did improve at Andersonville, although the weather
remained damp and chilly. Rations got a little better, though First Sergeant
Turrill of the Seventy-Second Ohio fumed when he saw a prisoner politely
ask Wirz for more corn bread, only to have a pistol thrust in his face and be

told, "God damn you, I will give you bullets for bread." Yet Wirz finally felt confident in January to allow a few men from each detachment to go out every day under heavy guard into the nearby woods to gather firewood. "From this time on," wrote Aslakson, "we suffered less from the cold." With Sherman rampaging through South Carolina and Lee immobilized in his entrenchments around Richmond and Petersburg, the end of the war seemed imminent even to some Rebels at Andersonville. Medkirk recalled a particularly revealing conversation with a guard:

> One bitter cold morning in January, 1865, when snow and ice were on the ground a rebel sergeant, known as crooked neck Smith, called for my mess to report to the gate for wood. I ran down to the south gate, reported and went out for wood. I soon lost all feeling in my feet and they puffed up to what seemed to be twice their natural size, and if it had not been for the kindness of the old man who was my guard I would not have been able to get any wood, but he waited until I hunted around and got a stick that I could carry. The old man watched his chance and then said to me that he hoped to God that Mr. Grant would soon get hold of Mr. Lee and whip the hell out of him as he was tired of the war. I told him that I fully concurred with him in his wish, and that he could rest assured that when Gen. Grant got his hands on Gen. Lee that Gen. Lee would get whipped like hell.

The prisoners rejoiced to learn from Macon newspapers regularly brought into camp that advancing Union armies were literally tearing the Confederacy asunder.[11]

On one of Aslakson's sessions outside the walls of Andersonville foraging for wood, he saw for the first time the cemetery where so many of his friends and comrades were buried. There were three large, rectangular zones, each filled with row upon depressing row of closely set wooden headboards—so many thousands of markers that one could scarcely take in the true extent of the vast number of dead interred there. It is not known whether by the time of Aslakson's visit the last member of the Ninth Minnesota to perish in Andersonville already rested in grave 12,656. Private Henry Fuchs of Company D, a twenty-eight-year-old German immigrant from Oshawa in Nicollet County, died in quarters on February 14 from chronic diarrhea.[12]

In late January Orderly Sgt. T. J. Sheppard of the Ninety-Seventh Ohio and Pvt. Joseph Quesnel of the Seventh New York Heavy Artillery moved in with Aslakson and Mattson in their shebang near the South Gate. Soon after his return to Andersonville, Reverend Sheppard had ailed with a severe cold and suffered greatly despite Quesnel's devoted care. Now with better shelter and "warmer suns," he recovered his "usual prison health." In February the religious meetings resumed and continued regularly thereafter. The early hour set for the "Sunday School," Sheppard quipped, "was not inconvenient in that place, as our couches possessed no attractions especially preventive of early rising." On March 13 his flock convened a special meeting where 155 signed a testimonial addressed to the governor of Ohio to honor "the faithful manner in which Brother Sheppard has voluntarily performed the duties of chaplain while among us." He was a "faithful and consistent Christian soldier" who was "eminently successful as a preacher of the gospel." The document became one of Sheppard's most treasured possessions.[13]

There were other signs of progress in Andersonville. In late February began construction of several barracks along the South Wall to match those built the previous September on the North Wall. Each structure was intended to house one division of five hundred men, although during bad rainstorms a thousand might crowd inside. Only five buildings were actually erected. Like the others they were only open sheds, but they did serve to keep the cold rain off. In March the Rebel surgeons began issuing a sort of "corn beer" from "corn fermented with water and molasses." Each prisoner was to receive one cupful daily as a possible medicine for scurvy. To Hutchinson the doses were "nothing but a slightly sour drink," but the prisoners, nonetheless, "eagerly" drank them. In March the weather at Andersonville grew warmer. That "balmy message of spring," wrote Aslakson, "renewed our hope of life and possibly a speedy liberation" for the 17 surviving prisoners from the Ninth Minnesota and their roughly 5,470 companions.[14]

COLONEL HILL'S TOBACCO WAREHOUSE

In the summer of 1864, at least 207 captives from the Ninth Minnesota entered Andersonville, and those who survived to September and beyond endured a dizzying series of moves throughout Georgia and the Carolinas. In stark contrast, all but 3 of the 18 prisoners consigned that summer to Cahaba prison in central Alabama stayed to the bitter end. There were other huge differences. By mid-March 1865 more than 125 of the 207 men who started out in Andersonville prison had died—a mortality rate of slightly more than 60 percent. Of the 18 imprisoned at Cahaba during approximately the same interval, just 1 died. If Andersonville and its sister camps represented hell on earth, grossly overcrowded Cahaba, though far from pleasant or even tolerable under any ordinary circumstances, treated its enlisted prisoners, writes historian William O. Bryant, "better" than "any other prison inside of the Confederate lines."[15]

Located ten miles south of Selma, at the confluence of the Alabama and Cahaba Rivers, Cahaba (also known as Cahawba) had in 1819 become the Alabama state capital. Seven years later after a catastrophic flood, the site was abandoned. By 1860 it seemed that Cahaba's fortunes were finally reviving as a vital transshipment point for cotton. A new railroad linked the town with Selma, and construction began on a large warehouse. Once the war started, the state lifted the rails from the track bed to use elsewhere, and the big cotton shed was never finished. Thus Cahaba reverted to its former status of "lifeless village." In 1863 a prison compound known unofficially as "Castle Morgan" was built there, but in May 1864 the Rebels closed the camp and forwarded its over 900 prisoners to Andersonville. In the early summer, though, a large new influx of captives caused Cahaba prison to be reopened. Indeed, as Bryant remarks, Bedford Forrest seemed personally "determined to keep Castle Morgan filled" with bluecoats he kept grabbing in Tennessee, Alabama, and Mississippi. In late June 1864, as previously noted, the first batch of 150 new prisoners arrived from Guntown. Five were from the Ninth Minnesota, including the youngest liberator, Allen Hilton. On August 11 when the party of nearly 100 wounded (13 from the Ninth Minnesota) and 7 orderlies reached Cahaba from Mobile, the prison held 400 men.[16]

The heart of Castle Morgan was "Colonel" Samuel Hill's cotton warehouse set between the town and the Alabama River. The stout red-brick building measured 193 feet by 116 feet. Its roof was never completed, leaving a large open space in the center, and the floor was dirt. Water from an artesian well was "good, and there was plenty of it." The overflow from a small reservoir serviced a few water closets in one corner of the building. Tiers of bunks accommodated five hundred men (the number for which the facility was originally intended), but no bedding was provided. "The prisoners received after the bunks were filled," wrote one inmate, "respected the rights of those who had possession and tried to content themselves with Alabama soil for a bed and sky for a covering." A plank stockade twelve feet high with a walkway along the top enclosed the warehouse and an adjacent yard. The customary deadline stood six feet inside of the walls, and a few cannons were strategically placed "to mow down the prisoners if a break was made for liberty." A few blocks away, the Bell Tavern, a former hotel, became a modest-sized hospital for both guards and prisoners. The camp administrators were "in the main, courteous."[17]

The prisoners were organized into divisions of one hundred men, subdivided into messes of ten. They would start the day by queuing up at "the barrels into which the artesian well water flowed, where the men waited their turn to wash up. The soap was not of the best quantity, so we did not bother much with it." After the first roll call, rations were issued, and the men were allowed into the yard to cook their food. Each mess possessed its own "skillet or Dutch oven," ten inches in diameter and three inches deep. There was a small daily allowance of green wood for fires. According to Thomas A. Edgerton of Company E, a twenty-five-year-old private from Mankato who had been badly wounded at Brice's Crossroads, "Our fare most of the time consisted of corn meal, not always of good quality, and water. Sometimes we had a little meat, bacon generally. Once for a little while we had some fresh beef." Prisoners with money could buy yams, watermelons and peaches, and other fruit from the guards. Edgerton described the "daily occupation" as picking "the lice from our clothes." The second roll call took place in the late afternoon. At night all prisoners were confined inside the warehouse behind another deadline patrolled by an interior guard force.[18]

Thus, in August the eighteen Minnesotans settled in for the long term at Cahaba. Dirty, damp, and vermin-ridden, Castle Morgan was far from jolly, though as yet it was not too crowded. All the Minnesotans appear to have had bunks. The rations were not particularly skimpy or especially poor in quality. A kind neighbor woman lent the prisoners plenty of books and magazines to help while away the time. The men were still fairly healthy, with "homesickness" the "worst malady." Not long after arriving at Cahaba, Melville Robertson, the medical orderly from the Ninety-Third Indiana, philosophically recorded in his diary, "I eat my corn-bread, smoke my pipe and look forward to something better." In September Pvt. Henry Howard of Company F described his condition in a letter home. "I have had plenty of hard corn and meat to eat. I am nearly naked; I have one poor shirt, a ragged pair of pants, and an old cap and one old quilt to lay on. My wound has not healed yet."[19]

By September 8, with 750 prisoners at Cahaba, the crowding began to affect inmate health. The "ague [was] becoming quite common," Robertson recorded, as patients filled the small hospital at Bell Tavern. On October 4 he noted that "last night or rather this morning at half past 1 o'clock Hugh Roberts of the 9th Minn died in the bunk I sleep in." A thirty-four-year-old Company E private from Mankato, Hugh R. Roberts had been badly wounded in the knee and was a former Mobile patient. Apparently because he perished inside the warehouse, he was not included in the hospital death register and was thus buried as unknown. Only Robertson's diary marked the time and place of his demise. Just a week later, the compound ballooned to 1,745 prisoners—"very much crowded—rapidly becoming very unhealthy," according to Robertson. Soon over 2,300 souls were packed inside. Even the Rebels understood that was the maximum capacity. "We were so thick," Edgerton recalled, "we could hardly move." To give an idea of how little room the prisoners had inside the warehouse, Andersonville at its densest (on June 30, the day before the addition to the stockade opened) allowed roughly thirty square feet per prisoner, whereas in Cahaba the corresponding figure was six and one-half square feet.[20]

During October, the Cahaba stockade was enlarged, relieving the overcrowding during the day, though at night the prisoners were still jammed back into the warehouse. Moreover, at the end of October, over six hundred prisoners were shipped out of Cahaba to Millen. Syvert Ellefson of Company F, a Norwegian immigrant from Rochester also wounded at Brice's Crossroads, was included. He died somewhere on the way to Georgia, date and place of burial not known. Of the eighteen Ninth Minnesota prisoners in Cahaba, only Roberts and Ellefson died before being exchanged.[21]

A much more fortunate member of the Ninth Minnesota who also left Cahaba early was Henry Seelye of Company A. The twenty-six-year-old native of New Brunswick, Canada, who had relocated to St. Anthony, was another of Dr. Dixon's former patients. In December Seelye passed through Jackson, Mississippi, and into Federal lines. He and twenty others were formally paroled on December 31 at Baton Rouge. In September 1864 General Washburn in Memphis had negotiated with Confederate authorities to secure the parole of 350 prisoners from the Sixteenth Corps held at Cahaba, most of whom, it was said, had been "taken in the Sturgis raid." Predictably, the War Department, at Grant's direction, refused permission. Even so, General Canby arranged for the December exchange in return for Rebels he intended to deliver to Mobile. Seelye proceeded to Benton Barracks near St. Louis and from there on furlough to Minnesota.[22]

Little of note disturbed Cahaba for the rest of the year. Some clothing from the North was distributed in early December. Robertson received "shoes, pants and blouse." Soon afterward he was admitted to the prison hospital, where on Christmas Day to his surprise and delight he savored a turkey dinner, just like home. By mid-January 1865 the number of inmates had again risen to a bone-crushing 2,300. At that time, wrote one prisoner, "many could not find room to lie down at night, and those could not, passed the night in stamping the ground to keep from freezing, and lucky was the man who had a friend that would let him take his place a portion of the time under his blanket. Those who remained up at night would sleep a portion of the daytime, and sunny days it was quite warm. Those who had blankets would 'double up,' and by frequent 'spooning' (turning) manage to get some sleep." Such close quarters spread vermin, but this time certain prisoners took direct action against others "unable or unwilling to take care of themselves." Their clothing was removed and washed, their scalps were shaved, and they themselves were immersed in vats and "thoroughly scrubbed with a brush." Nothing like that had ever been possible in Andersonville.[23]

Around 3 A.M. on January 20, a small group of prisoners assaulted the guards stationed inside the warehouse in the hope of sparking a mass escape. That extremely reckless plan was the brainchild of Capt. Hiram S. Hanchett of the Sixteenth Illinois Cavalry, a prisoner who had recently come to Cahaba masquerading, unwisely, as a civilian. Hanchett and a small cadre of frustrated prisoners hoped to overpower the interior guard by stealth, seize the whole stockade, and make a run for the Union lines at Pensacola. By the desperate expedient of flinging blankets over the heads of the Rebels and muscling away their muskets, ten or twelve prisoners managed, amazingly, to capture and disarm all nine interior guards without hurting them. The Rebel corporal, however, got away, slammed the door shut, and spread the alarm. At the same time, Hanchett shouted for help from the other prisoners to storm the door. "I want a hundred men, men of courage, to fall in immediately!" So few of the other inmates had known of the impending escape that his sudden cry went largely unanswered. The Rebels quickly wheeled a cannon up to the door, flung it open, and threatened to blast the prisoners unless they released the guards unharmed and surrendered unconditionally. Bowing to the inevitable, the conspirators, hoping to remain anonymous, blended back into the general population. The uprising was, in Robertson's word, merely a "fizzle," but to camp administrators it was foul mutiny. They spent several days, during which they issued no rations, fruitlessly trying to identify the ringleaders. "Some of the men died from the hardship," according to Edgerton. "One day we buried seven."[24]

One of the tiny group of conspirators was Pvt. Godfrey Hammerberg of Company H, who had been shot in the face at Brice's Crossroads and miraculously recovered. Many years later he recalled the attempted escape and the immediate aftermath:

> One night when we had mugged the rebel guards (all but one, who gave us away), the Johnnies rolled in a howitzer in front of the gate to blow us up if we did not give up the guns that we had captured from the inside guards. We had to march single file thru Johnny officers, protected by rebel soldiers with fixed bayonets. We had been ordered to disrobe, and our rags held over our heads, we had to turn around before the Surgeons, who examined us to see if anyone had a flesh wound received [from] the rebel guard, who got away, thinking if they could find him they would compel him to tell who the ringleader of the mutiny was. They threatened that unless the ringleader was given up we should

all starve. How hungry we all were, for even our scanty ration was held up for three days and nights.

Finally informers among the prisoners gave away Hanchett, Hammerberg, and six others, who were clapped in irons. Remanded to the county jail, they were stuffed into a dark dungeon six feet square, where all could not even lie down at the same time. After several harrowing weeks, all but Hanchett were released and returned in rough shape to Castle Morgan. Despite Union demands for his release, Hanchett was held as a spy until the end of the war, when he was mysteriously murdered. His body was never found.[25]

Aside from the abortive escape, the other significant event at Cahaba in early 1865 was the flood. On March 1 the site fully lived up to its reputation when the Alabama River rose over the banks and penetrated the stockade yard. By the morning of March 3, water had seeped inside the warehouse and gradually rose several feet. Inmates whose bunks were still dry, including apparently all the Minnesotans, had to remain in them, while those who ordinarily slept on the floor or in the lowest tier of bunks, wrote Robertson, "passed the night on their feet half a leg deep in water." Finally the Rebels allowed the bedraggled men to "pass out to the levee, at which place there was piled large quantities of cord-wood. Each prisoner selected a stick or two, and would propel it into the prison yard, where his messmates would criss-cross the wood, holding it down by their weight until built out of the water, then, laying others on top, they had a dry place to rest in." Because the men could not cook their rations, hardtack "made of ground rice and peas was brought in by skiffs." Two per day were issued to each man, "just enough . . . to sustain life, and no more," but yet, as Edgerton noted, "This was about the best food we had."[26]

During the inundation, the prison became an even more terrible place than before. "At that time human offal & everything else was mixed up together," recalled Edgerton. "That happened for several days. Ordinarily, however, we were able to move most of the offal & stuff out of the prison." The immersion in cold, filthy water and the tainted drinking water tipped the balance for prisoners who had otherwise been relatively healthy. Diarrhea and worse maladies became rampant. Private Edson M. Rice of Company C wrote his family on March 27 that he had been "in good health" until "the river rose 2–5' deep in prison. The [Colonel, commanding] would not take us out of the water, so it made a great many of us sick. I have been very much unwell since." According to historian Bryant, "the plight of the prisoners even touched some of the guards," who petitioned the commander, Lt. Col. Sam Jones, to move them to dry ground. The reply was "No! Not if every damn Yankee drowns." It took ten days for the waters to recede completely from Castle Morgan, and they left a terrible mess in their wake. Despite Jones's intransigence, substantial numbers of prisoners were in fact removed from Cahaba to Selma. For the others, including the fifteen remaining from the Ninth Minnesota, the whiff of possible exchange was in the air, and they expected soon to be set free.[27]

CHAPTER EIGHTEEN

The War Is Won

PREPARING FOR BATTLE

The grave threat that drew Smith's Guerrillas and the Ninth Minnesota back across the Mississippi River in late November 1864 was the battered but still unbowed Confederate Army of Tennessee. Once Sherman roared toward Savannah, Hood, just as aggressive, set the distant Ohio River firmly in his sights. He led his ragtag legions, some thirty-eight thousand strong, across the Tennessee River on November 21 and aimed for Nashville. Major General George Thomas, the "Rock of Chickamauga," needed time to gather an army to stop him. Hood missed the chance to trap two retreating corps under General Schofield (who had not yet gone to North Carolina) but caught them on November 30 at Franklin, twenty miles south of Nashville. Hood foolishly launched a frontal assault that failed despite incredible bravery and ferocity. The horrible losses virtually tore the heart out of his army. Schofield escaped to Thomas's main position at Nashville, which Hood approached and claimed to besiege. After detaching Forrest to take Murfreesboro, Hood massed twenty-two thousand exhausted, poorly equipped, and dispirited men in front of Nashville.

Hood's one remaining chance for victory was to tempt Thomas to make rash attacks into the teeth of the Rebel defenses. Instead, Thomas patiently assembled fifty-four thousand men to counterattack, with another twelve thousand in the Nashville garrison. He knew Hood could never take Nashville and had no real chance to slip past into Kentucky and Ohio. To take full advantage of the rare opportunity to annihilate an entire Rebel army, Thomas prepared Maj. Gen. James H. Wilson's powerful cavalry corps of twelve thousand men to pursue Hood once he was defeated. To mount and properly equip Wilson's horsemen required several days. During that time, ironically, Thomas was in more danger from panicky superiors than from Hood himself. Numerous telegrams demanded that Thomas immediately attack, but he steadfastly refused to move until he was ready.[1]

After reaching Nashville on December 1, the Ninth Minnesota moved into line two miles south of town and dug in comfortably for a siege. Markham and Chaplain Kerr came up from Memphis with 150 convalescents. Among 13 officers and 289 enlisted men present for duty were 16 liberators. In Company C in addition to Sergeant Merchant, who was in command, were Corporal Epler, Bullard, Hartley, McCain, Padden, Slocum, Stewart, Vaughan, and John Watkins. Peterman and Evan Watkins had been invalided out, Arnold was sick in Minnesota, Lagree was in the hospital at Jefferson Barracks in St. Louis, and Williams was sick in Nashville. Lieutenant Capon's Company K included Corporal Ehmke, Heilmann, Jansen, Lüthye, Pike, and Raymond. Fenstermacher was with division headquarters, but Buck was sick in St. Louis, and Mickel was home on sick leave.[2]

On December 6, once Thomas learned the so-called Right Wing of the Sixteenth Army Corps had been disbanded, he gave Smith's force (now three divisions) the bland designation "Detachment of the Army of the Tennessee." No matter their unit's name, the Minnesotans were deeply proud. For the first time, three Minnesota regiments, the Fifth and Ninth in Colonel Hubbard's Second Brigade and the Tenth in Colonel McMillen's First Brigade, were arrayed in one continuous line of battle, while the Seventh Minnesota was nearby in Col. Sylvester G. Hill's Third Brigade. The next day the Eighth Minnesota under Lt. Col. Henry C. Rogers (the original captain of Company C) helped deliver a rare thrashing to Forrest at Murfreesboro.[3]

The weather at Nashville, which had been fairly decent until the night of December 8, turned first to rain, then to sleet and snow, followed by deep cold. By that time Wilson's cavalry was ready to fight, but for nearly a week thick sheets of ice covered the area. Only on December 14 did the sun emerge from the clouds and begin melting the ice and snow. Thomas issued attack orders for the next day. The battle would open to the east with a diversionary attack against the Confederate right, while the main effort, nearly forty thousand men, smashed the west end of the Rebel line. As part of that deployment, Smith's detachment and a portion of Wilson's cavalry were to maneuver far around Hood's left flank. When Smith's three divisions were in position, Brig. Gen. Thomas Wood's Fourth Corps would pin down the Rebel center and left, while together Smith and Wilson smashed the far left flank. Schofield's Twenty-Third Corps would support Smith and Wood.

NASHVILLE: THE FIRST DAY

Fog on the morning of December 15 greatly obscured visibility over the battlefield. After some confusion, McArthur's First Division sortied from the Nashville defenses with the rest of Smith's detachment. Cutting southeast across hilly country, Smith aimed for the flank of Lt. Gen. A. P. Stewart's Rebel corps that was deployed along the Hillsboro Pike. The advance through muddy fields was slow. Eventually pivoting to the east, McArthur deployed his three brigades in echelon with Hubbard's Second Brigade (with the Ninth Minnesota) in the center. Smith's two other divisions went into action off to the north, while a division of Wilson's cavalry drew up to the south on McArthur's right. Capon's Company K, with half the liberators, pressed ahead as part of a strong line of skirmishers, while Merchant's Company C with the rest was in line with the regiment. After 12 P.M. the haze suddenly dispersed to reveal a line of enemy redoubts occupying the hills in front of the Hillsboro Pike, which slanted across Smith's front. Nearest to Hubbard's brigade was Redoubt No. 4, an isolated fort defended by Capt. Charles Lumsden's Alabama Battery (four guns) and one hundred infantry from the Twenty-Ninth Alabama. Sited on a higher elevation about five hundred yards farther south was Redoubt No. 5 (with two rifled cannons from Capt. Edward Tarrant's Alabama Battery) that directly overlooked the Hillsboro Pike. For an hour the opposing batteries dueled, while Union skirmishers and dismounted cavalry pushed back a thin line of Rebel infantry and worked "through a marsh and a clearing covered with stumps and fallen trees" toward No. 4. In the meantime Schofield's corps fanned out on McArthur's right. A Confederate colonel marveled at the size of the Union force now opposing the Rebel left flank. "The whole face of creation seemed to be covered with bluecoats. I counted flags to estimate their strength until I was tired."[4]

The Rebel infantry falling back toward Redoubt No. 4 "passed us in retreat, going on both sides of our battery," wrote one of Lumsden's artillery sergeants, "leaving the bushy hollow in our front and to our right full of Federal sharpshooters." In that band of timber, Company K enjoyed front row seats for the gun duel. Lumsden's brave artillerymen were seriously outmatched. Near 3 P.M., after one of their caissons exploded, the nearest Union skirmishers and dismounted troopers seized the moment. As Capon led his men forward out of the wood, "the fort on the hill to the right [Redoubt No. 5] opened with terrific force," recalled liberator E. W. Pike, and caught the Minnesotans "between two fires." Nonetheless, they did not slacken their pace. McArthur's division charged. McMillen's First Brigade and the dismounted cavalry brigade rapidly converged on Redoubt No. 4, while Hubbard's brigade swung around to the north. "The order was received with a 'Minnesota yell' by the boys," wrote Color Sergeant Macdonald, "and on they rushed, under a terrible fire, down and across a muddy field, over a marsh, and up the hillside through a clearing covered with stumps and fallen trees." As "we drew near the battery and its support, volley after volley was poured in [the Rebel] ranks, which soon gave way, and shortly our colors were wavering over the rebel works." McMillen and the cavalry stormed into the redoubt about the time Hubbard's skirmishers, including Company K, entered its northeast side. Overwhelmed, most of the valiant defenders fled. The cavalry quickly turned all four guns against the retreating Rebels.[5]

McArthur swiftly launched McMillen's brigade against the second fort on top of a steep, higher hill. Hubbard again supported his left flank. Curving south, Capon and the First Platoon of Company K joined the rush toward Redoubt No. 5, while First Sergeant Hays led the Second Platoon against distant Rebel infantry forming out ahead. The redoubt fell swiftly, and two more guns were taken. While McMillen consolidated his men around the fort, Hubbard's brigade halted to catch its breath near the Hillsboro Pike. Capon returned Company K to its place in line, turned over command to Hays, and led out Company G as skirmishers. Sunset was only forty minutes off. Out of sight to the north, Wood's Corps and the rest of Smith's detachment had seized the other three Rebel redoubts and had begun rolling up Hood's main line. To the south, Schofield's corps, after forming up beyond Redoubt No. 5, advanced east across the Hillsboro Pike. Two Rebel divisions desperately formed behind a stone wall to protect several hills that dominated the Granny White Pike, the main retreat route for the whole Confederate left and center.[6]

To assist Schofield's attack, Hubbard's brigade, despite being well out in front of the rest of Smith's corps, charged the Rebels behind the wall. "Soon the enemy was discovered in force, with his line of battle formed along the crest of a hill, in a very strong position of considerable natural advantage," wrote Macdonald. "To reach his lines we were compelled to advance through an open wood and across a field of nearly a mile in length, in the face of a sharp and effective fire of musketry and artillery. But soon the hill was reached, and up it charged the veterans of the Second Brigade, flushed with victory, and with bayonets fixed." Hubbard's men collided with Brig. Gen. Daniel H. Reynolds's all-Arkansas brigade from Maj. Gen. Edward C. Walthall's division. "The battle was short, sharp and deadly," according to Macdonald. "The enemy recoiled under our withering fire and retreated in disorder. In the pursuit his retreat became a rout. Killed and wounded covered the ground and squads of rebels were captured at every step of the advance. Over 400

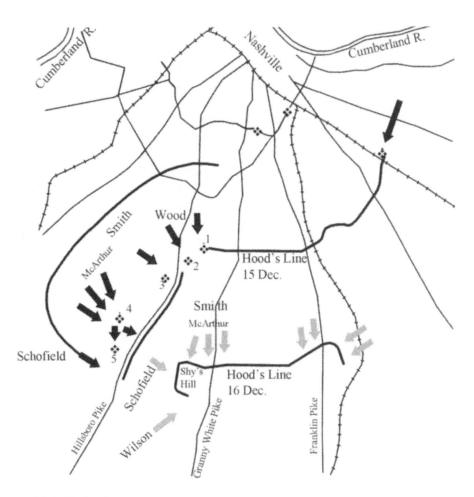

Nashville Battle

prisoners were taken in these movements. We pursued him closely to the Granny White pike, where two more pieces of artillery were captured, the enemy abandoning them in his hasty flight." One Confederate artilleryman noted that once Hubbard flanked the Razorbacks, they "broke," and thereafter "it was one perfect stampede for a mile."[7]

By sundown Hubbard's brigade was far out ahead of the rest of the First Division, indeed the whole army. "The men were supplied with shovels and spades, instructed to intrench, and directed to sleep upon their arms. We were so close to the enemy's lines that the bullets from his pickets whistled about our ears rather uncomfortably." Company G rejoined the Ninth Minnesota, but without Capon, who, it was reported, was last seen sprawled in a bloody heap after taking a bullet in the head. Marsh sent a sorrowful detail from Company K back over the now dark battlefield to find and bury their lieutenant. To their great surprise and delight, Capon was quite alive, suffering only an intense headache. The bullet had struck him a glancing blow above the left eye and had just stunned him. Marsh praised Capon, who "behaved nobly" and "gallantly" in the fight. The only fatal casualty was a soldier of Company G killed in the final charge. In the same charge, a bullet mangled Cpl. Lorin Cray's left shoulder and permanently crippled his arm. Even so, he would be the only one of the eight particular "soldier boys" of Company D to survive the war.[8]

BULLY FOR THE SNOW DIGGERS!

Overnight from December 15 to 16, McArthur faced his division to the south. Hubbard's Second Brigade, on the west edge of the Granny White Pike, held the center, McMillen's First Brigade took the right to the west, and the Third Brigade (now under Colonel Marshall of the Seventh Minnesota) was on the left across the pike. Hood anchored the flanks of his new line, a mile and three-quarters south of the original, on two high hills. The westernmost hill (directly in front of McMillen's brigade) was an "abrupt knob with a front so precipitous that it seemed foolhardy to attempt its capture by direct assault." It became known as Shy's Hill, after a Rebel colonel killed there that day. Schofield's corps, including a division borrowed from Smith, and much of Wilson's cavalry corps already ringed Shy's Hill to the west and southwest. Consequently, Hood shifted most of Maj. Gen. Benjamin F. Cheatham's corps from his right to his extreme left to defend that vital ground.[9]

Dawn was bright and clear, although showers were in the offing. The already mild temperatures rose into the sixties. Around 8 A.M., while the Union left wing moved up, McArthur brought his own line forward, descending a half mile across mushy farmer's fields until about three hundred yards from the main enemy position. "This movement," wrote Marsh, "was made in the face of a galling fire from a well-protected foe, and not without loss to us." The skirmishers edged within one hundred yards of the Rebels. The Ninth Minnesota dug in quickly, using mess kits because the shovels had been left behind. To avoid becoming prominent targets, the field officers sent their horses back. "The rebel sharpshooters annoyed us considerably," Marsh reported. Four men, including Capt. Harrison Jones of Company A, were badly wounded. Directly ahead of Hubbard's brigade, across a cornfield "as open and level as a threshing floor," Walthall's Rebel Division (minus the battered Arkansas brigade) hunched behind a "heavy stonewall" that they had reinforced with wood, stones, and dirt.[10]

The Ninth Minnesota endured steady sniping. Around noon rain turned the ground, already muddy, into a quagmire. Schofield, poised opposite the Rebel left flank, was supposed to open the general assault, but he fretted that Hood was about to strike him and beseeched Thomas for more troops. Finally, about 2 P.M. the shovels reached the Ninth Minnesota. "We soon made ourselves safe by throwing up sod," recalled Pvt. Milton Stubbs of Company B, "but we knew that the hour was soon coming for a charge." Shortly after 3 P.M., the artillery thundered in earnest. "Every gun in the army was set at work, firing with the utmost rapidity," wrote Macdonald. "The rebel guns responded with spirit, and the result was one of the grandest artillery battles of the war. The air over the heads of the men was filled with shot and shell flying in opposite directions, and the very earth seemed to tremble under the terrible concussion in the atmosphere above."[11]

After nearly an hour, Schofield had not moved, and the order to charge had still not been given to McArthur's division. Thomas's secondary attack against Peach Orchard Hill on the Confederate right flank was sharply repulsed. With sundown quickly approaching, the prospects for defeating Hood that day rapidly waned. Taking the bit in his teeth, McArthur sent word to his three brigade commanders to prepare to advance in echelon. Only then did he dispatch a staff officer to tell Smith and Thomas, who happened to be conferring on a hill behind the Second Brigade. Before his superiors could respond, McArthur ordered the charge. It was the decisive moment of the Battle of Nashville, and the four Minnesota regiments would play a key role in the dramatic victory.[12]

On the right, McMillen's First Brigade (with the Tenth Minnesota) opened the attack by scaling steep Shy's Hill. As McArthur foresaw, the rough terrain sheltered their approach to some extent from enemy fire. When McMillen was about halfway to his objective, Hubbard took the Second Brigade forward against the stone wall. The Ninth Minnesota gave a shout that Marsh thought "might be heard for miles away." The Ninth Minnesota and Fifth Minnesota were the first line, the Eighth Wisconsin and Eleventh Missouri, the second. "We had to go about 80 rods across a cornfield and the mud was half knee deep," wrote Stubbs. "Many of our boys fell exhausted before they reached the works. The Rebels opened two masked batteries on us and Oh! how the grape and canister whistled. I would have hated to have been a cornstalk for it seemed as though every one was falling to the ground." Sergeant Frank Warner of Company F marveled how the "bullets flew like hail" and came "so fast and so much they cut the corn stalks off." He was soon "covered with mud from head to toe. The cannon balls would strike the mud and splatter our faces and our eyes full, but 'Forward' was the cry and 'Give it to 'em!'" Major Strait called it "the heaviest fire I ever experienced." Nonetheless, "our men went forward with a will and determination that knows no such thing as falter. . . . I have no idea how I passed through without getting hit. Bullets went past me zip! zip! every moment. They struck in the ground close to my feet, but none, thank God, hit me." The Fifth Minnesota and Eleventh Missouri, on the left of the brigade, suffered greatly from raking fire. To the east across Granny White Pike, Marshall's Third Brigade (with the Seventh Minnesota) attacked when he saw the other two brigades in motion. Lieutenant Colonel John H. Stibbs of the Twelfth Iowa admired how Hubbard's men, ahead and to his right, advanced "with their line as perfect as on parade." They were "under a terrific fire," with "no wavering or halting until their line, or what was left of it, had secured possession of the stone wall in their front."[13]

Strait found by the time he neared the stone wall his men "were completely exhausted and overdone. If the rebels had stuck to their works in our front and not yielded them at our approach, we would have suffered much greater loss, for our men were in no condition to engage in a hand to hand encounter." Instead, "when we got up close to their works [the defenders] held up white handkerchiefs[,] old rags and everything that they could get hold of that looked in any ways white, in token of surrender." Stubbs concurred. "As soon as our boys got near the works the Rebels jumped over and commenced waving their white flags. The day was won along the whole line." McMillen's perfect assault had pierced the Shy's Hill position and threw its defenders into complete confusion. That effect rippled along the Confederate line in front of Hubbard's and Marshall's brigades. Most of the Rebels took off running or surrendered en masse. The flags of the Fifth Minnesota and the Ninth Minnesota appear to have reached the stone wall about the same instant, though each colonel swore his was first. Macdonald, who bore

Lucius Hubbard, 1865

Taken at close of Civil war 1865

the stars and stripes of the Ninth, had no doubt whatsoever. "The colors of the Ninth were first planted thereon!" Strait marveled that "so many men lived to cross the field." When he himself passed over the wall, one of the Rebels who had surrendered said, "'You are the bravest men I ever saw; the world can't beat you.'" Marshall's gallant Third Brigade also broke the enemy line to its front.[14]

Witnessing McArthur's sudden strike, Thomas roused Schofield's corps to attack. The entire Confederate left flank soon dissolved in a mad rush to escape. Wilson's cavalry hastened to block the Granny White Pike, leaving the Rebels only the Franklin Pike to the southeast. The Ninth Minnesota snapped up two battle flags and hundreds of prisoners. When Smith rode up, Warner saw him slap his hat "down on his horse's neck" and shout, "Bully for the snow diggers!" one of his nicknames for his "Minnesota boys." Hubbard waved Marsh after the fleeing Rebels with the Ninth Minnesota and Eighth Wisconsin and turned the rest of the brigade sharply east to join Marshall in flanking the main line. The attackers were exhausted, but "when we put the Johnnies to flight every man seemed to take a new life." Marsh dropped off some men to guard the many prisoners and with the rest chased the Rebels southeast across the Granny White Pike toward the hills beyond.[15]

Strait's left wing forged ahead of the rest of the army. "After pushing across the field and gaining their works we did not halt but for a moment to get our scattered fragments together and then pushed on picking up prisoners in our front, on our right and left and in every direction where they could find a fence or a stone pile to conceal themselves you would find them hid." It was the retreat from Guntown all over again, but this time the shoe was on the other foot. The Ninth Minnesota nabbed another 150 fugitives, including 60 forlorn South Carolinians, and along with the Eighth Wisconsin captured three guns. Near sundown "a brigade staff officer galloped up to the front of the pursuit and exclaimed, 'My God, Maj. Strait, you cannot capture Hood's whole army with that handful of men!' The gallant major halted, looked at the rapidly retreating Confederates, and replied, 'No, I guess not; they run a damned sight faster than we can!'" A rear guard of sorts had formed on a hill ahead and "kept up a lively fusillade," wrote Macdonald. "Our men gained a good position in the deep bed of a creek, which formed a natural breastwork, and from which, as one of the regiment remarked, 'we shelled the hills with our musket so hotly that the enemy soon fell back and disappeared'" into the darkness.[16]

Whether the Battle of Nashville was truly "decisive" as Stanley F. Horn declares, the Tennessee campaign without doubt shattered Hood's Army of Tennessee. Union casualties at Nashville were just over 3,000 killed, wounded, and missing. Seeing the backs of thousands of Rebels fleeing in panic was immensely satisfying to the Guntown veterans, though the spectacle was costly. Hubbard's brigade went into battle on December 15 with about 1,500 officers and men and in two days suffered 315 killed, wounded, and missing. The Ninth Minnesota lost 1 officer and 5 enlisted men killed, and 3 officers and 47 enlisted men wounded, of whom 1 officer and 10 enlisted men subsequently died. The vast majority of the casualties occurred during the grand charge. Of 250 men in the ranks that morning, only 188 answered the next day's roll call. Three liberators from Company C sustained minor wounds on the sixteenth: Merchant, right hand; Hartley, right hip; and John Watkins, right hand. Company K liberator Frederick "Fritz" Heilmann, a twenty-seven-year-old farmer from Hesse-Darmstadt, Germany, suffered more serious wounds from shell fragments that tore up his right hand and thigh.[17]

THE WANDERING TRIBE OF ISRAEL

The pursuit of the Rebels began on December 17, but for once Smith's detachment followed at an easy pace. "Along the whole line of march," wrote Stubbs, "we found guns scattered in every direction." On the third day, the Ninth Minnesota passed through Franklin, scene of the "exceedingly sanguinary engagement" three weeks before. The ground was "awfully torn up by graves, men and horses." It seemed to Nicholas Schreifels that "every house in the town was filled up with wounded." On December 23 Strait wrote home: "We are still in pursuit of Hood, but are making very slow progress. It has rained every day since we started, weather very cold, roads bad and streams high. Hood, of course, destroys all the bridges possible and retards our progress to the best of his ability." Reports placed Hood "forty miles distant and increasing the distance as fast as he can."[18]

Crossing Duck River on Christmas Eve, the Ninth Minnesota marched through Columbia, a pretty, formerly prosperous town known for its culture and refinement. There Company C liberator Noah McCain fell out of the ranks. None of his comrades saw where he went, but there was no evidence of foul play. Listed initially as absent without leave, McCain was branded a deserter on January 29, 1865. On the official form where it was asked where the deserter might have fled, someone opined, "No idea." At any rate, McCain was the second liberator to desert. It would be interesting to know his reasons.[19]

By the time Smith's detachment slogged into Pulaski, fifteen miles north of the Tennessee-Alabama line, Hood's army had escaped. Thomas shifted gears and sent Smith seventy-five miles west to Clifton, on the Tennessee River. On January 9 the Ninth Minnesota clambered on board the transport *Tyrone,* chugged upriver (south) past the old battlefield at Shiloh, and went ashore that evening at Eastport, Mississippi, an isolated locale on the Alabama line, twenty-five miles east of Corinth. Smith's Guerrillas built log huts and settled in, ostensibly for the rest of the season.[20]

"In winter quarters we expected better things," complained one officer. In mid-January after a boat full of corn for animal fodder arrived by mistake instead of the normal supply vessel, the men went on half rations. Soon a hard freeze and snow choked river traffic. "Most of us were sick and hungry," recalled Schreifels, "and we had almost nothing to still the gnawing hunger." By January 25 the men were down to one ratty ear of corn apiece, with no proper way to grind it. For two days some had no food at all. "Myself with others considered ourselves lucky," A. J. Carlson confessed, "when we found a few kernels of corn in the offal from the mules and horses which we cleaned by washing several times, then roasting or frying, and in this way we could make out a scanty meal." Some even wrote home begging for food shipments. On February 2 a few transports reached Eastport with proper rations, but not nearly enough.[21]

Understandably, few at Eastport regretted sudden orders on February 5 to prepare to embark. The next day as the Minnesotans boarded their transport, five more inches of snow bade them farewell. Smith was to proceed via the Mississippi River to sunny New Orleans. After a fast trip north along the

Tennessee River, the transports stopped at Cairo, Illinois, where thick masses of ice clogged the Ohio and the Mississippi. "I am now," Smith informed Washington, "without a heading or identity for my command. Unless I receive a number or a name for my command, I must style myself the Wandering Tribe of Israel. Please telegraph me immediately and give me a number." Amused, Halleck replied, "Continue on in your exodus as the Wandering Tribe of Israel. On reaching the land of Canby you will have a number and a name." General Canby subsequently designated Smith's command the Sixteenth Army Corps.[22]

New Orleans and Dauphin Island

After a short sojourn at balmy Vicksburg, the Ninth Minnesota passed through the rich bottomland south along the Mississippi. William Dean marveled at the parade of lavish sugar plantations replete with the huge mansions and rude slave quarters so emblematic of the Rebel cause. "O, it serves them right," meaning their calamitous decline, "for the planters here must have lived like lords for their places to be destroyed and confiscated for they lived too well on the labor of the poor negro. But they have suffered for their foolhardiness for inaugurating this vast rebellion, which I think will soon be crushed to the earth to rise no more, for if they come back the constitution will be amended. Slavery is dead."[23]

Reaching New Orleans on February 22, the Ninth Minnesota camped on the old, soggy Chalmette battlefield where Andrew Jackson defeated the British fifty years before. There were "orange groves all around our camp," wrote Markham, "and the trees as full as they will sustain of large, ripe fruit." After going hungry at Eastport, the Minnesotans savored the vaunted culinary excellence of the exotic Creole city. The "oysters [are] as big as your hand and as fat as butter all alive and kicking and as plentiful as blackberries. For the present, good-bye salt pork and old horse yclept beef."[24]

Waiting at New Orleans were Sergeant Major Clapp and other former prisoners exchanged in November at Savannah. All told vivid accounts of their imprisonment. While on leave Clapp had published in local newspapers his partial list of midwesterners who had died at Andersonville. For many families he brought the first actual confirmation of the death of loved ones. The response was so great that Clapp resolved to write a pamphlet on Andersonville. "My meeting with my dear old comrades [in New Orleans]," he later wrote, "I cannot describe." It dawned on the other Minnesotans how many of their unfortunate captive comrades "sleep the sleep that knows no waking until the great day," and that most survivors would never be physically fit to serve again. "I wish I could think our government was free from blame in the matter," Markham observed. Many deeply suspected the motives behind the seeming stubborn reluctance of the federal government to countenance an immediate exchange of all prisoners.[25]

News from home in January and February concerned political matters that would have interested the liberators. Senator Wilkinson, who championed their cause in the Senate and who was erroneously credited with their release, failed to gain reelection despite Lincoln's strong support. In January the Republican caucus of the state legislature finally selected, after twenty-nine ballots, Daniel S. Norton of Winona. Wilkinson lost not because of his radical, anti-slavery positions, but because of his abrasive personality and style. He subsequently served a term in Congress (1869–71). Failing to garner renomination by the Republican Party, he switched to the Democrats and was twice elected to the state senate. Wilkinson died in 1894 at the age of seventy-five. On February 23, 1865, Minnesota became the seventeenth state to ratify the Thirteenth Amendment to the Constitution, which prohibited slavery and involuntary servitude. That same month the state legislature passed a bill, introduced by Charles Griswold, representative from Winona, to authorize a referendum to set aside the "white" qualification in the suffrage clause of the state constitution and give the vote to black males. The referendum failed in November 1865 and again in 1867 but passed in 1868.[26]

The Sixteenth Corps was not brought all the way down to New Orleans simply for sunshine and rich food. General Canby was under great pressure from Washington to finish off Mobile and take the war into central Alabama. At the same time, in southern Tennessee, Wilson prepared a huge cavalry raid against Selma and Montgomery. Mobile, the second-biggest cotton port on the Gulf of Mexico after New Orleans, was thirty miles inland at the head of shallow Mobile Bay. Admiral Farragut had kicked open the front door in August 1864 when he defeated naval forces defending the narrow entrance to the bay. The seizure of Mobile itself would be a much more difficult undertaking.[27]

In early March 1865, the Sixteenth Corps ventured 240 miles across the Gulf of Mexico to one of the barrier islands separating Mobile Bay from the gulf. Dauphin Island was "a rather barren piece of land," Macdonald recalled, of "white sand with very little vegetation. There were a few pine trees to break the monotony." The troops delightedly discovered rich oyster beds in adjacent waters. "Soon bivalves on the half-shell were the regular bill of fare." Carlson and his comrades regularly hiked two miles to the bay, and with a "gunnybag" suspended around the neck, they waded in the "quite cold water" until nearly neck deep. Toes were the principal means of locating the tasty mollusks, and in three hours a two-man team could easily fill a pail.[28]

At Dauphin the Ninth Minnesota numbered nearly 350 men. The five company officers present became six on March 13 when Sergeant Merchant received his long-awaited promotion to first lieutenant of Company C. He could not advance to captain because the absent Edwin Ford held the slot. So in Company K did David Wellman, notwithstanding Jules Capon's excellent combat record. As engineer officer on the division staff, Wellman was highly esteemed for his competence and wide experience. Counting Merchant, just eleven of the original thirty-eight liberators were present. Epler, Bullard, Hartley, Padden, Slocum, and Stewart were in Company C, Buck, Jansen, Lüthye, and Raymond in Company K, while Fenstermacher remained in division headquarters as a teamster or orderly.[29]

BESIEGING MOBILE

Against Canby's forty-five thousand men, Mobile could only muster nine thousand defenders, but they counted on stout earthworks and strong artillery to even the odds. Canby planned to cross to the east side of Mobile Bay, strike north, cut the rail line to Montgomery, and assault the city from the northeast. On the east edge of the bay, two large fortifications barred the way: Spanish Fort and Fort Blakely, five miles to the north. One Union corps (thirteen thousand men) was to march northwest from Pensacola directly against Fort Blakely, while Canby and thirty-two thousand men of the Sixteenth Corps and Thirteenth Corps traversed the bay to take on Spanish Fort from the south.[30]

Hubbard's brigade with the Ninth Minnesota left Dauphin Island on March 20 for the mouth of the shallow Fish River and the next day rode ten miles upriver to a landing eighteen miles south of Spanish Fort. On March 25 Canby's entire force, with the Ninth Minnesota in the lead as skirmishers, pushed north into rough, heavily forested country laced with creeks and swamps. Warily proceeding two miles, Marsh encountered Rebel cavalry and some infantry in line of battle. Pressing steadily ahead for six miles without pause, the Ninth Minnesota, at the cost of two wounded, cleared the road and attained the designated campsite. "Oh! How handsomely," admired a soldier of the Seventh Minnesota, "did they drive the rebels through the pines to their sand holes." Giving the nod to Company G's Ojibwe, he particularly praised "the splendid shooting of the half-breeds in that regiment."[31]

On the morning of March 27, Canby's main body slowly drew within a mile of its objective. On a high bluff overlooking Mobile Bay, Spanish Fort comprised several large earthwork redoubts linked by an extensive network of rifle pits and gun positions. The defenses stretched for a mile and a half, with both flanks firmly anchored on the water. The landward approach, sloping down from the Rebel position, was stripped bare of cover and well protected by deep ditches and other obstacles, including "torpedoes" (an early type of land mine). "Altogether, it was an ugly-looking fortification to assault," wrote Macdonald. The garrison eventually comprised four thousand men, including many Nashville veterans, and forty artillery pieces. The Union troops anticipated immediate attack orders, but to their great relief, Canby, reluctant to risk heavy casualties, decided on a siege.[32]

Canby's forces dug in. Shovels became as important as rifles, and sweat more important than blood. Siege tactics called for establishing trench lines parallel to the enemy fortifications. Snaking out from the parallels, a series of saps, or trenches, would be dug toward the enemy position until attaining suitable ground for the second parallel. The process would be repeated until the troops drew close enough for a successful assault. Both sides harassed the other with artillery and sharpshooters. Consequently, excavation or repair of positions in exposed areas had to be done at night. McArthur's division manned the center of the Union line, and Hubbard's brigade found itself directly opposite a Rebel redoubt (Battery No. 4) known as Red Fort, from the reddish soil. The besiegers took cover "behind logs & stumps," Dean wrote, laboring "nearly all night on works to protect ourselves, as they cannot see us at night.... We then lay in them during the day. We have root houses [bomb proof dugouts] ... and very high works, though there [are] stray shots sometimes that will hit somebody[,] there being so many moving about."[33]

On rainy March 28, men from the Ninth Minnesota not on trench duty relaxed behind the Second Iowa Battery, which kept a steady fire on one of the Rebel gun positions. "We had plenty of music all day," wrote Carlson, "with shells exploding among us and solid shot flying over our heads." At the same time, there was always the worry "the keen eye of a sharpshooter would detect an exposure perhaps impossible to prevent." That afternoon, only a few feet from where Carlson was sitting, liberator George Bullard, a thirty-seven-year-old Mower County farmer from New York, happened to be "boiling his coffee in a little can held over the fire" when "a minie-ball from the fort hit his arm and broke the bone so he dropped his coffee in the fire." The heavy lead slug smashed Bullard's left arm just below the shoulder. At the corps field hospital, Assistant Surgeon Francis H. Mulligan of the Tenth Minnesota, a well-known Wabasha physician, speedily removed the arm. Such amputations of extremities were among the most common operations performed during the Civil War. Proper surgical techniques did not yet exist to repair a shattered bone like the humerus and to restore proper circulation. With the strong possibility of gangrene, amputation of the affected limb was nearly always the only safe recourse. When Bullard was well enough to travel, he was taken to the General Hospital in New Orleans. His wound was truly a freak occurrence, for he was the only casualty in Hubbard's entire brigade that day.[34]

The next day when the brigade started digging saps toward the enemy lines, Merchant suffered a close call, receiving a slight wound in the ankle. Two days later work began on the second parallel to bring the lines within three hundred yards of Red Fort itself. During daylight, Hubbard manned his forward trenches with 250 sharpshooters, drawn mostly from the best shots in the Fifth Minnesota and Ninth Minnesota. As before, Rebel artillery and marksmen warmly reciprocated. Dean wrote on April 3 of the "deadly bullets that are at all times flying about. We lay behind works as high as a man's head, built of logs & dirt. . . . When they fire many shells we get into [the bombproof] and are safe. . . . Some have to work every night, a detail went out last night and worked up very close to the forts, they dig bigger holes for the skirmishers to stop in. Skirmishers is mostly one company from each regiment put ahead as guards so the enemy cannot surprise us." Red

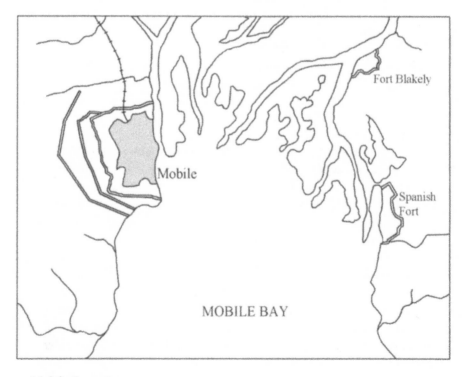

Mobile Campaign

Fort was truly a place where "a Christian can feel and pray to God continuously, for he [sees] danger ever present with him and that he is liable at any moment to be struck by the missile of death."[35]

Canby visited the brigade on the fourth, wrote Carlson; "examining everything, his pleasant manner and kind words gave hope and encouragement to the boys in blue." Starting at 5 P.M. a huge bombardment rocked Spanish Fort for two hours. "Such a roar of thunder I had never heard and never expect to hear again, the very foundation of the earth was trembling." When the firing slackened, Carlson "crept out, saw [the] last of [the] shelling, two or three guns were silenced on immediate front, and logs, sand-bags and earth was flying high in the air. The boys begun to cheer and in a few minutes it was general over the whole line which extended about three miles." They all expected orders to storm Spanish Fort, but Canby was not yet ready.[36]

On the evening of April 6, Capon and a dozen "picked men," most likely including some liberators, experienced quite an adventure that fortunately went off much better than might have been expected. That afternoon it looked as if the Rebels might be evacuating Spanish Fort. Shortly after sundown, Hubbard sent Capon, "a brave and enterprising officer," to reconnoiter. He "succeeded in getting his men through the abatis and to the ditch of the Red fort, without arousing attention, and remained there long enough to become satisfied the works were still occupied in force. In withdrawing, he was fired upon, but none of the party were hit."[37]

By April 8 Hubbard's brigade had shoveled its way closer to Rebel lines than any other unit in the Sixteenth Corps. The head of one sap leading from the second parallel was only sixty yards from Red Fort, and work had begun on the third parallel. It was only a matter of time before Spanish Fort fell. That night the Confederates hastily withdrew most of their forces along a secret path north through the swamps to Fort Blakely. Aware something was up, the division on the right of the Sixteenth Corps stormed the enemy works after a short bombardment and captured part of the rear guard. Hubbard's sharpshooters infiltrated Red Fort and nabbed more prisoners. McArthur followed with a full attack. "Orderlies [first sergeants] came running all along our line, ordering the whole line to advance at once and take possession of the Fort," wrote Carlson. "We went pell mell over ditches, logs, torpedoes, trenches and earthworks and were soon inside the works." The "Rebels had taken away everything movable and spiked their guns. The interior of the Fort exhibited marks of our bombardment. Guns were dismounted; caissons exploded; pieces of artillery knocked here and there." Carlson and Andrew Wallace, one of his Guntown companions, "ventured down in the darkness

to the bottom of one of their bomb-proof huts, 6 or 8 feet below the surface."
The dugout was a battery headquarters that, a struck match revealed, had live
artillery shells "strewn over the floor." The two beat a hasty retreat, but not
before snatching up a basket of "edibles," including a delicious "American
mince-pie." Inside the fort Stubbs discovered "sacks of meal flour and ham,
tobacco, sugar and other things too tedious to mention. Some of the boys
dressed up in Rebel uniforms."[38]

On April 9 the Sixteenth Corps moved on Fort Blakely, which fell in the
afternoon to assault by the corps that had come up from Pensacola. Nearly
eight hundred miles to the northeast in Virginia, Lee surrendered the Army
of Northern Virginia to Grant at Appomattox, effectively ending the war, but
Smith's troops did not know that yet. On April 10, while the First Division
rested in camp, over three thousand Confederate prisoners, the defenders of
Fort Blakely, trudged sullenly past. Carlson was especially struck by the high
percentage of men who looked sixty or older and boys who were younger
than fifteen. The South had run out of soldiers, but the war persisted. "There
are some more heavy works around Mobile but they are bound to come,"
Stubbs wrote home that day. "We'll dig them out. We are meeting with such
success that we won't be surprised any day to hear of peace." The following day persistent shelling by Rebel gunboats compelled the division to shift
camp, but artillery soon drove the vessels off. "Today we heard the last cannon of the rebellion fired but we were not then aware of it," recalled Carlson.
The next day Mobile surrendered, and on April 13 Smith's Guerrillas started
north for Montgomery in hot, muggy weather that was all too reminiscent of
the Guntown raid.[39]

By late afternoon on April 19, the Sixteenth Corps was still fifty miles short
of Montgomery. "Near the close of a very hot day," wrote Hubbard, "the
troops had made a march, over dusty roads, and were feeling sore and tired
out. The column had halted for a rest, and the men were seeking protection
from the heat in the corners of fences and on the friendly side of an occasional
stump or tree." In the distance, "suddenly," there came "a faint cheer toward
the rear of the column," Macdonald recalled. "It was repeated more distinctly,
and gradually grew nearer and nearer, swelling in volume as it approached."
The men wondered what could be happening. "A courier bearing dispatches
rode up rapidly from the rear," wrote Hubbard, and announced that Lee had
surrendered and the war was over. There had been rumors to that effect, but
nothing had been confirmed. Now "followed a scene it was a delight to witness. The heat, dust and fatigue were forgotten; the weary became rested and
the footsore suddenly cured. Officers and soldiers abandoned themselves to
the most extravagant demonstrations of joy. Everybody cheered and shouted

until they were hoarse. The men disregarded orders and discipline, fired a salute with their muskets on their own account. They pulled and hustled each other about, stood on their hands, rolled in the dirt and were guilty of innumerable other absurd performances." A. J. Carlson "thanked God our heavenly Father that this bloody war had now terminated, and through the victory, 4,000,000 slaves were now free."[40]

CHAPTER NINETEEN

Coming Home

VIA THE RIVER

By mid-March 1865, with Robert E. Lee besieged in Richmond and Petersburg, and Joe Johnston scrambling in North Carolina to protect his rear, the general exchange of prisoners that emptied Florence, Salisbury, and Columbia finally spread to other prisons deep within the rapidly shrinking Confederacy. Outside of Virginia and Texas, the vast majority of remaining Federal captives, perhaps nine thousand men, languished at Andersonville, Cahaba, and Meridian. Of the thirty-one from the Ninth Minnesota, sixteen, including liberators Frahm, Gordon, and Rodier, endured in Andersonville, while the rest (among them liberator Hilton) dried out after the flood at Cahaba.

Mobile appeared the likeliest site for an exchange of Andersonville and Cahaba inmates, but complications soon arose. Fortuitously, in February local negotiations opened for an exchange in Vicksburg, a location convenient for swapping more than three thousand Union prisoners at Cahaba and Meridian for captive Rebels brought down the Mississippi. On March 16 the authorities agreed on a neutral zone to extend eleven miles east along the railroad from Four-Mile Bridge (four miles east of Vicksburg) to the Big Black River. Federal forces at Four-Mile Bridge would erect a special tent city, Camp Fisk, to detain their own paroled prisoners under Confederate control (but fed and supplied by the North) until the Union released the equivalent number of Rebels.[1]

The decision to establish Camp Fisk proved wise, for by March 16 the Confederates, eager to close out the remaining camps, had already started thousands of prisoners on the arduous trek west to Vicksburg. By March 18 the Cahaba stockade had largely been evacuated. The former inmates journeyed, mostly by rail, through Meridian to Jackson, Mississippi. Beyond Jackson the rail link to Vicksburg no longer existed, forcing the hapless prisoners to hike thirty miles to the Big Black River. That hard slog proved especially difficult for sick men who were poorly clothed and lacked proper food. The roads were "terrible," especially in the rain, and fording the many overflowing rivers and creeks cost several lives.[2]

On March 18 the first prisoners joyously crossed the Big Black River over a newly built pontoon bridge, where black soldiers welcomed them warmly. The starving men could not resist the stacks of hardtack boxes and barrels of whiskey stockpiled in neutral territory, and a few died from overeating. The survivors rode the recently restored railroad to Four-Mile Bridge and the relative luxury of Camp Fisk. For Melville Robertson, the medical orderly from the Ninety-Third Indiana, the march from Jackson to the Big Black River commenced in a downpour on March 19 and lasted two days. Edson Rice of Company C departed Cahaba around March 16 with the final group and reached Camp Fisk only on March 26 as the last of the fifteen from the Ninth Minnesota. He was very glad, he wrote home, that the "black-hearted rebs" no longer censored his letters but added that he still felt "very much unwell," as his "hand trembles" and could "scarcely hold my pen."[3]

The Rebels in the meantime decided unilaterally against any exchanges through Mobile because of the increasing military threat to the city. Instead they also began shipping Andersonville inmates westward to Vicksburg. As of March 18 Camp Sumter held 5,746 prisoners: 4,470 in the stockade and 1,276 in the hospital. In the next ten days, over 2,400 inmates left, including the entire Ninth Minnesota contingent except, for reasons now unknown, John Gordon. With priority ostensibly accorded the infirm, about half of the discharged inmates came out the hospital. While most of the others were also sick, some did get out by bribing Rebel sergeants as much as twenty U.S. dollars. Five dollars secured Uriah Karmany of the Second Minnesota a place on the third train. It is doubtful anyone from the Ninth Minnesota had much to pay guards. One who certainly lacked funds was Aslakson, who refused to believe he might be exchanged until he was actually on a westbound train. During the stopover at Meridian, he was delighted finally to be "quartered in barracks" and "served wheat bread for the first time since we were taken prisoners."[4]

Only on March 23 did the Rebels bother to inform the authorities at Vicksburg that thousands of Andersonville prisoners, too, were en route. They warned if Vicksburg refused to accept all the prisoners—as had recently happened for a short time at Wilmington—the "suffering that will attend to the turning of them back will be without a parallel." Perhaps "one-fourth of them will die and be killed." Determined to maintain control, the Rebels vowed not to reveal to the prisoners that they would be going back to Cahaba and Andersonville until enough guards were on hand "to shoot all who try to escape." General Napoleon Dana, in charge at Vicksburg, agreed to take all whom the Confederates could deliver.[5]

The Rebel commander at Jackson submitted an unusual request for help. Appalled at reports of the poor physical condition of the Andersonville prisoners, apparently in much worse shape than those from Meridian and Cahaba, he feared many were incapable of walking from Jackson to the Big Black River. Prisoners were already "dying on the roadside with no food and no one to feed them." Dana swiftly dispatched his chief surgeon with fifteen ambulances and twenty wagons under flag of truce to Jackson to help transport the weakest men. The Federal convoy rolled into the Mississippi capital on the evening of March 24 at the same time as the first Andersonville contingent from Meridian. "During the night, eleven of the poor sufferers died from want of food and exhaustion," according to one report. Six more succumbed on the march to the Big Black River. When the first Andersonville group finally attained neutral territory on March 27 and saw the old flag, wrote Simon Peter Obermier of the Seventy-Second Ohio, "shout after shout went up from the boys, many crying like children for Joy." Dana confirmed that most Andersonville prisoners were far more debilitated than their peers from Cahaba. Some were "permanently and incurably diseased, some, from excessive fasting and want of food, have lost all taste and relish for it and are but moving skeletons, if perchance they can move."[6]

To the paroled prisoners, Camp Fisk's spartan facilities seemed positively sumptuous. Rations were carefully measured to prevent dangerous overindulgence, but there was always plenty of hot coffee. Even so, the first party discovered an all-too-familiar army ploy. "Our quartermaster at Vicksburg could not resist the temptation to make some money by feeding us on condemned hardtack so alive with vermin as to be almost unfit for a dog to eat." When Dana inspected the camp, the men indignantly displayed the contaminated crackers, "and after that fresh bread was furnished to us daily." Robertson himself received the "kindest treatment" at Camp Fisk. Delicacies and personal goods, such as "combs, spoons, tobacco and pipes" donated by the Christian Commission and the citizens of Vicksburg, worked wonders. Plenty of soap was furnished for bathing in nearby creeks, but getting sufficient new clothing to equip everyone took longer than expected. Once the new uniforms arrived, the men tossed their old rags into large piles and set them on fire. Wearing the regulation blue greatly raised morale.[7]

It appears that by April 2 all thirty of the Ninth Minnesota's prisoners from Cahaba and Andersonville had reached Camp Fisk, along with more than four thousand others. Orders called for them to be forwarded as soon as possible to Benton Barracks near St. Louis for processing and furloughs. Most, though, would not be leaving any time soon. The Confederate commissioners demanded that they remain at Camp Fisk until the Southerners for whom they had been exchanged were delivered to Vicksburg. Dana had to petition Washington for Rebel captives to be brought in from Rock Island or Alton, but that would require considerable time.[8]

Most of the returned prisoners from the Ninth Minnesota, whether from Andersonville or Cahaba, were in very poor health. Nearly all suffered from chronic diarrhea, while advanced scurvy ravaged several. Half the returnees, including Frahm, Hilton, and Rodier, were soon transferred to the hospital in Vicksburg. Aslakson himself never actually entered Camp Fisk. On March 31 one of the surgeons who met the train bringing his group from the Big Black River diagnosed him with severe scurvy and forwarded him directly to the newly arrived hospital ship *R. C. Wood* waiting at Vicksburg. Dana had secured permission from the Rebel commissioners to send four hundred of the sickest paroled prisoners, or at least those who could still be moved, to St. Louis. Joining Aslakson on board were two former Cahaba prisoners, Ed Rice, with chronic diarrhea, and Pvt. John Stockholm of Company D, who like Aslakson was crippled by scurvy. Another patient described how on board the *R. C. Wood* they were put "to bed in the main salon, where long rows of cots were placed. It may be imagined how little life was left in us, when it is stated that a teaspoonful of milk punch every half hour was all that they dare give us." The *R. C. Wood* sailed on April 2 and reached St. Louis five days later. Twenty patients died while on the river, and the rest went to the large hospital at Jefferson Barracks. Once there, Aslakson recalled, "we were cleaned up and received all possible care and nursing. One must have lived through the horrors of Andersonville to be able to appreciate what a hot bath and decent food is like after ten months in such a prison. Many a prayer of thanksgiving and many a tear of pure joy was shed in gratefulness to God that through His mercy we were again free and safe under a Star Spangled Banner."[9]

Only a portion of the huge percentage of sick at Camp Fisk could be hospitalized even in Vicksburg. On April 3 Cpl. John Chase of Company A, a former Cahaba prisoner, died in camp. In mid-April Dana arranged for another transport of nearly four hundred sick on the hospital steamer *Baltic*. Five were from the Ninth Minnesota, including Hilton and Frahm, who was the only former Andersonville prisoner among the five. Robertson, who ailed from typhoid fever, joined them. He left his diary for safekeeping with a fellow Hoosier at Vicksburg. Robertson died on April 22 while still on board. The next day the *Baltic*'s passengers joined their comrades at Jefferson Barracks.[10]

The paroled prisoners waiting at Camp Fisk did not seem particularly impatient to leave. They were content to live quietly for the time being and regain their strength. "The agents of the Sanitary and Christian Commission[s] cared for us," wrote Corporal McLean. "Our sick were tenderly administered to by them; the reading material they furnished us was a rare treat; besides we had many little extras, there, which made the place seem almost heavenly." Word of Lee's surrender elicited the same joyous reaction as elsewhere among Northerners, but the report, a few days later, of Lincoln's assassination plunged Camp Fisk into deepest gloom. The Rebel commissioners immediately fled lest they be attacked by vengeful Union soldiers.[11]

Following the surrender at Appomattox, the Confederate government announced the release of all Federal prisoners at Vicksburg in exchange for their own men being freed in Virginia. Dana declared they would be "sent north as rapidly as possible" in order according to their states. After the *Baltic* sailed, twenty-two paroled prisoners from the Ninth Minnesota (including Rodier) remained at Camp Fisk or in the Vicksburg hospital. Private George W. Kearney of Company I, another former Cahaba inmate, died on April 19 in the hospital. On April 22 the remaining Minnesotans joined 1,300 men from Wisconsin, Iowa, and Illinois who were crowded on board the large side-wheeler *Henry Ames*. Dana himself saw the steamboat off that evening. After a fast, uneventful trip the happy passengers disembarked on April 25 at St. Louis, where they paraded on the levee. "Their appearance on various streets of the city, on the march to Benton Barracks, attracted general attention and drew many crowds of spectators. From their dress and general appearance of good health and spirits," judged the *Missouri Republican*, "it is evident that since their release from their respective prisons they have been kindly cared for by the Federal authorities." The steamer *Olive Branch* reached St. Louis a few days later with six hundred more men, mostly from Mid-Atlantic and northeastern states.[12]

Fate spared the formerly captive Minnesotans one final incredible catastrophe. The last big group of paroled prisoners at Camp Fisk, over 2,000 men from Indiana, Kentucky, Michigan, Ohio, Tennessee, and West Virginia, were ordered to Camp Chase at Columbus, Ohio. The Vicksburg authorities thoughtlessly jammed nearly all of them on board the big steamboat *Sultana*. Early on the morning of April 27, shortly after passing Memphis, a boiler exploded and engulfed the grossly overcrowded vessel in flames. Those who were not killed by the blast or burned to death took to the cold, dark river, where hundreds more drowned. Of the nearly 2,300 passengers (almost all ex-prisoners) and crew on board, over 1,700 died (the exact number is not known) in what remains the worst maritime disaster in American history. The dead included a substantial number who had been captured at Brice's Crossroads, even some who were refused their freedom the previous September in Georgia. It was a horrific end for so many brave soldiers who had endured so much. By a strange twist of fortune, one surviving *Sultana* passenger was the anonymous friend entrusted with Robertson's diary. He took the papers into the river, thus saving them for the young man's family and for posterity.[13]

At Benton Barracks all the paroled prisoners fit for travel received thirty-day furloughs. On May 6 most of the Minnesota "boys," including Rodier and Hilton, left for home. The small number of Minnesotans remaining at Jefferson Barracks for treatment included three who did not survive: Stockholm died on May 5, Rice on the sixth, and Frahm on the ninth. George Frahm succumbed to chronic diarrhea before his disability discharge could even reach him. He was the ninth and final liberator to die during the war. Toward the end of May, several patients from the Ninth Minnesota were released from the hospital and put on the steamboat *Muscatine*. Reaching St. Paul on May 29, they were simply dropped off without ever having been paid or any arrangements being made for their care. The still much weakened men slept outdoors and were discovered the next morning "sitting on the sidewalk eating dry bread begged from a bakery." Ashamed city officials immediately saw to their needs and set up a "soldiers' home" to house and feed casuals and returning sick.[14]

Aslakson stayed in the hospital. Visiting Jefferson Barracks in May 1865 while awaiting his own discharge after being exchanged in March at North East Ferry, Allen Tiffany, Aslakson's lieutenant, found him to be "a mere wreck of a man scarcely able to get about, sorely troubled with diarrhea scurvy & rheumatism." Aslakson received his discharge on July 14 in the hospital. "I cannot describe the joy I felt at boarding the steamboat which was to take me to St. Paul where I could for good say 'Farewell' to army life with its horrors and constraints and be again with my loved ones at home. May the Lord be praised for all, both the chastisement and the deliverance."[15]

VIA THE SEA

On March 28, the day the last Andersonville prisoners departed for Vicksburg, Camp Sumter retained over 3,400 inmates. Liberator John Gordon was the only member of the Ninth Minnesota among them. Another shipment for Vicksburg was expected to leave shortly, but the route to the west was no longer open after Wilson's cavalry corps, heading for Selma and Montgomery, totally disrupted Rebel communications throughout central Alabama. Although disappointed not to have gone with the others, the remaining Andersonville prisoners expected Wilson to free them. "The whole camp seemed cheerful and confident that we would soon get out, in some way."[16]

With Mobile already ruled out and Vicksburg no longer accessible, nearby Florida seemed the only likely place to exchange the rest of the Andersonville prisoners. The Union commander at Jacksonville was willing. "Although I have received no instructions in references to exchanges," Brig. Gen. Eliakim P. Scammon advised the Confederates on March 29, "I will not hesitate to receive the prisoners whom you propose to parole for exchange and receipt therefore." Thus, between April 4 and 6, Andersonville dispatched 3,425 prisoners, including Gordon, to Albany by rail, leaving behind only 15 others too sick to be moved. The plan was to march the men, in three batches, the sixty miles to Thomasville and from there twenty-two miles to Monticello, Florida, where trains would shuttle them east toward Jacksonville. Starting south on April 5 from Albany, the lead group found the mud from the recent rains especially hard going and straggled into Thomasville late on the seventh. The second group left on April 6 and plodded fifteen miles that day, but bad news canceled the departure of the third batch. The Yankees at Jacksonville would not, after all, accept any prisoners. Scammon's superior, Maj. Gen. Quincy A. Gillmore, refused to sanction any exchanges until he received permission from Grant. Given the difficulties of communication, he expected that would take more than two weeks. The prisoners already at Thomasville had to retrace their steps and trudge a grueling 120 miles to no purpose. By the thirteenth nearly 3,400 incredibly disheartened prisoners, including Gordon, had returned to Andersonville. "The boys are very mad," wrote Cpl. John Whitten of the Fifth Iowa. "We are nearly all sick with disappointment."[17]

With Florida seemingly out of the picture, the only recourse was somehow to forward the prisoners to Savannah. On April 18 and 19, three trains started the process by hauling 3,100 men north to Macon. At the same time, Johnston met with Sherman in North Carolina to arrange the surrender of the last large organized Confederate force east of the Mississippi. Expecting the arrival of Wilson's raiders momentarily, Macon was bedecked with white flags as Rebel troops prepared to evacuate. "The town is full of paroled rebels," Whitten found, "and they cuss the rebel Govt. for starving us fellows and not giving us any clothing." The prisoners could go no farther than Macon, nor could they remain there. Trains hauled them back to Andersonville, but to their great relief, they stopped there only briefly before continuing to Albany. Most hospital patients soon followed.[18]

From Albany, starting on April 20, the first batch of prisoners once again hiked the all-too-familiar route to Thomasville, but this time the road was "a good deal drier than before." At Thomasville they learned the exchange was going forward after all. Told to be ready to go, the prisoners were too excited to sleep. As events transpired, they did not have to march to Monticello but proceeded to Jacksonville in a more roundabout way. Jammed onto flat cars, the prisoners rolled northeast to Lawton on April 23, then scooted south across the Florida state line to Live Oak, on the direct rail line to Jacksonville. By the twenty-fifth, 3,300 prisoners were camped in a grove of pines at Lake City, where they signed new parole papers. While waiting there the next two days, they heard of Lincoln's assassination and rumors that the war was over. Early on April 28, trains shuttled them to Baldwin, nineteen miles west of Jacksonville. There they were turned loose to reach Union lines as best they could along the abandoned railroad right of way.[19]

"Like the children of Israel in Bible times," recalled Jacob Hutchinson, "we were afraid Pharaoh might change his mind and try to recapture us, and we were anxious to be off." The marchers split up, "the strong outstripping the weak, and the sick and cripples from scurvy struggling along as best they could, some with crutches and some with canes." The "sand burs were as thick as they could lay," Whitten noted, and for "about two-thirds of us [who] were barefoot, myself among the number, it was like walking on needles." The worst obstacle was an "immense swamp." Hutchinson particularly dreaded crossing a stripped railroad bridge. "Each sill of the trestle was filled with feeble tottering men, weak from the miseries of prison life and scarcely able to walk the solid ground, much less this dizzying height."[20]

The lead group of about three hundred prisoners stumbled into the Federal picket line late that afternoon. "We saw the *Old Stars and Stripes* waving over the city," wrote Whitten, "and then such cheering as the boys done. It appeared as if they would never got through. The Pickets were colored boys, and they cursed the rebels when they saw us, they gave us all their rations as we were awfully hungry." The surprised Federal commander rounded up wagons to pick up stragglers and arranged for a train to wait at the terminus of the track. Shortly before sundown on the twenty-eighth, the first prisoners filtered into town and "took a course straight for the river, as if by instinct," noted one local newspaper. "Their appearance as they passed was pitiful in the extreme. Their clothing was in tatters; their faces were begrimed with dirt and black smoke from pine wood; they nearly were all without shoes; many were without hats. Large numbers were affected with scurvy." Soap was issued and a camp set up for them along the St. Johns River. "We were treated well," Whitten added, "and got all we could eat and more too." Over the next several days, many more paroled men straggled into town. "As each wagon load of ragged, famished wretches came in," wrote Hutchinson, "the ex-prisoners were instructed to go to a pond of clear water near the camp, where a good wash could be taken, and as much of the southern confederacy pine-knot smut rubbed off as possible. Each man then had his hair cut close, and we looked like new-shorn sheep. New clothes were then furnished us, and we began to look like Uncle Sam's boys once more." The surgeon in charge, Dr. Oliver T. Bundy, found "nearly all were in an extreme state of emaciation, terribly filthy, and covered with vermin." Starting on May 1, he placed about 350 "of the worst cases" in a special hospital. "Many were idiotic and insane," Bundy testified in 1868 to Congress. "Many presented the appearance of living skeletons, with scarcely enough muscular fiber left to control the movements of the body. These men had no disease apparently but were literally starved. We had to treat them as children in giving them food, and we found in almost all cases treated that a good nourishing diet was all that they required."[21]

It is not known when John Gordon himself reached Jacksonville, but on May 9 he, too, entered Bundy's hospital. A week later he left, probably on a coastal steamer for Fernandina, thirty miles northeast, where he boarded the hospital transport *S. R. Spaulding*. On May 29, while disembarking at Annapolis, Gordon had the misfortune to fall and break his collarbone. He received his discharge in the hospital on June 26 and left for Winona. Upon enlistment in 1862 he had weighed 188 pounds, but now, even after nearly two months of good food, he still only attained 120 pounds. After Gordon and a few other Minnesotans from different regiments were freed at Jacksonville, only one more prisoner from the state remained in Rebel captivity, and he came out of Camp Tyler in Texas late in May 1865.[22]

The Confederate Minnesotans

Five members of the Ninth Minnesota found a way out of the horrible Rebel prisons other than by death, exchange, or escape. They joined the Rebel army. It was inevitable that the Confederacy, starved of troops, looked greedily at the thousands of starving Union soldiers held in its prisons. Recruitment began at Millen in late October, where the charismatic, Irish-born John G. O'Neill, colonel of the Tenth Tennessee, C.S.A., trolled for recruits for Tennessee regiments in Hood's Army of Tennessee. By mid-November two privates from Company B, youngsters DeWitt C. Handy and George E. Day,

John Gordon

and Pvt. Pat Connell of Company D had signed on along with nearly five hundred other prisoners. Just why the three Minnesotans enlisted is not known, but the general reasons can easily be surmised. Years later Day wrote "the filth and death at Andersonville were more than I can speak of. Over half our men died." At Andersonville Handy had given his dying father, Joel, his promise to do everything he could to survive. Prisoners exchanged in November and December reported that the three had deserted to the Rebel army. Many in the Ninth Minnesota were inclined to be understanding. In January 1865 Milton Stubbs explained how the two from Company B, his friends Day and Handy, were "in the Rebel Army to keep from starving."[23]

On Christmas Day 1864, Connell, Day, and Handy found themselves in Mobile in an ad hoc combat unit of ex-Millen prisoners known as O'Neill's (universally misspelled "O'Neal's") Regiment. Even more shocking was that they soon hastened north to fight Grierson's Union cavalry raiding along the railroad south of Corinth. On December 28 O'Neill's Regiment and other Rebel troops lost to Grierson in a surprisingly fierce encounter at tiny Egypt Station, thirty miles south of Tupelo. Connell, Day, and 252 former Union soldiers were captured. The prisoners, one of Grierson's men wrote, "were in a miserable plight, badly clothed to meet the pitiless pelting of the winter's blast, and many were barefoot. Especially was this the case with a number of our own men—captives from our own army—who had been induced to fight with the rebels." At some point, possibly even before the battle, Handy had jumped from a Rebel train and lit out for the woods. After a long, lonely trek, he reached Memphis on February 6, 1865. He reported that he was a former Andersonville inmate who had fled from a Rebel prison. Twelve days later he caught up with the Ninth Minnesota at Vicksburg. His successful escape erased any concern about his having deserted to the Rebels.[24]

Sent to the military prison at Alton, Illinois, the toughest in the Federal system, Connell, Day, and their luckless cohorts faced charges of desertion, with the added disgrace of going over to the enemy. The penalty could be death, for both armies regularly executed deserters found in enemy ranks. In the summer of 1864, the U.S. Army had started recruiting Confederate prisoners of war to serve in special volunteer regiments in the West, defending settlers from Indians all along the frontier. Those ex-Rebels became known as "Galvanized Yankees," although that term was first applied by the Confederates themselves to Union prisoners of war who joined their army. In March 1865 the War Department devised an elegant solution to the dilemma of the true Galvanized Yankees like Connell and Day by enlisting most of them in the newly formed Fifth U.S. Volunteers. That spring the Fifth U.S. Volunteers settled in Fort Riley, Kansas. Connell deserted on July 16 from Lake Sibley, Kansas, and was never apprehended. On August 13 Day, too, left after learning the Ninth Minnesota was being sent home. For the rest of his long life (he died in 1937 just short of his ninety-second birthday), Day tried in vain to clear his name and secure his pension, but the government never relented.[25]

On January 23 dapper Colonel O'Neill resumed his recruiting efforts at Andersonville. "The rebels are enlisting our boys in the rebel army," wrote Iowan John Whitten. "There is a good many of the boys taking the oath. Some of [them] I do not blame for they are nearly naked, and they cannot stand it here much longer, and a man will do almost anything to save his life." In fact nearly two hundred desperate prisoners volunteered, including 1st Sgt. Frank Weber and Pvt. John Da Rusha. Just why they took that drastic step is not known. They were the only survivors of the twelve comrades from Company G, eight of whom had died in Andersonville, one at Savannah, and the last in Millen. Little is known about subsequent service of Weber and Da Rusha in the Rebel army. On April 3 Weber stumbled into Union lines outside of Savannah and reported he was an escaped prisoner of war from Andersonville. He prudently said nothing of his recruitment by O'Neill, but that was later revealed in captured Andersonville records. Weber was one of the very few of O'Neill's former recruits who succeeded in having his record cleared, and he received a disability pension. His longtime comrade Da Rusha had not escaped with him to Savannah. Da Rusha's subsequent movements remain a complete mystery. Somehow by June 19, he had gotten all the way north to the general hospital at Alexandria, Virginia, where on July 21 he was mustered out of the service. With that event, every surviving former prisoner of the Ninth Minnesota was finally accounted for.[26]

Occupation Duty

On April 25 Smith's Guerrillas completed their triumphal march to Montgomery. The first Confederate capital did not seem like "much of a town" to William Dean, but A. J. Carlson greatly enjoyed seeing the room where Jefferson Davis had been inaugurated in February 1861. Stacks of suddenly worthless Rebel currency proved "irresistible souvenirs." The victory celebrations were dampened on the thirtieth when a boat coming up the Alabama River from Mobile confirmed the previous rumors of Lincoln's assassination. "The news fell with stupefying weight upon the command, casting a gloom over every countenance," recalled Macdonald. "The rage which filled every breast was of that kind which thirsteth for revenge—blood!" Dean wrote the folks that the president's death "cast sorrow in almost every heart, for even the men that was against him wished to see him finish the war."[27]

On May 7 another boat from Mobile brought a substantial number of healed sick and wounded men and a few more returned prisoners of war. One was Nate Palmeter, who joined the thirteen liberators still present in the ranks: First Lieutenant Merchant, Corporal Epler, Hartley, Padden, Slocum, Stewart, Vaughan, and John Watkins in Company C; Buck, Fenstermacher, Jansen, Lüthye, and Raymond in Company K. Beset by a "general feebleness of Constitution," Reverend Arnold of Company C had received his disability discharge on April 25 at Fort Snelling. After the amputation of his left arm, Bullard was a convalescent in New Orleans. Lagree had gotten his disability discharge on February 20 in St. Louis, while Williams was sick at home. From Company K, Corporal Ehmke and Pike were sick at Memphis, while Mickel ran the "Negro Quarters" at Gayoso General Hospital. Recovering from his wounds, Heilmann was in Swift General Hospital in Prairie du Chien, Wisconsin.[28]

"Well, this cruel war is over," Dean explained to his parents, "but we have to stop here till the regular army is got in order and railroads running. Law and order established that will remain supreme." Smith's Guerrillas went on occupation duty in central Alabama to keep order, protect the freed slaves, and safeguard former Confederate public property, such as military installations and equipment and stockpiles of food and cotton. Marching to Perry County northwest of Selma, the Ninth Minnesota penetrated the heart of the famous "Black Belt" of dark, rich soil. Carlson was impressed by "the most prosperous country we had yet seen in the South. Large fields of Corn and Cotton were not wanting. Oh, what a beautiful country this would be if not disgraced by slavery." In 1860 the slaves in Perry County had outnumbered white residents nearly two to one, and that ratio had scarcely changed in the interval.[29]

On May 20 the Minnesotans moved into Marion, the Perry County seat, twenty-six miles from Selma. A "very aristocratic place," according to Dean, the town was known as the "Athens of Alabama" because of numerous colleges and schools. The sole military institution was a hospital with a "large number of maimed CS soldiers." Except for a cavalry detachment that rode through the week before, the Ninth Minnesota were the first Yankees the residents had seen. According to Markham, the town was "one of the most bitter, if not the very most, in the entire South. [Its citizens] are just as rebellious at heart to-day as they were four years ago. It does me good to see them pass under the stars and stripes as they pass along the side-walk." Dean was amused that some of the young women "will not look at us . . . but they keep peeping sometimes." Carlson, too, remarked of the "Rebel spirit, especially the ladies." The first Sunday there, he and a few comrades attended a Methodist church. "It was quite interesting to see the embarrassment, as no one would invite us to a seat we helped ourselves the best we could for the time being. There was not too many Hallelujas at that meeting." At first the stores were tightly shut, but the shopkeepers reopened once they realized there would be no looting. The newly paid Minnesotans spread some greenbacks around, particularly, as Markham noted, "now that we have the money, we have no way of sending it to our families, as the Express does not yet reach us."[30]

The new freedmen most decidedly did not share the defiant attitude of the whites. "The news had spread far and near among the negroes that the Yankees were at Marion, and they flocked in on Sunday afternoon to see us," Macdonald recalled. "They were of all ages, color, sizes and sexes. Those from the village were stylishly dressed, especially many of the young women, not a few of whom were nearly white." Indeed, Markham explained, "The country is full of [freedmen], just from their homes; some left to better their condition; others, because they were free and they could not realize the fact until they got away from the old plantation." Planter Hugh Davis Jr., a resentful former slaveholder who lived near Marion, complained that "orders have been issued vouchsafing freedom to negroes and they have all become monomaniacs on the subject of freedom—As soon as the order was issued thousands of them flocked to Selma to be free, to embrace the *nigger lovers*" [Davis's emphasis].[31]

The blacks of Perry County "are ready to die for a Yankee, the whole of them," wrote Markham. "They bring us all kinds of fruits, vegetables, chickens and everything else that they have any idea we can make any use of." In June, as Carlson described, "the negro population arranged for a festival and invited our whole Regiment to partake." The men, "with the exception of a few that were leaning toward copperheadism, attended, more for curiosity. [There were] not too many delicacies; many of us brought our own hardtack and coffee along in order to help them out and show the whites it was a success. Oh, how happy were those ignorant slaves, that they had been set at liberty. They tried in every conceivable way to show their gratitude of our services in their behalf, as their hearts were overflowing with joy." The blacks "gave the whole regiment a supper one night last week," Markham noted, "and it would have paid you for the trip from Rochester here to see the evidence of pure enjoyment among these poor, unsophisticated creatures. The bare idea of a whole Yankee regiment taking supper with them, with the Lt. Colonel, Chaplain, Adjutant, and all the Captains and Lieutenants in the regiment present, was a great event in their lives."[32]

"Our duty here," recalled Macdonald, "consisted of taking it easy, and enjoying the fruits of a well-earned rest. Aside from seizing all the cotton that could be found and shipping it by rail, the regiment had no particular duty to perform." The Minnesotans saw to the transportation of about five thousand bales of cotton. Inevitably, a few Yankee and ex-Rebel criminals could not resist trying to profit from such a valuable commodity. There were rumors of speculation and worse in the cotton market. It appears that even Marsh joined in the illegal activities, although nothing was ever proven. "Col. Marsh very busy getting in Confederate cotton," Chaplain Kerr noted on June 13. "There is much feeling as to the *manner* in which it is done." On July 20 Kerr learned of "an enormous amount of cotton stealing." One dealer had "52 bales of Govt and 15 of private cotton stolen last night. Many persons are engaged in it. Col. Marsh's course has been very unwise, to say the least." Four days later Kerr charged that "cotton stealing has been engaged to in an outrageous and shameful extent. Col. Marsh has acquired an infamous reputation." That fall, in fact, after his discharge, Marsh purchased two cotton plantations in adjacent counties and returned to reside in Marion. His recent behavior had so tarnished his reputation that years later Major Strait testified the former colonel, "a proud spirited man," was "not popular with the Regt and I could think it difficult to get any member of the Regt to volunteer any statement in his behalf."[33]

At the end of June, Markham led five companies fifty miles north to Tuscaloosa to relieve fifteen forlorn Hoosiers who dared not leave the sanctuary of a stone building. The summer heat was terrible. So was the reception in Tuscaloosa. "I do not remember any city in the whole south where the hatred to the soldiers showed itself so plainly as here," wrote Carlson. On the way into town, the Minnesotans were "jeered at, and called all sorts of names, but marching to the tune of 'Dixie' we soon arrived out of the hot bed, to our destination." Markham brooked no nonsense. "We planted the stars and stripes at the corner and strung one across the street," wrote Carlson. "Many negroes kissed our flag, as they were flocking around our quarters in great numbers." The garrison fired a Fourth of July salute and marched in a dress parade. "The street fronting our quarters was packed with humanity of the African race, singing, dancing and playing all day long. It was a grand sight." The black population of Tuscaloosa likewise invited the garrison to a dinner, which "came off in grand style. A more happy gathering of people I never saw." As on the earlier occasion in Marion, Markham gave a short speech of thanks. In turn, Chaplain Kerr did come to understand that relationships between slaves and masters could be complex. On the way to visit the troops in Tuscaloosa, he chanced to converse at length with a black man who was formerly the servant of a Confederate officer in Virginia. After his master died there, the slave willingly incurred a debt of $350 to bring the body back home for burial and had "since repaid the loan by his own labor."[34]

On July 19 the Tuscaloosa detachment started back to Marion, where the main body of the regiment was preparing to go home. It was high time. The Eleventh Missouri from the old "Eagle Brigade" was to replace them. Carlson had enjoyed chatting with former Confederate soldiers "who were generally of a friendly nature," but he understood that when they left "there were not many tears shed by our Southern friends." Dean wrote that he had "found some very fine people here. They are *union* and friends to us, they are sorry for our leaving." In October a young girl whose family had in particular befriended Dean wrote to tell him how "the inhabitants of Marion seemed to prefer the Eleventh Missouri much more than your regiment when they first came on but now, I think, they would gladly exchange them for the Ninth Minnesota if it lay in their power."[35]

"The question of how to manage the freedmen is the most troublesome one we have to solve now," Markham had commented earlier that summer. How would the millions of Southern blacks fare under the Reconstruction? Could a new society be created that would ensure their fundamental rights and the opportunity to advance themselves? Davis, the bitter plantation owner, boasted that most of his former slaves soon returned to their old digs. "Freedom nor the accursed Yankees were not exactly what they had supposed them to be—They know now they must work for a living." Markham especially feared the adoption of a "conciliatory policy" toward former hard-line Rebels by certain Northerners, "doughfaces and lick-spittles" who would accommodate the "extreme Southerners" by selling out the freedmen. In truth, he anticipated the ultimate failure of the Reconstruction. By casting aside the ideals of the Radical Republicans, the North thereby relinquished the full potential of the glorious freedoms that the war had brought at such a heavy cost in lives, black as well as white. That victory has yet to be fully achieved.[36]

HOME

The route the Ninth Minnesota took west from Marion via Demopolis to Meridian was only too familiar to the few among them who, in June 1864, had gone in the opposite direction to Andersonville. On July 27 the weather was so pitilessly hot on the open deck of the boat that carried the Minnesotans along the Tombigbee River to McDowell's Bluff that a veteran soldier of three years' service perished from heat stroke. Carlson could not believe the dilapidated condition of the railroad between McDowell's, Meridian, and Jackson. From Jackson the Minnesotans marched the well-trod thirty-mile stretch to the Big Black River and rode the train into Vicksburg. On July 31 seven former prisoners of war from Company C, including Palmeter, his close friend Breckon, Vandegrift, Rafferty, and Bourgard, unexpectedly received their discharges.[37]

That same day the Ninth Minnesota boarded the commodious *Henry Ames*. The big side-wheeler glided into St. Louis on the fifth of August. Thousands of troops milled around waiting to board the many steamboats jammed along the riverfront. That evening as the Minnesotans transferred to the steamer *Burlington*, they supposedly "broke loose from their guards on the levee," a New York newspaper correspondent claimed, and "raised a row among the storekeepers and whisky dealers by an indiscriminate pillaging of all places within reach. They frightened a small squad of police, and it was not until nearly a hundred men of the Provost guard appeared that they returned to the boat." Dean never mentioned the incident in his diary or letters, and all Carlson bothered to note was "after all the convalescents and stragglers had joined us, and the usual drunkards row with several arrests, had been attended to, we were ready to leave, and at 10: P.M. we headed for the Capitol of the North Star state."[38]

The regiments returning up the Mississippi received warm greetings all along the way. The Ninth Minnesota landed at St. Paul on August 11 to a huge celebration with a salute, parade, and grand dinner. The next day at

Fort Snelling, the men received furloughs and orders to report back later to be mustered out. Already at home were those who had received disability discharges. Bullard was discharged in New Orleans on May 14, Ehmke the next day in Memphis, Pike on May 23 in Memphis, Williams on June 26 at St. Louis, and Heilmann on June 30 at Prairie du Chien. Returning to St. Paul after their furloughs, Hilton and Rodier were both discharged on August 17.[39]

Some ex-prisoners sadly did not live long enough to receive discharges. Both Andersonville hospital survivors died at home. Looking "more like a skeleton than a man," Sgt. Andrew Mattson, who tented with Aslakson at Millen and Andersonville, returned on May 11 to Waconia, southwest of Minneapolis. He died on May 28 of "nervous fever." Sergeant Moses Chamberlin of Company K was gravely ill with chronic diarrhea when he reached Saratoga on May 10. A young neighbor serving in Chattanooga wrote home on May 28 to say he "was so sorry" to learn that Chamberlin was so sick. "I hope he will get better for I think when he has endured so much that I think it is pretty hard to come home and die." Chamberlin never rallied and died on July 17.[40]

Mustering Out

The formal disbanding of the Ninth Minnesota took place on August 24 at Fort Snelling. Of 1,076 men in the regimental roster, just 402 were present at the final muster, including 14 of the original 38 liberators. On parade with Company C were Merchant (recently promoted to captain), Corporal Epler, Hartley, Padden, Slocum, Stewart, Vaughan, and John Watkins. With Company K were Buck, Fenstermacher, Jansen, Lüthye, Mickel, and Raymond. Captain Wellman had resumed command of Company K (with George Hays as his new first lieutenant and Frank Lohr as second lieutenant), while Jules Capon became captain of Company G. In Company B, George Herrick became first lieutenant and Ernest Hainlin (the man with the healed teeth) second lieutenant, while Color Sergeant Macdonald rose to second lieutenant of Company I.[41]

Of the five infantry regiments (Sixth through Tenth) that Minnesota raised in the summer of 1862, the Ninth Minnesota sustained by far the greatest number of deaths to all causes: 263 fatalities in contrast to 177 in the Sixth Minnesota, the next highest. Combat-related deaths (killed in action or died of wounds) were also highest in the Ninth Minnesota. Only the longer serving First, Second, and Third Minnesota Regiments surpassed the Ninth in total deaths. Nine liberators perished: Augustus Whitney killed in action, David Felch of disease, and Jacob Bader to wounds, and Stephen Chandler,

Charles Dietrich, George Frahm, Zara Frisbie, John Morrison, and Jacob Thielen because of Rebel imprisonment. The 262 killed, wounded, and missing that the Ninth Minnesota incurred at Brice's Crossroads and during the calamitous retreat constituted the highest number of casualties suffered by a Minnesota regiment in a single battle that did not involve a simple surrender, such as the Third Minnesota at Murfreesboro. The next highest totals were the First Minnesota at First Bull Run (180), Antietam (147), and Gettysburg (205), and the Second Minnesota at Chickamauga (162), although both valiant regiments suffered many, many more killed and wounded, as opposed to the number of prisoners, than the Ninth Minnesota. Even so, 139 of the 228 enlisted men of the Ninth Minnesota captured in June 1864 ultimately succumbed, for a mortality of slightly over 60 percent. Renowned Minnesota historian William Watts Folwell, himself a Civil War veteran, eloquently recognized their sacrifice:

> Had these men fallen on the battle field, a monument, or at least a tablet in the rotunda of the Capitol, would commemorate their gallantry. The writer of these lines offers his humble tribute of gratitude to these men of Minnesota who gave up their lives and strength in the cause of their country as surely as if they had fallen charging a rebel division in battle.

Only eighteen regiments in the entire Union army exceeded the loss of the Ninth Minnesota in Confederate prisons.[42]

The newly discharged veterans remained in camp awaiting their final pay. On August 26 many of them went up to St. Paul to greet Grant on his triumphal tour of the Midwest. The scope of the ceremonies eclipsed even the tumultuous greetings accorded the returning regiments. At Fort Snelling later that afternoon, the men were paid, and afterward "many affectionate good-byes were said, mingled with emotions and even tears." The Ninth Minnesota Volunteer Infantry Regiment became only a memory.[43]

CHAPTER TWENTY

After the War

EXEUNT OMNES

The postwar experiences of the twenty-seven surviving liberators (nothing is known of the two deserters), as they faced the challenges of resuming their lives, earning a living, and raising families, might be seen as broadly representative of Union Civil War veterans. All but one eventually married. Several indeed tied the knot more than once, and one outlived five wives. All but one or two were blessed with children. At enlistment nineteen were farmers, one was a clergyman, six were in the trades, and one was a laborer. By 1870 agriculture in eastern Minnesota had changed drastically once the railroad traversed all the areas where the liberators lived. No longer did farmers need to haul their crops great distances or transport them by river to market. Yet in the latter decades of the nineteenth century, in common with the country as whole, the number of liberators who worked the land gradually declined. After the war just fourteen were farmers for all or substantial portions of their lives. Five practiced trades, at least two were entrepreneurs or merchants, three were laborers, two were industrial workers, and one became an architect and builder. It appears ten stayed in Minnesota the rest of their days, while five retired out of state. The other twelve sought their fortunes elsewhere in the familiar Midwest or, a few, far out West.

Many if not most of the liberators joined the Grand Army of the Republic, the most influential Union veterans' organization. The GAR lobbied quite successfully for generous pension rights for ex-soldiers. All but two applied for federal veteran disability pensions and gradually came onto the rolls according to the changing laws. Finally, just reaching a certain age constituted eligibility. Of the nine liberators who perished during the war, three left widows with young children who received pensions, as did two mothers and one father. Three liberators died in state or national soldiers' homes. So did, so far as is known, one widow, who was among twelve surviving spouses with pensions in their own right. The entire Civil War pension program, quite generous for its time, was a vital forerunner of Social Security and other government pension plans. In 1893, for example, 43 percent of Federal expenses were wrapped up in war pensions. The system was rife with corrupt practices, particularly for claiming disabilities that were not actually suffered.[1]

Most liberators experienced a ripe old age, and as a whole they well exceeded the average life expectancy in the post–Civil War era. Eight lived into their seventies, nine into their eighties, and two to their nineties. The last survivor was ninety-three-year-old Theobald B. Fenstermacher, who died on June 27, 1936, at Mill Grove in northern Missouri. At five feet three inches, he was one of the shortest men in the regiment. Soon leaving Mower County, he farmed in Iowa and after 1872 in Missouri. From 1892 until he retired, he worked on a railroad. His four sons were his pallbearers.[2]

Captain Francis Merchant, leader of the liberators, died in 1927 at age eighty-five in San Francisco, California. After the war he was a farmer in Mower County and in 1877 purchased the family farm in adjacent Freeborn County. In 1884 the post of county deputy sheriff lured him off the land. Two years later he became chief of police in Albert Lea, the Freeborn County seat. Exceptionally contentious local politics dogged his entire tenure. In December 1889, on being served with a huge frivolous lawsuit, he submitted a blistering letter of resignation that condemned some local officials for their "plot" against him, "bound by every means, however foul." Both the lawsuit and Merchant's countersuit for slander and libel were eventually dropped, but the legal fees impoverished him. He spent the next twenty years in Minneapolis as a streetcar driver and teamster and retired to the West Coast. Over the years Merchant stayed in close touch with his comrades in Company C and submitted numerous affidavits supporting their pension applications.[3]

Certainly worthy of the title "Honorary Liberator," Capt. Edwin W. Ford resided nearly all of his postwar life in La Crosse, Wisconsin, where he worked for the Chicago, Milwaukee & St. Paul Railroad and the city's board of public works, where he was familiarly known as "Uncle Ed." In 1904, deemed a "poor man in great need," he received a special pension increase through a private bill put through Congress. His last known occupation was janitor. A "staunch" Democrat "intensely interested" in politics, Ford prided himself on having voted in every presidential election between 1856 and 1924. He died in 1925 at age ninety-three in Chula Vista, California.[4]

After the war Capt. David W. Wellman resumed his successful practice of civil engineering. In 1898, at age seventy-three, he died at Los Gatos, California. Captain Jules Capon, the irrepressible "Big Frenchman," stayed in Wabasha, where he worked as a laborer and farmer. He was sixty-nine when he died in 1897. It was said that he "possessed all of the qualities of a brave soldier," that he "loved the American flag with a devotion immeasurable," and that he "was happiest when speaking of his exploits on the field of battle." Soon after the end of the war, to the regret of the citizens of Rochester, Lt. Col. William Markham moved to St. Louis and later to Aubrey, Kansas, where in October 1866, he died at age forty-two from typhoid fever and the rigors of wartime service. Colonel Josiah F. Marsh's tenure as an Alabama cotton planter proved brief, for by 1869 he had "lost his fortune." He tried various business ventures in Iowa, Ohio, and Indiana, but none were particularly successful. Marsh died in Chicago in 1886 at age sixty-two.[5]

Sergeant Major Edward L. Clapp became a grocer and postmaster in Franklin, Michigan, where he died in 1900 at age sixty-six. William Franklin Lyon was a longtime teacher of penmanship in the Detroit city schools and was seventy-five when he died in 1918 in Hart, Michigan. Bjørn Aslakson never recovered his health and died in 1888, at only fifty-seven, in Willmar, Minnesota, shortly after writing his Andersonville memoir in Norwegian. "When I think back to those days, my very soul seems to revolt and shudder." He would "often wake up in the night, shivering with fright and anguish, my body wet with clammy cold sweat," but relieved and thankful to God that the vision of the "deathly pale faces, the terrible gangrene infested sores, the insane look of despair" and the "moans of the dying" was "only a dream."[6]

Prolific Swedish diarist Andrew John Carlson was postmaster and ran a little newspaper in East Union, Minnesota, where, at age seventy-one, he died in 1909. William Johnston Dean became a successful Minneapolis businessman and aspiring politician. He died in 1910 at age sixty-seven. Myron Tower, who took good care of fellow prisoners at Andersonville and Florence, prospered in Lincoln, Nebraska. Surprisingly, he relocated to Texas, where he became mayor of La Porte, near Houston. He died in 1905 at age sixty-seven. Believed to be the final survivor of the Ninth Minnesota and certainly its last living prisoner of war, William Lovell of Sherburne County, Minnesota, who died in 1945 at age ninety-nine, was one of the last survivors of Andersonville.[7]

Reverend Thomas J. Sheppard of Ohio, beloved prisoner chaplain of Andersonville, completed his studies at Denison University after the war and continued as a Baptist pastor. He was chaplain of the Ohio Soldiers' and Sailors' Home as well as several veterans organizations. For years his many friends tried to get Congress to appoint him an honorary chaplain in the U.S. Army, an honor he richly deserved, but the politicians never took the appropriate action before his death in 1912 at age seventy-eight.[8]

Charles Willis Carter Walker, John's former master, died in 1880 at age fifty-nine on his Missouri farm. Brigadier General Egbert Benson Brown, who had ordered the arrest of the liberators, led a cavalry brigade in the fall of 1864 during Sterling Price's invasion of Missouri. That October, in the Battle of Westport, he was summarily relieved of command for not instantly obeying orders to attack. Tried by court-martial, he was acquitted and by the end of the war led the District of Rolla. He passed away in 1902 at age eighty-five in Cuba, Missouri. For some fantastic reason the 1994 *Civil War Book of Lists* named Brown the worst Union general of the war. Certainly many others (notably Samuel Sturgis) seem much more deserving of that particular honor. Captain Henry Wirz, the Andersonville commandant, was arrested soon after the war, tried by a military commission, and hanged on November 10, 1865. One of the crimes for which he was convicted was the murder of a certain Pvt. William Stewart of the Ninth Minnesota. There is no evidence William Stewart ever existed, and one must conclude the Indiana soldier who accused Wirz was a perjurer.[9]

Oddly enough, Otterville's only claim to fame today involves the saga of another eastbound train stripped by armed men of a precious cargo. On the evening of July 7, 1876, Jesse and Frank James, the three Younger brothers, and others halted a Missouri Pacific train at Rocky Cut, just east of Lamine Bridge, and removed $18,200. No one was killed, and the perpetrators got clean away. In another historical twist, the James gang subsequently, like the liberators at Brice's Crossroads, suffered a stinging defeat that led to death, wounds, and imprisonment for some of them. On September 7, 1876, the gang stormed the bank in Northfield, Minnesota, only to be shot to pieces by its citizens, who proved tougher than the famed desperadoes ever imagined.[10]

A Look at Some Liberators

Most of the liberators ended their days in quiet anonymity, their lives only faintly revealed through obituaries, censuses, and pension papers. For the most part, their personal triumphs and disasters remain private. However, some remarkable personal stories offer fuller portraits of nine liberators that enable them truly to emerge as personalities.

Born about 1824 in New York, Ira W. Padden brought his family from Canada in early 1856 to farm in Mower County. In three years of war, including three battles and one siege, he was never wounded or seriously ill. On

December 17, 1865, barely four months after he returned home to Austin, Minnesota, he and Patrick McEntee, a twenty-one-year-old Irishman from Lyndon Station, Wisconsin, were working the threshing machine on J. S. Decker's farm, two miles outside of town. McEntee, who was "feeding the machine," could not or would not match Padden's pace at stacking sheaves of wheat alongside. They exchanged "a few pleasant, unpleasant and irritable words." McEntee told Padden to put up his dukes, but he refused. McEntee stormed out but soon reappeared. "Padden [was] leaning on his fork" when "McEntee walked up" and shouted he was "ready to fight you now." Padden again shook his head. In front of six or seven witnesses, McEntee drew a revolver and shot him in the chest, killing him. None of the shocked bystanders restrained the murderer, who escaped, it was thought, back to Wisconsin. Although, commented the *Mower County Register,* Padden was "naturally very passionate and this passion caused him often to abuse his wife," there was "nothing here [that was] provocative." Padden's sudden death at age forty-one left his widow, Mary, to bring up their three young children. Oddly, she never applied for a federal veteran's pension. The state of Minnesota posted a five-hundred-dollar reward for McEntee's capture, but apparently he was never apprehended. Overcoming tough odds through talent and sheer hard work, Padden's seven-year-old son Ira became a prominent, prosperous, and highly respected citizen of Austin.[11]

Frederick Heilmann and John Henry Ehmke became casualties of the Industrial Age. Severely wounded in the right hand and thigh at Nashville, Fritz Heilmann spent over six months in the hospital. The government gave him a partial disability pension of four dollars per month. In 1870 he was working in a grist mill in southeastern Missouri when a terrible accident mangled his already injured right arm and forced its amputation above the elbow. He moved to Cherokee, Kansas, to be near his younger sister, Katharina Kiehl, who had a farm nearby. Over the years Heilmann, the sole surviving liberator who never married, also suffered the loss of his hearing. He became well known in Cherokee as "the one-arm deaf man." By 1880 he was boarding at and working on the farm of his good friend Jacob Roemick and had gradually saved enough money to buy several small adjoining lots in town.

On Sunday evening, September 10, 1882, Heilmann was walking on the railroad track south out of Cherokee toward nearby Scammonville and Roemick's place. He did not know there had been a change in schedule and that rapidly overtaking him was a passenger train making its first-ever Sunday trip. "The engineer of course saw him and supposed he would leave the track, but as the train got closer and he still remained on the track the warning was given, but too late. He didn't hear it and the engine was so near him and running so fast, about 33 miles an hour, that it was impossible to stop in time to save him." Heilmann "apparently saw or heard the train just as the engine was on him, and gave a jump up, the cowcatcher striking him, throwing him so that his head struck on the corner of the steam chest, smashing in the skull." Frederick Heilmann never regained consciousness and died on the afternoon of the twelfth at the Roemick house. He was forty-five years old. His sister inscribed his tombstone: "I have fought a good fight. I have finished my course. I have kept the faith."[12]

In 1865 Henry Ehmke resumed farming in Winona County, but he gave it up in 1872 for a partnership in a meat market on Main Street in Winona. In 1876 he sold his share of "Hass & Ehmke" and joined the L. C. Porter Milling Company, where he was a wheat inspector and weigh-master in charge of the elevator. In 1889 Ehmke's right leg "was torn off below the knee in the elevator machinery." The community held events to raise funds so the popular ex-soldier could afford the cost of an artificial limb. Unfortunately, the lawsuit against his powerful former employer apparently did not go as well. Ehmke was initially awarded $2,500 in compensation, but the defendant gained a new trial that evidently eliminated or severely limited any damages that were eventually paid. Severely strapped by his legal expenses, Ehmke had to take whatever jobs he could get. In 1900 he was working in Winona as a street sweeper. Three years later a private bill in Congress increased his federal disability pension to sixteen dollars per month. John Henry Ehmke finally retired in 1906 and died in 1929 at age eighty-eight in Winona.[13]

Enoch W. Pike and L. D. Stewart both chanced radical long-distance moves out West. After the war Pike returned to his father's farm in Winona County. The next year he married and became postmaster of tiny Lewiston. He hoped for much more. In the spring of 1867, he took what would be the biggest speculative plunge of all the liberators. In New Orleans he and his wife booked passage to Panama, crossed the disease-ridden isthmus, and sailed north along the Pacific coast to Oregon. After working as a carpenter in Salem, where his parents joined him, Pike bought a farm. A few years later, his savings were wiped out when a friend for whom he had guaranteed a loan "proved unreliable" and left him holding the bag.[14]

In May 1872 Pike took another great risk by once more pulling up stakes and shifting north across the Columbia River to the barren Klickitat country in southern Washington Territory. Taking advantage of the 1862 Homestead Act, he settled in the "bunch grass country" east of the town of Goldendale. The area was known for raising cattle, and no one yet had tried farming. "With a sick and discouraged wife, and a broken down team," Pike "found himself alone in that wild region. Laying his soldier's claim, however, and securing a little lumber, he erected the walls of his cabin, which an untimely snowstorm filled with drift before the roof was on. As the winter lingered he was obliged, in order to comply with the six months' clause of the [Homestead] law, to shovel out a room in the snow, and with robes, blankets and a rousing fire on the cellar-floor, to pass a night with his family in that storm-bound spot." Pike only scraped by that severe winter by carrying mail, "a very hard task." The next spring the ranchers, his nearest neighbors, confidently "predicted a failure of the crops. But believing that grain would grow where grass was luxurious," Pike "prepared a high, dry field, sowed it to grain, and planted it also with vegetables; and such was the success of his experiment that others followed his example." Through his innovative farming techniques, Pike greatly expanded his acreage and his fortune.[15]

In the spring of 1878, worried about Indian troubles because of the Bannock War raging south of the Columbia, the settlers around Goldendale formed a militia company, the "Klickitat Rangers," and elected Pike captain. That autumn angry residents of Yakima, north of Goldendale, arrested Chief Moses, longtime leader of the Sinkiuse-Columbia tribe, in connection with the murder of a white family. Deeply worried the elderly chief might be killed before he could even be tried, the Indian agent asked Pike's company to escort him to the Fort Simcoe jail. On the way Pike showed his steady nerves and cool temperament. "One member of the Klickitat Rangers proved that he was not above treachery by making an attempt on the life of the old chieftain, but the attention of the commander was attracted by the click of the gun as he cocked it to shoot Moses. Captain Pike was upon him in an instant, and he was easily overpowered and rendered harmless." Chief Moses was exonerated. Soon after he visited Washington, D.C., and met President Rutherford B. Hayes.[16]

In 1884 Pike moved to Goldendale, where he used nearly all his savings to build a livery stable, the "Red Barn." He soon handled important stage routes and mail contracts and dealt in wagons, farm implements, and tools. He helped found the first bank in Goldendale, and his growing wealth led to many investments in real estate and other ventures. Around 1890 he purchased the first telephone installed in town. In the meantime, in 1887 with the foundation of the Washington National Guard, Pike was elected lieutenant colonel of the Second Regiment. In 1890 he became its colonel and served in that post for eleven years. E. W. Pike retired in 1905 to Portland, Oregon, where he died in 1918. He was seventy-five years old.[17]

Marrying soon after the war, Latham Denison Stewart tried farming in Mower County and in Wisconsin before taking up a homestead in the wooded

Enoch W. Pike

lake country of far northwestern Minnesota. He built "a pretty little farm home in a grove of giant oaks" but "lived there just a few years longer than necessary to prove up his land," as "he did not like farming." In 1878 Stewart sought a fresh start as a carpenter in Bismarck, Dakota Territory. Eight years later he moved all the way west to Port Angeles on Puget Sound. Starting as a shipwright, he gradually switched to construction and eventually became a well-known local architect and building contractor. "Many of the early buildings in Port Angeles were built under and by him," including the opera house. In 1905 he bought a spread in nearby Dungess and discovered that farming was much more agreeable when one did not have to make a living by it. Stewart died in 1930 at age eighty-five in Port Angeles. His wife, Martha, who passed away in December 1947 at age ninety-six, was the last surviving liberator widow.[18]

The contrasting fortunes of Isaac Peterman and Hens G. Lüthye represent the ups and downs of family ties. In September 1864 Peterman, discharged due to deafness, came home to Mower County. He continued to farm there until the death of his wife, Barbara, in 1876, then bought a place near Marshalltown, Iowa. In 1882 at age sixty-two, he married Mary Ealy, who was thirty-one years younger than him. By 1887 Peterman keenly missed his children, who were all living elsewhere. "I am a goin to move to Wis," he advised the pension office. "I find as I grow old I must get near my Children. I have

3 in Wis and none hear. I have no home of my one [own]. Cant read nor rite
nor hear. I must go to my sons in Wisconsin where I can look to them for
help in my Old days." That October he and Mary relocated to Prairie Farm
near Rice Lake in northwestern Wisconsin. When his daughter Delana
Peterman Hall, who lived nearby, became deathly ill in early 1897, Peterman,
then probably seventy-six years old, "jumped on his horse and rode to Barron and back" to fetch a doctor. That ride of "36 miles in bitter winter cold
over roads that were snow covered" was "a feat that would be a challenge
for a young man in the top of condition." Sadly, Delana died two days later
on her forty-fifth birthday. In the 1900 census, Peterman, who certainly had
a sense of humor, gave his occupation as "capitalist." He died in 1902 at age
eighty-two at home.[19]

Isaac Peterman and sons

Hens (or Hans) Lüthye and his dysfunctional family became a saga all by themselves. The short (five feet five inches) and wiry German immigrant became famous in Winona as "Well Digger Hans," not only by excavating the vast majority of wells in and around town but also for a particular act of heroism. One Sunday morning in April 1874, Lüthye was bird hunting on the Wisconsin side of the Mississippi River when he witnessed a tragedy unfold. Five children of the John Schuler family had started across the river in a rowboat to attend church service in Winona when the fast current threw their boat against a snag and overturned it. The children "shrieked for help, which, by the greatest fortune," wrote the *Winona Daily Republican*, "was at hand, or all of them must have perished." Lüthye "ran with all his speed to his boat on the bank, sprang to the oars and pulled vigorously to the rescue, his boat going diagonally against the current." Eighteen-year-old Lina Schuler grasped her nine-year-old sister, Anna, but both girls swiftly sank in the swirling water. Joseph, twenty, Catherine, fourteen, and Charles, about eleven, held precariously on to the capsized boat. "Hans turned to catch the two girls as they rose to the surface. He saw something coming, but it proved to be only a bonnet. The two girls—the eldest and the youngest—never rose again." Lüthye grabbed Catherine "just as she was sinking" and rescued Joseph and Charles, who were "weak and suffering from cramp." He brought the boat "across to Winona, the girl wailing and bemoaning the sad fate of her sisters," who were never found.[20]

By 1885 Lüthye's own life had also gone drastically wrong. His second marriage failed, his wife, Barbara, would later claim, because of his "intemperate habits" and his failure to support her. The separation was not amicable. Their thirteen-year-old son, Ernest, eldest of three children, took things so hard that he ran away and completely disappeared. In 1889, crippled by severe rheumatism, Lüthye gained admittance to the beautiful new Minnesota Soldiers' Home outside Minneapolis. He died there in 1899 at age sixty-eight from vertigo caused by sunstroke, possibly an effect of the illness first incurred at Brice's Crossroads. When Barbara Lüthye, who in the interval had moved to Colorado, applied for her widow's pension, she received a nasty shock. When they married in 1869, Hens told her he had divorced his first wife, but he apparently never did. Thus, the second marriage was not legal, and the government denied Barbara a pension. In 1910 after years of insisting that she "has been abandoned by all of her children," she finally gained passage of a private pension bill through Congress, but by that time she was a patient in the Insane Ward of the Denver County Hospital.[21]

In the meantime, long-lost Ernest Lüthye turned up in 1907 in Winona along with "Jumbo," a massive python. They were one of the circus acts the town had booked for a huge celebration and street fair. He had quite a tale to tell his old hometown friends. Running away to join the circus was the fondest dream of many a disheartened child, but Ernest actually did it. He succeeded in being hired by the fabled Buffalo Bill Wild West Show in the era when Annie Oakley and Chief Sitting Bull were its principal performers. In 1887 he accompanied the show to Europe and stayed there when it returned to America in 1893. In Hamburg, Ernest was tattooed in intricate patterns all over his body—"certainly a very fine piece of work as can be seen upon looking at him," noted the *Winona Republican Herald*—and toured the continent with another show as "the tattooed man." Ten years followed in the Carl Hagenbeck Circus, the renowned animal trainers, where he learned to handle all kinds of critters but came to like reptiles best. Coming home to America about 1905, Ernest Lüthye continued to show snakes around the country. He married and eventually settled in Minnesota, where he became a merchant and farmer.[22]

It is deeply ironic that the oldest and youngest liberators—thirty-two years apart in age—were both tried in criminal court for dire felonies. In fact they were the only two known to have run seriously afoul of the law. In the case of the younger, guilt was not in question as he pled guilty. The same was manifestly not true for the elder, whose very life hung in the balance.

Allen S. Hilton went astray after returning to Winona in May 1865 when he was only seventeen or possibly still sixteen. Very likely he had a difficult time adjusting to his wartime experiences. The youngest Civil War soldiers were particularly vulnerable to developing "symptoms of diseases that have been linked to battlefield trauma." On April 17, 1867, two years to the day from when he was formally paroled at Vicksburg (he spent nearly a year at Cahaba), he was convicted of assault with intent to commit great bodily harm. No indication in the source is given as to why the attack took place. The judge had intended to sentence Hilton to a lengthy term in state prison, but "owing to the youth of the prisoner, and the earnest entreaties of his mother in his behalf," he instead set a fine of three hundred dollars. That sum was "immediately paid into court, and the prisoner was discharged." Such a stiff fine was a tremendous burden for Hilton's family. That summer his mother, Rohanna, and stepfather, James W. Curry, defaulted on their mortgage and lost their property. In the 1870 census, Hilton (age twenty-two, a house painter) was recorded as living in Winona with his twenty-year-old wife, Villie (a milliner), and his mother, who ran a boardinghouse. There was no mention of James Curry. That is the last trace of Allen Hilton and his family in any available source. Neither he nor a widow or dependent ever applied for a federal pension for his Civil War service.[23]

Reverend John Arnold's horrific encounter with the legal system came near the end of his very long life. A few years after the war, his second wife, Susan, died in Minnesota. In November 1868 he married Melissa Luick, a "grass widow" whose divorce was due to her first husband's infidelity. For a time they lived on her farm in northern Iowa, where they had a daughter. In 1869 when Arnold missed the North Iowa Annual Conference of the United Brethren, the presiding elder took back his license to preach and erased his name from the rolls, but there is no indication he was removed for cause. Arnold remained an ordained minister and certainly did not give up his religious work. In later years he worshiped in the Baptist Church.[24]

In the early 1870s, Arnold (who among all the liberators was the greatest wanderer) took his family to central California, where he bought a farm in Tulare County. For reasons not known, he and Melissa divorced in 1876. Their young daughter, Eva, stayed with her mother. Melissa Arnold died in 1883 in California. In the meantime, in 1880 John Arnold returned to his old home territory in Wellington, Ohio, and in May married Samantha, his fourth wife. She died in Ohio in 1889. Two years later, in Wellington, Arnold, at age seventy-five, wed another widow, Eliza Thompson, who was nine years younger than him. It was his fifth marriage and her fourth. For years Arnold operated a stand in Wellington that sold "candies, nuts, soft drinks etc." In addition he was well known for "frequently going out into the country to preach in school houses," as well as for performing weddings and officiating at funerals. He particularly enjoyed marching with the local Salvation Army group.[25]

In early 1892 Eliza Arnold came down with stomach cancer and by August was an invalid. At the beginning of December, Arnold gave up his candy business to devote full time to her care. During late morning on the twelfth, Eliza asked him for his penknife so she could pare her nails. A few minutes later, he noticed she was in great difficulty and appeared to be dying. He ran to the neighbors for help and sent for the doctor. Eliza passed away less than an hour later. She had one "very small wound in the throat," and when the doctor moved her, they could see that blood had soaked the bed beneath her. Arnold was stunned to realize she had stabbed herself to death. Thirty-seven years before, his first wife, Harriett had killed their youngest child and herself. In deep shock, he kissed Eliza, asked a neighbor to watch over the house and her body, and advised he would return the next morning. He left to rent a buggy to ride to the old family homestead at Kipton, eleven miles northwest of Wellington, where he would arrange for Eliza's burial in the family cemetery plot alongside his first and fourth wives.[26]

Among some of the neighbors, however, "strong suspicion was at once aroused that foul play had taken place, as Mr. Arnold had taken a penknife from his pocket covered with blood, in the presence of the persons who were first called in, which he claimed he had picked up on the bed when he went into the room and found her struggling, previous to calling the neighbors. Blood was also observed on his hands, while the hands of the deceased were perfectly clean." In Arnold's absence great alarm, almost mass hysteria, swept through Wellington. The mayor summoned the county coroner. When Arnold returned the next morning, "he was very much surprised upon learning of the mission of the [coroner] and insisted upon a thorough investigation." After conducting a postmortem and hearing witnesses, the coroner remanded the case to the prosecuting attorney. On December 15 Arnold was arrested and charged with murdering his wife by a single stab to the throat with a penknife, inflicting a fatal wound one quarter inch long and two inches deep. He pled not guilty.[27]

At the preliminary hearing, Arnold testified that Eliza had asked for his penknife and that ten minutes later he returned to find her "in obvious distress." Noticing his knife sitting on the bed, he absentmindedly returned it to his vest pocket. "I did everything I could to save her, but she died. I first thought of suicide when they called my attention to the cut or wound. I could see the cut though it was quite small. I had never seen anything in her conduct or actions to indicate disarrangement or insanity, though I thought she had been unusually quiet for a few days. I did not cut or wound her. I saw no blood on her hands or neck." Arnold affirmed that only "the most pleasant relations existed between himself and wife through their married life—never had any unpleasantness whatever." He was not believed. On December 17 he was bound over for trial and taken to the Cleveland jail. The court set bail at twenty thousand dollars—a fantastic sum for the time. Three friends, including a nephew, gave sureties to enable his release.[28]

Newspapers all over the country, intrigued by the drama of a minister being charged with the murder of his fifth wife, printed the notice of a real-life "Bluebeard." In February 1893 the grand jury indicted Arnold for premeditated murder with the death penalty. A Wellington newspaper remarked in March that "the man out on bail for wife murder, is seen at his old home occasionally, but does not meet with a very cordial reception from his former neighbors, especially those who are best acquainted with the details concerning his late wife's death."[29]

In late March the trial opened in Elyria, the Lorain County seat. Legal luminaries handled the prosecution and the defense. Over seventy-five witnesses had been summoned, and spectators crowded the courtroom. According to one reporter, Arnold sat "in court as stoical as an Indian, and no one would suspect he was on trial for his life." The state presented its case over four days, followed by the defense. In general Arnold testified in a "calm and deliberate manner," but "at times" he was "deeply affected and shedding tears," especially when the defense attorney asked, "Did you stab your wife in the neck?" One reporter wrote, the defendant "is evidently a man of strong determination and bears his trial with remarkable fortitude." He was a "good provider and a kind man." Arnold steadfastly denied any ill feelings toward his late wife or harming her in any way. Strong character witnesses supported his assertions. Further testimony brought out that his eyesight was poor and his hands were "very much palsied," which threw doubt on his ability to inflict the single, precise fatal blow that his wife suffered.[30]

On April 1 the jury retired to decide on a verdict. "During each day while the jury was deliberating on the question of his life or death, it was pitiful to see the old man sitting, often alone, in his place at the trial table, with his eyes fixed intently upon the door through which the jury departed." Finally on the fourth, the jury dramatically announced it was deadlocked, with eight for conviction and four for acquittal. Because "the state has failed to make a case against the accused," Arnold was released, though the terms of his bail were to remain in effect until the end of the current court session. The state had to decide whether to try him again. "So far as we have been able to learn," wrote the *Wellington Enterprise,* "a majority of the people in this place believe him to be guilty, but the jury heard all of the testimony and four of them took a different view of the matter."[31]

In May Arnold's bail was renewed at twenty thousand dollars. After having a chance to reflect, the *Enterprise* took a different stance. "Unless the state can produce additional evidence of guilt we are inclined to think the case had better be dropped." The "aged gentleman has been deprived of his liberty for five months and left penniless in the bargain. In view of the doubts existing in the case this would seem to be a sufficient punishment." In fact, if Arnold were truly innocent, there should have been no punishment at all.[32]

By October Arnold was "in very feeble health," and it was thought he would not survive "the ordeal of another trial." The prevailing opinion was the case would be dismissed, as "public opinion favors that disposition." Finally in November 1893—thirty years after the liberation of John's family in Missouri—all charges were dropped. At that time the *Lorain County Reporter* decided it was proper to comment at length on the indictment and the trial. "There were certain indices, plainly appearing in this case, which were conclusive proof that the defendant ought not to be condemned." Because of "some extravagance of thought and action" among neighbors and local officials, deep distrust had overpowered careful reasoning. "Little circumstances were magnified, first in their description and many times more in their repetition until such suspicions were aroused, that even the most natural and innocent acts of the accused [were] given a criminal coloring." The evidence was in fact "insufficient to justify a conviction." Testimony was firm that "Arnold had treated his wife with the utmost kindness, nursing her with tender care through a long and painful sickness. The wife had testified to this to her physician and many others who called upon her." Nor was it logical for him to have committed such a murder by violence since there was "morphine in the house sufficient to have killed ten persons [and] would have left no trace." Arnold, moreover, "was a feeble old man, almost blind and very clumsy." It was very unlikely he could have inflicted with surgical precision just such a single tiny wound to a vein without getting bloodstains on himself or his clothing. The original claim that he had blood on his hands and his clothes was not sustained by the evidence. Arnold had retained the knife, whereas a "murderer would have discarded it." There was "no evidence of preparation" or "anything which showed a disposition to conceal or cover up the evidence of his guilt." His wife was melancholic over her painful, fatal illness. "All circumstances strongly tended to show that the wound was self-inflicted." The newspaper concluded: "That he was not guilty we have always firmly believed and now more than ever when the State has also pronounced that verdict."[33]

After finally being freed, Arnold relocated to Chico in northern California where his daughter Ida (his and Susan's child) lived. His youngest daughter, Eva, was in Ione, 130 miles south. They appear to have been his only living children, but there were grandchildren as well. Reduced to a pauper by his legal expenses, Arnold was in 1900, at eighty-four, still working as a day laborer. At age eighty-nine, he died in Chico in June 1905, "after a long illness, principally from the infirmities of old age." Despite all the tragedies he endured, which culminated in a murder trial the *Lorain County Reporter* described as "a terrible ordeal second only to death," Rev. John Arnold never lost his faith in God. His obituary described his life's work as a "missionary preacher, which since engrossed his time."[34]

Thus the liberators completed the span of their years. They have gone on ahead along with the rest of the Civil War generation, including sadly, in complete anonymity, John and his entire family. We can only hope their full story will yet come to light.

CONCLUSION

Drops in the Sea of Blue

FIDELITY AND COURAGE

The saga of the thirty-eight liberators during the Civil War is a part of the greater story of the Ninth Minnesota Volunteer Infantry in the struggle to destroy Southern slavery and reunite the United States. The Minnesotans overcame the shame of one of the bitterest defeats of the war at Brice's Crossroads to triumph at Tupelo, Nashville, and Mobile. Over two hundred endured hell on earth at Andersonville and other Confederate prisons at a staggering cost of lives. Ultimately, though, the liberators, as with all their comrades in the Ninth Minnesota, were just drops in the vast sea of Yankee blue, sharing to one degree or another the fortunes, good and bad, of the more than a million Union men who fought and won that most terrible of American wars. It is the excellence of the surviving documentation that, 150 years later, fortunately allows a better understanding and appreciation of their specific contribution to that victory.

If their overall narrative is one of common experience in the Civil War, what the liberators did at Otterville on November 11, 1863, sets them apart in one vital respect. Their actions there help illuminate a fundamental controversy: Just why did Northern soldiers fight? The obvious answer is to put down the rebellious Southern states and preserve the Union. Waging war with such fervor and ferocity underscored the enmity most Northerners bore against the Southerners that matched the South's own hatred for the North. Still quite contentious are the extent of anti-slavery sentiment among the Northern soldiers and the true level of their support for emancipation. One school of thought holds that in fact a considerable and ever-growing percentage of Union soldiers came rather early to identify slavery as the predominant cause of the conflict and to readily accommodate, if not wholeheartedly cheer, emancipation. The other point of view counters that the current overwhelming "focus on emancipation and race" stresses contemporary values in the place of the original period beliefs and obscures what Union soldiers really thought at the time. As historian Gary W. Gallagher writes, only "a small minority of soldiers enthusiastically greeted news of emancipation as a moral accomplishment." Humanitarian considerations were at first only a minimal factor as to the way Union troops viewed black people in general and slaves in particular. Before the war many Northerners, Gallagher notes, "could go about their lives without encountering many, if any, African Americans." Sympathy for the slaves and freedmen grew only gradually as more bluecoats came to see and understand their plight.[1]

Where in light of these competing interpretations do the Ninth Minnesota and the incident at Otterville properly fit? It would seem the preponderance of evidence supports the contention that very few Northerners at the outset of the war would have put the destruction of slavery very high on their list of war goals. Only later did ending slavery emerge as a valuable tool in harming the Southern war effort and morale. It is evident, therefore, the anti-slavery sentiment of a high percentage of the Ninth Minnesota clearly differed from the vast majority of the Union army. In common with other Northern volunteers, the Minnesotans had enlisted in August 1862 consumed with the desire to punish the seceded states and restore the Union. The war effort had faltered and desperately needed their help. Slavery itself was at most a peripheral issue for nearly all of them. Reverend John Arnold was probably one of the very few members of the Ninth Minnesota who was a committed abolitionist prior to the war. The men, nonetheless, appear to have hewed strongly to the Republican Party and to the general concept of emancipation. They had a great distaste for slaveholders, no matter how loyally the masters might support the Union. Once they got their first actual look at the appalling reality of slavery in Missouri, they understood the baleful institution not only harmed the enslaved but degraded their masters. Many Union soldiers in Missouri and Kentucky, in particular, were completely disgusted at having to preserve slavery while the rest of the Union army did everything it could in the seceded Southern states to eradicate it. The furor surrounding the Missouri state elections only intensified Radical sympathies in the Ninth Minnesota for the swift and decisive end of slavery, a cause that resounded in numerous statements expressed by liberators and their comrades both before and following the rescue of John's family at Otterville.

Despite everything, however, the dramatic appearance of John himself at the Lamine camp transformed anti-slavery feelings into action. His sincere, emotional, and necessarily articulate plea to the soldiers to prevent his family from being shipped out of state, separated, and sold, affected Capt. Edwin Ford and the thirty-eight volunteers in a way no abstract declaration of rights could ever have. They personally could no longer abide such rank injustice and hastened to rectify the situation in disobedience of strict army orders. Despite the presence of superior officers who demanded they desist, the Minnesotans effected the liberation, tragically brief as it may have been, of Charles W. C. Walker's ten slaves. The Otterville outrage transformed the Ninth Minnesota from merely an exception with regard to emancipation into something quite exceptional and, in its own way, wonderful. When the call came for justice, the liberators of the Ninth Minnesota were not found wanting.

Yet there was more to the liberation than simply high-minded principles. The liberators were not magically cleansed of the race and class prejudices so prevalent in white America of that era. Afterward, when faced with serious charges and harsh punishment, there was equivocation and rationalization on the part of some and their champions. Nonetheless, a bond had formed at a basic human level between John and the liberators that transcended ideology.

It is supremely ironic that that primal connection would eventually be brought into sharper focus in a way no one could possibly have imagined in 1863 through John Arnold's own tragic ordeal thirty years later. Wellington, Ohio, where he lived many years and where he was arrested for the murder of his fifth wife, had witnessed one of the most famous and noble pre-war "forcible slave rescues." In 1858 abolitionists from there and nearby Oberlin stormed a hotel and in a bloodless coup freed the escaped slave John Price from his captors and spirited him to safety in Canada. Thirty-seven Ohio "liberators" were arrested, jailed, and indicted for Price's rescue. Two were ultimately convicted before all were subsequently released. They were then and are today justly honored in their communities for their selfless action in defense of liberty.

In 1893, while on trial in nearby Elyria, Ohio, John Arnold faced the hangman's noose in a legal process tainted by hysteria, unreason, and a precipitous rush to judgment. Many of his fellow Wellingtonians vehemently demanded his conviction and swift execution for a crime of which he was completely innocent. Only the refusal of the four anonymous jurors from Elyria to vote for conviction prevented a terrible miscarriage of justice. "That [Arnold] is alive today, innocent though he is," the *Lorain County Reporter* editorialized in November 1893, resulted solely from "the courage and firmness of the men who stood to their convictions with a fidelity and courage worthy of all praise." Those four particular jurors had shown a "firmness and conscientious charge of the duty, as they understand it" and "could not be coerced into rendering a verdict contrary to their sense of right and justice."[2]

Those handsome words could with equal justice have been applied to the rescuers of John Price in 1858 as well as to John Arnold and the other thirty-seven Minnesota soldiers who, in 1863, also defied authority to save one black family from another horrible fate. Redemption for John the escaped slave from Oberlin, John the Missouri slave, and John the Ohio minister ultimately rested on the honor, goodwill, and firm resolution of strangers who responded so magnificently in their hour of greatest need.

Acknowledgments

Many individuals, institutions, and organizations have graciously contributed their resources, expertise, and time to the creation of this book. The mere mention of some of them here can only be a token of my warmest gratitude for them all.

This project was originally supposed to result in an article for the Minnesota Historical Society, which had awarded me a research grant in 2002. A trip that fall to St. Paul and to several other historical societies in southern Minnesota swiftly persuaded me there was plenty of material on the Ninth Minnesota to justify a book. I am most grateful to MHS for its patience in seeing this project to its conclusion and particularly thank Deborah Miller, Sally Rubinstein, and Civil War historian Hampton Smith for their support. At the Minnesota Historical Society Press, Shannon Pennefeather and Ann Regan have been instrumental in the publication of this book, as has my editor, Andrea Rud.

In addition to the Minnesota Historical Society, institutions that have provided invaluable documents include the Mower County Historical Society, Olmsted County Historical Society, Winona County Historical Society (and Winona State University's tremendously useful Winona Newspaper Project online archive), and the Carver County Historical Society. I owe a special debt of gratitude to Nan Card, Curator of Manuscripts at the Rutherford B. Hayes Presidential Center. At the National Archives, archivists DeAnne Blanton and Juliette Arai have been most helpful. Professional genealogist Bonnie Cary has diligently copied numerous service records and pension files, and I am especially grateful to her. Other organizations of real value for my research are the Brice's Crossroads Visitors and Interpretive Center, headed by Edwina Carpenter; the Andersonville National Historic Site; the University of Iowa Special Collections; the State Historical Society of Iowa; the Wisconsin Historical Society; the John Nau III Civil War Collection; and the Wilson's Creek National Battlefield. At the Herrick Memorial Library in Wellington, Ohio, Lynne Welch was especially kind to provide newspaper accounts of the tragic misfortune of liberator John Arnold. This is my first book that has truly benefited from the myriad resources available on the Internet. Such online research organizations as Ancestry.com, Fold Three, Newspaper Archive, Genealogy Bank, the Library of Congress's Chronicling America, and the National Park Service Civil War Soldiers database are invaluable.

In exploring various aspects of the liberator story, I was greatly aided by other scholars and researchers. In Minnesota, I would like to thank Jerald Anderson, Roger Norland, and Stephen E. Osman. General Parker Hills has shared his unparalleled knowledge of the battlefield of Brice's Crossroads and is a good friend. We hope to work together in the near future. Tommy Lee, Dr. John Chisolm, and Bjorn Skaptason have also been helpful regarding Brice's Crossroads. Dr. Richard Sauers very kindly gave me the citations on Brice's Crossroads from his extensive index of the *National Tribune*. For the subject of Union soldiers in Confederate prisons, I could have had no better guide than John Lundquist and his wife, Carol. Jack showed me the ropes when it came to Andersonville and Cahaba. Other prison experts of great help have been Rev. Albert Ledoux, the authority on Florence Prison, and Robert S. Davis and Kevin Frye on Andersonville. Edmund Raus, a retired National Park Service historian, also aided my Minnesota research, and Frank Crawford shared his extensive work on the Ninety-Fifth Illinois. My old museum colleague H. Michael Madaus, a world-class authority on Civil War flags and weapons; renowned Civil War historian Lance Herdegen; and Dan Joyce, Director of the Kenosha Museum, also helped me to learn more about the Civil War.

A real pleasure has been making the acquaintance of descendants of soldiers of the Ninth Minnesota. Those who have provided extremely valuable documents and photographs include Dean B. Krafft, Helene Leaf, Brian and Janet Schumacher, Jeff Glover, Carol Jauregui, Dianne M. Bower Clegg and Susan N. Bower-Litzenberger, Dorene Conti, Hiram McCoy, Gay Wilhelm, Loren Rochester, Jean C. Pool, Richard Aslakson, David Beaulieu, Lois Paulson-Kvamme, Jerry Kagele, A. J. Jackson, and Margie Williams Jackson.

Richard Frank, Robert Mrazek, Dr. Craig Symonds, James Denny, and J. Michael Wenger have read all or portions of the manuscript, and I am most indebted to them for their comments and corrections. I am responsible for all errors of fact and interpretation that remain. My stalwart friends Bruce C.

Cazel, Craig Smith, Dr. Steve Ewing, Dr. Darek Ciemniewski, Robert H. G. Thomas, and James Rindt kindly served as sounding boards for my ideas, as often did my fellow museum curators Carter Lupton and Albert Muchka. The superb physical therapists and nurses of the rehabilitation wing of the Aurora–St. Luke's Medical Center in Milwaukee could not have been kinder during two long hospital stays. They referred to my room, with its piles of research books and documents, as my "office." Pastor George Richter also provided steadfast support.

My family has played a more important role in this research than in any of my previous books. My grandmother passed on the family Civil War letters to me. Mother strongly encouraged my research and writing. She had fervently hoped to read this book, but she departed this life too soon. Finally, I express my deepest appreciation to my dear wife, Sandy, and daughter, Rachel Lundstrom Gladis. Sandy, my closest associate in this and all my endeavors, read every word of every draft and provided invaluable counsel and support. This is also the fifth book for which she drew the maps. I simply could not do this work without her.

APPENDIX

The Liberators

THE LIBERATORS

Company C

John Arnold
Born probably March 1, 1816, Milton, Saratoga County, New York
Died June 4, 1905, Chico, Butte County, California
Chico Cemetery

George Henry Bullard
Born July 1827, Chautauqua County, New York
Died September 30, 1902, Red Bluff, Tehama County, California
Red Bluff Cemetery

Stephen N. Chandler
Born November 30, 1839, Sherbrooke County, Canada East (Quebec)
Died October 31, 1864, Millen, Georgia
Beaufort, South Carolina, National Cemetery, Plot 41–4804

Joshua C. Epler
Born February 5, 1840, Cape May, New Jersey
Died June 9, 1904, Great Falls, Montana
Old Highland Cemetery, Great Falls

David F. M. Felch
Born 1844, Racine, Wisconsin
Died September 30, 1864, Memphis, Tennessee
Memphis National Cemetery, Plot 3774

Zara Frisbie
> Born April 17, 1834, White Creek, Washington County, New York
> Died August 19, 1864, Andersonville, Georgia
> Andersonville National Cemetery, Grave 6191

John W. Hartley
> Born February 17, 1839, Warren County, Ohio
> Died March 6, 1903, Indiana State Soldiers' Home, Lafayette, Indiana
> Twin Cities Cemetery, Pennville, Jay County, Indiana

Joseph H. Lagree
> Born October 1840, Wisconsin
> Died December 29, 1908, Tomah, Wisconsin
> Greenfield Cemetery, Tunnel City, Monroe County, Wisconsin

Noah McCain
> Born c. 1840, Green County, Indiana
> Date and place of death unknown

Francis Merchant
> Born September 20, 1842, Toledo, France
> Died October 1, 1927, San Francisco, California
> Oakwood Cemetery, Austin, Mower County, Minnesota

Ira W. Padden
> Born c. 1824, New York
> Died December 17, 1865, Austin, Mower County, Minnesota
> Oakwood Cemetery

Nathan N. Palmeter
> Born June 17, 1843, Nova Scotia, Canada
> Died November 16, 1919, Mayfield, Grand Traverse County, Michigan
> Evergreen Cemetery

Isaac Peterman
> Born probably March 26, 1820, Ohio
> Died June 29, 1902, Prairie Farm, Barron County, Wisconsin
> Evergreen Cemetery

Erastus Slocum
> Born December 28, 1843, Cattaraugus County, New York
> Died February 3, 1916, Long Beach, California
> Long Beach Municipal Cemetery

Latham Denison Stewart
Born July 30, 1844, Western, Oneida County, New York
Died January 14, 1930, Port Angeles, Washington
Acacia Park Cemetery, Seattle, Washington

Daniel B. Vaughan
Born July 3, 1835, Red Ford, Clinton County, New York
Died February 4, 1921, Lansing, Mower County, Minnesota
Lansing Cemetery

Evan Watkins
Born May 25, 1840, Llanblisier, Radnorshire, Wales, United Kingdom
Died June 20, 1919, Austin, Mower County, Minnesota
Oakwood Cemetery

John Richard Watkins Jr.
Born February 16, 1836, Wales, United Kingdom
Died January 2, 1913, Mower County, Minnesota
Cedar City Cemetery

Augustus Whitney
Born c. 1835, New York
Died June 10, 1864, Brice's Crossroads, Mississippi
Location of grave unknown

Siloam Williams
Born July 23, 1833, Derby Center, Vermont
Died March 16, 1922, Oakland, Shawnee County, Kansas
White City, Kansas

Company K

Jacob Bader
Born c. 1844, Wurttemberg, Germany
Died July 4, 1864, Mobile, Alabama
Mobile National Cemetery, Plot 445

Hiram A. Buck
Born July 22, 1838, Delaware County, Ohio
Died November 8, 1913, Winnebago, Faribault Country, Minnesota
Riverside Cemetery

Charles Dietrich
Born December 14, 1843, Hasselrode, Prussia
Died October 17, 1864, Savannah, Georgia
Location of grave unknown

Pierre Demars
Born c. 1835, Canada East (Quebec)
Date and place of death unknown

John Henry Ehmke
Born December 24, 1840, Holstein, Germany
Died March 9, 1929, Winona, Minnesota
Woodlawn Cemetery

Theobald B. Fenstermacher
Born January 27, 1843, Cottawissa, Columbia County, Pennsylvania
Died June 27, 1936, Mill Grove, Mercer County, Missouri
Salem Cemetery

George Frahm
Born c. 1839, Germany
Died May 9, 1865, Jefferson Barracks, St. Louis, Missouri
Jefferson Barracks National Cemetery, Plot 45–0–1843

John Gordon
Born July 4, 1827, County Westmeath, Ireland
Died March 30, 1918, Houston County, Minnesota
Ridgway Cemetery

Frederick Heilmann
Born March 16, 1837, Hesse-Darmstadt, Germany
Died September 12, 1882, Scammonville, Cherokee County, Kansas
Cherokee Cemetery

Allen S. Hilton
Born c. 1848, Maine
Date and place of death unknown

Henry Jansen
Born May 31, 1832, Schleswig-Holstein, Germany
Died January 5, 1901, Winona, Minnesota
Woodlawn Cemetery

Hens G. Lüthye
Born c. 1831 (or c. 1834), Schleswig, Schleswig-Holstein, Germany
Died May 12, 1899, Minnesota Soldiers' Home, Minneapolis, Minnesota
Location of grave unknown

Samuel Mickel
Born September 18, 1833, Napoli, Cattaraugus County, New York
Died August 20, 1917, Ogden, Utah
Ogden City Cemetery

John Morrison
Born c. 1828, Scotland
Died November 11, 1864, Florence, South Carolina
Florence National Cemetery, unknown grave

Enoch W. Pike
Born April 13, 1842, Franklin County, Maine
Died March 19, 1918, Portland, Oregon
Rose City Cemetery

Lyman Raymond
Born March 13, 1844, Oneida, New York
Died December 29, 1925, Weiser, Idaho
Hillcrest Cemetery

Pierre Rodier
Born January 15, 1835, St. Hyacinth, St. Hyacinth County, Canada East
(Quebec)
Died March 17, 1914, Wabasha, Minnesota
Riverview Cemetery

Jacob Thielen
Born c. 1841, Germany
Died September 16, 1864, Andersonville, Georgia
Andersonville National Cemetery, Grave 9003

Notes

NOTES TO CHAPTER ONE

1. *The War of the Rebellion: A Compilation of the Official Records of the Union and Confederate Armies*, series 1–4, 70 vols. in 128 (Washington, D.C.: 1880–1901) (hereafter cited as *OR*); *OR*, ser. 3, vol. 2, 200, 295–96; *New York Evening Post*, 16 July 1862.

2. General sources on Minnesota history include William Watts Folwell, *A History of Minnesota*, vols. 1 and 2 (St. Paul: Minnesota Historical Society Press, 1956–61), and Theodore C. Blegen, *Minnesota: A History of the State*, 2nd ed. (St. Paul: University of Minnesota Press, 1975).

3. General sources on Minnesota in the Civil War include Minnesota, Board of Commissioners, *Minnesota in the Civil and Indian Wars 1861–1865*, 2nd ed., 2 vols. (St. Paul: Pioneer Press, 1891–99) (hereafter cited as *MICIW*), and Kenneth Carley, *Minnesota in the Civil War: An Illustrated History* (St. Paul: Minnesota Historical Society Press, 2000).

4. Folwell, *History of Minnesota*, 2:100–104; *Rochester City Post*, 26 July 1862.

5. *Winona Daily Republican*, 12 Aug. 1862; Franklyn Curtiss-Wedge, *The History of Mower County Minnesota* (Chicago: H.C. Cooper Jr., 1911), 332.

6. Folwell, *History of Minnesota*, 2:104; *Mankato Weekly Record*, 9 Aug. 1862; *Rochester City Post*, 16 Aug. 1862.

7. On the formation and history of the Ninth Minnesota, see the "Narrative of the Ninth Regiment" by Colin F. Macdonald in *MICIW*, 1:416–54, and the Ninth Minnesota's Record of Events in *Supplement to the Official Records of the Union and Confederate Armies*, vol. 32 (ser. no. 44) (Wilmington, N.C.: Broadfoot Publishing, 1996), 148–83; *St. Cloud Democrat*, 14 Aug. 1862.

8. *St. Cloud Times*, 21 Aug. 1912; *St. Cloud Daily Times*, 11 Aug. 1919; Loren Cray, "Experiences in Southwestern Minnesota 1859 to 1867," *Collections of the Minnesota Historical Society* 15 (1915): 444.

9. Curtiss-Wedge, *Mower County*, 152–54.

10. Ole Paulson, *Memoirs: Rev. Ole Paulson: Reminiscences of a Pioneer Pastor in America, 1850–1885*, trans. Torstein O. Kvamme (Wisconsin, 1981). A portion of the

memoir was also translated for the *Chaska Valley Herald* in 1933. The quotations in this and the following paragraph are from the 9 Mar. 1933 issue.

11. Fundamental sources on the U.S.–Dakota War include *MICIW,* Folwell, *History of Minnesota,* vol. 2, and Kenneth Carley, *The Dakota War of 1862: Minnesota's Other Civil War* (St. Paul: Minnesota Historical Society Press, 1976); Cray, "Experiences," 439.

12. *Chaska Valley Herald,* 30 Mar. 1933.

13. A. J. Carlson's extensive memoirs appeared in the *East Union News* (Carver County, Minn.) between 1895 and 1899; quotation here from 15 Jan. 1898 issue. I am much indebted to Helene Leaf for this excellent source. Pehr Carlson letters, 23 Sept. 1862 and 16 Apr. 1864, Pehr Carlson and Family Papers, Minnesota Historical Society, St. Paul.

14. *Chaska Valley Herald,* 9 Mar. 1933.

15. Burn [Bjørn] Aslakson's memoir *Ti Maaneders fangenskab i Andersonville* was published in Minneapolis in 1887. A translation by Richard Aslakson is in Torbjørn Greipsland, *Nordmenn i dødsleirene: Tusen norske soldater døde i den amerikanske borgerkrigen* [Norwegian Soldiers in the Prison Camps during the American Civil War] (Norway: Emigrantforlaget, 2005), 181–95. Quote from Greipsland, 181.

16. *MICIW,* 2:232.

17. Marion P. Satterlee, "Narratives of the Sioux War," *Collections of the Minnesota Historical Society* 15 (1915): 349–70; Roger Avery Stubbs, *Milton Aurelius and Elizabeth Eleanor Turnham Stubbs* (Long Lake, Minn.: Stubbs, 1938), 4–9; Folwell, *History of Minnesota,* 2:159–60, 416.

18. "Sample Letters of Immigrants," *Wisconsin Magazine of History* 20, no. 4 (June 1937): 437–38; *Winona Daily Republican,* 20 Jan. 1876.

19. *MICIW,* 2:270, 287–88. On the Felch family, Curtiss-Wedge, *Mower County,* 893–94; David F. M. Felch letter, 21 Nov. 1862, and Emma Hurlbut letter, 29 Oct. 1862, Charles H. Steffens and Family Papers, Minnesota Historical Society, St. Paul.

20. On Wilkin, see Alexander Wilkin and Family Papers, Minnesota Historical Society, St. Paul, and Ronald M. Hubbs, "The Civil War and Alexander Wilkin," *Minnesota History* 39, no. 5 (Spring 1965): 173–90; on the duel, see *New York Herald,* 2 June 1848; Hubbs, *Alexander Wilkin,* 174.

21. On Marsh, Compiled Military Service Record (CMSR) and Pension File No. 277,528. CMSRs are found in National Archives, Records of the Adjutant General Office, 1780's–1917, Book Records of Volunteer Union Organizations: Records of the Ninth Minnesota Infantry, 1863–1864, RG-94 (hereafter cited as NA RG-94). Pension Files are found in Records of the Department of Veterans Affairs, 1773–2001, RG-15; *Rochester City Post,* 29 Nov. 1862; Dean letter, 5 Jan. 1863, William Johnston Dean letters and diary, Dean Blackmar Krafft private collection (hereafter cited as Dean Papers).

22. Markham CMSR (Second and Ninth Minnesota); Joseph A. Leonard, *History of Olmsted County, Minnesota* (Chicago: Goodspeed Historical Association, 1910), 60; Ron Freeberg, "Hard Fighting, Hard Drinking Col. Markham," *Post-Bulletin* (Rochester, Minn.), 26 Oct. 1961; *Rochester City Post,* 3 and 17 May, 19 July, 23 Aug. 1862, and 27 Oct. 1866; Dean letter, 29 Jan. 1863.

23. There are two collections of James Woodbury letters, one in the Minnesota Historical Society collection and the other published in Leon Basile, "Letters of a Minnesota Volunteer: The Correspondence of James M. Woodbury," *Lincoln Herald,* pt. 1

(Summer 1980): 387–92, pt. 2 (Fall 1980): 438–46. The letter quoted here, 15 Dec. 1862, is in Basile, 1:391.

24. *Mankato Weekly Record,* 26 Dec. 1862 and 3 Jan. 1863; *Chaska Valley Herald,* 27 Apr. 1933.

25. *St. Peter (Minn.) Tribune,* 23 Feb. 1863; Joseph Kirkland, *The Captain of Company K* (Ridgewood, N.J.: Gregg Press, 1968), 83; Wilkin letter to Capt. T. H. Barrett, 11 Feb. 1863, and Regimental Circular, 4 Jan. 1863, both in Wilkin Papers; Dean letters, 13 Mar. and 26 Apr. 1863, Dean Papers; Cray "Experiences," 445.

26. *Fairmont (Minn.) Sentinel,* 29 June 1912; Martha Dieter, "A Pioneer Mother," Jacob Dieter Family Papers, Olmsted County Historical Society, Rochester, Minn. (hereafter cited as Dieter Papers).

27. *MICIW,* 2:297–304; Folwell, *History of Minnesota,* 2:266–80; Paulson, *Memoirs,* 94–103; Pehr Carlson letter, 4 July 1863, Carlson Papers.

28. Stubbs, *Milton Aurelius,* 12–13; for background on the black teamsters, see Earl Spangler, *The Negro in Minnesota* (Minneapolis: T. S. Denison, 1961), 50–52.

29. Wilkin letter to Van Cleve, 3 Sept. 1863, Wilkin Papers.

30. John Aiton letter, 7 Sept. 1863, John Felix Aiton Papers, Minnesota Historical Society, St. Paul (hereafter cited as Aiton Papers); *Fairmont Sentinel,* 29 June 1912.

31. *OR,* ser. 1, vol. 22, pt. 2, 496, 498–99, 516, 534, 538, 553–54.

32. *Mower County Register,* 8 Oct. 1863.

33. *Mower County Register,* 29 Oct. 1863. The letter is signed "J. A.," but the author is obviously John Arnold, not only because he was the only J. A. in Company C, but also because he later signed letters as J. A. while in confinement for the mutiny.

Notes to Chapter Two

1. *St. Paul Pioneer,* 9 Oct. 1863; Aiton letter, 9 Oct. 1863, Aiton Papers; Cray, "Experiences," 452; *Fairmont (Minn.) Sentinel,* 29 June 1912; *Rochester City Post,* 28 Nov. 1863.

2. *Rochester Republican,* 28 Oct. 1863.

3. Dean letter, 14 Oct. 1863, Dean Papers; *St. Paul Pioneer,* 15 Oct. 1863; *Mankato Weekly Union,* 30 Oct. 1863; Aiton letter, 9 Oct. 1863, Aiton Papers; *Mower County Register,* 29 Oct. 1863.

4. *Rochester City Post,* 19 Dec. 1863; *Mankato Weekly Union,* 30 Oct. and 6 Nov. 1863.

5. Albert Castel, *Winning and Losing in the Civil War: Essays and Stories* (Columbia: University of South Carolina Press, 1996), 51–62; *OR,* ser. 1, vol. 22, pt. 2, 512, 516, 521, 533, 534.

6. *OR,* ser. 1, vol. 22, pt. 2, 622–25, 629, 639, 640.

7. *Mankato Weekly Record,* 14 Nov. 1863; *OR,* ser. 1, vol. 22, pt. 2, 642; *Rochester Republican,* 28 Oct. 1863; *Mower County Register,* 29 Oct. 1863; Woodbury letter, 15 Oct. 1863, James M. Woodbury Papers, Minnesota Historical Society, St. Paul (hereafter cited as Woodbury Papers); *Mankato Weekly Union,* 30 Oct. 1863; Aiton letter, 14 Oct. 1863, Aiton Papers.

8. Dean letter, 14 Oct. 1863, Dean Papers; *OR,* ser. 1, vol. 22, pt. 1, 674, 678; James M. Denny, "The Battle of Marshall: The Greatest Little Battle That Was Never Fought," *Boone's Lick Heritage* 9, no. 3 (Sept. 2001): 4–13.

9. Felch letter, 11 Oct. 1863, Steffens Papers; Aiton letter, 14 Oct. 1863, Aiton Papers; *OR,* ser. 1, vol. 22, pt. 1, 678; *Mankato Weekly Union,* 30 Oct. 1863; George W.

Herrick letter, 22 Oct. 1863, George W. Herrick Papers, Vermont Historical Society, Barre (hereafter cited as Herrick Papers, VHS).

10. *Winona Daily Republican,* 11 Nov. 1863; *Rochester Republican,* 28 Oct. 1863; George W. Herrick letter, 3 Nov. 1863, Henry N. Herrick and Family Papers, Minnesota Historical Society, St. Paul (hereafter cited as Herrick Papers, MHS).

11. Aiton letters, 22, 24, and 31 Oct. 1863, Aiton Papers; *Mankato Weekly Union,* 13 Nov. 1863; Captain Clark F. Keysor interview, 15, John L. Nau III Civil War Collection, Houston, Texas (hereafter cited as Keysor Papers); Dean letters, 22 Oct. and 1 Nov. 1863, Dean Papers; *Winona Daily Republican,* 6 Nov. 1863.

12. Wilkin letter, 30 Oct. 1863, Wilkin Papers; Herrick letter, 3 Nov. 1863, Herrick Papers, MHS; Dean letter, n.d. (Oct. 1863), Dean Papers; Felch letter, n.d. (Oct. 1863), Steffens Papers.

13. *Rochester City Post,* 12 Dec. 1863; *Mankato Weekly Union,* 18 Dec. 1863.

14. *Mankato Weekly Union,* 30 Oct. and 13 Nov. 1863; Aiton letter, 19 Oct. 1863, Aiton Papers; Frank M. Harrington letter, 16 Oct. 1863, Harrington and Merrill Family Papers, Minnesota Historical Society, St. Paul; *Rochester City Post,* 26 Dec. 1863; Dean letter, 10 Nov. 1863, Dean Papers; Herrick letter, 22 Oct. 1863, Herrick Papers, VHS.

15. Herrick letter, 3 Nov. 1863, Herrick Papers, MHS; *OR,* ser. 1, vol. 22, pt. 1, 678.

16. Michael Fellman, *Inside War: The Guerrilla Conflict in Missouri during the American Civil War* (New York: Oxford University Press, 1989), 40–41, 211; *Mankato Weekly Union,* 13 Nov. 1863; *Missouri State Times* (Jefferson City), 7 Nov. 1863; *Winona Daily Republican,* 9 Nov. 1863; *Mankato Weekly Record,* 14 Nov. 1863; Wilkin letter, 30 Oct. 1863, Wilkin Papers.

17. Henry Clay Bruce, *The New Man: Twenty-Nine Years a Slave, Twenty-Nine Years a Free Man: The Recollections of H. C. Bruce* (Lincoln: University of Nebraska Press, 1996), 101; Aiton letters, 27 and 30 Oct. 1863, Aiton Papers; *Winona Daily Republican,* 6 Nov. 1863.

18. Among the best sources on the tortuous nature of Missouri wartime politics are the two works of William E. Parrish, *Turbulent Partnership: Missouri and the Union 1861–1865* (Columbia: University of Missouri Press, 1963) and *A History of Missouri, Vol. III, 1860 to 1875* (Columbia: University of Missouri Press, 1973). Bill R. Lee, "Missouri's Fight over Emancipation in 1863," *Missouri Historical Review* 45, no. 3 (Apr. 1951): 268.

19. Michael Burlingame, *Abraham Lincoln: A Life,* 2 vols. (Baltimore, Md.: John Hopkins University Press, 2008), 2:154.

20. Parrish, *History of Missouri,* 3:106–7; Parrish, *Turbulent Partnership,* 141–46.

21. John M. Schofield, *Forty-Six Years in the Army* (Norman: University of Oklahoma Press, 1998), 74–76.

22. "Frémont's Hundred Days in Missouri," *Atlantic Monthly* 9, no. 53 (Mar. 1862): 377. I am indebted to James M. Denny for this source. Samuel Bannister Harding, *Life of George R. Smith Founder of Sedalia, Mo.* (Sedalia, Mo., 1904), 305–6.

23. *OR,* ser. 1, vol. 22, pt. 2, 574–75, 585–86; Schofield, *Forty-Six Years,* 87, 89–91.

24. Burlingame, *Abraham Lincoln,* 2:545–50; Michael Burlingame, *At Lincoln's Side: John Hay's Civil War Correspondence and Selected Writings* (Carbondale: Southern Illinois University Press, 2000), 57–64; Michael Burlingame and John R. Turner Ettlinger, *Inside Lincoln's White House: The Complete Civil War Diary of John Hay* (Carbondale:

Southern Illinois University Press, 1997), 101; Harding, *Life of George R. Smith,* 351; Schofield, *Forty-Six Years,* 99.

25. August Scherneckau, *Marching with the First Nebraska: A Civil War Diary* (Norman: University of Oklahoma Press, 2007), 206; *OR,* ser. 1, vol. 22, pt. 2, 640.

26. Felch letter n.d. (Oct. 1863), Steffen Papers; Herrick letter, 22 Oct. 1863, Herrick Papers, VHS; Aiton letter, 14/19 Oct. 1863, Aiton Papers; *Mankato Weekly Union,* 30 Oct. and 14 Nov. 1863.

27. *Rochester Republican,* 2 Dec. 1863; Dean letter, n.d. (Oct. 1863), Dean Papers.

28. Theodore George Carter, "The Tupelo Campaign. As Noted at the Time by a Line Officer in the Union Army," *Publications of the Mississippi Historical Society* 10 (1909): 112–13; James M. McPherson, *For Cause & Comrades: Why Men Fought in the Civil War* (New York: Oxford University Press, 1997), 117.

29. Benjamin P. Thomas and Harold M. Hyman, *Stanton: The Life and Times of Lincoln's Secretary of War* (New York: Alfred A. Knopf, 1962), 231; James A. Wright, *No More Gallant a Deed: A Civil War Memoir of the First Minnesota Volunteers* (St. Paul: Minnesota Historical Society Press, 2001), 44; McPherson, *For Cause & Comrades,* 117–18; N. B. Martin, "Letters of a Union Officer: L. F. Hubbard and the Civil War," *Minnesota History* 35, no. 7 (Sept. 1957): 314–15; Earl J. Hess, *Liberty, Virtue, and Progress: Northerners and Their War for the Union* (New York: Fordham University Press, 1997), 98–110.

30. *Mankato Weekly Union,* 30 Oct. 1863; *Winona Daily Republican,* 11 Nov. 1863.

31. Parrish, *Turbulent Partnership,* 170–72; Herrick letter, 3 Nov. 1863, Herrick Papers, MHS; *Mankato Weekly Union,* 20 Nov. 1863; *Winona Daily Republican,* 19 Nov. 1863; Aiton letter, 29 Nov. 1863, Aiton Papers; *Rochester City Post,* 26 Dec. 1863.

NOTES TO CHAPTER THREE

1. National Archives, Records of the Adjutant General's Office, Regiment and Company Books of Civil War Volunteer Union Organizations, Ninth Minnesota Regimental Letter and Order Book, Ninth Minnesota, District of Central Missouri Special Order 69, 18 Oct. 1863, RG-94; *OR,* ser. 1, vol. 22, pt. 1, 664–68.

2. James M. Denny, "Civil War Entrenchment Near Otterville," *Boone's Lick Heritage* 7, no. 2 (June 1999): 4–9; Josiah W. Bissell, "The Western Organization of Colored People for Furnishing Information to United States Troops in the South," in *Glimpses of the Nation's Struggle,* Second Series, Minnesota Commandery, Military Order of the Loyal Legion of the United States (St. Paul: St. Paul Book and Stationery, 1890), 316.

3. *OR,* ser. 1, vol. 22, pt. 1, 626, 637, 673; Basile, "Letters," 1:441–42.

4. Pacific Railroad Company, *History of the Pacific Railroad of Missouri* (St. Louis, Mo.: Democrat Book and Job Printing House, 1865), 22–23; Herman Haupt, *Reminiscences of General Herman Haupt* (Milwaukee: Wright & Joy, 1901), 49.

5. Henry C. Levens and Nathaniel M. Drake, *A History of Cooper County, Missouri* (St. Louis, Mo.: Perrin & Smith, 1876), 171–72, 174. For a detailed history of Cooper County during the Civil War, see James F. Thoma, *This Cruel Unnatural War* (Memphis, Tenn.: James F. Thoma, 2003); David Lathrop, *The History of the Fifty-Ninth Regiment Illinois Volunteers* (Indianapolis: Hall & Hutchinson, 1865), 20; *OR,* ser. 1, vol. 22, pt. 1, 667–68.

6. Edwin W. Ford CMSR and Pension File No. 1,058,978; Felch letters, 24 Feb. and 27 June 1863, Steffen Papers; Woodbury letter, May 1863, Woodbury Papers.

7. *Winona Daily Republican,* 18, 20, 26 Aug., 9 and 10 Sept. 1862; David W. Wellman CMSR and Pension File No. 861,872.

8. *Winona Daily Republican,* 7 Nov. 1863; Muster Rolls of Volunteer Organizations during the Civil War, Ninth Minnesota, Co. C and Co. K, Nov.–Dec. 1863, NA RG-94.

9. *Winona Daily Republican,* 7 Nov. 1863.

10. On Capon, CMSRs Co. C, Second Minnesota, and Co. K, Ninth Minnesota; Pension File No. 174,099; *Wabasha Herald,* 2 Dec. 1897; *St. Peter (Minn.) Tribune,* 23 Feb. 1863.

11. Capon CMSR, Co. C, Second Minnesota.

12. *Winona Daily Republican,* 27 Nov. 1863.

13. Woodbury letter, 25 Nov. 1863, Woodbury Papers; National Archives, Records of Army Continental Commands, Entry 3378, District of Central Missouri Letters Received, Saunders, S. H., 25 Nov. 1863, RG-393 (hereafter cited as NA RG-393).

14. Ninth Minnesota Regimental Letter and Order Book, G. O. 13, 16 Oct. 1863, detailing General Calls, NA RG-94.

15. Basic documents on the Otterville incident are in National Archives, Records of the Office of the Secretary of War, Letters Received, 1864, File J445(128), RG-107 (hereafter cited as NA RG-107), which is partially reprinted in Ira Berlin, et al., *The Destruction of Slavery,* Freedom: A Documentary History of Emancipation 1861–1867, series 1, vol. 1 (Cambridge, Mass.: Cambridge University Press, 1985), 467–71, and *Letter of the Secretary of War, Communicating, In answer to a resolution of the Senate of the 11th of January 1864, information relating to the arrest and imprisonment, by the military authorities in Missouri, of soldiers belong to the Ninth Minnesota regiment,* 38th Cong., 1st sess., Mar. 4, 1864, S. Doc. No. 24.

16. "John" and his family are identified in the text of the slave pass included in the report of Capt. Levi Pritchard, 11 Nov. 1863, in File J445(128), NA RG-107, reproduced (with several typographical errors) in S. Doc. No. 24. For example, "Patsey" is rendered as "Patey." *Winona Daily Republican,* 27 Nov. 1863; Felch letter, 12 Nov. 1863, Steffens Papers.

17. I. MacDonald Demuth, *The History of Pettis County, Missouri, Including an Authentic History of Sedalia* (N.p., 1882), 750, 928, 942; Genevieve L. Carter, *Pioneers of Pettis and Adjoining Missouri Counties,* vol. 3 (Warrensburg, Mo.: Privately printed, 1987), 43; U.S. Census 1830, 1840, 1850, 1860, 1870, 1880; Berry-Thomson-Walker Family Papers, Western Historical Manuscripts Collection, Columbia, University of Missouri; Michael Cassity, *Defending a Way of Life: An American Community in the Nineteenth Century* (Albany: State University of New York Press, 1989), 8–9, 25–26; William B. Claycomb, *A History of North-East Pettis County, Missouri* (Dayton, Ohio: Morningside Press, 1996), 17–18; Harrison Anthony Trexler, *Slavery in Missouri 1804–1865* (Baltimore, Md.: John Hopkins Press, 1914), 19; Harding, *Life of George R. Smith,* 11–12, 17.

18. On the Civil War in Missouri in 1861, see James Denny and John Bradbury, *The Civil War's First Blood: Missouri, 1854–1861* (Boonville: Missouri Life, 2007); Harding, *Life of George R. Smith,* 301, 305–6, 316–17, 322–23, 317, 322; Cassity, *Defending a Way of Life,* 47–48; Demuth, *Pettis County,* 450–53.

19. Bruce, *New Man,* 103.

20. Berlin, *Destruction of Slavery,* 554–57; Berlin, *The Black Military Experience,* Freedom: A Documentary History of Emancipation 1861–1867, series 2 (Cambridge, Mass.: Cambridge University Press, 1982), 228–30; Bruce, *New Man,* 108–9.

21. Bruce, *New Man,* 99–100, 103.

22. Trexler, *Slavery in Missouri,* 39; Bruce, *New Man,* 102.

23. Berlin, *Black Military Experience,* 187–90; Dennis K. Boman, *Lincoln and Citizens' Rights in Civil War Missouri: Balancing Freedom and Security* (Baton Rouge: Louisiana State University Press, 2011), 199–201.

24. Berlin, *Destruction of Slavery,* 411; Berlin, *The Wartime Genesis of Free Labor: The Upper South,* Freedom: A Documentary History of Emancipation 1861–1867, series 1, vol. 2 (Cambridge, Mass.: Cambridge University Press, 1993), 584; text of Spec. Ord. No. 307 in File J445(128), NA RG-107; *Daily Missouri Republican,* 13 Nov. 1863.

25. Text of slave pass in File J445(128), NA RG-107, and S. Doc. No. 24; *Missouri Democrat,* 13 Nov. 1863, has the schedule for the Pacific Railroad mail trains.

26. Bruce, *New Man,* 64, 103.

27. Bruce, *New Man,* 74; Cassity, *Defending a Way of Life,* 8–9, 29; Harding, *Life of George R. Smith,* 17–20.

28. Bissell, "Western Organization of Colored People," 317–18.

29. *Winona Daily Republican,* 8 Dec. 1863, also cited in S. Doc. No. 24; *OR,* ser. 1, vol. 22, pt.2, 450, 585–86; *Rochester Republican,* 2 Dec. 1863.

30. John W. Hartley Pension File No. 1,032,964; *Mower County Register,* 10 Dec. 1863; Edward D. Neill, *History of Freeborn County* (Minneapolis: Minnesota Historical Company, 1882), 516.

31. *Mower County Register,* 17 Dec. 1863. The thirty-eight "liberators" are identified from the muster rolls of Co. C and Co. K, Nov.–Dec. 1863, NA RG-94; Henry Ehmke Pension File No. 191,318.

32. Report of Capt. Oscar B. Queen, 11 Nov. 1863, in File J445(128), NA RG-107, and S. Doc. No. 24.

33. The text of the slave pass from File J445(128), NA RG-107, as incorrectly reproduced in S. Doc. No. 24, can be read to add two unidentified children, presumably Rachel's, for a total of thirteen slaves. However, the original text shows the "two children" actually referred to the young aunts, Anna and Patsey. Some sources note that eleven slaves were rescued (that being the number of slaves listed in the pass), but the Felch letter, 12 Nov. 1863, Steffen Papers, and Walker's own total recorded in Pritchard's report in File J445(128), NA RG-107, both categorically state there were nine. *Mower County Register,* 10 Dec. 1863.

34. *Mower County Register,* 10 and 17 Dec. 1863.

35. On White, see 1860 U.S. Census for Jefferson City, Mo., and *History of Franklin, Jefferson, Washington, Crawford and Gasconade Counties, Missouri* (Chicago: Goodspeed, 1888), excerpt in: http://home.usmo.com/~momollus/FranCoCW/FC1860GS .htm; report of Levi Pritchard, 11 Nov. 1863, in File J445(128), NA RG-107, and S. Doc. No. 24; *Daily Missouri Republican,* 12 Nov. 1863.

36. Oscar B. Queen Pension File No. 313,183; Queen's Report, 11 Nov. 1863, File J445(128), NA RG-107; letter of an anonymous soldier of Co. C to H. J. Fisher, 3 Dec. 1863, in S. Doc. No. 24; *Daily Missouri Republican,* 12 Nov. 1863.

37. *Winona Daily Republican,* 23 Nov. 1863; Pritchard Report, 11 Nov. 1863, File J445(128), NA RG-107; Felch letter, 12 Nov. 1863, Steffens Papers; *Daily Missouri Republican,* 12 Nov. 1863.

38. *Mower County Register,* 17 Dec. 1863; Queen's Report, 11 Nov. 1863, File J445(128), NA RG-107; *Daily Missouri Republican,* 12 Nov. 1863.

39. Felch letter, 12 Nov. 1863, Steffens Papers; Queen's Report, 11 Nov. 1863, File J445(128), NA RG-107; *Winona Daily Republican,* 23 Nov. 1863.

40. Felch letter, 12 Nov. 1863, Steffens Papers; Latham D. Stewart Pension File No. 1,126,971.

41. Queen's Report, 11 Nov. 1863, and endorsements, in File J445(128), NA RG-107; Latham D. Stewart Pension File No. 1,126,971; Felch letter, 12 Nov. 1863, Steffens Papers; *Daily Missouri Republican,* 12 Nov. 1863.

42. John W. Hartley Pension File No. 1,032,964; *Rochester Republican,* 2 Dec. 1863; *Mower County Register,* 10 Dec. 1863; Aiton letter, 17 Dec. 1863, Aiton Papers.

43. Wilkin letter to Sibley, 13 Nov. 1863, Wilkin Papers; *St. Paul Press,* 28 July 1864.

44. Anthony L. Blair, "Democratization, Revivalism and Reform: The United Brethren in the Antebellum Era," *Journal of United Brethren History and Life* 1, no. 1 (Fall 2000): 37, 40; John Arnold Pension File No. 102,575; *Wellington (Ohio) Enterprise,* 5 Apr. 1893; *Elyria (Ohio) Republican,* 30 Mar. 1893; F. E. Weeks, *Pioneer History of Camden Township, Lorain County, Ohio* (Wellington, Ohio: Genealogical Workshop, 1983), 12; Demuth, *Pettis County,* 446–47.

45. *Religious Telescope* (Dayton, Ohio), 27 Aug. 1863.

46. Primary sources for the liberators are their CMSRs and the pension files for those who applied for them. For Stewart's connection to the *Mayflower,* see *Port Angeles (Wash.) Evening News,* 15 Jan. 1930.

47. War Department, *Revised United States Army Regulations of 1861* (Washington, D.C., 1863), 486; endorsements to Queen's Report, 11 Nov. 1863, File J445(128), NA RG-107; Woodbury letter, 25 Nov. 1863, Woodbury Papers; *Mower County Register,* 10 Dec. 1863.

Notes to Chapter Four

1. Victor B. Howard, *Black Liberation in Kentucky: Emancipation and Freedom, 1862–1884* (Lexington: University Press of Kentucky, 1983), 12–20; Berlin, *Destruction of Slavery,* 499–500.

2. William M. Fliss, "Wisconsin's 'Abolition Regiment': The Twenty-Second Volunteer Infantry in Kentucky, 1862–1863," *Wisconsin Magazine of History* (Winter 2002–03): 2–17; Howard, *Black Liberation,* 21–26; William H. Townsend, *Lincoln and the Bluegrass: Slavery and Civil War in Kentucky* (Lexington: University of Kentucky Press, 1955), 299–304.

3. Nicole Etcheson, *Bleeding Kansas: Contested Liberty in the Civil War Era* (Lawrence: University Press of Kansas, 2004), 228; "Frémont's Hundred Days in Missouri," 377–78.

4. Stephen Z. Starr, *Jennison's Jayhawkers: A Civil War Cavalry Regiment and Its Commander* (Baton Rouge: Louisiana State University Press, 1973), 17, 166, 173–83.

5. Queen's Report, 11 Nov. 1863, File J445(128), NA RG-107.

6. Don E. Fehrenbacher, *The Slaveholding Republic: An Account of the United States Government's Relations to Slavery* (New York: Oxford University Press, 2001), 231–36.

7. Fehrenbacher, *Slaveholding Republic,* 236–39; James I. Clark, *Wisconsin Defies the Fugitive Slave Law: The Case of Sherman M. Booth* (Madison: State Historical Society of Wisconsin, 1955), 6; Steven Lubet, *Fugitive Justice: Runaways, Rescuers, and Slavery on Trial* (Cambridge, Mass.: Belknap/Harvard, 2010), 159–228; Roland M. Bauman,

The 1858 Oberlin-Wellington Rescue: A Reappraisal (Oberlin, Ohio: Oberlin College, 2003), passim.

8. William D. Green, "Eliza Winston and the Politics of Freedom in Minnesota, 1854–60," *Minnesota History* 57, no. 3 (Fall 2000): 106–22.

9. Eric Foner, *The Fiery Trial: Abraham Lincoln and American Slavery* (New York: Norton, 2010), 6; Frank L. Byrne, *The View from Headquarters: Civil War Letters of Harvey Reid* (Madison: State Historical Society of Wisconsin, 1965), 15–16; Aiton letter, 5 Nov. 1863, Aiton Papers.

10. Foner, *Fiery Trial*, 131; "Frémont's Hundred Days in Missouri," 377–78; Bruce, *New Man*, 108.

11. Cited in *Winona Daily Republican*, 23 Nov. 1863.

12. *St. Paul Daily Press*, 21 Nov. 1863; *Rochester City Post*, 28 Nov. 1863.

13. *Rochester Republican*, 2 Dec. 1863.

14. *Religious Telescope* (Dayton, Ohio), 23 Dec. 1863; *Mower County Register*, 10 Dec. 1863; Letter to H. J. Fisher, 3 Dec. 1863, in S. Doc. No. 24.

15. Felch letter, 12 Nov. 1863, Steffens Papers.

16. Mower County Register, 10 Dec. 1863; *Religious Telescope*, 23 Dec. 1863; David M. Potter, *The Impending Crisis 1848–1861* (New York: Harper & Row, 1976), 102.

17. *Mower County Register*, 17 Dec. 1863; *St. Paul Daily Press*, 21 Nov. 1863; *Winona Daily Republican*, 27 Nov. and 8 Dec. 1863; Woodbury letter, 25 Nov. 1863, Woodbury Papers.

18. *Rochester Republican*, 2 Dec. 1863; *St. Paul Daily Press*, 28 Jan. 1864.

19. *Mower County Register*, 10 and 24 Dec. 1863; *Religious Telescope*, 23 Dec. 1863; *Central Republican* (Faribault, Minn.), 9 Dec. 1863.

20. Parrish, *Turbulent Partnership*, 172–73; Norma L. Peterson, *Freedom and Franchise: The Political Career of B. Gratz Brown* (Columbia: University of Missouri Press, 1965), 128–29; John G. Nicolay and John Hay, *Abraham Lincoln: A History*, vol. 8 (New York: Century Company, 1886), 470; Burlingame and Ettlinger, *Inside Lincoln's White House*, 125.

21. S. Doc. No. 24; undated petition in File J445(128), NA RG-107.

22. Ezra J. Warner, *Generals in Blue: Lives of the Union Commanders* (Baton Rouge: Louisiana State University Press, 1964), 47–48.

23. File J445(128), NA RG-107; S. Doc. No. 24; and Berlin, *Destruction of Slavery*, 469–70.

24. S. Doc. No. 24.

25. *Revised Army Regulations of 1861*, 498; Steven J. Ramold, *Baring the Iron Hand: Discipline in the Union Army* (DeKalb: Northern Illinois University Press, 2010), 322.

26. Ninth Minnesota Regt. Letter and Order Book, G. O. 19, 25 Nov. 1863, NA RG-94; *MICIW*, 1:419.

27. *St. Paul Daily Press*, 28 Jan. 1864; *Rochester City Post*, 26 Dec. 1863.

28. Felch letters, 2, 16, and 29 Dec. 1863, Steffens Papers; Pearl Frisbie Estee, "The Story of Zara Frisbie," Bonus Issue, *Bulletin of the Frisbee-Frisbie Family Association of America* 18 (May 1968): 7–9.

29. Woodbury letter, 16 Dec. 1863, Woodbury Papers; *Missouri Democrat*, 5 Jan. 1864; *St. Paul Daily Press*, 28 Jan. 1864.

30. *Missouri Democrat*, 5, 9, and 10 Jan. 1864.

31. Regiment and Company Books, Ninth Minnesota Order Book, Cos. A to K, 8 Jan. 1864, NA RG-94; *St. Paul Daily Press,* 28 Jan. 1864.

32. *Rochester Republican,* 27 Jan. 1864; Ramold, *Baring the Iron Hand,* 232; S. Doc. No. 24; Latham D. Stewart Pension File No. 1,126,971. The pension board had tried to reduce Stewart's credits for the time he was incarcerated in Jefferson City and thereby reduce his pension.

33. E. B. Brown letter, 21 Jan. 1864; *Letter of the Secretary of War,* S. Doc. No. 24.

34. Ninth Minnesota Order Book, Cos. A to K, 8 and 11 Jan. 1864, NA RG-94; *OR,* ser. 1, vol. 22, pt. 2, 749–50; James Woodbury letter, 7 Jan. 1864, Woodbury Papers; *OR,* ser. 1, vol. 34, pt. 2, 21.

35. *Congressional Globe,* 13 Jan. 1864, 145.

36. Sketch in Lucius F. Hubbard and Return I. Holcombe, *Minnesota in Three Centuries,* vol. 3. (Mankato: Publication Society of Minnesota, 1908), 86, and Edward D. Neill, *History of Ramsey County and the City of St. Paul* (Minneapolis: North Star Publications, 1881), 236; *OR,* ser. 1, vol. 22, pt. 2, 494; Theodore C. Blegen, "Campaigning with Seward 1860," *Minnesota Historical Quarterly* 8, no. 2 (June 1927): 166; Alan G. Bogue, *The Earnest Men: Republicans of the Civil War Senate* (Ithaca, N.Y.: Cornell University Press, 1981), 131; James H. Baker, "Lives of the Governors of Minnesota," *Minnesota Historical Society Collections* 8 (1908), 24.

37. *Congressional Globe,* 13 Jan. 1864, 145; *MICIW,* 1:419–20.

38. *Congressional Globe,* 13 Jan. 1864, 145–46, and 15 July 1862, 3333–34; Starr, *Jennison's Jayhawkers,* 181–83.

39. *Congressional Globe,* 13 Jan. 1864, 146.

40. Burlingame and Ettinger, *Inside Lincoln's White House,* 127.

41. *Letter of the Secretary of War,* S. Doc. No. 24.

42. *Congressional Globe,* 27 Jan. 1864, 273–75; Wilkinson's reminiscence, "Abraham Lincoln, A Statesman's Tact," *New York Tribune,* 12 July 1885; *Senate Executive Journal,* 12 May 1864, 541; Michael Burlingame, *An Oral History of Abraham Lincoln: John G. Nicolay's Interviews and Essays* (Carbondale: Southern Illinois University Press, 1996), 59–61.

43. *Letter of the Secretary of War,* S. Doc. No. 24; Latham D. Stewart Pension File No. 1,126,971.

44. Thomas and Hyman, *Stanton,* 245, wrongly assert that Stanton controlled where the prisoners were held "while he worked through his friends in Congress to have the whole matter dropped." There is no evidence that Stanton's intervention ever occurred.

45. *MICIW,* 1:419–20; *Rochester Republican,* 27 Jan. 1864; *Mower County Register,* 21 Jan. 1864.

46. Burlingame, *Abraham Lincoln,* 2:492–94.

47. *OR,* ser. 1, vol. 34, pt. 2, 277–78; Ninth Minnesota Record and Order Book, 11 Feb. 1864, NA RG-94; Ebenezer Clapp, *The Clapp Memorials: Record of the Clapp Family in America* (Boston: David Clapp & Son, Publisher, 1876), 338; Muster Rolls, Co. C and Co. K, Ninth Minnesota, Jan.–Feb. 1864, NA RG-94.

48. *Rochester City Post,* 27 Feb. 1864.

49. Felch letters, 12 Nov. and 28 Dec. 1863, Steffens Papers; Latham D. Stewart Pension File No. 1,126,971; District of Central Missouri Letters Received, 24 Nov. 1863, NA RG-393, Entry 3378.

50. John W. Hartley Pension File No. 1,032,964.

51. Berlin, *Destruction of Slavery*, 411–12.

52. Berlin, *Destruction of Slavery*, 410; Berlin, *Black Military Experience*, 188–90; *OR*, ser. 3, vol. 3, 1034–36; also Boman, *Lincoln and Citizens' Rights*, 200–201.

53. *Rochester City Post*, 26 Dec. 1863.

54. Berlin, *Destruction of Slavery*, 481–82; Berlin, *Wartime Genesis*, 410; Berlin, *Black Military Experience*, 242–44, 247.

Notes to Chapter Five

1. Harrington letter, 19 Dec. 1863, Harrington Papers; Aiton letter, 17 Jan. 1864, Aiton Papers; *St. Paul Daily Press*, 28 Jan. 1864.

2. Castel, *Winning*, 58–59.

3. *OR*, ser. 1, vol. 34, pt. 2, 321–22; Aiton letter, 19 Feb. 1864, Aiton Papers; Dieter letter, 17 Feb. 1864, Dieter Papers.

4. *OR*, ser. 1, vol. 22, pt. 2, 321–22; *OR*, ser. 1, vol. 34, pt. 2, 374.

5. *Rochester Republican*, 15 Apr. 1864; Dieter letter, 14 Mar. 1864, Dieter Papers.

6. *Rochester Republican*, 15 Apr. 1864; *Rochester City Post*, 14 May 1864; *St. Peter (Minn.) Tribune*, 4 May 1864.

7. *OR*, ser. 1, vol. 34, pt. 2, 374; *St. Peter Tribune*, 4 May 1864; Basile, "Letters," 2:444; Isaac Peterman CMSR and Pension File No. 405,701; Ninth Minnesota Letter and Order Book, 10 May 1864, NA RG-94.

8. *OR*, ser. 1, vol. 34, pt. 2, 238, Part 3, 51; Basile, "Letters," 2:445; Woodbury letter, 3 May 1864, Woodbury Papers; Felch letter, 1 May 1864, Steffens Papers.

9. Dieter letters, 11 Feb. and 6 Mar. 1864, Dieter Papers; Basile, "Letters," 2:444; William Doyle letter, 10 Mar. 1864, William Doyle Papers, Minnesota Historical Society, St. Paul (hereafter cited as Doyle Papers); Dean letter, 8 Apr. 1864, Dean Papers.

10. Paulson, *Memoirs*, 108.

11. Chauncey Hill's letters are in Chauncey J. Hill Family Papers, Minnesota Historical Society, St. Paul (hereafter cited as Hill Papers), and his diary was published in 1909 in the *Montevideo (Minn.) Leader*. The family history written by his widow, Sarah E. West, is courtesy of Gay Wilhelm private collection, Sarah E. West family history, 36–37; *Montevideo Leader*, 8 Jan. 1909; on Martin Shortt, see the *Mower County Transcript*, 15 Jan. 1902, cited in http://freepages.geneaology.rootsweb.ancestry.com/~sunnyann/obituary2:html#S; Dudley Perry CMSR, NA RG-94.

12. Hill letter, 25 Apr. 1864, Hill Papers; *Rochester City Post*, 14 May 1864; Wilkin letters, 27 Jan. and 7 Feb. 1864, Wilkin Papers; Harrington letter, 18 Feb. 1864, Harrington Papers; Basile, "Letters," 2:443.

13. *Rochester City Post*, 27 Feb. 1864; *OR*, ser. 1, vol. 34, pt. 3, 42, 62.

14. Hill letter, 21 May 1864, Hill Papers.

15. *Chaska Valley Herald*, 31 Oct., 7 Nov., and 12 Dec. 1863, and 2 and 30 Jan. and 11 June 1864; *St. Paul Press*, 8 Dec. 1864; *Rochester City Post*, 26 Dec. 1863; Paulson, *Memoirs*, 107–8.

16. *Winona Daily Republican*, 19 Nov. 1863; on Beaulieu's background, see *The Tomahawk* (Minn.), 12 May 1904; *St. Louis Republican* article cited in *St. Paul Pioneer*, 4 June 1864.

17. Woodbury letter, 23 May 1864, Woodbury Papers; *St. Paul Pioneer*, 3 June 1864; Hill letter, 23 May 1864, Hill Papers.

18. *St. Paul Pioneer,* 3 June 1864; Aiton letter, 27 May 1864, Aiton Papers; *MICIW,* 1:420.

19. Hill letter, 29 May 1864, Hill Papers; *MICIW,* 1:419; Castel, *Winning,* 59.

20. Pierre Demars CMSR, NA RG-94.

21. Frederick Way Jr., *Way's Packet Directory, 1848–1994* (Athens: Ohio University, 1994), 35–36; Dean letter, 30 May 1864, Dean Papers; Aiton letter, 27 May 1864, Aiton Papers; Felch letter, 9 June 1864, Steffens Papers; *Montevideo Leader,* 12 Feb. 1909.

22. *Montevideo Leader,* 19 Feb. 1909; Wilkin letter, 18 June 1864, Wilkin Papers.

23. Way, *Way's Packet,* 36.

Notes to Chapter Six

1. The primary source for the Battle of Brice's Crossroads is *OR,* ser. 1, vol. 39, pts. 1 and 2, which contain the battle reports, correspondence, and the Sturgis board of investigation. The Ninth Minnesota's report, however, is in *MICIW,* 2:464–68. Vital secondary sources include Edwin C. Bearss, *Forrest at Brice's Cross Roads* (Dayton, Ohio: Morningside Bookshop, 1979), 3–141, the most detailed study, and Parker Hills, "A Study in Warfighting: Nathan Bedford Forrest and the Battle of Brice's Crossroads," *The Papers of the Blue and Gray Education Society,* no. 2 (Fall 1995): 1–64, which offers crucial new insights. The Gustavus A. Gessner Papers in the Rutherford B. Hayes Presidential Center, Fremont, Ohio (hereafter cited as Gessner Papers), include many accounts of the battle by Union veterans, including part in an unpublished pamphlet, hereafter Gessner pamphlet.

2. *OR,* ser. 1, vol. 34, pt. 4, 73; *OR,* ser. 1, vol. 39, pt. 2, 73–74.

3. Joseph E. Harvey letter, 31 May 1864, Joseph E. Harvey Papers, Minnesota Historical Society, St. Paul (hereafter cited as Harvey Papers); Richard L. Fuchs, *An Unerring Fire: The Massacre at Fort Pillow* (Mechanicsburg, Pa.: Stackpole Books, 2002), passim.

4. Sketch in Ezra J. Warner, *Generals in Gray: Lives of the Confederate Commanders* (Baton Rouge: Louisiana State University Press, 1959), 92–93. Important biographies include John Allan Wyeth, *That Devil Forrest: Life of General Nathan Bedford Forrest* (Baton Rouge: Louisiana State University Press, 1989), Robert Selph Henry, *"First With The Most" Forrest* (Indianapolis: Bobbs-Merrill, 1944), and Brian Steel Wills, *The Confederacy's Greatest Cavalryman: Nathan Bedford Forrest* (Lawrence: University Press of Kansas, 1992). David Felch letter, 1 June 1864, Steffens Papers.

5. Wilkin letter, 18 June 1864, Wilkin Papers; *St. Paul Press,* 22 and 30 June 1864; Felch letter, 1 June 1864, Steffens Papers; CMSRs of the "liberators," NA RG-94.

6. Pehr Carlson letter, 29 June 1864, Carlson Papers; for great illustrations of Union uniforms and gear, see Time-Life, *Echoes of Glory: Arms and Equipment of the Union* (Alexandria, Va.: Time-Life Books, 1991), and for the life of the foot soldier, Gregory A. Coco, *The Civil War Infantryman: In Camp, on the March and in Battle* (Gettysburg, Pa.: Thomas Publications, 1996); Haversack quote: John D. Billings, *Hardtack & Coffee: The Unwritten Story of Army Life* (Lincoln: University of Nebraska Press, 1993), 276; Felch letter, 1 June 1864, Steffens Papers.

7. A fine survey of Civil War infantry weapons is Earl J. Coates and Dean S. Thomas, *An Introduction to Civil War Small Arms* (Gettysburg, Pa.: Thomas Publications, 1990); loading is described in 75–77. For the original drill, see War Department, *The 1863 U.S. Infantry Tactics* (Philadelphia: J. P. Lippencott, 1863), 77–82.

8. Melville Robertson, "Journal of Melville Cox Robertson," *Indiana Magazine of History* 28, no. 2 (June 1932): 124; Aiton letter, 15 June 1864, Aiton Papers; *Montevideo Leader,* 19 Feb. 1909; Wright, *No More Gallant a Deed,* 106–7.

9. Edmund Newsome, *Experience in the War of the Great Rebellion By a Soldier of the Eighty First Regiment of Illinois Volunteer Infantry* (Murphysboro, Ill.: Jackson County Historical Society, 1984), 157; Aiton letter, 9 June 1864, Aiton Papers; *Montevideo Leader,* 19 Feb. 1909; Hill letter, 2 June 1864, Hill Papers.

10. Warner, *Generals in Blue,* 486–87; Jacob Doleson Cox, *Military Reminiscences of the Civil War,* vol. 2 (New York: Charles Scribner's Sons, 1900), 117–18; William Garrett Piston and Richard W. Hatcher III, *Wilson's Creek: The Second Battle of the Civil War and the Men Who Fought It* (Chapel Hill: University of North Carolina Press, 2003), 305; Benjamin H. Grierson, *A Just and Righteous Cause: Benjamin H. Grierson's Civil War Memoir* (Carbondale: Southern Illinois University Press, 2008), 235; OR, ser. 1, vol. 39, pt. 1, 215–16.

11. Warner, *Generals in Blue,* 189–90; Bearss, *Forrest,* 326; D. Warren Lambert, *When the Ripe Pears Fell: The Battle of Richmond, Kentucky* (Richmond, Ky.: Madison County Historical Society, 1995), 86–87; Pvt. Alexander Almond (Seventy-Second Ohio) diary, 1 June 1864, courtesy of Richard D. Goff private collection, via Robert S. Davis (hereafter cited as Almond Papers); John B. Rice (Seventy-Second Ohio) letter, 17 June 1864, John B. Rice Papers, Rutherford B. Hayes Presidential Center, Fremont, Ohio (hereafter cited as Rice Papers).

12. Wilkin letter, 9 June 1864, Wilkin Papers; John Merrilies (Company E, First Illinois Artillery) diary, 3 June 1864, John Merrilies Papers, Chicago Historical Society, (hereafter cited as Merrilies Papers); OR, ser. 1, vol. 39, pt. 1, 181.

13. OR, ser. 1, vol. 39, pt. 1, 118, 120, 125; OR, ser. 1, vol. 32, pt. 1, 566–68.

14. Robertson, "Journal," 124; *East Union News,* 1 Feb. 1895; Pehr Carlson letter, 29 June 1864, Carlson Papers; Woodbury diary, 3 June 1864, Woodbury Papers; Almond diary, 3 June 1864, Almond Papers; William B. Halsey (Seventy-Second Ohio) diary, 3 June 1864, William B. Halsey Papers, Rutherford B. Hayes Presidential Center, Fremont, Ohio (hereafter cited as Halsey Papers).

15. OR, ser. 1, vol. 39, pt. 1, 159; Gustavus A. Gessner, "General Sturgis at Guntown, Miss. (1864)," unpublished pamphlet, 27, Gessner Papers; Merrilies diary, 3 June 1864, Merrilies Papers.

16. *East Union News,* 1 Feb. 1895; Aiton letter, 15 June 1864, Aiton Papers; Merrilies diary, 5 June 1864, Merrilies Papers.

17. Robertson, "Journal," 125.

18. Aiton letter, 15 June 1864, Aiton Papers; *East Union News,* 1 Feb. 1895; Almond diary, 6 June 1864, Almond Papers; Merrilies diary, 6 June 1864, Merrilies Papers.

19. *Montevideo Leader,* 19 Feb. 1909; Pehr Carlson letter, 29 June 1864, Carlson Papers; Merrilies diary, 7 June 1864, Merrilies Papers.

20. OR, ser. 1, vol. 39, pt. 1, 172; Merrilies diary, 8 June 1864, Merrilies Papers; Halsey diary, 8 June 1864, Halsey Papers; *East Union News,* 15 Feb. 1895.

21. OR, ser. 1, vol. 39, pt. 1, 207; Bearss, *Forrest,* 52.

22. Merrilies diary, 8 June 1864, Merrilies Papers.

23. OR, ser. 1, vol. 39, pt. 1, 91; Samuel Pepper, *My Dear Wife: The Civil War Letters of Private Samuel Pepper, Company G–95th Illinois Infantry 1862 to 1865* (Caledonia,

Ill.: Muffled Drum Press, 2003), 82–83; *MICIW*, 2:464; Woodbury diary, 9 June 1864, Woodbury Papers.

24. Wilkin letters, 9 and 18 June 1864, Wilkin Papers; *MICIW*, 2:464; Hill letter, 9 June 1864, Hill Papers.

25. *East Union News*, 15 Feb. 1895; *MICIW*, 2:465; Merrilies diary, 9 June 1864, Merrilies Papers; W. F. [William Franklin] Lyon, *In and Out of Andersonville Prison* (Detroit: George Harland, 1907), 12–13.

26. Lyon, *Andersonville*, 14–15; William F. Lyon CMSR and Pension File No. 451,787; *East Union News*, 15 Feb. 1895.

27. *OR*, ser. 1, vol. 39, pt. 1, 165; James Dinkins, "The Battle of Brice's Crossroads," *Confederate Veteran* (Oct. 1925): 380; Grierson, *Just and Righteous Cause*, 242–43; *Mower County Register*, 30 June 1864; Lyon, *Andersonville*, 15.

28. *OR*, ser. 1, vol. 39, pt. 1, 92, 104, 119, 167.

29. Marvin D. Layman, *The Bartlesons of Grand Chain*, rev. ed. (N.p.: Marvin D. Layman, 1998), 89; Merrilies diary, 10 June 1864, Merrilies Papers.

30. *Rochester City Post*, 2 July 1864; Bearss, *Forrest*, 61–66; Hills, "Study in Warfighting," 21–25.

31. *OR*, ser. 1, vol. 39, pt. 1, 192.

Notes to Chapter Seven

1. A. J. Carlson recalled, "We had all day marched in what is called left in front," *East Union News*, 15 Feb. 1895; *1863 U.S. Infantry Tactics*, 7–9; Dominic J. Dal Bello, *Parade, Inspection and Basic Evolutions of the Infantry Battalion*, 4th ed. (Santa Barbara, Calif.: Dominic Dal Bello, 1998), 18–19, 56.

2. *OR*, ser. 1, vol. 39, pt. 1, 92, 104.

3. John L. Satterlee, *The Journal & the 114th 1861 to 1865* (Springfield, Ill.: Phillips Brothers, 1979), 259; Dean affidavit in Josiah Cooper (Co. I) Pension File No. 500,567, courtesy of Arlene Gabel private collection; *National Tribune* (Washington, D.C.), 16 June 1887.

4. William F. Lyon Pension File No. 451,787.

5. *1863 U.S. Infantry Tactics*, 24–26; *New Albany (Ind.) Ledger*, 14 June 1864; George W. Herrick letter, 15 June 1864, courtesy of Carol Jauregui private collection; Aiton letter, 14 June 1864, Aiton Papers.

6. Wilkin letter, 18 June 1864, Wilkin Papers; John King letter to Gessner, 20 Feb. 1882, and Gessner pamphlet, 58, Gessner Papers; *OR*, ser. 1, vol. 39, pt. 1, 196.

7. *Mower County Register*, 30 June 1864; *OR*, ser. 1, vol. 39, pt. 1, 114, 116–17, 169, 173.

8. *Rochester City Post*, 25 June 1864; *Richmond (Minn.) Standard*, 5 Mar. 1909; *Montevideo Leader*, 19 Feb. 1909; George O. Jenkins Pension File No. 188,477; *Mankato Weekly Record*, 25 June 1864; Keysor interview, 29, Keysor Papers; Pehr Carlson letter, 29 June 1864, Carlson Papers.

9. Dean letter, 14 June 1864, Dean Papers; Herrick letter, 15 June 1864; Samuel Ennerson Pension File No. 261,079.

10. *MICIW*, 2:465; *1863 U.S. Infantry Tactics*, 8; Evan Watkins and John Watkins CMSRs; Arad Welch Pension File No. 417,206.

11. Grierson, *Just and Righteous Cause*, 248.

12. *OR*, ser. 1, vol. 39, pt. 1, 195–96; Merrilies diary, 10 June 1864, Merrilies Papers.

13. *MICIW*, 2:465; *East Union News*, 15 Feb. 1895; Herrick letter, 15 June 1864.

14. *OR*, ser. 1, vol. 39, pt. 1, 107; Aiton letter, 14 June 1864, Aiton Papers.

15. *OR*, ser. 1, vol. 39, pt. 1, 129, 132; Grierson, *Just and Righteous Cause*, 244–45; William Forse Scott, *The Story of a Cavalry Regiment: The Career of the Fourth Iowa Veteran Volunteers, from Kansas to Georgia 1861–1865* (New York: G. P. Putnam's Sons, 1893), 237.

16. *Indianapolis Sunday Star*, 9 June 1912; *OR*, ser. 1, vol. 39, pt. 1, 132; Grierson, *Just and Righteous Cause*, 244–45; George E. Waring Jr., *Whip and Spur* (New York: Doubleday and McClure, 1897), 136.

17. Bearss, *Forrest*, 71; Thomas Jordan and J. P. Pryor, *The Campaigns of Lieut.-Gen. N. B. Forrest, and of Forrest's Cavalry* (Dayton, Ohio: Press of the Morningside Bookshop, 1973), 468–70; Henry George, *History of the 3d, 7th, 8th and 12th Kentucky, C.S.A.* (Lyndon, Ky.: Mull-Wathen Historic Press, 1970), 92–93. R. R. Hancock, *Hancock's Diary; or, A History of the Second Tennessee Confederate Cavalry* (Dayton, Ohio: Morningside Press, 1999), 382–84. It is this author's belief that the strength of Forrest's army at Brice's Crossroads has been understated, hence the estimated figures given in this chapter. The detailed reasoning behind this assertion will appear in a forthcoming study of the battle.

18. Edward F. Winslow, "Episode 4. Expeditions from Memphis May and June 1864," unpublished Civil War memoir, Edward F. Winslow Papers, University of Iowa, Iowa City, 13 (hereafter cited as Winslow Papers).

19. *OR*, ser. 1, vol. 39, pt. 1, 132, 135, 137.

20. *OR*, ser. 1, vol. 30, pt. 1, 92–93; Grierson, *Just and Righteous Cause*, 246.

21. John Milton Hubbard, *Notes of a Private* (Memphis, Tenn.: E. H. Clark & Brother, 1909), 99; John Watson Morton, "Fighting under Forrest at the Battle of Brice's Crossroads," in *The New Annals of the Civil War*, eds. Peter Cozzens and Robert I. Girardi (Mechanicsburg, Pa.: Stackpole Books, 2004), 363–80.

22. *OR*, ser. 1, vol. 39, pt. 1, 119; Surgeon Dyer's account, dated 30 June 1864, in Frank Moore, *Rebellion Record: A Diary of American Events*, vol. 11 (New York: D. Van Nostrand, 1868), 168; Gessner pamphlet, 17, and James Mooney letter to Gessner, 20 Feb. 1882, Gessner Papers.

23. *OR*, ser. 1, vol. 39, pt. 1, 208; Gessner pamphlet, 62, Gessner Papers; *Indianapolis Sunday Star*, 9 June 1912; *National Tribune* (Washington, D.C.), 28 May 1896.

24. *OR*, ser. 1, vol. 39, pt. 1, 163; Winslow memoir, "Episode 4," 12–14, Winslow Papers.

25. *OR*, ser. 1, vol. 39, pt. 1, 104, 111, 117; John Satterlee, *Journal & 114th*, 259.

26. Grierson, *Just and Righteous Cause*, 247; Scott, *Cavalry Regiment*, 270–73; Louis Bir, "Remenecence of My Army Life," *Indiana Magazine of History* 101, no. 1 (Mar. 2005): 37.

27. Jordan and Pryor, *Lieut.-Gen. N. B. Forrest*, 471–72; Hubbard, *Notes of a Private*, 99; George, *History of the 3d*, 93; Hancock, *Hancock's Diary*, 385–86; John W. Carroll, *Autobiography and Reminiscences of John W. Carroll* (Harrah, Okla.: Brandy Station Bookshelf, 2003), 30; Nathaniel Cheairs Hughes Jr., *Brigadier General Tyree Bell, C. S. A.: Forrest's Fighting Lieutenant* (Knoxville: University of Tennessee Press, 2004), 142.

28. *OR*, ser. 1, vol. 39, pt. 1, 111, 169; *National Tribune* (Washington, D.C.), 16 June 1887; George, *History of the 3d*, 93.

29. John Satterlee, *Journal & 114th*, 259.

30. Newsome, *Experience in the War*, 160–61; Gessner pamphlet, 62–63.

31. *OR*, ser. 1, vol. 39, pt. 1, 209; an account by "One of Forrest's Escort," *Supplement to the Official Records of the Union and Confederate Armies*, 7:193; Winslow memoir, "Episode 4," 14, Winslow Papers.

32. *MICIW*, 2:465; *OR*, ser. 1, vol. 39, pt. 1, 194–95; Gessner pamphlet, 27, Gessner Papers. The order of the Ninth Minnesota's companies was determined by the seniority of the captains present and absent according to the regulations in *1863 U.S. Infantry Tactics*, 7–9, and confirmed in regimental accounts.

33. Aiton letter, 14 June 1864, Aiton Papers; *Mower County Register*, 30 June 1864; *Mankato Weekly Record*, 25 June 1864; *Rochester City Post*, 2 July 1864; *Montevideo Leader*, 19 Feb. 1909; Dean letter, 15 June 1864, Dean Papers.

34. *MICIW*, 2:465; *OR*, ser. 1, vol. 39, pt. 1, 209; Keysor interview, 29, Keysor Papers.

35. H. A. Tyler letter to E. W. Rucker, 22 June 1908, Edmund Winchester Rucker Papers, Birmingham Public Library, Birmingham, Ala. (hereafter cited as Rucker Papers); *1863 U.S. Infantry Tactics*, 164–65, 181–83; *Rochester City Post*, 25 June and 16 July 1864; George, *History of the 3d*, 93; *MICIW*, 2:465.

36. Tyler letter to Rucker, 22 June 1908, Rucker Papers; Aiton letters, 14 and 15 June 1864, Aiton Papers; *St. Peter Tribune*, 29 June 1864; Thomas Hughes, *Old Traverse des Sioux* (St. Peter, Minn.: Herald Publishing, 1929), 143.

37. *MICIW*, 2:465; Aiton letter, 14 June 1864, Aiton Papers; "One of Forrest's Escort," account, *Supplement to the Official Records*, 7:193.

38. *MICIW*, 2:465; *Rochester City Post*, 2 July 1864; *Mankato Weekly Record*, 25 June 1864; Wilkin letter, 18 June 1864, Wilkin Papers; Tyler letter to Rucker, 22 June 1908, Rucker Papers; *Daily Mississippian* (Jackson, Miss.), 7 July 1864; *OR*, ser. 1, vol. 39, pt. 1, 231.

39. Carroll, *Autobiography and Reminiscences*, 30; Hughes, *Brigadier General Tyree Bell*, 143–44; *Rochester City Post*, 2 and 16 July 1864; Herrick letter, 15 June 1864, private collection; *Montevideo Leader*, 19 Feb. 1864.

40. *MICIW*, 2:465–66; Wilkin letter, 18 June 1864, Wilkin Papers; Merrilies diary, 10 June 1864, Merrilies Papers; D. C. Thomas letter to Gessner, 9 Feb. 1882, Gessner Papers.

41. *MICIW*, 2:467–68; *Winona Daily Republican*, 30 June 1864; *St. Paul Press*, 1 Dec. 1864; Hiram A. Buck Pension File No. 307,919; Herrick letter, 15 June 1864, private collection; John Burns Pension File No. 162,758.

42. *MICIW*, 2:467–68; Godfrey Hammerberg Pension File No. 65,229; Felch letter, 15 June 1864, Steffens Papers; Nicholas Swab Pension File No. 78,650; Curtiss-Wedge, *Mower County*, 441; Augustus Whitney Pension File No. 92,398; Keysor interview, 29–30, Keysor Papers; *Rochester City Post*, 25 June 1864.

43. *Rochester City Post*, 2 July 1864; *MICIW*, 2:466; *OR*, ser. 1, vol. 39, pt. 1, 111–12; *New Albany (Ind.) Ledger*, 14 June 1864.

44. *OR*, ser. 1, vol. 39, pt. 1, 104–5; *St. Paul Press*, 19 Aug. 1865.

45. *OR*, ser. 1, vol. 39, pt. 1, 111, 209; Bearss, *Forrest*, 91.

46. Nathaniel Cheairs Hughes, *Brigadier General Tyree Bell*, 143; *Mobile Evening News*, 17 June 1864; Wilkin letter, 24 June 1864, Wilkin Papers; Jordan and Pryor, *Lieut.-Gen. N. B. Forrest*, 472; Morton, "Fighting," 369; Hancock, *Hancock's Diary*, 386–87.

47. Morton, "Fighting," 369; Nathaniel Cheairs Hughes, *Brigadier General Tyree Bell*, 143–44; Bearss, *Forrest*, 96–97; Merrilies diary, 10 June 1864, Merrilies Papers.

NOTES TO CHAPTER EIGHT

1. *MICIW*, 2:466; "One of Forrest's Escort," account, *Supplement to the Official Records*, 7: 193; *Rochester City Post*, 2 July 1864; Merrilies diary, 10 June 1864, Merrilies Papers; Samuel Ennerson Pension File No. 261,079.

2. *MICIW*, 2:466; Scott, *Cavalry Regiment*, 247.

3. *Mower County Register*, 30 June 1864; *Mankato Weekly Record*, 25 June 1864; Gessner pamphlet, 27, Gessner Papers; *Rochester City Post*, 16 July 1864; Arad Welch Pension File No. 417,206; Jules Capon Pension File No. 174,099; Joel D. Chamberlain Pension File No. 300,674.

4. Winslow Civil War memoir, "Episode 4," 14–15, Winslow Papers; *OR*, ser. 1, vol. 39, pt. 1, 137.

5. *OR*, ser. 1, vol. 39, pt. 1, 163, 195, 204.

6. On Buford, see Warner, *Generals in Gray*, 39; Mercer Otey, "Story of Our Great War," *Confederate Veteran* (Mar. 1901): 110; Jesse Hawes, *Cahaba: A Story of Captive Boys in Blue* (New York: Burr Printing House, 1888), 76; Hancock, *Hancock's Diary*, 386–87; Jordan and Pryor, *Lieut.-Gen. N. B. Forrest*, 473. Mooney letter to Gessner, 20 Feb. 1882, Gessner Papers; Morton, "Fighting," 370–71.

7. Edward M. Coffman, "Memoirs of Hylan B. Lyon Brigadier General, C.S.A.," *Tennessee Historical Quarterly* 18 (Mar. 1959): 43; Mooney letter to Gessner, 20 Feb. 1882, Gessner Papers; Henry Ewell Hord, "Brice's X Roads from A Private's View," *Confederate Veteran* (Nov. 1904): 529–30.

8. *OR*, ser. 1, vol. 39, pt. 1, 93, 105, 209; *Chicago Tribune*, 28 Feb. 1882.

9. *OR*, ser. 1, vol. 39, pt. 1, 105, 210.

10. Gessner pamphlet, 59, 62, Gessner Papers.

11. Gessner pamphlet, 40–41, Gessner Papers.

12. Moore, *Rebellion Record*, 11:168; *MICIW*, 2:467; John Summers Pension File No. 243,069; *East Union News*, 1 Mar. 1895.

13. *OR*, ser. 1, vol. 39, pt. 1, 145; Gessner pamphlet, 6, Gessner Papers.

14. *OR*, ser. 1, vol. 39, pt. 1, 195; Abial R. Abbott, "The Negro in the War of the Rebellion," in *Military Essays and Recollections*, vol. 3, Illinois Commandery, Military Order of the Loyal Legion of the United States (Chicago: Dial Press, 1899), 376–77; *Belvidere (Ill.) Standard*, 5 July 1864; John Satterlee, *Journal & 114th*, 261; *MICIW*, 2:467.

15. George, *History of the 3d*, 94.

16. *Indianapolis Sunday Star*, 9 June 1912; *OR*, ser. 1, vol. 39, pt. 1, 125, 182; Grierson, *Just and Righteous Cause*, 249; Moore, *Rebellion Record*, 11:168.

17. Morton, "Fighting," 372; Moore, *Rebellion Record*, 11:168; Lyon, *Andersonville*, 17; *East Union News*, 1 Mar. 1895.

18. Moore, *Rebellion Record*, 11:168; William F. Lyon Pension File No. 451,787.

19. *East Union News*, 1 Mar. 1895.

20. Lyon, *Andersonville*, 18; *OR*, ser. 1, vol. 39, pt. 1, 133, 903; Grierson, *Just and Righteous Cause*, 248–49; Hancock, *Hancock's Diary*, 390–92; Morton, "Fighting," 372–73 J. Harvey Mathes, *General Forrest* (New York: Appleton, 1902), 240, map.

21. *OR*, ser. 1, vol. 39, pt. 1, 125–26, 177; Gessner pamphlet, 21, Gessner Papers; Parker Hills, "A Study in Warfighting," 38–42, is invaluable for understanding the

course of the battle on the west bank of Tishomingo Creek and the retreat through the successive positions up through sunset.

22. Morton, "Fighting," 373; *OR,* ser. 1, vol. 39, pt. 1, 182; *Indianapolis Sunday Star,* 9 June 1912; *Fremont (Ohio) Journal,* 14 June 1889; John Satterlee, *Journal & 114th,* 255; *National Tribune* (Washington, D.C.), 20 Apr. 1916.

23. *OR,* ser. 1, vol. 39, pt. 1, 126, 182, 184, 213; Morton, "Fighting," 373.

24. John Watkins Pension File No. 225,874; *Rochester City Post,* 2 July 1864; Morton, "Fighting," 373; *Mower County Register,* 30 June 1864; Parker B. Pillow letter to Gessner, 31 Jan. 1882, Gessner Papers.

25. *Rochester City Post,* 2 July 1864; *MICIW,* 1:422, 2:466; *Mower County Register,* 30 June 1864.

26. *Montevideo Leader,* 19 Feb. 1909; *Rochester City Post,* 2 July 1864; *Mankato Weekly Record,* 25 June 1864.

27. Aiton letter, 14 June 1864, Aiton Papers; *Fremont (Ohio) Journal,* 14 June 1889. Robert Medkirk erred in calling it the Tenth Minnesota, but the Tenth did not join the First Brigade until late June 1864; *OR,* ser. 1, vol. 39, pt. 1, 903.

28. Morton, "Fighting," 373; *Montevideo Leader,* 19 Feb. 1909; *OR,* ser. 1, vol. 39, pt. 1, 124, 182, 903–4; Pillow letter to Gessner, 31 Jan. 1882, Gessner Papers; William S. Blackman, *The Boy of Battle Ford and the Man* (Marion, Ill.: Egyptian Press Printing, 1906), 84.

29. *OR,* ser. 1, vol. 39, pt. 1, 182; Lyman Raymond Pension File No. 1,094,810; *Montevideo Leader,* 19 Feb. 1909; *Mower County Register,* 30 June 1864.

30. Morton, "Fighting," 373; Taliesin Williams Pension File No. 316,440, courtesy of Jean C. Pool private collection; Josiah Cooper Pension File No. 500,567; *Montevideo Leader,* 19 Feb. 1909; Albert Downing Pension File No. 1,060,928.

31. *MICIW,* 1:422; *Chaska Valley Herald,* 24 Dec. 1864; Andrew Bangston Pension File No. 312,320; *St. Paul Press,* 8 Dec. 1864.

32. *MICIW,* 2:466; Morton, "Fighting," 373.

33. *OR,* ser. 1, vol. 39, pt. 1, 93, 115.

34. *OR,* ser. 1, vol. 39, pt. 1, 108, 211; *National Tribune* (Washington, D.C.), 16 June 1887.

35. *OR,* ser. 1, vol. 39, pt. 1, 108.

36. *OR,* ser. 1, vol. 39, pt. 1, 904; Morton, "Fighting," 373–74.

37. *OR,* ser. 1, vol. 39, pt. 1, 126, 904; Morton, "Fighting," 374.

38. Morton, "Fighting," 374; Layman, *Bartlesons,* 92; J. J. Fitzgerrell letter to Gessner, n.d. (Feb. 1882), Gessner Papers; *National Tribune* (Washington, D.C.), 16 June 1887 and 23 Mar. 1916.

39. Morton, "Fighting," 374; *MICIW,* 2:466; *St. Paul Press,* 7 July 1864; *Montevideo Leader,* 19 Feb. 1909; Herrick letter, 15 June 1864, private collection; Dean letter, 16 June 1864, Dean Papers; John Satterlee, *Journal & 114th,* 259, 261.

40. *OR,* ser. 1, vol. 39, pt. 1, 108; Wilkin letter, 18 June 1864, Wilkin Papers; Aiton letter, 14 June 1864, Aiton Papers.

41. Samuel A. Agnew, "Battle of Tishomingo Creek," *Confederate Veteran* (Sept. 1900): 402; *OR,* ser. 1, vol. 39, pt. 1, 904; Morton, "Fighting," 374–75; "One of Forrest's Escorts," account, *Supplement to the Official Records,* 7:194; Mamie Yeary, *Reminiscences of the Boys in Gray 1861–1865* (Dayton, Ohio: Morningside, 1986), 767.

42. Hord, "Brice's X Roads," 531; *OR*, ser. 1, vol. 39, pt. 1, 904; *Rochester City Post,* 2 July 1864; Edward Bouton, *Events of the Civil War* (Los Angeles: Kingsley, Moles and Collins, 1906), 67. William A. Drobak's *Freedom by the Sword: The U.S. Colored Troops, 1862–1867* (Washington, D.C.: Center of Military History, U.S. Army, 2011), 214, pointedly fails to include the Ninth Minnesota in citing the praise of the rear guard in McMillen's report; OR, ser. 1, vol. 39, pt. 1, 105–6.

43. *MICIW*, 1:422, 2:466; Yeary, *Reminiscences,* 767; John Satterlee, *Journal & 114th,* 259; *OR*, ser. 1, vol. 39, pt. 1, 904.

44. Evan Watkins Pension File No. 50,774; Jacob Bader and Charles Dietrich CMSRs, NA RG-94; Myron Tower Pension File No. 60,987; *Portrait and Biographical Album of Lancaster County, Nebraska* (Chicago: Chapman Brothers, 1888), 589–91; Wilbur Fisk Stone, *History of Colorado,* vol. 3 (Chicago: S. J. Clarke Publishing, 1918), 688–90; *Rochester City Post,* 25 June 1864; *Mankato Weekly Union,* 24 June 1864; *National Tribune* (Washington, D.C.), 19 Mar. 1903; Matice Scherrer Pension File No. 70,486.

45. *OR*, ser. 1, vol. 39, pt. 1, 105–6; *Mower County Register,* 30 June 1864; Herrick letter, 15 June 1864, private collection; Dean letter, 14 June 1864, Dean Papers; *MICIW*, 1:422.

46. *St. Paul Press,* 7 July 1864; *OR*, ser. 1, vol. 39, pt. 1, 94, 205.

Notes to Chapter Nine

1. *Mankato Weekly Record,* 25 June 1864; John Satterlee, *Journal & 114th,* 261; *Richmond (Minn.) Standard,* 5 Mar. 1909; *State Atlas* (Minneapolis), 22 June 1864. For Lucius Babcock, see Edmund Raus, *Where Duty Called Them: The Story of the Samuel Babcock Family of Homer, New York, in the Civil War* (Daleville, Va.: Schroder Publications, 2001), 14.

2. *OR*, ser. 1, vol. 39, pt. 1, 109; Moore, *Rebellion Record,* 11:169; Merrilies diary, 10 June 1864, Merrilies Papers; Lyon, *Andersonville,* 18; *National Tribune* (Washington, D.C.), 23 Mar. 1916; *East Union News,* 1 Mar. 1895; Newsome, *Experience in the War,* 162–63.

3. *OR*, ser. 1, vol. 39, pt. 1, 109, 205, 214; Moore, *Rebellion Record,* 11:169.

4. Mooney letter to Gessner, 9 Mar. 1882, Gessner Papers; *OR*, ser. 1, vol. 39, pt. 1, 109; Bjorn Skaptason, ed., "West Tennessee U.S. Colored Troops and the Retreat from Brice's Crossroads: An Eyewitness Account by Major James C. Foster (USA)," *The West Tennessee Historical Society Papers* 60 (2006): 83; James C. Foster letter to Gessner, 10 Mar. 1882, Gessner Papers; Merrilies diary, 10 June 1864, Merrilies Papers; Taliesin Williams Pension File No. 316,440.

5. Skaptason, "West Tennessee," 83; *MICIW*, 1:423; *Montevideo Leader,* 19 Feb. 1909; Jules Capon Pension File No. 174,099; *Rochester City Post,* 2 July 1864.

6. Aiton letter, 15 June 1864, Aiton Papers; Seth Wheaton letter to Gessner, 20 Mar. 1882, Gessner Papers; Herrick letter, 15 June 1864, private collection; *MICIW*, 1:423; *Montevideo Leader,* 19 Feb. 1909; *Mankato Weekly Record,* 3 Sept. 1864.

7. Herrick letter, 15 June 1864, private collection; Lyman Raymond Pension File No. 1,094,810; *MICIW*, 1:423; *Richmond (Minn.) Standard,* 5 Mar. 1909; *Mower County Register,* 30 June 1864; Ebenezer Clapp, *Clapp Memorials,* 338; *Rochester City Post,* 2 July 1864; *Montevideo Leader,* 19 Feb. 1909; *Mankato Weekly Record,* 25 June 1864.

8. Lyman Raymond Pension File No. 1,094,810; Herrick letter, 15 June 1864, private collection.

9. Matice Scherrer Pension File No. 70,486; Albert Downing Pension File No. 1,060,928.

10. Robert Selph Henry, *As They Saw Forrest* (Jackson, Tenn.: McCowat-Mercer Press, 1956), 127–28; John Watson Morton, *The Artillery of Nathan Bedford Forrest's Cavalry* (Marietta, Ga.: R. Bemis Publishing, 1995), 181; Frank Moore, *Anecdotes, Poetry and Incidents of the War: North and South 1860–1865* (New York: Publication Office, Bible House, 1867), 451; John Milton Hubbard, *Notes of a Private*, 105.

11. Herrick letter, 15 June 1864, private collection.

12. *OR*, ser. 1, vol. 39, pt. 1, 109, 138; *MICIW*, 1:423; Scott, *Cavalry Regiment*, 255.

13. Moore, *Rebellion Record*, 11:168–69; John Satterlee, *Journal & 114th*, 255; Fremont (Ohio) *Journal*, 14 June 1889; *OR*, ser. 1, vol. 39, pt. 1, 94.

14. Lyman Raymond Pension File No. 1,094,810; *St. Paul Press*, 23 June 1864, with the list of officers who came in with Markham.

15. Waring, *Whip and Spur*, 132; Moore, *Rebellion Record*, 11:169; *National Tribune* (Washington, D.C.), 13 Mar. 1903; John C. Dixon Pension File No. 943,746; *National Tribune*, 22 Jan. 1914; *St. Paul Press*, 7 July 1864.

16. *Fremont (Ohio) Journal*, 14 June 1889.

17. Skaptason, "West Tennessee," 84; *MICIW*, 2:466; Wilkin letter, 18 June 1864, Wilkin Papers.

18. Hancock, *Hancock's Diary*, 393–94; *OR*, ser. 1, vol. 39, pt. 1, 127, 182–83; Foster letter to Gessner, 10 Mar. 1882, Gessner Papers; Blackman, *Boy of Battle Ford*, 85.

19. Jordan and Pryor, *Lieut.-Gen. N. B. Forrest*, 478–79; Mooney letter to Gessner, 9 Mar. 1882, Gessner Papers; Herrick letter, 15 June 1864, private collection; *Mankato Weekly Record*, 25 June 1864; *OR*, ser. 1, vol. 39, pt. 1, 138; John Satterlee, *Journal & 114th*, 260.

20. Grierson, *Just and Righteous Cause*, 251–52; Blackman, *Boy of Battle Ford*, 85; Foster letter to Gessner, 10 Mar. 1882, Gessner Papers; *OR*, ser. 1, vol. 39, pt. 1, 182–83.

21. Merrilies diary, 11 June 1864, Merrilies Papers.

22. Bearss, *Forrest*, 124–25; Merrilies diary, 11 June 1864, Merrilies Papers; Scott, *Cavalry Regiment*, 262; *National Tribune* (Washington, D.C.), 19 Mar. 1903.

23. *Mower County Register*, 30 June 1864; Lyon, *Andersonville*, 18–19; *MICIW*, 1:423; *East Union News*, 15 Mar. 1895; *St. Peter Tribune*, 29 June 1864.

24. *OR*, ser. 1, vol. 39, pt. 1, 112; Hancock, *Hancock's Diary*, 395–96; Mobile (Ala.) *Evening News*, 17 June 1864; Newsome, *Experience in the War*, 163.

25. Jordan and Pryor, *Lieut.-Gen. N. B. Forrest*, 478–79; *National Tribune* (Washington, D.C.), 28 May 1896; Edward A. Davenport, *History of the Ninth Regiment Illinois Cavalry Volunteers* (Chicago: Donohue & Henneberry, 1888), 112; *Rochester City Post*, 2 July 1864; Ebenezer Clapp, *Clapp Memorials*, 338; *Fremont (Ohio) Journal*, 14 June 1889.

26. *OR*, ser. 1, vol. 39, pt. 1, 112, 116; *Daily Herald* (Cleveland, Ohio), 23 June 1864; *National Tribune* (Washington, D.C.), 30 June 1887.

27. *Montevideo Leader*, 19 Feb. 1909; *Rochester City Post*, 25 June 1864; Taliesin Williams Pension File No. 316,440; Herrick letter, 15 June 1864, private collection; Ebenezer Clapp, *Clapp Memorials*, 338.

28. Davenport, *Ninth Regiment Illinois*, 113; *OR*, ser. 1, vol. 39, pt. 1, 113; John Watkins Pension File No. 225,874.

29. Merrilies diary, 11 June 1864, Merrilies Papers; Lyman Raymond Pension File No. 1,094,810; *Mankato Weekly Record*, 3 Sept. 1864.

30. *OR*, ser. 1, vol. 39, pt. 1, 120; *Montevideo Leader*, 19 Feb. 1909; Varnum Hadley letter to Mrs. Jacob Dieter, 15 June 1864, Dieter Papers.

31. Onley Andrus, *The Civil War Letters of Sergeant Onley Andrus* (Urbana: University of Illinois Press, 1947), 87; *St. Paul Press*, 7 July 1864; *Daily Herald* (Cleveland, Ohio), 23 June 1864; *Rochester City Post*, 2 July 1864.

32. *St. Paul Press*, 30 June 1864; *Woodstock (Ill.) Sentinel*, 29 June 1864; David Ellis Pension File No. 40,770; *Richmond (Minn.) Standard*, 5 Mar. 1909; Lyman Raymond Pension File No. 1,094,810.

33. *OR*, ser. 1, vol. 39, pt. 1, 203; Grierson, *Just and Righteous Cause*, 253.

34. *OR*, ser. 1, vol. 39, pt. 1, 109; "George A. Woodruff's Account of the Battle of Brice's Cross Roads Written June 10th, 1897," courtesy Randy Morford, at: http://www.34hotrod.com/geneaology/red_willow-co/george_woodruff.htm.

35. Theodore George Carter, "Tupelo Campaign," 95.

36. *OR*, ser. 1, vol. 39, pt. 1, 109; Foster letter to Gessner, 10 Mar. 1882, Gessner Papers; Skaptason, "West Tennessee," 88–89; Abial Abbott, "Negro in the War," 379.

37. Colin F. Macdonald, "The Battle of Brice's Cross Roads," in *Glimpses of the Nation's Struggle*, vol. 6, Minnesota Commandery, Military Order of the Loyal Legion of the United States (Minneapolis: August Davis Publishing, 1909), 456–57; Herrick letter, 15 June 1864, private collection.

38. *OR*, ser. 1, vol. 39, pt. 1, 109; *National Tribune* (Washington, D.C.), 22 Jan. 1914; in Skaptason, "West Tennessee," 89, Foster stated the command did move at midnight, but that is an error; Blackman, *Boy of Battle Ford*, 87; Herrick letter, 15 June 1864, private collection; *Mankato Weekly Record*, 25 June 1864; Aiton letter, 15 June 1864, Aiton Papers; Dean letter, 14 June 1864, Dean Papers.

39. *O.R.*, ser. 1, vol. 39, pt. 1, 109; Wilkin letter, 18 June 1864, Wilkin Papers; Woodruff account; Hancock, *Hancock's Diary*, 397; Herrick letter, 15 June 1864, private collection; *Woodstock (Ill.) Sentinel*, 29 June 1864; Wilkin letter, 14 June 1864, Wilkin Papers.

40. Wilkin letter, 18 June 1864, Wilkin Papers; Mooney letter to Gessner, 9 Mar. 1882, Gessner Papers; Abial Abbott, "Negro in the War," 379–80; Skaptason, "West Tennessee," 90.

41. Wilkin letter, 18 June 1864, Wilkin Papers; Herrick letter, 15 June 1864, private collection; *MICIW*, 1:424; Mooney letter to Gessner, 9 Mar. 1882, and Gessner pamphlet, 46, Gessner Papers.

42. Herrick letter, 15 June 1864, private collection; Skaptason, "West Tennessee," 91–92; *Mower County Register*, 30 June 1864; George Hays Pension File No. 234,462; Wilkin letter, 14 June 1864, Wilkin Papers; Mooney letter to Gessner, 9 Mar. 1882, Gessner Papers.

43. *OR*, ser. 1, vol. 39, pt. 1, 109; *Woodstock (Ill.) Sentinel*, 29 June 1864; Wilkin letter, 18 June 1864, Wilkin Papers.

44. Wilkin letter, 18 June 1864, Wilkin Papers; *MICIW*, 1:424; *Mankato Weekly Record*, 25 June 1864; *Mower County Register*, 30 June 1864.

45. John Satterlee, *Journal & 114th*, 260; Herrick letter, 15 June 1864, private collection; *Woodstock (Ill.) Sentinel*, 29 June 1864.

46. Mooney letter to Gessner, 9 Mar. 1882, and Gessner pamphlet, 4, Gessner Papers; *OR*, ser. 1, vol. 39, pt. 2, 115.

47. *OR*, ser. 1, vol. 39, pt. 2, 115, 118; Herrick letter, 15 June 1864, private collection; Wilkin letter, 14 June 1864, Wilkin Papers.

48. Grierson, *Just and Righteous Cause*, 254; *Transcript* (Peoria, Ill.), 22 June 1864.

49. Herrick letter, 15 June 1864, private collection; Keysor interview, 32, Keysor Papers; Felch letter, 15 June 1864, Steffens Papers; *St. Paul Press*, 30 June 1864.

NOTES TO CHAPTER TEN

1. Wilkin letter, 14 June 1864, Wilkin Papers; *OR*, ser. 1, vol. 39, pt. 1, 110; Dean letter, 20 June 1864, Dean Papers; "List of Killed and Missing of the Ninth Reg. Minn. Vols. in the battle of Guntown and Ripley, Miss., June 15, 1864, amended to evening of 17th.," in Minnesota State Archives, Office of the Adjutant General, Reports and Records, Ninth Minnesota Volunteer Infantry, Minnesota Historical Society, St. Paul, is the basic source of the Ninth Minnesota's casualties. The revised list is in *MICIW*, 2:467–68.

2. Taliesin Williams Pension File No. 316,446; Albert Downing Pension File No. 1,060,928; *History of Winona and Olmsted Counties* (Chicago: H. H. Hill, 1883), 652–53.

3. Thomas E. Hughes, ed., *The History of the Welsh in Minnesota, Foriston and Lime Springs, Ia.* (Mankato, Minn.: Free Press Print, 1895), 51–52, 163; *Mankato Weekly Record*, 2 July and 3 Sept. 1864.

4. *Mankato Weekly Record*, 3 Sept. 1864.

5. *Mankato Free Press*, 27 Apr. 1908.

6. A. J. Carlson's story of the return of the three is in the *East Union News*, 15 Mar., 1 Apr., and 1 May 1895; see also the *Chaska Valley Herald*, 2 July 1864, and A. J. Carlson's obituary in the *Enterprise* (Cokato, Minn.), 25 Mar. 1909.

7. *St. Paul Press*, 21 July 1864; Aiton letter, 11 July 1864, Aiton Papers; *Burlington (Iowa) Hawkeye*, 16 July 1864; on Miller, see *A Biographical Record of Calhoun County, Iowa* (New York: S. J. Clarke Publishing, 1902), 229–30; *Daily Clarion* (Meridian, Miss.), 8 July 1864, citing the *Grenada Picket*.

8. *Rochester City Post*, 2 July 1864; *MICIW*, 2:467–68; *St. Paul Press*, 8 Dec. 1864.

9. Cos. C and K muster rolls, May–June 1864, NA RG-94; Company order books, NA RG-94; CMSRs of the liberators, NA RG-94.

10. *OR*, ser. 1, vol. 39, pt. 1, 95, 225, 230–31; Quartermaster General, *Roll of Honor (No. XX.) Names of Soldiers Who Died in Defense of the American Union, interred in the National Cemeteries at Corinth, Mississippi, Pittsburgh Landing, Tennessee and Jefferson Barracks, Missouri* (Washington, D.C.: G.P.O., 1869), 49–50.

11. Abial Abbott, "Negro in the War," 381; Newsome, *Experience in the War*, 243; *Winona Daily News*, 15 Mar. 1964.

12. *Rochester City Post*, 2 July 1864; Aiton letter, 15 June 1864, Aiton Papers; Herrick letter, 15 June 1864, private collection; Dean letter, 20 June 1864, Dean Papers; Grierson, *Just and Righteous Cause*, 254, 256; *OR*, ser. 1, vol. 39, pt. 1, 89, pt. 2, 121; Samuel D. Sturgis, *The Other Side as Viewed by Generals Grant, Sherman and Other Distinguished Officers* (Washington, D.C., 1882), 15.

13. Warner, *Generals in Blue*, 487; Gessner pamphlet, 16, 27, 28, 32, Gessner Papers; Grierson, *Just and Righteous Cause*, 256; Cox, *Military Reminiscences*, 2:118.

14. Aiton letter, 15 June 1864, Aiton Papers; Herrick letter, 15 June 1864, private collection; *St. Paul Press*, 30 June 1864; Davenport, *Ninth Regiment Illinois*, 116; John Satterlee, *Journal & 114th*, 272; Wilkin letter, 24 June 1864, Wilkin Papers.

15. *Rochester City Post*, 2 July 1864; Wilkin letter, 24 June 1864, Wilkin Papers; *MICIW*, 2:481.

NOTES TO CHAPTER ELEVEN

1. "Forrest's Guntown Victory," *Confederate Veteran* (Oct. 1905): 464; Henry, *As They Saw Forrest*, 133–34; Dabney H. Maury, "Recollections of Nathan Bedford Forrest," in *Battles and Leaders of the Civil War*, vol. 5, ed. Peter Cozzens (Urbana-Champaign: University of Illinois Press, 2002), 144–45; *Macon (Ga.) Telegraph*, 24 June 1864.

2. Ebenezer Clapp, *Clapp Memorials*, 338–39; *Rochester Republican*, 29 June 1864; E. L. Clapp, *Andersonville: Six Months a Prisoner of War* (Milwaukee: Daily Wisconsin Steam Printing House, 1865), 16–17; *Winona Daily Republican*, 18 Jan. 1876; John E. Warren, "Civil War Reminiscences," 6, Warren Papers, Wisconsin Historical Society, Madison; an abridged version was published as John E. Warren, "Release from the Bull Pen – Andersonville, 1864," *The Atlantic*, Nov. 1958, 130–38.

3. Lyon, *Andersonville*, 20–24.

4. *Montevideo Leader*, 19 Feb. 1909.

5. Lyon, *Andersonville*, 24–25.

6. Riley V. Beach, "Record and Extr. From Diaries of Army Life of Rev. Riley V. Beach of Co. 'B,' 113th Ills Inft Vols.," 32, courtesy of Terry and Peg McCarty private collection; James H. Dennison, *Dennison's Andersonville Diary* (Kankakee, Ill.: Kankakee County Historical Society, 1987), 38; *Harper County (Kans.) Times*, 21 Apr. 1881; Gustavus W. Dyer and John Trotwood Moore, *The Tennessee Civil War Veterans Questionnaires* (Easley, S.C.: Southern Historical Press, c. 1985), 1:375.

7. Jacob Hutchinson, "Glimpses of a Prisoner's Life," *The Ohio Soldier* 2, no. 5 (15 Sept. 1888): 69; Lyon, *Andersonville*, 26; *Harper County (Kans.) Times*, 28 Apr. 1881; *Montevideo Leader*, 19 Feb. 1909.

8. Wheaton letter to Gessner, 20 Mar. 1882, Gessner Papers; Robertson, "Journal," 127.

9. Samuel A. Agnew diary, 4:307, 309, Agnew Papers; William B. Woolverton, "A Sketch of Prison Life at Andersonville," *The Firelands Pioneer* 7 (1894): 63.

10. *Woodstock (Ill.) Sentinel*, 30 Nov. 1864; Samuel A. Agnew, *Historical Sketch of the Associated Reformed Presbyterian Church of Bethany, Lee County, Mississippi* (Louisville, 1881); extracts at: http://rootsweb.ancestry.com/~mslee/bethanyhist.html; Hughes, *Old Traverse*, 136.

11. Harkness Lay diary, 13 June 1864, courtesy of Richard D. Goff private collection, via Robert S. Davis (hereafter cited as Lay Papers); Layman, *Bartlesons*, 95; Lyon, *Andersonville*, 27.

12. Godfrey Hammerberg Pension File No. 65,229; *Montevideo Leader*, 19 Feb. 1909; *East Union News*, 1 Mar. 1895; John Gordon CMSR, NA RG-94.

13. Robertson, "Journal," 127; Agnew diary, 4:310, Agnew Papers.

14. *Montevideo Leader*, 26 Feb. 1909.

15. Hill letter, 17 June 1864, Hill Papers; *St. Paul Press*, 7 July 1864; *MICIW*, 1:157.

16. William Best Hesseltine, *Civil War Prisons: A Study in War Psychology* (Columbus: Ohio State University Press, 1998), 69–113; Charles W. Sanders Jr., *While in the*

Hands of the Enemy: Military Prisons of the Civil War (Baton Rouge: Louisiana State University Press, 2005), 118–220.

17. Lay diary, 14 June 1864, Lay Papers.

18. Hawes, *Cahaba*, 116; Woolverton, "Sketch," 63–64; *Daily Clarion* (Meridian, Miss.), 15 June 1864; *Macon (Ga.) Telegraph*, 24 June 1864.

19. *Rochester Republican*, 29 June 1864; *Winona Daily Republican*, 30 June 1864; Stephen N. Chandler letter, 15 June 1864, Stephen N. Chandler Papers, Mower County Historical Society, Austin, Minn. (hereafter cited as Chandler Papers).

20. *Montevideo Leader*, 26 Feb. 1909; Lay diary, 15 June 1864, Lay Papers.

21. Lay diary, 16 June 1864, Lay Papers; Warren, "Reminiscences," 7, Warren Papers; *Selma Daily Reporter*, 18 June 1864; E. L. Clapp, *Andersonville*, 18; Lyon, *Andersonville*, 27.

22. *Fremont (Ohio) Journal*, 18 June 1889.

23. *Fremont (Ohio) Journal*, 18 June 1889; Lay diary, 19 June 1864, Lay Papers; *Harper County (Kans.) Times*, 5 May 1881; Lyon, *Andersonville*, 28.

24. *Winona Daily Republican*, 20 Jan. 1876, 3 Dec. 1879; on von Braida, see also *National Tribune* (Washington, D.C.), 28 May 1925.

25. *Montevideo Leader*, 26 Feb. 1909; *Mobile (Ala.) Evening News*, 17 June 1864; *Macon (Ga.) Telegraph*, 21 June 1864.

26. Hill letter, 17 June 1864, Hill Papers.

27. *Montevideo Leader*, 26 Feb. 1864; John H. Lundquist, *Andersonville Prison Headcount Rosters: Monthly Roster by Month and Day as Maintained by the Confederate Army* (Minneapolis, 2004), also lists all the shipments to and from Andersonville, based on the camp records in National Archives, Records of the Commissary General, 1861–1905, RG-249. The late Jack Lundquist was a superb and enthusiastic researcher of Union prisoners held in Confederate camps.

28. A. O. Abbott, *Prison Life in the South* (New York: Harper & Brothers, 1865), 73–74.

29. Lonnie R. Speer, *Portals to Hell: Military Prisons of the Civil War* (Mechanicsburg, Pa.: Stackpole Books, 1997), 266–68; A. O. Abbott, *Prison Life*, 58–68; Newsome, *Experience in the War*, 177–80; *Fremont (Ohio) Journal*, 14 June 1889.

30. Newsome, *Experience in the War*, 173–76; William R. Lovell narrative, 1937, William R. Lovell Papers, Minnesota Historical Society, St. Paul (hereafter cited as Lovell Papers).

31. *Report on the Treatment of Prisoners of War by the Rebel Authorities during the War of the Rebellion*, 40th Cong., 3rd sess., H. Rep. No. 45, 1132 (hereafter cited as "Shanks Report"); Myron Tower Pension File No. 60,987; *Biographical Album of Lancaster County*, 590; Stone, *History of Colorado*, 3:668–70.

32. John Morrison CMSR, NA RG-94; James Strachan letter, 3 Aug. 1864, private collection.

33. Thomas Edgerton Pension File No. 147,587; Hawes, *Cahaba*, 48–50; Robertson, "Journal," 128; *Winona Daily Republican*, 26 Oct. 1864; *Macon (Ga.) Telegraph*, 24 June 1864.

34. Hawes, *Cahaba*, 52–53; *OR*, ser. 2, vol. 7, 423, 467.

35. Robertson, "Journal," 129; Jacob Bader CMSR and Pension File No. 376,712.

36. *Winona Daily Republican*, 26 Oct. 1864; Robertson, "Journal," 129–31; Hawes, *Cahaba*, 21.

37. *Rochester Republican*, 29 June 1864.

NOTES TO CHAPTER TWELVE

1. Principal sources on Andersonville: (1) surviving camp records in "Selected Records of the War Department Commissary General of Prisoners relating to Federal Prisoners of War confined at Andersonville, Georgia," RG-249, M1303, 6 rolls of microfilm, and online at Ancestry.com. Camp records include partial registers of prisoner departures (which also serve as a nominal roll from Dec. 1864). Additional sources are consolidated monthly strength reports, burial registers, and the hospital register. (2) *The Trial of Henry Wirz*, 40th Cong., 2nd sess. H. Doc. No. 23. (3) general histories of the camp, most notably, William Marvel, *Andersonville: The Last Depot* (Chapel Hill: University of North Carolina Press, 1994); Ovid L. Futch, *History of Andersonville Prison*, rev. ed. (Gainesville: University Press of Florida, 2011); and Robert Scott Davis, *Andersonville Civil War Prison* (Charleston, S.C.: History Press, 2010). Edwin C. Bearss, *Andersonville National Historic Site: Historical Resource Study and Historical Base Map* (Washington, D.C.: National Park Service, 1970), is a very useful guide to the physical layout and routine at the camp.

2. William N. Tyler, *The Dispatch Carrier*, 2nd ed. (Port Byron, Ill.: Port Byron "Globe" Print, 1892), 10.

3. Greipsland, *Nordmenn*, 181–82; *Fremont (Ohio) Journal*, 14 June 1889.

4. Andrew C. McCoy, 1898 speech on Andersonville, Andrew C. McCoy Papers, Andersonville National Historic Site, Andersonville, Ga. (hereafter cited as McCoy Papers); see also *Rochester Post*, 13 May 1898, which described McCoy's presentation. On Wirz, see Marvel, *Andersonville*, 35–38.

5. Greipsland, *Nordmenn*, 181; Layman, *Bartlesons*, 96; *The Trial of Henry Wirz*, H. Doc. No. 23, 556; Lyon, *Andersonville*, 29; James Madison Page, *The True Story of Andersonville Prison: A Defense of Major Henry Wirz* (New York: Neale Publishing, 1908), 80.

6. E. L. Clapp, *Andersonville*, 18–19; Marvel, *Andersonville*, 51–52. Composition of squads is derived primarily from the Andersonville Hospital Register (NA RG-249), which usually noted the detachment and squad of those who were admitted or who had died in the camp. The many dead from the Ninth Minnesota permit an analysis of the squads to which they and their comrades belonged. Thus, in combination with other sources on specific prisoners, it is possible to give a tentative arrangement of the squads.

7. *St. Cloud Democrat*, 17 Nov. 1864; Frank Weber CMSR, NA RG-94; Brian Schumacher, "Frank Weber," *Civil War Times* 44, no. 5 (Dec. 2005): 12. *OR*, ser. 2, vol. 7, 620, has a list of the detachment sergeants who signed a petition on 20 July 1864. One of the signers is given as "F. Webers, Company G, 9th Maine." This is clearly a misreading of the handwritten text for "Minn.," as there was no Sergeant Webers or Weber in the Ninth Maine. Weber provided Nicholas Schreifels some recollections of Andersonville in the *Richmond (Minn.) Standard*, 5 Mar. 1909. E. L. Clapp, *Andersonville*, 19. Woolverton, "Sketch," 64, gives his squad as "166," which was actually 66/1 after the reorganization on July 4.

8. John L. Hoster diary, 90, John L. Hoster Papers, Emory University, Atlanta, Ga. (hereafter cited as Hoster Papers); E. L. Clapp, *Andersonville*, 19.

9. "Shanks Report," H. Rep. No. 45, 1133; Woolverton, "Sketch," 64.

10. Greipsland, *Nordmenn*, 182; "Shanks Report," H. Rep. No. 45, 1099; McCoy speech, McCoy Papers; Layman, *Bartlesons*, 96; William Styple, ed., *Andersonville*

Giving Up the Ghost: A Collection of Prisoners' Diaries, Letters & Memoirs (Kearney, N.J.: Belle Grove Publishing, 1996), 30; Robert H. Kellogg, *Life and Death in Rebel Prisons* (Hartford, Conn.: L. Stebbins, 1866), 143.

11. McCoy speech, McCoy Papers; John H. Lundquist, *Andersonville Prison Headcount Rosters: Monthly Roster by Month and Day as Maintained by the Confederate Army* (Minneapolis, 2004), June 1864.

12. Lyon, *Andersonville*, 33–34; E. L. Clapp, *Andersonville*, 19–20; Warren, "Reminiscences," 8–9, Warren Papers.

13. John McElroy, *Andersonville: A Story of Rebel Military Prisons* (Toledo, Ohio: D. R. Locke, 1879), 190.

14. Greipsland, *Nordmenn*, 182, 184; Warren "Reminiscence," 8, Warren Papers; *Fremont (Ohio) Journal,* 14 June 1889.

15. E. L. Clapp, *Andersonville*, 12; David Kennedy diary, 20 June 1864, courtesy of Stephen E. Osman private collection (hereafter cited as Kennedy Papers); Warren, "Reminiscences," 9, Warren Papers; Layman, *Bartlesons*, 96; McCoy speech, McCoy Papers; Hoster diary, 90, Hoster Papers.

16. E. L. Clapp, *Andersonville*, 20; *Fremont (Ohio) Journal,* 14 June 1889; *Harper County (Kans.) Times,* 19 May and 2 June 1881; Henry Devillez, "Reminiscences of the Civil War: Andersonville," *Indiana Magazine of History* 11 (1915): 144.

17. McCoy speech, McCoy Papers; Marvel, *Andersonville*, 101.

18. Lundquist, *Headcount,* June 1864; McElroy, *Andersonville*, 629, which is part of Thomas J. Sheppard's recollections (628–38); William Lovell narrative, Lovell Papers; David Kennedy's papers include his original roster for Squad 42/1 (later 24/1), which notes Rafferty, Kennedy Papers.

19. *Mankato Union,* 23 June 1865; *Mankato Free Press,* 30 Jan. 1891.

20. E. L. Clapp, *Andersonville*, 21, Warren, "Reminiscences," 9, Warren Papers; Lyon, *Andersonville*, 64; McCoy speech, McCoy Papers.

21. McCoy speech, McCoy Papers; *Chaska Valley Herald,* 24 Dec. 1864; Bearss, *Andersonville*, 24–25; Lyon, *Andersonville*, 35.

22. *Montevideo Leader,* 26 Feb. 1909; *Mankato Union,* 23 June 1865; Warren, "Reminiscences," 8, Warren Papers; Marvel, *Andersonville*, 55–57.

23. *Montevideo Leader,* 26 Feb. 1909; Greipsland, *Nordmenn*, 183; E. L. Clapp, *Andersonville,* 37.

24. *Richmond (Minn.) Standard,* 5 Mar. 1909; *Lake Benton Valley News,* 5 Mar. 1913; McCoy speech, McCoy Papers.

25. Warren, "Reminiscences," 11–12, Warren Papers; File on George W. Daigh, 114th Illinois, George W. Daigh Papers, Andersonville National Historic Site, Andersonville, Ga.; Lay diary, 5 July 1864, Lay Papers.

26. E. L. Clapp, *Andersonville*, 31; *Richmond (Minn.) Standard,* 5 Mar. 1909; Lovell narrative, Lovell Papers; McCoy speech, McCoy Papers; Lyon, *Andersonville*, 44.

27. E. L. Clapp, *Andersonville*, 30–31; McCoy speech, McCoy Papers; *Mankato Union,* 23 June 1865.

28. McCoy speech, McCoy Papers; Woolverton, "Sketch," 65–66; *Lake Benton Valley News,* 26 Feb. 1913; *Richmond (Minn.) Standard,* 5 Mar. 1909; Greipsland, *Nordmenn,* 184; Lyon, *Andersonville*, 44.

29. Greipsland, *Nordmenn,* 184; McCoy speech, McCoy Papers; Lyon, *Andersonville*, 44; E. L. Clapp, *Andersonville*, 21–22.

30. Lyon, *Andersonville*, 58; McCoy speech, McCoy Papers; *Richmond (Minn.) Standard*, 5 Mar. 1909.

31. E. L. Clapp, *Andersonville*, 24; *Chaska Valley Herald*, 24 Dec. 1864; *Montevideo Leader*, 26 Feb. 1909; Greipsland, *Nordmenn*, 183–84.

32. McCoy speech, McCoy Papers; Greipsland, *Nordmenn*, 184; Lyon, *Andersonville*, 63; *OR*, ser. 2, vol. 7, 427; *Mankato Free Press*, 18 Jan. 1891.

33. Atwater's testimony in the "Shanks Report," H. Rep. No. 45, 1026; Jacob Dieter letter, 22 June 1864, Dieter Papers.

34. *Montevideo Leader*, 26 Feb. 1909; Lay diary, 28 June 1864, Lay Papers; Ronald G. Watson, ed., *From Ashby to Andersonville: The Civil War Diary and Reminiscences of Private George A. Hitchcock, 21st Massachusetts Infantry* (Campbell, Calif.: Savas Publishing, 1997), 236; George O. Jenkins's Andersonville notes, George O. Jenkins Papers, courtesy Jeff Glover private collection; Greipsland, *Nordmenn*, 186.

35. Marvel, *Andersonville*, 96–99; Hoster diary, 92, Hoster Papers; Watson, *From Ashby*, 238; Greipsland, *Nordmenn*, 186–87. Robert Scott Davis, *Ghosts and Shadows of Andersonville* (Macon, Ga.: Mercer University Press, 2006), 231–48, includes a unique, detailed account of the trial.

36. Bearss, *Andersonville*, 28; E. L. Clapp, *Andersonville*, 9; Warren, "Reminiscences," 10, Warren Papers.

37. E. L. Clapp, *Andersonville*, 9–10; *Montevideo Leader*, 26 Feb. 1909.

38. *Lake Benton Valley News*, 26 Feb. 1913; Watson, *From Ashby*, 238–39; E. L. Clapp, *Andersonville*, 9–10; Lay diary, 1 July 1864, Lay Papers.

39. E. L. Clapp, *Andersonville*, 11; McCoy speech, McCoy Papers; *Lake Benton Valley News*, 26 Feb. and 5 Mar. 1913.

40. E. L. Clapp, *Andersonville*, 23–25.

41. Lyon, *Andersonville*, 57–58; Edward A. Todd Pension File No. 812,098.

42. E. L. Clapp, *Andersonville*, 24–25; Lyon, *Andersonville*, 48, 50–51.

43. *Montevideo Leader*, 26 Feb. 1909; Marvel, *Andersonville*, 105; Willie D. Hammack's testimony in *The Trial of Henry Wirz*, H. Doc. No. 23, 496–511, quotes here from 498, 505.

44. *The Trial of Henry Wirz*, H. Doc. No. 23, 505, 508; *OR*, ser. 2, vol. 7, 393; On Hammack, see also Georgia State Archives, "Reminences [*sic*] of Confederate Soldiers and Stories of the War 1861–1865, Collected and Bound by the Georgia Division, Daughters of the Confederacy," vol. 2 (1940); "Reminiscences—Rev. Wm. David Hammack," 306–10; and "Randolph County, Georgia, Biographies: Biography of Rev. Willie (William D.) Hammack 1842–1936" in: http://files.usgwarchives.net/ga/randolph/bios/whammack.txt; Woolverton, "Sketch," 67–68; McElroy, *Andersonville*, 156.

45. Marvel, *Andersonville*, 105.

46. Marvel, *Andersonville*, 106; David Kennedy Papers; Alfred D. Burdick diary, 1 June and 14 July 1864, Alfred D. Burdick Papers, Wisconsin Historical Society, Madison; Watson, *From Ashby*, 239–40; Hoster diary, 93, Hoster Papers; *Montevideo Leader*, 26 Feb. 1909.

47. Lay diary, 6 July 1864, Lay Papers; E. L. Clapp, *Andersonville*, 26; Lyon *Andersonville*, 65; Basil Meek, *Twentieth Century History of Sandusky County* (Chicago: Richmond-Arnold Publishing, 1909), 920.

48. Lyon, *Andersonville*, 108–9.

49. Lundquist, *Headcount,* July 1864; H. Clavreul, *Diary of Rev. H. Clavreul* (Waterbury: Connecticut Association of Ex-Prisoners of War, 1910), 15.

50. Watson, *From Ashby,* 241; Greipsland, *Nordmenn,* 188; Lyon, *Andersonville,* 70–71; *Montevideo Leader,* 26 Feb. 1909.

51. Greipsland, *Nordmenn,* 188; McCoy speech, McCoy Papers; Hoster diary, 96, Hoster Papers.

52. *Montevideo Leader,* 26 Feb. 1909; E. L. Clapp, *Andersonville,* 26; *Richmond (Minn.) Standard,* 5 Mar. 1909.

53. E. L. Clapp, *Andersonville,* 23.

54. Lyon, *Andersonville,* 66–67; E. L. Clapp, *Andersonville,* 26.

55. *Montevideo Leader,* 26 Feb. 1909; Helen M. White, *The Tale of the Comet and Other Stories* (St. Paul: Minnesota Historical Society Press, 1984), 64; Gerald F. Linderman, *Embattled Courage: The Experience of Combat in the American Civil War* (New York: Free Press, 1987), 259; John L. Ransom, *John Ransom's Andersonville Diary* (Middlebury, Vt.: Paul S. Eriksson, 1986), 62; Steven E. Woodworth, *While God Is Marching On: The Religious World of Civil War Soldiers* (Lawrence: University Press of Kansas, 2001), 308n35. See also George C. Rable, *God's Almost Chosen Peoples: A Religious History of the American Civil War* (Chapel Hill: University of North Carolina Press, 2010), 469n48.

56. Helen White, *Tale,* 63; *National Tribune* (Washington, D.C.), 26 Aug. 1882; Greipsland, *Nordmenn,* 191.

57. Peter J. Meaney, O.S.B., *Father Whelan of Fort Pulaski and Andersonville,* reprinted from the *Georgia Historical Quarterly* 71, no. 1 (Spring 1987): 15–20; Clavreul, *Diary,* 5–6, 9; Kellogg, *Life and Death,* 163–64; Hospital Register, NA RG-249.

58. Helen White, *Tale,* 63–64; H. B. Turrill, "Andersonville Prison in 1864: Reminiscences of Religious Services," from the text in handbill for "What I Saw at Andersonville," and a lecture by the "Andersonville Chaplain Rev. T. J. Sheppard," c. 1886, Ohio Historical Society, Columbus.

59. *Bucyrus (Ohio) Evening Telegraph,* 14 Aug. 1912; McElroy, *Andersonville,* 629–30; Watson, *From Ashby,* 240–41; *Montevideo Leader,* 26 Feb. 1909.

60. McElroy, *Andersonville,* 632; Greipsland, *Nordmenn,* 191.

61. McElroy, *Andersonville,* 630; Turrill, "Andersonville"; Solon Hyde, *A Captive of War* (Shippensburg, Pa.: Burd Street Press, 1996), 113.

62. Kellogg, *Life and Death,* 180, 239; *Vermont Chronicle* (Bellow Falls), 18 Mar. 1865.

63. McElroy, *Andersonville,* 636; George Atkinson Pension File No. 50,455; Dean letter, 24 July 1863, Dean Papers; *Lake Benton Valley News,* 5 Mar. 1913; George A. Pomeroy Pension File No. 291,834; John Worrell Northrop, *Chronicles from the Diary of a War Prisoner in Andersonville and Other Military Prisons of the South in 1864* (Wichita: privately printed, 1904), 93.

64. Rable, *Chosen Peoples,* 367; McElroy, *Andersonville,* 636–37; Hyde, *Captive,* 113–14.

65. McCoy speech, McCoy Papers; E. L. Clapp, *Andersonville,* 27. Clapp does not identify the brothers by name, but there is little doubt that he is referring to them, as he would have known them.

66. Woolverton, "Sketch," 69–70.

67. E. L. Clapp, *Andersonville,* 50; Woolverton, "Sketch," 70–71; Julian W. Merrill, *Records of the 24th Independent Battery, N. Y. Light Artillery, U. S. V.* (West Falls, N.Y.: B. Conrad Bush, 2000), 239; Clavreul, *Diary,* 7.

68. E. L. Clapp, *Andersonville,* 50; Warren, "Reminiscences," 20, Warren Papers; John H. Lundquist's *Andersonville Prison, Sumter County, Georgia: A Record of Recorded and "Reported" Deaths February 27, 1864 to May 6, 1865* (Minneapolis, 2000) provides the most useful list of Andersonville dead. The Andersonville Hospital Register (NA RG-249), ledger page 63, noted the hospital admission number for O. Geer as 5523 and gave the cause of death as "unknown." It also noted he died "in quarters." In the list of dead published in 1865 by Dorence Atwater, reprinted as *Prisoners Who Died at Andersonville Prison: Atwater List* (Andersonville, Ga.: National Society of Andersonville, 1981), 26, Geer's cause of death was given as "scorbutus" (scurvy), which is a later, erroneous emendation that does not appear in any of the original prison records.

Notes to Chapter 13

1. Greipsland, *Nordmenn,* 189; *Montevideo Leader,* 26 Feb. 1909.

2. Eugene Forbes, *Death Before Dishonor: The Andersonville Diary of Eugene Forbes 4th New Jersey Infantry* (Kearney, N.J.: Belle Grove Publishing, 1995), 88; Lay diary, 14 July 1864, Lay Papers.

3. Lundquist, *Headcount,* July 1864; Watson, *From Ashby,* 242, 249; Styple, *Giving Up the Ghost,* 95.

4. Marvel, *Andersonville,* 151–52; *Montevideo Leader,* 26 Feb. 1909.

5. Bearss, *Andersonville,* 29–30, 97–100; Forbes, *Dishonor,* 100; Watson, *From Ashby,* 245.

6. *Montevideo Leader,* 26 Feb. 1909; Lundquist, *Deaths,* 19; *Memorial Record of the Counties of Faribault, Martin, Watonwan and Jackson, Minnesota* (Chicago: Lewis Publishing, 1895), 86.

7. E. L. Clapp, *Andersonville,* 44; Woolverton, "Sketch," 68; McElroy, *Andersonville,* 635.

8. Bearss, *Andersonville,* 132–33; Ludoviso Bourgard Pension File No. 87,309; E. L. Clapp, *Andersonville,* 44; William E. Walker Pension File No. 86,608; Henry A. C. Thompson Pension File No. 347,691; *Seattle Daily Times,* 13 Oct. 1906.

9. Woolverton, "Sketch," 68–69; McElroy, *Andersonville,* 635–36.

10. Woolverton, "Sketch," 68; Hospital Register, 3 June 1864, NA RG-249; Woodbury diary, 24–26 July 1864, Woodbury Papers; *Montevideo Leader,* 26 Feb. 1909; Watson, *From Ashby,* 244.

11. Marvel, *Andersonville,* 168–71; Hospital Register, 1–6 Aug. 1864, NA RG-249; *Montevideo Leader,* 26 Feb. 1909.

12. Research in Andersonville Hospital Register, NA RG-249; Warren, "Reminiscences," 17–18, Warren Papers.

13. Warren, "Reminiscence," 18–19, Warren Papers; Hospital Register, NA RG-249.

14. Bearss, *Andersonville,* 121–23; Merrill, *24th Independent Battery,* 238–39; Warren, "Reminiscences," 19–21, Warren Papers.

15. Warren, "Reminiscences," 18, 20, Warren Papers; *OR,* ser. 2, vol. 7, 774.

16. Warren, "Reminiscences," 20, Warren Papers.

17. McCoy speech, McCoy Papers; Watson, *From Ashby,* 248; Meek, *Sandusky County,* 921.

18. Bearss, *Andersonville*, 36–37, 42; E. L. Clapp, *Andersonville*, 12–13.

19. Lundquist, *Headcount*, Aug. 1864; Lyon, *Andersonville*, 53–54; Bearss, *Andersonville*, 31–32; E. L. Clapp, *Andersonville*, 13; Marvel, *Andersonville*, 177–78.

20. *OR*, ser. 2, vol. 7, 588–90; E. L. Clapp, *Andersonville*, 13–14.

21. E. L. Clapp, *Andersonville*, 13; Lyon, *Andersonville*, 54; Watson, *From Ashby*, 249; Bearss, *Andersonville*, 43–44.

22. Lyon, *Andersonville*, 54–55; Greipsland, *Nordmenn*, 191; Bearss, *Andersonville*, 46–47.

23. E. L. Clapp, *Andersonville*, 31; Hoster diary, 100–101, Hoster Papers; Watson, *From Ashby*, 244.

24. Research in Hospital Register (NA RG-249) and in Lundquist, *Deaths*, which breaks down the names by regiments. The Seventy-Second Ohio's Andersonville contingent is mostly well documented. As a start, the *Fremont (Ohio) Journal*, 8 July 1864, has a full list of 200 who were at Meridian on June 15; the enlisted men went into Andersonville on the nineteenth. For the 113th Illinois, see Dennison, *Andersonville Diary*, 41.

25. Hospital Register (NA RG-249), which is the authoritative source. In some instances the Atwater List arbitrarily added causes of death where the original Hospital Register entry was "unknown." *National Tribune* (Washington, D.C.), 8 Mar. 1888; Woolverton, "Sketch," 70.

26. Hospital Register, NA RG-249; Greipsland, *Nordmenn*, 189.

27. Woodbury diary, 7 Aug. 1864, Woodbury Papers; Lyon, *Andersonville*, 108, does not identify the dead comrade, but his name can be determined through his enlistment details and the 1860 U.S. Census for Olmsted County. Only Wilson fits the criteria.

28. Hospital Register, NA RG-249; *Richmond (Minn.) Standard*, 5 Mar. 1909.

29. Hospital Register, NA RG-249; *Lake Benton Valley News*, 5 Mar. 1913; Chaplain Aaron H. Kerr's "List of Officers and Men of the 9th Regt. Min Vols.," in Minnesota State Archives, Office of the Adjutant General, Reports and Records, Ninth Minnesota Volunteer Infantry, Minnesota Historical Society, St. Paul; Herrick Family History notes, George W. Herrick and Herrick-Handy Family Papers, courtesy of Carol Jauregui private collection (hereafter cited as Herrick-Handy Papers).

30. Hospital Register, NA RG-249.

31. Hospital Register, NA RG-249; *Montevideo Leader*, 26 Feb. 1909; Manning letter, Hill Papers; information on George Jenkins, Jenkins Papers.

32. Woodbury diary, 16, 18, 23, and 28 Aug. and 1 Sept. 1864, Woodbury Papers; Francis Rafferty Pension File No. 191,803; Stephen N. Chandler Pension File No. 55,060.

33. *History of Winona and Olmsted Counties*, 651; McCoy speech, McCoy Papers.

34. Lundquist, *Headcount*, Aug. 1864; *Portrait and Biographical Record of Winona County, Minnesota* (Chicago: Chapman Publishing, 1895), 414–15.

35. *National Tribune* (Washington, D.C.), 12 Aug. 1882; Woodbury diary, 6 Sept. 1864, Woodbury Papers; Watson, *From Ashby*, 253.

36. Marvel, *Andersonville*, 198–201; Lundquist, *Headcount*, Sept. 1864; Woodbury diary, 8–10 Sept 1864, Woodbury Papers.

37. Lundquist, *Headcount*, Sept. 1864. For an example of a high-numbered detachment leaving Andersonville on Sept. 12, see Charles A. Smith, *Recollections of Prison Life at Andersonville, Georgia and Florence, South Carolina* (Raleigh, S.C.: Martini

Print Media, 1997), 33, 66–67. Smith entered Andersonville on July 29 with the 118th Detachment (later renumbered 113th). Watson, *From Ashby*, 255; Styple, *Giving Up the Ghost*, 102.

38. *OR*, ser. 2, vol. 7, 784, 791–92, 808; Andersonville Register of Prison Departures, C's, exchanged 19 Sept. 1864, Atlanta; Dwight Card Pension File No. 870,428.

39. *OR*, ser. 2, vol. 7, 857; Lundquist, *Headcount*, Sept. 1864; Watson, *From Ashby*, 255; *National Tribune* (Washington, D.C.), 19 Aug. 1882.

40. Forbes, *Dishonor*, 120; Marvel, *Andersonville*, 203–4; Lyon, *Andersonville*, 72–73; Watson, *From Ashby*, 254; Hospital Register, NA RG-249; Jacob Thielen CMSR (misspelled "Theilen").

41. Lyon, *Andersonville*, 73, 75; *OR*, ser. 2, vol. 8, 603.

42. Hospital Register, NA RG-249; Ebenezer Clapp, *Clapp Memorials*, 239; *Rochester City Post*, 7 Jan. 1865; *Milwaukee Daily Sentinel*, 18 Jan. 1865; Hyde, *Captive*, 127; Edward L. Clapp Pension File No. 719,399.

43. *Rochester City Post*, 7 Jan. 1865; *Milwaukee Daily Sentinel*, 18 Jan. 1865; on Atwater, his testimony in the "Shanks Report," H. Rep. No. 45, 1023–30; *National Tribune* (Washington, D.C.), 2 Sept. 1882.

44. Curtiss-Wedge, *Mower County*, 905; Marvel, *Andersonville*, 203; Pvt. U. W. Byram, Co. F, 1st Regt. Georgia Reserves (Fannin's), CMSR, NA RG-94; Andersonville Register of Prisoner Departures, NA RG-249; Lundquist, *Headcount*, Sept. 1864.

45. Marvel, *Andersonville*, 203–4; *The Trial of Henry Wirz*, H. Doc. No. 23, 179.

46. *St. Paul Press*, 20 Apr. 1865; Hyde, *Captive*, 132.

47. Watson, *From Ashby*, 256–57; Lundquist, *Headcount*, Sept. and Oct. 1864; Andersonville Register of Prisoner Departures, NA RG-249.

48. Lyon, *Andersonville*, 52; Joseph Lagree CMSR, NA RG-94.

49. Lyon, *Andersonville*, 75–76.

50. *Lake Benton Valley News*, 5 Mar. 1913; Daniel McArthur CMSR, NA RG-94.

51. *Lake Benton Valley News*, 5 Mar. 1913; *OR*, ser. 1, vol. 39, pt. 3, 362, 382–83.

52. *Lake Benton Valley News*, 5 Mar. 1913.

53. *National Tribune* (Washington, D.C.), 2 Sept. 1882; Watson, *From Ashby*, 260, 261, 264; William B. Smith, *On Wheels: And How I Came There: The True Story of a 15-year-old Yankee Soldier and Prisoner in the American Civil War* (College Station, Tex.: Virtualbookworm.com, 2002), 132.

54. *Fremont (Ohio) Journal*, 14 June 1889.

55. Lundquist, *Headcount*, Oct. and Nov. 1864; Andersonville Register of Prisoner Departures, which are complete from 31 Oct. through 15 Nov. 1864; William Bruce and Edward S. Evans CMSRs.

56. Andersonville Register of Prisoner Departures; *Rochester City Post*, 7 Jan. 1865; Hospital Register, NA RG-249.

57. Thomas E. Hughes, *Welsh*, 239–40; Lundquist, *Deaths*, 64, and *Headcount*, Nov. 1864.

Notes to Chapter Fourteen

1. Arch Frederic Blakey, *General John H. Winder C.S.A.* (Gainesville: University of Florida Press, 1990), 193–94; William Giles, *Disease, Starvation & Death: Personal Accounts of Camp Lawton, the South's Largest Prison* (Magnolia Springs State Park, Ga.: Lulu Press, 2005), 12–13.

2. Blakey, *Winder*, 194–95; McElroy, *Andersonville*, 401; Walter J. Fraser Jr., *Savannah in the Old South* (Athens: University of Georgia Press, 2003), 336–37.

3. Blakey, *Winder*, 194; McElroy, *Andersonville*, 402, 423; Greipsland, *Nordmenn*, 192.

4. Simon Peter Obermier diary, 36, 37, Simon Peter Obermeir Papers, Rutherford B. Hayes Presidential Center, Fremont, Ohio; Hutchinson, "Glimpses," 70; *OR*, ser. 2, vol. 7, 846, 851–52; *The Trial of Henry Wirz*, H. Doc. No. 23, 173; Lee Kennett, *Marching through Georgia: The Story of Soldiers & Civilians during Sherman's Campaigns* (New York: HarperCollins, 1995), 212; Amos W. Ames diary, 22 Sept. 1864, Amos W. Ames Papers, State Historical Society of Iowa, Des Moines.

5. *OR*, ser. 2, vol. 7, 606–7, 685, 846.

6. Greipsland, *Nordmenn*, 192; McCoy speech, McCoy Papers; Lyon, *Andersonville*, 78–79.

7. Ransom, *Andersonville Diary*, 136–41, 144–45, 150; for the Savannah Hospital Death Book, see *New York Times*, 17 Dec. 1864; Clavreul, *Diary*, 13. Father Clavreul became sick at Andersonville in September and had to leave.

8. Ludoviso Bourgard Pension File No. 8,309; Blakey, *Winder*, 195; Greipsland, *Nordmenn*, 192.

9. Charles Dietrich Pension File No. 132,078; Fraser, *Savannah*, 337. Quartermaster General, *Roll of Honor (XIV.)*, 313, lists only two Federal deaths in Savannah, both during Sherman's March to the Sea.

10. Fraser, *Savannah*, 337; Henry M. Davidson, *Fourteen Months in Southern Prisons* (Milwaukee: Daily Wisconsin Printing House, 1865), 326.

11. *History of Winona and Olmsted Counties*, 652; for the history of Salisbury, see Louis A. Brown, *The Salisbury Prison: A Case Study of Confederate Military Prisons 1861–1865* (Wilmington, N.C.: Broadfoot Publishing, 1992); Dieter's entry in the dead book as "Deter," 292. Benjamin F. Booth and Steve Meyer, *Dark Days of the Rebellion: Life in Southern Military Prisons* (Garrison, Iowa: Meyer Publishing, 1996), 117; Martha Dieter, "A Pioneer Mother," Dieter Papers.

12. *OR*, ser. 2, vol. 7, 869–70; Giles, *Disease*, 13–15; George M. Shearer diary, 29 Oct.–2 Nov. 1864, George Shearer Papers, State Historical Society of Iowa, Des Moines, and Amos W. Ames diary, 2 Nov. 1864, Ames Papers.

13. McCoy speech, McCoy Papers; Lyon, *Andersonville*, 80.

14. Lyon, *Andersonville*, 80; Greipsland, *Nordmenn*, 192; Watson, *From Ashby*, 268; E. L. Clapp, *Andersonville*, 15; Merrill, *24th Independent Battery*, 235.

15. Washington K. Latimer letter, 14 Nov. 1864, Washington Kays Latimer Papers, Minnesota Historical Society, St. Paul (hereafter cited as Latimer Papers).

16. Latimer letter, 14 Nov. 1864, Latimer Papers; Lyon, *Andersonville*, 81–82.

17. M. B. Patterson, "Remarkable Case of Replantation," *The Dental Cosmos* 17, no. 3 (Mar. 1875): 168.

18. Dennison, *Andersonville Diary*, 78; Davidson, *Fourteen Months*, 332; Ames diary, 23 Oct. 1864, Ames Papers.

19. George Chandler, *The Chandler Family* (Worcester, Mass.: Charles Hamilton, 1883), 1225; Stephen N. Chandler Pension File No. 55,060; Curtiss-Wedge, *Mower County*, 702–3.

20. Robert Knox Sneden, *Eye of the Storm: A Civil War Odyssey* (New York: Simon & Schuster, 2000), 270; Robert Knox Sneden, *Images from the Storm* (New York: Free

Press, 2001), 228. On the Millen dead, see also United States Christian Commission, *Record of the Federal Dead Buried from Libby, Belle Isle, Danville & Camp Lawton Prisons and at City Point and in the Field before Petersburg and Richmond* (Philadelphia: James B. Rogers, Printer, 1866), 159–68, and Quartermaster General, *Roll of Honor (XIV.)*, 293–313.

21. Latimer letter, 14 Nov. 1864, Latimer Papers.

22. Speer, *Portals*, 213–15, 248–52.

23. *Chaska Valley Herald*, 25 Mar. 1865; *Fremont (Ohio) Journal*, 14 June 1889; John C. Dixon Pension File No. 943,746; *Winona Daily Republican*, 26 Oct. 1864; *Vista (Calif.) Press*, 12 Feb. 1931.

24. Kellogg, *Life and Death*, 290; Noah Grant Pension File No. 434,095.

25. Myron Tower Pension File No. 60,987; Stone, *History of Colorado*, 3:690.

26. *OR*, ser. 2, vol. 7, 817, 894. For the history of Florence Prison, see G. Wayne King, "Death Camp at Florence," *Civil War Times Illustrated* 12, no. 9 (Jan. 1974): 34–42; Speer, *Portals*, 273–77. An excellent memoir by a Florence prisoner is Ezra Hoyt Ripple's *Dancing along the Deadline* (Novato, Calif.: Presidio Press, 1996).

27. Woodbury diary, 1–28 Sept. 1864, Woodbury Papers; *OR*, ser. 2, vol. 7, 841; Forbes, *Dishonor*, 128; George Cummings Pension File No. 65,995.

28. Forbes, *Dishonor*, 131–32; *OR*, ser. 2, vol. 7, 972, 1098.

29. *OR*, ser. 2, vol. 7, 973, 1098; "Shanks Report," H. Rep. No. 45, 1132, 1133; William E. Walker Pension File No. 186,608.

30. Information on the Sanitary Commission's distribution of clothing at Florence is through the kindness of Rev. Albert Ledoux, who is seeking to identify all of the Union dead at Florence and is writing a comprehensive history of the prison. "Shanks Report," H. Rep. No. 45, 1132; Kellogg, *Life and Death*, 325–26.

31. John Morrison Pension File No. 63,154; Tower Affidavit in John Morrison Estate Probate File, 10 Dec. 1867, Olmsted County Historical Society, Rochester, Minn.; on the assigning of the date and place of death to Morrison, see Minnesota State Archives, Office of the Adjutant General, Reports and Records, Ninth Minnesota Volunteer Infantry, "Report of men who have died or have been discharged during the month of April 1865 in the 9th Regt. Infty," which notes five men from Company K said to have died on Oct. 31, 1864, at Savannah. Perhaps three or four of them actually did die at Savannah, but not John Morrison.

32. "Shanks Report," H. Rep. No. 45, 982–85; Quartermaster General, *Roll of Honor (XIV.)*, 252; Rev. Albert Ledoux personal communications.

33. "Shanks Report," H. Rep. No. 45, 1132; Frederick F. Field Pension File No. 393,432.

NOTES TO CHAPTER FIFTEEN

1. *MICIW*, 1:426; Gary D. Joiner, *Through the Howling Wilderness: The 1864 Red River Campaign and the Union Failure in the West* (Knoxville: University of Tennessee Press, 2006), 51; Warner, *Generals in Blue*, 338–39, 454–55.

2. *OR*, ser. 1, vol. 39, 249; liberator CMSRs, NA RG-94. For the Tupelo Campaign, see in addition to the reports and correspondence in *OR*, ser. 1, vol. 39, pts. 1 and 2, Bearss, *Forrest*, 143–233, and Michael B. Ballard, "The Battle of Tupelo," *The Papers of the Blue and Gray Education Society*, no. 3 (Winter 1996): 1–57. Helen White, *Tale*, 56, 58; *Daily Herald* (Cleveland, Ohio), 1 Aug. 1864.

3. Felch Letter, undated, [July 1864], Steffens Papers; *Rochester City Post,* 13 Aug. 1864.

4. *OR,* ser. 1, vol. 39, pt. 1, 259, 346–47; Hancock, *Hancock's Diary,* 417–18.

5. *OR,* ser. 1, vol. 39, pt. 1, 265, 266–67; *Rochester City Post,* 13 Aug. 1864.

6. *OR,* ser. 1, vol. 39, pt. 1, 259, 330; Carroll, *Autobiography and Reminiscences,* 31.

7. *Rochester City Post,* 13 Aug. 1864; *OR,* ser. 1, vol. 39, pt. 1, 251–52, 265–66, 349; *MICIW,* 1:427.

8. *OR,* ser. 1, vol. 39, pt. 1, 252, 322–23, 326–27; Dean letter, 22 July 1864, Dean Papers; *Richmond (Minn.) Standard,* 5 Mar. 1909.

9. *OR,* ser. 1, vol. 39, pt. 1, 267; Felch letter, 26 July 1864, Steffens Papers; Enoch W. Pike Pension File No. 1,097,068; Samuel Mickel Pension File No. 860,551.

10. *Rochester City Post,* 13 Aug. 1864; *OR,* ser. 1, vol. 39, pt. 1, 253, 268; *MICIW,* 2:494; Harrington letter, 30 July 1864, Harrington Papers; Dean letter, 26 July 1864, Dean Papers; Hubbs, *Alexander Wilkin,* 190. The county was first known as Toombs County, after Georgia Senator Robert Toombs, but once Toombs joined the Confederacy, the name became Andy Johnson County in 1862, in honor of loyalist Tennessee Senator Andrew Johnson. In 1868 in disgust with President Johnson's impeachment, it was renamed Wilkin County. Warren Upham, *Minnesota Place Names: A Geographical Encyclopedia* (St. Paul: Minnesota Historical Society Press, 2001), 627.

11. Felch letter, undated [July 1864], Steffens Papers.

12. Felch letter, 26 July 1864, Steffens Papers; *OR,* ser. 1, vol. 39, pt. 1, 252, 257–58.

13. *OR,* ser. 1, vol. 39, pt. 1, 266, 267, 303; Felch letter, 26 July 1864, Steffens Papers.

14. Dean letter, 22 July 1864, Dean Papers; *OR,* ser. 1, vol. 39, pt. 1, 256; *Rochester City Post,* 13 Aug. 1864; *Mankato Weekly Record,* 13 Aug. 1864.

15. *OR,* ser. 1, vol. 39, pt. 1, 249; *Mankato Weekly Record,* 13 Aug. 1864.

16. Dean letter, 31 Aug. 1864, Dean Papers; *East Union News,* 1 June 1895.

17. Sources for the operations in Missouri include the reports and correspondence in *OR,* ser. 1, vol. 41, pts. 1, 3, and 4, and Albert Castel, *General Sterling Price and the Civil War in the West* (Baton Rouge: Louisiana State University Press, 1993), 208–56, and *OR,* ser. 1, vol. 41, pt. 3, 62; John M. Williams, *"The Eagle Regiment," 8th Wis. Inf'ty Vols* (Belleville, Wis.: "Recorder" Print, 1890), 30, 73.

18. *MICIW,* 1:428; Liberator CMSRs, NA RG-94; *East Union News,* 15 June 1895.

19. *MICIW,* 1:428; *St. Paul Press,* 8 Dec. 1864.

20. David W. Reed, *Campaigns and Battles of the Twelfth Regiment Iowa Veteran Volunteer Infantry* (Evanston?, Ill., 1903), 179.

21. *MICIW,* 1:428; Liberator CMSRs, NA RG-94.

22. *OR,* ser. 1, vol. 41, pt. 3, 714, 741; *St. Paul Press,* 8 Dec. 1864.

23. *St. Paul Press,* 8 Dec. 1864; *MICIW,* 1:428–29.

24. Leslie Anders, *The Twenty-First Missouri: From Home Guard to Union Regiment* (Westport, Conn.: Greenwood Press, 1975), 196; *MICIW,* 1:429; Dean letter, 7 Nov. 1864, Dean Papers; *St. Paul Press,* 8 Dec. 1864.

25. *OR,* ser. 1, vol. 41, pt. 4, 306; David Reed, *Twelfth Regiment Iowa,* 189; Warner, *Generals in Blue,* 288–89; Society of the Army of the Tennessee, *Report of the Proceedings of the 42nd and 43rd Reunions* (Cincinnati: Bacharach Press, 1915), 43.

26. *MICIW,* 1:429; Williams, *"Eagle Regiment,"* 32, 93; *St. Paul Press,* 8 Dec. 1864.

27. *St. Paul Press,* 8 Dec. 1864; David Reed, *Twelfth Regiment Iowa,* 184.

28. *MICIW*, 1:429; Liberator CMSRs, NA RG-94; *East Union News*, 1 and 15 July 1895; *St. Paul Press*, 1 Dec. 1864.

29. Felch letters, undated [July 1864] and 10 Sept. 1864, Aaron H. Kerr letters, 21 Sept. and 28 Oct. 1864, Surgeon Adams letter, 3 Oct. 1864, Steffens Papers, Minnesota Historical Society, St. Paul; Felch CMSR, NA RG-94. The official date of Felch's death, 1 Oct. 1864, is actually the day of his burial in the Memphis cemetery.

30. *St. Paul Press*, 8 Dec. 1864.

Notes to Chapter Sixteen

1. Obermier diary, 45, Obermier Papers; Warren, "Reminiscences," 24, Warren Papers; Kellogg, *Life and Death*, 330.

2. Hesseltine, *Civil War Prisons*, 226–28; *OR*, ser. 2, vol. 7, 793, 872, 1070, 1090, 1120.

3. Warren, "Reminiscences," 24, Warren Papers; Lundquist, *Headcount*, Nov. 1864; E. L. Clapp, *Andersonville*, 15.

4. McCoy speech, McCoy Papers; Lyon, *Andersonville*, 84.

5. William F. Lyon Pension File No. 451,787; Lyon, *Andersonville*, 84–86; August Arndt Pension File No. 212,263; McCoy speech, McCoy Papers.

6. McCoy speech, McCoy Papers; Lyon, *Andersonville*, 86–87.

7. Lyon, *Andersonville*, 87–91; McCoy speech, McCoy Papers; *St. Peter Tribune*, 7 Dec. 1864. The CMSRs of surviving prisoners include a form giving the date and place of parole, NA RG-94.

8. Lyon, *Andersonville*, 91–92; Warren, "Reminiscences," 25, Warren Papers; *OR*, ser. 2, vol. 7, 1149.

9. Edward L. Clapp Pension File No. 719,399; Ebenezer Clapp, *Clapp Memorials*, 339.

10. *OR*, ser. 2, vol. 7, 1148, 1169; Noah Andre Trudeau, *Southern Storm: Sherman's March to the Sea* (New York: Harper, 2008), 263, 324–26.

11. *OR*, ser. 2, vol. 7, 1204; Greipsland, *Nordmenn*, 193; J. A. Mowris, *A History of the One Hundred and Seventeenth Regiment, N. Y. Volunteers, (Fourth Oneida,) from the Date of Its Organization, August 1862, Till That of Its Muster Out, June, 1865* (Hamilton, N.Y.: Edmonston Publishing, 1996), 309; Hutchinson, "Glimpses," 70. For Blackshear, see Speer, *Portals*, 279–81.

12. Watson, *From Ashby*, 272–75; Obermier diary, 48, Obermier Papers; *National Tribune* (Washington, D.C.), 28 Sept. 1882.

13. *OR*, ser. 2, vol. 7, 1170, 1204; Northrup, *Chronicles*, 179–80; George W. Bailey, *The Civil War Diary and Biography of George W. Bailey* (Colleyville, Tex.: G. R. Post, 1990), 94.

14. *OR*, ser. 2, vol. 7, 1203, vol. 8, 424; Nathan M. Palmeter CMSR, NA RG-94; *National Tribune* (Washington, D.C.), 25 Sept. 1882; Watson, *From Ashby*, 282.

15. Palmeter CMSR, NA RG-94, and Pension File No. 184,047; *National Tribune* (Washington, D.C.), 16 May 1907; Isaac Peterman Pension File No. 342,960.

16. *Mower County Register*, 22 Dec. 1864; Basile, "Letters," 2:446.

17. On Columbia, see Speer, *Portals*, 270–73; A. O. Abbott, *Prison Life*, 132–33, Newsome, *Experience in the War*, 196–98; *Fremont (Ohio) Journal*, 14 June 1889; *Chaska Valley Herald*, 24 Mar. 1865.

18. A. O. Abbott, *Prison Life*, 149, 152–55; Newsome, *Experience in the War*, 204–5; *Fremont (Ohio) Journal*, 14 June 1889.

19. *Fremont (Ohio) Journal,* 14 June 1889; *Chaska Valley Herald,* 24 Mar. 1865.

20. *OR,* ser. 2, vol. 8, 137, 160–61; Hoster diary, 128–31, Hoster Papers.

21. *History of Winona and Olmsted Counties,* 650; "Shanks Report," H. Rep. No. 45, 1133; Edward Todd Pension File No. 812,098.

22. *History of Winona and Olmsted Counties,* 650–51; Alpheus Merritt CMSR, NA RG-94; Louis A. Brown, *Salisbury Prison,* 305, where in the death record Merritt is listed separately as Alpheus Merrett and A. G. Merritt; "Shanks Report," H. Rep. No. 45, 983; Forbes, *Dishonor,* 162.

23. Blakey, *Winder,* 201; *OR,* ser. 2, vol. 8, 206, 449; Hoster diary, 131, Hoster Papers; Leonard, *Olmsted County,* 646–47; Henry Etzell Pension File No. 219,937; Goveneur K. Ives Pension File No. 747,380.

24. "Shanks Report," H. Rep. No. 45, 1133.

25. Hoster diary, 131, Hoster Papers; Chris E. Fonvielle Jr., *The Wilmington Campaign: Last Rays of Departing Hope* (Mechanicsburg, Pa.: Stackpole Books, 1997), 446.

26. John Arndt Pension File No. 147,152; A. O. Abbott, *Prison Life,* 180–81; Bernhard Domschcke, *Twenty Months in Captivity: Memoirs of a Union Officer in Confederate Prisons* (Rutherford, N.J.: Farleigh Dickinson University Press, 1987), 119; *Fremont (Ohio) Journal,* 14 June 1889.

27. Hoster diary, 131, Hoster Papers; *OR,* ser. 2, vol. 8, 358; Fonvielle, *Wilmington Campaign,* 447–48.

28. William H. Carlton CMSR, NA RG-94.

29. Helen M. Goodale Hargrave, *Carleton-Carlton Forebears* (N.p., 1977), 65–66.

30. *History of Winona and Olmsted Counties,* 650; Henry Niles CMSR, NA RG-94.

31. Henry Niles Pension File No. 235,176; *History of Winona and Olmsted Counties,* 653; *Rochester Republican,* 17 Aug. 1864.

32. Henry Niles Pension File No. 235,176; *Rochester Weekly Post,* 24 June 1876.

NOTES TO CHAPTER SEVENTEEN

1. Hutchinson, "Glimpses," 70; Greipsland, *Nordmenn,* 193.

2. Barry L. Brown and Gordon R. Elwell, *Crossroads of Conflict: A Guide to Civil War Sites in Georgia* (Athens: University of Georgia Press, 2010), 177; Greipsland, *Nordmenn,* 193; *OR,* ser. 2, vol. 7, 1238.

3. Georgia State Historical Marker, Thomasville, at http://www.civilwaralbum.com /misc12/Thomasville1.htm; Hutchinson, "Glimpses," 70; *Mankato Union,* 23 June 1865; Obermier diary, 51, Obermier Papers.

4. Greipsland, *Nordmenn,* 194; Mowris, *One Hundred and Seventeenth,* 310.

5. Lundquist, *Headcount,* Dec. 1864; *Fremont (Ohio) Journal,* 14 June 1889.

6. Obermier diary, 51, Obermier Papers; Mowris, *One Hundred and Seventeenth,* 311; Greipsland, *Nordmenn,* 194.

7. Andersonville Register of Prisoner Departures, which from this point includes all the names organized by division and detachment, NA RG-249; *National Tribune* (Washington, D.C.), 15 June 1893; Hutchinson, "Glimpses," 70; Francis J. Hosmer, *A Glimpse of Andersonville and Other Writings* (Springfield, Mass.: Loring & Axtell, 1896), 48; Greipsland, *Nordmenn,* 194; *Fremont (Ohio) Journal,* 14 June 1889; Marvel, *Andersonville,* 227–28.

8. Bearss, *Andersonville,* 37–38, 125–27; Hospital Register, NA RG-249; *The Trial of Henry Wirz,* H. Doc. No. 23, 34.

9. *Fremont (Ohio) Journal,* 14 June 1889; Hutchinson, "Glimpses," 70; Greipsland, *Nordmenn,* 194.

10. *Wabasha Herald,* 19 Mar. 1914; Pierre Rodier CMSR, NA RG-94, and Pension File No. 140,293; George L. Wheelock Pension File No. 729,212; *History of Winona and Olmsted Counties,* 1034–35.

11. *The Trial of Henry Wirz,* H. Doc. No. 23, 171; Greipsland, *Nordmenn,* 194; *Fremont (Ohio) Journal,* 14 June 1889.

12. Greipsland, *Nordmenn,* 194; Lundquist, *Deaths,* 38.

13. McElroy, *Andersonville,* 634–35; *Bucyrus (Ohio) Evening Telegraph,* 14 Aug. 1912.

14. *The Trial of Henry Wirz,* H. Doc. No. 23, 270; Hutchinson, "Glimpses," 70; Greipsland, *Nordmenn,* 194.

15. William O. Bryant, *Cahaba Prison and the Sultana Disaster* (Tuscaloosa: University of Alabama Press, 1990), 49.

16. Bryant, *Cahaba Prison,* 16–20, 101; Hawes, *Cahaba,* 6.

17. Detailed reports in *OR,* ser. 2, vol. 7, 998–1002, 1088–89; *National Tribune* (Washington, D.C.), 26 Sept. 1889; Bryant, *Cahaba Prison,* 64–65.

18. *National Tribune,* 26 Sept. 1889; John Kern Pension File No. 272,210.

19. *National Tribune,* 26 Sept. 1889; Robertson, "Journal," 131; *Rochester City Post,* 29 Oct. 1864.

20. Robertson, "Journal," 132–33; John Kern Pension File No. 272,210; Lundquist, *Headcount,* n.p. (unpaginated page 2).

21. Syvert Ellefson CSMR (NA RG-94), which gives the date he was last seen as Nov. 18, 1864, but all indications are that he actually left Cahaba at the end of October with the shipment to Millen.

22. Henry E. Seelye CMSR, NA RG-94, and Pension File No. 136,068; *OR,* ser. 2, vol. 7, 895–96, vol. 8, 364–65.

23. Robertson, "Journal," 133–34; *National Tribune* (Washington, D.C.), 26 Sept. 1889; *Hamilton (Ohio) Journal,* 19 May 1961.

24. *OR,* ser. 2, vol. 8, 117–22; Bryant, *Cahaba Prison,* 103–6; *National Tribune* (Washington, D.C.), 26 Sept. 1889; Hawes, *Cahaba,* 387–438; Robertson, "Journal," 134; John Kern Pension File No. 272,210.

25. *National Tribune* (Washington, D.C.), 21 Nov. 1912; Bryant, *Cahaba Prison,* 107–8.

26. Bryant, *Cahaba Prison,* 108–11; Robertson, "Journal," 134–35; *National Tribune* (Washington, D.C.), 26 Sept. 1889; John Kern Pension File No. 272,210.

27. John Kern Pension File No. 272,210; *Mower County Register,* 13 Apr. 1865; Bryant, *Cahaba Prison,* 109.

NOTES TO CHAPTER EIGHTEEN

1. Basic sources on the Battle of Nashville include the reports and correspondence in *OR,* ser. 1, vol. 45, pts. 1 and 2; James Lee McDonough, *Nashville: The Western Confederacy's Final Gamble* (Knoxville: University of Tennessee Press, 2004); Wiley Sword, *The Confederacy's Last Hurrah: Spring Hill, Franklin & Nashville* (Lawrence: University Press of Kansas, 1993); David R. Logsdon, *Eyewitnesses at the Battle of Nashville* (Nashville: Kettle Mills Press, 2004); Mark Zimmerman, *Guide to Civil War Nashville* (Nashville: Battle of Nashville Preservation Society, 2004); for Minnesota's participation, *MICIW,* vols. 1 and 2, and Carley, *Minnesota,* 149–59.

2. *MICIW*, 1:430; Ninth Minnesota regimental books in NA RG-94; CMSRs, NA RG-94.

3. *OR*, ser. 1, vol. 45, pt. 2, 73; *St. Paul Press*, 30 Dec. 1864.

4. *MICIW*, 1:430; *OR*, ser. 1, vol. 45, pt. 1, 452–53; Logsdon, *Eyewitnesses*, 45, 61; *St. Paul Press*, 30 Dec. 1864; Zimmerman, *Guide*, 54–55. There is controversy over the order in which Redoubts No. 4 and No. 5 were attacked, but as McDonough, *Nashville*, 187–92, 323–25, ably demonstrates (and sources from the Ninth Minnesota confirm), No. 4 was taken first. William Lee White and Charles Denny Runion, *Great Things Are Expected of Us: The Letters of Colonel C. Irvine Walker, 10th South Carolina Infantry, C.S.A* (Knoxville: University of Tennessee Press, 2009), 181.

5. Logsdon, *Eyewitnesses*, 51, 55; *National Tribune* (Washington, D.C.), 28 Aug. 1890; *MICIW*, 1:431.

6. *OR*, ser. 1, vol. 45, pt. 1, 445–46; Logsdon, *Eyewitnesses*, 62, 63; *National Tribune* (Washington, D.C.), 31 July and 26 Aug. 1890.

7. *MICIW*, 1:431; Logsdon, *Eyewitnesses*, 64–65; Kate Cumming, *A Journal of Hospital Life in the Confederate Army* (Louisville, Ky.: John P. Morton, 1866), 162.

8. *MICIW*, 1:431; *OR*, ser. 1, vol. 45, pt. 1, 453; *Mankato Free Press*, 15 Dec. 1921.

9. Society of the Army of the Tennessee, *Report of the Proceedings of the 42nd and 43rd Reunions*, 48.

10. *OR*, ser. 1, vol. 45, pt. 1, 453, pt. 2, 215; Zimmerman, *Guide*, 57.

11. Stubbs, *Milton Aurelius*, 24; *MICIW*, 1:432.

12. McDonough, *Nashville*, 246–52; Society of the Army of the Tennessee, *Report of the Proceedings of the 42nd and 43rd Reunions*, 49.

13. *OR*, ser. 1, vol. 45, pt. 1, 447, 453; Stubbs, *Milton Aurelius*, 24; *Billings (Mont.) Gazette*, 16 Feb. 1969; *Shakopee Argus*, 14 Jan. 1865; *St. Paul Press*, 7 Jan. 1865; Society of the Army of the Tennessee, *Report of the Proceedings of the 42nd and 43rd Reunions*, 49.

14. *Shakopee Argus*, 14 Jan. 1865; Stubbs, *Milton Aurelius*, 24; *OR*, ser. 1, vol. 45, pt. 1, 723; *MICIW*, 1:432.

15. *Rochester City Post*, 28 Jan. 1865; *Billings (Mont.) Gazette*, 16 Feb. 1969.

16. *Shakopee Argus*, 14 Jan. 1865; *MICIW*, 1:432.

17. Stanley F. Horn, *The Decisive Battle of Nashville* (Baton Rouge: Louisiana State University Press, 1956), n.p.; *OR*, ser. 1, vol. 45, pt. 1, 448–49, 454; *Billings (Mont.) Gazette*, 16 Feb. 1969; Chaplain Kerr's "List of Officers and Men of the 9th Regt. Min. Vols.," Minnesota State Archives; CMSRS, NA RG-94.

18. Stubbs, *Milton Aurelius*, 24; *Richmond (Minn.) Standard*, 5 Mar. 1909; *Shakopee Argus*, 14 Jan. 1865.

19. Noah McCain, CMSR, NA RG-94; Ninth Minnesota regimental records; *MICIW*, 1:443, wrongly lists McCain as deserting in Nov. 1862.

20. *MICIW*, 1:434.

21. *St. Paul Press*, 1 Apr. 1865; *Richmond (Minn.) Standard*, 5 Mar. 1909; *East Union News*, 1 Jan. 1896; *Shakopee Argus*, 25 Mar. 1865.

22. *Rochester City Post*, 22 Apr. 1865; *OR*, ser. 1, vol. 49, pt. 1, 669.

23. Dean letter, 24 Feb. 1865, Dean Papers.

24. *Rochester City Post*, 18 Mar. and 22 Apr. 1865.

25. *Rochester City Post*, 7 Jan. and 22 Apr. 1865; *Milwaukee Daily Sentinel*, 18 Jan., 14 and 17 Mar. 1865; Ebenezer Clapp, *Clapp Memorials*, 339.

26. Folwell, *History of Minnesota,* 2: 340–42; William D. Green, "Minnesota's Long Road to Black Suffrage 1849–1868," *Minnesota History* 56, no. 2 (Summer 1998): 78–79.

27. Chester G. Hearn, *Mobile Bay and the Mobile Campaign* (Jefferson, N.C.: McFarland, 1993), 60–158.

28. *MICIW,* 1:434; *East Union News,* 15 Apr. 1896.

29. *Rochester City Post,* 22 Apr. 1865; CMSRs, NA RG-94; *OR,* ser. 1, vol. 49, pt. 1, 234.

30. Basic sources on the Mobile Campaign are reports and correspondence in *OR,* ser. 1, vol. 49, pts. 1 and 2 (no report for the Ninth Minnesota can be found); Christopher C. Andrews, *History of the Campaign of Mobile* (New York: D. Van Nostrand, 1867); and Hearn, *Mobile Bay.*

31. *OR,* ser. 1, vol. 49, pt. 1, 239; *St. Paul Pioneer,* 16 Apr. 1865.

32. Andrews, *Campaign of Mobile,* 48–49; *MICIW,* 1:434.

33. Dean letter, 29 Mar. 1865, Dean Papers.

34. Bullard CMSR, NA RG-94; *East Union News,* 1 June 1896; Andrews, *Campaign of Mobile,* 63.

35. *OR,* ser. 1, vol. 49, pt. 1, 239; Merchant CMSR, NA RG-94; Dean letter, 3 Apr. 1865, Dean Papers.

36. *East Union News,* 15 July 1896.

37. Andrews, *Campaign of Mobile,* 145.

38. *OR,* ser. 1, vol. 49, pt. 1, 239–40; *East Union News,* 1 Aug. 1896; Stubbs, *Milton Aurelius,* 27.

39. *East Union News,* 15 Aug. 1896; Stubbs, *Milton Aurelius,* 27; *MICIW,* 1:435.

40. Martin, "Letters of a Union Officer," 318; *MICIW,* 1:435; *East Union News,* 1 Sept. 1896.

NOTES TO CHAPTER NINETEEN

1. *OR,* ser. 2, vol. 8, 404–5.

2. Gene Eric Salecker, *Disaster on the Mississippi: The Sultana Explosion, April 27, 1865* (Annapolis, Md.: Naval Institute Press, 1996), 18–20; *National Tribune* (Washington, D.C.), 22 June 1893.

3. *National Tribune* (Washington, D.C.), 22 June 1893; Robertson, "Journal," 136; *Mower County Register,* 13 Apr. 1865.

4. Lundquist, *Headcount,* Mar. 1865; Andersonville Register of Prisoner Departures, NA RG-249; *Mankato Union,* 23 June 1865; Greipsland, *Nordmenn,* 194–95.

5. *OR,* ser. 2, vol. 8, 425–26.

6. *OR,* ser. 2, vol. 8, 437; *New Orleans Times-Picayune,* 4 Apr. 1865; Obermier diary, 53, Obermier Papers.

7. *Hamilton (Ohio) Journal,* 19 May 1961; Robertson, "Journal," 136.

8. *OR,* ser. 2, vol. 8, 477.

9. CMSRs, NA RG-94; *St. Paul Press,* 14 and 20 Apr. 1865; Greipsland, *Nordmenn,* 195; *National Tribune* (Washington, D.C.), 22 June 1893; *OR,* ser. 2, vol. 8, 477.

10. *Missouri Democrat,* 2 May 1865; Robertson, "Journal," 116–17, 136–37.

11. Mowris, *One Hundred and Seventeenth,* 314; Howard A. M. Henderson, "Lincoln's Assassination and Camp Fisk," *Confederate Veteran* 15 (Apr. 1907): 170–71.

12. *OR,* ser. 2, vol. 8, 492; Salecker, *Disaster,* 36–37; *Missouri Republican,* 26 Apr. 1865.

13. The best study of the *Sultana* disaster is Salecker; Robertson, "Journal," 116–17.

14. *St. Paul Press*, 11 May 1865; CMSRs, NA RG-94; Walter N. Trenerry, "When the Boys Came Home," *Minnesota History* 38, no. 6 (June 1963): 289.

15. Aslakson Pension File No. 179,129 (using the name "Burns Arlakson"); Greipsland, *Nordmenn*, 195.

16. Lundquist, *Headcount*, Mar. 1865; John B. Vaughter ["Sergeant Oats"], *Prison Life in Dixie* (Chicago: General Book Concern, 1880), 173.

17. *OR*, ser. 2, vol. 8, 445, 465, 470; Lundquist, *Headcount*, Apr. 1865; John Whitten diary, 32, John Whitten Papers, State Historical Society of Iowa, Des Moines (hereafter cited as Whitten Papers).

18. Lundquist, *Headcount*, Apr. 1865; Whitten diary, 33, Whitten Papers.

19. *OR*, ser. 1, vol. 47, pt. 3, 284, 343; Whitten diary, 33–34, Whitten Papers.

20. Hutchinson, "Glimpses," 71; Whitten diary, 34, Whitten Papers.

21. Whitten diary, 33–35, Whitten Papers; Daniel L. Schafer, *Thunder on the River: The Civil War in Northeast Florida* (Gainesville: University Press of Florida, 2010), 236–37; Hutchinson, "Glimpses," 71; "Shanks Report," H. Rep. No. 45, 967–70.

22. Gordon CMSR, NA RG-94, and Pension File No. 262,965; "Shanks Report," H. Rep. No. 45, 970.

23. Connell and Day CMSRs, NA RG-94, for Ninth Minnesota and Tenth Tennessee, C.S.A.; *St. Paul Press*, 23 Mar. 1865; Thelma Jones, *Once Upon a Lake: A History of Lake Minnetonka and Its People* (Minneapolis: Ross and Haines, 1957), 149; Herrick Family History notes, Herrick-Handy Papers; Davidson, *Fourteen Months*, 334; Kerr's "List of Officers and Men of the 9th Regt. Min Vols," Minnesota State Archives; Stubbs, *Milton Aurelius*, 24.

24. Connell and Day CMSRs, NA RG-94, Tenth Tennessee, C.S.A.; *OR*, ser. 1, vol. 45, pt. 1, 846, 848–49, 861–63, 870; *Milwaukee Daily Sentinel*, 16 Jan. 1865; Herrick Family History notes, Herrick-Handy Papers; Handy CMSR, NA RG-94.

25. *OR*, ser. 1, vol. 45, pt. 1, 847, ser. 2, vol. 8, 358–59, 554; Dee Brown, *The Galvanized Yankees* (Lincoln: University of Nebraska Press, 1986), 9, 11–16, 120–21; Connell and Day CMSRs, Fifth U.S. Volunteers, NA RG-94; George E. Day Pension File Application, Ind. Sur 10448; *Minnetonka Record*, 12 Feb. 1937.

26. CMSRs, NA RG-94; Andersonville Register of Prisoner Departures, NA RG-249; Weber Pension File No. 437,617; Da Rusha Pension File Application No. 1,008,228.

27. Dean letters, 30 Apr. and 2 May 1865, Dean Papers; *East Union News*, 1 Oct. 1896; *MICIW*, 1:435.

28. CMSRs, NA RG-94; John Arnold Pension File No. 102,575.

29. Dean letter, 16 May 1865, Dean Papers; *East Union News*, 15 Oct. 1896; 1860 U.S. Census.

30. Dean letters, 22 and 25 May, 25 June, and 16 July 1865; *Rochester City Post*, 15 July 1865; *East Union News*, 15 Nov. 1896.

31. *MICIW*, 1:436; *Rochester City Post*, 15 July 1865; Weymouth T. Jordan, *Hugh Davis and His Alabama Plantation* (Tuscaloosa: University of Alabama Press, 1948), 160.

32. *Rochester City Post*, 15 July 1865; *East Union News*, 15 Nov. 1896.

33. *MICIW*, 1:436; Kerr diary, 13 June, 20 and 24 July 1865, Kerr Papers; Josiah Marsh Pension File No. 277,528; *East Union News*, 15 Nov. 1896.

34. *East Union News*, 1 Dec. 1896; Kerr diary, 11 July 1865, Kerr Papers.

35. *East Union News,* 15 Nov. 1896 and 1 Jan. 1897; Dean letter, 16 July 1895, and Gardner letter, 16 Oct. 1865, both Dean Papers.

36. *Rochester City Post,* 15 July 1865; Jordan, *Hugh Davis,* 160.

37. *East Union News,* 15 Jan. 1897; CMSRs, NA RG-94.

38. *MICIW,* 1:436–37; *New York Herald Tribune,* 11 Aug. 1865; *East Union News,* 1 Mar. 1897.

39. *MICIW,* 1:437; Trenerry, "Boys," 290, on the ceremonies for the returning regiments; CMSRs, NA RG-94.

40. CMSRs, NA RG-94; *East Union News,* 1 May 1895; Robert Strachan letter, 28 May 1865, private collection.

41. *MICIW,* 1:436–37; CMSRs, NA RG-94.

42. Figures in Regimental Histories in *MICIW,* vol. 1; Folwell, *History of Minnesota,* 2: 306; William F. Fox, *Regimental Losses in the American Civil War 1861–1865* (Albany, N.Y.: Albany Publishing, 1889), 524.

43. *East Union News,* 15 Apr. 1897; Trenerry, "Boys," 293–95.

NOTES TO CHAPTER TWENTY

1. The National Archives has two massive card files for the Civil War–era Federal Pension Files: the General List (1861–1934), which is alphabetical by name, and the Organizational Index by regiment and company (1861–1900), both RG15. Both are required to check for a specific pensioner. James Marten, *Sing Not War: The Lives of Union & Confederate Veterans in Gilded Age America* (Chapel Hill: University of North Carolina Press, 2011), 17.

2. Theobald B. Fenstermacher Pension File No. 1,029,634. Obituary in *Princeton (Mo.) Post,* 1 July 1936.

3. Francis Merchant CMSR, NA RG-94, and Pension File No. 274,560; Neill, *Freeborn County,* 516; *Freeborn County Standard,* 9 Jan. 1884, 12 May and 25 Aug. 1886, 19 and 26 Dec. 1888, 3 Jan. and 12 Sept. 1889; *Oakland (Calif.) Tribune,* 2 Oct. 1927.

4. Edwin W. Ford Pension File No. 1,058,978; Committee on Pensions, *Edwin W. Ford,* 58th Cong., 2nd sess., March 7, 1904, S. Rep. No. 1328; *La Crosse (Wis.) Tribune,* 22 Oct. 1906; *La Crosse (Wis.) Tribune and Leader Press,* 11 May 1925.

5. David W. Wellman Pension File No. 861,872; *Wabasha Herald,* 2 Dec. 1897; *Rochester City Post,* 27 Oct. 1866; Josiah S. Marsh Pension File No. 277,528.

6. Edward L. Clapp Pension File No. 719,399; *Oceana (Mich.) Herald,* 17 Jan. 1918, courtesy Roger Norland; "Burns Arlakson" Pension File No. 179,129; Greipsland, *Nordmenn,* 189.

7. *The Enterprise,* 25 Mar. 1909; notes on William Dean from Dean Blackmar Krafft; Stone, *History of Colorado,* 3:690–91; Lovell Reminiscences, Lovell Papers.

8. *Bucyrus (Ohio) Evening Telegraph,* 14 Aug. 1912.

9. Genevieve Carter, *Pioneers,* 43; Warner, *Generals in Blue,* 48; Combined Books, ed., *Civil War Book of Lists* (New York: Da Capo Press, 1994), 143; Marvel, *Andersonville,* 240–47; *The Trial of Henry Wirz,* H. Doc. No. 23, 397–403; Page, *True Story,* 194, 208, 239. This author is writing a detailed analysis of the question of Wirz and "William Stewart."

10. T. J. Stiles, *Jesse James: Last Rebel of the Civil War* (New York: Knopf, 2002), 312–15.

11. Curtiss-Wedge, *Mower County*, 442–43, 683; *Mower County Register*, 21 Dec. 1865 and 4 Jan. 1866. See also http://www.rootsweb.ancestry.com/~mnmower/bios/paddeniraw_new.htm.

12. Frederick Heilmann Pension File No. 80,014; *Cherokee Sentinel on the Border* (Crawford County, Kans.), 15 Sept. 1882; Fritz Heilman Probate Record, Crawford County, Kansas, 15 Sept. 1884; letter to author from Crawford County Genealogical Society, 2 Nov. 2007.

13. Henry Ehmke Pension File No. 191,318; Committee on Invalid Pensions, *Henry Ehmke*, 57th Cong., 2nd sess., 15 Dec. 1902, H. Rep. No. 2861; *Winona Daily Republican*, 19 Mar. 1875, 1 May 1882, 15 June and 23 Dec. 1889; 1900 U.S. Census; *Winona Republican Herald*, 11 Mar. 1929.

14. Enoch W. Pike Pension No. 1,097,068; *An Illustrated History of Klickitat, Yakima and Kittitas Counties* (Chicago: Interstate Publishing, 1904), 381–82; Elwood Evans, *History of the Pacific Northwest: Oregon and Washington,* (Portland, Ore.: North Pacific History, 1889), 2:523.

15. Evans, *Pacific Northwest,* 2:523.

16. *An Illustrated History of Klickitat,* 170; Robert Ballou, *Early Klickitat Days* (Goldendale, Wash.: Goldendale Sentinel, 1938), 341–44.

17. *Klickitat County (Wash.) News,* 31 Oct. 1925; *Goldendale (Wash.) Sentinel,* 21 Mar. and 11 Apr. 1918.

18. Latham D. Stewart Pension File No. 1,126,971; *Port Angeles (Wash.) Evening News,* 15 Jan. 1930.

19. Isaac Peterman Pension File No. 405,701; Sherman Scott Crane, *The Crane Family Genealogy* (Grand Rapids, Minn.: Presto Print, 1991), 23–29; 1900 U.S. Census; *Barron County (Wis.) Herald,* 4 July 1902.

20. *Winona Republican Herald,* 12 Sept. 1907; *Winona Daily Republican,* 27 Apr. 1874.

21. Hans Luthye Pension File No. 325,502; Committee on Invalid Pensions, *Barbara Luthye,* 61st Cong., 3rd sess., 8 Dec. 1910, H. Rep. No. 1743, H. R. 21574; 1910 U.S. Census.

22. *Winona Republican Herald,* 12 Sept. 1907; 1930 U.S. Census.

23. Hilton CMSR, NA RG-94; Marten, *Sing Not War,* 89; *Winona Daily Republican,* 18 Apr. and 21 Aug. 1867; 1870 U.S. Census.

24. Further biographical sources on John Arnold are Pension File No. 102,575; 1865 Minnesota State Census; 1870, 1880, and 1900 U.S. Census; *Lorain County (Ohio) Reporter,* 1 Apr. 1893; and *Elyria (Ohio) Republican,* 30 Mar. 1893. For the date of his marriage to Melissa Luick, see Wright County, Iowa, Marriages at http://www.onentofl.com/chmarriawright.html. Letter to author from Randy Neuman, Archivist, United Brethren Historical Society, 23 Sept. 2002.

25. *Wellington (Ohio) Enterprise,* 11 Mar. 1891 and 21 Dec. 1892. For the important articles from the *Wellington (Ohio) Enterprise,* I am indebted to Lynne Welch, Herrick Memorial Library, Wellington, Ohio.

26. *Wellington (Ohio) Enterprise,* 14 Dec. 1892.

27. *Wellington (Ohio) Enterprise,* 14 and 21 Dec. 1892.

28. *Wellington (Ohio) Enterprise,* 21 Dec. 1892.

29. See, for example, *New York Times,* 17 Dec. 1892. *Lorain County (Ohio) Reporter,* 18 Mar. 1893.

30. *Elyria (Ohio) Republican,* 23 and 30 Mar. 1893; *Lorain County (Ohio) Reporter,* 1 Apr. 1893.

31. *Lorain County (Ohio) Reporter,* 8 Apr. 1893; *Wellington (Ohio) Enterprise,* 5 Apr. 1893.

32. *Wellington (Ohio) Enterprise,* 12 Apr. and 10 May 1893; *Plain Dealer* (Cleveland, Ohio), 31 Oct. 1893.

33. *Lorain County (Ohio) Reporter,* 25 Nov. 1893.

34. 1900 U.S. Census; *Semi-Weekly Record* (Chico, Calif.), 6 June 1905; *Lorain County (Ohio) Reporter,* 25 Nov. 1893.

NOTES TO CONCLUSION

1. Chandra Manning, *What this Cruel War Was Over: Soldiers, Slavery and the Civil War* (New York: Alfred A. Knopf, 2007), passim; Gary W. Gallagher, *The Union War* (Cambridge, Mass.: Harvard University Press, 2011), 4, 43, 102. See also Eric Foner's review of the Gallagher book, *New York Times,* 29 Apr. 2011.

2. *Lorain County (Ohio) Reporter,* 25 Nov. 1893.

Bibliography

GOVERNMENT AND MILITARY DOCUMENTS

Congressional Globe. 38th Congress, 1st Session, 13 Jan. 1864; 22 Jan. 1864; 3 Feb. 1864.

Minnesota State Archives. Office of the Adjutant General. Reports and Records, Ninth Minnesota Volunteer Infantry. Minnesota Historical Society, St. Paul.

National Archives. Records of the Adjutant General Office, 1780's–1917. Book Records of Volunteer Union Organizations: Records of the Ninth Minnesota Infantry, 1863–1864. RG-94.

———. Records of the Department of Veterans Affairs, 1773–2001. RG-15.

———. Records of the Office of the Commissary General, 1861–1905. RG-249.

———. Records of the Office of the Secretary of War, 1791–1947. File J445 (January 1864). RG-107.

———. Records of the U.S. Army Continental Commands, 1817–1940. Records of the District of Central Missouri, 1863–1864. RG-393.

Quartermaster General. *Roll of Honor (No. XIV.) Names of Soldiers Who in Defense of the American Union Suffered Martyrdom in the Prison Pens Throughout the South.* Washington, D.C.: Government Printing Office, 1868.

———. *Roll of Honor (No. XX.) Names of Soldiers Who Died in Defense of the American Union, interred in the National Cemeteries at Corinth, Mississippi, Pittsburgh Landing, Tennessee and Jefferson Barracks, Missouri.* Washington, D.C.: Government Printing Office, 1869.

Senate Executive Journal. 38th Congress, 1st Session, 12 May 1864 [18 May 1864].

United States Census, 1840, 1850, 1860, 1870, 1880, 1900, 1910, 1920, 1930.

United States Congress. House of Representatives. Committee on Invalid Pensions. *Barbara Luthye.* 61st Congress, 3rd Session, 8 Dec. 1910. House Report No. 1743, H. R. 21574.

———. House of Representatives. Committee on Invalid Pensions. *Henry Ehmke.* 57th Congress, 2nd Session, 15 Dec. 1902. H. Rep. No. 2861.

———. House of Representatives. *Report on the Treatment of Prisoners of War by the Rebel Authorities during the War of the Rebellion.* 40th Congress, 3rd Session. House

Report No. 45. Washington, D.C.: Government Printing Office, 1869. ["Shanks Report"]

———. House of Representatives. *The Trial of Henry Wirz.* 40th Congress, 2nd Session. House Executive Document No. 23. Washington, D.C.: Government Printing Office, 1868.

———. Senate. Committee on Pensions. *Edwin W. Ford.* 58th Congress, 2nd Session, 7 March 1904. Senate Report No. 1328.

———. Senate. *Letter of the Secretary of War, Communicating, In answer to a resolution of the Senate of the 11th of January 1864, information relating to the arrest and imprisonment, by the military authorities in Missouri, of soldiers belong to the Ninth Minnesota regiment.* 38th Congress, 1st Session, 4 March 1864. Senate Executive Document No. 24.

———. Senate. *Letter of the Secretary of War in Obedience to Law, The Report of the Inspector of the National Cemeteries of the United States for 1869.* 41st Congress, 2nd Session, 15 March 1870. Senate Executive Document No. 62.

War Department. *The 1863 U.S. Infantry Tactics.* Philadelphia: J. P. Lippencott, 1863.

———. *Revised United States Army Regulations of 1861 with an Appendix containing the Changes and Laws affecting Army Regulations and Articles of War to June 25, 1863.* Washington, D.C.: Government Printing Office, 1863.

———. *The War of the Rebellion: A Compilation of the Official Records of the Union and Confederate Armies.* Series 1–4, 70 volumes in 128. Washington, D.C.: 1880–1901.

PERSONAL PAPERS

Agnew, Samuel A., Papers. University of North Carolina, Chapel Hill.

Aiton, John Felix, Papers. Minnesota Historical Society, St. Paul.

Almond, Alexander, Papers. Richard D. Goff (via Robert Scott Davis) private collection.

Ames, Amos W., Papers. State Historical Society of Iowa, Des Moines.

Bartleson, John Wool, Papers. Andersonville National Historic Site, Andersonville, Ga.

Beach, Riley V., Papers. Terry and Peg McCarty private collection.

Bell, Tyree H., Papers. Duke University, Durham, N.C.

Berry-Thomson-Walker Family Papers. Western Historical Manuscripts Collection–Columbia, University of Missouri.

Bond, Daniel C., Papers. Minnesota Historical Society, St. Paul.

Burdick, Alfred D., Papers. Wisconsin Historical Society, Madison.

Carlson, Pehr (Peter), and Family Papers. Minnesota Historical Society, St. Paul.

Chandler, Stephen N., Papers. Diane M. Bower Clegg and Susan N. Bower-Litzenberger private collection.

Chandler, Stephen N., Papers. Mower County Historical Society, Austin, Minn.

Cooper, Josiah, Papers. Arlene Gable private collection.

Daigh, George W., Papers. Andersonville National Historic Site, Andersonville, Ga.

Dean, William Johnston, Papers. Dean Blackmar Krafft private collection.

Dieter, Jacob, and Family Papers. Olmsted County Historical Society, Rochester, Minn.

Doyle, William, Papers. Minnesota Historical Society, St. Paul.

Epler, Joshua C., Papers. Diane M. Bower Clegg and Susan N. Bower-Litzenberger private collection.

Gessner, Gustavus A., Papers. Rutherford B. Hayes Presidential Center, Fremont, Ohio.

Halsey, William B., Papers. Rutherford B. Hayes Presidential Center, Fremont, Ohio.

Hammack, William David, Papers. Georgia State Archives, Morrow.

Harrington and Merrill Family Papers. Minnesota Historical Society, St. Paul.

Harvey, Joseph E., Papers. Minnesota Historical Society, St. Paul.

Herrick, George W., and Herrick-Handy Family Papers. Carol Jauregui private collection.

Herrick, George W., Papers. Diane M. Bower Clegg and Susan N. Bower-Litzenberger private collection.

Herrick, George W., Papers. Vermont Historical Society, Barre.

Herrick, Henry N., and Family Papers. Minnesota Historical Society, St. Paul.

Hill, Chauncey J. [*sic*, I.], and Family Papers. Minnesota Historical Society, St. Paul.

Hoster, John L., Papers. Emory University, Atlanta, Ga.

Jenkins, George O., Papers. Jeff Glover private collection.

Kennedy, David, Papers. Stephen E. Osman private collection.

Kerr, Aaron H., Papers. Minnesota Historical Society, St. Paul.

Keysor, Clark F., Papers. John L. Nau III Civil War Collection, Houston, Tex.

Latimer, Washington Kays, Papers. Minnesota Historical Society, St. Paul.

Lay, Harkness, Papers. Richard D. Goff (via Robert Scott Davis) private collection.

Lovell, William R., Papers. Minnesota Historical Society, St. Paul.

McCoy, Andrew C., Papers. Andersonville National Historic Site, Andersonville, Ga.

Merrilies, John, Papers. Chicago Historical Society.

Obermier, Simon Peter, Papers. Rutherford B. Hayes Presidential Center, Fremont, Ohio.

Rice, John B., Papers. Rutherford B. Hayes Presidential Center, Fremont, Ohio.

Rucker, Edmund Winchester, Papers. Birmingham Public Library, Birmingham, Ala.

Shearer, George, Papers. State Historical Society of Iowa, Des Moines.

Sheppard, Thomas J., Papers. John White Johnson Collection. Rochester Museum and Science Center, Rochester, N.Y.

Sheppard, Thomas J., Papers. Ohio Historical Society, Columbus.

Steffens, Charles H., and Family Papers. Minnesota Historical Society, St. Paul.

Strachan, James, Papers. John B. Lundstrom private collection.

Strachan, Robert, Papers. John B. Lundstrom private collection.

Warren, John E., "Civil War Reminiscences," Warren Papers. Wisconsin Historical Society, Madison.

Weber, Frank, Papers. Brian Schumacher private collection.

West (formerly Hill), Sarah E., Family History, Gay Wilhelm private collection.

Whitten, John, Papers. State Historical Society of Iowa, Des Moines.

Wilkin, Alexander, and Family Papers. Minnesota Historical Society, St. Paul.

Williams, Taliesin, Papers. Jean C. Pool private collection.

Williams, William, Papers. Jean C. Pool private collection.

Winslow, Edward F., Papers. University of Iowa, Iowa City.

Woodbury, James M., Papers. Minnesota Historical Society, St. Paul.

BOOKS AND ARTICLES

Abbott, A. O. *Prison Life in the South.* New York: Harper & Brothers, 1865.

Abbott, Abial R. "The Negro in the War of the Rebellion." In *Military Essays and Recollections,* vol. 3, 373–84. Illinois Commandery, Military Order of the Loyal Legion of the United States. Chicago: Dial Press, 1899.

Agnew, Samuel A. "Battle of Tishomingo Creek." *Confederate Veteran,* September 1900, 401–3.

——. *Historical Sketch of the Associated Reformed Presbyterian Church of Bethany, Lee County, Mississippi.* Louisville, 1881. Extracts at: http://www.rootsweb/com/~mslee/bethanyhist.html.

Anders, Leslie. *The Twenty-First Missouri: From Home Guard to Union Regiment.* Westport, Conn.: Greenwood Press, 1975.

Andrews, Christopher C. *History of the Campaign of Mobile.* New York: D. Van Nostrand, 1867.

Andrus, Onley. *The Civil War Letters of Sergeant Onley Andrus.* Urbana: University of Illinois Press, 1947.

Aslakson, Burns [Bjørn]. *Ti Maaneders fangenskab i Andersonville.* Minneapolis: Augsburg Pub., c. 1887.

Atwater, Dorence. *Prisoners Who Died at Andersonville Prison: Atwater List.* Andersonville, Ga.: National Society of Andersonville, 1981.

Bailey, George W. *The Civil War Diary and Biography of George W. Bailey.* Colleyville, Tex.: G. R. Post, 1990.

Baker, James H. *Lives of the Governors of Minnesota.* Vol. 8 of *Minnesota Historical Society Collections.* St. Paul: Minnesota Historical Society, 1908.

Ballard, Michael B. "The Battle of Tupelo." *The Papers of the Blue and Gray Education Society,* no. 3 (Winter 1996): 1–57.

Ballou, Robert. *Early Klickitat Days.* Goldendale, Wash.: Goldendale Sentinel, 1938.

Basile, Leon, ed. *The Civil War Diary of Amos E. Stearns, a Prisoner at Andersonville.* Rutherford, N.J.: Fairleigh Dickinson University Press, 1981.

——."Letters of a Minnesota Volunteer: The Correspondence of James M. Woodbury." *Lincoln Herald* Part 1 (Summer 1980): 387–92; Part 2 (Fall 1980): 438–46.

Bauman, Roland M. *The 1858 Oberlin-Wellington Rescue: A Reappraisal.* Oberlin, Ohio: Oberlin College, 2003.

Bearss, Edwin C. *Andersonville National Historic Site: Historical Resource Study and Historical Base Map.* Washington, D.C.: National Park Service, Office of Eastern and Historic Architecture, Eastern Service Center, 1970.

——. "The Battle of Brice's Cross Roads." *Blue & Gray* 16, no. 6 (Summer 1999): 6–21, 44–53.

——. *Forrest at Brice's Cross Roads.* Dayton, Ohio: Morningside Bookshop, 1979.

Berlin, Ira, ed. *The Black Military Experience.* Freedom: A Documentary History of Emancipation 1861–1867, series 2. Cambridge, Mass.: Cambridge University Press, 1982.

——. *The Destruction of Slavery.* Freedom: A Documentary History of Emancipation 1861–1867, series 1, vol. 1. Cambridge, Mass.: Cambridge University Press, 1985.

——. *The Wartime Genesis of Free Labor: The Upper South.* Freedom: A Documentary History of Emancipation 1861–1867, series 1, vol. 2. Cambridge, Mass.: Cambridge University Press, 1993.

Billings, John D. *Hardtack & Coffee: The Unwritten Story of Army Life.* Lincoln: University of Nebraska Press, 1993. Reprint of 1887 edition.

Biographical Record of Calhoun County, Iowa. New York: S. J. Clarke Publishing, 1902.

Bir, Louis. "Remenecence of My Army Life." *Indiana Magazine of History* 101, no. 1 (March 2005): 15–57.

Bissell, Josiah W. "The Western Organization of Colored People for Furnishing Information to United States Troops in the South." In *Glimpses of the Nation's Struggle*. Second Series, 314–21. Minnesota Commandery, Military Order of the Loyal Legion of the United States. St. Paul: St. Paul Book and Stationery, 1890.

Blackman, William S. *The Boy of Battle Ford and the Man*. Marion, Ill.: Egyptian Press Printing, 1906.

Blair, Anthony L. "Democratization, Revivalism and Reform: The United Brethren in the Antebellum Era." *Journal of United Brethren History and Life* 1, no. 1 (Fall 2000): 30–51.

Blakey, Arch Frederic. *General John H. Winder C.S.A.* Gainesville: University of Florida Press, 1990.

Blegen, Theodore C. "Campaigning with Seward 1860." *Minnesota Historical Quarterly* 8, no. 2 (June 1927): 150–71.

———. *Minnesota: A History of the State*. 2nd ed. St. Paul: University of Minnesota Press, 1975.

Bogue, Alan G. *The Earnest Men: Republicans of the Civil War Senate*. Ithaca: Cornell University Press, 1981.

Boman, Dennis K. *Lincoln and Citizens' Rights in Civil War Missouri: Balancing Freedom and Security*. Baton Rouge: Louisiana State University Press, 2011.

———. *Lincoln's Resolute Unionist: Hamilton Gamble, Dred Scott Dissenter and Missouri's Civil War Governor*. Baton Rouge: Louisiana State University Press, 2006.

Booth, Benjamin F., and Steve Meyer. *Dark Days of the Rebellion: Life in Southern Military Prisons*. Garrison, Iowa: Meyer Publishing, 1996.

Bouton, Edward. *Events of the Civil War*. Los Angeles: Kingsley, Moles and Collins, 1906.

Brown, Andrew. *History of Tippah County, Mississippi: The First Century*. Ripley, Miss.: The Tippah County Historical and Genealogical Society, 1998.

Brown, Barry L., and Gordon R. Elwell. *Crossroads of Conflict: A Guide to Civil War Sites in Georgia*. Athens: University of Georgia Press, 2010.

Brown, Dee. *The Galvanized Yankees*. Lincoln: University of Nebraska Press, 1986.

Brown, Louis A. *The Salisbury Prison: A Case Study of Confederate Military Prisons 1861–1865*. Wilmington, N.C.: Broadfoot Publishing, 1992.

Bruce, Henry Clay. *The New Man: Twenty-Nine Years a Slave, Twenty-Nine Years a Free Man: The Recollections of H. C. Bruce*. Lincoln: University of Nebraska Press, 1996.

Bryant, William O. *Cahaba Prison and the Sultana Disaster*. Tuscaloosa: University of Alabama Press, 1990.

Burlingame, Michael. *Abraham Lincoln: A Life*. 2 vols. Baltimore, Md.: Johns Hopkins University Press, 2008.

———, ed. *An Oral History of Abraham Lincoln: John G. Nicolay's Interviews and Essays*. Carbondale: Southern Illinois University Press, 1996.

———, ed. *At Lincoln's Side: John Hay's Civil War Correspondence and Selected Writings*. Carbondale: Southern Illinois University Press, 2000.

Burlingame, Michael, and John R. Turner Ettlinger. *Inside Lincoln's White House: The Complete Civil War Diary of John Hay*. Carbondale: Southern Illinois University Press, 1997.

Byrne, Frank L. *The View from Headquarters: Civil War Letters of Harvey Reid*. Madison: State Historical Society of Wisconsin, 1965.

Carley, Kenneth. *The Dakota War of 1862: Minnesota's Other Civil War*. St. Paul: Minnesota Historical Society Press, 1976.

———. *Minnesota in the Civil War: An Illustrated History*. St. Paul: Minnesota Historical Society Press, 2000.

Carroll, John W. *Autobiography and Reminiscences of John W. Carroll*. Harrah, Okla.: Brandy Station Bookshelf, 2003. Reprint of 1898 edition.

Carter, Genevieve L. *Pioneers of Pettis and Adjoining Missouri Counties*, vol. 3. Warrensburg, Mo.: Privately printed, 1987. Reprint of 1966 edition.

Carter, Theodore George. "The Tupelo Campaign. As Noted at the Time by a Line Officer in the Union Army." *Publications of the Mississippi Historical Society* 10 (1909): 91–113.

Cassity, Michael. *Defending a Way of Life: An American Community in the Nineteenth Century*. Albany: State University of New York Press, 1989.

Castel, Albert. *General Sterling Price and the Civil War in the West*. Baton Rouge: Louisiana State University Press, 1993.

———. *Winning and Losing in the Civil War: Essays and Stories*. Columbia: University of South Carolina Press, 1996.

Castle, Henry A. *Minnesota: Its Story and Biography*, vol. 1. Chicago: Lewis Publishing, 1915.

Chandler, George. *The Chandler Family*. Worcester, Mass.: Charles Hamilton, 1883.

Clapp, E. L. [Edward L.] *Andersonville: Six Months a Prisoner of War*. Milwaukee: Daily Wisconsin Steam Printing House, 1865.

Clapp, Ebenezer. *The Clapp Memorials: Record of the Clapp Family in America*. Boston: David Clapp & Son, Publisher, 1876.

Clark, James I., *Wisconsin Defies the Fugitive Slave Law: The Case of Sherman M. Booth*. Madison: State Historical Society of Wisconsin, 1955.

Clavreul, H. *Diary of Rev. H. Clavreul*. Waterbury: Connecticut Association of Ex-Prisoners of War, 1910.

Claycomb, William B. *A History of North-East Pettis County, Missouri*. Dayton, Ohio: Morningside Press, 1996.

Coates, Earl J., and Dean S. Thomas. *An Introduction to Civil War Small Arms*. Gettysburg, Pa.: Thomas Publications, 1990.

Coco, Gregory A. *The Civil War Infantryman: In Camp, on the March and in Battle*. Gettysburg, Pa.: Thomas Publications, 1996.

Coffman, Edward M. "Memoirs of Hylan B. Lyon Brigadier General, C.S.A." *Tennessee Historical Quarterly* 18 (March 1959): 35–53.

Cogley, Thomas S. *History of the Seventh Indiana Cavalry Volunteers*. Dayton, Ohio: Morningside Press, 1991.

Combined Books, ed. *Civil War Book of Lists*. New York: Da Capo Press, 1994.

Cowden, Robert. *A Brief Sketch of the Organization and Services of the Fifty-Ninth Regiment of United States Colored Infantry and Biographical Sketches*. Dayton, Ohio: United Brethren Publishing House, 1883.

Cox, Jacob Doleson. *Military Reminiscences of the Civil War*. 2 vols. New York: Charles Scribner's Sons, 1900.

Crane, Sherman Scott. *The Crane Family Genealogy*. Grand Rapids, Minn.: Presto Print, 1991.

Cray, Loren. "Experiences in Southwestern Minnesota 1859 to 1867." *Collections of the Minnesota Historical Society* 15 (1915): 435–54.

Cross, David Faris. *A Melancholy Affair at the Weldon Railroad: The Vermont Brigade, June 23, 1864.* Shippensburg, Pa.: White Mane Press, 2003.

———. "What Killed the Yankees at Andersonville?" *North & South* 6, no. 6 (September 2003): 26–32

Cumming, Kate. *A Journal of Hospital Life in the Confederate Army.* Louisville, Ky.: John P. Morton, 1866.

Curtiss-Wedge, Franklyn. *The History of Mower County Minnesota.* Chicago: H. C. Cooper Jr., 1911.

Dal Bello, Dominic J. *Parade, Inspection and Basic Evolutions of the Infantry Battalion.* 4th ed. Santa Barbara, Calif.: Dominic Dal Bello, 1998.

Davenport, Edward A. *History of the Ninth Regiment Illinois Cavalry Volunteers.* Chicago: Donohue & Henneberry, 1888.

Davidson, Henry M. *Fourteen Months in Southern Prisons.* Milwaukee: Daily Wisconsin Printing House, 1865.

Davis, Robert Scott. *Andersonville Civil War Prison.* Charleston, S.C.: History Press, 2010.

———. *Ghosts and Shadows of Andersonville: Essays on the Secret Social Histories of America's Deadliest Prison.* Macon, Ga.: Mercer University Press, 2006.

Demuth, I. MacDonald. *The History of Pettis County, Missouri, Including an Authentic History of Sedalia.* N.p., 1882.

Dennison, James H. *Dennison's Andersonville Diary.* Kankakee, Ill.: Kankakee County Historical Society, 1987.

Denny, James M. "The Battle of Marshall: The Greatest Little Battle That Was Never Fought." *Boone's Lick Heritage* 9, no. 3 (September 2001): 4–13.

———. "Civil War Entrenchment Near Otterville," *Boone's Lick Heritage* 7, no. 2 (June 1999): 4–9.

Denny, James M., and John Bradbury. *The Civil War's First Blood: Missouri, 1854–1861.* Boonville, Mo.: Missouri Life, 2007.

Devillez, Henry. "Reminiscences of the Civil War: Andersonville." *Indiana Magazine of History* 11 (1915): 144–47.

Dinkins, James. "The Battle of Brice's Crossroads." *Confederate Veteran*, October 1925, 380–82.

Domschcke, Bernhard. *Twenty Months in Captivity: Memoirs of a Union Officer in Confederate Prisons.* Rutherford, N.J.: Fairleigh Dickinson University Press, 1987.

Drabak, William A. *Freedom by the Sword: The U.S. Colored Troops, 1862–1867.* Washington, D.C.: Center of Military History, U.S. Army, 2011.

Dyer, Gustavus W., and John Trotwood Moore. *The Tennessee Civil War Veterans Questionnaires.* 5 vols. Easley, S.C.: Southern Historical Press, c.1985.

Estee, Pearl Frisbie. "The Story of Zara Frisbie." Bonus Issue, *Bulletin of the Frisbee-Frisbie Family Association of America* 18 (May 1968): 7–9.

Etcheson, Nicole. *Bleeding Kansas: Contested Liberty in the Civil War Era.* Lawrence: University Press of Kansas, 2004.

Evans, Elwood. *History of the Pacific Northwest: Oregon and Washington.* 2 vols. Portland, Ore.: North Pacific History, 1889.

Everett, Homer. *History of Sandusky County Ohio, With Portraits and Biographies of Prominent Citizens and Pioneers.* Cleveland, Ohio: H. Z. Williams & Bro., 1882.

Fehrenbacher, Don E. *The Slaveholding Republic: An Account of the United States Government's Relations to Slavery.* New York: Oxford University Press, 2001.

Fellman, Michael. *Inside War: The Guerrilla Conflict in Missouri during the American Civil War.* New York: Oxford University Press, 1989.

Fliss, William M. "Wisconsin's 'Abolition Regiment': The Twenty-Second Volunteer Infantry in Kentucky, 1862–1863." *Wisconsin Magazine of History,* Winter 2002–2003, 2–17.

Folwell, William Watts. *A History of Minnesota,* vols. 1 and 2. St. Paul: Minnesota Historical Society, 1956–61.

Foner, Eric. *The Fiery Trial: Abraham Lincoln and American Slavery.* New York: Norton, 2010.

Fonvielle, Chris E., Jr. *The Wilmington Campaign: Last Rays of Departing Hope.* Mechanicsburg, Pa.: Stackpole Books, 1997.

Forbes, Eugene. *Death Before Dishonor: The Andersonville Diary of Eugene Forbes 4th New Jersey Infantry.* Kearney, N.J.: Belle Grove Publishing, 1995.

"Forrest's Guntown Victory." *Confederate Veteran,* October 1905, 463–65.

Fox, William F. *Regimental Losses in the American Civil War 1861–1865.* Albany, N.Y.: Albany Publishing, 1889.

Fraser, Walter J., Jr. *Savannah in the Old South.* Athens: University of Georgia Press, 2003.

Freeberg, Ron. "Hard Fighting, Hard Drinking Col. Markham." *Post-Bulletin* (Rochester), October 26, 1961.

"Frémont's Hundred Days in Missouri." *Atlantic Monthly* 9, no. 53 (March 1862): 372–85.

Fuchs, Richard L. *An Unerring Fire: The Massacre at Fort Pillow.* Rev. ed. Mechanicsburg, Pa.: Stackpole Books, 2011.

Futch, Ovid L. *History of Andersonville Prison.* Gainesville: University Press of Florida, 1999.

Gallagher, Gary W. *The Union War.* Cambridge, Mass.: Harvard University Press, 2011.

George, Henry. *History of the 3d, 7th, 8th and 12th Kentucky, C.S.A.* Lyndon, Ky.: Mull-Wathen Historic Press, 1970.

Giles, William. *Disease, Starvation & Death: Personal Accounts of Camp Lawton, the South's Largest Prison.* Magnolia Springs State Park, Ga.: Lulu Press, 2005.

Green, William D. "Eliza Winston and the Politics of Freedom in Minnesota, 1854–60." *Minnesota History* 57, no. 3 (Fall 2000): 106–22.

———. "Minnesota's Long Road to Black Suffrage 1849–1868." *Minnesota History* 56, no. 2 (Summer 1998): 68–84.

Greipsland, Torbjørn. *Nordmenn i dødsleirene: Tusen norske soldater døde i den amerikanske borgerkrigen* [Norwegian Soldiers in the Prison Camps during the American Civil War]. Odins, Norway: Emigrantforlaget, 2005.

Grierson, Benjamin H. *A Just and Righteous Cause: Benjamin H. Grierson's Civil War Memoir.* Carbondale: Southern Illinois University Press, 2008.

Hancock, R. R. *Hancock's Diary; or, A History of the Second Tennessee Confederate Cavalry.* Dayton, Ohio: Morningside Press, 1999.

Harding, Samuel Bannister. *Life of George R. Smith Founder of Sedalia, Mo.* Sedalia, Mo., 1904.

Hargrave, Helen M. Goodale. *Carleton-Carlton Forebears.* N.p., 1977.

Haupt, Herman. *The Reminiscences of General Herman Haupt.* Milwaukee: Wright & Joy, 1901.

Hawes, Jesse, M.D. *Cahaba: A Story of Captive Boys in Blue.* New York: Burr Printing House, 1888.

Hearn, Chester G. *Mobile Bay and the Mobile Campaign.* Jefferson, N.C.: McFarland, 1993.

Henderson, Howard A. M. "Lincoln's Assassination and Camp Fisk." *Confederate Veteran* 15 (April 1907): 170–71.

Henry, Robert Selph. *As They Saw Forrest.* Jackson, Tenn.: McCowat-Mercer Press, 1956.

———. *"First With The Most" Forrest.* Indianapolis: Bobbs-Merrill, 1944.

Hess, Earl J. *Liberty, Virtue, and Progress: Northerners and Their War for the Union.* New York: Fordham University Press, 1997.

Hesseltine, William Best. *Civil War Prisons: A Study in War Psychology.* Columbus: Ohio State University Press, 1998.

Hills, Parker. "A Study in Warfighting: Nathan Bedford Forrest and the Battle of Brice's Crossroads." *The Papers of the Blue and Gray Education Society,* no. 2 (Fall 1995): 1–64.

History of Franklin, Jefferson, Washington, Crawford and Gasconade Counties, Missouri. Chicago: Goodspeed, 1888. Excerpt in http://home.usmo.com/~momollus/FranCo CW/FC1860GS.htm.

History of Winona and Olmsted Counties. Chicago: H. H. Hill, 1883.

Hord, Henry Ewell. "Brice's X Roads from A Private's View." *Confederate Veteran,* November 1904, 529–30.

Horn, Stanley F. *The Decisive Battle of Nashville.* Baton Rouge: Louisiana State University Press, 1956.

Hosmer, Francis J. *A Glimpse of Andersonville and Other Writings.* Springfield, Mass.: Loring & Axtell, 1896.

Howard, Victor B. *Black Liberation in Kentucky: Emancipation and Freedom, 1862–1884.* Lexington: University Press of Kentucky, 1983.

Hubbard, John Milton. *Notes of a Private.* Memphis, Tenn.: E. H. Clark & Brother, 1909.

Hubbard, Lucius F., and Return I. Holcombe. *Minnesota in Three Centuries,* vol. 3. Mankato: Publication Society of Minnesota, 1908.

Hubbs, Ronald M. "The Civil War and Alexander Wilkin." *Minnesota History* 39, no. 5 (Spring 1965): 173–90.

Hughes, Nathaniel Cheairs, Jr. *Brigadier General Tyree Bell, C. S. A.: Forrest's Fighting Lieutenant.* Knoxville: University of Tennessee Press, 2004.

Hughes, Thomas [E.]. *Old Traverse des Sioux.* St. Peter, Minn.: Herald Publishing, 1929.

Hughes, Thomas E., ed.. *The History of the Welsh in Minnesota, Foriston and Lime Springs, Ia.* Mankato, Minn.: Free Press Print, 1895.

Hutchinson, Jacob. "Glimpses of a Prisoner's Life." *The Ohio Soldier* 2, no. 5 (15 September 1888): 69–71.

Hyde, Solon. *A Captive of War.* Shippensburg, Pa.: Burd Street Press, 1996.

Illustrated History of Klickitat, Yakima and Kittitas Counties. Chicago: Interstate Publishing, 1904.

Joiner, Gary D. *Through the Howling Wilderness: The 1864 Red River Campaign and the Union Failure in the West.* Knoxville: University of Tennessee Press, 2006.

Jones, Thelma. *Once Upon a Lake: A History of Lake Minnetonka and Its People*. Minneapolis: Ross and Haines, 1957.

Jordan, Thomas, and J. P. Pryor. *The Campaigns of Lieut.-Gen. N. B. Forrest, and of Forrest's Cavalry*. Dayton, Ohio: Press of the Morningside Bookshop, 1973.

Jordan, Weymouth T. *Hugh Davis and His Alabama Plantation*. Tuscaloosa: University of Alabama Press, 1948.

Keenan, Jerry. *Wilson's Cavalry Corps*. Jefferson, N.C.: McFarland, 1998.

Kellogg, Robert H. *Life and Death in Rebel Prisons*. Hartford, Conn.: L. Stebbins, 1866.

Kennett, Lee. *Marching through Georgia: The Story of Soldiers & Civilians during Sherman's Campaigns*. New York: HarperCollins, 1995.

King, G. Wayne. "Death Camp at Florence." *Civil War Times Illustrated* 12, no. 9 (January 1974): 34–42.

Kirkland, Joseph. *The Captain of Company K*. Ridgewood, N.J.: Gregg Press, 1968. Reprint of 1891 edition.

Klement, Frank. "The Abolition Movement in Minnesota." *Minnesota History* 32 (March 1951), 15–33.

Lambert, D. Warren. *When the Ripe Pears Fell: The Battle of Richmond, Kentucky*. Richmond, Ky.: Madison County Historical Society, 1995.

Lathrop, David. *The History of the Fifty-Ninth Regiment Illinois Volunteers*. Indianapolis: Hall & Hutchinson, 1865.

Layman, Marvin D. *The Bartlesons of Grand Chain*. Rev. ed. N.p.: Marvin D. Layman, 1998.

Lee, Bill R. "Missouri's Fight over Emancipation in 1863." *Missouri Historical Review* 45, no. 3 (April 1951): 256–74.

Lee, Stephen D. "Battle of Brice's Cross Roads or Tishomingo Creek, June 2nd to 12th, 1864." *Publications of the Mississippi Historical Society* 6 (1902): 26–37.

Leonard, Joseph A. *History of Olmsted County, Minnesota*. Chicago: Goodspeed Historical Association, 1910.

Levens, Henry C., and Nathaniel M. Drake. *A History of Cooper County, Missouri*. St. Louis, Mo.: Perrin & Smith, 1876.

Linderman, Gerald F. *Embattled Courage: The Experience of Combat in the American Civil War*. New York: Free Press, 1987.

Logsdon, David R. *Eyewitnesses at the Battle of Nashville*. Nashville: Kettle Mills Press, 2004.

Lubet, Steven. *Fugitive Justice: Runaways, Rescuers, and Slavery on Trial*. Cambridge, Mass.: Belknap/Harvard, 2010.

Lundquist, John H. *Andersonville Prison, Sumter County, Georgia: A Record of Recorded and "Reported" Deaths February 27, 1864 to May 6, 1865*. [Minneapolis?], 2000.

——. *Andersonville Prison Headcount Rosters: Monthly Roster by Month and Day as Maintained by the Confederate Army*. [Minneapolis?], 2004.

Lyon, W. F. [William Franklin]. *In and Out of Andersonville Prison*. Detroit: George Harland, 1907.

Macdonald, Colin F. "The Battle of Brice's Cross Roads." In *Glimpses of the Nation's Struggle*, vol. 6, 443–62. Minnesota Commandery, Military Order of the Loyal Legion of the United States. Minneapolis: August Davis Publishing, 1909.

Manning, Chandra. *What This Cruel War Was Over: Soldiers, Slavery and the Civil War*. New York: Alfred A. Knopf, 2007.

Marten, James. *Sing Not War: The Lives of Union & Confederate Veterans in Gilded Age America*. Chapel Hill: University of North Carolina Press, 2011.

Martin, N. B. "Letters of a Union Officer: L. F. Hubbard and the Civil War." *Minnesota History* 35, no. 7 (September 1957): 313–19.

Marvel, William. *Andersonville: The Last Depot*. Chapel Hill: University of North Carolina Press, 1994.

Mathes, J. Harvey. *General Forrest*. New York: D. Appleton, 1902.

Maury, Dabney H. "Recollections of Nathan Bedford Forrest." In *Battles and Leaders of the Civil War*, vol. 5, edited by Peter Cozzens, 139–52. Urbana-Champaign: University of Illinois Press, 2002.

McCarty, Terry, with Margaret Ann Chatfield McCarty. *The Chatfield Story: Civil War Letters and Diaries of Private Edward L. Chatfield of the 113th Illinois Volunteers*. Georgetown, Tex.: privately printed, 2009.

McDonough, James Lee. *Nashville: The Western Confederacy's Final Gamble*. Knoxville: University of Tennessee Press, 2004.

McElroy, John. *Andersonville: A Story of Rebel Military Prisons*. Toledo, Ohio: D. R. Locke, 1879.

McPherson, James M. *For Cause & Comrades: Why Men Fought in the Civil War*. New York: Oxford University Press, 1997.

Meaney, Peter J., O.S.B. *Father Whelan of Fort Pulaski and Andersonville*. Reprinted from the *Georgia Historical Quarterly* 71, no. 1 (Spring 1987).

Meek, Basil. *Twentieth Century History of Sandusky County*. Chicago: Richmond-Arnold Publishing, 1909.

Memorial Record of the Counties of Faribault, Martin, Watonwan and Jackson, Minnesota. Chicago: Lewis Publishing, 1895.

Merrill, Julian W. *Records of the 24th Independent Battery, N. Y. Light Artillery, U. S. V.* West Falls, N.Y.: B. Conrad Bush, 2000.

Minnesota, Board of Commissioners. *Minnesota in the Civil and Indian Wars 1861–1865*. 2 vols., 2nd ed. St. Paul: Pioneer Press, 1891–99.

Minnesota Commission. *Report of the Minnesota Commission Appointed to Erect Monuments to Soldiers in the National Military Cemeteries at Little Rock, Arkansas, Memphis, Tennessee, and Andersonville, Georgia*. St. Paul, c. 1916.

Moore, Frank. *Anecdotes, Poetry and Incidents of the War: North and South 1860–1865*. New York: Publication Office, Bible House, 1867.

———. *Rebellion Record: A Diary of American Events*, vol. 11. New York: D. Van Nostrand, 1868.

Morton, John Watson. *The Artillery of Nathan Bedford Forrest's Cavalry*. Marietta, Ga.: R. Bemis Publishing, 1995. Reprint of 1909 edition.

———. "Fighting under Forrest at the Battle of Brice's Crossroads." In *The New Annals of the Civil War*, edited by Peter Cozzens and Robert I. Girardi, 363–80. Mechanicsburg, Pa.: Stackpole Books, 2004.

Moseley, T. M. "The Eighth Mississippi Cavalry at Brice's Crossroads." *Confederate Veteran* 33 (1925): 462–63.

Mowris, J. A. *A History of the One Hundred and Seventeenth Regiment, N. Y. Volunteers, (Fourth Oneida,) from the Date of Its Organization, August 1862, Till that of Its Muster Out, June, 1865*. Hamilton, N.Y.: Edmonston Publishing, 1996.

Neill, Edward D. *History of Freeborn County*. Minneapolis: Minnesota Historical Company, 1882.

———. *History of Ramsey County and the City of St. Paul*. Minneapolis: North Star Publications, 1881.

Newsome, Edmund. *Experience in the War of the Great Rebellion By a Soldier of the Eighty First Regiment of Illinois Volunteer Infantry*. Murphysboro, Ill.: Jackson County Historical Society, 1984.

Nicolay, John G., and John Hay. *Abraham Lincoln: A History*, vol. 8. New York: Century Company, 1886.

———. *Complete Works of Abraham Lincoln*, vols. 8 and 9. New York: F. D. Tandy, c. 1905.

Norland, Roger A. *"Boys In Blue": Blue Earth County in the Civil and Indian Wars 1861–1865*. Mankato, Minn., 1989.

Northrop, John Worrell. *Chronicles from the Diary of a War Prisoner in Andersonville and Other Military Prisons of the South in 1864*. Wichita: privately printed, 1904.

Otey, Mercer. "Story of Our Great War." *Confederate Veteran*, March 1901, 107–10; April 1901, 153–55.

Pacific Railroad Company. *History of the Pacific Railroad of Missouri*. St. Louis, Mo.: Democrat Book and Job Printing House, 1865.

Page, James Madison. *The True Story of Andersonville Prison: A Defense of Major Henry Wirz*. New York: Neale Publishing, 1908.

Parrish, William E. *A History of Missouri, Vol. III, 1860 to 1875*. Columbia: University of Missouri Press, 1973.

———. *Turbulent Partnership: Missouri and the Union 1861–1865*. Columbia: University of Missouri Press, 1963.

Patterson, M. B. "Remarkable Case of Replantation." *The Dental Cosmos* 17, no. 3 (March 1875): 168.

Paulson, Ole. *Memoirs: Rev. Ole Paulson: Reminiscences of a Pioneer Pastor in America, 1850–1885*. English translation by Torstein O. Kvamme. Wisconsin: privately printed, 1981.

Pepper, Samuel. *My Dear Wife: The Civil War Letters of Private Samuel Pepper, Company G–95th Illinois Infantry 1862 to 1865*. Caledonia, Ill.: Muffled Drum Press, 2003.

Peterson, Norma L. *Freedom and Franchise: The Political Career of B. Gratz Brown*. Columbia: University of Missouri Press, 1965.

Piston, William Garrett, and Richard W. Hatcher III. *Wilson's Creek: The Second Battle of the Civil War and the Men Who Fought It*. Chapel Hill: University of North Carolina Press, 2003.

Portrait and Biographical Album of Lancaster County, Nebraska. Chicago: Chapman Bros., 1888.

Portrait and Biographical Record of Winona County, Minnesota. Chicago: Chapman Publishing, 1895.

Potter, David M. *The Impending Crisis 1848–1861*. New York: Harper & Row, 1976.

Rable, George C. *God's Almost Chosen Peoples: A Religious History of the American Civil War*. Chapel Hill: University of North Carolina Press, 2010.

Ramold, Steven J. *Baring the Iron Hand: Discipline in the Union Army*. DeKalb: Northern Illinois University Press, 2010.

"Randolph County, Georgia, Biographies: Biography of Rev. Willie (William D.) Hammack 1842–1936." http://files.usgwarchives.net/ga/randolph/bios/whammack.txt.

Ransom, John L. *John Ransom's Andersonville Diary*. Middlebury, Vt.: Paul S. Eriksson, 1986.

Raus, Edmund. *Where Duty Called Them: The Story of the Samuel Babcock Family of Homer, New York, in the Civil War*. Daleville, Va.: Schroder Publications, 2001.

Reed, David W. *Campaigns and Battles of the Twelfth Regiment Iowa Veteran Volunteer Infantry*. [Evanston?] Ill., 1903.

Reed, Joseph R. "Guntown and Tupelo." In *War Sketches and Incidents*, vol. 2, 300–324. Iowa Commandery, Military Order of the Loyal Legion of the United States. Des Moines, Iowa: Kenyon, 1898.

Ripple, Ezra Hoyt. *Dancing along the Deadline*. Novato, Calif.: Presidio Press, 1996.

Robertson, Melville. "Journal of Melville Cox Robertson." *Indiana Magazine of History* 28, no. 2 (June 1932): 116–37.

Roth, Dave. "The General's Tour: The Battle of Brice's Cross Roads." *Blue & Gray* 16, no. 6 (Summer 1999): 54–64.

Sabre, G. E. *Nineteen Months a Prisoner of War*. New York: American News, 1865.

Salecker, Gene Eric. *Disaster on the Mississippi: The Sultana Explosion, April 27, 1865*. Annapolis, Md.: Naval Institute Press, 1996.

"Sample Letters of Immigrants." *Wisconsin Magazine of History* 20, no. 4 (June 1937): 437–46.

Sanders, Charles W., Jr. *While in the Hands of the Enemy: Military Prisons of the Civil War*. Baton Rouge: Louisiana State University Press, 2005.

Satterlee, John L. *The Journal & the 114th, 1861 to 1865*. Springfield, Ill.: Phillips Brothers, 1979.

Satterlee, Marion P. "Narratives of the Sioux War." *Collections of the Minnesota Historical Society* 15 (1915): 349–70.

Schafer, Daniel L. *Thunder on the River: The Civil War in Northeast Florida*. Gainesville: University Press of Florida, 2010.

Scherneckau, August. *Marching with the First Nebraska: A Civil War Diary*. Norman: University of Oklahoma Press, 2007.

Schofield, John M. *Forty-Six Years in the Army*. Norman: University of Oklahoma Press, 1998. Reprint of 1897 edition.

Schumacher, Brian. "Frank Weber." *Civil War Times* 44, no. 5 (December 2005): 12.

Scott, William Forse. *The Story of a Cavalry Regiment: The Career of the Fourth Iowa Veteran Volunteers, from Kansas to Georgia 1861–1865*. New York: G. P. Putnam's Sons, 1893.

Skaptason, Bjorn, ed. "West Tennessee U.S. Colored Troops and the Retreat from Brice's Crossroads: An Eyewitness Account by Major James C. Foster (USA)." *The West Tennessee Historical Society Papers* 60 (2006): 74–107.

Smith, Charles A. *Recollections of Prison Life at Andersonville, Georgia and Florence, South Carolina*. Raleigh, S.C.: Martini Print Media, 1997.

Smith, William B. *On Wheels: And How I Came There; The True Story of a 15-year-old Yankee Soldier and Prisoner in the American Civil War*. College Station, Tex.: Virtualbookworm.com, 2002.

Sneden, Robert Knox. *Eye of the Storm: A Civil War Odyssey*. New York: Simon & Schuster, 2000.

———. *Images from the Storm*. New York: The Free Press, 2001.

Society of the Army of the Tennessee. *Report of the Proceedings of the 42nd and 43rd Reunions*. Cincinnati: Bacharach Press, 1915.

Spangler, Earl. *The Negro in Minnesota*. Minneapolis: T. S. Denison, 1961.

Speer, Lonnie R. *Portals to Hell: Military Prisons of the Civil War*. Mechanicsburg, Pa.: Stackpole Books, 1997.

Starr, Stephen Z. *Jennison's Jayhawkers: A Civil War Cavalry Regiment and Its Commander*. Baton Rouge: Louisiana State University Press, 1973.

Stevenson, R. Randolph. *The Southern Side; or, Andersonville Prison*. Baltimore, Md.: Turnbull Brothers, 1876.

Stibbs, John Howard. "Andersonville and the Trial of Henry Wirz." *Iowa Journal of History and Politics* 9 (1911): 33–56.

Stiles, T. J. *Jesse James: Last Rebel of the Civil War*. New York: Knopf, 2002.

Stone, Wilbur Fisk. *History of Colorado*, vol. 3. Chicago: S. J. Clarke Publishing, 1918.

Stubbs, Roger Avery. *Milton Aurelius and Elizabeth Eleanor Turnham Stubbs*. Long Lake, Minn.: Stubbs, 1938.

Sturgis, Samuel D. *The Other Side as Viewed by Generals Grant, Sherman and Other Distinguished Officers*. Washington, 1882.

Styple, William, ed.. *Andersonville Giving Up the Ghost: A Collection of Prisoners' Diaries, Letters & Memoirs*. Kearney, N.J.: Belle Grove Publishing, 1996.

Supplement to the Official Records of the Union and Confederate Armies. 100 vols. Wilmington, N.C.: Broadfoot Publishing, 1993–2000.

Sword, Wiley. *The Confederacy's Last Hurrah: Spring Hill, Franklin & Nashville*. Lawrence: University Press of Kansas, 1993.

Thoma, James F. *This Cruel Unnatural War*. Memphis, Tenn.: James F. Thoma, 2003.

Thomas, Benjamin P., and Harold M. Hyman. *Stanton: The Life and Times of Lincoln's Secretary of War*. New York: Alfred A. Knopf, 1962.

Time-Life. *Echoes of Glory: Arms and Equipment of the Union*. Alexandria, Va.: Time-Life Books, 1991.

Townsend, William H. *Lincoln and the Bluegrass: Slavery and Civil War in Kentucky*. Lexington: University of Kentucky Press, 1955.

Trenerry, Walter N. "When the Boys Came Home." *Minnesota History* 38, no. 6 (June 1963): 287–97.

Trexler, Harrison Anthony. *Slavery in Missouri 1804–1865*. Baltimore, Md.: John Hopkins Press, 1914.

Trudeau, Noah Andre. *Southern Storm: Sherman's March to the Sea*. New York: Harper, 2008.

Turrill, H. B. "Andersonville Prison in 1864: Reminiscences of Religious Services." From the text in handbill for "What I Saw at Andersonville," and a lecture by the "Andersonville Chaplain Rev. T. J. Sheppard." (1886) Ohio Historical Society, Columbus.

Tyler, William N. *The Dispatch Carrier*. 2nd ed. Port Byron, Ill.: Port Byron "Globe" Print, 1892.

United States Christian Commission. *Record of the Federal Dead Buried from Libby, Belle Isle, Danville & Camp Lawton Prisons and at City Point and in the Field before Petersburg and Richmond*. Philadelphia: James. B. Rogers, Printer, 1866.

Upham, Warren. *Minnesota Place Names: A Geographical Encyclopedia*. St. Paul: Minnesota Historical Society Press, 2001.

Vaughter, John B. ["Sergeant Oats"] *Prison Life in Dixie*. Chicago: General Book Concern, 1880.

Waring, George E., Jr. *Whip and Spur*. New York: Doubleday and McClure, 1897.

Warner, Ezra J. *Generals in Blue: Lives of the Union Commanders*. Baton Rouge: Louisiana State University Press, 1964.

———. *Generals in Gray: Lives of the Confederate Commanders*. Baton Rouge: Louisiana State University Press, 1959.

Warren, John E. "Release from the Bull Pen—Andersonville, 1864." *The Atlantic*, November 1958, 130–38.

Watson, Ronald G., ed. *From Ashby to Andersonville: The Civil War Diary and Reminiscences of Private George A. Hitchcock, 21st Massachusetts Infantry*. Campbell, Calif.: Savas Publishing, 1997.

Way, Frederick, Jr. *Way's Packet Directory, 1848–1994*. Athens: Ohio University, 1994.

Weeks, F. E. *Pioneer History of Camden Township, Lorain County, Ohio*. Wellington, Ohio: Genealogical Workshop, 1983. Reprint of 1927 edition.

White, Helen M. *The Tale of the Comet and Other Stories*. St. Paul: Minnesota Historical Society Press, 1984.

White, William Lee, and Charles Denny Runion. *Great Things Are Expected of Us: The Letters of Colonel C. Irvine Walker, 10th South Carolina Infantry, C.S.A.* Knoxville: University of Tennessee Press, 2009.

Williams, John M. *"The Eagle Regiment," 8th Wis. Inf'ty Vols.* Belleville, Wis.: "Recorder" Print, 1890.

Wills, Brian Steel. *The Confederacy's Greatest Cavalryman: Nathan Bedford Forrest*. Lawrence: University Press of Kansas, 1992.

Wood, Wales W. *A History of the Ninety-Fifth Regiment Illinois Infantry Volunteers*. Belvidere, Ill.: Boone County Historical Society, 1993.

Woodruff, George A. "George A. Woodruff's Account of the Battle of Brice's Cross Roads Written June 10th 1897," transcribed by Randy Morford. http://www.34hot rod.com/geneaology/red_willow-co/george_woodruff.htm.

Woodworth, Steven E. *While God Is Marching On: The Religious World of Civil War Soldiers*. Lawrence: University Press of Kansas, 2001.

Woolverton, William B. "A Sketch of Prison Life at Andersonville." *The Firelands Pioneer* 7 (1894): 62–71.

Wright, James A. *No More Gallant a Deed: A Civil War Memoir of the First Minnesota Volunteers*. St. Paul: Minnesota Historical Society Press, 2001.

Wyeth, John Allan. *That Devil Forrest: Life of General Nathan Bedford Forrest*. Baton Rouge: Louisiana State University Press, 1989.

Yeary, Mamie. *Reminiscences of the Boys in Gray 1861–1865*. Dayton, Ohio: Morningside, 1986.

Young, John P. *The Seventh Tennessee Cavalry (Confederate): A History*. Dayton, Ohio: Morningside Bookshop, 1976. Reprint of 1890 edition.

Zimmerman, Mark. *Guide to Civil War Nashville*. Nashville, Tenn.: Battle of Nashville Preservation Society, 2004.

Index

Page numbers in *italic* refer to illustrations.
Brice's Crossroads is abbreviated as BCR

Image Credits

One Drop in a Sea of Blue is set in the Minion Pro typeface family.

Book design and typesetting by
BNTypographics West Ltd., Victoria, B.C., Canada.

Printed by Versa Printing, East Peoria, Illinois.

CPSIA information can be obtained
at www.ICGtesting.com
Printed in the USA
BVHW070951110919
558157BV00001B/27/P